Frommer's®

Norway

5th Edition

by Roger Norum

WILEY
A John Wiley and Sons, Ltd, Publication

Published by:
WILEY PUBLISHING, INC.

John Wiley & Sons Ltd
The Atrium
Southern Gate
Chichester
West Sussex PO19 8SQ, UK
Telephone (+44) 1243 779777
Email (for orders and customer service enquiries): cs-books@wiley.co.uk. Visit our Home Page on www.wiley.com

UK Publisher: Sally Smith
Project Manager: Daniel Mersey
Commissioning Editor: Fiona Quinn
Development Editor: Myka Carroll
Content Editor: Erica Peters
Cartography: Roberta Stockwell
Photo Editor: Jill Emeny

Front cover photo: Description: Small island near Bergen, Western Fjords/© Peter Adams / awl-images
Back Cover photo: Description: Timbered buildings in Bergen's Bryggen district/© Doug Pearson / awl-images

Wiley also publishes its books in a variety of electronic formats. Some content that appears in print may not be available in electronic books.

For information on our other products and services or to obtain technical support, please contact our Customer Care Department within the U.S. at 877/762-2974, outside the U.S. at 317/572-3993 or fax 317/572-4002.

British Library Cataloguing in Publication Data
A catalogue record for this book is available from the British Library
ISBN 978-0-470-97242-7 (pbk); 978-1-119-99373-5 (ebk); 978-1-119-99450-3 (epub); 978-1-119-99466-4 (emobi)
Typeset by Wiley Indianapolis Composition Services

Printed and bound in the United States of America

5 4 3 2 1

CONTENTS

4 SUGGESTED NORWAY ITINERARIES 75

5 SETTLING INTO OSLO 89

6 EXPLORING OSLO 125

7 SIDE TRIPS FROM OSLO 171

8 LILLEHAMMER & THE PEER GYNT ROAD 190

9 SOUTHERN NORWAY 220

10 STAVANGER 241

11 BERGEN 258

12 THE WEST COAST FJORD COUNTRY 298

13 TRONDHEIM 347

14 TROMSØ 377

15 THE ROUTE TO THE NORTH CAPE 394

LIST OF MAPS

ABOUT THE AUTHOR

Award-winning writer and photographer **Roger Norum** studied Norwegian literature at the University of Tromsø before reading for a PhD in Social Anthropology at the University of Oxford. After a life as a computer programmer and would-be Internet mogul, Roger worked as a translator, authored guidebooks and taught creative writing. He currently makes his home in London, where he covers travel and food for a range of publications. See some of his work at www.rogernorum.com.

ACKNOWLEDGMENTS

Roger would like to thank the genial, knowledgable and ever-outdoorsy Hanne Knudsen at Innovation Norway for help organising research logistics and tips on what's best and new in Norway. Expert kayaker and information coordinator Annett Brohmann at Visit Oslo was also extra helpful with supplying information, advice and tips on the capital. General assistance and insight was also offered by tourist officers, hoteliers and restauranteurs across the country, including Marit Giske, Gunhild Bellsli Reinskou, Malin Backlund, Ove Skylstad, Rigmor Myhre, Linn Kjos Falkenberg, Gunhild Lundblad, Ann-Kristin Robstad Jørgensen, Jens Fredrik von der Lippe, Silje Havikhagen, Lene Berge Forland, Elisabeth Farkvam, Gyri Midveit, Marianne Paulsen, Synnøve Henden, Simone Beck, Laila Immel, Anne Grethe Bakke, Hege Anita Eilertsen, Elin Kvale, Bente Saxon, Tone Tveit, Lars Bakkom, Ragnhild Magerøy, Hege Anita Moen, Anne-Marie Øydivn, Henriette Martinsen, Inga Bjotveit, Hilde Opedal, Anne Farnes, Lone Olsen, Eivind Ødegård, Bente Fekene, Marianne Supphellen, Marianne Olsen, Anne Grete Loland, Noralv Distad, Marit Hæreid Sandstad, Finn Andresen, Elisabeth Niekel and Knut Slinning. Thanks too to best friends forever Marie and Ingrid Sølverud and Jarle Kjepso, who have always opened their hearts and homes to me while I've been in Norway. Finally, gratitude and love to my Norwegian relatives in the US and the homeland—especially my grandpa and dad, who never missed an opportunity to careen around the house sporting a plastic viking helmet and drinking a pewter stein of wassail.

HOW TO CONTACT US

In researching this book, we discovered many wonderful places—hotels, restaurants, shops, and more. We're sure you'll find others. Please tell us about them, so we can share the information with your fellow travelers in upcoming editions. If you were disappointed with a recommendation, we'd love to know that, too. Please email frommers@wiley.com or write to:

Frommer's Norway, 5th Edition
Wiley Publishing, Inc. • 111 River St. • Hoboken, NJ 07030-5774

AN ADDITIONAL NOTE

Please be advised that travel information is subject to change at any time—and this is especially true of prices. We therefore suggest that you write or call ahead for confirmation when making your travel plans. The authors, editors, and publisher cannot be held responsible for the experiences of readers while traveling. Your safety is important to us, however, so we encourage you to stay alert and be aware of your surroundings. Keep a close eye on cameras, purses, and wallets, all favorite targets of thieves and pickpockets.

FROMMER'S STAR RATINGS, ICONS & ABBREVIATIONS

Every hotel, restaurant, and attraction listing in this guide has been ranked for quality, value, service, amenities, and special features using a **star-rating system.** In country, state, and regional guides, we also rate towns and regions to help you narrow down your choices and budget your time accordingly. Hotels and restaurants are rated on a scale of zero (recommended) to three stars (exceptional). Attractions, shopping, nightlife, towns, and regions are rated according to the following scale: zero stars (recommended), one star (highly recommended), two stars (very highly recommended), and three stars (must-see).

In addition to the star-rating system, we also use **seven feature icons** that point you to the great deals, in-the-know advice, and unique experiences that separate travelers from tourists. Throughout the book, look for:

special finds—those places only insiders know about

fun facts—details that make travelers more informed and their trips more fun

kids—best bets for kids and advice for the whole family

special moments—those experiences that memories are made of

overrated—places or experiences not worth your time or money

insider tips—great ways to save time and money

great values—where to get the best deals

The following abbreviations are used for credit cards:

AE	American Express	DISC	Discover	V	Visa
DC	Diners Club	MC	MasterCard		

TRAVEL RESOURCES AT FROMMERS.COM

Frommer's travel resources don't end with this guide. Frommer's website, **www.frommers.com**, has travel information on more than 4,000 destinations. We update features regularly, giving you access to the most current trip-planning information and the best airfare, lodging, and car-rental bargains. You can also listen to podcasts, connect with other Frommers.com members through our active-reader forums, share your travel photos, read blogs from guidebook editors and fellow travellers, and much more.

THE BEST OF NORWAY

1

The "Land of the Midnight Sun" offers a truly unique and unforgettable travel experience. Norwegians view their scrub-covered islands, snow-crested peaks, and glacier-born fjords as symbols of a strong wilderness culture. The majestic scenery inspired the symphonies of Grieg, the plays of Ibsen, and the paintings of Munch. The landscape has also shaped the Norwegians' view of themselves as pastoral dwellers in one of the world's most splendid countrysides.

Norway is a land of tradition, exemplified by its rustic stave churches and its folk dances. But Norway is also an extremely modern place. This technologically advanced nation is rich in petroleum and hydroelectric energy. Norwegians enjoy a well-developed national social insurance system that provides pensions, health insurance, unemployment insurance, and rehabilitation assistance.

One of the last great natural frontiers of the world, Norway invites exploration. So that you don't exhaust yourself with difficult decisions on where to go, I've compiled the best deals and once-in-a-lifetime experiences in this chapter. What follows is the best of the best.

THE most unforgettable TRAVEL EXPERIENCES

- **Enjoying Nature:** Norway is one of the last major countries of the world where you can experience a close encounter with nature in one of the planet's last largely unspoiled wildernesses. The country extends 1,770km (1,100 miles) from south to north (approximately the distance from New York to Miami). Norway is filled with 20,000km (12,000 miles) of fjords, narrows, and straits. It's a land of contrasts, with soaring mountains, panoramic fjords, ice-blue glaciers, deep-green forests, fertile valleys, and rich pastures. The glowing red midnight sun and the Northern Lights have fueled the imaginations of artists and craftspeople for centuries.

The Best of Natural Norway

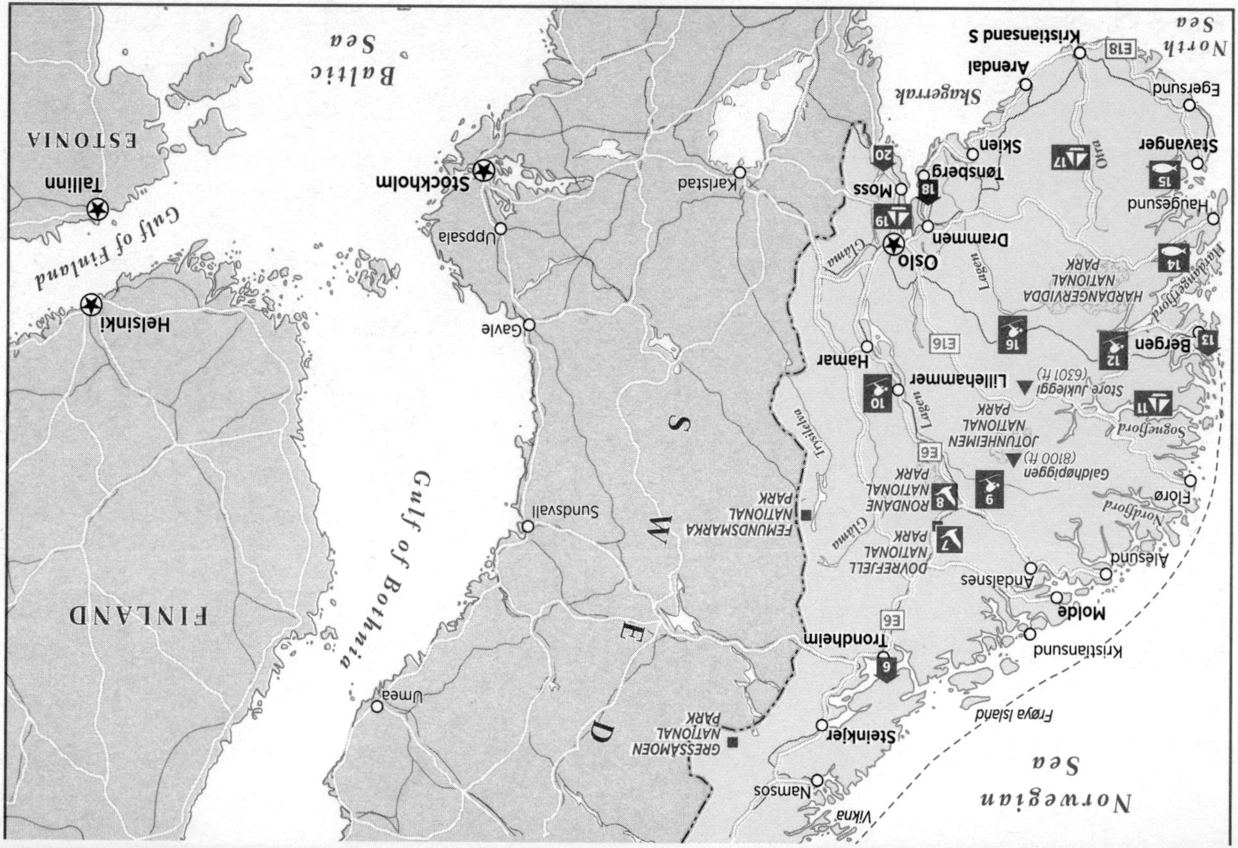

Norwegian Sea
North Sea
Baltic Sea
Gulf of Bothnia
Gulf of Finland
Skagerrak
FINLAND
ESTONIA
SWEDEN
Helsinki
Tallinn
Stockholm
Uppsala
Gavle
Sundsvall
Umeå
Karlstad
GRESSÅMOEN NATIONAL PARK
FEMUNDSMARKA NATIONAL PARK
Trysilelva
Glåma
Namsos
Vikna
Steinkjer
Trondheim
E6
Frøya Island
Kristiansund
Molde
Åndalsnes
Ålesund
Nordfjord
Florø
DOVREFJELL NATIONAL PARK
RONDANE NATIONAL PARK
Galdhøpiggen (8100 ft)
JOTUNHEIMEN NATIONAL PARK
Store Jukleggi (6301 ft)
Sognefjord
Lagen
Lillehammer
Hamar
E16
Bergen
Hardangerfjord
HARDANGERVIDDA NATIONAL PARK
Haugesund
Stavanger
Egersund
Otra
E18
Oslo
Drammen
Moss
Tønsberg
Skien
Arendal
Kristiansand S
6 7 8 9 10 11 12 13 14 15 16 17 18 19 20

- **Experiencing "Norway in a Nutshell":** One of Europe's great train rides, this 12-hour excursion is Norway's most exciting. The route encompasses two arms of the Sognefjord, and the section from Myrdal to Flåm—a drop of 600m (2,000 ft.)—takes you past seemingly endless waterfalls. Tours leave from the Bergen train station. If you have limited time but want to see the country's most dramatic scenery, take this spectacular train trip. See "Flåm: Stopover on Europe's Most Scenic Train Ride," in chapter 12.
- **Visiting the North Cape:** For many, a trip to one of the northernmost inhabited areas of the world will be the journey of a lifetime. Accessible by ship, car, or air, the North Cape fascinates travelers in a way that outweighs its bleakness. Ship tours began in 1879 and, except during wartime, have gone to the Cape ever since. Hammerfest, the world's northernmost town of significant size, is an important port of call for North Cape steamers. See chapter 15.
- **Exploring the Fjord Country:** Stunningly serene and majestic, Norway's fjords are some of the world's most awe-inspiring sights. The fjords are reason enough for a trip to Norway. Bergen can be your gateway; two of the country's most famous fjords, the Hardangerfjord and the Sognefjord, can easily be explored from here. If you have time for only one, my vote goes to the Sognefjord for its sheer, lofty walls that rise to more than 1,000m (3,300 ft.) along its towering cliffs. Sheer cliff faces and cascading waterfalls create something of a fantasy landscape. As Norway's longest fjord, the Sognefjord can be crossed by express steamer to Gudvangen. You can go on your own or take an organized tour, which will probably include the dramatic Folgefonn Glacier. See p. 298.
- **Seeing the Midnight Sun at the Arctic Circle:** This is one of the major reasons visitors go to Norway. The Arctic Circle marks the boundary of the midnight sun of the Arctic summer and the sunless winters of the north. The midnight sun can be seen from the middle of May until the end of July. The Arctic Circle cuts across Norway south of Bodø, from where bus excursions visit the circle. The adventurous few who arrive in the winter miss the midnight sun but are treated to a spectacular display of the aurora borealis, the flaming spectacle of the Arctic winter sky. See chapter 14.

THE best SCENIC TOWNS

- **Fredrikstad:** Founded in 1567 at the mouth of the River Glomma, Fredrikstad preserved its Old Town, which had become a fortress by 1667. Today Fredrikstad (97km/60 miles south of Oslo) offers a glimpse of what a Norwegian town looked like several hundred years ago. The old buildings in the historic district have been converted into studios for craftspeople and artisans, while maintaining their architectural integrity. After a visit here, you can drive along Oldtidsveien (the "Highway of the Ancients"), the most concentrated collection of archaeological monuments in Norway. See "Fredrikstad: Norway's Oldest Fortified Town," in chapter 7.
- **Tønsberg:** On the western bank of the Oslofjord is Norway's oldest town. It was founded in 872, a year before King Harald Hårfagre (Fairhair) united parts of

Norway and the Viking town became a royal coronation site. Its hill fortress is sometimes called "the Acropolis of Norway." Its ancient district, Nordbyen, is filled with well-preserved homes, and the folk museum houses a treasure trove of Viking-era artifacts. See "Tønsberg: The First Settlement," in chapter 7.

- **Bergen:** The gateway to Norway's fjord country, this town is much more scenic than the capital of Oslo. In fact, it was the capital of Norway for 6 centuries and a major outpost of the medieval Hanseatic merchants. The town's biggest event is the Bergen International Music Festival, but there are also many year-round attractions. Many visitors come to explore Bergen's museums (including Edvard Grieg's former home) as well as its diverse environs—especially fjords, mountains, and waterfalls. See chapter 11.
- **Trondheim:** Norway's third-largest city traces its history from 997, when the Vikings flourished. Norway's kings are crowned at the ancient Nidaros Domkirke (Trondheim Cathedral). Scandinavia's largest medieval building, the cathedral was erected over the grave of St. Olav, the Viking king. Trondheim is the popular stopover for travelers from Oslo to destinations north of the Arctic Circle. See chapter 13.
- **Bodø:** Lying 1,305km (809 miles) north of Oslo, this far-northern seaport, the terminus of the Nordland railway, is the gateway to the Arctic, which lies just south of this breezy town. Another excellent place to observe the midnight sun, from June 1 to July 13, Bodø is the capital of the Nordland province. From the center, you can also explore the environs, filled with glaciers and "bird islands." Bodø is also a gateway to the remote Lofoten Islands. See "Bodø: Gateway to the North," in chapter 15.

THE best FESTIVALS

For more details on these events, see "Norway Calendar of Events" in chapter 3.

- **Bergen International Festival:** This European cultural highlight, which takes place in late May and early June, ranks in importance with the Edinburgh and Salzburg festivals. Major artists from all over the world descend on the small city to perform music, drama, opera, ballet, folkloric presentations, and more. The works of Bergen native Edvard Grieg dominate the festival, and daily concerts are held at his former home, Troldhaugen. Contemporary plays are also performed, but the major focus is on the works of Ibsen. See p. 40.
- **Molde International Jazz Festival:** In this "City of Roses," Norway's oldest jazz festival is held every summer, usually around mid-July. Some of the best jazz artists in the world wing in for this event. People stay up most of the night listening to foot-stomping music and drinking beer. Oftentimes the best concerts are the impromptu jam sessions in smoky little clubs. See "Molde: City of Roses" (p. 41).
- **Holmenkollen Ski Festival:** This large ski festival takes place in March at the Holmenkollen ski jump, on the outskirts of Oslo. The agenda is packed with everything from international ski-jumping competitions to Norway's largest cross-country race for amateurs. See p. 40.

THE best ACTIVE VACATIONS

- **Fishing:** The cold, clear waters of Norway's freshwater streams are renowned for their salmon and trout, and the storm-tossed seas off the coast have traditionally provided enough cod and mackerel to satisfy most of the nation's population. Serious anglers sometimes end up losing themselves in the majesty of the scenery. Tips on fishing in and around the Norwegian fjords are provided by the **Bergen Sportsfiskere (Bergen Angling Association),** Damsgaardveien 106, Bergen (✆ **55-34-18-08;** www.bergensportsfiskere.no), and the tourist information offices in Oslo and Bergen. Rural hotels throughout the nation can also give pointers on good spots. For a truly unusual fishing experience, **Borton Overseas** (✆ **800/843-0602;** www.bortonoverseas.com) can arrange treks and accommodations in old-fashioned fishermen's cottages in the isolated Lofoten Islands. The rustic-looking, fully renovated cottages are adjacent to the sea. Rentals are for 3 days and include bed linens, maid service, boat rentals, and fishing equipment. For my favorite fishing-hole recommendations, refer to "The Best Fishing." See p. 8.
- **Hiking:** The woods *(marken)* around Oslo boast thousands of kilometers of trails, many of which are lit for nighttime use. If you don't want to leave the city, Frogner Park also has many navigable paths. Any Norwegian regional tourist bureau can advise you about hiking. In Bergen, for example, get in touch with the **Bergen Touring Club** (p. 292), whose members have spent years hiking through the western fjord country and can advise about the best trails. For my favorite hikes, refer to "The Best Hikes." See below.
- **Skiing:** Considering that "ski" is a Norwegian word, it isn't surprising that this is the undisputed top winter sport in Norway, attracting expert skiers and neophytes alike from around the world. Norway is also a pioneer in promoting skiing as a sport for people with disabilities. If you're a serious skier, consider the best winter resorts, in Voss, Geilo, and Lillehammer (site of the 1994 Winter Olympics). See "Lillehammer of Olympic Glory," in chapter 8; "Voss: A Winter Playground," in chapter 12; and "Geilo: A Winter Wonderland," in chapter 12. For my choices of the best downhill skiing and the best cross-country skiing. See below.
- **Mountain Climbing:** Local tourist offices can offer advice. What I like best are guided hikes to the archaeological digs of the 8,000-year-old Stone Age settlements near the Hardangerjøkulen (Hardanger Glacier). The digs are about an hour's drive north of the mountain resort of Geilo. For information, contact the **Geilo Tourist Office** (✆ **32-09-59-00;** www.geilo.no). See "Geilo: A Winter Wonderland," in chapter 12.

THE best HIKES

- **Besseggen Ridge:** In the Jotunheimen Nasjonalpark, Norway's greatest park, you'll find a landscape of glaciers, mountains, lakes, and waterfalls, crowned by two towering peaks: Glittertind, at 2,452m (8,043 ft.), and Galdhøpiggen, at 2,469m (8,098 ft.), the highest peak in northern Europe. This park also boasts the country's most justifiably popular hike, across Besseggen Ridge, towering over a beautiful lake, Gjende, which earned the praise of Henrik Ibsen, among others. The trail along the ridge links the remote mountain lodges of Memurubo and Gjendesheim. See p. 211.

- **Preikestolen:** Outside the city of Stavanger, on the western coast of Norway, you can take one of the most memorable hikes in this part of the world, through scenic fjord country with mountain landscapes as a backdrop. The ultimate goal is Pulpit Rock (its English name), with a vertical drop of 609m (1,998 ft.) over the stunningly blue Lysefjord. You can drive to a rock parking lot to begin a hike of 4km (2½ miles). The hike has a height difference of 350m (1,150 ft.); it begins steeply, climbing past rocky, even boggy sections before the final ascent. The cliffs are exposed and extremely windy, but all this is part of the Norwegian experience. Despite an alarming crack in the rock, making it look as if you're about to plunge to your death in the fjord below, geologists claim it will take thousands of years for the rock to break apart. Once on the rock, looking down at the 42-km (26-mile) fjord, you'll perhaps understand why poets have praised its "ethereal light." See p. 257.
- **Lofoten Fishing Villages:** The best hikes in Norway don't always have to be up steep mountains. In the remote Lofoten Islands in the north of Norway, while based on the glaciated island of **Moskenesøy,** I like to hike along a seascape of little fishing villages stacked up one after the other like a string of pearls. The mountain peak of Hermannsdalstind, rising to 1,029m (3,375 ft.), offers a scenic backdrop. Begin in the north, at the little fishing village of Hamnøy, and then hike southward to other quaint settlements at Sakrisøy, Reine, Moskenes, Sørvägen, and the curiously named Å. To extend the hike at Sørvägen for another 2 hours, you can hike inland along a signposted ramblers' trail to get acquainted with the handsome interior of a Lofoten island. See "The Lofoten Islands: The Soul of Norway," in chapter 15.

THE best DOWNHILL SKIING

- **Lillehammer:** It may not be Switzerland, but Norway has carved out its own alpine skiing, a lot of it centered at Lillehammer. The skiing at Lillehammer, Norway's oldest ski resort, is so superb that the 1994 Olympic committee chose the resort as the site of its winter games. **Hafjell Alpine Center** lies 9.3km (5¾ miles) north of the center and was the main venue for the Olympic alpine competitions, offering seven lifts and 20km (12 miles) of alpine slopes. The longest slope at Hafjell is 7km (4¼ miles) long, and there's a wide range of alpine slopes for different levels of skiing proficiency. The Lillehammer mountains lie 850m (2,800 ft.) above sea level. See "Lillehammer of Olympic Glory," in chapter 8.
- **Geilo:** Superior to Voss but not an Olympic ski spectacle like Lillehammer, Geilo features five different ski centers. The best is the Geilo Skiheiser, with 24km (15 miles) of slopes, many as exciting as those in Gstaad, Switzerland. The area is also equipped with 18 lifts and a "ski-board" tunnel. Cable cars will take you to the top of the resort at 1,060m (3,480 ft.) above sea level. From that point, marked trails split off in many directions. See "Geilo: A Winter Wonderland," in chapter 12.
- **Voss:** This excellent winter resort has eight chairlifts and an aerial cableway carrying passengers up to a peak of 788m (2,625 ft.). In all, there are 40km (25 miles) of alpine slopes that have been compared favorably to those in western Austria. One ski lift climbs 900m (3,000 ft.) from Traastolen to the top of the mountain of Slettafjell, with a wide and varied choice of downhill runs. See "Voss: A Winter Playground," in chapter 12.

THE best CROSS-COUNTRY SKIING

- **Lillehammer:** The Olympic resort in central Norway boasts 402km (249 miles) of prepared cross-country tracks, 6km (3¾ miles) of which are illuminated. From mid-December, cross-country skiers arrive from all over Europe, and sometimes America, to test out the well-groomed trails. The landscape here is even more beautiful than that found in Geilo (see below). Lillehammer is set in an area of Norway that contains its highest mountains and its best-known Nasjonalpark (National Park), making it a cross-country-skiing paradise as you glide across the dramatic Hardanggervidda Plateau. See "Lillehammer of Olympic Glory," in chapter 8.
- **Peer Gynt Ski Area:** Consistently, Norwegian skiers rate this beautiful countryside as one of the best venues for cross-country skiing. Because it's a part of the same region, the landscape encountered cross-country is virtually the same as for Lillehammer. This vast ski region in central Norway is most suitable for those skiers who would like to combine cross-country skiing with alpine-esque slopes. For cross-country skiers, there are 460km (285 miles) of well-prepared trails; in winter, floodlit trails in Espedalen and in Gålå make it possible to go cross-country skiing at night. A ski bus links all the main resorts, such as Espedalen, Fefor, and Gålå. See p. 205.
- **Geilo:** For more than a century, Geilo, in a central location in southern Norway, has excelled as a ski resort. At 800m (2,600 ft.) above sea level, it lies halfway between Bergen and Oslo, and is even more dramatically situated than Voss, its major competitor. The Hallingskarvet Mountain—frosted with several small glaciers—is its "backbone," and it stands on the largest mountain plateau. Cross-country skiers will find a total of 220km (140 miles) of well-groomed and well-marked trails through forests, hills, and moors. You'll traverse the Hardangervidda Nasjonalpark, which is 3,430 sq. km (1,330 sq. miles) in area. This is some of the most beautiful and protected tundra in Norway and home of Norway's largest herds of wild reindeer, called caribou. See "Geilo: A Winter Wonderland," in chapter 12.

THE best FISHING

- **Alta:** In the north of Norway, 1,989km (1,233 miles) north of Oslo, this frontier outpost is known for having the best salmon-fishing waters in the world. Hook up with **AKU,** Storengveien 26 (✆ **78-43-48-40;** www.aku-finnmark.com), which leads salmon-fishing trips. It also offers deep-sea fishing and can arrange outings for fishing below glaciers, along with boat rentals and fishing tackle. See "Alta: City of Northern Lights," in chapter 15.
- **Suldalslågen:** Lying to the north of the western port city of Stavanger, this is the longest salmon river in the west. No license is required if you're angling for saltwater fish. Founded more than a century ago, **Lindum** (✆ **52-79-91-61;** www.lakseslottet.no) is the best fishing lodge in Norway. The salmon season here lasts from July to September. See p. 250.

- **Fjord Fishing:** Bergen and its environs lay claim to the best fjord fishing in the west. The area is known for its catches of haddock, coalfish, cod, and mackerel. You can fish in the sea without a permit, though fishing in freshwater streams and ponds requires a permit, arranged through the **Bergen Angling Association** (p. 291).

THE most scenic BOAT TRIPS

- **Sognefjord:** If you take only one fjord trip in your life, make it the panoramic Sognefjord in western Norway. Excursions depart the harbor at Bergen (p. 297). As you sail along, it's like a fantasy view of Norway, as the deep blue fjord waters are broken by many waterfalls. Sognefjord is the longest fjord in Norway, stretching for a distance of 205km (127 miles) up to the mountains of the Jotunheimen Nasjonalpark. (But most fjord excursions end long before you reach Jotunheimen.) Along the banks of this fjord—best explored in the late spring and summer—are farms, 19th-century villages, and lush landscapes. In springtime plum, pear, apple, and cherry trees grow profusely.
- **Oslofjord:** A web of cays, skerries, sandbars, and towering rocky banks parades before you as you head out on one of the Båtservice sightseeing boats that make summer trips from Oslo along this historic old fjord, the former stamping grounds of the Vikings. You'll sail aboard one of a trio of sloops with 19th-century rigging, one dating from 1892. Included in the cost are large buckets of Norwegian shrimp served buffet style. See p. 153.
- **Telemark Canal:** Norway's answer to the Panama Canal, the 1892 Telemark Canal carries boats from its gateway, the southern city of Skien. As you sail along, you'll penetrate deep into the panoramic countryside of Norway, with its lakes, rivers, and dark forests that you just know are inhabited by trolls. You can also see some of the marvelous feats of engineering that made such a boat ride possible. See p. 229.
- **Coastal Steamer to the North Cape:** One of the sea voyages of a lifetime, the route along the west coast of Norway from Bergen to the remote northern frontier town of Kirkenes is plied regularly by elegantly comfortable coastal steamers. Passengers and cargo are carried to 34 ports. Along the way, ships sail through some of the lesser-known but most beautiful fjords in the country. Passengers are allowed to make excursions into the mountains and across glacier country. The highlight of the sea voyage—with the most evocative scenery—is a visit to the Nordkapp (North Cape), at the top of Europe. See p. 261 and 397.

THE most memorable LANDSCAPES & DRIVES

- **Overland Route Oslo/Bergen:** The mountainous drive from Oslo to Bergen is one of the great scenic trips of Europe. You'll venture through mountain passes and even make a ferry crossing here and there. Along the way, you'll pass fjords and snowcapped mountains, along with waterfalls, fjord villages, and an ancient stave church. The most memorable stopover is at the town of Flåm, which lies on the Aurlandsfjord, a tip of the Sognefjord, the most scenic fjord in Norway (p. 297). If time allows, I recommend that you allow at least 2 days for this memorable motor tour. Faced with a choice of the northern or southern route, I prefer the southern. See "Flåm: Stopover on Europe's Most Scenic Train Ride," in chapter 12, for specific directions.

- **Electric Train from Myrdal to Flåm:** In my view, there is no more scenic train ride in Europe—the bahns of Switzerland included—than from Myrdal to the village of Flåm. There's no railway line anywhere in the world steeper than this one; the train and track were designed so that they would lock into each other with greater adhesion than smooth tracks. The trip is 19km (12 miles) long and takes 50 minutes. During that time you'll travel an elevation of 883m (2,896 ft.) up a steep mountain gorge and down again. Picture 20 tunnels and spectacular waterfalls in what I rate as the most beautiful and lushest mountain scenery in Norway. See p. 318.
- **The Route to the North Cape:** If you're up for it, you can leave Bergen and drive to the Arctic Circle in a relatively relaxed 3 days. To push on, you can even drive from Bergen to the North Cape in 5 days. Locals call the northern route the Arctic Highway. The road, which is well maintained, allows you to experience the majestic beauty of the far north of Norway as you move toward polar-bear country. Those who've driven in the far north of Alaska will roughly know what to expect. Fertile fields in the south in the fjord country give way to lakes and dark forests. In summer, you'll be driving into the land of the midnight sun. The Arctic Highway is faster, but the Kystriksveien Coast Route allows the most dramatic views of the landscape and seascape. As for what to see and where to stop over along the route, see chapter 15 for suggestions.
- **Hardangerfjord:** For the best fjordside motoring, try the Hardangerfjord, centered in the town of Lofthus i Hardanger, former retreat of composer Edvard Grieg and other well-known artists. You can take in the scenery here by either a boat ride or a motor trip along the shores. The fjord stretches a total distance of 179km (111 miles), and there are panoramic waterfalls on each of its banks. Along the way are superb views of the Folgefonna, Norway's third-largest glacier, stretching for 37km (23 miles). See p. 303.

THE best WILDLIFE VIEWING

- **Dovrefjell Nasjonalpark:** Dovrefjell (p. 213), in central Norway, is one of Norway's great national parks. You can spot reindeer in the park, and it's also a habitat for the wolverine and the arctic fox, but don't count on seeing these elusive creatures. Many visitors come here just for a glimpse of the musk ox. While this unusual species almost vanished during World War II, careful breeding has brought it back in limited herds. To see the rare animal, which may not make it through the century, you need to go on one of the safaris conducted by **Moskus Safari Dovrefjell.** See p. 214.
- **Rondane Nasjonalpark:** Entered through the little town of Jeska, this national park was the first ever to open in Norway, having been created in 1962. Peppered with little lakes and rivers, the park is famous throughout Norway for being inhabited

by more than two dozen types of animals, including reindeer. Rondane is also home to some 125 different species of birds, making it a favorite for birders. See p. 213.

- **The Puffins of Værøy:** In the remote Lofoten Islands in the north of Norway is one of Europe's great bird-watching retreats. The thinly populated island is the nesting place for more than 1.5 million seabirds, including sea eagles, auks, guillemots, kittiwakes, cormorants, the arctic tern, petrels, gulls, and other species, which breed from May to August. Many birders come here just to see the famous puffins at the seabird rookeries. See p. 423.

THE best HOTELS

- **Clarion Collection Hotel Grand Olav** (Trondheim; ✆ **73-80-80-80;** www.choicehotels.no): This is still the most stylish hotel in Norway's medieval capital, a tasteful enclave of comfort and good living. Located next to the city's concert house, the property is modern, filled with amenities, and imaginatively decorated. See p. 350.
- **Dr. Holms Hotel** (Geilo; ✆ **32-09-57-00;** www.drholms.com): One of Norway's most famous resort hotels, this establishment was opened by Dr. Holms in 1909. It still stands for elegance, comfort, and tradition, all of which are especially evident during the winter ski season. The hotel offers beautifully furnished rooms with classic styling, as well as a swimming complex. Renowned Norwegian musical artists often perform here. See p. 322.
- **Grand Hotel** (Oslo; ✆ **23-21-20-00;** www.grand.no): This has long been Norway's premier hotel, and is the last of Oslo's classic old-world palaces. It opened in 1874 and is still going strong; it's very popular with North American tour groups. Ibsen and Munch were regular visitors. The opulent suites house the Nobel Peace Prize winner every year. See p. 99.
- **Grims Grenka** (Oslo; ✆ **23-10-72-00;** www.grimsgrenka.no): Set near Akershus Castle, Oslo's only boutique and design hotel is definitely worth its *havsalt* (sea salt). It offers 50 low-key but colorful rooms with large beds on raised platforms, shag carpets, freestanding marble baths, and custom toiletries. A downstairs bar serves organic teas, top-shelf drinks—and caviar. The restaurant is also excellent. See p. 99.
- **Radisson BLU Hotel Norge** (Bergen; ✆ **800/333-3333** in the U.S., or 55-57-30-00; www.radissonblu.com): This grand hotel on Norway's west coast is sleek, modern, and cosmopolitan. It is located on the city's park, and offers every modern amenity you could ever expect from an upscale hotel, including free Wi-Fi. The staff and service are excellent. See p. 266.
- **Rica Ishavshotel** (Tromsø; ✆ **77-66-64-00;** www.rica.no): Although chain-owned and -operated, this is the best hotel in the chilly north of Norway. From its dramatic perch, the hotel provides views in all directions. Looking like a space-age yacht, it nicely houses guests near the pier where the coastal steamers stop. See p. 380.
- **Skagen Brygge Hotell** (Stavanger; ✆ **51-85-00-00;** www.skagenbryggehotell.no): Southwestern Norway's most architecturally impressive hotel at the harborfront replicates the look of a string of antique warehouses that used to stand here. Some of the preferred bedrooms are in the original 19th-century core.

Accommodations in the newer section contain large windows and more modern furnishings. See p. 244.

- **Solstrand Hotel & Bad** (Os, outside Bergen; © **56-57-11-00;** www.solstrand.com): This is the finest hotel in the fjord district around the city of Bergen. Dating back to 1896, the hotel evokes the nostalgia of the Belle Epoque era, and you'll be coddled in comfort in cheerfully decorated bedrooms. Come here for a vacation retreat instead of merely an overnight stopover. See p. 270.

THE best INNS & RESORTS

- **Dalen Hotel** (Dalen I Telemark; © **35-07-90-00;** www.dalenhotel.no): At the terminus of the Telemark Canal, the Dalen Hotel's architecture is studded with "dragon heads" and Viking-inspired gingerbread. Built in 1894 and still going strong, it has kept abreast of the times. It's the kind of nostalgic and evocative Norwegian decor that I like, filled with comforting but also whimsical features—including towers, turrets, and wide verandas. You'll be wined and dined royally here—after all, the King of Siam was once a guest. See p. 230.
- **Fretheim Hotel** (Flåm; © **57-63-63-00;** www.fretheim-hotel.no): Set in the midst of an impressive scene of mountains and waterfalls, this 1866 hotel opens onto a panoramic vista of fjord waters. Long renowned for its hospitality and now equipped with a modern annex, it houses you comfortably in attractive and well-maintained bedrooms. Salmon is the chef's specialty in the hotel's first-class restaurant. See p. 319.
- **Hotel Mundal** (Fjærland; © **57-69-31-01;** www.hotelmundal.no): On the banks of the Fjærlandsfjord, a scenic branch of the greater Sognefjord, this hotel has been run by the same family since it opened its doors back in 1891. With its peaked roofs, wooden scrollwork, round tower, and cavernous dining room, it is one of Norway's most classic hotel examples of Victorian architecture. Modern updates and improvements have ensured that it's still a wonderful choice to base yourself in one of the most scenic parts of the western fjord country. See p. 326.
- **Hotel Ullensvang** (Lofthus i Hardanger; © **53-67-00-00;** www.hotel-ullensvang.no): My favorite inn within the fjord country, the Ullensvang, from 1846, lies on the bank of the Hardangerfjord. It was once the retreat of the composer Edvard Grieg, whose piano is still in a cottage on the grounds. Expanded over the years, the hotel has been run by the same family for four generations. These family members extend a hearty Norwegian welcome to their guests, whom they feed and house most comfortably. See p. 304.
- **Juvet Landscape Hotel** (Alstad; © **95-03-20-10;** www.juvet.com): Opened in 2009, these seven singular, freestanding rooms are carved out of spruce and placed smack in the Gudbrandsjuvet, a canyon deep in the fjords inland from Ålesund. The individual pod-like structures, each constructed on 14 steel pylons built into the bedrock, feature south-facing walls made entirely of double-paned glass that give guests unfettered views of the gushing Valldøla River below and the spectacular alpine peaks that soar above it. The effect is something like watching an IMAX documentary from your bedroom.
- **Union Hotel** (Geiranger; © **70-26-83-00;** www.hotelunion.no): Located at one of the most majestic fjords in Norway, the Geirangerfjord, this is a celebrated 1891 family-style hotel. Kings, queens, and kaisers have found lodgings here in

the beautifully furnished bedrooms, many with private balconies opening onto the water. The hotel's restaurant is one of the best and most traditional in the area, featuring a huge classic Norwegian buffet. See p. 334.

THE best DINING EXPERIENCES

- **Bygdøy Allé** (Oslo; ✆ **40-00-38-34;** www.bygdøyallerestaurant.no): Also known rather simply as "Bar," this superb new spot comprises an excellent Asian-inspired restaurant as well as several intimate bars and even a small nightclub. Since it opened in 2009, it has quickly become one of Oslo's hippest places to come for a meal and a drink. Gregarious, gorgeous clientele dine from the eclectic menu, and then stick around for both *vorspiel* (a pre-party drink) and *nachspiel* (a late-night after-party).
- **Emma's Drømmekjøkken** (Tromsø; ✆ **77-63-77-30;** www.emmasdrommekjokken.no): Anne Brit, known locally as "Emma," operates this dream kitchen and is one of northern Norway's best-known culinary personalities. Although she uses ingredients primarily from the north—often fish from Arctic waters—she scours the globe for her flavors, which include everything from chili powder to wasabi. See p. 383.
- **Finnegaardsstuene** (Bergen; ✆ **55-55-03-00;** www.finnegaarden.no): In a converted Hanseatic League warehouse, this Norwegian-French restaurant is one of the finest in western Norway. The cuisine revolves around only the freshest ingredients, especially fish. The kitchen uses classical French preparation methods to create such delectable items as lime-marinated turbot in caviar sauce or breast of duck in lime-and-fig sauce. See p. 271.
- **Hanne På Høyden** (Bergen; ✆ **55-32-34-32;** http://hannepaahoeyden.wordpress.com). Run by Chef of the Year Hanne Frosta, this outstanding organic, farm-to-plate restaurant has become one of the country's biggest. Everything about it screams ecological, and special attention is paid to the tender meat and succulent fish dishes. Also try the great organic juices. See p. 274.
- **Oro** (Oslo; ✆ **23-01-02-40;** www.ororestaurant.no): A hyperstylish restaurant, Oro is just about as hip as it gets in Norway's capital, ranking right up there with the country's best restaurants. The Continental cuisine at this first-class dining citadel evokes the best of Paris's restaurants, but the decor feels very Scandinavian. Try a well-priced four-, five-, or six-course menu (and sample the excellent salmon), or the brasserie next door. See p. 109.
- **Statholdgaarden** (Oslo; ✆ **22-41-88-00;** www.statholdergaarden.no): Gourmets from all over Norway have flocked here to sample chef Bent Stiansen's interpretation of modern Norwegian cooking. Stiansen is almost fanatically tuned to what's best in any season, and here he has teamed up with culinary master Torbjørn Forster to create inspired Michelin-starred dishes—everything from grilled scallop and langoustine salad with coriander-marinated mango to mustard-glazed filet of lamb served with chanterelles and root vegetable *millefeuille*. See p. 116.
- **Tjuvholmen Sjømagasin** (Oslo; ✆ **23-89-77-77;** www.sjomagasinet.no): Opened on newly reclaimed land at the Aker Brygge waterfront, this chic seafood

restaurant serves outstanding lobster, king crab, and fish in a sprawling dining room with panoramic views of Oslofjord harbor—and of the open kitchen. Pick your catch straight from steel casks, then hand it to the team of chefs. The restaurant is run by Bjørn Tore Furset, a local wunderkind whose empire includes city eateries Havsmak, Ekeberg, and Argent. See p. 119.

THE best MUSEUMS

- **Det Hanseatiske Museum** (Bergen): Depicting commercial life on the wharf in the early 18th century, this museum is housed in one of the city's best-preserved wooden buildings. German Hanseatic merchants lived in similar medieval houses near the harbor. See p. 281.
- **Edvard Munch Museum** (Oslo): Here you'll find the most significant collection of the work of Edvard Munch (1863–1944), Scandinavia's most noted artist. The museum, his gift to the city, contains a staggering treasure trove: 1,100 paintings, 4,500 drawings, and about 18,000 prints—including *The Scream,* which was restored after theft and vandalism several years ago. See p. 129.
- **Norwegian Folk Museum** (Oslo): Some 140 original buildings from all over Norway were shipped here and reassembled on 14 hectares (35 acres) at Bygdøy. Although Scandinavia is known for such open-air museums, this one is the best. The buildings range from a rare stave church, constructed around 1200, to one of the oldest wooden buildings still standing in Norway. Old-time Norwegian life is captured here like nowhere else. See p. 130.
- **Vigelandsparken** (Oslo): This stunning park in western Oslo displays the lifetime work of Gustav Vigeland, the country's greatest sculptor. In 30-hectare (74-acre) Frogner Park, you can see more than 200 sculptures in granite, bronze, and iron, including *Angry Boy,* his most celebrated work. See p. 131.
- **Viking Ship Museum** (Oslo): Three stunning burial vessels from the Viking era were excavated on the shores of the Oslofjord and are now displayed in Bygdøy, Oslo's "museum island." The most spectacular is the *Oseberg,* from the 9th century, a 20-m (66-ft.) dragon ship with a wealth of ornaments. See p. 132.

THE best BUYS

Most of the products mentioned below are also available at shops in Oslo and Bergen; see "Shopping" in chapters 6 and 11.

- **Ceramics:** In the 1960s and 1970s, Norway earned a reputation among potters and stoneware enthusiasts for its chunky, utilitarian pottery. The trend today is to emulate the fragile, more decorative designs popular in France, England, and Germany, so Norwegian ceramists are producing thinner, more delicate, and more ornate forms. The best selection is found at **Tilbords Interiør Bergen Storsenter** (**© 55-55-33-41**) in Bergen. See p. 293.
- **Costumes:** Norway boasts more than 450 regional costumes, especially in the coastal communities. The original fishermen's sweater was knit of naturally colored wool (beige, brown, black, or off-white) in a deliberately large size and then washed in hot water so that it shrank. The tightly woven sweater could then resist water. Modern versions of these sweaters are known for their nubby texture,

sophisticated patterns, and varying shades of single colors. The best purveyor of Norwegian costumes and folk dress from various parts of the country is **Heimen Husflid** in Oslo (© **23-21-42-00**). See p. 159.

- **Crystal:** In Norway you can buy flawless crystal that is as clear as a Nordic iceberg. Norwegian tastes tend toward the clean and uncluttered, stressing line, form, and harmony. Crystal is sold at many stores, especially in Bergen and Oslo, but I've consistently been impressed with the selection on display at the prestigious **Norway Designs** (© **23-11-45-10**) in Oslo. See p. 157.
- **Knitwear:** Many visitors eagerly seek out Norwegian knitwear. Among the best buys are hand-knit or "half-handmade" garments. The latter, knit on electric looms, are so personalized and made in such small quantities that they're very hard to distinguish from handmade items. The tradition of women hand-knitting sweaters while rocking a cradle or tending a fire thrives in rural Norway, especially during the long winter. Beautifully made Norwegian knitwear is on sale at **Norway Designs** (© **23-11-45-10;** p. 157) in Oslo, and there's an especially large selection at the **Oslo Sweater Shop** (© **22-11-29-22;** www.oslosweatershop.com; p. 160), also in Oslo.

THE best OF NORWAY ONLINE

- **Cruise Norway** (www.cruisenorway.com): This site previews the best itineraries for those who'd like to cruise the fjords of Norway or take various Scandinavian cruises in general. Independent vacation packages are highlighted.
- **Explore Fjord Norway** (www.fjordnorway.com): This site focuses on one of Scandinavia's most visited attractions, the fjord country of western Norway. It provides information on fjord trips and cruises, with details for the active vacationer on climbing, walking, and cycling, plus information about fjord culture.
- **Norway.com** (www.norway.com): This is a solid website for the country, covering all the major cities, not just Oslo and Bergen, but Ålesund, Tønsberg, Hamar, Kristiansand S, and Lillehammer, among others. Travel-planning data is highlighted, as are the best travel deals. There are also news items about the country and a regularly updated blog.
- **Norwegian Tourist Board** (www.visitnorway.com): This is the country's official travel guide to Norway, with plenty of tips on attractions and special interests, accommodations, dining, and entertainment, along with maps and notes on the weather.
- **Official Site for Bergen** (www.visitbergen.com): Norway's second city is explored in some detail on this site, with a comprehensive database on maps, restaurants, shops, sports, sightseeing, transportation, accommodations, and other useful information.
- **Official Site for Trondheim** (www.trondheim.com): The first capital of Norway—today a modern university city—is explored in this databank, with pictures, useful information, a city map, and details about accommodations and attractions.
- **Official Site of the Oslo Tourist Office** (www.visitoslo.com): The site explores the city in detail, with tips on attractions, restaurants, activities, accommodations, and shopping.

- **Skiing Norway and Lillehammer** (www.lillehammer.com): This site is loaded with details about Norway's oldest sports resort, which was a venue for the 1994 Winter Olympics. The skiing terrain is previewed, along with tips on activities, accommodations, and attractions.
- **Visit Flåm** (www.visitflam.com): This site offers information about charming Flåm in the heart of the Sognefjord district. It's a major stop on the Flåm Railway, the world's most spectacular and panoramic line. It also offers information on the extremely popular "Norway in a Nutshell" tour.

NORWAY IN DEPTH

2

Norway is an ancient land of myth and legend, mountains, and nature. It also has a strong folklore tradition.

As children, Norwegians grow up on stories of *huldres* (see "A Long-Tailed Seducer," below) and trolls. Trolls—who can be either good or evil and who come in all shapes and sizes—have become part of the folklore of the country. And in their secret hearts, many Norwegians still believe in them. Trolls never come out in sunlight; if they should happen to appear during the day, they burst and are petrified as mountains. That's why Norway has so many mountains—or so the legend goes.

Go to Norway for an experience not only of folklore but also of the great outdoors. Spain and Italy overflow with legendary, treasure-filled cities, but Norway has nothing to equal them. England has preserved the crooked old architecture from the days of Samuel Johnson, while Norway's wooden villages have burned to the ground, for the most part. Many of Norway's towns along the coast—such as Bodø—were destroyed during World War II. But for sheer scenic beauty, Norway is about the greatest thing this side of Valhalla. Norway is a land of waterfalls and rapids, majestic mountains and glaciers, green islands, crystal lakes, pine and spruce forests, secluded valleys, craggy cliffs, and peaceful fjords.

Contemporary Norway is a blend of the ancient and the modern. How curious but how common it is to see a Sami grandmother—attired in a brightly colored braided costume, bonnet, and deer-hide moccasins with turned-up toes—waiting to board an airplane at the Tromsø airport. Search long and hard enough, and you might turn up a sod-roofed house, where old Grandfather Per—wearing high trousers—sits in a tub-chair in the corner downing his curds-and-whey. On the other hand, his grandson, clad in swimming trunks, will probably be sunning himself on a rock, listening to American music.

NORWAY TODAY

This long, narrow country stretches some 1,770km (1,100 miles) north to south, but rarely more than 96km (60 miles) east to west. Norway is a land of raw nature. It occupies the western and extreme northern portion of the Scandinavian peninsula, bordering Finland, Sweden, and Russia. In the west, it's 21,342km (13,232 miles). Along the country's western edge, some 60,896km (37,839 miles) of rugged coastline confront the often-turbulent North Atlantic Ocean.

There's plenty of breathing room for everybody. When you factor in the Arctic desolation of the north, Norway averages about 8 people per sq. km (20 people per sq. mile). Most of the four million inhabitants are concentrated in the swag-bellied south, where the weather is less severe. Even so, the population of Oslo, the capital, is less than half a million. Aside from Oslo, there are no really big cities; the populations of Bergen and Trondheim are 210,000 and 135,000, respectively.

Norway does not want to be a melting pot, and immigration is strictly controlled. The largest minority group is the Sami, who live in the far north; they have broad powers of self-government, including their own parliament. Although many people have emigrated from Norway—about one million to America alone—immigration to Norway from other countries has been limited. About 3.2% of the population originally came from Great Britain, Denmark, and Sweden.

Norway is a constitutional monarchy. Though without political power, Norway's royal family enjoys the subjects' unwavering support. The real power is in the Storting, or parliament. Women play a major role in government. Some 40% of all elected officials are women, and women head several government ministries. Many industries—especially energy—are fully or partially state-controlled. Oil from the North Sea is a vital resource; the government has a Ministry of Oil and Energy. The government grants large subsidies to agriculture and fisheries.

As a result of their natural surroundings, Norwegians are among the most athletic people in Europe. Nearly every Norwegian child learns to ski as readily as he learns to walk. They are also among the best-educated people in the world. Norway's educational standard has risen considerably since World War II, and some 90% of Norwegian young people take a 3-year course in higher education or vocational school after completing their compulsory education.

A Long-Tailed Seducer

At a cafe in Oslo, a woman picked up a fork, leaned over the table, and tapped her husband on the knuckles: "Keep your eyes off the *huldre*, darling."

The "*huldre*" was a tall blonde in pants at least three sizes too small.

In Norwegian folklore, a *huldre* is supposed to be a most beautiful woman—but she has a cow's tail tucked under her skirt, perhaps tied around her waist. And this bovine appendage is always dropping out at the most inopportune times. For her tail to drop off completely, she has to marry a man in a church.

The *huldre* makes a clever housewife and is resented—for that and other reasons—by Norwegian women. The Anna, Noram, or Birgit who wants to hang on to her husband is not averse to warning him against accepting an invitation to go home with a *huldre* for the night. The *huldre* has the power of stretching that night out for 7 years. At least, that's what many an errant Olav has claimed when he finally stumbles back to his spouse.

(Frankly, the tall blonde singled out probably wasn't a real *huldre*. It was impossible for her to conceal a caudal appendage under those pants. But that didn't matter. The wife knew her to be a *huldre*—and that was that.)

About 90% of the population belongs to the national Lutheran Church, of which the king is the titular head. Freedom of worship is guaranteed to all.

Because the economy depends significantly on foreign trade, most business is conducted in English. Norway has two official languages, Riksmal and Landsmal, both of Danish origin. The Sami, the indigenous people of the north, have their own language.

Cultural activities are important in Norway. The government subsidizes book publishing, guaranteeing sales of 1,000 copies of each book published for distribution to public libraries. Encouraging Norwegian writers helps preserve the language. Movie production, limited by population and language, fares poorly, however. Opera is fairly new to the country, and Norway didn't acquire a professional ballet ensemble until 1948. Folk music, however, has roots going back to Norse times and is still very much alive. Norway encourages the arts by providing a guaranteed income to active artists whose work has achieved and maintained a high standard over a period of years.

LOOKING BACK AT NORWAY

Norway has been inhabited since the end of the last ice age. The earliest Scandinavian settlers hunted reindeer and other game in these northern lands. Some 5,000 to 6,000 years ago, the inhabitants turned to agriculture, especially around the Oslofjord. Artifacts show that in the Roman era, Norway had associations with areas to the south.

The Age of the Vikings

Prehistory ended during the Viking era, roughly A.D. 800 to 1050. Much of what is known about this era wasn't written down, but has been conveyed through sagas passed by word of mouth or revealed by archaeological finds. Some scholars consider the looting of the Lindisfarne monastery in northern England in 793 the beginning of the "age of the Vikings."

DATELINE

793–1066 The age of the Vikings, when Norsemen terrorized the coasts of Europe.

872 Harald Fairhair conquers many small provinces and reigns as first king.

1001 Leif Eriksson discovers America (or so the sagas claim).

1030 Christianity is firmly established; Olav II is declared a saint.

1066 The Viking Age ends with the defeat of Harald III in England.

1350 The Black Death wipes out much of the population.

1397 Margaret becomes queen of Norway, Denmark, and Sweden at the Union of Kalmar.

1439 Danish rule is imposed on Norway.

1814 Norway breaks from Denmark and adopts a constitution, but comes under Swedish rule.

1905 The Norwegian parliament breaks from Sweden and declares independence.

continues

"The Vikings are coming!" became a dreadful cry along the coasts of Europe. The victims expected fire and sword. Scandinavian historians are usually kinder to the Vikings, citing the fact that they often went abroad to trade and colonize. From Norway, the Vikings branched out to settle in the Orkney and Shetland Islands (now part of Scotland). They also settled in the Scottish Hebrides and on the Isle of Man. Viking settlements were established on Greenland and Iceland, which had previously been uninhabited. The Norse communities on Greenland eventually died out. The sagas claim that in 1001, Leif Eriksson discovered "wineland of the good," a reference to the American continent. Many scholars, however, claim that the Vikings' long ships reached America long before Leif Eriksson.

The road to unification of Norway was rough. In 872, Harald Fairhair, after winning a battle near Stavanger, conquered many of the provinces; but other battles for unification took decades. Harald was followed by his son, Eric I—"Bloody Axe," to his enemies. Eric began his reign by assassinating two of his eight brothers and later killed five other brothers. His one surviving brother, Haakon, succeeded him as king in 954. Haakon tried unsuccessfully to convert Norway to Christianity. After he died in the Battle of Fitjar (960), Harald II Graafell, one of Eric's sons, became king of Norway. Cruel and oppressive, he died in battle in 970.

Haakon, son of Sigurd of Lade, became the next king of Norway. He resisted Danish attacks and ruled for about 25 years, but died in a peasant riot in 995. After the Battle of Swold in 1000, Norway was divided between Denmark and the Jarl of Lade.

Olaf II Haraldsson was a Viking until 1015, when he became king of Norway. Although oppressive and often cruel, he continued to spread Christianity. Canute of Denmark invaded Norway in 1028, sending Olav fleeing to England. Canute's son, Sweyn, ruled Norway from 1028 to 1035. Sweyn was forced out when Olav II was proclaimed a saint and his son, Magnus I, was made king. Magnus was also king of Denmark, a position he lost when Canute's nephew led a revolt against him and he was killed. Olav's sainthood firmly established Christianity in Norway.

1914	Norway declares its neutrality in World War I.
1920	Norway joins the League of Nations, ending its isolation.
1940	Nazi troops invade Norway; the king and government flee.
1945	Norway regains independence and executes its Nazi puppet ruler, Quisling.
1960s	An oil boom hits Norway.
1986	The Labor Party installs the first female prime minister, Gro Harlem Brundtland.
1989	A center-right coalition regains power.
1990	Brundtland becomes prime minister again.
1991	Harald V becomes king.
1994	Lillehammer plays host to XVII Olympic Winter Games.
1995	Norway wins Eurovision Song Contest, an annual cultural event observed by 600 million viewers.
1996	Eurovision Song Contest is held in Oslo; Norway takes second place.
1998	Oil prices fall, but Norway plunges ahead with costly engineering projects.
2001	U.N. group votes Norway the most desirable place to live in the world.

Harald Sigurdsson (known as Harald III) ruled Norway from 1046 until his death in 1066. His death marks the end of the Viking Age.

The Middle Ages

Wars with Denmark continued, and civil wars raged from 1130 to 1227. Norwegian towns and the Church continued to grow. Under Haakon V in the 13th century, Oslo became the capital of Norway. The Black Death reached Norway in 1350 and wiped out much of the population.

From 1362 to 1364, Norway and Sweden had a joint monarch, Haakon VI (1340–80), son of the Swedish king, Magnus Eriksson. Haakon married Margaret, daughter of the Danish king Valdemar Atterdag. Their son, Olav, was chosen to be the Danish king upon Valdemar's death in 1375. He inherited the throne of Norway after his father died in 1380, bringing Norway into a union with Denmark. The union lasted until 1814.

Union with Denmark

When Olav died at the age of 17, Margaret became regent of Norway, Denmark, and Sweden. She ruled through her nephew, Eric of Pomerania, who had become king of Norway in 1389. He was recognized as a joint ruler at Kalmar. Margaret was actually the power behind the throne until her death in 1412. Eric of Pomerania tried to rule the three countries, but Sweden and Norway rebelled. Eric fled in 1439 and Christopher III of Bavaria became the ruler, imposing Danish rule.

Denmark led Norway into the Seven Years' War of the North in 1563 and took unfair advantage of its position in trade, in the military, and even in surrendering Norwegian land to Sweden.

During the Napoleonic Wars (1807–14), Denmark and Norway were allied with France, although it created much economic hardship. Famine was widespread. In 1814, Frederik VI of Denmark surrendered to Napoleon's opponents and handed Norway over to Sweden. That officially ended 434 years of Danish rule over Norway.

2004	Princess Ingrid Alexandra, a possible future queen, is born
2005	New bridge links Sweden and Norway.
2008	Norway turns to the Barents Sea in its search for oil fields.
2010	Norway is named the sixth-best place in the world to live by *Newsweek* magazine.

Secession from Sweden

On May 17, 1814, an assembly adopted a constitution and chose Christian Frederik as the Norwegian king. May 17 is celebrated as Norwegian National Day. The Swedes objected and launched a military campaign, eventually subduing Norway. The Swedes accepted the Norwegian constitution, but only within a union of the two kingdoms. Christian Frederik fled.

Soon thereafter, Norway suffered through one of its greatest economic depressions. Norway's parliamentary assembly, the Stortinget, engaged in repeated conflicts with the Swedish monarchs. Bernadotte ruled over both Norway and Sweden as Charles XIV from 1818 to 1844.

By the 1830s, the economy of Norway had improved. The first railway line was laid in 1854. Its merchant fleet grew significantly between 1850 and 1880.

From the 1880s on, the Liberals in the Storting brought much-needed reform to the country. But by the end of the century, the conflict with Sweden was growing as more and more Norwegians demanded independence.

In August 1905, the Storting decided to dissolve the union with Sweden. Sweden agreed to let Norway rule itself. In October 1905, Norway held an election, and the son of Denmark's king was proclaimed king of Norway. He chose the name Haakon VII.

An Independent Norway

Free at last, Norway enjoyed peace and prosperity until the beginning of World War II. Even though the economy was satisfactory, thousands of Norwegians emigrated to the United States around the turn of the 20th century. In 1914, Norway joined Sweden and Denmark in declaring a policy of neutrality. Despite the declaration, around 2,000 Norwegian seamen lost their lives in the war because of submarine attacks and underwater mines.

In 1920, Norway joined the League of Nations, ending its policy of isolation. At the outbreak of World War II, Norway again declared its neutrality. Nonetheless, Allied forces mined Norway's waters in 1940, and the Nazis attacked on April 9, 1940. Great Britain and France provided some military assistance, but Norway fell after a 2-month struggle. The government and the royal family fled into exile in England, taking 1,000 ships of the Norwegian merchant fleet. In spite of the resistance movement, Nazis occupied Norway until the end of the war in 1945. Vidkun Quisling, the Norwegian minister of defense in the 1930s, served the Nazis as leader of the puppet government.

Quisling was executed following the Nazi retreat from Norway. On June 7, 1945, the government-in-exile returned from Britain. The retreating Nazis had followed a scorched-earth policy in the Finnmark region of the north, destroying almost everything of value. In the late 1940s, Norway began to rebuild its shattered economy.

After an abortive attempt to form a Nordic defense alliance, Norway and Denmark joined NATO in 1949. The Communist Party tried to secure recognition in Norway but failed.

By the 1960s, oil prospecting in the North Sea had yielded rich finds, which led to a profound restructuring of Norwegian trade and industry. In 1972, Norway voted not to enter the Common Market, following a bitter political dispute.

Norway had a non-Socialist government from 1981 to 1986. In 1986, Labor Party leader Gro Harlem Brundtland headed a minority government as Norway's first female prime minister. She introduced seven women into her 18-member cabinet.

Norway Just Grows & Grows

Without conquering other nations, it's almost impossible for a country to expand its coastline by 25,600km (15,900 miles), but Norway has done just that without invading its neighbors, as the Vikings did in days of yore. Today the conqueror is a computer.

Norwegian mapmakers in 2002 announced that computer programs are able to measure thousands of tiny inlets and islands in Norway, something that was virtually impossible 3 decades ago. The old figures gave Norway a coastline of 56,928km (35,373 miles) on the mainland; 35,586km (22,112 miles) around the islands. The new figures suggest that Norway's mainland coastline is actually 3,968km (2,460 miles) longer than previously believed and that the coastline around the islands is greater by 21,872km (13,590 miles).

"We are still the same," Tore Hegheim, a resident of Tromsø, said over the state radio network, NRK, "only our country got much bigger."

Soon, however, tumbling oil prices and subsequent unemployment led to a recession. The Labor government lost the 1989 elections. A center-right coalition assumed control of government. In November 1990, Brundtland returned to office as prime minister, this time with nine women in her 19-member cabinet. In 1991, Olav V died and was succeeded by his son, Harald V.

Although some Conservatives objected, Norway applied for membership in the European Union (E.U.) in 1993. The country also began to assert itself more on the international scene. Thorvald Stoltenberg, the minister of foreign affairs, was named peace negotiator for ravaged Bosnia-Herzegovina and, in clandestine meetings held outside Oslo, helped effect a rapprochement between the PLO and Israel. All these history-making events were eclipsed by the XVII Olympic Winter Games, held in Lillehammer in February 1994. In November 1994, Norwegians rejected a nonbinding referendum on E.U. membership. Following that, everyone waited for the Norwegian parliament to vote on whether the country would join. The parliament deliberately avoided the issue and did not vote on the matter. The referendum, though nonbinding, remains in force, and Norway is still not a member of the E.U. But that does not mean the country has no economic links with the rest of Europe. In 1994, Norway reinforced its commitments to membership in the EEAA (European Economic Area Agreement), an association initiated in 1992 to ensure its access to the E.U.'s single market. It includes cooperation in a variety of cultural and economic areas.

By 1998, Norway was having its share of troubles, as oil prices plunged to their lowest levels in a decade. Turmoil in financial markets knocked its currency, the krone, lower and prompted the central bank to double interest rates to 10%. The popular prime minister Kjell Magne Bondevik, who took over the office in 1997, stunned the country by taking a temporary leave from office. His doctors said he was having a "depressive reaction" to too much work and stress. In late 1998, Bondevik came back to his job—and is now running the country.

Norway has recently pushed forward with major engineering projects. The country is connecting its sparsely inhabited outcroppings and linking its interior fjord-side villages in an effort to stem the flow of people to larger towns and villages. At Hitra,

VIKINGS WERE people TOO

Throughout its early history, Norway had much contact with the outside world, but it was with the beginning of the so-called Viking Age that the country really became part of European history. Spanning roughly 300 years from A.D. 793 to 1066, the Viking Age saw few defined differences in national identity among Norwegians, Danes, and Swedes. Still, there tended to be three general geographic trajectories for the Vikings: Those based in Sweden headed east, those from Denmark ventured south and southwest, and those in Norway tended to sail west. Norwegians first became most notorious abroad in the guise of Viking marauders who plundered churches and monasteries. But behind this rather one-sided picture there lies a far more complex interplay of political and cultural factors. As fierce, unyielding warriors, the Vikings came to affect nearly every region to which they sailed, but the Vikings also played determining roles in the social and cultural life of Europe and beyond. As expert shipbuilders, they set up thriving coastal market centers, establishing the first towns and cities of Ireland; they were the first to settle Iceland, the first non-Inuit to set up communities on Greenland, and the first Europeans to "discover" North America.

WHY DID THE RAIDING BEGIN?

Though the earliest historical records are sparse in the information they offer, it is presumed that the first Vikings ventured out on their first expedition from Viken (they became known as Víkingar or "Vikings" on account of this provenance), a small bit of land flanking the Oslofjord in present-day Norway, on quick raids to the coast of places like Sheppey, Somerset, the Hebrides, Brittany, and Frisia. Maritime piracy had grown in Europe around the end of the 7th century as a result of an increase in trade between the Continent and England, which encouraged the development of several large trading centers in towns and cities including Hamwic (Southampton), York, London, and Quentovic (near Boulogne). Arctic fur pelts became one of the most prized commodities for wealthy Europeans, and by the middle of the 8th century several trading posts had been established in Norwegian and Danish towns which imported fur, animal hides, feathers, and whale bone from Sami communities in the north. Contact with western European merchants familiarized Scandinavians with European sailing and shipbuilding methods and gave them glimpses of the growing pockets of wealth in Europe. Most importantly, however, it allowed them to witness first-hand the internal conflicts plaguing numerous European kingdoms—political feuds and schisms from which Vikings were later able to profit.

The Scandinavian rulers and chieftains who profited most from the growth of the new trade were those who maintained control over the shipping routes and entrances to the trading centers—namely the early Norwegian and Danish kings, ruling from positions in and around southern Norway and Denmark in sites that allowed them to control the strategically important waterway entrances to the Baltic Sea. They often served as overlords, exacting tolls and tariffs on the sales and purchases of goods. Many subjects soon became envious of the gross amounts of income seized by these kings, and instead of accepting overlordship, chose exile to the seas to follow the trading routes to the origin of the wealth entering the country.

VIKING EXPANSION

The Vikings quickly set out on extensive raids, first around the North Sea and mainland Europe, invading territories as diverse as the British Isles, Iceland, and Greenland, then moving on to the Iberian peninsula, western Europe, and North Africa. When Viking activity in western Europe was curtailed in the 10th century, they shifted their eyes east to new trading posts such as Staraya Ladoga and Constantinople, and smaller markets on the Caspian Sea and Dnepr River were stores for the masses of Islamic Samanid silver that had made its way to Russia via Transoxania (modern-day central Asia). At their peak, the Vikings' rule extended from the eastern seaboard of North America to the Volga Bend and the regions surrounding the Black and Caspian seas, and from North Cape south to the Straits of Gibraltar.

The last major Viking expedition took place in 1066 at the Battle of Stamford Bridge, when their leader, Harald Harđráđi, lost to the King of England. Harđráđi's successors back in Norway subsequently abandoned their expansionist policy and focused on maintaining domestic order and ruling over the Norse islands of the Faroes, the Hebrides, and Iceland, while the kingdoms of Denmark and Sweden went on to experience new periods of prosperity after they pursued expansion into pockets of the Baltic. With centuries of maritime assault and unprecedented expansion having drawn to a close, the Vikings had left their mark on the peoples of Europe and beyond.

IN DEFENSE OF THE VIKINGS

While they will invariably be most remembered for the havoc they wreaked on the peoples they sought to conquer, it is nevertheless important to remember that Vikings were people too. The most common conception of the Vikings locates them as ruthless, burly, helmeted barbarians, sword and battle-axe in hand, careening from their ships onto foreign soil, engaging in bloody battle, raiding churches, kidnapping local women, and generally wreaking havoc all around. But the image of the Viking as plunderer, pillager, rapist, conqueror, and colonizer is only one side of the story.

Vikings regularly settled in the lands they conquered, set up farmsteads and cultivated the land, and integrated—if they didn't assimilate completely—with the local population. Much of this one-sidedness in popular arguments stems from the overwhelming reliance on the primary sources themselves. The non-Scandinavian chronicles that many historians often cite focus themselves invariably on the mass destruction and gross social upheaval which the Vikings inflicted upon their victims. Such sources neglect to consider the Vikings' enduring influence on trade, language, and the political and cultural institutions of the countries and peoples with which they interacted. The Vikings won their battles not because they were superb militiamen, but because they were excellent sailors. Their ships—flat-bottomed vessels with a draught of only 1m (39 in.)—could easily sail close to the coasts and through shallow canals. And like any other people, they tilled the soil, raised cattle, and hunted and fished.

A SIFTER OF VIKING secrets

The world press gave scant attention to the death, in 1997, of Norwegian archaeologist Anne-Stine Ingstad, but she was a pioneer, sifting through the sandy soil above a Newfoundland beach to uncover the remains of a Viking outpost.

She was the wife of Helge Ingstad, whose discovery of the site in 1961 produced the first conclusive evidence that Vikings had made a North American beachhead 500 years before Columbus. Vikings sailed from a colony in Greenland to reach the North American continent in what is today Canada. Icelandic sagas had described the voyages in detail, and few scholars doubted that Leif Eriksson and other Vikings had made such voyages and explorations. But until the Ingstads made their startling discoveries, no hard evidence of a Viking presence existed—only a spate of spurious artifacts.

The initial discovery was met with skepticism. But once Anne-Stine Ingstad started to dig, most doubts evaporated. Her husband had used vivid geographic descriptions in Icelandic sagas to find the camp described by Eriksson and others. Once the site was discovered, she carried out excavations over several months. In time, she uncovered the foundations of eight buildings, including a large house almost identical to Eriksson's great hall in Greenland.

In 1964, she unearthed a tiny stone spinning wheel, suggesting that female Vikings had used the camp. In 1980, UNESCO designated the settlement, L'Anse aux Meadows, a World Heritage Site.

a largely barren island off the west coast, a 5.5-km (3½-mile) tunnel (the world's deepest road tunnel) has been built at a cost of more than NOK1 billion. It links mainland Norway to a hamlet with some 4,100 residents. On the North Cape, at Norway's Arctic tip, a $140 million bridge and tunnel were constructed to Mager Island, home to only 3,600 people (and more than that many reindeer). An additional $135 million went into the earth in the mountains east of Bergen to link the towns of Aurland (pop. 1,900) and Lærdal (pop. 2,250). At 24km (15 miles), this is the longest road tunnel in the world. A more artistic bridge opened in December 2001. The designer? None other than Leonardo da Vinci. The 99-m (325-ft.) laminated timber bridge links Norway and Sweden at the town of Aas, 26km (16 miles) south of Oslo.

The year 2001 also was witness to the marriage of Crown Prince Haakon and Mette-Mari Tjessem Hoiby, a single mom who lived with the royal before marrying him. The crown prince and princess became parents to a daughter in 2004. Ingrid Alexandra may become the first reigning queen of Norway since 1412, when Margaret I reigned (1388–1412).

In 2009, Norway was the sixth-biggest exporter of oil in the world, just behind Kuwait. The country's petroleum production has been gradually declining as its oil fields have matured. Faced with exhaustion of resources in the North Sea, oil and gas companies have turned to the vast Barents Sea; in 2009, an unprecedented 65 wells were drilled and an unheard-of 28 well discoveries were made. State petroleum company Statoil announced in 2010 that it is investing US$3.4 billion to increase oil recovery in its existing wells by 25%. Additional wells are being drilled and new pipelines built. The oilmen, predictably, are engaged in fights with environmental groups, who want to protect the fragile environment and its major fishing waters.

Norway's established state Petroleum Fund, which will finance government programs after oil and gas resources are depleted, exceeded US$457 billion in early 2010. Furthermore, the country is enjoying extremely large foreign trade surpluses thanks to relatively high oil prices. And the country's unemployment rate has remained remarkably low—3.3% in 2010—despite the global financial crisis.

This oil-fueled economy has made Norway a magnet for young Swedes, because their own economy has lagged far behind. Long the poor cousin of Scandinavia, Norway has forged ahead, and thousands of Swedes are flocking there to work, many in menial jobs. The number of Swedes living and working in Norway doubled between 1990 and 2008.

THE LAY OF THE LAND

Norway is one of nature's last great frontiers in Europe—mountains, glaciers, and lakes cover 70% of its land. Less than 4% of its territory, mostly in the south-central area, is arable. Within Norway's Jotunheimen range are the highest mountain peaks in Europe north of the Alps. Norway has about 17,000 glaciers. Along the western coast, some 50,000 islands protect the mainland from some of the worst storms in the North Atlantic.

Norway has a varied and changing climate. The coastal zones in the west and east normally experience cool summers and temperate winters. Inland, summers are warm, and winters cold and dry. In the extreme north, 100 days of snowfall each year isn't uncommon.

The fjords are not only a distinguishing feature of Norway's landscape, but also a special attraction to visitors. These were created thousands of years ago when the ocean flowed into glacial valleys. These "fingers" of water cut deep into the landscape. The most intriguing of the fjords, the Sognefjord, is 205km (127 miles) long and extremely deep.

Norway's rivers tend to be short and volatile. A smooth flow of water is often "agitated" by waterfalls and patches of white water. Because they're not suited for transportation, rivers are primarily sources of food, principally salmon. The longest river in Scandinavia, the Glomma (or Gløma), runs through southwestern Norway.

Norway's position on the globe has earned it the nickname "Land of the Midnight Sun." Towns in northern Norway, such as Tromsø, experience 24 hours of sunshine in summer, and 24 hours of darkness in winter. Even in southern Norway, the summer days are long, and the winter nights may last more than 17 hours.

Thick birch and pine forests cover the mountains; in the lowlands, oak forests abound. Spruce forests cover the southeast and middle regions. The steep mountains in the east are among the tallest in Europe and the site of some of the world's most challenging alpine ski runs. There is excellent hiking in the Vassafaret district around Fløm, where the mountains are rounded, gentle, and dotted with alpine lakes and rivers.

The mountains are also home to ravens, eagles, grouse, and gyrfalcons. They serve as a migratory home to the pure-white snowy owl. Norway's countryside and forests teem with Arctic animals such as reindeer, arctic fox, wolves, bears, lynx, elk, beavers, and otters. Along the coast are nesting grounds for puffins and cormorants; whales, salmon, and cod frolic in the icy seas offshore. Through Norway's conservation efforts and strict regulations regarding the environment, these animals and fish flourish much as they have in the past.

ART & ARCHITECTURE

From the Age of the Vikings, Norway has given the world art and architecture, ranging from its famous wooden stave churches to the paintings of Edvard Munch, Scandinavia's most celebrated artist.

Art

Just before the Viking period, carved stones bearing runic inscriptions began appearing in Norway from the 3rd century A.D. on.

The Vikings may not have been the insensitive barbarians their reputation has it, as they showed a high artistic skill as reflected by the decorations on the Oseberg burial ship at the Vikingskiphuset (Viking Ship Museum) in Oslo (p. 132). The ship has a carved likeness of a ferocious beast, a traditional feature of Viking boats. The Vikings seemed to have been inspired by Carolingian art, which stemmed from Byzantine traditions.

Not much is left of Christian art in Norway. The country converted to Christianity in the 10th century. In early art, human figures were not often represented, the early Norwegians preferring to stick to the dragonlike heads as seen on the prows of Viking ships that terrified western Europe.

It took a long time before art firmly established itself in Norway. Cut off from the cultural life of Europe, Norwegian art experienced a long slumber from the 15th to the 18th centuries. The coming of the plague and the loss of political independence are blamed for this decline.

Local painters showed little originality, preferring to copy more famous examples established by artists in the south or central Europe.

As a decorative motif, the painted rose swept the country in the mid-1700s, introducing a striking use of color for the first time in Norwegian art. Later, the rose was combined with the acanthus leaf as a motif. The trend was toward abstract design in most Norwegian popular art.

Even as late as the beginning of the 1800s, there was little noteworthy art. The most original artist was Johan Christian Clausen Dahl (1788–1857), a major landscape painter who drew his inspiration from the North German Romantic School. His cloud studies are still viewed as brilliant art today.

French influence in painting made itself known in the works of the painter Christian Krohg (1852–1925). But with the birth of Edvard Munch (1863–1944), Norway was to experience an artist who became the most celebrated painter in Scandinavia. His works can be seen at, among other places, the Munch Museet (Edvard Munch Museum) in Oslo (p. 129).

Munch became the leading force in the creation of the Expressionist style. *The Scream* (1895) remains one of the most reproduced paintings on Earth. In this masterpiece, he used form and color (reds and yellows) to convey his deep personal vision of the horror of existence. In his works Munch explored the themes of life, love, fear, melancholy, and death. He portrayed women either as frail, innocent sufferers or the reason for jealousy and despair.

Other notable artists that you'll see in the museums of Norway include Christian Skredsvig (1854–1924), whose most famous work is the neoromantic *The Sallow Flute* (1889), and Adolph Tidemand (1814–1876), who became known for his paintings of old Norwegian farm culture. The Nasjonalgalleriet (National Gallery) in Oslo (p. 129) owns more than 100 of his works.

Another Norwegian painter, Nikolai Astrup (1880–1928), was also a neoromantic, preferring clear, strong colors in his landscapes. A pioneer among female artists was Harriet Backer (1845–1932), who was influenced by Impressionism, though most of her work is classified as realist.

Another woman is among the most distinguished of all Norwegian artists today. Born in 1971, Marianne Aulie sells works for millions of Norwegian kroner, although the art historian Stig Andersen calls her paintings "soft pornography." Her repertoire includes everything from abstract paintings to Madonnas and images of clowns. She likes to bathe her paintings in champagne to get a particular texture from the alcohol reacting with acrylic paint.

Sculpture in Norway first appeared as dragons on bedposts, carved chairs, and drinking vessels shaped like Viking ships, and on reliquaries in the form of churches. The first Norwegian sculptor who enjoyed an international reputation was Adolf Gustav Vigeland (1869–1943), whose great works remain the statuary groups he created for Vigelandsparken (p. 131) in Oslo. The chief treasure here is his Vigeland Monolith. Naked figures, entwined and struggling, cover the obelisk.

A distinguished Norwegian-Danish sculptor, Stephan (Abel) Sinding (1846–1922), was considered "too modern" by many traditional Norwegian art critics. But Danish beer baron Carl Jacobsen thought otherwise, and that is why the largest collection in the world of Sinding sculptures reside today in the Ny Carlsberg Glyptotek in Copenhagen. However, you can see the Sinding statue of Henrik Ibsen at the National Theater in Oslo.

Architecture

As a sparsely populated country on the northern edge of Europe, Norway did not distinguish itself in architecture the way countries such as Germany and Italy did. Little survives of early Christian architecture in Norway. Constructed in the 11th century, the first building of importance was Nidaros Domkirke (p. 362) in Trondheim. This cathedral was reconstructed (1282–1320) in the late Norman style, at which time it incorporated many Gothic features.

Norwegian architecture flourished in the country's *stavkirker* (stave churches), which were built before the Reformation, using as inspiration ancient pagan temples. The churches were constructed on a framework of staves, or heavily wooded posts, supporting the walls and roofs. There are 28 well-preserved stave churches remaining today, constituting Norway's most important contribution to world architectural history.

These churches were characterized by their many-storied and steeply sloping roofs. Gables, pinnacles, and cupolas were used in abundance. After the construction of these churches, Norwegian architecture fell into a slumber that lasted 3 centuries.

In the early part of the 1800s, architecture in Norway fell under the influence of the Swedish monarch Charles XIV (1763–1844). Norway was locked into a political union with Sweden, which dominated the country. In the development of Christiania (later Oslo) as the capital of Norway, the king imposed a neoclassical style in architecture.

DID YOU KNOW?

- Norwegians have one of the highest per-capita incomes in the world.
- While medieval alchemists were trying to make gold, they discovered *akevitt* (aquavit, or schnapps), the national "firewater" of Norway.
- Norway has the world's largest foreign trade per capita.
- The average population density is only 13 inhabitants per sq. km (34 per sq. mile), compared to 96 per sq. km (249 per sq. mile) for Europe as a whole.
- Norway and Russia share a short land border and have disputed control of a sea area the size of Belgium, Switzerland, and Austria combined.
- Hammerfest is the world's northernmost town with a population of more than 5,000.

However, in the countryside, vernacular architecture consisted mainly of wood structures, which can still be seen in many open-air museums throughout the country, including the Norsk Folkemuseum (p. 130) in Oslo and the Maihaugen Museum (p. 198) in Lillehammer.

Around the turn of the 20th century, *Jugendstil,* a variant of Art Nouveau, came into vogue, especially when the port of Ålesund, which had burned to the ground, was almost entirely rebuilt in that style. In the 1920s, modernism prevailed, which in Norway was called *funkis.* This simplified functional style would prevail until 1940, when Norway was conquered by Nazi Germany.

After the war, modern buildings were often multistoried, with wings, using timber or brick. New housing developments were set in long rows rather than in rectangular blocks to maximize light and sunshine.

The architecture of the 21st century can be daringly avant-garde, as evoked by the futuristic Oslo Opera House, designed by the Norwegian architecture firm Snøhetta (the same company designing the Bibliotheca Alexandrina in Egypt), and opened in 2008. With its marble-clad surface and enormous glass facade sporting solar panels, the building evokes a Norwegian iceberg rising out of—or slipping into—the cold Arctic Sea.

NORSE MYTHOLOGY

Prior to the arrival of Christian monks in 826, the inhabitants of Scandinavia—and the Vikings who had settled elsewhere—clung strongly to their beliefs in a pagan religion, a system which has been passed down largely through the Old Norse sagas and *eddas* written down several centuries after Christianization of the region. Norse mythology is a multilayered world of contradictions, with many marked resemblances to Greek and other myth systems.

The Gods

Power and omniscience in Norse mythology were ascribed to a fixed number of deities, split between the *Æsir* ("Sky Gods") who symbolize power, wisdom, and war, and the *Vanir* ("Earth Gods"), associated with wealth and fertility. Their cosmology is a disc-shaped world surrounded by the sea, at the center of which is Midgard

(Miðgarðr in Old Norse), the home of mankind, with the gods' home lying just above in Asgard (Ásgarðr). Below this realm are the worlds of Niflheim and Hel, and across the sea is Utgard (Útgarðar), the home of the adversarial Jotunheim giants.

Though fewer in number, Norse gods are somewhat akin to the coterie of Roman gods, and the Germanic languages—English among them—derive four days of the week from the names of Norse gods: Tiu (Tuesday), Odin (Wednesday), Thor (Thursday), and Freya (Friday). The chief god, Odin, leader of gods, warriors, and kings, is the most powerful and best known for his unabashed warrior ethic: Though he knew he was destined to die at Ragnarök, he embraced his fate and entered battle with guns ablaze. In addition to serving as the god of war, magic, wisdom, and poetry, he ruled over the Valkyries (literally, "choosers of the slain"), minor female deities who served him as warriors and who, according to the stories in the famous tome entitled *Prose Edda*, were charged with "serving drink and looking after the tableware and drinking vessels." Although Valkyries are often depicted in mythologically inspired artwork as strapping blonde maidens armed with spears, shields, and helmets, and riding winged horses, written sources more often portrayed them as riding on the backs of the wolves which vultured raven-like about the corpses of dead warriors. Their formidable role was to select the most heroic of soldiers, *Einherjar*, men who had died valiantly in battle, and transport them to Valhalla ("Hall of the Slain"), Odin's paradise-cum-military training ground. Odin anticipated the need for trained warriors to assist him at Ragnarök, and once in Valhalla the *Einherjar* would train from dawn to dusk. Soldiers who didn't fare so lucky as to make it to Valhalla ended up in the home of the dead, Hel, a shivering shadowy place said to consist of a grand hall with a roof made from the spines of serpents whose poison drips down onto those who wade in the rivers of blood below, undead beings nourished only by the excrement from goats. Hel is situated well below the underworld of Niflheim.

Odin was married to Frigga, goddess of marriage, home, and family, and had several sons, the most beloved of whom was Thor, god of fire, thunder, and lightning and the main enemy of the giants. Thor was also widely worshipped for fertility, as were Freya and her brother Frey, who also maintained a monopoly on the virtues of love and healing. Other gods include Njord, god of the sea; Tyr, preserver of justice; Skadi, goddess of anger and hunting; and the handsome, gold-toothed Heimdall, whose call will signal the onset of the apocalypse (though his most enviable trait is that he could go for years on end without a wink of sleep). The Norse gods are not immortal in the traditional sense of the term: They will be destroyed in the apocalypse in a battle with the giants, led by Loki, a giant bound by Promethean chains who presides over fire, mischief, and trickery and is said to have killed one of Odin's sons. Other minor gods include a coterie of elves, dwarves, and giants, many of whom were arch-enemies of the main gods.

Creation & Apocalypse

The Norse accounts of the beginning and end of the world are described in the *Völuspá* ("The Seeress's Prophesy"), the first and best-known poem in the sensational *Poetic Edda*, the 65-stanza verse history of Norse mythological civilization. The text exists as a sort of sacred book of Scandinavian religion, composed in the late 10th century at a time when Scandinavia's pagan religious practices were being thwarted by the onset of Christianity. The *Völuspá* is recounted by a seeress so old she remembers the beginning of the world and so wise that she can see forth to its demise, *Ragnarök*

("Doom of the Gods"), the prophesied battle at the end of the world, a momentous, fiery struggle during which nearly all the world's gods, monsters, and mortals will perish and the universe will be destroyed. The verses are rich with descriptive attention to detail and rank as some of the most impassioned in all of religious history.

NORWAY IN POPULAR CULTURE

Books

If runic inscriptions, dating from the 1st and 2nd centuries A.D., are to be counted, Norway has the oldest literary tradition of all the Scandinavian countries. The Vikings had a poetic tradition that was almost entirely oral. Legends were told by each generation, sagas of great heroes and mighty adventures, mostly at sea.

Court minstrels, called *scalds,* wrote down compositions to be sung before kings, including Harald I (850–933), the first king of Norway.

The Vikings, by Johannes Brondsted (Pelican Books), is one of the best written documents about the age of the Vikings. Viking fans will also be drawn to ***The Vinland Sagas: The Norse Discovery of America,*** translated by Magnus Magnusson and Hermann Palsson (Penguin Classics), an incredible saga detailing how Viking-Age Norwegians sailed in their long ships to the eastern coast of "Vinland" (America) in the 10th century.

The Middle Ages in Norway brought the spread of Christianity, with a large body of literature. In the secular realm, stories from the Arthurian cycle and French romances were adopted. Following Norway's union with Denmark at the end of the 14th century, a cultural decline began. Danes abolished the Old Norse tongue. When the Reformation came, many ancient Norwegian manuscripts were destroyed. Only the peasants kept national culture alive. The country didn't even have a printing press until 1643.

In the 18th century, a towering figure emerged in Norwegian literature in the form of Ludvig Holberg (1684–1754). Norway's voice in the Age of Reason, Holberg was a satirist, poet, playwright, and prose writer. Living mainly in Denmark, this Norwegian had a tremendous impact on Danish drama. His literary influence in Norway centered on historical writings and essays.

By the 19th century, Norwegian writing began to be appreciated by the world. ***The Governor's Daughter,*** by Camilla Collett, published in 1854, became the first modern Norwegian novel. Two towering writers emerged: Playwright Henrik Ibsen (1828–1906) and Bjornstjerne Björnson (1832–1910).

Ibsen was the first Norwegian to devote himself entirely to theater writing. His verse-plays, ***Brand*** and ***Peer Gynt,*** established his greatness, and these were followed by a number of plays, the most famous of which are ***A Doll's House, Hedda Gabler,*** and ***The Master Builder.*** Ibsen's plays today are performed all over the world and are available in various editions in book form.

Björnson won the Nobel Prize for literature in 1903. A poet, playwright, journalist, and politician, he was also deeply involved in social and religious problems. There are English translations of some of his most evocative creations, including his celebrated rustic novel ***Arne,*** first published in 1859, and ***The Fisher Maiden,*** published in 1868.

The best female novelist to emerge between the two world wars was Sigrid Undset (1882–1949). She was awarded the Nobel Prize for literature in 1928. She was a Christian writer, and her values were not political. Today she is mainly praised for her three-volume masterpiece ***Kristin Lavransdatter*** (Penguin Classics, 2005), which tells of love and religion in medieval Norway. Her later works include such widely known books as ***Ida Elisabeth,*** in 1932, and ***The Faithful Wife,*** in 1936. With the coming of the Nazis, her books were banned and she fled Norway.

Norwegian travel writing has been linked to voyages of discovery. Both Fridtjof Nansen (1861–1930) and Roald Amundsen (1872–1928) published detailed accounts of their travels. Nansen's books, such as ***The First Crossing of Greenland*** (1890), are still widely read, as are the works of Amundsen, including ***The South Pole*** (1912).

The Kon-Tiki Expedition by Thor Heyerdahl details the saga of a modern-day Viking, who set out on a balsa raft with five comrades and sailed 6,920km (4,290 miles) in 1947—all the way from Peru to Polynesia. ***Kon-Tiki Man: An Illustrated Biography of Heyerdahl,*** by Thor himself, highlights his attempt to document his idea that Polynesia was settled by people migrating west from South America.

Among contemporaries, the bestselling author today is Norwegian fantasy writer Margit Sandemo, whose novel ***Spellbound*** (The Tagman Press, 2008) has been translated into English. Some 40 million copies of her novels are in print. Two other popular writers today are Dag Solstad, who has a great ability to describe modern consciousness, and Herbjørg Wassmo, who enjoys international acclaim for her novels such as ***Dina's Book*** (Arcade Publishing, 1994), which was made into a film in 2002 with French actor Gérard Depardieu.

During the 1980s and 1990s, a number of Norwegian novels were noticed by international audiences, including Jostein Gaarder's ***Sophie's World,*** Lars Saabye Christensen's ***Beatles,*** and Ingvar Ambjørnsen's ***Hvite Niggere.*** Additionally, playwright Jon Fosse has seen no small amount of international acclaim.

More recently, author Per Petterson's compelling (if melancholic) novel ***Out Stealing Horses*** received rave reviews when its English translation by Anne Born was released in 2007. The story deals with the confusion, regret, and pain of a man who is forced to confront his past during a period of self-exile in a cabin in rural eastern Norway. Other authors to keep an eye out for include Hans Herbjørnsrud, Ingvar Ambjørnsen, and Frode Grytten, a Bergen-based sports journalist, author, and poet. For some real insight into very recent modern Norwegian literature in English translation, pick up a copy of *McSweeney's* issue #35 (available at www.mcsweeneys.net), which offers nearly a dozen short stories by contemporary authors.

Film

The Norwegian film industry has lagged far behind those in Sweden and Denmark. In olden days, talented Norwegian film directors ended up in Hollywood.

One of the first Norwegian films to attract worldwide attention was the 1951 *Kon-Tiki,* exploring the epic voyage of Thor Heyerdahl. It received the Academy Award that year for a documentary. It wasn't until 2006 that another Norwegian film won another Oscar, this time for Best Animated Short Film, *The Danish Poet,* narrated by Norwegian screen legend Liv Ullman.

Another great Norwegian film, Nils Gaup's *Pathfinder,* made in 1987, was based on the legend of the Lapps. It was an enormous international success and the second Norwegian film nominated for an Oscar.

Peter and the Wolf, produced in Norway, received an Oscar for Best Animated Short Film in 2008.

FAMOUS norwegians

Bjørnstjerne Bjørnson (1832–1910): A major Norwegian writer, he recorded and adapted into literary forms many of the folk tales that later inspired Henrik Ibsen. In 1857, he took over Ibsen's post as director of the Bergen Theater. His historical plays brought him world acclaim, and he became radically involved in Norwegian nationalism, campaigning for a country politically independent of its colonial links with Denmark. One of his poems was adopted as the national anthem of Norway, "Ja, Vi Elsker Dette Lanet" ("Yes, I Love This Land"). He won the Nobel Prize in 1903.

Kirsten Flagstad (1895–1962): The greatest Wagnerian singer in the history of opera was born in Hamar, Norway. Her 1933 performance at the Wagner Festival in Bayreuth, Germany, brought her world acclaim. She made her debut at the Metropolitan Opera House in New York City in 1935 as Sieglinde in *Die Walküre.*

Edvard Grieg (1843–1907): Norway's national composer, aka the "Chopin of the North," became famous for adapting musical themes from Norwegian folk tunes, as in *The Peer Gynt Suite,* for example. He was born in Bergen to an English father and a Norwegian mother.

Knut Hamsun (1859–1952): In 1888, a Danish magazine published a portion of his novel, *Hunger.* Hamsun was 19 years old. This novel, along with *Growth of the Soil* and *The Women at the Well,* earned him international fame. In 1920, he won the Nobel Prize for literature.

Thor Heyerdahl (1914–2002): In 1937, this Norwegian ethnologist began laying the groundwork for a series of research expeditions to the Pacific, the most important of which, in 1947, involved the *Kon-Tiki* expedition from Peru to the islands of Polynesia. In 1951, he won an Academy Award for his documentary (see "Kon-Tiki Museum" in chapter 6, p. 139). In 1969 and 1970, he led two *Ra* expeditions, which sailed from Morocco to Barbados and proved that early mariners were able to cross the Atlantic. Many of his books have become bestsellers, including *Aku-Aku,* a study of the tribal ethnologies of Easter Island, eventually translated into 32 languages.

Henrik Ibsen (1828–1906): One of the greatest modernist-realist playwrights,

More and more Norwegian films are finding world audiences, including world releases of such films as Alexander Rosler's *Mendel,* Pal Sletaune's *Junk Mail,* and Erik Skoldbjærg's *Insomnia.* In recent years, there have been the Norwegian horror comedy *Død Snø* (2009) and the gangster comedy *Tomme Tønner* (2010). Some film critics have hailed this avalanche of new films as a "Norwave in cinema."

Music

Norwegian music made little impact on the world until the 19th century. Ole Bull (1810–80) attracted major attention and even performed on a concert tour in America. He was one of the finest violinists of his time, composing mainly virtuoso pieces for the violin.

Norway's first composer to achieve world renown, however, was Edvard Grieg (1843–1907). He produced a specifically Norwegian type of music as evoked by his he was the author of *A Doll's House, Hedda Gabler, The Master Builder,* and *Peer Gynt.*

Trygve Lie (1896–1968): Lie was a leading Labor party lawyer and politician. In 1940, he was named foreign minister of a Norwegian government in exile during the Nazi occupation. In 1946, he was elected secretary-general of the United Nations, serving for 5 years. In 1950, he undertook a "great peace mission," which proposed controls of atomic energy and arms and the creation of a UN body for prevention of violence outbreaks; he met with Truman, Stalin, UK Prime Minister Attlee, and French President Vincent Auriol. He also supported the United Nations' effort to send troops to Korea. In 1951, his term was extended as secretary-general, but he resigned because of ongoing Soviet refusal to recognize him.

Edvard Munch (1863–1944): The greatest Scandinavian painter's most famous works include the gut-wrenching *The Scream* (1893) and *The Bridge* (1901), each conveying a sense of horror that became consistent with the philosophies of the existentialists. His murals are on display at Oslo University.

Fridtjof Nansen (1861–1930): A world explorer, he dreamed of crossing the ice caps of Greenland, a remarkable feat that brought him glory in 1889. He led the Norwegian delegation to the first assembly of the League of Nations in 1920, and in 1922 was awarded the Nobel Peace Prize for his work repatriating prisoners of war.

Liv Ullmann (b. 1938): The famous Norwegian actress made her stage debut in 1957 and became known in the 1960s for her work with the National Theater. World acclaim came through roles in the films of Ingmar Bergman, her lover at the time. These included *Cries and Whispers, Scenes from a Marriage,* and *Persona.* She has appeared on Broadway and has written two volumes of memoirs.

Sigrid Undset (1882–1943): *Kristen Lavransdatter* is considered this writer's masterpiece.

Adolf Gustav Vigeland (1869–1943): This sculptor, whose monumental works viewed collectively are one of Oslo's major sights, was a controversial artist—some claim a genius, others a madman. See his obelisk in Frognerpark (p. 29).

"Peer Gynt Suite" (1888). His piano "Concerto" and three sonatas for violin and piano are his finest works.

After Grieg's death, the major composer was Christian Sinding (1856–1941), who achieved fame for his composition for piano, "Rustle of Spring."

The most distinguished composer of the 20th century was Fartein Valen (1887–1952), who is known for his contribution to atonal music.

In the countryside, Norway has been known for centuries for its folk music tradition. Folk music is usually performed by soloists, with instrumentals commonly played on the Hardanger fiddle, the national musical instrument of Norway.

Norwegian musicians today have an impact on the international music scene, and Norwegian jazz festivals are attended by audiences worldwide. Pop, rock, hip-hop, metal, R&B, and electronic enjoy wide popularity. Metal traditionally has been one of Norway's biggest musical exports, with such bands as Red Harvest and Enslaved.

EATING & DRINKING IN NORWAY

MEALS & DINING CUSTOMS Working Norwegians rarely go out to lunch; instead they grab a quick open sandwich, or *smørbrød*, at the office. In major towns and cities, lunch is generally served from 1 to 3pm. The *middag*, the main meal of the day, is generally eaten between 4:30 and 6pm. Many restaurants serve this popular *middag* from 1 to 8pm. In late-closing restaurants, it's possible to dine much later, until around midnight in Oslo. Long after *middag* time, a Norwegian family will have *aftens*, a *smørbrød* supper that will see them through the night.

THE CUISINE The chief criticism leveled against Norwegian cooking is that it lacks strong flavors. The food is always abundant (Norwegians are known for their second helpings), substantial, and well prepared—but no threat to the French for a Cordon Bleu prize. As recently as a few years ago, Norwegians turned to the Continent or Asia to satisfy their tastebuds, resulting in the many foreign restaurants found in larger Norwegian cities. However, there has been a recent back-to-basics trend, and the cutting edge of Norwegian cuisine is being honed by the knives of local chefs championing the use of organic local products. In counterreaction to fast-food culture, Norway is experiencing a return to longstanding local food traditions, and people are once again consulting their grandmothers' recipe books.

Norwegians are proud—and rightly so—of many of their tempting specialties, ranging from boiled cod (considered a delicacy) to reindeer steak smothered in brown gravy and accompanied by tart little lingonberries, which resemble wild cranberries.

Norway relies on fish, both freshwater and saltwater, for much of its food supply. Prepared in countless ways, fish is usually well cooked and always fresh—a good bet indeed. Try, in particular, the aforementioned boiled cod; it's always—emphasis on *always*—served with boiled potatoes.

In early summer, *kokt laks* (boiled salmon) is a highly rated delicacy. *Kreps* (crayfish) is another big production (as it is in Finland), and *ørret* (mountain trout), preferably broiled and served with fresh lemon, is a guaranteed treat. A recommendation for top-notch fare: *Fiske-gratin* (fish soufflé), delicately seasoned.

Norwegians love their fatty smoked eel *(roket al)*, although many foreigners have a tendency to whip by this one on the *smörgåsbord* table. The national appetizer is brine-cured herring with raw onions.

You may want to try *får i kål* (reindeer steak), the national dish, a heavily peppered cabbage-and-mutton stew served with boiled potatoes. A fisher's or a farmer's favorite is *lapskus* (meat and potato hash, to us), prepared with whatever's left over in the kitchen. The North American palate seems to take kindly to *kjøttkaker,* the Norwegian hamburger—often pork patties—served with sautéed onions, brown gravy, and boiled potatoes.

The boiled potato is ubiquitous. Incidentally, the Norwegian prefers it without butter—just a bit of parsley. Nowadays fresh vegetables and crisp salads are a regular feature of the Norwegian diet as well.

Rumgraut is a sour-cream porridge covered with melted butter, brown sugar, and cinnamon. If they're in season, try the good-tasting, amber-colored *muiter* (cloudberries). An additional treat, well made in Norway, is a pancake accompanied by lingonberries.

Frommer's Smart Traveler: Restaurants

Value-conscious diners may want to consider the following when eating in Norwegian restaurants:

- **Look for the dagens menu or daily special, which is reasonably priced and usually prepared fresh each day.**
- **Order a fixed-price menu, especially at lunch. Often, you can dine in some of the most expensive restaurants by patronizing them at lunch and ordering from the set menu.**
- **Do as the Norwegians do: Order one or two *smørbrød* (open sandwiches) for lunch.**
- **Go easy on the booze—it can add greatly to the cost of any meal.**
- **Go ethnic—there are hundreds of affordable foreign dining spots. "Norwegian" or Nordic restaurants tend to be on the expensive side.**
- **The best bet for a quick and inexpensive meal is a *konditori,* or bakery tearoom. Look for self-service cafeterias as well.**
- **Fill up at the traditional Norwegian *koldtbord* (cold board) at breakfast buffets, so you'll need only a light lunch.**

Frokost (breakfast) is often a whopping *koldtbord,* the famous cold board, consisting of herring and goat's-milk cheese, and such fare as salmon and soft-boiled eggs, plus *wienerbrød* (Danish pastry). At this time, most visitors encounter the ever-popular *flatbrød,* paper-thin crisp rye bread. Many visitors may not want to spend the extra kroner for this big spread, but those going on glacier expeditions need this early-morning fortification.

Incidentally, *smörgåsbord* and *smørbrød* are very popular in Norway, although they seem to be served here without the elaborate ritual typical of Denmark and Sweden. Customarily, *smörgåsbord* in Norway is only a prelude to the main meal.

DRINK Norway has strict laws regarding the sale of alcohol. Beer and wine may be served in hotels and restaurants 7 days a week, but hard liquor can be sold only between 3 and 11:45pm—and never on Sunday. Visitors can buy the precious stuff from the Vinmonopolet, the state liquor-and-wine monopoly (see below). The restriction on hard liquor may be a bonus for budgeters, as Norwegian prices are sky-high, in line with all the Scandinavian countries. ***Warning:*** Unless you ask for a favorite brand of gin or scotch, you may be served a sour-tasting Norwegian home-brew.

The Norwegians, like the Danes, are essentially beer drinkers. *Pils,* a light lager, is fairly low in alcohol content, but *lagerøl* is so low in alcoholic content (less than 2.5%) that it's a substitute only for water. The stronger Norwegian beer is called Export and is available at higher prices. Two other types of beer are Brigg and Zero.

The other national drink is *akevitt* (aquavit or schnapps). Who would ever think that potatoes and caraway seeds could knock a person under the table? It's that potent, although it's misnamed the "water of life." Norwegians gulp down beer as a chaser. Aquavit (try Linie Akevitt) is sloshed around in oak vats all the way to Australia and back—which ostensibly is what gives it the rich flavor.

The stores of **Vinmonopolet,** the monopoly that sells wines and spirits, are open Monday through Wednesday from 10am to 5pm, Thursday from 9am to 6pm, and Friday from 9am to 5pm. The Vinmonopolet is closed on Saturday in all towns except Kirkenes, Bodø, Ålesund, Trondheim, Haugesund, and Arendal. Liquor is not sold to anyone under 20 years of age; for beer and wine, the legal age is 18.

PLANNING YOUR TRIP TO NORWAY

3

The question isn't whether you should go to Norway, but when. What is the best time to visit, and which destinations should you visit? How can you preplan a trip and find cheap deals and other tantalizing offers? In the pages that follow, we've compiled the essentials of what you need to know about the practical details of planning your trip—airlines, events, currency, and more.

For additional help in planning your trip and for more on-the-ground resources in Norway, please see chapter 16, "Fast Facts: Norway."

WHEN TO GO

In the summer, the average temperature in Norway ranges from 13 to 18°C (57–65°F). In January, it hovers around 2°C (27°F), ideal weather for winter sports.

The Gulf Stream warms the west coast, where winters tend to be temperate. Rainfall, however, is often heavy here. Above the Arctic Circle, the sun shines night and day from mid-May until late July. For about 2 months every winter, the North Cape is plunged into darkness.

From May to mid-June, the scenery in Norway is at its most spectacular, with fruit trees in blossom, snow in the mountains, and meltwater swelling the waterfalls. There are several public holidays in May, and the Norwegians make full use of them to celebrate springtime after a long winter. In particular, National Day, on May 17, is marked by parties, music, and street parades, with many people dressed in beautiful national costumes. Low-season rates apply during this period.

Late June to early August is the high season in Norway, when the weather is warmest and the schools are on holiday. The most popular tourist places can be busy, but finding peace and quiet, if you wish, is easy. All the manmade tourist attractions are open, and public transportation services are more frequent.

Mid-August to October is a time when accommodations and ferries are at mid- or low-season rates. There is so little traffic that you may feel as if you have the whole country to yourself. The temperature drops slowly through September, making for good berry- and mushroom-picking weather. The glorious colors of fall are at their best in October.

Norway's summer weather is variable and unpredictable, with a number of surprising features. The Gulf Stream keeps the western fjord area and the coast up into the Arctic North much warmer than you might expect. The west coast receives the most rain, but the area farther east is drier. The sea temperature can reach 18°C (64°F) or higher on the south coast, where swimming is a popular pastime. Surprisingly, the water is often calm, as most of the inhabited places in Norway are sheltered from the prevailing wind by mountains and forest.

The warmest and most stable weather is found on the eastern side of the southern mountains, including the south coast between Mandal and Oslo. Even in the north, summer temperatures are pleasantly warm; however, as nearly all of this area is near the west coast, the weather can be wet and changeable. Be sure to take waterproof clothing. If you should be unlucky with the weather, remember a wise Norwegian saying: "There is no such thing as bad weather, only bad clothing."

From November to April, much of Norway is transformed into a snow-clad paradise. Undoubtedly, the best way to enjoy it is on skis, but there are many other things to do as well. Just sitting by the fire in a warm and cozy log cabin is a pleasure for some, as is the friendly, relaxed atmosphere of the hotel bar. Children of all ages (and many grown-ups) never get tired of just playing in the snow. Active types can go tobogganing, skating, ice fishing, ice climbing, dog sledding, and more.

Land of the Midnight Sun

In these locations, you can see the whole disk of the sun for 24 hours on the given dates:

Place	From	To
Nordkapp (North Cape)	May 13	July 29
Hammerfest	May 16	July 26
Vardo	May 17	July 25
Tromsø	May 20	July 22
Harstad	May 24	July 18
Svolvær	May 28	July 14
Bodø	June 3	July 8

THE MIDNIGHT SUN In the summer, the sun never fully sets in northern Norway; and even in the south, the sun may set around 11pm and rise at 3am. Keep in mind that although the sun shines at midnight, it's not as strong as at midday. Always bring a warm jacket or sweater.

Norway's Average Daytime Temperatures (°C/°F)

		JAN	FEB	MAR	APR	MAY	JUNE	JULY	AUG	SEPT	OCT	NOV	DEC
OSLO	TEMP. (°C)	-2	-1	2	7	14	18	20	19	14	8	2	-1
	TEMP. (°F)	28	30	36	45	57	64	68	66	57	46	36	30
BERGEN/	TEMP. (°C)	3	3	5	8	13	15	17	16	13	10	6	3
STAVANGER	TEMP. (°F)	37	37	41	46	55	59	63	61	55	50	42	38
TRONDHEIM	TEMP. (°C)	-2	-1	2	5	11	13	15	15	11	7	2	-1
	TEMP. (°F)	28	30	36	41	52	55	59	59	52	45	35	31

Norway Calendar of Events

Dates are approximate. Check with the local tourist office before making plans to attend a specific event. For an exhaustive list of events beyond those listed here, check http://events.frommers.com, where you'll find a searchable, up-to-the-minute roster of what's happening all over the world.

JANUARY

Northern Lights Festival, Tromsø. Classical and contemporary music performances by musicians from Norway and abroad. Visit www.nordlysfestivalen.no for details. Late January.

FEBRUARY

Kristiansund Opera Weeks. Featuring Kristiansund Opera's productions of opera and ballet, plus art exhibitions, concerts, and other events. Visit www.oik.no for details. Early February.

MARCH

Holmenkollen Ski Festival, Oslo. One of Europe's largest ski festivals, with World Cup Nordic skiing and biathlons, international ski-jumping competitions, and Norway's largest cross-country race for amateurs. Held at Holmenkollen ski jump on the outskirts of Oslo. To participate, attend, or request more information, visit www.oslo2011.no. Early March.

Narvik Winter Festival. Sports events, carnivals, concerts, and opera performances highlight this festival dedicated to those who built the railway across northern Norway and Sweden. Visit www.vinterfestuka.no for details, or call ✆ **76-95-03-50.** Late March to early April.

Birkebeiner Race, Rena to Lillehammer. This historic international ski race, with thousands of participants, crosses the mountains between Rena and Lillehammer, site of the 1994 Olympics. It's a 53-km (33-mile) cross-country trek. For details, call ✆ **41-77-29-00** or go to www.birkebeiner.no. Mid-March.

APRIL

Voss Jazz Festival. Three days of jazz and folk music performances by European and American artists. Visit www.vossajazz.no, or call ✆ **56-52-99-11** for details. Mid-April.

MAY

Norwegian Book Town (Bokby), Fjærland. You'll find thousands of secondhand bookstores in this small rural town. ✆ **57-69-22-10;** http://bokbyen.no/en/. May to September.

National Day (Syttende Mai). The May 17 celebrations in Norway are bigger than Christmas. Hundreds of thousands of Norwegians parade through the streets of towns and cities to the sound of brass bands and celebration, blowing whistles, waving flags, singing songs and eating ice-cream. All through the country there are *barnetog*, parades composed of schoolchildren, and other parades of all kinds. Everywhere you turn you are bound to catch glimpses of the beautiful national costumes or *bunad* from the various regions of the country. May 17.

Bergen International Festival (Bergen Festspill). A world-class music event, featuring artists from Norway and around the world. This is one of the largest annual musical events in Scandinavia. Held at various venues in Bergen. For information, contact the Bergen International Festival, Slottsgaten 1, 4055, Dregen N-5835 Bergen (✆ **55-21-06-30;** www.fib.no). Late May to early June.

JUNE

Exxon Mobil Bislett Games, Oslo. International athletic competitions are staged in Oslo, with professional participants from all over the world. For details, call ✆ **22-59-17-59** or visit www.bislettgames.com. Early June.

Færder Sailing Race. The Færderseilasen is the world's largest overnight regatta, with more than 1,100 boats taking part. The race ends in Borre, by the Oslofjord. Call ✆ **23-27-56-00,** or go to www.kns.no for details. Mid-June.

Emigration Festival, Stavanger. A festive commemoration of Norwegian emigration to North America, with exhibitions, concerts, theater, and folklore. Mid-June.

Midsummer Night, nationwide. Celebrations and bonfires take place all over Norway in honor of the midnight sun. June 23.

Emigration Festival, Kvinesdal. Commemorates the Norwegian emigration to the United States. Visit www.sorlandetutvandrersenter.no for more information. Late June to early July.

Midnight Sun Marathon, Tromsø. This marathon in northern Norway starts at midnight and draws eager runners from over 30 countries. For details, call ✆ **77-67-33-63** or go to www.msm.no. Mid-June.

Solstice Bookfair, Fjærland. This massive second-hand book sale draws antiquarian-lovers from all over Scandinavia and the world.

JULY

Kongsberg Jazz Festival. International artists participate in one of the most important jazz festivals in Scandinavia, with open-air concerts and performances all over town. Call ✆ **32-73-31-66,** or visit www.kongsberg-jazzfestival.no for details. Early July.

Molde International Jazz Festival. The "City of Roses" is the site of Norway's oldest jazz festival. It attracts international stars from both sides of the Atlantic every year and is held at venues in Molde for 6 days. For details, contact the Molde Jazz Festival, Box 415, N-6401 Molde (✆ **71-20-31-50;** www.moldejazz.no). Mid-July.

Norway Cup International Youth Soccer Tournament, Oslo. The world's largest youth soccer tournament attracts 1,000 teams from around the world to Oslo. Call ✆ **22-28-90-57,** or visit www.norwaycup.no. Late July to early August.

Telemark International Folk Music Festival, Bø. An international festival of folk music and folk dance takes place in the homes of many famous fiddlers, dancers, and singers. Call ✆ **33-95-19-19,** or visit www.telemarkfestivalen.no. Late July.

AUGUST

Peer Gynt Festival, Vinstra. Art exhibitions, evenings of music and song, parades in national costumes, and other events honor Ibsen's fictional character. Call ✆ **95-90-07-70,** or visit www.peergynt.no for details. Early August.

International Church Music Festival, Kristiansand. One of the best places in the world to hear religious music, played at venues all over the city, including some gorgeous churches (www.kirkefestspill.no). Early August.

Oslo Jazz Festival. This annual festival features music from the earliest years of jazz (1920–25), as well as classical concerts, opera, and ballet. For details, call ✆ **22-42-91-20,** or visit www.oslojazz.no. Third week of August.

Chamber Music Festival, Oslo. Norwegian and foreign musicians perform at Oslo's Akershus Castle and Fortress, which dates from A.D. 1300. Call ✆ **23-10-07-30,** or visit www.oslokammermusikkfestival.no for details. Mid-August.

SEPTEMBER

Oslo Marathon. This annual event draws some of Norway's best long-distance runners. Call ✆ **22-95-50-50,** or visit www.oslomaraton.no. Late September.

DECEMBER

Nobel Peace Prize Ceremony, Oslo. A major event on the Oslo calendar, attracting world attention. Attendance is by invitation only. For information, contact the Nobel Institute, Henrik Ibsen Gate 51, N-0255 Oslo 2 (✆ **22-12-93-00;** http://nobelprize.org). Held at Oslo City Hall. December 10.

ENTRY REQUIREMENTS

Passports, Visas & Other Documents

Citizens of the United States, Canada, Ireland, Australia, and New Zealand need a valid **passport** to enter Norway. British citizens traveling to Norway will need either a passport or a European Identity Card. Visitors from other European countries that are part of the Schengen Area may be required to show only a European Identity Card when entering Norway for 90 days or fewer.

For information on how to get a passport, go to "Passports" in chapter 16—the websites listed provide downloadable passport applications and current fees. For an up-to-date, country-by-country listing of passport requirements around the world, go to the "Foreign Entry Requirement" Web page of the U.S. State Department at **http://travel.state.gov**.

Citizens of the United States, Canada, the United Kingdom, Australia, and most European nations may visit Norway for a maximum of 90 consecutive days without a visa. Check the Norwegian Directorate of Immigration website at **www.udi.no** for up-to-date information about visa requirements if you are traveling to Norway for longer than 3 months or for reasons other than vacation.

In an effort to prevent international child abduction, many governments require a parent or legal guardian (or someone other than the parent) traveling alone with a child to provide documentary evidence of relationship and travel permission. Having such documentation on hand can facilitate entry/departure if Immigration requests it, although it is not always required. Inquire when booking your airline ticket about updated entry/departure procedures for children.

Your current domestic **driver's license** is acceptable in Norway. An international driver's license is not required.

Medical Requirements

There are no vaccination requirements for entering Norway.

Customs

WHAT YOU CAN BRING INTO NORWAY

With certain food exceptions (such as meat, meat products, and cheese), personal effects intended for your own use can be brought into Norway. You can also bring in cameras, binoculars, radios, portable TVs, and the like, as well as fishing and camping equipment, if you plan to take the items with you when you leave. Visitors of all nationalities can bring in 200 cigarettes, or 250 grams of tobacco and 200 sheets of cigarette paper, or 50 cigars; and 1 liter of spirits or 1 liter of wine.

WHAT YOU CAN TAKE HOME FROM NORWAY

U.S. Residents

Returning U.S. residents who have been away for at least 48 hours are allowed to bring back, once every 30 days, $800 worth of merchandise duty-free. You'll be charged a flat rate of 4% duty on the next $1,000 worth of purchases. Any dollar amount beyond that is dutiable at whatever rates apply. On mailed gifts, the duty-free limit is $200. Be sure to have your receipts or purchases handy to expedite the declaration process. ***Note:*** If you owe duty, you are required to pay on your arrival in

Visitor Information

General Information In the **United States,** contact the **Scandinavian Tourist Board,** 655 Third Avenue, Suite 1810, New York, NY 10017 (© **212/885-9700;** www.goscandinavia.com), at least 2 months in advance for maps, sightseeing pointers, ferry schedules, and other information.

In the **United Kingdom,** contact the **Norwegian Tourist Board** (which generally does business as Innovation Norway), Charles House, 5 Lower Regent St., London SW1Y 4LR (© **020/7839-8800,** 50p per min.). You might also try the tourist board's official website, **www.visitnorway.com.**

In **Canada,** you can reach Innovation Norway at 2 Bloor Street West, Suite 504, Toronto, Ontario M4W 3E2 (© **416/920-0434;** www.emb-norway.ca).

Maps Many tourist offices supply free maps of their district. You can also contact the Norwegian Automobile Federation, Storgata 2, N-0155 Oslo 1 (© **92-60-85-05**), which offers free or inexpensive road maps. Some of Norway's most reliable maps are published by Cappelen.

the United States, by cash, personal check, government or traveler's check, or money order, or in some locations by Visa or MasterCard.

To avoid having to pay duty on foreign-made personal items you owned before you left on your trip, bring along a bill of sale, insurance policy, jeweler's appraisal, or receipts of purchase. Or you can register items that can be readily identified by a permanently affixed serial number or marking—think laptop computers, cameras, and CD players—with Customs before you leave. Take the items to the nearest Customs office or register them with Customs at the airport from which you're departing. You'll receive, at no cost, a Certificate of Registration, which allows duty-free entry for the life of the item.

With some exceptions, you cannot bring fresh fruits and vegetables into the United States. For specifics on what you can bring back and the corresponding fees, download the invaluable free pamphlet *Know Before You Go* online at **www.cbp.gov**. Or contact the **U.S. Customs & Border Protection (CBP),** 1300 Pennsylvania Avenue NW, Washington, DC 20229 (© **877/287-8667**), and request the pamphlet by snail-mail.

Canadian Residents

For a clear summary of Canadian rules, write for the booklet *Be Aware and Declare,* issued by the **Canada Border Services Agency** (© **800/461-9999** in Canada, or 204/983-3500; www.cbsa-asfc.gc.ca). Canada allows its residents a C$750 exemption, and adults are allowed to bring back duty-free one carton of cigarettes, one can of tobacco, 40 imperial ounces of liquor, and 50 cigars. In addition, you're allowed to mail gifts to Canada valued at less than C$60 a day, provided they're unsolicited and don't contain alcohol or tobacco (write on the package "Unsolicited gift, under C$60 value"). Declare all valuables on a Y-38 form before departure from Canada, including serial numbers of valuables you already own, such as expensive foreign cameras. ***Note:*** The C$750 exemption can be used only once a year and only after an absence of 7 days.

TRACING YOUR NORWEGIAN roots

If you're of Norwegian ancestry, you can get information on how to trace your family history from the nearest Norwegian consulate. In Norway, contact the **Norwegian Emigration Center,** Strandkaien 31, N-4005 Stavanger (✆ **51-53-88-60;** www.emigrationcenter.com), for a catalog of information about Norwegian families who emigrated abroad.

In the United States, the **Family History Library of the Church of Jesus Christ of Latter-Day Saints,** 35 North West Temple, Salt Lake City, UT 84150 (✆ **801/240-2331;** www.familysearch.org), has extensive records of Norwegian families that emigrated to the United States and Canada. The library is open to the public without charge for genealogical research, and much of this information has been put online for you to access, also without charge. Additionally, you can freely access their hard-copy resources at over 4,500 family history centers in 70 countries.

U.K. Residents

U.K. residents who are **returning from a European Union country** go through a separate Customs exit (the "Blue Exit") especially for E.U. travelers. In essence, there is no limit on what you can bring back from an E.U. country—Norway, while not a member of the E.U., is included in this—as long as the items are for personal use (this includes gifts) and you have already paid the necessary duty and tax. However, Customs law sets out guidance levels. If you bring in more than these levels, you may be asked to prove that the goods are for your own use. Guidance levels on goods bought in the E.U. for your own use are 3,200 cigarettes, 200 cigars, 400 cigarillos, 3 kilograms of smoking tobacco, 10 liters of spirits, 90 liters of wine, 20 liters of fortified wine (such as port or sherry), and 110 liters of beer.

For information, contact **HM Customs & Excise** at ✆ **0845/010-9000** (from outside the U.K., +44 20/8929-0152), or visit www.hmce.gov.uk.

Australian Residents

The duty-free allowance in Australia is A$900. Residents can bring in 250 cigarettes or 250 grams of loose tobacco, and 2.25 liters of alcohol. If you're taking valuables you already own, such as foreign-made cameras, you should file form B263. A helpful brochure available from Australian consulates or Customs offices is *Know Before You Go*. For more information, call the **Australian Customs Service** at ✆ **1300/363-263,** or from outside Australia +61 2-6275-6666, or go to www.customs.gov.au.

New Zealand Residents

The duty-free allowance for New Zealand is NZ$700. Residents 18 and over can bring in 200 cigarettes, 50 cigars, or 250 grams of tobacco (or a mixture of all three, if their combined weight doesn't exceed 250g); plus 4.5 liters of wine and beer or 1.125 liters of liquor. New Zealand currency does not carry import or export restrictions. Fill out a certificate of export listing the valuables you are taking out of the country; that way, you can bring them back without paying duty. Most questions are answered in a free pamphlet available at New Zealand consulates and Customs offices: *New Zealand Customs Guide for Travellers, Notice No. 4*. For more information, contact **New Zealand Customs Service,** the Customhouse, 17–21 Whitmore St., Box 2218, Wellington (✆ **0800/428-786** or, from outside New Zealand, +64-9300-5399; www.customs.govt.nz).

GETTING THERE & GETTING AROUND

Getting to Norway

BY PLANE

From North America

All transatlantic flights from North America land at Oslo's Fornebu Airport. **SAS** (www.flysas.com) flies non-stop daily from Newark to Oslo. The trip takes about 7½ hours. Most other SAS flights from North America go through Copenhagen. Flying time from Chicago is 11 hours; from Seattle, it's 12 hours, not including the layover in Copenhagen. From New York, **Continental** (www.continental.com) flies from New York (Newark) to Oslo.

If you fly to Norway on another airline, you'll be routed through a gateway city in Europe and will sometimes continue on a different airline. **British Airways** (www.britishairways.com), for example, has dozens of daily flights from many North American cities to London, where you can continue to Oslo. **Icelandair** (www.icelandair.com) can be an excellent choice, with connections through Reykjavik. **KLM** (www.klm.com) serves Oslo through Amsterdam.

From the U.K.

For passengers from the U.K., **British Airways** operates at least four daily nonstops to Oslo from Heathrow. **SAS** runs four daily flights from Heathrow to Oslo, as well as from Heathrow to Stavanger; it also flies from Gatwick to Bergen. **Eastern Airways** (www.easternairways.com) flies to Oslo, Bergen, and Stavanger airports from Aberdeen and Newcastle throughout the year, with connecting flights onto other U.K. regional airports such as Bristol and Southampton. Budget airline **Norwegian** (www.norwegian.com) flies from Gatwick to Oslo Torp, Oslo Rygge, Bergen, Stavanger, Tromsø, and Trondheim, and also from Edinburgh to Oslo. **Ryanair** (www.ryanair.com) flies from Stansted and Liverpool to Oslo Torp, and from Stansted, Liverpool, and Newcastle to Oslo Rygge, and from Stansted (and during the summer from Edinburgh) to Haugesund. Norwegian airline **Widerøe** (www.wideroe.no) flies 6 days a week from Aberdeen and Newcastle to Stavanger and also from Aberdeen to Bergen. Flying time from London to Oslo on any airline is around 2 hours, and from Scotland to Norway around 1 hour.

BY CAR

If you're driving from the Continent, you must go through Sweden. From **Copenhagen,** take the E47/55 express highway north to Helsingør and catch the car ferry to Helsingborg, Sweden. From there, the E6 runs to Oslo. From **Stockholm,** drive across Sweden on the E18 to Oslo.

BY TRAIN

Copenhagen is the main rail hub for services between Scandinavia and the rest of Europe. There are three daily trains from Copenhagen to Oslo. All connect with the Danish ferries operating to Norway through either Helsingør or Hirtshals.

Most rail traffic from Sweden into Norway follows the main corridors between Stockholm and Oslo and between Gothenburg and Oslo.

If you plan to travel a great deal on Norwegian railroads, it's worth securing a copy of the annually updated ***Thomas Cook European Timetable of European Passenger Railroads.*** It's available online at www.thomascooktimetables.com.

Thousands of trains run from Britain to the Continent, and at least some of them go directly across or under the Channel, through France or Belgium and Germany into Denmark, where connections can be made to Norway. For example, a train leaves London's Victoria Station daily at 14:34am and arrives in Copenhagen the next day at 10:06am. This train goes under the Chunnel via Brussels and Cologne, though other routes make use of the Dover–Ostende ferry. Once you're in Copenhagen, you can make rail connections to Oslo. Because of the time and distances involved, many passengers rent a couchette (sleeping berth). Designed like padded benches stacked bunk-style, they're usually clustered six to a compartment. First-class carriages generally have two-bed-per-berth arrangements.

Rail Passes for North American Travelers

EURAIL PASS The Eurail Pass permits unlimited first-class rail travel in any country in western Europe except the British Isles (good in Eire). Passes are available for purchase online (www.eurail.com) and at various offices/agents around the world. Travel agents and railway agents in such cities as New York, Montreal, and Los Angeles sell Eurailpasses. You can purchase them at the North American offices of CIT Travel Service, the French National Railways, the German Federal Railway, and the Swiss Federal Railways. It is strongly recommended that you purchase passes before you leave home as not all passes are available in Europe; also, passes purchased in Europe will cost about 20% more. Numerous options are available for travel in France.

The **Eurail Global Pass** allows you unlimited travel in 20 Eurail-affiliated countries. You can travel on any of the days within the validity period; available validity periods are 15 days, 21 days, 1 month, 2 months, 3 months, and some other possibilities as well. Prices for first-class adult travel are $659 for 15 days; $855 for 21 days; $1,059 for 1 month; $499 for 2 months; and $1,849 for 3 months. Children 4 to 11 pay half-fare; those 3 and under travel for free.

A **Eurail Global Pass Saver,** also valid for first-class travel in 20 countries, offers a special deal for two or more people traveling together. This pass costs $559 for 15 days; $725 for 21 days; $899 for 1 month; $1,275 for 2 months; and $1,579 for 3 months.

A **Eurail Global Youth Pass** for those 12 to 25 allows second-class travel in 18 countries. This pass costs $429 for 15 days; $555 for 21 days; $689 for 1 month; $975 for 2 months; and $1,205 for 3 months.

The **Eurail Select Pass** offers unlimited travel on the national rail networks of any three, four, or five bordering countries out of the 22 Eurail nations linked by train or ship. Two or more passengers can travel together for big discounts, getting 5, 6, 8, 10, or 15 days of rail travel within any 2-month period on the national rail networks of any three, four, or five adjoining Eurail countries linked by train or ship. A sample fare: For 5 days in 2 months you pay $410 for three countries. **Eurail Select Pass Youth** for travelers under 26 allows second-class travel within the same guidelines as Eurail Select Pass, with fees starting at $267. **Eurail Select Pass**

Saver offers discounts for two or more people traveling together—first-class travel within the same guidelines as Eurail Select Pass—with fees starting at $348.

WHERE TO BUY RAIL PASSES Travel agents in all towns and railway agents in major North American cities sell all these tickets, but the best supplier is **Railbookers** (✆ **020/3327-0800** in the U.K.; www.railbookers.com), which can sell you tickets and also recommend and book hotels and other excursions. Another option is **Rail Europe** (✆ **877/272-RAIL;** www.raileurope.com).

Many different rail passes are available in the United Kingdom for travel in Britain and continental Europe. Stop in at the **International Rail Centre,** Victoria Station, London SWIV 1JY (✆ **0845/748-4950** in the U.K.). Some of the most popular passes, including InterRail and Euro Youth, are offered only to travelers under 26 years of age; these allow unlimited second-class travel through most European countries.

EURAIL SCANDINAVIA PASS If your visit to Europe will be primarily in Scandinavia, Eurail's Scandinavia pass may be better and cheaper than the Eurail Pass. This pass allows its owner a designated number of days of free rail travel within a larger time block. You can choose a total of any 5 days of unlimited rail travel during a 15-day period, 10 days of rail travel within a 1-month period, or 1 month of unlimited rail travel. The pass, which is valid on all lines of the state railways of Denmark, Finland, Norway, and Sweden, offers discounts or free travel on some (but not all) of the region's ferry lines as well. The pass can be purchased only in North America. It's available from any office of **Rail Europe** (✆ **800/848-7245**) or **ScanAm World Tours,** 108 North Main St., Cranbury, NJ 08512 (✆ **800/545-2204;** www.scandinaviantravel.com), as well as direct from **Eurail.com**.

Depending on whether you choose first- or second-class rail travel, 5 days in 2 months costs $255 to $339, 8 days out of 2 months costs $319 to $425, and 10 days out of 2 months costs $355 to $475.

Rail Passes for British Travelers

If you plan to do a lot of exploring, you may prefer one of the three rail passes designed for unlimited train travel within a designated region during a predetermined number of days. These passes are sold in Britain and several other European countries.

An **InterRail Pass** is available to passengers of any nationality, with some restrictions—they must be under age 26 and able to prove residency in a European or North African country (Morocco, Algeria, or Tunisia) for at least 6 months before buying the pass. It allows unlimited travel through Europe, except Albania and the republics of the former Soviet Union. Prices are complicated and vary depending on the countries you want to include. For pricing purposes, Europe is divided into eight zones; the cost depends on the number of zones you include. For ages 25 and under, the most expensive option (£399) allows 1 month of unlimited travel in all eight zones and is known to the staff as a "global." The least expensive option (£159) allows 5 days of travel within 10 days.

Passengers aged 26 and older can buy an **InterRail 26-Plus Pass.** The cost varies from £399 to £599 for 15 days to £599 to £899 for 1 month. Passengers must meet the same residency requirements that apply to the InterRail Pass (described above).

For information on buying individual rail tickets or any of the just-mentioned passes, contact **National Rail Inquiries,** Victoria Station, London (✆ **0845/748-4950**). Tickets and passes also are available at any of the larger railway stations, as well as selected travel agencies throughout Britain and the rest of Europe.

BY SHIP & FERRY

FROM DENMARK The trip to Oslo from the northern port of Frederikshavn in Jutland takes 12 hours and costs from NOK230. Call **Stena Line** (✆ **96-20-02-00;** www.stenaline.com) for general reservations.

FROM SWEDEN The daily crossing in summer from Strømstad, Sweden, to Sandefjord, Norway, takes 2½ hours. Bookings can be made through **Color Line,** Tollbugata 5, N-3210 Sandefjord (✆ **47-22-94-44-00;** www.colorline.com).

FROM ENGLAND **SeaEurope Holidays,** 6801 Lake Worth Road, Suite 107, Lake Worth, Florida 33467 (✆ **800/533-3755;** www.seaeurope.com), is a U.S.-based company that will arrange a variety of seagoing options for you, all before you land in mainland Europe.

BY CRUISE SHIP

Norway's fjords and mountain vistas are among the most spectacular panoramas in the world. Many shipowners and cruise lines offer excursions along the Norwegian coast.

One of the most prominent lines is **Cunard** (✆ **800/7CUNARD** in the U.S. and Canada, or ✆ **0845-071-0300** in the U.K.; www.cunard.com).

Ten-day cruises are offered on the new Cunard flagship, *Queen Mary* 2 (from $2,220 in summer). This vessel re-creates the grandeur of those old queen liners, *Queen Mary* and *Queen Elizabeth,* but on a larger, more modern scale. The 150,000-ton ship carries a total of 2,620 passengers.

Departing from Southampton, England, the ship calls at Oslo and Bergen and cruises the North Sea. En route it also stops at the most frequently visited fjords, including the Eidfjord. Prices for the 7-day cruise (starting at $944 in summer) do not include round-trip airfare.

In its tour of Baltic capitals, **Norwegian Cruise Line** (www.ncl.com) stops at Helsinki, Stockholm, and Copenhagen, but, ironically, doesn't go as far as Norway itself.

Getting Around

BY PLANE

The best way to get around Norway is either to purchase flights on a discount airline such as Norwegian or Widerøe, or to take advantage of air passes that apply to the whole region. If you're traveling extensively, special European passes are available.

SAS'S "VISIT SCANDINAVIA" FARE The vast distances encourage air travel between Norway's far-flung points. One of the most worthwhile promotions is SAS's **Airpass Scandinavia/Nordic Airpass.** Available only to travelers who fly SAS across the Atlantic, it gives you discounts on SAS flights within or between Denmark, Norway, and Sweden. The pass is especially valuable if you plan to travel to the far northern frontiers of Sweden or Norway; in that case, the savings over the price of a regular economy-class ticket can be substantial. For information on buying the pass, contact **SAS** (www.flysas.com).

WITHIN NORWAY Norway has excellent domestic air services. In addition to SAS (www.sas.com) and Norwegian, an independent airway, **Widerøe,** provides quick and convenient ways to get around a large country with many hard-to-reach areas. For more information, call ✆ **75-11-11-11** or visit www.wideroe.no.

BY TRAIN

Norway's network of electric and diesel-electric trains runs as far as Bodø, 100km (62 miles) north of the Arctic Circle. (Beyond that, visitors must take a coastal steamer, flight, or bus to Tromsø and the North Cape.) Upgraded express trains (the fastest in the country) crisscross the mountainous terrain between Oslo, Stavanger, Bergen, and Trondheim. For information and reservations, contact the **Norwegian State Railways** (NSB; ✆ **81-50-08-88;** www.nsb.no).

The most popular and most scenic run covers the 483km (299 miles) between Oslo and Bergen. Visitors with limited time often choose this route for its fabled mountains, gorges, white-water rivers, and fjords. The trains make frequent stops for passengers to enjoy breathtaking views.

Second-class travel on Norwegian trains is recommended. In fact, second class in Norway is as good as or better than first class anywhere else in Europe, with reclining seats and lots of unexpected comforts. Of course, first-class train travel in Norway is better, though not necessarily *that* much better, than second class. For those who want the added comforts and can afford it, first class is the way to go.

The one-way second-class fare from Oslo to Bergen is NOK775. Another popular run, from Oslo to Trondheim, costs NOK852 one-way in second class. First class from Oslo to Bergen costs NOK865, and from Oslo to Trondheim NOK942.

One of the country's obviously scenic trips, from Bergen to Bodø, is not possible by train because of the terrain. Trains to Bodø leave from Oslo. Express trains are called *expresstog,* and you have to read the fine print of a railway schedule to figure out whether an *expresstog* is much faster than a conventional train.

On express and other major trains, you must reserve seats at the train's starting station. Sleepers are priced according to the number of berths in each compartment. Children 4 to 15 years of age and seniors are granted reduced fares.

There are special compartments for persons with disabilities on most medium- and long-distance trains. People in wheelchairs and others with physical disabilities, and their companions, may use the compartments. Some long-distance trains offer special playrooms ("Kiddie-Wagons") for children, complete with toys, games, and books.

EURAIL NORWAY PASS A restricted rail pass applicable only to the state railway lines, the Eurail Norway Pass is available for 3 to 8 days of unlimited rail travel in 1 month. It's suitable for anyone who wants to cover the long distances that separate Norwegian cities. The pass is available in North America through **Rail Europe** (✆ **800/848-7245;** www.raileurope.com). The cost is $265 for adults in second class for any 3 days in 1 month. For 4 days travel in 1 month, the second-class cost is $289; for 5 days $319; for 6 days $365; and for 8 days it's $405. Children 4 to 15 years of age pay half the adult fare, and those under 4 ride free. Discount passes are available for youth aged 16 to 25 (Norway Youth Pass).

MINIPRIS TICKETS NSB's regional trains offer unlimited travel for NOK199 to NOK399. The offer is valid for a limited number of seats. You can purchase the ticket by logging onto www.nsb.no. Tickets tend to sell out at least a week or so in advance—they must be purchased at least 1 day before travel—so make reservations as soon as possible. At this price, tickets are not refundable and a change of reservation is not possible. A supplement of NOK90 will grant you access to the NSB "Komfort" section.

BY BUS

Where the train or coastal steamer stops, passengers can usually continue on a scenic bus ride. Norway's bus system is excellent, linking remote villages along the fjords. Numerous all-inclusive motorcoach tours, often combined with steamer travel, leave from Bergen and Oslo in the summer. The train ends in Bodø; from there you can get a bus to Fauske (63km/39 miles east). From Fauske, the Polar Express bus spans the entire distance along the Arctic Highway, through Finnmark to Kirkenes, near the Russian border, and back. The segment from Alta to Kirkenes is open only from June to October, but there's year-round service from Fauske to Alta. Passengers are guaranteed hotel accommodations along the way..

Buses have air-conditioning, toilets, adjustable seats, reading lights, and a telephone. Reservations are not accepted on most buses, and payment is made to the driver onboard. Fares depend on the distance traveled. Children under 4 travel free, and children 4 to 16 and seniors pay half-price.

For more information about bus travel in Norway, contact **Nor-Way Bussekspress AS,** Karl Johans Gate (✆ **81-54-44-44;** www.nor-way.no) in Oslo.

BY CAR & FERRY

Dazzling scenery awaits you at almost every turn while driving through Norway. Some roads are less than perfect (dirt or gravel is frequent), but all are passable (you'll even be able to drive to the North Cape). Most mountain roads are open by May 1; the so-called motoring season lasts from mid-May to the end of September. In western Norway, hairpin curves are common, but if you're willing to settle for doing fewer than 240km (150 miles) a day, you needn't worry. The easiest and most convenient touring territory is in and around Oslo and south to Stavanger.

Bringing a car into Norway is relatively uncomplicated. If you own the car you're driving, you need only present your national driver's license, car registration, and proof that the car is insured. (This proof usually takes the form of a document known as a "green card," which Customs agents will refer to specifically.) If you've rented a car in another country and want to drive it into Norway, be sure to verify at the time of rental that the registration and insurance documents are in order—they probably will be. Regardless of whether you own or rent the car you're about to drive into Norway, don't assume that your private North American insurance policy will automatically apply. Chances are good that it will, but in the event of an accident, you may have to cope with a burdensome amount of paperwork.

If you're driving through any of Norway's coastal areas, you'll probably have to traverse one or more of the country's famous fjords. Although more and more bridges are being built, Norway's network of privately run ferries is essential for transporting cars across hundreds of fjords and estuaries. Motorists should ask the tourist bureau for the free map *Norway by Car* and a timetable outlining the country's dozens of car-ferry services. The cost for cars and passengers is low.

RENTALS The major car rental firms are represented in Norway, including **Budget** (www.budget.com), **Hertz** (www.hertz.com), and **Avis** (www.avis.com). They offer well-serviced, well-maintained fleets of rental cars. Prices and terms tend to be more favorable for those who reserve vehicles from home before their departure. The major competitors' prices tend to be roughly equivalent, except for promotional deals scheduled from time to time.

The prices quoted here include the 23% government tax. Despite pressure from the telephone sales representative, it pays to ask questions and shop around before you commit to a prepaid reservation. Each company maintains offices at the Oslo airport, in the center of Oslo, and at airports and city centers elsewhere around the country.

Note: Remember that prices and the relative merits of each company can and will change during the lifetime of this edition, depending on promotions and other factors.

An auto supplier that might not automatically come to mind is **Kemwel** (**✆ 877/820-0668;** www.kemwel.com), a U.S.-based auto-rental broker that monitors the availability of rental cars in markets across Europe, including Norway. Originally established in 1908 and now operating in close conjunction with its affiliated company, **Auto Europe** (www.autoeurope.com), which also has offices in the U.K., it offers convenient, prepaid access to thousands of cars, from a variety of reputable car-rental outfits throughout Europe; sometimes you'll find more favorable rates than those you might have gotten by contacting those companies directly.

Most car rentals are reserved and prepaid, in dollars or pounds, prior to your arrival in Norway, thereby avoiding the confusion of unfavorable currency conversions and government tax add-ons that you might discover after your return home. You're given the option at the time of your booking to include collision-damage and other forms of insurance. Most rental cars can be picked up either at the airport or at a downtown office in cities throughout Norway, though there is occasionally an added fee for one-way rentals.

DRIVING RULES Driving is on the right, and the law requires that you keep your headlights on at all times. Every passenger, including infants, must wear seat belts. Children 5 years of age and under must ride in the back. A driver must yield to cars approaching from the right. On most major highways, the maximum speed limit is 90km/h (55 mph). On secondary routes, the speed limit ranges from 70km/h (43 mph) to 80km/h (50 mph). Do not drink and drive: Norway has perhaps the strictest laws in Europe about drinking and driving, and there are roadside checks. Speeding is also severely punished, and most highways are monitored by radar and cameras.

FUEL There are plenty of fuel stations in Norway, and unleaded *(blyfri bensin)* and diesel fuel are sold from self-service pumps. Those pumps labeled *kort* are open day and night. Most of them accept regular bank credit cards and oil company credit cards. In the countryside, hours of operation vary widely.

Winter Motoring in Norway

If you're going to drive in Norway in winter, you must be prepared for the conditions. Most of the main roads are kept open by snowplows year-round, but the road surface will often be hard-packed snow and ice. Journey times will be much longer than in summer, typically 50km (30 miles) per hour, and in bad weather there can be long delays over mountain passes. Most Norwegians use winter tires with metal studs, which come with all rental cars. Temperatures as low as –3°C (25°F) are common. A good ice scraper and snow brush are essential, and a diesel engine is highly recommended.

MONEY & COSTS

The Norwegian currency is the **Norwegian krone** (plural: **kroner**), written "NOK." There are 100 **øre** in 1 krone. Banknotes are issued in denominations of 50, 100, 200, 500, and 1,000 kroner. Coins are issued in denominations of 50 øre, 1 krone, and 5, 10, and 20 kroner.

Currency Exchange

Banks offer the best rates for currency exchange. Most hotels will exchange money but usually at an unfavorable rate or with a commission.

Many hotels in Norway simply will not accept dollar- or pound-denominated personal checks; those that do will certainly charge for making the conversion. In most cases, a hotel will accept a credit or debit card. On occasion, some will accept countersigned traveler's checks.

ATMs

Plus, Cirrus, and other networks connecting automated teller machines (ATMs, or *bankomat* in Norwegian) operate throughout Norway. The easiest and best way to get cash while you're away from home is from an ATM. The **MasterCard/Cirrus/Maestro** (www.mastercard.com) and **Visa/Plus** (www.visa.com) networks span the globe; look at the back of your bank card to see which network you're on, and then call or check online for ATM locations at your destination. Be sure you know your personal identification number (PIN) before you leave home, and be sure to find out your daily withdrawal limit before you depart. Also keep in mind that many banks impose a fee every time a card is used at a different bank's ATM, and that fee can be higher for international transactions than for domestic ones. On top of this, the bank from which you withdraw cash may charge its own fee. For international withdrawal fees, ask your bank.

You can also get cash advances on your credit card at an ATM. Keep in mind that credit card companies try to protect themselves from theft by limiting the funds cardholders can withdraw outside their home country (sometimes per day, sometimes as a total sum), so call your credit card company before you leave home. And keep in mind that you'll pay interest from the moment of your withdrawal, even if you pay your monthly bills on time.

EMERGENCY CASH—THE fastest WAY

If you need emergency cash over the weekend, when all the banks and American Express offices are closed, you can have money wired to you via **Western Union** (www.westernunion.com). You must present valid ID (best is a passport) to pick up the cash at the destination Western Union office. However, in some countries you can pick up a money transfer if you don't have valid identification, provided you answer a test question provided by the sender; in this case be sure to let the sender know in advance that you don't have ID. If you need to use a test question instead of ID, the sender must take cash to his or her local Western Union office rather than transfer the money over the phone or online.

WHAT THINGS COST IN OSLO	NOK
Taxi from Gardermoen airport to the city center	120.00
Bus from Gardermoen airport to the city center	26.00
Double room at the Grand Hotel (very expensive)	420.00
Double room at the Thon Hotel Cecil (moderate)	359.00
Double room at the Cochs Pensjonat (inexpensive)	144.00
Lunch for one at Brasserie France (moderate)	78.00
Lunch for one at Mamma Rosa (inexpensive)	50.00
Dinner for one, without wine, at ***restauranteik*** (expensive)	90.00
Dinner for one, without wine, at 3 Brødre (moderate)	45.00
Dinner for one, without wine, at Santino's Spaghetteria (inexpensive)	12.00
Pint of beer (draft pilsner) in a bar	9.00
Coca-Cola in a restaurant	4.50
Cup of coffee in a bar or cafe	4.00
Admission to the Viking Ship Museum	10.00
Movie ticket	18.00
Theater ticket	30.00

Important note: Make sure that the PINs on your bank cards and credit cards will work in Norway. You'll need a **four-digit code** (six digits won't work); if you have a six-digit code, you'll have to go into your bank and get a new PIN for your trip. If you're unsure about this, contact Cirrus or Plus (see above). Be sure to check the daily withdrawal limit at the same time.

Credit Cards

In general, major credit cards (including Diners Club) are accepted at most establishments in Norway, although the Discover card's popularity is somewhat on the wane. Credit cards provide a convenient record of all your expenses, and they generally offer relatively good exchange rates. You can also get cash advances from your credit card at banks or ATMs, provided you know your PIN. If you've forgotten yours, or didn't even know you had one, call the number on the back of your credit card and ask the bank to send it to you. It usually takes 5 to 7 business days, though some banks will provide the number over the phone if you tell them your mother's maiden name or some other personal information. Keep in mind that when you use your credit card abroad, most banks assess a 2% fee above the 1% fee charged by Visa, MasterCard, or American Express for currency conversion on credit charges. But credit cards still may be the smart way to go when you factor in such things as exorbitant ATM fees and higher traveler's check exchange rates (and service fees).

Some organizations also offer prepaid, reloadable debit cards, a safe and convenient alternative to traveler's checks and cash. They can be used everywhere Visa and MasterCard credit and debit cards are accepted, and are useful if you don't have a credit card or don't want to risk it getting stolen.

For tips, and telephone numbers to call, if your wallet or purse is stolen or lost, see "Lost & Found" in chapter 16.

Traveler's Checks

Although they are infrequently used now that ATMs are available everywhere, you can still buy traveler's checks at most banks. Generally, you'll pay a service charge ranging from 1% to 4%.

The most popular traveler's checks are offered by **American Express** (www.amex.com). If you are a cardholder, then you can call collect, and Amex gold and platinum cardholders may be exempted from the 1% fee. AAA (American Automobile Association) members can obtain American Express traveler's checks for no fee at most AAA offices. Other popular providers include **Visa** (www.visa.com). **American Express, Thomas Cook, Visa,** and **MasterCard** offer **foreign currency traveler's checks,** which are useful if you're traveling to one country, or to the euro zone; they're accepted at locations where US dollar checks may not be.

If you carry traveler's checks, keep a record of their serial numbers, separately from your checks, in the event that the checks are stolen or lost. You'll get a refund faster if you know the numbers.

HEALTH

Staying Healthy

Norway is viewed as a "safe" destination, although problems, of course, can and do occur anywhere. You don't need to get shots, most food is safe, and the water in cities and towns is potable. It is easy to get a prescription filled in towns and cities, and nearly all places throughout Norway contain hospitals with English-speaking doctors.

If you suffer from a chronic illness, consult your doctor before your departure. Pack prescription medications in your carry-on luggage, and carry them in their original containers, with pharmacy labels—otherwise they won't make it through airport security. Carry the generic name of prescription medicines, in case a local pharmacist is unfamiliar with the brand name.

Specific Health Concerns

Although Norway is a fairly safe country, certain outdoor activities are not without risks.

Although summers are far from sweltering in Norway, the sun can often be very bright and it's important to take precautions against **sunburn** and **heat stroke.** If you're wearing a T-shirt or shorts, or swimming in a fjord, be responsible and put on sunblock; a strength of SPF 30 or above should be adequate protection against the Scandinavian sunshine. If you are glacier skiing, be sure to wear goggles or sunglasses to combat **sun blindness.**

Altitude sickness (or acute mountain sickness) is a condition that results from ascending a hillside or mountain. It is believed to result from changes in the body's response to changes in air pressure and decreased levels of oxygen. Altitude sickness can occur as low as 2,500m (8,000 ft.), but as most mountains in Norway are not of

Avoiding "Economy-Class Syndrome"

Deep vein thrombosis, or as it's known in the world of flying, "economy-class syndrome," is a blood clot that develops in a deep vein. It's a potentially deadly condition that can be caused by sitting in cramped conditions—such as an airplane cabin—for too long. During a flight (especially a long-haul flight), get up, walk around, and stretch your legs every 60 to 90 minutes to keep your blood flowing. Other preventive measures include frequent flexing of the legs while sitting, drinking lots of water, and avoiding alcohol and sleeping pills. If you have a history of deep vein thrombosis, heart disease, or another condition that puts you at high risk, some experts recommend wearing compression stockings or taking anticoagulants when you fly; always ask your physician about the best course for you. Symptoms of deep vein thrombosis include leg pain or swelling, or even shortness of breath.

Everest heights, it is unlikely to affect you. Still, be aware of the symptoms, which include headache, nausea, vomiting, and fatigue. The best way to prevent altitude sickness is to ascend slowly (over a period of several days) and avoid overexerting yourself physically until you have time to acclimate. The condition generally resolves itself with rest, hydration, and general pain medication. If your altitude sickness worsens, it is recommended to descend to a lower altitude.

Hypothermia occurs when the internal body temperature drops below 35°C (95°F). It need not be extremely cold for hypothermia to settle in; the condition can happen anytime you're exposed to cool, damp conditions, and elderly people tend to be more susceptible. The symptoms include shivering, loss of coordination, confusion, pale skin, drowsiness, and reduced heart or breathing rate. To treat hypothermia, get indoors and remove all wet clothes, and drink warm fluids (but nothing with caffeine or alcohol). Cover the body with warm blankets, a sleeping bag, or (in severe cases) aluminum-coated emergency warming foils. Avoid using outside heat sources such as radiators or hot water baths, as this is likely to slow the rate of the temperature increase in the body's core. Lastly, avoid any strenuous muscle exertion until you've recovered.

If You Get Sick

For travel abroad, you may have to pay all medical costs up front and be reimbursed later. Before leaving home, find out what medical services your health insurance covers. To protect yourself, consider buying medical travel insurance.

If a medical emergency arises, your hotel staff can usually put you in touch with a reliable doctor. If not, contact your hotel, embassy, or a consulate; each one maintains a list of English-speaking doctors.

For U.S. visitors, very few health insurance plans pay for medical evacuation (which can cost $75,000 and up from a foreign country). A number of companies offer medical evacuation services anywhere in the world. If you're ever hospitalized more than 150 miles from home, **MedjetAssist** (✆ **800/527-7478;** www.medjetassistance.com) will pick you up and fly you to the hospital of your choice virtually anywhere in the world in a medically equipped and staffed aircraft 24 hours a day,

> **Healthy Travels to You**
>
> **The following government websites offer up-to-date health-related travel advice.**
>
> - **Australia: www.dfat.gov.au/travel**
> - **Canada: www.hc-sc.gc.ca**
> - **U.K.: www.nhs.uk/healthcareabroad**
> - **U.S.: www.cdc.gov/travel**

7 days a week. Annual memberships are $250 individual, $385 family; you can also purchase short-term memberships.

U.K. and European residents will need a **European Health Insurance Card** (EHIC; ✆ **0845/606-2030;** www.ehic.org.uk) to receive free or reduced-cost health benefits during a visit to a European Economic Area (EEA) country (European Union countries plus Iceland, Liechtenstein, and Norway) or Switzerland. For advice, ask at your local post office or see www.nhs.uk/healthcareabroad.

Hospital and **emergency numbers** are listed under "Emergencies" and "Hospitals" in chapter 16.

SAFETY

Norway has a relatively low crime rate, with rare but increasing instances of violent crime. Most crimes involve the theft of personal property from cars or residences or in public areas. Pickpockets and purse-snatchers often work in pairs or groups, with one distracting the victim while another grabs valuables. Often they operate in or near major tourist attractions such as those in central Oslo—especially at restaurants, museums, and bars—and on buses and subway trains. Hotel breakfast rooms and lobbies can attract professional, well-dressed thieves who blend in with guests and target purses and briefcases left unguarded by unsuspecting visitors and business travelers. Valuables should never be left unguarded in parked vehicles.

The loss or theft abroad of a passport should be reported immediately to the local police and your nearest embassy or consulate. U.S. citizens may refer to the Department of State's pamphlet, *A Safe Trip Abroad,* for ways to promote trouble-free journeys. The pamphlet is available via the Bureau of Consular Affairs website at http://travel.state.gov/travel/tips/safety.

SPECIALIZED TRAVEL RESOURCES

Travelers with Disabilities

Norway has been in the vanguard of providing services for people with disabilities. In general, trains, airlines, ferries, department stores, and malls are accessible. For information about wheelchair access, ferry and air travel, parking, and other matters, contact the appropriate tourist board (see "Visitor Information," earlier in this chapter). The **Norwegian Association of the Disabled,** Schweigaards gate 12, 9217 Grønland, 0185 Oslo (✆ **24-10-24-00;** www.nhf.no), also provides useful information.

If you're flying around Norway or Europe in general, the airline can help with such things as reserving seats with enough space, while ground staff can help you on and off your flights, but you must arrange for this assistance *in advance* through the airline.

For information on organizations that offer resources to travelers with disabilities, go to www.frommers.com/planning.

Gay & Lesbian Travelers

As one of the most developed countries on the planet, it would follow that Norway is also one of the most gay-friendly. While this isn't entirely the case—much of rural Scandinavia, remember, is fairly conservative, politically speaking—most Norwegians are tolerant of the lifestyles and sexual preferences of others. Obviously, an urban center such as Oslo will accommodate a more openly gay life than smaller, more remote areas.

In Norway, gays and lesbians have the same legal status as heterosexuals, with the exception of adoption rights. Legislation passed in 1981 protects gays and lesbians from discrimination. In 1993, a law was passed recognizing the "partnerships" of homosexual couples—in essence, a recognition of same-sex marriages. The age of consent for both men and women in Norway is 16 years of age.

For more gay and lesbian travel resources, visit Frommers.com.

Senior Travel

Mention the fact that you're a senior when you first make your travel reservations. All major airlines and many Norwegian hotels offer discounts for seniors. In Norway, people over age 67 are entitled to 50% off the price of first- and second-class train tickets. Ask for the discount at the ticket office.

Frommers.com offers more information and resources on travel for seniors.

Family Travel

Norwegians like kids but don't offer a lot of special amenities for them. Many Norwegian hoteliers will let children aged 12 and under stay in a room with their parents for free; some will not. Sometimes this requires a little negotiation at the reception desk. A kids' menu in a restaurant is a rarity. However, you can order a half-portion, and most waiters will oblige. At attractions—even if it isn't specifically posted—inquire whether a kids' discount is available. European Union citizens under 18 are admitted free to all state-run museums.

People to People: Reaching Out

Established in 1971, Friends Overseas matches American visitors and Norwegians with similar interests and backgrounds. For more information, visit www.friendsoverseas.org.

Babysitting services are available through most hotel desks or by applying at the tourist information office in the town where you're staying. Many hotels have children's game rooms and playgrounds.

To locate those accommodations, restaurants, and attractions that are particularly kid-friendly, refer to the "Kids" icons throughout this guide.

For a list of family-friendly travel resources, visit www.frommers.com/planning.

Multicultural Travelers

Norway is one of Europe's most culturally and ethnically homogenous countries, with very little foreign immigration and a government that has been less progressive than neighboring Sweden when it comes to immigration quotas. Larger cities such as Oslo and Bergen have a somewhat different countenance, however. Over 25% of Oslo's population is of immigrant background, and many immigrants claim that the capital's neighborhood of Grønland is more Muslim than the countries they emigrated from. The number of immigrants in Norway in 2010 was approximately 552,000—roughly 11.4% of the total population—232,000 of whom have Norwegian citizenship. The largest ethnic groups are Polish, Swedish, Pakistani, Iraqi, and Somali.

Norwegians on the whole consider themselves rather progressive, liberal thinkers, although strains of conservativism are not absent. In general, travelers of non-Caucasian backgrounds will be met with rather little prejudice or harassing behavior, especially from younger Norwegians, many of whom have traveled extensively to less developed parts of the world and are often very aware of other multicultural societies. While it's not inconceivable that someone with a Middle Eastern, South Asian, or African background may experience some level of passive-aggressive behavior, this is by far the exception rather than the rule.

Women Travelers

Norway is one of the most progressive countries in the world when it comes to gender equality, and female travelers (even those traveling on their own) should experience little, if any, harassment. For general travel resources for women, go to www.frommers.com/planning.

RESPONSIBLE TOURISM

Responsible tourism is conscientious travel. It means being careful with the environments you explore, and respecting the communities you visit. Two overlapping components of sustainable travel are **ecotourism** and **ethical tourism.** The **International Ecotourism Society (TIES)** defines ecotourism as responsible travel to natural areas that conserves the environment and improves the wellbeing of local people. TIES suggests that ecotourists follow these principles:

- Minimize environmental impact.
- Build environmental and cultural awareness and respect.
- Provide positive experiences for both visitors and hosts.
- Provide direct financial benefits for conservation and for local people.
- Raise sensitivity to host countries' political, environmental, and social climates.
- Support international human rights and labor agreements.

You can find some eco-friendly travel tips and statistics, as well as touring companies and associations—listed by destination under "Travel Choice"—at the **TIES** website, www.ecotourism.org. Also check out **Ecotravel.com**, which lets you search for sustainable touring companies in several categories (water-based, land-based, spiritually oriented, and so on).

While much of the focus of eco-tourism is about reducing impacts on the natural environment, ethical tourism concentrates on ways to preserve and enhance local economies and communities, regardless of location. You can embrace ethical tourism by staying at a locally owned hotel or shopping at a store that employs local workers and sells locally produced goods.

FROMMERS.COM: THE COMPLETE travel RESOURCE

It should go without saying, but we highly recommend **Frommers.com**, voted Best Travel Site by *PC Magazine.* We think you'll find our expert advice and tips; independent reviews of hotels, restaurants, attractions, and preferred shopping and nightlife venues; vacation giveaways; and an online booking tool indispensable before, during, and after your travels. We publish the complete contents of over 128 travel guides in our **Destinations** section, covering nearly 4,000 places worldwide to help you plan your trip. Each weekday, we publish original articles reporting on **Deals and News** via our free **Frommers.com Newsletter,** to help you save time and money and travel smarter. We're betting you'll find our new **Events** listings (http://events.frommers.com) an invaluable resource; it's an up-to-the-minute roster of what's happening in cities everywhere—including concerts, festivals, lectures, and more. We've also added weekly **podcasts, interactive maps,** and hundreds of new images across the site. Check out our **Travel Talk** area, featuring **Message Boards** where you can join conversations with thousands of fellow Frommer's travelers and post your trip report once you return.

Green Traveller (www.greentraveller.co.uk) is an excellent resource for ideas on how to travel in an eco-friendly fashion; the founder is co-author of a bestselling book on environmentally responsible travel. **Responsible Travel** (www.responsibletravel.com) is a great source of sustainable travel ideas; the site is run by a spokesperson for ethical tourism in the travel industry. **Sustainable Travel International** (www.sustainabletravelinternational.org) promotes ethical tourism practices, and manages an extensive directory of sustainable properties and tour operators around the world.

In the U.K., **Tourism Concern** (www.tourismconcern.org.uk) works to reduce social and environmental problems connected to tourism. The **Association of Independent Tour Operators** (**AITO;** www.aito.co.uk) is a group of specialist operators leading the field in making holidays sustainable.

Lending a Helping Hand

Volunteer travel has become popular among those who want to venture beyond the standard group-tour experience to learn languages, interact with locals, and make a positive difference while on vacation. Volunteer travel usually doesn't require special skills—just a willingness to work hard—and programs vary in length from a few days to several weeks. Some programs provide free housing and food, but many require volunteers to pay for travel expenses, which can add up quickly. For general information on volunteer travel, visit **www.idealist.org**.

Before you commit to a volunteer program, it's important to make sure any money you're giving is truly going back to the local community, and that the work you'll be doing will be a good fit for you. **Volunteer International** (www.volunteerinternational.org) has a helpful list of questions to ask to determine the intentions and the nature of a volunteer program.

Dining in Good Conscience

Although fans of Santa and Rudolph may take issue with eating reindeer meat, reindeer is an abundant species in Norway and perfectly safe (and ethical) to eat. Most Norwegians don't even think twice about ordering reindeer at a restaurant.

Whales, however, may be a different story. Man has hunted whales for millennia, but the practice was much more common when whale oil had strong commercial value. Today, it is the whales' meat that is considered a delicacy, particularly in Japan. In Norway, whaling is only permitted from the minke whale species, the smallest of the baleen whales. The minke population consists of some 180,000 animals in the central and northeast Atlantic and 700,000 around Antarctica. Although government officials have determined that this is a large enough and sustainable population for commercial whaling, foreign animal rights groups protest the industry's activities, as well as the popular consumption of the meat.

Norway objected to the International Whaling Commission's moratorium on commercial whaling, and as a result resumed whaling in 1993 (Faroe Islands, Iceland, and Japan are the other countries that also presently whale). Catches in Norway, which occur between early May and late August, have ranged in quantity from 218 whales (in 1995) to 646 (in 2003). In 2009 Norway's whale catch fell to the lowest number in over a decade. The decline was due in large part to the global financial crisis and an attendant lower demand for such meat products. Despite a total of 484 minke whales being caught in 2009, the quota was raised in April 2010 to 1,286 per year—a quota that has never been reached. Frozen whale meat tends to cost around NOK130 per kilo, a price that is rather less expensive than reindeer or beef.

Good Buying

While in Norway consider picking up some handicrafts produced by the Sami in the north. Sami artisans produce a number of excellent housewares and handcrafted goods, including wooden curios (often with a reindeer theme), knives, colorful wool mittens, handknit sweaters, and silver (traditional jewelry is very popular).

In terms of heath concerns, there is nothing wrong with eating whale or seal meat. Whaling and sealing processes throughout Norway are strictly controlled. Many Norwegians themselves are divided, and you'll want to decide for yourself on which side of the whaling argument you stand before ordering a scrumptious whale filet for dinner.

PACKAGE TOURS FOR THE INDEPENDENT TRAVELER

For travelers who feel more comfortable if everything is prearranged—hotels, transportation, sightseeing excursions, luggage handling, tips, taxes, and even meals—a package tour is the obvious choice, and it may even help save money.

FROM THE U.S. One of the best tour operators to Norway is **ScanAm World Tours** (**© 800/545-2204;** www.scanamtours.com). Its best and most highly sought-after itinerary is its **Norway in a Nutshell Fjord Tours.** These tours,

IT'S EASY BEING green

Here are a few simple ways you can help conserve fuel and energy when you travel:

- Each time you take a flight or drive a car greenhouse gases are released into the atmosphere. You can help neutralize this danger to the planet through "carbon offsetting"—paying someone to invest your money in programs that reduce their greenhouse gas emissions by the same amount you've added. Before buying carbon-offset credits, just make sure that you're using a reputable company, one with a proven program that invests in renewable energy. Reliable carbon-offset companies include **Carbonfund** (www.carbonfund.org), **TerraPass** (www.terrapass.org), and **CoolClimate** (coolclimate.berkeley.edu).
- Whenever possible, choose nonstop flights; they generally require less fuel than indirect flights that stop and take off again. Try to fly during the day—some scientists estimate that nighttime flights are twice as harmful to the environment. And pack light—each 15 kilograms (13 lb.) of luggage on a 5,000-mile flight adds up to 50 kilograms (110 lb.) of carbon dioxide emitted.
- Where you stay during your travels can have a major environmental impact. To determine the green credentials of a property, ask about trash disposal and recycling, water conservation, and energy use; also question whether sustainable materials were used in the construction of the property. The website **www.greenhotels.com** recommends green-rated member hotels around the world that fulfill the company's stringent environmental requirements. Also consult **www.environmentallyfriendlyhotels.com** for more green accommodations ratings.
- At hotels, request that your sheets and towels not be changed daily. (Many hotels already have programs like this in place.) Turn off the lights and air-conditioner (or heater) when you leave your room.
- Use public transportation where possible—trains, buses, and even taxis are more energy-efficient than driving. Even better is to walk or cycle; you'll produce zero emissions and stay fit and healthy on your travels.
- If renting a car is necessary, ask the rental agent for a hybrid, or rent the most fuel-efficient car available. You'll use less gas and save money at the tank.
- Eat at locally owned and operated restaurants that use produce grown in the area. This contributes to the local economy and cuts down on greenhouse gas emissions associated with transportation of food.

which cost $208 to $619 per person from May to September, take either a full day or 2 days and 1 night. They include a tour on the famous Flåm mountain railway (p. 318) and a 2-hour cruise on the Aurlandsfjord and the Nærøyfjord. Tours are operated from Oslo to Bergen or vice versa. The company also operates many other tours, the most useful being the 9-day, 8-night tour of Oslo and Bergen plus the fjord country, for those wanting to cover just the highlights of Norway. Prices include only land travel and cost around $1,000 per person.

Grand Circle Travel (✆ **800/959-0405;** www.gct.com) offers 17-day tours of the Norwegian fjords and Lapland, with carefully chosen hotels and big Norwegian breakfasts. Highlights of this tour are Bergen, Trondheim, the Lofoten Islands, and Geirangerfjord. Although **American Express** (✆ **800/335-3342**) doesn't offer package deals to Norway, Amex agents can customize a special package just for you.

For a vast array of other tours of Norway, many of them appealing to the active vacationer and special-interest traveler, refer to "The Active Vacation Planner," below.

FROM THE U.K. The oldest travel agency in Britain, **Cox & Kings,** Gordon House 10, Greencoat Place, London SW1P 1PH (✆ **020/7873-5000;** www.coxandkings.co.uk), was established in 1758. Today the company specializes in first-class and unusual, if pricey, holidays. Its offerings in Norway include cruises through the spectacular fjords and waterways, bus and rail tours through sites of historic and aesthetic interest, and visits to the region's best-known handicraft centers, Viking burial sites, and historic churches. The company is noted for its focus on tours of ecological and environmental interest.

Another reliable tour operator is **Nordic Experience, Inc.** (✆ **012/0670-8888;** www.scantours.co.uk).

THE ACTIVE VACATION PLANNER

From dog-sled racing to canoeing, from curling to speed skating to skiing, Norway is the most sports-oriented country in Europe. Nearly half of the four million people of Norway are members of the Norwegian Sports Federation, and three out of four Norwegian children take part in sporting activities. Winter sports are dominated by skiing, of course, along with ice hockey and curling. In the too-short summer, virtually all Norwegians head for the outdoors while the sun shines. They sail, swim, or canoe, and trails fill with hikers or mountain bikers.

SKIING Norway is the birthplace of skiing, predating the sport in Switzerland or Austria. It boasts some 30,000km (19,000 miles) of marked ski trails.

From November until the end of May, cross-country and downhill skiing are both available, but don't expect the brilliant sun of the Alps. The days get long just before Easter, when skiing is best. Lights illuminate many of the tracks for winter skiers, proving to be especially helpful in January and February.

From December to April, daylight is limited, but it's still possible to have a full day's skiing if you start early. The bigger resorts have at least one floodlit downhill slope, and many towns and villages have a floodlit cross-country track *(lysløype)*. The days lengthen rapidly in January and February. Mid-February is the most popular period, and accommodations prices are higher then. Early March offers a combination of good skiing conditions and low prices. Easter time is popular with Norwegians, and hotel prices are very high then. Beginning Easter Monday, low-season rates apply again. Skiing in the higher elevations is possible until May, and you can even ski all summer in a few places. For information about summer skiing, get in touch with **Stryn Sommerski Senter** (✆ **57-87-79-00;** www.strynefjellet.com). The largest mainland glacier in Europe is at Jostedalsbreen, near Stryn.

Snowboard and skiing facilities in the country are excellent overall. The winter season is longer than in southern Europe. The bigger resorts in Norway have plenty to interest beginners and intermediate skiers for a week or more, and there are many black-diamond runs for the more experienced. Families can find free lift passes and helmets for kids under 7, plus plenty of nursery slopes and day-care centers. Lift passes are relatively inexpensive, rental equipment is often cheaper than in other ski countries, lines are usually short, and the slopes are uncrowded.

Norway is best known for its cross-country skiing, which is superb at ski resorts everywhere. An endless network of marked trails *(skiløyper)* crosses rolling hills, forests, frozen lakes, and mountains. Numerous small ski centers offer inexpensive ski rentals and tuition. All the downhill resorts also have extensive trail networks.

Norwegian ski resorts are known for their informality, which is evident in the schools and the atmosphere. The emphasis is on simple pleasures, not the sophistication often found at alpine resorts. (Incidentally, the word *ski* is an Old Norse word, as is *slalom.*)

Geilo and **Hemsedal** are the best-known downhill resorts for keen downhill skiers. Geilo has the most extensive lift system, but Hemsedal has steeper runs and more spectacular scenery. There is also good cross-country skiing near both resorts. The huge mountain area of **Golsfjellet,** between Hemsedal, Gol, and Valdres, is excellent for experienced cross-country skiers. The main railway between Oslo and Bergen serves Geilo directly and Hemsedal via a bus connection from Gol (3–4 hr.).

Geilo is my favorite ski resort in Norway because you can step off a train and onto a ski lift. Voss, its rival, has more folklore and better architecture. A lot of Geilo consists of large structures that evoke army barracks. But, in winter, the white snow is all-forgiving, and you will have arrived at an alpine paradise. The best slope at Geilo is the Skiheiser, with 24km (15 miles) of some of the best skiing this side of the Swiss Alps. With 18 lifts and 33 ski runs, Geilo is competitive with any resort in Norway.

Trysil, in eastern Norway, is less famous than Geilo and Hemsedal, but it also offers good downhill skiing and a particularly fine choice of self-catering chalets and apartments with skiable access to the lifts. Trysil is easy to reach by a direct express bus service from Oslo airport (3 hr.). Of course, Trysil is more of a backwater and doesn't possess the après-ski life of more established resorts such as Voss and Geilo.

The Cradle of Skiing

A 4,000-year-old rock carving from Nordland shows that Norwegians were already using skis then. Telemark region is regarded as the "cradle of skiing," because Sondre Nordheim from Morgedal created an interest in the sport there in the 1870s and 1880s. He devised a binding that made it possible to turn and jump without losing the skis, and also designed a ski with inwardly curved edges—the Telemark ski—that became the prototype of all subsequent skis.

The **Valdres** area between Hemsedal and Lillehammer is famous for its scenery of rolling forested hills with high mountains in the distance. The Aurdal ski center has the unbeatable combination of superb cross-country terrain and good downhill facilities. A good base for both is one of the excellent chalets at the top of the downhill slopes. A direct bus service connects Valdres to central Oslo (3 hr.).

The owners of ski resorts in Voss, Geilo, and Lillehammer are hardly socking money away for when Valdres takes over all their business (it hasn't happened so far). But many world-class skiers are increasingly frequenting this resort to avoid the crowds and to enjoy slopes at a more leisurely pace.

Impressions

Skiing is the most Norwegian of all our sports, and a glorious sport it is; if any merits being called the sport of sports, this is surely the one.

—Explorer Fridtjof Nansen, after crossing Greenland on skis in 1880

Lillehammer has been well known since the Winter Olympics in 1994, and the competitive facilities are world-class. The main downhill slopes are at **Hafjell,** 15km (9¼ miles) north of Lillehammer. The cross-country skiing through the gentle hills, scattered forests, and lakes of the Sjusjøen area is endless and particularly good for beginners. Lillehammer itself is more cosmopolitan than the other ski towns and has a wide range of shops and places to eat and drink.

Though I love Geilo's small-scale winter charm, no other resort in Norway can compete with the multifarious offerings of Lillehammer. Facilities here are more wide-ranging and better organized than in Voss or Geilo. Lillehammer might lack charm, but it more than makes up for that with experienced instructors in its ski schools, good lifts and smooth alpine slopes, and sheer vastness. (It has 402km/249 miles of prepared, illuminated cross-country tracks.)

North of Lillehammer is the Gudbrandsdal Valley, surrounded by extensive cross-country areas linked by two long-distance trails: "Troll løype" to the east and "Peer Gynt løype" to the west. Skiers of all abilities enjoy this area, and downhillers find several good ski centers. This region, including **Gålå** and **Fefor,** is especially well served by mountain hotels.

For those traveling with their own car, the **Telemark** area is easily accessible from Haugesund or Kristiansand (3–5 hr.). **Gaustablikk,** near the town of Rjukan, is the best all-around center, with several lifts and downhill runs of all standards, plus many kilometers of cross-country trails to suit all abilities. Although the skiing is good here, it lacks much in après-ski life, restaurants, and hotels.

Voss is well known and easily reached from Bergen in about 90 minutes by car or train, but the location near the west coast suffers from unreliable weather, particularly early and late in the season. It is well worth considering for a short break, though, or if you want to combine skiing with a winter visit to the fjord area.

Even though it's trying hard, Voss still has a long way to go before it overtakes either Geilo or Lillehammer. Nonetheless, it offers ski lifts, chairlifts, and an aerial cableway that can carry skiers up to 788m (2,585 ft.). I am especially fond of Mjølfjell, reached by going up the Raundalen Valley. This area offers some of the best cross-country skiing in Norway. Voss also emphasizes Norwegian folklore more than either Geilo or Lillehammer.

BIKING For the serious cyclist, there are two great routes in Norway: The North Sea Cycleway and the Rallarvegen (Old Navvy Road). Each of them is only partially paved. The coastal route is much easier, whereas the Old Navvy Road runs across open mountains, passing through pastures and meadows en route down to the nearest fjord. Pick up detailed maps of routes and how to reach them in tourist offices throughout Norway.

The North Sea Cycleway stretches for 296km (184 miles) and is mostly rural, with woodland, moors, and crags, passing many a meadow. It runs through such ports as Flekkefjord and Egersund, passing such larger towns as Sandnes and Stavanger.

The Old Navvy Road was built from 1895 to 1902, starting in the tree-lined east and climbing into the open mountains, with panoramic views of snow-covered slopes; high-altitude, incredibly blue lakes; and the Hardangerjøkulen Glacier. The most dramatic point along the route is from Vatnahalsen, where the road descends the 21 hairpin bends of Myrdalskleiva, continuing down the Flamsdal Valley to Flåm. The road has been a cycle track since the 1970s. Because it follows the Bergen–Oslo train tracks for most of the way, the usual starting point is Haugastøl, known for its herring and jazz.

Bike rentals abound in Norway. Inquire at your hotel or the local tourist office. The Norwegian Mountain Touring Association (see "Hiking," below) provides inexpensive lodging for those on overnight bike trips. To cycle through the splendors of Norway, you can join Britain's oldest (1878) and largest association of bicycle riders, the **Cyclists' Touring Club,** CTC Parklands, Railton Road, Guildford, Surrey GU2 9JX (✆ **0844/736-8450;** www.ctc.org.uk). The fees for membership start at £37, which includes information, maps, a subscription to a newsletter packed with practical information and morale boosters, plus recommended cycling routes through virtually every country in Europe. The organization's knowledge of scenic routes is especially comprehensive. Membership can be arranged over the phone with a credit card.

One of the best bets for mountain biking is the Setesdal region, with its many small roads and forest trails. **TrollAktiv** (✆ **37-93-11-77;** www.troll-mountain.no), 7km (4¼ miles) north from Evje on the main road (Rte. 9), is an expert in the area, offering both guided trips and bikes for rent (with helmets) from mid-April to late October.

The Øyer Mountains are also excellent for cycling, and the scenery is splendid. For more information, including suggested cycle tours in the Øyer Mountains, consult the **Øyer tourist office** (✆ **61-27-70-00**).

BIRD-WATCHING Some of Europe's most noteworthy bird sanctuaries are on islands off the Norwegian coast or on the mainland. Rocky and isolated, the sanctuaries offer ideal nesting places for millions of seabirds that vastly outnumber the local human population during certain seasons. Foremost among the sanctuaries are the **Lofoten Islands**—particularly two of the outermost islands, Værøy and Røst—and the island of Runde. An almost .5km (¼-mile)-long bridge (one of the longest in Norway) connects **Runde** to the coastline, a 2½-hour drive from Ålesund. Runde's year-round human population is about 150, and the colonies of puffins, cormorants, razor-billed auks, guillemots, gulls, and eider ducks number in the millions. Another noteworthy bird sanctuary is at **Fokstumyra,** a national park near Dombås.

FROMMER'S FAVORITE offbeat ADVENTURES

- **Dog Sledding:** Traveling over the frozen tundra or through snowbound forests at dog speed can be one of the great experiences of the Nordic world. You can be a passenger bundled aboard a sled or a driver urging on a team of huskies. An outfitter that specializes in the experience, usually as part of midwinter camping trips under a canopy of stars, is **Muir's Tours,** Nepal House, 97A Swansea Road, Reading, Berkshire RG1 8HA, England (✆ **0118/950-2281;** www.nkf-mt.org.uk). Five-day all-inclusive tours are conducted in winter (Dec–May) for £802 per person. You're given your own team of four to six huskies for this safari. As you ride along, you'll likely see reindeer along your trail. Longer tours are also available.
- **Observing Musk Oxen:** A vestige of the last ice age, the musk ox had become nearly extinct by the 1930s. Between 1932 and 1953, musk oxen were shipped from Greenland to the Dovrefjell (a national park roughly 1 hour's train ride south of Trondheim), where about 60 of them still roam. On a safari you can observe this thriving herd—take along some binoculars—as well as Norway's purest herd of original mountain reindeer. The park's landscape, also a survivor from the last ice age, is Europe's most bountiful wildflower mountain. Accommodations in or near the park can be arranged through **Borton Overseas** in the U.S. (✆ **800/843-0602;** www.borton overseas.com).
- **Rafting:** Norway's abundant snow and rainfall and its steep topography feed dozens of roaring white-water streams. Experience these torrents first-hand as part of white-water treks downriver. One of Norway's most respected river outfitters is **Norwegian Wildlife and Rafting AS,** Varphaugen Gard, N-2670 Ofta (✆ **47-66-06-80;** www.sjoa raftingsenter.no). Based in central Norway, about a 90-minute drive north of Lillehammer, the company has a flotilla of devices suitable for helping you float, meander, or shoot down the rapids. Whatever conveyance you

The isolated island of **Lovund** is a 2-hour ferry ride from the town of Sandnesjøen, south of Bødo. Lovund ("the island of puffins") has a human population of fewer than 270 and a bird population in the hundreds of thousands. You can visit Lovund and the other famous Norwegian bird-watching sites on your own, or sign up for one of the organized tours sponsored by **Borton Overseas,** 5412 Lyndale Avenue, Minneapolis, MN 55419 (✆ **800/843-0602** or 612/882-4640; www.bortonoverseas.com).

Brochures and pamphlets are available from the tourist board **Destination Lofoten** (✆ **76-06-98-00;** www.lofoten.info).

CANOEING, KAYAKING & RAFTING Canoeing and kayaking, two increasingly popular sports, allow visitors to reach places that are otherwise almost inaccessible. Both activities offer a unique opportunity to observe Norway's animals and birds without frightening them away with the sound of an engine.

can imagine (paddle boards, kayaks, canoes, or inflatable rafts), this company can provide it. Trips last from 1 to 8 days.

- **Trekking the Fjords:** Two respected U.S.-based outfitters, **Borton Overseas** (see above) and **Five Stars of Scandinavia** (✆ **800/722-4126;** www.5stars-of-scandinavia.com), offer 7- and 8-day treks through Norway, designed to acquaint you with the country's heritage and its thousands of scenic wonders. Amid the cliffs and waterfalls of the fjords, you can participate in point-to-point guided treks that average around 24km (15 miles) per day. En route you'll visit wooden churches, mountain hamlets, and, in some cases, snowfields and slow-moving glaciers. Depending on your budget and your tastes, overnight accommodations range from first-class hotels to simple mountain huts favored by rock climbers and many trekkers.
- **Bicycling in Lofoten:** Some of the weirdest and most isolated tundra and lichen-covered rock formations in Norway lie within the Lofoten archipelago, north of the Arctic Circle. Berkeley, California-based **Backroads Travel** (✆ **800/462-2848;** www.backroads.com) conducts 6-day hiking-and-biking (they refer to them as "multisport") tours of the isolated archipelago at least twice a year, during July and August, with an emphasis on ecology and natural beauty. **Five Stars of Scandinavia** (p. 68) offers comparable tours and tends to be cheaper than Backroads. Both operators house their participants in simple mountain huts and lodges.
- **Going on a Moose Safari:** Norway's largest animal, the moose, can weigh up to 600 kilograms (1,323 lb.). These forest dwellers are shy of people and best spotted at night. If you'd like to go on a moose safari, contact **Dæsbekken Villmarksenter** in Finneskogen (✆ **62-95-48-57;** www.villmarksenter.hm.no), east of Oslo, near the Swedish border. Individual visitors can arrange tours from July to September; otherwise, it's strictly group bookings.

Some of my best experiences out on a canoe have been with **TrollAktiv** (✆ **37-93-11-77;** www.trollaktiv.no), 7km (4¼ miles) north from the village of Evje on the main road (Rte. 9). The region of Setesdal, known for its mountains, rivers, and varied wildlife, contains a stunning stretch of the River Otra—ideal for canoeing—extending from the rafting center south to Evje. En route you'll pass several osprey nests and beaver lodges. The center is also the best place in southern Norway for white-water rafting from mid-April to late October. From late June until September, water temperatures can reach 20°C (68°F), which makes the River Otra the warmest in Norway. Both half-day and full-day trips can be arranged. **Crossing Latitudes,** 420 West Koch St., Bozeman, MT 59771 (✆ **406/585-5356;** www.crossinglatitudes.com), is another source for sea-kayaking and backpacking expeditions.

If you'd like to go rafting on the Sjoa River, billed as "the wildest in Norway," you can obtain full information from the **Jotunheimen Reiseliv** (✆ **61-21-29-90;**

www.visitjotunheimen.com), which also provides information about horseback riding, mountain and glacier climbing, mountain biking, and canoeing.

The rivers around Voss resort, in Norway's fjord country, have some of the finest river rafting. **Voss Rafting Center** (© **56-51-05-25;** www.vossrafting.no) offers rafting and other watersports such as river-boarding and canyoning. Overnight stays in the wild along with meals can be arranged.

FISHING With one of the most extensive coastlines in the world—some 57,458km (35,702 miles) including fjords and bays—Norway offers plenty of opportunities for sea fishing.

Norway has long been famous for its salmon and trout fishing, with more than 100 salmon rivers flowing into its fjords. The best months for salmon are June, July, and sometimes August. Sea-trout fishing takes place from June to September and is best in August. The brown-trout season varies with altitude.

Fishing in the ocean is free. To fish in lakes, rivers, or streams, anyone over 16 must have a fishing license. The cost of a day license to fish begins at NOK250. National fishing licenses can be purchased at local post offices. For more information, contact the **Bergen Angling Association,** Wernerholmsvegen 33, 5221 Nesttun (© **55-34-18-08;** www.bergensportsfiskere.no).

A U.S.-based company that can arrange fishing (as well as hunting) excursions anywhere within Norway and the rest of Scandinavia is **Five Stars of Scandinavia,** 225A 93rd Avenue S.E., Tumwater, WA 98501 (© **800/722-4126;** www.5stars-of-scandinavia.com). For a truly unusual fishing experience, consider renting one of their old-fashioned fishermen's cottages in the isolated Lofoten Islands. The rustic-looking, fully renovated cottages each lie adjacent to the sea and evoke 19th-century isolation. Five Stars will rent you a cottage for as little as 1 night, but I recommend a minimum stay of 3 nights to appreciate this offbeat adventure.

Norwegian Summers: 23 Hours of Daylight

The Norwegian summer has magnificent, long, sunny days. Temperatures often reach 30°C (86°F). Daylight on the longest days can last 23 hours, warming the lakes and fjords for all watersports.

The River Gudbrandsdalslågen, running through a beautiful valley and the ski resort of Hafjell Hunderfossen, is one of the best fishing rivers of Europe, set against a backdrop of the Øyer Mountains, with its many fishing lakes and rivers. The main types of fish caught are burbot, trout, char, and grayling. Many lakes in the mountains have rowboats for free use, and permits are easily obtainable at gas stations, grocery stores, hotels, or inns. For more information, contact the **Øyer tourist office** at © **61-27-70-00.**

GOLFING Norway has more than two dozen 18-hole golf courses, and the **Norwegian Golf Federation** (© **21-02-91-50;** www.golfforbundet.no) can provide information on all of them. Many golf clubs are open to foreign guests. Greens fees tend to be moderate. My two favorite clubs are the 18-hole **Oslo Golf Klubb,** at Bogstad, Oslo (© **22-51-05-60;** www.oslogk.no), and the 18-hole **Meland Golf Club,** Meland/Frekhaug (© **56-17-46-00;** www.melandgolf.no), 36km (22 miles) north of Bergen.

HIKING Norway's mountains and wilderness are among the most spectacular in the world. The **Norwegian Mountain Touring Association,** Storgata 3, N-0101 Oslo (✆ **22-82-28-22;** www.turistforeningen.no), maintains affiliations with all the hiking associations of Norway and provides maps and advice. The association offers guided hikes of 5 to 8 days. They cost from around NOK700, including meals and lodging. Local associations mark the routes and operate a network of cabins for hikers to share.

In the U.S., **Blue Marble Travel,** 350 Ramapo Valley Road, Suite 18-131, Oakland, NJ 07436 (✆ **201/465-2567;** www.bluemarble.org), features reasonably priced biking and hiking trips in Norway. **European Walking Tours,** 1401 Regency Drive East, Savoy, IL 61874 (✆ **800/231-8448** or 217/398-0058; www.walkingtours.com), sponsors walking tours for the mature traveler in Norway. The operator, Jacqueline Tofté, is a native of the Swiss Alps and has charted routes across meadows, through remote valleys, over mountain passes, and alongside serene lakes. The tours include searches for wildflowers, birds, and mountain animals, with lessons in local architecture, traditions, and history thrown in.

HORSEBACK RIDING Throughout Norway you'll find riding schools with horses for rent. Many country hotels in Norway also keep a few horses for the use of guests. Many organizations offer horseback tours of Norway's wilderness, enabling visitors to see some of the more spectacular scenery. Tours can range from a few hours to a full week. Luggage is transported by car. One tour organizer is **Borton Overseas,** 5412 Lyndale Avenue, Minneapolis, MN 55419 (✆ **800/843-0602** or 612/882-4640; www.bortonoverseas.com).

Our favorite place to go mountain riding is **Voss Fjellhest,** outside the resort of Voss (✆ **90-75-48-40;** www.vossfjellhest.no). In panoramic fjord and mountain scenery, you'll be taken on day or weekend rides with everything arranged for you, including accommodations and meals.

SAILING Norway's long coast can be a challenge to any yachting enthusiast. The most tranquil havens are along the southern coast. To arrange sailing or rafting trips, various boat rentals, or evening parasailing, contact **SeaAction** (✆ **33-33-69-93;** www.seaaction.no).

WHALE-WATCHING In Norway, you can catch a glimpse of 20-m (70-ft.), 40,000-kilogram (88,000-lb.) sperm whales, the largest-toothed whales in the world. You can also see killer whales, harbor porpoises, minke whales, and white-beaked dolphins. Whale researchers conduct 6-hour whale-watching tours in the Arctic Ocean.

For information and bookings, contact **Borton Overseas,** 5412 Lyndale Avenue, Minneapolis, MN 55419 (✆ **800/843-0602** or 612/882-4640; www.bortonoverseas.com).

STAYING CONNECTED

Telephones

Norway's country code is **47.** Norwegian landline and cellphone numbers consist of eight digits. The first digit generally determines the region the phone is registered in (for example, 2 tends to be Oslo, 5 is Bergen, and 7 is for the north). Cellphone numbers begin with either 4 or 9.

For more telephone dialing tips, see "Telephones" in chapter 16.

ONLINE traveler's TOOLBOX

Veteran travelers usually carry some essential items to make their trips easier. Following is a selection of handy online tools to bookmark and use.

- **Airplane Food** (www.airlinemeals.net)
- **Airplane Seating** (www.seatguru.com; www.airlinequality.com)
- **Foreign Languages for Travelers** (www.travlang.com; www.bbc.com/languages)
- **Maps** (maps.google.com; www.mapquest.com)
- **Time and Date** (www.timeanddate.com)
- **Travel Warnings** (http://travel.state.gov; www.fco.gov.uk/travel; www.voyage.gc.ca; www.smartraveller.gov.au)
- **Universal Currency Converter** (www.xe.com/ucc)
- **Visa ATM Locator** (www.visa.com), **MasterCard ATM Locator** (www.mastercard.com)
- **Weather** (www.intellicast.com; www.weather.com)

Cellphones (Mobile Phones)

Because nearly everyone in Norway has a cellphone, landline use is on the decline; even some businesses today only use cellphones. On the whole, cellphone coverage in Norway is excellent. Even in some of the more remote places, you will find good phone reception (though in some of the more remote, mountainous areas you may have trouble getting consistent reception). Norway has three main cellphone operators: Telenor Mobil, Netcom, and Network Norway. Mobile calls in Norway tend to be charged per minute, but there is frequently a *startpris,* a higher charge that is assessed for the first minute of the phone call.

Having a cellphone while traveling is both wise and affordable, especially since the charges for using a hotel phone are often extremely expensive. The easiest way to make calls is to use your own cellphone from home, though this can be pricey. You will need to let your home carrier know that you will be traveling abroad, as this "roaming" service must often be enabled, and you will also need to make sure that you have a multi-frequency GSM phone that will work in European countries. Be sure, too, to get the per-minute rate before you go so you know what you'll be spending. An alternative is to use your own cellphone with a local SIM card purchased once you're in Norway. For this to work, your phone will need to be SIM-unlocked, which your phone provider should be able to do for a small fee (or for free).

Buying a phone abroad can be economically attractive, as many nations have cheap prepaid phone systems (*kontantkort* in Norwegian). The two primary mobile companies offering this service are Telenor Mobil and Netcom. You will be assigned a local Norwegian number and will be charged at local rates. All your incoming calls are free, no matter where they originate. When you run out of credit you can easily top up your account with extra minutes at cellphone shops and kiosks. Because the air time you use is prepaid, you have full control over how much you spend and can easily stay within budget. Once you arrive in Norway, stop by a local cellphone shop and get the cheapest package; you're likely to spend under NOK500 for a phone and a starter calling card that includes a nominal number of minutes. Local calls may cost under NOK1 per minute.

Wilderness adventurers might consider renting a **satellite phone** ("satphone"). It's different from a cellphone in that it connects via satellite and works where there's no cellular signal or ground-based tower. You can rent a satphone from Road-Post (www.roadpost.com). InTouch USA (www.intouchusa.com) offers a wider range of satphones but at higher rates. Per-minute call charges can be even cheaper than roaming charges with a regular cellphone, but the phone itself is more expensive. Satphones are outrageously expensive to buy, so don't even think about that.

Voice over Internet Protocol (VoIP)

If you have Web access while traveling, consider a broadband-based telephone service (in technical terms, **Voice over Internet Protocol,** or **VoIP**) such as Skype (www.skype.com), Line 2 (www.line2.com), or Vonage (www.vonage.com), which allow you to make free international calls from your laptop or in a cybercafe. Neither service requires the people you're calling to also have that service (though there are fees if they do not). Check the websites for details.

Internet & E-mail

WITH YOUR OWN COMPUTER

More and more hotels, cafes, and retailers are signing on as Wi-Fi (wireless fidelity) "hot spots." To find public Wi-Fi hot spots at your destination, go to **www.jiwire.com**; its Hotspot Finder holds the world's largest directory of public wireless hot spots.

Most hotels offer cable or Wi-Fi connections for laptops.

WITHOUT YOUR OWN COMPUTER

Cybercafes are found in all large cities, especially Oslo and Bergen, but they do not tend to cluster in any particular neighborhoods because of competition. To find cybercafes, check **www.cybercaptive.com** and **www.cybercafe.com**. Aside from formal cybercafes, most **youth hostels** and **public libraries** have Internet access.

TIPS ON ACCOMMODATIONS

Hotel passes (see below) can save you big money. In addition, there are several imaginative lodging possibilities other than hotels that are not only workable, but a lot of fun and a change of pace.

For tips on surfing for hotel deals online, visit www.frommers.com/planning.

BOOKING A HOTEL The Norwegian Tourist Board does not provide a hotel-booking service. Your local travel agency will be able to do this for you, or you can ask a tour operator. Alternatively, you can book accommodations directly by post, fax, or telephone. Practically everyone in Norway speaks English, so you will rarely encounter any difficulty communicating. If you're traveling in the high season (mid-June to mid-Aug), it's advisable to book in advance. Tourist offices in Norway often have a reservation service. You can also make bookings at the website **www.visitnorway.com**.

HOTEL PASSES In Norway, you can get discounts on hotel rooms by purchasing the **Norway Fjord Pass,** Fjord Tours, Strøm gate 4, NO-5015 Bergen (✆ **81-56-82-22;** www.fjordtours.no), which offers discounts on nearly 170 hotels all over the country. The pass costs NOK120 and is valid for two adults and accompanying children under the age of 15. The pass is valid throughout the year. One hotel chain, Scandic, also offers their own discount card for guests who stay for several nights at their hotels. Contact **Scandic Stamgjest Membership Program,** Scandic Booking Services (✆ **23-15-50-00;** www.scandic-hotels.no).

CHALET HOLIDAYS Norway offers one of the least expensive vacation bargains in all of Europe. Ideal for outdoors-loving families or groups, log-cabin chalets are available throughout the country, on the side of a mountain or by the sea, in a protected valley or woodland, or by a freshwater lake. Some lie in what are known as chalet colonies; others are set on remote and lofty peaks. At night, by paraffin lamplight or the glow of a log fire, you can enjoy aquavit or an early supper, as many Norwegians do. Some cabins are fully equipped with hot and cold running water, showers, and electricity; others are more primitive, evoking pioneer living. Naturally, the price of the rental varies according to the amenities, as well as the size (some come with as many as three bedrooms, most with tiered bunks). The price range is NOK3,000 to NOK10,000 weekly, the latter price for completely modern structures. There are chalets in most parts of the country—in the mountains, near lakes, along the coast, and in the fjord country. For a catalog with prices, locations, and other data, write to **Novasol,** Nedre Vollgate 3, N-0103 Oslo (✆ **81-54-42-70;** www.novasol.com).

FISHERMEN'S CABINS In Lofoten in northern Norway, you can rent a traditional former fisherman's cabin, called a *rorbu*. The fishermen used to come to Lofoten from other parts of the coast for the winter cod-fishing season from January to April and would make these cabins their temporary homes for the duration. Most have been modernized, and a number of them have their own shower and toilet. Nowadays you also find newly built fishermen's cabins. Although most *rorbuer* are in the Lofoten Islands, you can rent these cabins all along the coast of Norway from north to south. The cabins are by the seashore and, therefore, boast excellent fishing. Prices range from as low as NOK100 all the way up to NOK1,200 and higher per night, depending on the size and level of comfort. Local and regional tourist boards will supply you with further information.

THE B&B WAY The B&B system in Norway isn't as highly developed as it is in such countries as England. Generally, when you arrive at a town in Norway, you can go to the local tourist office, which will give you a list of private homes that receive guests. Most often they can book you into one of these accommodations for a small fee. Or you can look for signs displayed along roads or directly outside houses, reading ROM or HUSROM.

In larger towns, private rooms are priced from NOK650 to NOK900 for a double, breakfast included. A B&B guidebook for Norway titled *Bed & Breakfast Norway* has full details; copies are available in Norway at general bookshops. For more information, contact **B&B Norway AS,** Østbyfaret 9D, N-0690 Oslo (✆ **99-23-77-99;** www.bbnorway.com).

The list of private homes serving as B&Bs can change from week to week. Also, Norwegians will sometimes open their homes only briefly for the few weeks that summer lasts. Therefore, recommending permanent B&Bs that receive guests year-round is not always reliable. Actually, some of the best B&Bs are located in ugly industrial towns. As such, they tend to attract mainly commercial clients and not the adventurous visitor who wants to explore Norway's scenery.

Clarion Collection Hotel Gabelshus (p. 107) is one of my favorite places to stay in Oslo. In other parts of Norway, other favorites include: **Gjestehuset Ersgård** in the summer and winter ski resort of Lillehammer; **Ullensvang Gjesteheim** (p. 305), at Loftus, one of the best B&Bs in the western fjord country;

Ulvik Fjord Pensjonat (p. 311), another idyllic B&B in the fjord country; **Norrøna,** in the far northern city of Bodø beyond the Arctic Circle; and **Gamle Prestegård** (p. 424) in the remote Lofoten Islands.

FARM HOLIDAYS Farm holidays in Norway are many and varied, but all serve as escapist (and often isolated) destinations for those who want to venture into the remote hinterlands to discover what is called "the real Norway." Farms all over the country offer accommodations, ranging from western farms in the mountains, sometimes with impressive fjord views, to farms in northern Norway facing the open sea. Guests usually stay in their own comfortable cabin or house, complete with kitchen facilities, in or near the farmhouse. Some farms provide breakfast. Many offer the chance to participate in activities and aspects of daily life on the farm. Standards, activities, and prices vary a great deal. Contact the local tourist information office, or visit www.visitnorway.com.

I've stayed in enough farmhouses to have some particular favorites. **Hardanger Fjord og Fjellferie BA,** Sjusetevegan 145, N-5610 Øystese (✆ **56-55-58-65;** www.hff.no), is actually a complex where five owners offer 14 units for rent in restored farmhouses and modern cabins in Øystese and Norheimsund in the Hardangerfjord district (one of Norway's most beautiful fjords). You can also visit www.hff.no for more information.

Outside Bergen, I recommend **No. 17 Grønnestølen Gård,** Grønnestølsveinen 17, N-5073 (✆ **55-28-66-00;** www.no17.biz). Lying about 4km (2½ miles) from the center, this complex of wood-sided buildings in tranquil surroundings lies in beautiful countryside.

In the Telemark district in the south of Norway, my favorite is a typical old farm with log houses and turfed roofs, the **Uppigard Natadal,** Flatdal, N-3841 Flatdal (✆ **35-06-59-00;** www.natadal.no).

Another real charmer is **Kårøyan Fjellgård,** Kårøydalen, N-7203 Vinjeøra (✆ **72-45-44-60;** www.karoyan.no), lying in the beautiful, rugged countryside at the end of the Kårøydalen Valley. This place is ideal for families. You'll get rustic accommodations and country food, with plenty of farm animals to see. Mountains and white-water rapids lie nearby for walking and rafting outings.

A final favorite is **Lilland Gård,** Lilland, N-4120 Tau (✆ **51-74-20-00;** www.lilland.no), a farm dating from the Viking Age. The king, Erik "Blood-Axe," had his estate nearby. In idyllic surroundings, you can enjoy rustic accommodations and an old-fashioned Norwegian breakfast.

CAMPING Norway has more than 12,000 campsites, so you're sure to find somewhere to stay in the area you want to visit. The sites are classified with one to five stars, depending on standards, facilities, and activities available. There is no standard price, and rates vary. Normally, the fixed charge per site for two to three stars is NOK85 to NOK170, and for four to five stars NOK120 to NOK350, with additional charges per person.

Many campsites have cabins that can be booked in advance. Most cabins have electricity and heating, but note that you may need to bring bedding. Check when making your booking.

The **Camping Card (Norsk Campingkort)** entitles you to a faster check-in service, along with special deals. The Camping Card can be ordered before traveling from the Norwegian Hospitality Association (Reiselivsbedriftenes Landsforening, or RBL), Essendrops gate 6, N-0305 Oslo (✆ **23-08-86-20;** fax 23-08-86-21;

www.camping.no). The 1-year stamp can be purchased from participating campsites for NOK110. RBL also provides a camping guide with extensive information.

A favorite campsite in Norway is **Lone Camping,** located between Espeland and Haukeland, Hardangerveien 697, Haukeland (✆ **55-39-29-60;** www.lonecamping.no), because it lies among some of the most dramatic landscapes in the fjord country. If you tire of the country, you can always head for Bergen, which is 20km (12 miles) away and is reached by public bus no. 900. The bus runs to town every half-hour during the day.

While you're in the area, you might also check out **Bratland Camping,** Bratlandsveien 6, Haukeland (✆ **55-10-13-38;** www.bratlandcamping.no), which lies nearby and is also reached by bus no. 900. Here you can rent tent sites or simply furnished cabins, costing from NOK290 to NOK1,290. This site is well equipped and lies 4km (2½ miles) south of the town of Lone.

Still in fjord country, a final favorite takes you to the summer resort and winter ski center at **Voss** (p. 311). **Voss Camping,** Prestegårdsalléen 40 (✆ **56-51-15-97;** www.vosscamping.no), has a lakeside location and is convenient to the attractions and sports of the resort (p. 313). Cabins cost NOK600 and tent sites cost NOK140 to NOK190. In the same area, **Tvinde Camping** (✆ **56-51-69-19;** www.tvinde.no) is one of the most scenic campsites in central Norway, as it lies beside a waterfall, 12km (7½ miles) from the center of Voss (p. 313). Both tent sites and cabins are rented here. Cabins cost NOK375 to NOK495, and tent sites are NOK130. This camp is reached by the public bus marked VOSS-GUNVANGEN.

HOMESTAYS **Friendship Force International** (www.friendshipforce.org) is a nonprofit organization that encourages friendship among people worldwide. Dozens of branch offices arrange visits, usually once a year. Because of group bookings, the airfare to the host country is usually less than the cost of individual APEX tickets. Each participant spends 2 weeks in the host country, the first as a guest in the home of a family and the second traveling in the host country.

Servas (www. usservas.org or servasbritain.org) is an international nonprofit, nongovernmental, interfaith network of travelers and hosts whose goal is to help promote world peace, goodwill, and understanding. Servas hosts offer travelers hospitality for 2 days. Travelers pay an annual fee and a list deposit after filling out an application and being approved by an interviewer. They then receive Servas directories listing the names and addresses of Servas hosts.

HOME EXCHANGES One of the most exciting breakthroughs in modern tourism is the home exchange. Sometimes the family vehicle is even included. Of course, you must be comfortable with the idea of having strangers in your home, and you must be content to spend your vacation in one place. One potential problem, though, is that you may not get a home in the area you request—depending on your desired time of exchange.

Intervac (www.intervac-homeexchange.com) is part of the largest worldwide exchange network. It offers over 10,000 homes in at least 36 countries. Members contact each other directly. The cost includes the purchase of three of the company's catalogs, plus the inclusion of your own listing in whichever catalog you select. If you want to publish a photograph of your home, there is an additional charge.

The Invented City (www.invented-city.com) publishes home-exchange listings three times a year. For the membership fee, you can list your home with your own written descriptive summary.

Home Link (www.homelink.org) will send you five directories a year for a fee.

SUGGESTED NORWAY ITINERARIES

4

Vacation time is becoming more and more precious, and a pared-down schedule is often necessary if you want to experience the best of any country in a condensed time. If you're a time-pressed traveler, with only 1 or 2 weeks for Norway, you may find these first two suggested itineraries most helpful, as they take in the best of either eastern or western Norway. If you have time for only a 1-week driving tour, make it to the western district, as that contains the fjord country, one of the greatest tourist attractions in all the world.

THE REGIONS IN BRIEF

WESTERN NORWAY Western Norway is fabled for its fjords, saltwater arms of the sea that stretch for miles inland toward soaring alpine peaks. Many date from the end of the last ice age. Some fjords cut into mountain ranges as high as 1,000m (3,300 ft.). The longest fjord in western Norway is the Sognefjord, north of Bergen, which penetrates 205km (127 miles) inland. Other major fjords in the district are the Nordfjord, Geirangerfjord, and Hardangerfjord.

The capital of the fjord district is **Bergen,** the largest city on the west coast. **Lofthus,** a collection of farms extending along the slopes of Sørfjorden, offers panoramic views of the fjord and the **Folgefonna Glacier.** Hiking is the primary activity in this region.

The area north of the **Hardangerfjord** is a haven for hikers. Here you'll find Hardangervidda Nasjonalpark, on Europe's largest high-mountain plateau, home to Norway's largest herd of wild reindeer and a place where summertime glacier skiing is one of the most unique experiences you'll have. The town of **Voss** is surrounded by glaciers, fjords, rivers, and lakes.

CENTRAL NORWAY Fjords are also common in central Norway; the two largest are the Trondheimsfjord and Narnsfjord. It's not unusual for roads to pass waterfalls that cascade straight down into the water. Many thick forests and snowcapped peaks fill central Norway.

The town of **Geilo,** placed halfway between Bergen and Oslo, is one of Norway's most popular ski resorts, with more than 130km (80 miles) of cross-country trails.

Trondheim, central Norway's largest city, is home to Nidaros Domen, the 11th-century cathedral that was once the burial place for Nordic kings. **Røros** is a well-preserved 18th-century mining town. The medieval city of **Molde,** Norway's capital during World War II, plays host to one of Europe's largest jazz festivals. **Geiranger,** site of the Seven Sisters waterfall, is one of the country's most popular resorts.

EASTERN NORWAY On the border with Sweden, eastern Norway is characterized by clear blue lakes, rolling hills, and green valleys. In some ways, it's the most traditional part of the country. Because of its countless fertile valleys, it was one of the earliest areas to be settled. Some of the largest valleys are Valdres, Østerdal, Hallingdall, Numedal, and Gudbrandsdalen. Campers and hikers enjoy the great forests of the Hedmark region, site of Norway's longest river, the Glomma (or Gløma), which runs for about 580km (360 miles).

The area has many ski resorts, notably **Lillehammer,** site of the 1994 Winter Olympics. Norway's most visited destination is its capital, **Oslo,** which rises from the shores of the Oslofjord. The city of **Fredrikstad,** at the mouth of the Glomma, was once the marketplace for goods entering the country. Its 17th-century Kongsten Fort was designed to defend Norway from Sweden. **Tønsberg,** Norway's oldest town, dates from the 9th century. This area is also the site of the **Peer Gynt Road,** of Ibsen fame, and the mountainous region is home to numerous ski resorts.

SOUTHERN NORWAY Southern Norway is sometimes referred to as "the Riviera" because of its unspoiled and uncrowded—but chilly—beaches. It's also a favorite port of call for the yachting fraternity.

Stavanger, the oil capital of Norway, is the largest southern city and is also quite popular. There's much to explore in the Telemark region, which is filled with lakes and canals popular for summer canoeing and boating. **Skien,** birthplace of the playwright Henrik Ibsen, is primarily an industrial town. In Skien, you can board a lake steamer to travel through a series of canals.

The southern part of **Kristiansand** links Norway with continental Europe. Close by is 10-km (6¼-mile)-long **Hamresanden Beach,** one of the longest uninterrupted beaches in Europe. More fjords lie along the western half of the district, notably the Lysefjord, Sandefjord, and Vindefjord.

NORTHERN NORWAY The "Land of the Midnight Sun" is a region of craggy cliffs that descend to the sea and of deep, fertile valleys along the deserted, wild plains. It also holds islands with few, if any, inhabitants, where life has remained relatively unchanged for generations.

The capital of the Nordland region is **Bodø,** which lies just north of the Arctic Circle; it's a base for Arctic fishing trips and visits to the wild Glomfjord. Norway's second-largest glacier, the **Svartisen,** is also in this region, as is the city of **Narvik,** a major Arctic port and the gateway to the stunning **Lofoten Islands.** The islands, which have many fishing villages, make up one of the most beautiful areas of Norway. Visitors come here from all over the world for sport fishing and bird-watching.

Norway Regions

TROMS Troms is the name of the province, and **Tromsø,** from where polar explorations are launched, is its capital. Troms contains one of Norway's most impressive mountain ranges, the Lyngs Alps, which attracts winter skiers and summer hikers. **Alta,** site of the Altafjord, is renowned for having the best salmon-fishing waters in the world.

FINNMARK At the very top of Norway is the Finnmark region, home of the Sami—Norway's indigenous, reindeer-herding nomads. Settlements here include the Sami town of **Kautokeino** and **Hammerfest,** one of the world's northernmost towns. Most tourists come to Finnmark to see the **North Cape,** site of Europe's northernmost giftshop (and arguably its northernmost point) and an ideal midnight-sun viewing spot. **Vardø** is the only Norwegian mainland town in the Arctic climate zone. In the 17th century, Vardø was the site of more than 80 witch burnings. The town of **Kirkenes** lies 274km (170 miles) north of the Arctic Circle and just paces from the Russian border.

EASTERN NORWAY IN 1 WEEK

Before commencing any driving tour, you'll want to spend at least 2 or 3 days in **Oslo** (see chapters 5 and 6). Use the following itinerary to make the most of a week in eastern Norway, but feel free to skip a place or two if you require some downtime. One week provides just enough time to see some of the significant sights of this region, from dramatic parks to fabled old Viking towns along the Oslofjord.

The highlights of the north include the Olympic resort of **Lillehammer** (one of the most famous towns in Norway) and some of the country's greatest national parks—**Jotunheimen** and **Rondane.** Time is also allotted for a visit to **Røros,** Scandinavia's most colorful mining town, which is on the UNESCO list of World Heritage Sites.

Heading back to Oslo (going south along the Oslofjord), you can take in other attractions, including **Fredrikstad,** Norway's oldest fortified town, and **Tønsberg,** the ancient Viking town and a former royal coronation site.

Day 1: Olympic Resort of Lillehammer ★★

On the morning of Day 1, depart Oslo and head north to the winter and summer resort of Lillehammer, at the northern end of Lake Mjøsa, where the 1994 Winter Olympics were staged. The trip is a drive of 169km (105 miles). From Oslo, follow the E6 express highway to Lillehammer, where you can stay for the night. The major attraction here is the open-air Maihaugen Museum (p. 198), which will take roughly 2 hours. If you have time remaining on the clock, hook up with an 1850s' paddle steamer, the *White Swan* (or *Skibladner)* of Lake Mjøsa (for more details, see "Sailing on Norway's Oldest Paddle Steamer," p. 193).

Day 2: Jotunheimen National Park ★★★

Leave Lillehammer on the morning of **Day 2,** heading northwest toward the resort of **Lom,** a distance of 180km (112 miles), by continuing along the E6 until you reach the junction of Route 15. Here you will head west for the final

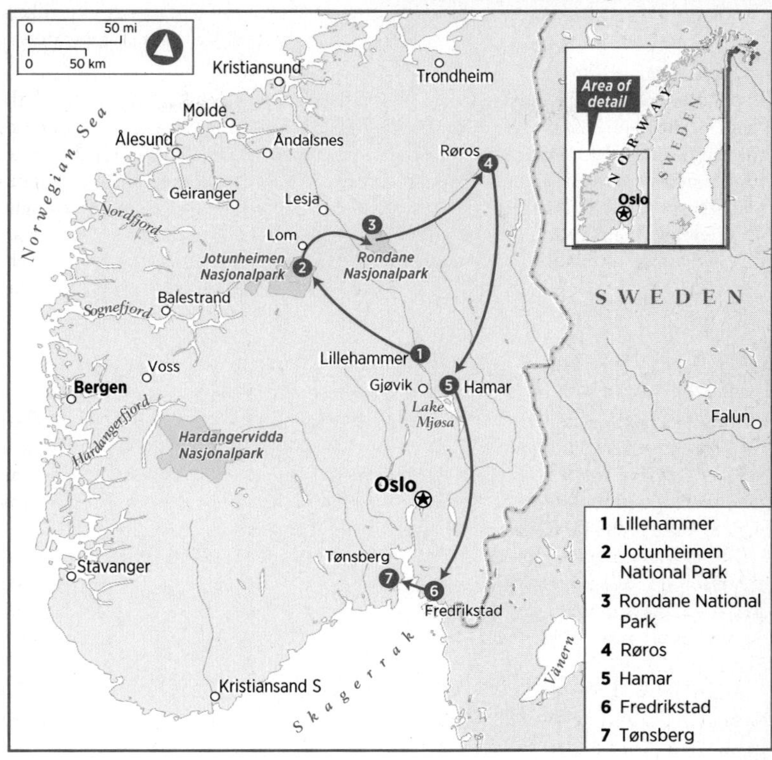

stretch into Lom, where you can easily stay overnight in the small town itself or somewhere nearby.

Lom lies in the center of **Jotunheimen,** with its foreboding glaciers and towering mountain peaks. This is the prize jewel among the national parks of Norway. For details about experiencing the best of the park in a short time, refer to "Jotunheimen Nasjonalpark: 'Home of the Giants'" (p. 210).

Day 3: The Ice Age Park of Rondane ★★

Leave Lom on the morning of **Day 3** and drive all the way to the village of **Lesja,** a distance of 159km (99 miles). To reach Lesja, exit Lom via Route 15 east, then enter the E6 express highway, heading northwest. At the roundabout, connect to the E136 heading west into Lesja. Check into one of the region's hotels for the night. With its towering peaks, deep valleys, and waterfalls, **Rondane Nasjonalpark** is one of the most visited parks in Norway. See p. 213.

Day 4: The Ancient Mining Town of Røros ★★

On the morning of **Day 4,** leave Lesja and head for the old mining town of **Røros,** a distance of 193km (120 miles). Take the E136 east, then the E6 northeast, entering Route 29 as the road continues east. At the junction with Route 3, head north, continuing on the highway as it turns into Route 30, which will take you into Røros. Thankfully, Røros is signposted along these complicated routes.

Check in to a hotel for the night and set out to explore Scandinavia's most famous old mining town, with its collection of 80 antique houses, some of which date from the 1600s. For a survey of the attractions, including the first smelting works in the area, the **Røros Museum-Smelthytta,** see the reviews beginning on p. 217.

Day 5: Røros ★★ to Hamar

On the morning of **Day 5,** leave Røros and drive 275km (171 miles) to the resort of **Hamar,** the gateway to central Norway's **Lake Mjøsa,** an area of serious beauty. At this point, you'll be only 134km (83 miles) north of Oslo. From Røros, take Route 30, heading southwest to the junction with Route 3. Route 3 will take you south to the junction with Route 25, which you follow southeast into Hamar. Stay in one of Hamar's several fetching hotels for the night. Mostly you come here to enjoy the beauty of the lake. But if you have time for any of the minor sights, visit the **Hedmarksmuseet** and **Domkirke-odden** (p. 192), and the **Kirsten Flagstad Museum** (p. 193). Of minor interest is the **National Railway Museum** (p. 193).

Day 6: Hamar to Fredrikstad ★

To conclude this 1-week tour, continue south of Oslo to the two oldest and most intriguing cities along the Oslofjord, **Fredrikstad** and **Tønsberg.** Leave Hamar on the morning of **Day 6,** following the E6 south to Fredrikstad, a driving distance of 216km (134 miles). Check in to a hotel in Fredrikstad for the night. What brings you here is **Gamlebyen,** the Old Town of Fredrikstad, at the mouth of the Glomma River. The oldest fortified town in Norway, this is one of the best preserved old quarters in eastern Norway. You should allow a good 3 hours to tour its precincts, including stopovers at the **Fredrikstad Museum** (p. 172) and **Fredrikstad Domskirke** (p. 174). The Old Town is also known as a center for artisans and highly skilled craftspeople. You'll want to devote part of your time to exploring local shops, which sell some of the most desirable handcrafted jewelry, housewares, and objets d'art in Norway.

Day 7: Fredrikstad ★ to Tønsberg ★

For your final look at eastern Norway, you will have to cross from the east bank of the broad Oslofjord to the west bank. On the morning of **Day 7,** say goodbye to Fredrikstad and head for the fjord town of Moss, a distance of 39km (24 miles). From Fredrikstad, follow the E6 north to the junction with Route 19, which you will take west into Moss. Once there, head for the port, where you can board one of the frequent ferries crossing the fjord to the port of Horten on the west bank.

At Horten, take Route 19 south into **Tønsberg,** a distance of only 18km (11 miles), where you'll stay at a hotel for your final night. Tønsberg, a former Viking settlement, is Norway's oldest town. In the late morning, you can take in its major sights, including **Slottsfjellet** (p. 182), hailed as the "Acropolis of Norway"—the views from the **Slottsfjelltårnet** are a real show-stealer. You can spend an hour wandering through the **Nordbyen** (p. 182), the Old Town, with its historic houses; drop in also to see **Sem Church** (p. 182), the oldest in Vestfold county. With its Viking and whaling treasures, **Vestfold Fylkesmuseum** (p. 183) is most intriguing. After an overnight in Tønsberg, you can drive back to Oslo, which, most likely, is your transportation hub for making your way home.

WESTERN FJORD COUNTRY IN 1 WEEK

This driving tour of the fjords of western Norway, one of the world's greatest tourist attractions, is far more scenic than the environs of Oslo in the east. The last ice age carved a wonderland of nature into this region. One of the best ways to experience this part of the country is by boat, traversing the most scenic of the fjords, such as Sognefjord.

If the coastlines of all the fjords were laid out in a straight line, they would measure 21,347km (13,235 miles), roughly the distance between the north and south poles. Add in Europe's largest glacier, little fjordside farming villages, and jagged snow-capped peaks, and you've got one of the most gorgeous landscapes on the planet.

Day 1: Ålesund ★★: Top of the Fjord Country

Spread over three islands and opening onto two bright blue fjords, **Ålesund,** lying 1,186km (735 miles) northwest of Oslo, is a good launch pad for a driving tour of the fjord country. Because it is such a long distance from Oslo (and because there are no rail lines to Ålesund), it's best to fly here and rent a car before beginning your tour.

Before heading out from Ålesund, you can explore the rebuilt Art Nouveau town, including its most important attraction, the **Sunnmøre Museum** (p. 338), one of the fjord country's best open-air museums.

Day 2: Åndalsnes & Romsdalsfjord ★

Leave Ålesund on the morning of **Day 2,** and drive east to the resort of **Åndalsnes,** a distance of 127km (79 miles), following the A69. Once here, check in to a hotel for the night. At Åndalsnes, try to hook up with a summer excursion, especially one involving a hike through the **Romsdalen Alps** (p. 335) that envelop the town. The summit of **Nesaksla Mountain** towers over Åndalsnes at 715m (2,345 ft.). You can ask about the boat trips on **Romsdalsfjord,** one of the most beautiful waterways in western Norway.

Day 3: The Trollstigveien ★ to Geirangerfjord ★★★

On the morning of **Day 3,** leave Åndalsnes and head south on one of the greatest road trips in Norway, the **Trollstigveien,** a 20-hour drive along Route 63 to the fjord resort of **Geiranger** (p. 331), a distance of 85km (53 miles) from Åndalsnes. At one point, the highway climbs a breathtaking 620m (2,034 ft.). When it opened in 1952, the **Ørnevein,** or Eagle's Road, section of Route 63 was heralded as a marvel of engineering—and so it is today. Nearly one dozen hairpin turns await you, opening onto panoramic views over **Geirangerfjord.**

Once at the resort town of **Geiranger,** explore the area in the afternoon after checking in to a hotel for the night. Its waterfalls, such as the **Seven Sisters,** are among the world's most dramatic. If it's summer and you arrive late, an evening tour of the Geirangerfjord is available.

Day 4: A Trio of Resorts: Stryn, Loen & Olden

On the morning of **Day 4,** leave Geiranger and take the ferry across the Geirangerfjord to Hellesylt, a scenic hour's boat ride. At Hellesylt, follow the signs south along Route 60 to **Stryn,** a distance of 50km (31 miles). You can check in to a hotel for the night at Stryn, or at Loen or Olden, all close together.

From your home base in Stryn, you are poised to explore one of the natural wonders of Norway, the ice plateau of **Jostedalsbreen Nasjonalpark.** See p. 328 for details on how to tour this wonder that lies between Sognefjord and Nordfjord. The glacier is the largest in Europe, and you must have a qualified guide to tour it.

Day 5: Fjærland ★★

On the morning of **Day 5,** head 60km (37 miles) to the south to **Fjærland,** where you can book a hotel room for the evening. For directions, see "Getting There," under Fjærland (p. 324). Once at Fjærland, you can spend the afternoon touring **Bøyaøyri Estuary,** a protected nature reserve north of the village. Have some more time? You can also take in the exhibits at the **Norwegian Glacier Museum** (p. 325).

Day 6: Balestrand ★★ & the Sognefjord ★★★

On the morning of **Day 6,** leave Fjærland and journey by car ferry to **Balestrand;** the scenic boat ride takes about 45 minutes. Check your luggage in to a hotel for the night before setting out to explore one of the world's deepest and most beautiful fjords, the famous **Sognefjord.** This fjord stretches for 205km (127 miles), and a scenic boat ride on it will comfortably fill your afternoon.

Day 7: Voss ★: Summer Fun in a Winter Playground

On **Day 7,** it's just a 90-km (56-mile) drive south to Voss, where you can choose from any number of hotels for the night. Route 13 links Balestrand to Voss, but the section between Vanganes and Balestrand is serviced by car ferry. A wide range of activities awaits you in Voss; refer to "What to See & Do" (p. 312) and "Other Outdoor Pursuits" (p. 313) for the full array of choices.

Western Fjord Country in 1 Week

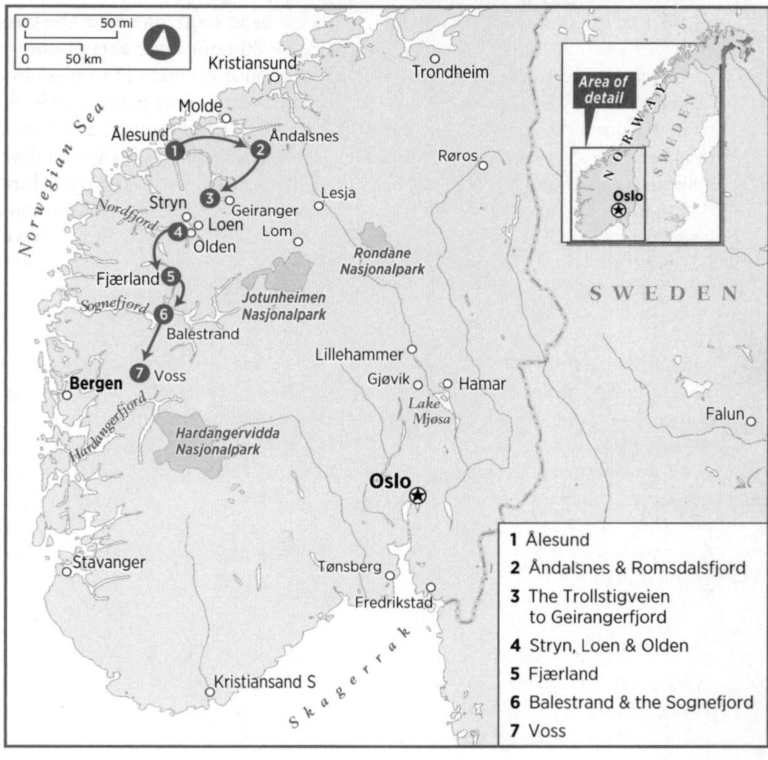

Voss is also a good connecting point for travel back to either Bergen or Oslo, one of which can be your point of departure from Norway.

THE ROUTE TO THE NORTH CAPE ★★ IN 1 WEEK

The drive from **Trondheim** to the **North Cape,** along a narrow and very long strip of land, is one of the most scenic and dramatic in northern Europe. This itinerary should be undertaken only in summer, when the midnight sun will light your way.

That said, the weather along this coast has been called "wild and unpredictable," even in summer. Except for the long drive between **Trondheim** and **Mo i Rana,** we've paced the stopovers between towns so that you won't have long treks every day. Many motorists begin this drive in Oslo, but that makes for a 552-km (342-mile) jaunt to Trondheim. To eliminate that long trek, many visitors take a train or else fly to Trondheim, where they rent a car before setting out to points north.

Day 1: Trondheim ★★★: Norway's Most Historic City

Arriving in **Trondheim** for **Day 1,** drop your bags off at your hotel room, and then set out to see the city. Begin at Scandinavia's grandest cathedral, **Nidaros Domkirke (Trondheim Cathedral)** (p. 362), dating from the 11th century, followed by a visit to the nearby **Erkebispegården (Archbishop's Palace)** (p. 359). These two sights alone will fill your morning schedule. In the afternoon, you can explore the eclectic collections of the **Nordenfjeldske Kunstindustrimuseum** (p. 363) and wander the grounds of one of Norway's finest folk-culture museums, the **Sverresborg Trøndelag Folk Museum** (p. 374).

Day 2: Mo i Rana: Arctic Circle

Leave Trondheim on the morning of **Day 2** and head north for 450km (279 miles). Obviously, most of the day will be spent on the highway, taking in the scenery as you motor along the E6 express highway. **Mo i Rana,** the third-largest city in the cold north of Norway, is your gateway to the Arctic, which slices the city's boundaries from east to west. The city itself is nothing to write home about, but its setting offers high drama in towering mountains, stark glaciers, and coastline—as rugged as you'll find anywhere in Maine or Scotland. Overnight at Mo i Rana before setting out the next morning on your northward journey.

Day 3: Bodø ★: Gateway to the North

Leave Mo i Rana on the morning of **Day 3** and head for the major stopover and refueling stop of **Polarsirkelsenteret,** which lies along the E6, just 80km (51 miles) north of Mo i Rana. In this bleak countryside, stop at the Polarsirkelsenteret, or Arctic Circle Center, in the Saltfjellet mountains. It's a bit corny, but many motorists pick up a certificate showing that they've crossed the Arctic Circle, just in case the folks back home need proof.

From Polarsirkelsenteret, it is still a drive of 174km (108 miles) north to **Bodø.** After leaving Polarsirkelsenteret, follow the route north to Fauske and cut onto Route 80 west, which will take you along the Skjerstadfjord into Bodø, where you can check into a hotel for the night.

The major attraction here is the famous **Maelstrom** (p. 401). This is one of the most powerful maelstroms in the world and is one of the most dramatic natural sights in the north of Europe. If time remains in your day, you can also explore the **Norwegian Aviation Museum** (p. 400), which is the best flight-related museum in Norway.

Day 4: Narvik: World War II Battleground

On the morning of **Day 4,** leave Bodø and travel for 301km (187 miles) north-east to **Narvik,** an ice-free seaport on the Ofotfjord, which was the scene of one of the infamous sea battles of World War II on April 9 and 10, 1940, when the British attacked the Nazis there. A rebuilt Narvik awaits you today.

To reach Narvik from Bodø, drive east once again along Route 80 until you reach Fauske, at which point you head north along the E6 to Bognes. Here you transfer to a car ferry taking you to the opposite bank and the beginning of the

The Route to the North Cape in 1 Week

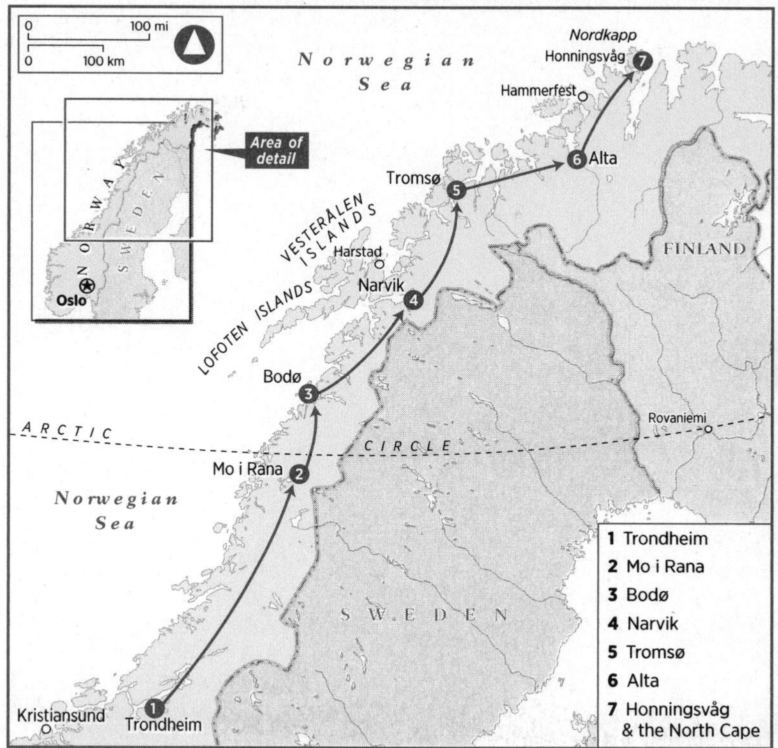

E10. This will carry you northeast into Narvik, where you can check into a hotel for the night.

You should still have time to take a ride on the **Gondolbanen cable car** (p. 405), transporting you to the top of **Fagernesfjell mountain,** at 640m (2,100 ft.), for a panoramic view. If you still have some energy, you can pay a visit to the **War Museum** (p. 405).

Day 5: Tromsø ★★: North Sea Boomtown

On the morning of **Day 5,** leave Narvik heading north to **Tromsø,** a distance of 421km (262 miles). Take the E6 from Narvik, cutting northwest at the junction with the E8, leading directly into Tromsø.

Book your room, stow your bags, and set out to explore Norway's gateway to the Arctic, the port from which famous explorers have set forth—and to which some have, sadly, never returned. Take the cable car to **Fjellheisen** (p. 385) for one of the most panoramic views in all of Norway. Later you can knock off the major attractions of Tromsø, including the **Arctic Cathedral** (p. 385),

Mack's Brewery, the northernmost brewery in Norway (p. 386), and the Disney-esque **Polaria** (p. 387). If time remains, visit the **Polarmuseet** (p. 388).

Day 6: Alta: City of Northern Lights

On the morning of **Day 6,** leave Tromsø and set out for a long drive of 329km (204 miles) to the far northern outpost of **Alta.** From Tromsø, follow the E8 southeast to the junction with the E6, heading northeast along the rugged coast into Alta, where you can check in to a hotel for the night. Spend a day taking in its sights, which include prehistoric rock carvings at **Hjemmeluft** (p. 425) and a riverboat excursion up the Alta River to **Sautso-Alta Canyon** (p. 425), the "Grand Canyon of Scandinavia."

Day 7: Honningsvåg & the North Cape ★★

On the morning of **Day 7,** leave Alta and drive northeast along the E6 to the junction with the E69, which leads north into **Honningsvåg,** the world's northernmost town, a distance of 210km (130 miles) from Alta.

Once your lodging is secured, set out to explore the **North Cape.** In addition to the cape itself, you can visit such satellite attractions as the visitor center at **Nordkapphallen** (p. 434) and the **Nordkappmuseet** (p. 435).

If you made arrangements in Trondheim to return your car in Tromsø, you can fly back to Oslo for your transportation connection to destinations worldwide. Otherwise, prepare for a long—but inarguably beautiful—drive back from the North Cape.

NORWAY FOR FAMILIES IN 1 WEEK

Norway is loaded with attractions that the entire family can enjoy. Oslo and Bergen tend to be the favorite stops for travelers with children. From Viking ships to open-air folkloric parks, from cable-car rides into the mountains to thriving amusement parks, Norway is filled with summer fun. The only problem may be that at midsummer the sun never sets, and it may be hard to get kids to go to bed.

Beginning in **Oslo** in the east, this itinerary traverses the south coast of Norway, with overnight stopovers in **Kristiansand S** and **Stavanger** before heading to **Bergen,** where you'll spend 3 nights. Using Bergen as a base will allow time to explore Norway's greatest attraction, the fjord district, which appeals to all ages.

Days 1 & 2: Oslo ★★★: Gateway to Norway

Flying into Oslo, you can spend 2 busy days having fun before renting a car to explore the southern regions and the fjord district in the west, centered on Bergen. After checking into an Oslo hotel for 2 nights, head out on a Viking adventure. Reached by ferry from the harbor at Oslo, Bygdøy is your best bet. Once on this peninsula, you can spend 3 to 4 fun-filled hours and also have lunch here. This will allow you to explore the polar exploration ship ***Fram*** (p. 139), the world-famous balsa log raft ***Kon-Tiki*** (p. 139), the **Norwegian Maritime Museum** (p. 140), the **Norwegian Folk Museum** (p. 130), and the **Viking Ship Museum** (p. 132). The latter holds a special fascination for

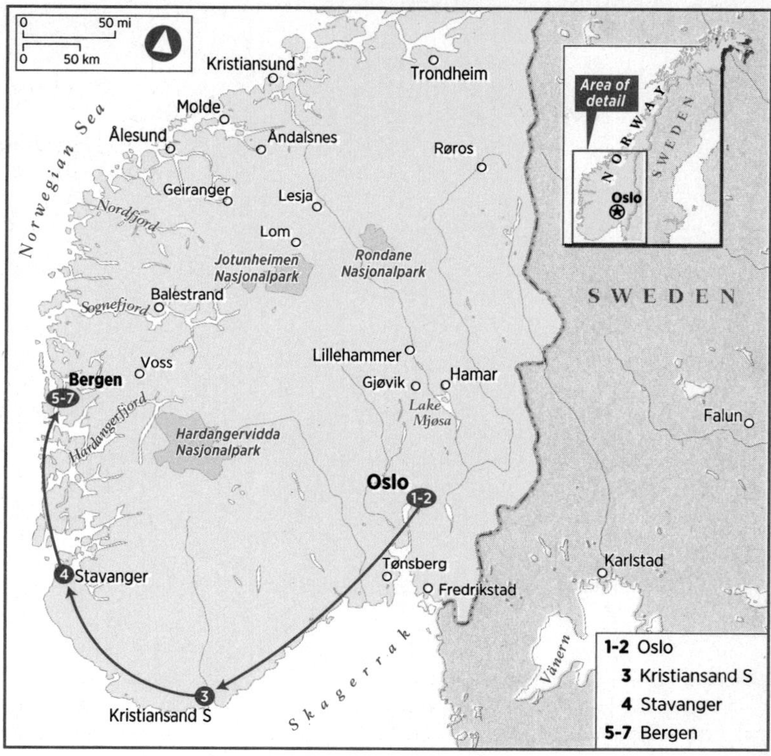

kids of all ages. In the afternoon, head for **Tryvannstårnet** (p. 140), the highest lookout tower in Scandinavia, with a viewing gallery at 570m (1,870 ft.). You can even see all the way to Sweden in the east, and the views of the Oslofjord are panoramic.

In the early evening, take the entire family for a walk along the complex of restaurants and shops that line the harbor at **Aker Brygge.** This is one of the most colorful parts of the city and an ideal place to have a Norwegian seafood dinner. The restaurants serve meat, too, though kids may balk at eating reindeer, a meat as popular in Norway as steak in Texas.

On the morning of **Day 2,** plan a 2-hour **summer cruise** (see "Norway Yacht Charter," p. 152), which will take in the blue beauty of the Oslofjord, with its islands and narrow sounds. You'll be back in Oslo in time for lunch. After a meal, take kids to see the **Children's Art Museum** (p. 144), designed especially for them. Later go for a stroll along the precincts of **Akershus Castle & Fortress** (p. 138). Cap the afternoon by going to **Norgesparken Tusenfryd** (p. 144), the largest amusement park in Norway. It's a smaller version of Copenhagen's fabled Tivoli Gardens.

Day 3: Kristiansand S ★: The Summer City

Get an early start on the morning of **Day 3** and prepare for a long but scenic drive along the southeastern coast of Norway—all the way to the country's fifth-largest city, **Kristiansand S,** lying 342km (212 miles) southwest of Oslo. Kristiansand is reached by following the E18 all the way.

After lunch, set out for some summer fun by booking a ticket on the **Setesdalsbanen** in Grovane (p. 237), an 1894 locomotive running on a narrow-gauge track for 4.8km (3 miles). Follow that up with a stroll through the **Agder Museum of Natural History & Botanical Garden** (p. 234) before rounding off the late afternoon and early evening with a visit to the **Kristiansand Zoo & Amusement Park** (p. 235), the biggest family attraction in the south. It's been called Norway's version of Disneyland. Overnight in Kristiansand before heading west the following day.

Day 4: Stavanger ★★: Capital of the Southwest

On the morning of **Day 4,** leave Kristiansand and drive northwest along the E18 into **Stavanger,** a distance of 247km (153 miles). Anchor at a hotel for the night and set out to explore. The most important pilgrimage is to **Preikestolen** (p. 257), or "Pulpit Rock," towering 609m (1,998 ft.) over beautiful Lysefjord. It's more scenic to take the boat trip instead of a bus or car to the destination. Back in Stavanger, you can spend 2 hours exploring **Gamle Stavanger** (p. 252), the Old Town, one of the northern Europe's best-preserved old quarters, with a visit to its **Domkirke** (p. 250) or cathedral. You can visit the **Norwegian Children's Museum** (p. 252), the greatest playpen in Norway for kids 5 to 12 years old.

Days 5, 6 & 7: Bergen ★★★, Queen of the Fjords

On the morning of **Day 5,** leave Stavanger and head for **Bergen,** a journey by car and ferry that locals can do in 4½ hours, although most foreign visitors spend at least 6½ hours because of stopovers. The trip is complicated but the most scenic in the southwest of the country. For detailed instructions, see "Getting There" in chapter 11.

Once you finally arrive in Bergen, you'll have your pick of hotels: Check into one for 3 nights. If you arrive in the late afternoon, you'll still have time to take the **Fløibanen funicular** to the top of Fløien, one of Bergen's famous seven hills. Follow up with an early-evening stroll along the historic **Bryggen waterfront,** where you'll find a number of places perfect for a family dinner.

On the morning of **Day 6,** explore some of the major attractions of Bergen, beginning with the **Bergen Aquarium** (p. 276) and **Gamle Bergen** (p. 282), the latter a collection of wooden houses from the 18th and 19th centuries set in a park. In the afternoon, visit **Troldhaugen** (p. 286), outside of town, Edvard Grieg's beautiful Victorian summer villa, which makes a pleasant excursion.

On the morning of **Day 7,** go out with a bang: Take a 1-day tour, lasting 12 hours, through some of Norway's most dramatic fjords and towering mountain peaks. This will be one of the most scenic journeys of your lifetime. For details on how to do this, see "Norway in a Nutshell" (p. 297).

In Bergen, you can make bus, train, or plane connections back to Oslo, which will most likely be your departure point from Norway.

SETTLING INTO OSLO

Over the years, Oslo, the capital of Norway, has grown from a sprawling country town into a sophisticated metropolis fueled by oil money from the "black gold" of the North Sea. Oslo today is permeated with a Nordic *joie de vivre* in contrast to its staid, dull reputation of times past.

Although the city has experienced population growth and urban sprawl, Oslo still manages, in spite of its growing numbers, to have more green belts than any other European capital. There are still virgin forests in Oslo and hundreds of hiking trails that lead you to fjords or mountains. No slouch in the cultural department, either, Oslo has some of the greatest museums in all of northern Europe. The only real shortcoming is that Oslo is one of the most expensive cities in the world. Proceed with caution if you're on a strict budget.

Oslo was founded in the mid-11th century by a Viking king and became the capital around 1300 under Haakon V. In the course of its history, the city burned down several times; most recently, fire destroyed it in 1624. The master builder Christian IV, king of Denmark and Norway, ordered the town rebuilt near the Akershus Castle. He named the new town Christiania (after himself), its official name until 1924, when the city reverted to its former name. In 1814, Norway split from Denmark and united with Sweden, a fruitful union that lasted until 1905. During that period, the Royal Palace, the House of Parliament, the old university, the National Theater, and the National Gallery were built. After World War II, Oslo grew to 454 sq. km (177 sq. miles); it now has nearly 600,000 inhabitants. That makes it one of the largest of world capitals in acreage—not in population.

Oslo is also one of Europe's most heavily forested cities, and its citizens relish this standing. Oslovians love nature in both summer and winter. When the winter snows fall, they bundle up and take to their nearby ski slopes. During their brief summer, they're quick to shed their clothes and head to the pine-covered hills in the north for long hikes and picnics, or else for sails on the blue waters of Oslofjord to the south. After a long winter slumber, the fjord suddenly becomes clogged with hundreds of sailboats, motorboats, and windsurfers, and dozens of sunbathers stripped down on the rocks, taking in the few precious days of summer sun Oslovians are granted.

ORIENTATION

Arriving

BY PLANE

Airlines from all over the world fly into **Oslo International Airport** at Gardermoen (© **06400** or 91-50-64-00), about 50km (31 miles) east of downtown Oslo, a 45-minute drive from the center. All domestic and international flights coming into Oslo arrive through this much-upgraded airport, including those of SAS, British Airways, Norwegian, and Ryanair. Two smaller airports, **Torp** (© **33-42-70-00;** www.torp.no) and **Rygge** (© **69-23-00-00;** www.ryg.no), both south of Oslo city center, serve various European discount airlines.

There's a regular bus service from all three airports into downtown Oslo. The bus service for Gardermoen is maintained by **SAS** (© **81-50-01-76;** www.flybussen.no), whose buses deliver passengers to Oslo Sentralstasjon (Oslo Central railway station) and to most of the Radisson BLU hotels in Oslo. The cost is NOK130 per person. For Rygge, contact **Rygge Expressen** (www.rygge-ekspressen.no); the ticket price is NOK130. For Torp, contact **Torp Expressen** (www.torpekspressen.no); the ticket price is NOK190. There's also a high-speed railway service, **Flytoget** (© **81-50-07-77;** www.flytoget.no), between Gardermoen airport and Oslo Central station, taking only 19 minutes and departing approximately every 10 minutes, priced at NOK140 per person each way. There are also local trains to both Rygge and Torp airports. If you want to take a taxi, be prepared for a minimum of NOK700 for up to four passengers plus luggage to Gardermoen; the other airports will cost significantly more. If you need a "maxi-taxi" (a minivan suitable for 5 to 15 passengers plus luggage) you'll be assessed NOK900.

High-Speed Link from Stockholm

A high-speed train between Stockholm and Oslo takes only 4 hours 50 minutes between these Scandinavian capitals. Depending on the day, there are two to three trains daily in each direction. This high-speed train now competes directly with air travel.

BY TRAIN

Trains from the Continent, Sweden, and Denmark arrive at **Oslo Sentralstasjon (Oslo Central railway station),** Jernbanetorget 1 (© **81-50-08-88** for train information), located at the beginning of Karl Johans Gate in the center of the city. The station is open daily from 4:30am to 1am. From here, trains leave for Bergen, Stavanger, Trondheim, Bodø, and all other rail links in Norway. You can also take trams to all major parts of Oslo. Lockers and a luggage office are available at the station, where you can exchange money, if needed.

BY BUS

Buses from and to cities all over Norway—as well as international departure points—arrive and depart Oslo's central bus station, located next to the railway station. For route information, contact Nor-Way Bussekspress (© **81-54-44-44;** www.nor-way.no).

BY CAR

If you're driving from mainland Europe, the fastest way to reach Oslo is to take the car ferry from Frederikshavn, Denmark. From Frederikshavn, car ferries run to several towns near Oslo and to Gothenburg, Sweden. You can also take a car ferry from Copenhagen to several points in western Sweden, or from Helsingør, Denmark, to Helsingborg, Sweden. Highway E6 runs the length of Sweden's western coast from Malmö through Helsingborg and Gothenburg, right up to Oslo. If you're driving from Stockholm to Oslo, take the E3 west to Örebro, where it connects with the E18 to Oslo. Once you near the outskirts of Oslo from any direction, follow the signs into the *sentrum* (center).

BY FERRY

Ferries from Europe arrive at the Oslo port, a 15-minute walk (or a short taxi ride) from the center. From Denmark, Scandinavia's link with the Continent, ferries depart for Oslo from Copenhagen, Hirtshals, and Frederikshavn.

The daily summer crossing from Strømstad, Sweden, to Sandefjord, Norway, takes 2½ hours; from Sandefjord, it's an easy drive or train ride north to Oslo.

Visitor Information

Assistance and information for visitors are available at the **Tourist Information office,** at Fridtjof Nansens Plass 5 near City Hall. You'll be able to pick up free maps and brochures, and book hotel accommodation, sightseeing tickets, and guide services. The office is open June to August daily 9am to 7pm, April to May and September Monday to Saturday 9am to 5pm, and October to March Monday to Friday 9am to 4pm. There is an additional information office at **Oslo Sentralstasjon (Central railway station),** Jernbanetorget 1, which is open daily from May to September 8am to 8pm and October to April daily 8am to 6pm. The centralized phone number for all the tourist offices in Oslo is ✆ **81-53-05-55** or go to www.visitoslo.com.

City Layout

See the "Oslo Attractions" map on p. 126 for a breakdown of these neighborhoods.

MAIN ARTERIES & STREETS Oslo lies at the mouth of the Oslofjord, which is 97km (60 miles) in length. Opening onto the harbor is **Rådhusplassen (City Hall Square),** dominated by the modern City Hall, a major attraction. Guided bus tours leave from this point, and the launches that cruise the fjords depart from the pier facing the municipal building. You can catch Bygdøy-bound ferries from the quay at Rådhusplassen. On a promontory to the east is **Akershus Castle.**

Karl Johans Gate, Oslo's main street (especially for shopping and strolling), is north of Rådhusplassen. This boulevard begins at Oslo Central railway station and stretches all the way to the 19th-century Royal Palace at the western end.

A short walk from the palace is the famed **Studenter Lunden (Students' Grove),** where seemingly everybody gathers on summer days to socialize. The University of Oslo is nearby. Dominating this center is the National Theater, guarded by statues of Ibsen and Bjørnson, the two greatest names in Norwegian theater. South of the theater, near the harbor, is **Stortingsgaten,** another shop-filled street.

The main city square is **Stortorvet,** though the hub of city life is actually along Karl Johans Gate.

FINDING AN ADDRESS Street numbers begin on the southern end of streets running north–south and on the eastern end of streets running east–west. Odd numbers are on one side of the street, and even numbers on the other. Where large buildings hold several establishments, different addresses are designated with A, B, and C.

STREET MAPS Maps of Oslo are distributed free at the tourist office (see "Visitor Information," above). For extensive exploring, especially of some back streets, you may need a more detailed map. Opt for a pocket-size map with a street index that can be opened and folded like a wallet. Such maps are sold at most newsstands in the central city. If you can't find a map, go to the city's most central bookstore, **Tanum Karl Johan,** Karl Johans Gate 43 (✆ **22-41-11-00;** www.tanumbokhandel.no).

Neighborhoods in Brief

Oslo is made for walking—in fact, you can walk from Oslo Central railway station all the way to the Slottet (Royal Palace) in a straight line. Except for excursions to the museum-loaded Bygdøy Peninsula and the Holmenkollen ski jump, most attractions can be covered on foot.

Oslo is not neatly divided into separate neighborhoods or districts. It consists mainly of **central Oslo,** with Oslo Central railway station to the east of the city center and the Royal Palace to the west. Karl Johans Gate, the principal street, connects these two points. Central Oslo is the heart of the city—the most crowded and traffic-congested, but also the most convenient place to stay. Those on the most rushed of schedules—the average visitor spends only 2 days in Oslo—will want to book accommodations in the center. It's not a real neighborhood per se, but it's the core of the city, as Piccadilly Circus is to London. Most Oslo hotels and restaurants are here, as are almost 50 museums and galleries—enough to fill plenty of rainy days. The best of the lot include Akershus Castle, the Historical Museum, and the National Gallery.

The streets Drammensveien and Frognerveien lead northwest to Frogner Park (Frognerparken), whose main entrance is on Kirkeveien. This historical area is the site of the Vigeland Sculpture Park, which displays some of Gustav Vigeland's masterpieces.

The **Old Town** (or Gamlebyen) lies south of the Parliament building (the Stortinget) and Karl Johans Gate. This section contains some of the city's old-fashioned restaurants, along with the Norwegian Resistance Museum and the Old Town Hall. A stay here is the same as staying in central Oslo (see above). The only difference is that the streets of the Old Town have more old-fashioned Norwegian flavor than the more modern parts of central Oslo.

Aker Brygge is one of Oslo's newest neighborhoods, an excellent place for dining and diversions, but with few hotels. For sights along the waterfront, it's the best place for long walks to take in the harbor life. It emerged near the mouth of the Oslofjord in the old wharf area formerly used for shipbuilding yards. Fueled by oil wealth, steel-and-glass buildings now rise from what had been a relatively dilapidated section. Some of the best shops, theaters, restaurants, and cultural attractions are located here.

The main attractions in **Eastern Oslo** are the Botanisk Hage (Botanical Garden), the Zoological Museum, and the Edvard Munch Museum in Tøyen—little more is worth seeing here. Unless you're interested in seeing those sights mentioned, you might skip eastern Oslo. However, thousands of visitors head here just to see the Edvard Munch Museum (p. 129).

The **West End** is a chic residential area graced with some of the city's finest hotels and restaurants. It's a more tranquil setting than the center and only 15 minutes away by public transportation. Many visitors who stay here don't mind the short commute and prefer this area to the more traffic-clogged center. However, for walking and sightseeing, central Oslo and its port are more alluring. There is little to see in the West End unless you like walking up and down pleasant residential streets.

Farther west—6km (3¾ miles) by car, but better reached by car ferry—is the **Bygdøy Peninsula.** Here you'll find such attractions as the Norwegian Folk Museum, the Viking ships, the polar ship *Fram,* and the *Kon-Tiki* Museum. Break up your sightseeing venture with a meal here, but plan to stay elsewhere.

The suburb of **Frogner** begins 0.8km (½ mile) west of Oslo's center and stretches for a mile or so. Unless you specifically have business here, you can probably skip this section of the city.

Lying behind Oslo Central railway station is the **Grønland district,** where many Oslovians go for ethnic dining and great nightlife. There is little of sightseeing interest here, though the large immigrant population has given it some real local appeal, with some great budget Indian and Pakistani restaurants. Come here for affordable dining, not for long, leisurely walks. On a hurried visit, you could afford to skip Grønland entirely.

At last, once-staid Oslo has grown big and diverse enough to have its own trendy, counterculture district. Lying in east Oslo is **Grünerløkka,** which most of its inhabitants refer to affectionately as "Løkka." This once-run-down sector of Oslo traditionally was known as the worker's district. Today many professional Oslovians are moving in to restore apartments, and the district is the site of several fashionable cafes and restaurants. If you're young, with a roving eye at night, you might want to check out some of the establishments in this area.

Many Oslo neighborhoods lie along the **Oslofjord,** which stretches more than 97km (60 miles) north from the Skagerrak to Oslo. Basins dotted with islands fill the fjord. (There are 40 islands in the immediate Oslo archipelago.) Chances are, you won't be staying or dining along the fjord, but might consider a boat trip, as it's a grand attraction on a summer day.

Nearly all visitors want to see **Holmenkollen,** a wooded range of hills northwest of the city rising to about 226m (741 ft.). You can reach it in 35 minutes by electric train from the city center. Skiers might want to stay here in winter, lodging at the Holmenkollen Park Hotel Rica (p. 108). Otherwise, visit for the view and perhaps make it a luncheon stopover, then head back to the historic core.

Marka, Oslo's forest, is a sprawling recreation area with hiking, bicycle riding, skiing, fishing, wild-berry picking, jogging trails, and more. It contains 343 lakes, 500km (310 miles) of ski trails, 623km (386 miles) of trails and roads, 11 sports chalets, and 24 ski jumps and alpine slopes. If you like to go for long walks on summer days, Marka's the spot for you. It's also one of the best places in greater Oslo for a picnic.

GETTING AROUND

By Public Transportation

Oslo has an efficient citywide network of buses, trams (streetcars), and subways. Buses and electric trains take passengers to the suburbs. From mid-April to October, ferries to Bygdøy depart from the harbor in front of the Rådhuset (City Hall).

Oslo Public Transportation

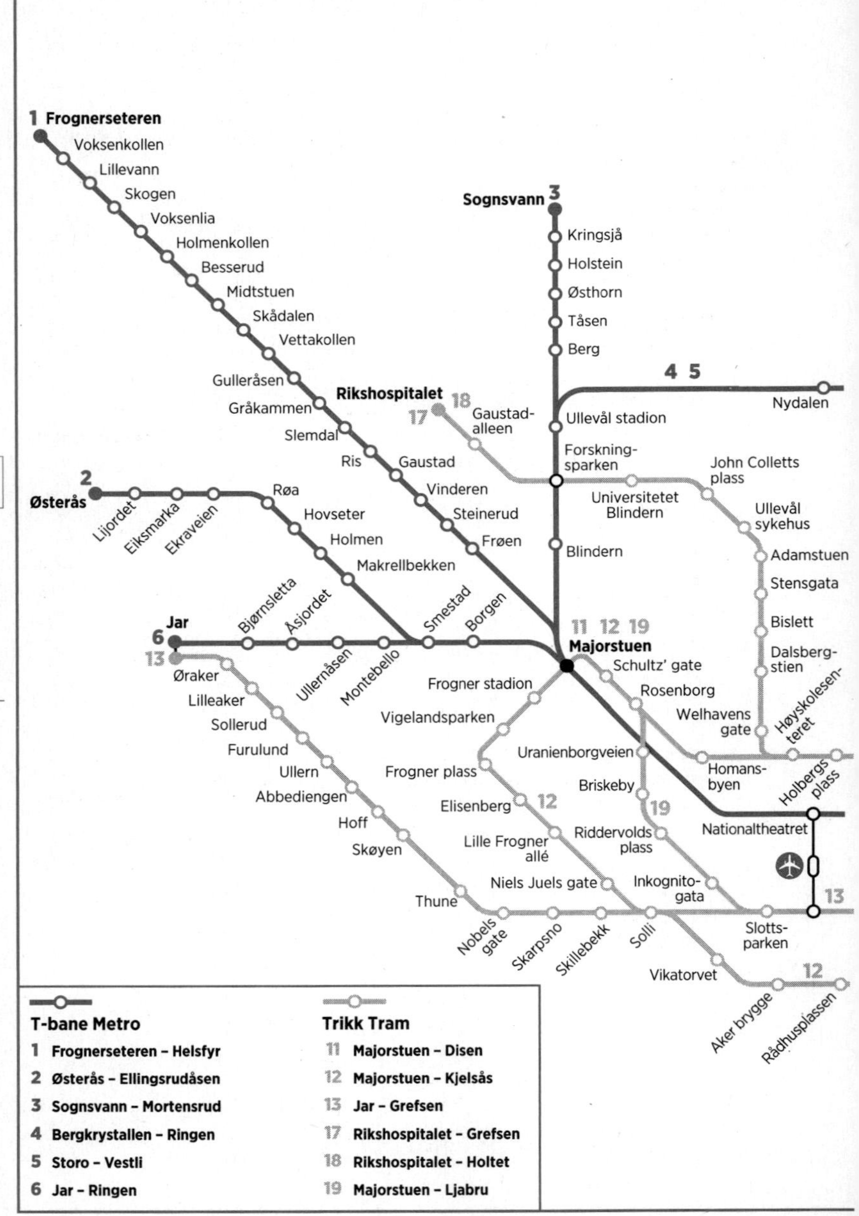

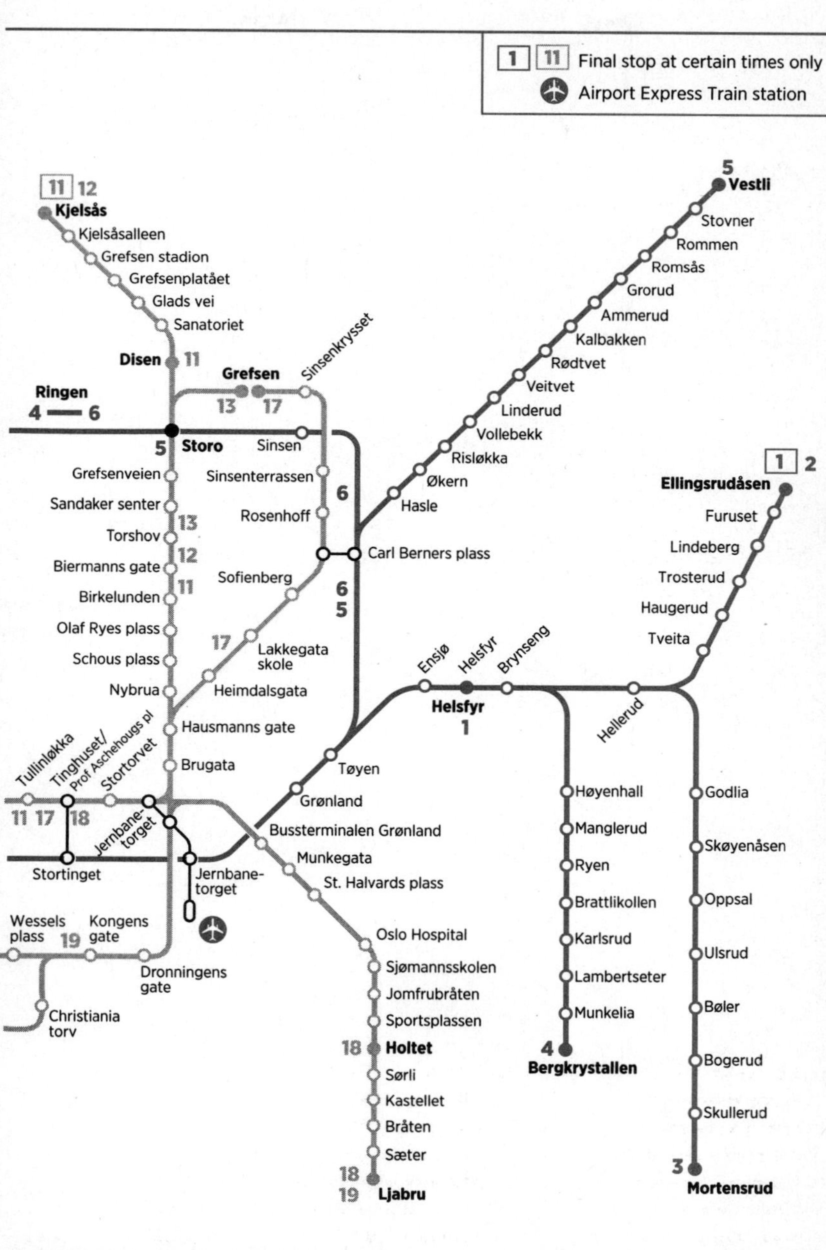

1
11
Final stop at certain times only
Airport Express Train station
11 12
Kjelsås
Kjelsåsalleen
Grefsen stadion
Grefsenplatået
Glads vei
Sanatoriet
Disen 11
Grefsen
13 17
Sinsenkrysset
Ringen
4 — 6
5 Storo
Sinsen
Grefsenveien
Sandaker senter
Torshov
Biermanns gate
Birkelunden
Olaf Ryes plass
Schous plass
Nybrua
13
12
11
Sinsenterrassen
Rosenhoff
6
Carl Berners plass
Sofienberg
6
5
17
Lakkegata skole
Heimdalsgata
Hausmanns gate
Brugata
Tullinløkka
Tinghuset/ Prof Aschehougs pl
Stortorvet
11 17 18
Jernbane-torget
Stortinget
Jernbane-torget
Wessels plass
Kongens gate
19
Dronningens gate
Christiania torv
5
Vestli
Stovner
Rommen
Romsås
Grorud
Ammerud
Kalbakken
Rødtvet
Veitvet
Linderud
Vollebekk
Risløkka
Økern
Hasle
Tøyen
Grønland
Bussterminalen Grønland
Munkegata
St. Halvards plass
Oslo Hospital
Sjømannsskolen
Jomfrubråten
Sportsplassen
18 Holtet
Sørli
Kastellet
Bråten
Sæter
18
19 Ljabru
Ensjø
Helsfyr
Brynseng
Helsfyr
1
Hellerud
Høyenhall
Manglerud
Ryen
Brattlikollen
Karlsrud
Lambertseter
Munkelia
4
Bergkrystallen
1 2
Ellingsrudåsen
Furuset
Lindeberg
Trosterud
Haugerud
Tveita
Godlia
Skøyenåsen
Oppsal
Ulsrud
Bøler
Bogerud
Skullerud
3
Mortensrud

DISCOUNT PASSES The **Oslo Pass** can help you become acquainted with the city at a fraction of the usual price. It allows free travel on public transportation, free admission to museums and other top sights, discounts on sightseeing buses and boats, a rebate on your car rental, and special treats in restaurants. You can purchase the card at hotels, fine stores, and tourist information offices; from travel agents; and in the branches of Sparebanken Oslo Akershus. Adults pay NOK230 for a 1-day card, NOK340 for 2 days, and NOK430 for 3 days. Children's cards cost NOK100, NOK120, and NOK160, respectively.

BY BUS, TRAM & SUBWAY Jernbanetorget is Oslo's major **bus and tram** terminal station. Most buses and trams passing through the heart of town stop at Wessels Plass, next to the Parliament, or at Stortorvet, the main marketplace. Many also stop at the National Theater or University Square on Karl Johans Gate, as well as stopping throughout Oslo's suburbs. At a subway stop near the National Theater, you can catch an electric train to **Tryvannstårnet,** the loftiest lookout in Scandinavia, and to the **Holmenkollen ski jump.**

The **subway (T-banen)** has four branch lines to the east. The Western Suburban subway route (including Holmenkollen) has four lines to the residential sections and recreation grounds west and north of the city. Subways and trains leave from near the National Theater on Karl Johans Gate.

For schedule and fare information, call **Trafikanten** (✆ **81-50-01-76;** www.trafikanten.no). Automated machines on board stamp and validate tickets. Drivers sell single-trip tickets for NOK40; children travel for half-fare, though you can save money if you buy these ahead of time at various ticket machines. An eight-coupon **Flexi card** costs NOK190 and is half-price for children. **Maxi cards** can be used for unlimited transfers for 1 hour from the time the ticket is stamped.

By Taxi

Hiring a taxi is very expensive in Oslo. Tariffs start at NOK46 (flagfall) for a taxi hailed in the street or at NOK50 if you summon one in advance. In addition to regular fares, there are pricey surcharges between 5 and 10pm; these increase even further between 10pm and 6am. If you need a taxi, call ✆ **23-23-23-23,** available 24 hours a day; reserve at least an hour in advance.

Taxis can be hailed on the street, provided they're more than 91m (298 ft.) from a taxi rank. When a cab is available, its roof light goes on. The most difficult time to hail a taxi is Monday to Friday 8:30 to 10am and 3 to 5pm, and Saturday 8:30 to 10am.

By Car

Driving is not a practical way to get around Oslo because parking is limited. The efficient public transportation system makes a private car unnecessary. You can reach even the most isolated areas by public transportation.

Among the multistory parking lots in the city center, the best is **Vestre Vika P-hus,** Dronning Mauds Gate (✆ **81-53-21-32**). The cost of parking a car in a public garage is NOK60 per hour or NOK195 for 24 hours. Illegally parked cars are towed away. For car problems, call the **NAF Alarm Center** (✆ **22-34-14-00**), available 24 hours a day.

By Ferry

Beginning in mid-April, ferries depart for Bygdøy from pier 3 in front of the Rådhuset. For schedules, call **Båtservice** (✆ **23-35-68-90**). For Bygdøy the ferry or bus is a good choice because parking there is limited. Other ferries leave for various parts of the Oslofjord. Inquire at the **tourist information office,** Fridtjof Nansens Plass 5 (✆ **24-14-77-00**).

[FastFACTS] OSLO

American Express American Express Reisebyrå, Maribores Gate 13 (✆ **22-98-35-00**), is open Monday to Friday 9am to 6pm, Saturday 10am to 4pm.

Babysitters Hotels can often enlist the help of a housekeeper for "child-minding." Give at least a day's notice, or two if you can. You can also contact the tourist office (see "Visitor Information," above), which keeps a list of available sitters on file.

Bookstores Oslo has many bookstores. The most central and one of the best stocked is **Tanum Karl Johan,** Karl Johans Gate 43 (✆ **22-41-11-00**).

Currency Exchange **Banks** will exchange most foreign currencies or cash traveler's checks. Bring your passport for identification. If the banks are closed, try the automated machines at the Oslo Central railway station. Alternatively, go to **Forex,** Oslo Central station, Jernbanetorget 1 (✆ **22-17-60-80**), open Monday to Friday 8am to 8pm and Saturday 9am to 5pm.

Dentists If you have a dental emergency, you can contact either of these organizations during extended hours for the address of a dentist who can take a new client on short notice: **Volvat Medisinske Senter (Volvat Medical Center),** Borgenveien 2A (✆ **22-95-75-00**); and **Oslo Legevakt (Oslo Emergency Hospital),** Storgten 40 (✆ **22-11-80-80;** ask for emergency services).

Doctors Some larger hotels have arrangements with doctors in case a guest becomes ill, or you can try the 24-hour **Legevaktsentralen (Emergencies),** Storgata 40 (✆ **22-93-22-93**). A privately funded alternative is **Oslo Akutten,** Nedre Vollgate 8 (✆ **22-00-81-60**), located two blocks from the Stortinget (Parliament building). For more routine medical assistance, you can contact the biggest hospital in Oslo, **Ullevål,** Kirkeveien 166 (✆ **02770** or 22-11-80-80). To consult a private doctor (nearly all of whom speak English), check the telephone directory or ask at your hotel for a recommendation.

Drugstores A 24-hour pharmacy is **Jernbanetorvets Apotek,** Jernbanetorget 4A (✆ **22-41-24-82**).

Embassies & Consulates See "Embassies & Consulates" in chapter 16.

Emergencies Dial the Oslo **police** at ✆ **112;** to report a **fire,** call ✆ **110;** call an **ambulance** at ✆ **113.**

Eyeglass Repair **Synsam Karl Johan,** Karl Johans Gate 2 (✆ **23-00-05-50**), is a big eyeglass supplier. Most contact lenses are in stock, too. Unusual prescriptions take about 2 days. Hours are Monday and Wednesday to Friday 9am to 5pm, Tuesday 9am to 6pm, and Saturday 10am to 3pm.

Internet Access You can log on for free at the Rådhuset (City Hall) on Rådhusplassen (✆ **23-46-16-00**).

Laundry & Dry Cleaning Washing and drying can usually be completed in an hour at laundromats. You must have exact change. Dry cleaning is extremely expensive in Oslo—prohibitively so in hotels—and many establishments can take more than a week to return clothing. Try **American Lincoln Norge,** Østmarkveien 25 (✆ **22-27-24-50**), which promises 24-hour service.

Lost Property If you've lost anything of value, the two most obvious places to begin your search are the Lost Property office at Gardermoen Airport (✆ **64-81-34-77**), which is open daily 7am to 6pm, and the Lost Property office at Oslo Central railway station (✆ **81-56-83-40**), open Monday to Friday midnight to 5pm.

Luggage Storage & Lockers Facilities for luggage storage are available at **Oslo Central railway station,** Jernbanetorget 1 (✆ **81-50-08-88**). It's open daily 4:30am to 1am. Lockers cost NOK40 to NOK70 per day, depending on size.

Newspapers & Magazines English-language newspapers and magazines are sold—at least in the summer months—at kiosks throughout Oslo. International editions, including the *International Herald Tribune* and *USA Today,* are always available, as are the European editions of *Time* and *Newsweek.*

Photographic Needs Try **Preus Foto,** Stovner Senter 3 (✆ **22-42-98-04**), for supplies, including black-and-white and color film. Film from negatives or digital memory cards can be developed in 1 hour. It's open Monday to Friday 9am to 5pm, and Saturday 10am to 3pm.

Police Dial ✆ **112.**

Post Office The **Oslo General Post Office** is at Dronningensgatan 15 (✆ **23-14-90-00** for information). Enter at the corner of Prinsensgate. It's open Monday to Friday 8am to 5pm and Saturday 9am to 2pm; it's closed Sunday and public holidays. You can arrange for mail to be sent to the main post office c/o General Delivery. The address is Poste Restante, P.O. Box 1181-Sentrum, Dronningensgatan 15, N-0101 Oslo, Norway. You must show your passport to collect it.

Safety Of the four Scandinavian capitals, Oslo is widely considered the safest. However, it is still a major city, so don't be lulled into a false sense of security. Be careful, and don't carry your wallet visibly exposed or sling your purse over your shoulder.

Taxes Oslo has no special city taxes. You'll pay the same value-added tax throughout the country (see "Taxes," in chapter 16).

Taxis See "Getting Around," above.

Toilets Clean public toilets can be found throughout the city center, in parks, and at all bus, rail, and air terminals. For a detailed list, contact the tourist information office.

Weather See "When to Go," in chapter 3.

WHERE TO STAY

By the standards of many North American and European cities, hotels in Oslo are very expensive. Oslovian hotels lose most of their business travelers, their main revenue source, during the peak tourist months in midsummer. July is always a month for discounts. Some hotels' discounts begin from June 21. Regular pricing usually resumes in mid-August.

Hotels also slash prices on weekends—usually Friday and Saturday, and sometimes Sunday. Again, hotels often change their policies, so it's best to check when you make your reservations. Don't always expect a discount—a quickly arranged conference could lead hotels to increase their prices.

The most economy-minded visitors can cut costs by staying at one of the old-fashioned hotels that offer some rooms without private bathrooms. Sometimes a room will have a shower but no toilet. Even rooms without bathrooms usually have a sink with hot and cold running water.

HOTEL RESERVATIONS The worst months for finding a place to stay in Oslo are May, June, September, and October, when many business conferences are held. July and August are better, though that's the peak of the summer tourist invasion.

If you happen to arrive in Oslo without a reservation, head for the **Oslo tourist information office** by City Hall at Fridtjof Nansens Plass 5 (✆ **81-53-05-55;** www.visitoslo.com), where the staff can help you find a room. The minimum stay is 2 days. Don't try to phone—the service is strictly for walk-ins who need a room on the night of their arrival.

Note: Rates quoted below include service charge and tax. Breakfast—usually a generous Norwegian buffet—is almost always included. Unless otherwise indicated, all the recommended accommodations have private bathrooms.

Central Oslo

VERY EXPENSIVE

First Hotel Grims Grenka ★ ☺ While this sleek spot once played second fiddle to the First Hotel Millennium (see below), this is now one of the city's most desirable addresses. This elegant boutique hotel, in which the lobby has a seven-story glassed-in atrium with Oriental carpets, columns, and a fireplace, has a personalized feel and excellent, professional staff. This is one of the few hotels anywhere where I prefer the regular rooms to the oddly laid-out, curiously spartan suites, where lots of room might be devoted, say, to an interior hallway. Each of the suites is thematically decorated, based on the life of a famous Scandinavian, such as opera and ballet personalities Kirsten Flagstad, Ingrid Bjoner, and Indra Lorentzen. Rooms and suites are accessed via a labyrinthine pathway of stairs and angled hallways.

Kongensgate 5, N-0153 Oslo. ✆ **23-10-72-00.** Fax: 23-10-72-10. www.grimsgrenka.no. 45 units. NOK1,495–NOK2,195 double; from NOK2,495–NOK2,995 suite. Rates include breakfast. AE, DC, MC, V. Parking NOK100–NOK170 per night. T-banen: Stortinget. **Amenities:** Nightclub; fitness room; wellness center; outdoor Jacuzzi on roof terrace; sauna. *In room:* A/C, TV, kitchenette, Wi-Fi (free), minibar.

Grand Hotel ★★★ ☺ Norway's most famous guests still arrive at the country's premier hotel, and there's a chance you'll catch glimpse of CEOs, Nobel Prize winners, or movie stars. Tradition and style reign supreme here, as they did when the Grand opened its doors in 1874 in a Louis XVI revival–style building imbued with touches of Art Nouveau. Constant modernization has not managed to erase the original character of the hotel, which stands on the wide boulevard leading to the Royal Palace. In fact, the stone-walled hotel with its mansard gables and copper tower is now one of the most distinctive landmarks of Oslo. Guest rooms are in the 19th-century core or in one of the tasteful modern additions. Newer rooms contain plush facilities and electronic extras, and the older ones have been completely modernized. An eight-story extension contains larger, brighter doubles. Children enjoy the indoor heated pool, and the reception staff keeps a list of activities going on in Oslo that will amuse kids. The hotel has several restaurants that serve international and Scandinavian food. The Palm Court, the Restaurant Julius Fritzner (p. 112), and the Grand Café (p. 112), the most famous cafe in Oslo, all offer live entertainment.

Karl Johans Gate 31, N-0159 Oslo. ✆**23-21-20-00** or 800/223-5652 in the U.S. Fax: 23-21-21-00. www.grand.no. 292 units. NOK1,495–NOK2,400 double; from NOK9,000–NOK25,000 suite. Rates include

Where to Stay in Oslo

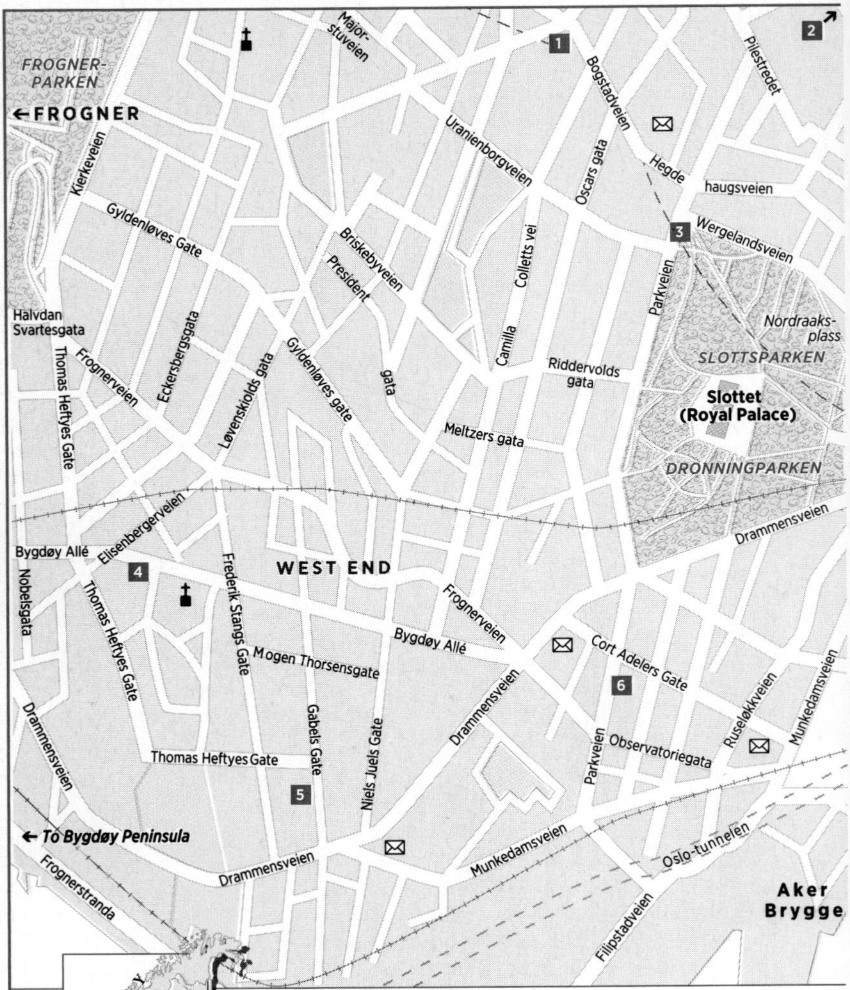

Best Western Hotell Bondeheimen **12**
Best Western Karl Johan Hotell **14**
Clarion Collection Hotel Gabelshus **5**
Clarion Collection Hotel Savoy **9**
Clarion Hotel Royal Christiania **15**
Cochs Pensjonat **3**
First Hotel Grims Grenka **21**
First Hotel Millennium **20**

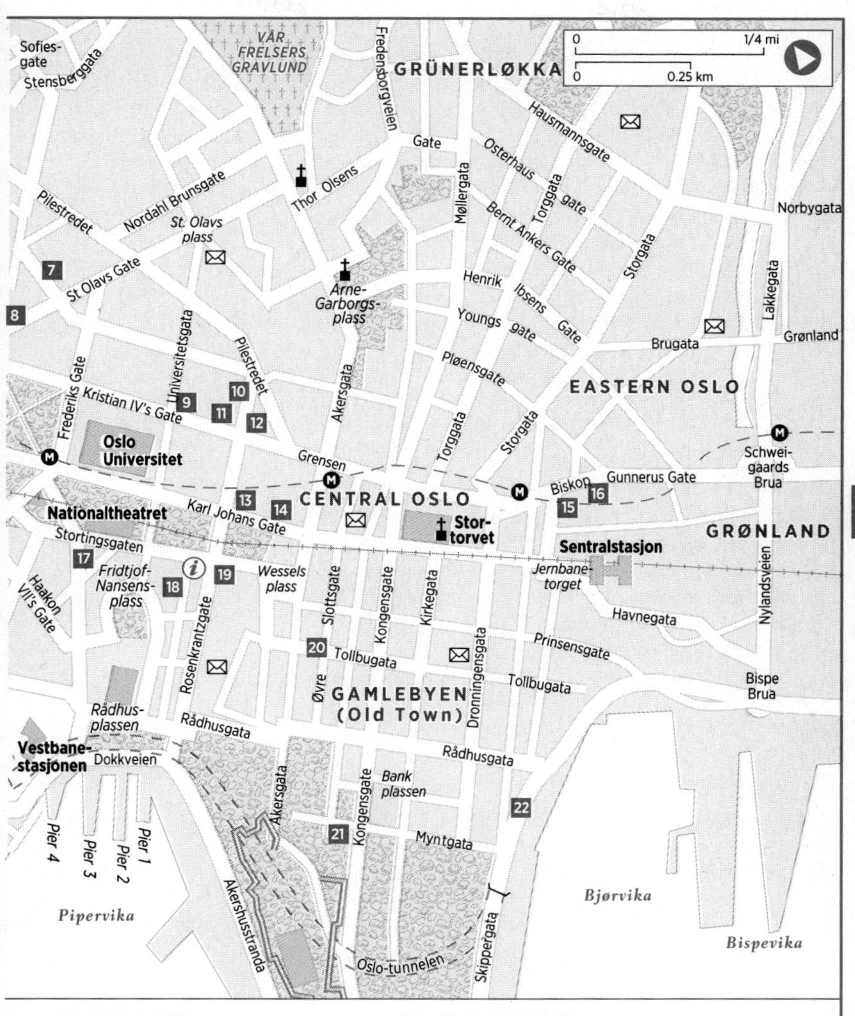

Grand Hotel **13**
Hotel Bastion **22**
Hotel Bristol **11**
Hotel Continental **17**
Radisson BLU Airport Hotel **2**
Radisson BLU Plaza Hotel **16**
Radisson BLU Scandinavia Hotel **8**
Rica Hotel Bygdøy Allé **4**
Rica Victoria Hotel **18**
Scandic KNA Oslo City Hotel **6**
Thon Hotel Cecil **19**
Thon Hotel Europa **7**
Thon Hotel Gardermoen **2**
Thon Hotel Gyldenløve **1**
Thon Hotel Stefan **10**

Church
Information
Post Office
Metro
Railway

buffet breakfast. AE, DC, MC, V. Parking NOK330. T-banen: Stortinget. **Amenities:** 3 restaurants; 2 bars; nightclub; babysitting; indoor heated pool; fitness center; health club; sauna; room service. *In room:* A/C, TV, minibar, hair dryer, Wi-Fi (free).

Hotel Continental ★★★ This deluxe hotel is beautifully appointed and somewhat edgier than the Grand, attracting its share of the entertainment industry crowd. Although it's been around since 1900, and is still one of Norway's grand old hotels, it is the only Norwegian member of the Leading Hotels of the World. It's the only major hotel in Oslo that's still mostly owned by an individual family, making it cozy, a bit inbred, and thoroughly welcoming in its approach to virtually everything. Expect lots of personalized touches, such as a masterful collection of framed original lithographs and woodcuts by Edvard Munch in a salon near the reception area. Bedrooms are plush and extremely well decorated, often with textured wallpaper and upper-crust touches, sometimes evoking comfortable bedrooms in private homes. The suites rival those at the Grand. The hotel is entirely nonsmoking.

Stortingsgaten 24-26, N-0117 Oslo. ✆ **22-82-40-00.** Fax: 22-82-96-89. www.hotel-continental.no. 154 units. Sun–Thurs NOK2,450–NOK3,000 double, NOK4,580–NOK8,970 suite; Fri–Sat from NOK2,680 double, NOK3,300–NOK5,485 suite. Rates include breakfast buffet. AE, DC, MC, V. Parking NOK360. T-banen: Nationaltheatret. **Amenities:** 2 restaurants; 2 bars; 2 cafes; babysitting; gym; room service; smoke-free rooms. *In room:* A/C, TV, hair dryer, minibar, Wi-Fi (free).

Thon Hotel Cecil ★ This contemporary hotel enjoys a central location, with many restaurants, sights, and shops within a short walk of its main entrance. Dating from 1989, it was constructed on the site of a previous hotel destroyed by fire. As if inspired by a much grander Hyatt, most of its rooms are built to open onto a central atrium. Only four rooms on each of the eight floors overlook the street (the sometimes rowdy—at least, at night—Rosenkrantzgate). The well-maintained rooms are cozy and contain neatly kept bathrooms.

Stortingsgate 8 (entrance on Rosenkrantzgate), N-0130 Oslo. ✆ **23-31-48-00.** Fax: 23-31-48-50. www.thonhotels.com/cecil. 111 units. NOK1,545–NOK2,295 double; NOK2,145–NOK3,595 suite. AE, DC, MC, V. Parking NOK235. T-banen: Stortinget. **Amenities:** Breakfast room' smoke-free rooms. *In room:* A/C, TV, hair dryer, minibar, Wi-Fi (free).

EXPENSIVE

Best Western Karl Johan Hotell ★★ For the sake of this hotel's reputation, it is regrettable that it was built across the street from the finer Grand, to which it is often unfavorably compared. However, put that aside and you'll find a winning address, charm, and grace. As you wander about its stylish public rooms, taking in the stained glass and circular staircase, you'll think you've stumbled into Belle Epoque Paris. The five-story hotel itself is in a renovated building that dates from the late 18th century. The owners have done much to imbue the hotel with some real character, filling the rooms with Norwegian folk art and installing antiques in every room, both public and private. The medium-size bedrooms have a classic decor with excellent fabrics, double glazing on the windows to cut down on the noise outside, and tiny but marble-clad bathrooms. I prefer the rooms that open onto the front and contain French windows.

Karl Johans Gate 33, N-0162 Oslo. ✆ **23-16-17-00.** Fax: 22-42-05-19. www.karljohan.no. 111 units. NOK995–NOK2,495 double; year-round daily from NOK3,300 suite. Rates include breakfast. AE, DC, MC, V. Parking NOK180 in nearby public garage. T-banen: Nationaltheatret or Stortinget. **Amenities:** Breakfast room; smoke-free rooms. *In room:* TV, hair dryer, minibar, Wi-Fi (free).

FAMILY-FRIENDLY hotels

First Hotel Grims Grenka The chain-run hotel offers rooms with small kitchenettes for preparing quick meals for the family, as well as suites with a fairytale theme for your little prince or princess. See p. 99.

First Hotel Millennium The other "First" in town, the Millennium, offers some of the best family rooms in Oslo, with spacious living areas and even a separate bedroom should you want some privacy from your brood. See below.

Grand Hotel The Grand's indoor heated pool provides an outlet for your child's energy. The "solve-everything" concierge can recommend baby-sitting services as well as diversions for young people. See p. 99.

Hotel Bristol One of the most elegant and comfortable hotels in Oslo welcomes children and lets those under 15 stay free in their parents' room. The chef will even put a "junior steak" on the grill. See below.

First Hotel Millennium ★★ ☺ Because there are two "First" hotels in Oslo, a choice has to be made. The Millennium is one of Oslo's "personality" hotels, known for its cozy atmosphere and character. In 1998, the owners took over a 1930s' office building, successfully transforming it into this comfortable refuge. Rising nine floors behind a pale pink facade, the hotel is noted for a stylish kind of minimalism. Rooms range from standard to superior, and most are very spacious, with many Art Deco touches. On the top floor are a dozen accommodations with their own large balconies opening onto cityscape views. Family rooms are also very spacious, with a separate bedroom and living area. All bedrooms feature hardwood flooring.

Tollbugate 25, N-0157 Oslo. ✆ **21-02-28-00.** Fax: 21-02-28-30. www.firsthotels.com/millennium. 112 units. NOK850–NOK1,695 double. AE, DC, MC, V. No on-site parking. T-banen: Stortinget. **Amenities:** Restaurant; bar; babysitting, room service; smoke-free rooms. *In room:* TV, hair dryer, minibar, Wi-Fi (free).

Hotel Bristol ★★★ ☺ Imbued with character, this 1920s-era hotel competes aggressively and gracefully with two other historic properties, the Grand and the Continental. Of the three, the Bristol consistently emerges as the hippest and the most accessible. Set in the commercial core of Oslo, one block north of Karl Johans Gate, the Bristol is warm, rich with tradition, and comfortable. It also isn't as formal as either the Grand or the Continental, attracting the media, arts, and showbiz communities, with a sense of playfulness and fun that's unmatched by either of its rivals.

Bedrooms are comfortable and dignified, but not as plush or as intensely "decorated" as the rooms in either of its grander competitors. Lavish public areas still evoke the Moorish-inspired Art Deco heyday in which they were built. There's enormous life and energy in this hotel, thanks to active restaurants such as the Bristol Grill (p. 113), piano bars, and a sense of elegant yet unpretentious conviviality.

Kristian IV's Gate 7, N-0164 Oslo 1. ✆ **22-82-60-00.** Fax: 22-82-60-01. www.thonhotels.com/bristol. 252 units. NOK2,650–NOK3,200 double; year-round daily NOK8,000 suite. Rates include breakfast buffet. AE, DC, MC, V. Parking NOK300. Tram: 10, 11, 17, or 18. **Amenities:** 2 restaurants; 2 bars; nightclub/dance bar; small exercise room & fitness center; spa & Turkish bath; room service; all smoke-free rooms. *In room:* A/C, TV, hair dryer, minibar, Wi-Fi (free).

Radisson BLU Plaza Hotel ★ If for no other reason, we'd check in here for the panoramic views of the city and the Oslofjord. With an exterior sheathed in blue-tinted glass, and a needle-nosed summit that soars high above everything else in Oslo, this is the tallest building in Norway, and the largest hotel in northern Europe. The hotel struggles to permeate its vast, impersonal interior with a sense of intimacy and individuality. Guests do a lot of high-velocity elevator riding, and stay in fairly predictable but comfy rooms high above the city's commercial core, almost immediately next to the city's bus and railway stations. The high-altitude views are sublime, and the comfortable, well-decorated rooms have flair and original works of art. The bar on the 34th floor, 34 Skybar (p. 168) has a panoramic view, and is the perfect place to watch the sunset over the city.

Sonja Henies Plass 3, N-0134 Oslo. ✆ **22-05-80-00.** Fax: 22-05-80-10. www.radissonblu.com/plazahotel-oslo. 673 units. NOK995–NOK2,095 double; from NOK3,900 suite. Rates include breakfast. AE, DC, MC, V. Parking NOK300. T-banen: Jernbanetorget. **Amenities:** 2 restaurants; bar; indoor pool; sauna; room service; all smoke-free rooms. *In room:* A/C, TV, hair dryer, minibar, Wi-Fi (free).

Radisson BLU Scandinavia Hotel ★ As the sun sets over Oslo, it's great to gather with friends at Summit (p. 168), a bar on the 21st floor, for one of the grandest vistas of Oslo. This black, angular hotel doesn't quite escape the impersonal curse of its 1975 construction, but it tries nobly and succeeds rather well on its interior. With 22 floors, this is Oslo's third-biggest hotel (after the Radisson BLU Plaza Hotel and the Clarion Hotel Royal Christiana), the second-tallest building, and the first hotel that most Oslovians think of when they hear the name "Radisson Hotel." Bedrooms are relatively large, very comfortable, and come in about a dozen different styles, including Scandinavian, Japanese, Art Deco, and a nautical style inspired by Norway's maritime traditions.

Holbergsgate 30, N-0166 Oslo. ✆ **23-29-30-00.** Fax: 23-29-30-01. www.radissonblu.com/scandinaviahotel-oslo. 488 units. NOK1,295–NOK2,095 double; from NOK3,500 suite. Rates include breakfast. AE, DC, MC, V. Parking NOK360. T-banen: Nationaltheatret. Smoke-free hotel. **Amenities:** 3 restaurants; bar; indoor heated pool; fitness room; sauna; kids' playroom; room service. *In room:* A/C, TV, hair dryer, minibar, Wi-Fi (free).

Rica Victoria Hotel ★ If your heart is set on one of the Radissons (see above), this hotel may come as a bit of a letdown. But its interior offers cozy comfort in spite of its foreboding facade. This hotel, built in 1991, enjoys an enviable position midway between the Aker Brygge restaurant and office complex and the Norwegian Parliament. Some of the best rooms are on the ninth (uppermost) floor, where the sloping walls of the Mansard-style roof add a general coziness. Regardless of their location within the hotel, rooms have wood flooring and tile-covered bathrooms. Rooms are conservatively decorated but comfortable enough, with non-standard fittings such as rounded corners, reproduction antiques, and circa-1900s' brass lamps.

Rosenkrantzgate 13, N-0121 Oslo. ✆ **24-14-70-00.** Fax: 24-14-70-01. www.rica-hotels.com. 199 units. NOK895–NOK1,760 double; NOK2,500–NOK3,500 suite. Rates include breakfast. AE, DC, MC, V. Parking NOK280 per night. Tram: 10, 12, 15, or 19. **Amenities:** Restaurant; bar; babysitting; smoke-free rooms. *In room:* TV, hair dryer, minibar, Wi-Fi (free).

Thon Hotel Europa Of the Thon hotels in Oslo, the Cecil is a better choice, but this well-run hotel has a lot going for it as well. Few other hotels enjoy a position as quiet yet as convenient to Karl Johans Gate as this red-brick member of the chain. The building faces a large patch of greenery and the front entrances of two of Oslo's museums, the Norse Teknisk Museum (Norwegian Technological Museum) and the Nasjonalgalleriet (National Gallery). The hotel was originally built as a complex of private apartments before being transformed in the 1970s into this efficient and well-managed hotel. Bedrooms are small but comfortable, with burl-grained walnut veneers and writing desks.

St. Olavs Gate 31, N-0166 Oslo. ✆ **23-25-63-00.** Fax: 23-25-63-63. www.thonhotels.com/europa. 167 units. NOK1,400–NOK1,800 double; year-round daily from NOK2,990 suite. AE, DC, MC, V. No on-site parking. T-banen: Stortinget. **Amenities:** Restaurant/bar; smoke-free rooms. *In room:* A/C, TV, hair dryer, minibar, Wi-Fi (free).

Thon Hotel Gyldenløve ★ The "Golden Lion" was once a dowdy *hospits* (an inexpensive hotel, but better than a youth hostel). Lying only a 10-minute walk from the Royal Palace, it stands on a tree-lined street in the West End, a highly desirable neighborhood. In its latest reincarnation as part of the ever-growing Thon chain, it has become one of the city's most desirable addresses. Midsize bedrooms are in a modernistic Nordic design, combining a light, airy feeling with Scandinavian pastels.

Bogstadveien 20, N-0355 Oslo. ✆ **23-33-23-00.** Fax: 23-33-23-03. www.thonhotels.com/gyldenlove. 164 units. NOK995–NOK1,795 double. Rates include breakfast. AE, DC, MC, V. Parking NOK150. Tram: 11, 19. **Amenities:** Breakfast room; smoke-free rooms. *In room:* TV, hair dryer, minibar, Wi-Fi (free).

Thon Hotel Stefan As "Thons" go, this is the low man on the totem pole, but it's a recommendable choice if its siblings are fully booked. We've seen bigger and better hotels in Oslo, but very few that offer comparable comfort at such affordable rates. In an excellent location in the center of the city, this unpretentious hotel never claims to be more than it is. Built in 1952, it has been modernized and much improved over the years. The color-coordinated guest rooms are traditional in style and well furnished and maintained. From May until September 1, weekend rates are granted only to those who make reservations less than 48 hours before arrival.

Rosenkrantzgate 1, N-0159 Oslo 1. ✆ **23-31-55-00.** Fax: 23-31-55-55. www.thonhotels.com/stefan. 150 units. NOK1,195–NOK1,995. Rates include buffet breakfast. AE, DC, MC, V. Parking NOK180. Tram: 10, 11, 17, or 18. **Amenities:** Coffee shop/bar; smoke-free rooms. *In room:* A/C, TV, hair dryer, minibar, Wi-Fi (free).

MODERATE

Best Western Hotell Bondeheimen This is one of the safest and most reliable choices in town. Guests here are more interested in value (not to mention values) than in frills. In the city center, a short block from the Students' Grove at Karl Johans Gate, the Bondeheimen was built in 1913. A cooperative of farmers and students established this hotel, now a Best Western, to provide affordable, teetotalist-friendly accommodations when they visited Oslo from the countryside. Although small, the compact rooms are comfortably furnished, often with Norwegian pine pieces. Bedrooms are larger than standard, with tasteful furniture. All rooms are nonsmoking.

Rosenkrantzgate 8 (entrance on Kristian IV's Gate), N-0159 Oslo 1. ✆ **23-21-41-00** or 800/633-6548 in the U.S. Fax: 23-21-41-01. www.bondeheimen.com. 127 units. NOK895–NOK2,500 double. Rates include buffet breakfast. AE, DC, MC, V. Parking NOK180. Tram: 7 or 11. **Amenities:** Restaurant; smoke-free hotel. *In room:* TV, hair dryer, minibar, Internet (free).

Clarion Collection Hotel Savoy ★ This hotel has a tough act to follow now that it's joined that small, select group, Clarion Collection, which operates the superior

Hotel Bastion (p. 106). First, try for the Bastion; if no rooms are available there, the Savoy is a viable alternative, though it draws mixed reviews. One former guest found his room "the smallest I have ever stayed in." Another couple loved their room, finding the Savoy "great value, great location," the latter a reference to it standing opposite the National Gallery. My conclusion is that how much you end up liking the Savoy depends on your room assignment, so be specific when booking. Some of the bedrooms are spacious and stylishly furnished. The building itself is classic, a traditional-looking structure that was built in the early 20th century, but has been frequently renovated since. On-site is restauranteik (p. 112), serving well-prepared Norwegian and international dishes in a smoke-free atmosphere. The soft upholstered chairs of the hotel's Savoy Bar also attract many nonguests for evening cocktails. The hotel is entirely nonsmoking.

Universitesgata 11, N-0164 Oslo. ✆ **23-35-42-00.** Fax: 23-35-42-01. www.clarionhotel.com. 93 units. NOK950–NOK2,895 double. Rates include buffet breakfast. AE, DC, MC, V. Parking NOK180. Tram: 11, 13, 18, or 19. **Amenities:** Restaurant; bar; room service; smoke-free rooms. *In room:* TV, hair dryer, Wi-Fi (free)

Clarion Hotel Royal Christiania ★ Opposite Oslo Central railway station, this is one of the leading business and leisure hotels in Oslo, though its largesse means that it's less a personalized affair than the Grand or the Continental. This is the second-largest hotel in Norway, a soaring 14-story tower built to house athletes and administrators during the 1952 Winter Olympics. Refurbished in 2010, the luxury hotel is now comparable to the nearby Radisson BLU Plaza Hotel (p. 104), but without so much drama. The medium-size guest rooms are as quiet, conservatively decorated, and blandly tasteful as you'd expect from an international chain.

Biskop Gunnerus' Gate 3, N-0106 Oslo. ✆ **23-10-80-00.** Fax: 23-10-80-80. www.clarionroyalchristiania.com. 532 units. NOK1,395–NOK2,600 double; NOK4,700 suite. Rates include buffet breakfast. AE, DC, MC, V. Parking NOK350. Bus: 30, 31, or 41. **Amenities:** 4 restaurants; bar; indoor heated pool; fitness center & sauna; room service; all smoke-free rooms. *In room:* TV, hair dryer, Wi-Fi (free).

Hotel Bastion ★★ Several years ago, this boutique hotel became a member of the Clarion Collection, a chain of small individual hotels with a personal touch. In this reincarnation, it is the closest rival to the Bristol (see above), which still retains the cutting edge. In the Old Town of Oslo, within walking distance of Karl Johans Gate, this is a warm, inviting, residential-style property, a true bastion of comfort. The midsize-to-spacious bedrooms are tastefully stylish, yet are also intimate and unpretentious; they were designed in part by Anemone W. Våge, one of the best-known Norwegian designers, who even decorated the apartments of the royal family nearby. If you want to go more upmarket, you can ask for one of the junior suites or deluxe suites, among the best in the capital. The hotel is entirely nonsmoking.

Skippergaten 7, N-0152 Oslo. ✆ **22-47-77-00.** Fax: 22-33-11-80. www.hotelbastion.no. 99 units. NOK980–NOK2,995 double; NOK2,095–NOK3,995 suite. Rates include buffet breakfast. AE, DC, MC, V. T-banen: Jernbanetorget. **Amenities:** Restaurant; bar; fitness center; Jacuzzi; sauna; room service; all smoke-free rooms. *In room:* A/C, TV, hair dryer, minibar, Wi-Fi (free).

Scandic KNA Oslo City Hotel This hotel looks deceptively new, thanks to a futuristic-looking mirrored facade that was added in the 1970s to an older core that was originally built in the 1940s by the Norwegian Auto Club. Inside, you'll find a cozy lobby-level bar and restaurant serving Norwegian food, and a deeply entrenched kind of informality. Bedrooms are simple, well maintained, and a bit spartan-looking. If you're a self-motivated kind of traveler with a clear idea of what you want to see and where you want to go in Oslo, without much need for attention or advice from the staff, this might be an appropriate choice.

Parkveien 68, N-0254 Oslo. ✆ **23-15-57-00.** Fax: 23-15-57-11. www.scandic-hotels.com/KNA. 189 units. Sun–Thurs NOK900–NOK1,990 double; Fri–Sat NOK900–NOK1,800 double. Rates include buffet breakfast. AE, DC, MC, V. No on-site parking. Tram: 12 or 15. **Amenities:** Restaurant; bar; babysitting; health club & sauna; room service; smoke-free rooms. *In room:* TV, hair dryer, minibar, Wi-Fi (free).

INEXPENSIVE

Cochs Pensjonat One of Norway's bestselling and most-translated novelists, Lars Saabye Christensen, once claimed in an interview: "I often went past Cochs Pensjonat in my childhood and I always slackened my pace. But I never went in. You couldn't see in. I imagined all sorts of things happening behind the entrance door." He was so impressed that he wrote a novel, *The Half Brother,* in which one of his main characters stayed in room 502 at Cochs for 4,982 days. There's nothing secretive going on inside. Rather, Cochs is the most famous and most enduring boardinghouse in Oslo, having been launched in 1927 by the Coch sisters. The building has an ornate facade curving around a bend in a boulevard that banks the northern edge of the Royal Palace. This is a comfortable but simple lodging whose newer rooms are high-ceilinged, spartan but pleasant, and outfitted with birchwood furniture. I much prefer looking out onto Slottsparken from the "Royal Rooms," which were created in 1996 when a large apartment was incorporated into the guesthouse. Expect very few, if any, amenities and services at this hotel—rooms are without telephones. Breakfast is served at KafeCaffé, Parkveien 21.

Parkveien 25, N-0350 Oslo. ✆ **23-33-24-00.** Fax: 23-33-24-10. www.cochspensjonat.no. 88 units. Rooms w/private bathroom & kitchenette NOK780 double, NOK990 triple, NOK1,120 quad; rooms w/ shared bathroom & no kitchenette NOK680 double, NOK870 triple, NOK1,060 quad. MC, V. No on-site parking. Tram: 11 or 12. *In room:* TV, kitchenette (in some), no phone.

West End

MODERATE

Clarion Collection Hotel Gabelshus ★ This member of the Clarion Collection chain may not be as first-class as its previously recommended brethren (see the Savoy, p. 105, or the Bastion, p. 106), but in some ways I prefer it because of its location. A brisk 15-minute walk from the city center, it sits in a tranquil location on a tree-lined street. Since its opening as a guesthouse back in 1912, it has greatly expanded through its takeover of an adjoining building. Discreetly conservative, it calls to mind an English manor house, laced with climbing ivy. The public rooms are filled with antiques, art, burnished copper, and working fireplaces. Guest rooms are decorated with tasteful colors and textiles, and some have terraces. You'll have a choice of Scandinavian modern furniture or traditional styling.

Gabels Gate 16, N-0272 Oslo 2. ✆ **23-27-65-00.** Fax: 23-27-65-60. www.clarionhotel.com. 114 units. Mon–Thurs NOK1,580 double; Fri–Sun NOK1,300 double; NOK3,000–NOK4,000 suite. Rates include buffet breakfast. AE, DC, MC, V. Free parking. Tram: 10. **Amenities:** Restaurant; exercise room; sauna; steam room; smoke-free rooms. *In room:* TV, hair dryer, Wi-Fi (free).

Rica Hotel Bygdøy Allé ★ This upscale hotel is better equipped than the Gabelshus (see above), but you'll pay more for the privilege of lodging here. The intimate hotel, the smallest in the Rica chain, has the air of an artsy boutique hotel. Its designers shoehorned it into the framework of a late-19th-century Flemish-revival brick structure in Oslo's well-heeled West End. Each of the bedrooms is different in its layout, corresponding to the already-existing towers and gables of the older structure. Room nos. 206, 214, 406, and 414 are among the most sought-after because of their Victorian-era curved walls and bay windows. Other than that, the decor is conservative and predictably upscale—and a bit bland, usually in pastel tones.

Bygdøy Allé 53, N-0265 Oslo. ✆ **23-08-58-00.** Fax: 23-08-58-08. www.rica-hotels.com. 57 units. Sun–Thurs NOK1,760–NOK2,145 double; Fri–Sat NOK795–NOK1,200 double. Rates include buffet breakfast. AE, DC, MC, V. No on-site parking. Tram: 10. Bus: 30, 31, 32, or 33. **Amenities:** Restaurant; bar; room service; smoke-free rooms. *In room:* TV, hair dryer, Wi-Fi (free).

Holmenkollen

EXPENSIVE

Holmenkollen Park Hotel Rica ★ If you stay here, you'll be both in the city of Oslo and in the country. Just how far out in the country are you? Let's put it this way: At sundown, you are likely to see elks in the distance. On a panoramic hillside crowning Oslo, this hotel sits on forested land that's devoted to recreation, cross-country skiing, and hiking. Its location is a short walk from the Holmenkollen ski jump, at the terminus of tram line no. 1. The hotel was built in 1894, rebuilt after a fire in 1904, reconstructed again in 1948 after a 4-year occupation by the Nazis, and then massively enlarged with four new wings in 1982, when it was taken over by the Rica hotel chain. Today the oldest part of the hotel (a richly detailed log-and-timber building designed in the Viking revival "dragon" style) is used for check-ins and for convention facilities; the remainder contains modern, comfortable rooms and all the facilities you'd expect in a resort hotel. Ranging from comfortable and spacious standards to classically decorated deluxe units, bedrooms are cozy, with lots of exposed wood and hints of chalet styling.

Kongeveien 26, N-0390 Oslo. ✆ **22-92-20-00.** Fax: 22-14-61-92. www.holmenkollenparkhotel.no. 220 units. Mon–Thurs NOK1,695–NOK1,995 double; Fri–Sun NOK1,325–NOK1,735 double; from NOK2,895–NOK3,595 suite. Rates include breakfast. AE, DC, MC, V. Parking NOK150. Tram: 1. **Amenities:** 2 restaurants; cafe; bar; babysitting; indoor heated pool; health club; Jacuzzi; sauna; smoke-free rooms. *In room:* A/C, TV, hair dryer, Jacuzzi (in some), minibar, Wi-Fi (free).

At the Airport

VERY EXPENSIVE

Radisson BLU Airport Hotel ★ To go between the arrivals terminal and the hotel, designed as an integral part of the Gardermoen airport, wheel your luggage along a series of sloping cement ramps and across a busy access road. The architecture is futuristic and well conceived, and rapid checkout (via your TV screen) eliminates a lot of the fuss. Bedrooms have carved headboards in a Southeast Asian style, as well as writing tables, plus sleek, white-tiled bathrooms. Like any airport hotel, this one is somewhat impersonal.

Hotellvegen, Box 163, N-2061 Gardermoen. ✆ **63-93-30-00.** Fax: 63-93-30-30. www.radissonblu.com/hotel-osloairport. 503 units. NOK1,595–NOK2,095 double; NOK1,995 junior suite; from NOK3,900 suite. Rates include buffet breakfast. AE, DC, MC, V. Free parking. **Amenities:** 2 restaurants; bar; babysitting, health club & sauna; room service; smoke-free rooms. *In room:* A/C, TV, hair dryer, minibar, Wi-Fi (free).

INEXPENSIVE

Thon Hotel Gardermoen The Thon chain strikes again with the first budget hotel (opened in 2006) at Gardermoen airport. In spite of its smart, stylish decor, it is an affordable choice, with a shuttle bus running between the hotel and the airport, 5 minutes away. Admittedly, it's so large it's something of a bed factory. But the rooms are comfortably furnished, albeit a bit small. Rated at three stars by the government, its bedrooms are spread out over 13 two-story buildings. The standard singles feature just one bed, but most rooms are doubles with two single beds.

Balder Allé 22, N-2065 Gardermoen. ✆ **64-00-45-00.** Fax: 63-92-94-01. www.thonhotels.com/osloairport. 435 units. NOK925–NOK1,075 double. AE, DC, MC, V. Free parking. **Amenities:** Restaurant; bar; health club & spa; room service; smoke-free rooms. *In room:* TV, hair dryer, minibar, Wi-Fi (free).

WHERE TO DINE

You can now dine internationally without leaving the city of Oslo. The influx of immigrants in recent years has led to the growth of Mexican-, Turkish-, Moroccan-, Chinese-, Greek-, and American-style restaurants. Among European cuisines, French and Italian are the most popular. The largest concentration of restaurants is at Aker Brygge. This former shipbuilding yard on the harborfront is now the smartest dining and shopping complex in Norway.

Not all restaurants in Oslo are newcomers. Some have long been associated with artists and writers—the Grand Café, for example, was the stamping ground of Henrik Ibsen and Edvard Munch.

At most restaurants, a 15% service charge and 25% value-added tax are included in the bill. It's customary to leave some additional small change if the service has been satisfactory. Wine and beer can add a lot of money onto your final bill, so be careful.

Central Oslo

VERY EXPENSIVE

Oro ★★★ CONTINENTAL/MEDITERRANEAN Is this the best restaurant in Oslo, as some critics maintain? I won't go that far, but Oro is among the top five choices. This very stylish Michelin-star winner is run by chef Mads Larsson, who directs the kitchen of a three-faceted establishment that includes a European gourmet restaurant, a separate section called Oro Bar & Grill, and a boutique-style deli (Mon–Fri 11:30am–3pm) for enthusiasts who want to haul some of its raw ingredients back home. The restaurant is a curvaceous, slick-looking testimonial to stainless steel and warm-toned hardwoods. I recommend the fixed-price menus, although be warned that each of them will be prepared only for every member of the table at the same time. One option includes a five-course vegetarian menu at NOK545. Representative dishes, each one delectable, include pasta with truffle, codfish with spinach and hazelnut, deer with mushroom and foie gras, and pigeon with cabbage and bacon.

Tordenskiolds 6A (entrance on Kjeld Stubs Gate). ✆ **23-01-02-40.** www.ororestaurant.no. Reservations required. Fixed-price menus: NOK545–NOK795 for 5 courses. AE, DC, MC, V. Mon–Sat 11am–3pm & 5–10pm. T-banen: Stortinget.

Where to Dine in Oslo

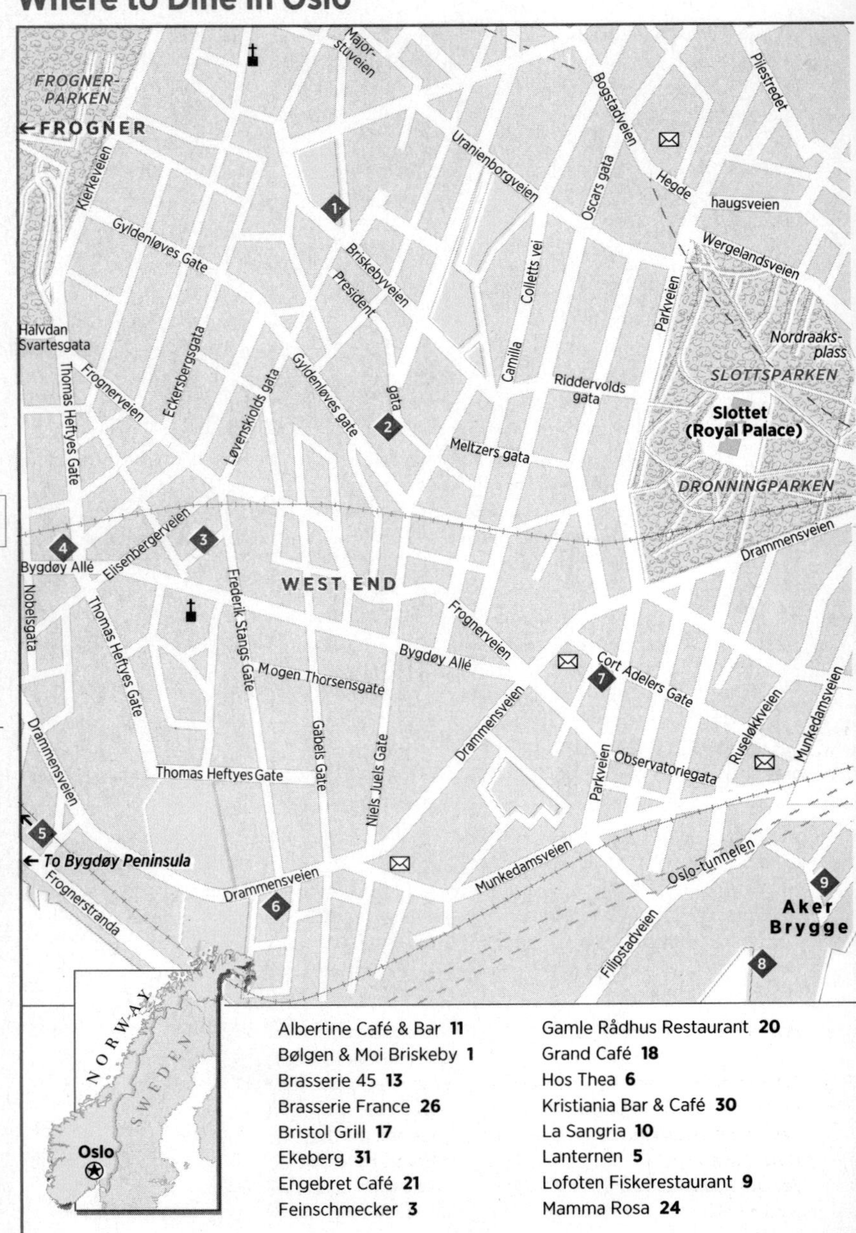

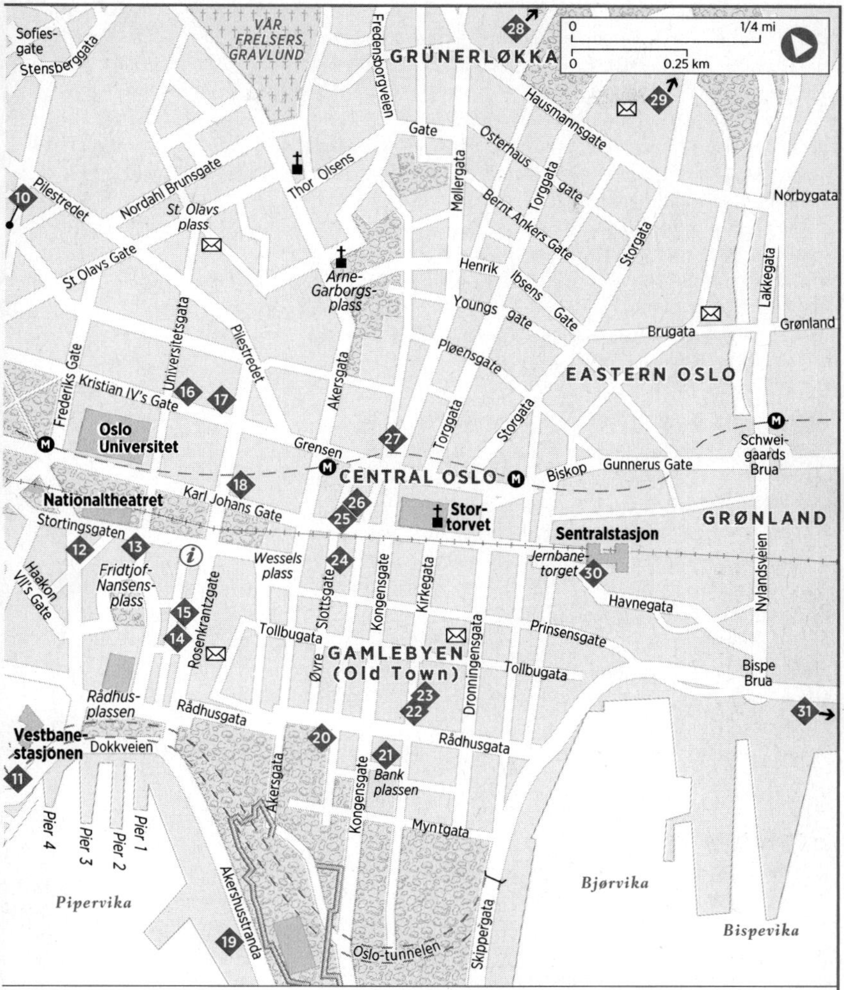

Markveien Mat og Vinhus **28**
Oro **15**
Palace Grill **7**
Restaurant Julius Fritzner **18**
Restaurant Le Canard **2**
restauranteik **16**
Santino's Spaghetteria **14**
Solsiden **19**
Statholderens Krostue **22**
Statholdergaarden **23**
Stortorvets Gjæstgiveri **27**
Südøst **29**
Theatercafeen **12**
3 Brødre **25**
Tjuvholmen Sjømagasin **8**
Village **4**

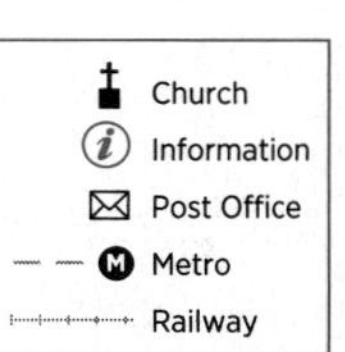

Restaurant Julius Fritzner ★★ NORWEGIAN/CONTINENTAL Its namesake, pastry chef Julius Fritzner, opened the Grand Hotel in 1874, so it's only fitting that the present-day owners have named this deluxe restaurant in his honor. Dining at the Grand has long been a marker of tradition. When Roald Amundsen returned to Oslo after his successful expedition to the South Pole in 1912, a banquet here honored him. One of the best and most impressive restaurants in Oslo, it opened in 1995 to rave reviews, and the accolades just keep coming. The venue is conservative, with a battalion of impeccably trained waiters who maintain their humor and personal touch despite the sophisticated setting. The dishes, all made with the finest Scandinavian ingredients, change with the season and the chef's inspiration. Some of the best dishes are orange and pepper-crusted trout with a parsley purée, and smoked rabbit with forest mushrooms and parsnips. Desserts, which are occasionally theatrical, include a terrine of chocolate with a compote of peaches and sorbet flavored with basil and cinnamon.

In the Grand Hotel, Karl Johans Gate 31. ✆ **23-21-20-00.** www.grand.no. Reservations recommended. Main courses NOK295–NOK395; 5 courses including wine pairings & aperitif NOK1,490. AE, DC, MC, V. Mon–Sat 5–10:30pm. Closed June 21–Aug 11. T-banen: Stortinget.

restauranteik ★ INTERNATIONAL Located within the Clarion Collection Hotel Savoy (p. 105), one floor above street level, immediately adjacent to Oslo's National Gallery, this is a hip, trendy, expensive, and highly visible restaurant that has attracted such big names as the prime minister of Norway since its opening in 2003. A color scheme of very pale pink and gray offsets a starkly minimalist decor that includes floors and an entire wall that's paneled in walnut. The five on-staff chefs are given free rein to express their creativity in the form of food that's inspired by Thai, Chinese, Japanese, American, Continental, or all-Norwegian culinary motifs. Some dishes that win over palates include pan-fried redfish served with pea purée, orange-braised fennel, a lightly pickled tomato, and shellfish sauce; and the grilled lamb cutlets, served with risotto-style orzo pasta and a concentrated rosemary sauce.

Universitesgata 11. ✆ **22-36-07-10.** www.restauranteik.no. Reservations recommended. Set-price menus: NOK465 for 5 courses. AE, DC, MC, V. Tues–Sat 6–11pm (last seating). Closed 1 week at Easter, 1 week at Christmas, & 4 weeks in midsummer. T-banen: Tullenløkka.

EXPENSIVE

Grand Café ★★ NORWEGIAN Over the decades, this 1874 cafe has served as the living and dining room for the elite of Christiania (an old name for Oslo). The country's greatest artists have dined here with foreign diplomats, kings, and explorers. While it's not as chic as it once was, I am still loyal to it and view a night here as part of my Norwegian experience. A large mural on one wall depicts Ibsen and Edvard Munch, along with other, less famous, former patrons. The atmosphere and tradition here are sometimes more compelling than the cuisine, but if you like solid, honest flavors, this is the place to eat. The menu relies on Norwegian country traditions (how many places still serve elk stew?). Representative dishes include chicken with green asparagus, sun-dried tomatoes, and a basil cream pasta; or herb-marinated monkfish with beans, rice pilaf, and a demi-glace of figs.

In the Grand Hotel, Karl Johans Gate 31. ✆ **23-21-20-00.** www.grand.no. Reservations recommended. Main courses NOK165–NOK320. AE, DC, MC, V. Mon–Fri 11am–11pm; Sat noon–11pm; Sun 1–10pm. T-banen: Stortinget.

Theatercafeen ★ INTERNATIONAL The *New York Times,* with a great deal of justification, listed this cafe as among the 10 most famous on the planet. If you like to eat and drink in opulence, head here for your grand fix. The last of the grand Viennese cafes in northern Europe, this long-standing favorite was founded a century ago to rival the Grand Café. Each has its devotees, although I like this one better because of its old world *schmaltz.* Serenaded by piano and a duet of violins, the style might well have pleased Habsburg Emperor Franz Josef had he ever ventured this far north. With soft lighting, antique bronzes, cut-glass lighting fixtures, and Art Nouveau mirrors, it's the type of place that encourages lingering, and it attracts present-day *boulevardiers* and businesspeople. The entire establishment was renovated in 2010, adding a private dining room for 38 guests, as well as a new smaller eatery and bar. Menu items are well prepared and traditional, and are adjusted accordingly to get the best flavors out of each season. That might mean butter-roasted turbot with toasted bacon, chives, and boiled potatoes; or breast of duck with spinach and madeira sauce.

In the Hotel Continental, Stortingsgaten 24. ✆ **22-82-40-50.** www.hotel-continental.no. Reservations recommended. Main courses NOK235–NOK295; open-faced sandwiches NOK130 at lunch. AE, DC, MC, V. Mon–Sat 11am–11pm; Sun 3–10pm. T-banen: Stortinget.

MODERATE

Brasserie France ★ FRENCH One of my favorite restaurants in town is this most typical of all French bistros with its Art Nouveau decor, French posters, and waiters in long white aprons. The decor is that of a typical French brasserie, the kind you'd find beside the road in Alsace, complete with tables spilling out onto the sidewalk during the summer months. The brasserie is known for serving Oslo's freshest oysters. Treat yourself to such dishes as confit of duck leg with cherry tomatoes and green asparagus; or grilled rib-eye with French green beans and a Béarnaise sauce. The best of local ingredients and a strong technique in the kitchen combine to turn out such dishes as shellfish soup with panfried scallops, fennel fried cod with forest mushrooms and shellfish sauce, and black mullet and grilled gambas served with cauliflower purée and green tomatoes.

Øvre Slottsgate 16. ✆ **23-10-01-60.** www.brasseriefrance.no. Reservations required. Main courses NOK225–NOK350; 3-course menu NOK495. AE, DC, MC, V. Mon–Fri 4–10:30pm; Sat noon–10:30pm. Bus: 27, 29, 30, 41, or 61.

Bristol Grill ★★ CONTINENTAL This is the premier dining room of the Hotel Bristol (p. 103), one of Oslo's most prestigious hotels. You'll find old-world charm, formal service without a lot of flash or frenzy, and elegant decor that evokes a baronial hunting lodge from the 1920s, when the restaurant was founded. In the '30s, the place evolved into the dining venue you'll see today, with a gentleman's-club allure that eventually welcomed big-name entertainers. You'll pass through a cozy, woodsy-looking piano bar to reach the restaurant. With a culinary focus that has radically improved over the years, the menu continues to be one of the finest in the Norwegian capital as it beautifully adjusts to take advantage of the best ingredients in all four seasons, including winter. There's a spectacular version of bouillabaisse, prepared with Nordic (not Mediterranean) fish and seasoned with saffron, which can be ordered as either a starter or a main course. One of the chef's most successful specialties is medallions of venison sautéed with vanilla and bacon, served on a bed of mushrooms with a terrine of potatoes.

In the Hotel Bristol, Kristian IV's Gate 7. ✆ **22-82-60-20.** www.thonhotels.com. Reservations recommended, especially at night. Main courses NOK220–NOK295; 3-course menu NOK410. AE, DC, MC, V. Daily 5–11pm. Tram: 10, 11, 17, or 18.

La Sangria ★ SPANISH Established in 1992 in a location across the street from the Radisson BLU Scandinavia Hotel (p. 104), within a dining room sheathed with roughly textured stucco and hand-painted Iberian porcelain, this is the best Spanish restaurant in Oslo. It was launched by two hard-working brothers (Fernando and Juan-Carlos) from Madrid, whose appreciation of both bullfighting and soccer, especially the Real Madrid team, is obvious, to judge by the posters, memorabilia, and photos displayed. Here you can enjoy all the old tapas favorites—snails in garlic butter, fried chorizo sausage, sautéed chicken in garlic. Entrees include paella; shrimp with garlic; Serrano ham with Manchego cheese and chorizo sausage; gazpacho; *bacalhau* (dried cod) alla Vizcaina; and, my favorite, boneless chicken stuffed with ham and cheese in a white-wine sauce. Don't miss the outstanding large paella plates (NOK229).

Holbergsgate 19. ✆ **22-11-63-15.** www.lasangria.no. Reservations recommended. Main courses NOK218–NOK289. AE, DC, MC, V. Mon–Sat 3–11pm; Sun 3–10pm. Closed Dec 23–Jan 2. Tram: 11 or 19.

INEXPENSIVE

Brasserie 45 ★ ☺ CONTINENTAL After taking in an Ibsen play at the National Theater, this is the perfect nearby restaurant for dinner. Airy and stylish, this second-story bistro overlooks the biggest fountain along downtown Oslo's showplace promenade. It is a family business, and the hard-working owners employ a certain discerning taste to treat you to the best of Mother France's kitchen. In recent years they have added Asian inspiration to their menu: Onion soup and chocolate mousse, naturally, appear on the menu but the uniformed staff also bears steaming platters of less-traditional cuisine—king prawns in a spicy Thai sauce, anyone? The Norwegian kitchen isn't neglected, either, with dishes such as smoked moose and baked filet of cod with stir-fried vegetables, or oven-baked leg of lamb with mushroom sauce. Marinated chicken breast comes with a creamy tomato-glazed sauce and roast potatoes. For dessert in summer, what really beats freshly picked blackberries with ice cream? Great kids' menu too.

Stortingsgaten 20. ✆ **22-41-34-00.** www.brasserie45.no. Reservations recommended. Main courses NOK139–NOK235; fixed-price menu NOK295–NOK335. AE, DC, MC, V. Mon–Thurs 3–11:30pm; Fri–Sat 2pm–midnight; Sun 2–10pm. T-banen: Centrum.

Kristiania Bar & Café CONTINENTAL Set within the oldest part of Oslo's railway station (the Østbanehallen, or East Wing), this late-19th-century cafe has one of the grandest decors of any cafe in Oslo, though it's hardly a rival of Theatercafeen. You'll dine and drink beneath a soaring ceiling dotted with cavorting cherubs and elaborate plaster reliefs, at a dark-stained Victorian-era bar that's an antique in its own right. Even this cafe's toilets are historically important and, consequently, ferociously protected against architectural changes. Surprisingly for such a lavish setting, the food is relatively simple and much less expensive than at such equally historic cafes as the Grand Café. Menu items focus on burgers, salads, club sandwiches, pastas, milkshakes, and specials of the day. If the weather is fine, opt for a table on this cafe's very large outdoor terrace. It's sunnier and brighter than the more

DINING secrets OF OSLO

One of Oslovians' favorite pastimes is visiting **Aker Brygge** (www.akerbrygge.no). Formerly a dilapidated shipbuilding yard, the futuristic complex now combines more shopping, entertainment, and dining diversions in one area than anywhere else in Norway. Many visitors, some with children, come here to check out the restaurants and cafes, watch the people, and listen to music in the bars. Part of the fun is strolling through the complex and picking a restaurant. Norwegian food is served along with a representative selection of foreign food offerings, including American. In the summer visitors and locals fill the outdoor tables overlooking the harbor. There are also many nightlife options (see "Oslo After Dark," in chapter 6). To reach Aker Brygge, take bus no. 27 or walk down from the center west of the Rådhuset.

A local favorite here is the **Albertine Café & Bar,** Stranden 3 (✆ **22-83-00-60;** www.cafealbertine.no), an informal place on the wharf's edge, offering a panoramic view over the harbor and Akershus fortress. This place consistently serves some of the freshest and tastiest oysters in Oslo. You can drop in for anything from a hamburger to a full Norwegian seafood dinner. It's also an easy place for meeting singles. It is named after the character in a popular Norwegian novel.

In front of the Rådhuset, you can join Oslovians for a special picnic treat. From 7 to 8am, **shrimp fishermen** pull their boats into the harbor after having caught and cooked a fresh batch of shrimp during their night at sea. You can order shrimp in a bag (it comes in two sizes). Seafood aficionados take their shrimp to the dock's edge, remove the shells, and feast. The fishermen usually stick around until they've sold the last batch, saving just enough for their families.

expensive cafes on nearby narrower, darker streets, and it enjoys a close-up view over one of Oslo's most stunning and monumental fountains.

Østbanehallen, Jernbanetorget 1. ✆ **22-17-50-30.** www.kristianiacafe.no. Main courses NOK95–NOK170. AE, DC, MC, V. Mon–Thurs 11am–midnight; Fri 11am–3am; Sat 11am–1am; Sun 2–11pm. Food service until 9pm Mon–Sat & 7pm on Sun. T-banen: Jernbanetorget.

Santino's Spaghetteria ☺ ITALIAN This overlooked, inexpensive Italian restaurant lies smack in the center of one of the most expensive neighborhoods in Europe. The decor is whimsical—a hallucinogenic, rainbow-hued interpretation of a carnival setting in Venice, with warm-colored tones of polished stone, a big circular bar, and a tutti-frutti color scheme run amok. Begin with an antipasto, mussels steamed in garlic white wine sauce, or melon and Parma ham, always a winner. A fresh minestrone is made daily. The pastas (almost all of which are homemade) are among Oslo's best, with a wide range of tagliatelle, spaghetti, lasagna, penne, and tortellini, along with fusilli and ravioli. The pizzas emerge piping hot from the oven topped with virtually anything. A special treat is the alla Romana pizza with tomato sauce, mozzarella, smoked baby pork, and arugula.

Tordensskiolds 8. ✆ **22-41-16-22.** www.santinos.no. Reservations recommended. Main course pizza & pasta NOK119–NOK159. No credit cards. Mon–Fri 11am–11pm; Sat 1–11pm; Sun 3–10:30pm. T-banen: Stortinget.

Old Town (Gamlebyen)

VERY EXPENSIVE

Statholdergaarden ★★ NORWEGIAN I know of no grander and more tranquil setting in Oslo for a luxury restaurant than this restored 17th-century house offering a first-floor dining room with original decor. Beautifully laid tables are placed under period stucco ceilings, whose motifs reappear on the china. At this century-old restaurant (set in a building dating from 1640), menu items change frequently, according to what's in season. Some of the best examples of the cuisine here include fried sea bass with petit pois-truffle cremé, chanterelles, and cabbage; and herb-infused filet of lamb served with mushrooms, bean ragout, and Chevre-pecan nut croquette. Other great bets? The grilled scallop and langoustine salad with coriander-marinated mango, and a mustard-glazed filet of lamb served with chanterelles and root vegetable *millefeuille*. Don't confuse this upscale and prestigious site with the less-expensive bistro Statholderens Krostue (see below), which occupies the building's vaulted cellar.

Rådhusgate 11. ✆ **22-41-88-00.** www.statholdergaarden.no. Reservations recommended. Main courses NOK385–NOK395; 4-course fixed-price menu NOK895; 5-course fixed-price menu NOK980; 6-course fixed-price menu NOK1,050. AE, DC, MC, V. Mon–Sat 6pm–midnight. Tram: 11, 15, or 18.

EXPENSIVE

Gamle Rådhus Restaurant ★ NORWEGIAN One of the oldest restaurants in Oslo, Det Gamle Rådhus is in Oslo's former Town Hall (1641). This is strictly for nostalgia buffs, as the restaurant is not at all cutting-edge. It's there for those wanting to see Oslo the way it used to be, who won't mind that the fires of innovation died a long time ago. You'll dine within a network of manorial-inspired rooms with dark wooden panels and Flemish, 16th-century-style wooden chairs. In the spacious dining room, a full array of open-faced sandwiches is served on weekdays only. A la carte dinner selections can be made from a varied menu that includes fresh fish, game, and Norwegian specialties. If you want to sample a dish that Ibsen might have enjoyed, check out the house specialty (and acquired taste), *lutefisk*—but hold your nose. This traditional Scandinavian dish is eaten just before Christmas and is made from dried fish that has been soaked in lye and then poached in broth. More to your liking might be smoked salmon (cured right on the premises), a parfait of chicken livers, freshwater pikeperch from nearby streams sautéed in a lime sauce, filet of reindeer with lingonberry sauce, or Norwegian lamb coated with herbs and baked with a glaze.

Nedre Slottsgate 1. ✆ **22-42-01-07.** www.gamleraadhus.no. Reservations recommended. Main courses NOK210–NOK345. AE, DC, MC, V. Mon–Fri 11:30am–3pm & 4–10pm; Sat 1–3pm & 4–10pm; Kroen Bar Mon–Sat 4pm–midnight. Closed last 3 weeks in July. Bus: 27, 29, 30, 41, or 61.

Statholderens Krostue ★ SWEDISH/DANISH Here you can have a happy return to the culinary past known to Henrik Ibsen. This relatively uncomplicated cellar-level bistro is associated with Statholdergaarden, one of Oslo's most prestigious restaurants (see above). Unlike its more sophisticated sibling, it's open for lunch as well as dinner and features relatively uncomplicated food that's mostly based on traditional Swedish and Danish recipes. The cuisine provides many original and rewarding combinations of ingredients. Beneath the vaulted Renaissance-era ceiling, you can order *frikadeller* (meatballs), minced veal patties in creamy dill

FAMILY-FRIENDLY restaurants

Brasserie 45 This traditional-with-a-twist bistro has a good menu for little ones, especially the picky eaters among them. See p. 114.

Mamma Rosa The best place to fill up on pasta dishes or on one of 10 kinds of pizzas, each a meal in itself. See below.

Santino's Spaghetteria Delectable pasta and pizza, served in a quirky setting that kids should love. See p. 115.

sauce, steak with fried onions, fried eel with potato-and-herb dumplings, or grilled salmon with saffron-flavored noodles. Lunch specialties include platters piled high with Danish or Norwegian ham, herring, boiled eggs, and vegetables, and a selection of *smørbrød* (Danish open-faced sandwiches).

Rådhusgate 11. ✆ **22-41-88-00.** www.statholdergaarden.no. Reservations recommended. Main courses NOK240–NOK300. AE, DC, MC, V. Tues–Sat 11:30am–10pm. Closed for lunch June 22 to Aug 30. Tram: 11, 15, or 18.

MODERATE

Engebret Café NORWEGIAN Regrettably, it's no longer possible to sit, eat, and drink the night away with Henrik Ibsen, Edvard Grieg, and Bjørnstjerne Bjørnson, former patrons of this cafe. A favorite since 1857, this restaurant sits directly north of Akershus Castle in two buildings that have been joined together to form this establishment. The facade of the buildings has been preserved as an architectural landmark. It has an old-fashioned atmosphere and good food, served in a former bohemian literati haunt. During lunch, a tempting selection of open-faced sandwiches is available. The evening menu is more elaborate; you might begin with a terrine of game with blackberry port-wine sauce, or Engebret's always reliable fish soup. Main dishes include a truly savory dish, red wild boar with whortleberry sauce. Or you can try Norwegian reindeer, salmon Christiania, or Engebret's big fish pot. For dessert, try the cloudberry parfait.

Bankplassen 1. ✆ **22-82-25-25.** www.engebret-cafe.no. Reservations recommended. Main courses NOK235–NOK345; 3-course lunch menu NOK275. AE, DC, MC, V. Mon–Fri 11:30am–11pm. Bus: 27, 29, or 30.

Mamma Rosa ☺ ITALIAN This basic trattoria is good for a change of taste and texture. Established by two Tuscan brothers, they have done up the second-floor dining room in a good approximation of reproduction rococo. You can order a dozen types of pizza and pastas, as well as fried scampi and squid, rigatoni, grilled steaks, and gelato. Families, both foreign and Oslovian, frequent this restaurant in large numbers nightly. Children can always find something on the menu to fill up on, especially the pizzas and pastas.

Øvre Slottsgate 12. ✆ **22-42-01-30.** www.mamarosaoslo.no. Main courses NOK128–NOK258; pizzas NOK98–NOK125. AE, DC, MC, V. Mon–Sat noon–11:30pm; Sun 3–10:30pm. T-banen: Stortinget.

Stortorvets Gjæstgiveri ★ NORWEGIAN Many legends surround this nostalgic dining room. It is the oldest restaurant in Oslo, composed of a trio of wood-framed buildings, the most antique of which dates from the 1700s. The inn's upstairs bedchambers with their wood-burning stoves are virtually unchanged since their original construction, although they're now used as private dining rooms. This restaurant changes radically throughout the day: Expect a cafe near the entrance; an old-fashioned, charming, and usually packed restaurant in back; and outside dining in good weather. Menu items are traditional, well prepared, and flavorful, and include steamed mussels in white wine and garlic; poached salmon in a creamy butter sauce with horseradish; or pan-fried trout served with asparagus in parma ham, mushrooms, and mussel sauce. A specialty is roast reindeer in a port sauce spiked with wild berries.

Grensen 1. © **23-35-63-60.** www.stortorvet.no. Reservations recommended. Small platters & snacks NOK98–NOK145; main courses NOK179–NOK349. AE, DC, MC, V. Cafe & restaurant Mon–Sat 11am–10:30pm. Tram: 12 or 17.

3 Brødre ★ MEXICAN Diners once came here for old-fashioned Norwegian fare, but "Three Brothers" now serves food from south of the border—the U.S. border, that is. In their heyday in the 19th century, the "brothers" (the glove manufacturers who once occupied this building) were said to have kept more fingers from freezing off than any other manufacturer in Norway. The food served now is zesty and well prepared, and you'll get hearty portions at reasonable prices. Get those fajitas you've been hungering for, including one version made with jumbo prawns, or dig into double-cheese enchiladas and burritos. The entire street level houses the bustling bar, while a piano bar is the upstairs attraction. Lighter meals, such as snacks and sandwiches, are available on the outside dining terrace in the summer.

Øvre Slottsgate 13. © **23-10-06-70.** www.3brodre.com. Main courses NOK168–NOK246. AE, DC, MC, V. Mon–Sat 7pm–midnight. Street-level bar Mon–Sat 11pm–2:30am. Piano bar Wed–Sat 5pm–2am. Bus: 27, 29, or 30.

Aker Brygge

EXPENSIVE

Lofoten Fiskerestaurant ★★ SEAFOOD This is the Aker Brygge district's most appealing—and best—seafood restaurant. Opening onto the waterfront, the interior sports nautical accessories that evoke life on an upscale yacht. In good weather, tables are set up on an outdoor terrace lined with flowering plants. Menu items change according to the available catch, with few choices for meat-eaters. The fish is served in generous portions, and always very fresh. Look for culinary inspirations from Italy and France, and an ample use of such Mediterranean flavors as pesto. Old-guard diners don't find their tried-and-true dishes on the menu but are introduced to Norwegian fish enriched with various sauces and accompaniments, including baked halibut with garlic cream. Other temptations include seabass baked with spices, filet of beef with rosemary *jus* and pimientos, and baked salmon with horseradish butter.

Stranden 75. © **22-83-08-08.** www.lofoten-fiskerestaurant.no. Reservations recommended. Main courses NOK140–NOK265 lunch; NOK185–NOK325 dinner. AE, DC, MC, V. Mon–Sat 11am–11pm; Sun noon–10pm. Bus: 27.

Solsiden ★ NORWEGIAN/SEAFOOD The degree to which this wildly popular summer restaurant is known throughout Oslo seems way out of proportion to its size and season—it's only open for 4 months of the year. Part of its fame involves its location within a homely, cement-sided warehouse opening onto a pier that's directly across the harbor from the larger, glossier restaurants of the Aker Brygge complex, directly below the imposing bulk of Akershus castle. It's especially appealing on sunny midsummer evenings when sunlight streams onto the pier, while many of the restaurants of Aker Brygge lie in the shadows. The venue features an open kitchen, wide views of Oslo's harbor, the setting sun, and a hard-working staff. Menu items include only fish and shellfish, with no meat of any kind on the menu. The highly theatrical house specialty is a platter of shellfish, prepared for a minimum of two diners at a time, artfully draped with seaweed. Perennial favorites are chorizo-gratinated catfish with cauliflower purée and veal-and-garlic sauce, and pan-fried redfish with thyme risoni. Instead of settling for one of the fancier dishes—such as grilled tuna with lemon grass and sesame onions—it's best to simply ask for *dagens fisk* (the catch of the day).

Søndre Akershus Kai 34. ✆ **23-33-36-30.** www.solsiden.no. Reservations required. Main courses NOK265–NOK295; 3-course fixed-price menu NOK445. May–Aug Mon–Sat 5–10pm; Sun 5–9pm. Closed Sept–Apr. Tram: 10 or 15.

Tjuvholmen Sjømagasin ★★ SEAFOOD Recently opened on a stretch of reclaimed land at the far end of Aker Brygge, this chic, silvery seafood restaurant is run by Bjørn Tore Furset, the local wunderkind restauranteur whose empire includes city eateries Havsmak, Ekeberg, and Argent. His philosophy is all about fresh, locally sourced ingredients. The heralded restaurant seats up to 300 diners—from well-heeled locals to in-the-know tourists—in a sprawling dining room that offers panoramic views of Oslofjord harbor. You can pick your catch right out of the casks that greet you as you walk in, then hand them to the team of chefs manning the open kitchen, and watch them cook your food. Or try a dish from the seafood bar, where things are a bit more informal. The restaurant serves excellent grilled lobster (Norwegian- or American-caught), Varanger king crab, and charcoal-grilled Hordaland trout.

Tjuvholmen Allé 14. ✆ **23-89-77-77.** www.sjomagasinet.no. Main courses NOK270–NOK395; 3-course fixed-price menu NOK465; 5-course fixed-price menu NOK595. Mon–Sat 11am–midnight. Bus: 27.

West End

EXPENSIVE

Bølgen & Moi Briskeby ★ CONTINENTAL When this restaurant's kitchen is firing on all cylinders, it can turn out cooking to match the best you'll find in Oslo. This is a showcase branch of a chain that's now scattered throughout the urban centers of Norway. Backed by the creative zest of two Norway-born chefs and entrepreneurs (Mr. Bølgen and Mr. Moi), the chain is known for being creative and stylish, and as a haven for the discreetly rich and the sometimes famous denizens of Norway. It's set in the Oslovian suburb of Briskeby, within a redesigned industrial building, which is lined with original paintings and photographs by avant-garde artists, most of them Norwegian. The fussiest, most prestigious, and most experimental venue here is the gourmet restaurant, one floor above street level, where only about seven tables accommodate diners for elaborate, drawn-out meals. Frankly, I prefer the street-level brasserie; it's a wee bit less self-consciously grand, and the food is good enough to satisfy all but the most jaded palates. Well-flavored examples include pork marinated in tamarind with lemon grass glacé; halibut with pickled lemon; or fresh lobster gratinée with a shellfish reduction.

Løvenskioldsgate 26, Briskeby. ✆ **24-11-53-53.** www.bolgenogmoi.no. Reservations recommended (required for the gourmet restaurant upstairs). Brasserie main courses NOK225–NOK325; fixed-price menus NOK465–NOK595. AE, DC, MC, V. Mon–Fri 7:30am–12:30am; Sat 9am–12:30am; Sun 11am–4:30pm. Brasserie closed 3 weeks in July. Gourmet restaurant closed July to mid-Aug. Tram: 19.

Feinschmecker ★★ SCANDINAVIAN An old local friend, a savvy food critic, once proclaimed this the best restaurant in Oslo, and I concede that it ranks near the top. One of the most prestigious restaurants in Oslo, Feinschmecker will entertain you with the same style and verve it's produced for such guests as King Harald and Queen Sonja. The dining room's antique furniture and small-paned windows evoke old-time style despite the building's modernity. Menu items change frequently, but there are a few favorites that regularly reappear. Dishes are immaculately presented with a high degree of finish. I found that the quality of materials shines throughout, particularly in such dishes as grilled scallops with crispy potatoes. Even better is the sautéed ocean crayfish tails with apple cider, wild rice, and sun-dried tomatoes. A particularly sought-after main course, and rightly so, is rack of Norwegian lamb.

Balchensgate 5. ✆ **22-12-93-80.** www.feinschmecker.no. Reservations recommended. Main courses NOK325–NOK395; fixed-price 4-course menu NOK745; fixed-price 7-course menu NOK925. AE, DC, MC, V. Mon–Sat 4:30–11pm. Closed 3 weeks in July. Tram: 12 or 19 to Ilesberg.

MODERATE

Hos Thea ★ 🎁 SCANDINAVIAN/SPANISH This century-old building, once a private home, lies in a West End neighborhood 3km (1¾ miles) south of Oslo's center. Is it worth the trip? A lot of foreign foodies who read about this place in European gourmet magazines think so. The stylish, well-managed restaurant also attracts a loyal crowd of people active in the media and the arts. The waitstaff and chefs share duties, so the person who prepares your meal is likely to carry it to your table as well. Depending on the staff's mood and the season, the superbly prepared menu items might include filet of hardanger mountain trout with herbed crème fraiche, or Røros reindeer with traditional cream sauce and Russian peas. The venison, which comes from the north of Norway, is handled delicately and served with a sauce of mixed Nordic summer berries.

Gabelsgate 11 (entrance on Drammensveien). ✆ **22-44-68-74.** www.hosthea.no. Reservations recommended. Main courses NOK245–NOK275; fixed-price 4-course menu NOK465; fixed-price 6-course menu NOK665. AE, DC, MC, V. Daily 4:30–11pm. Tram: 10 or 13.

Village ★ INDIAN You can spend a lot of time admiring the weavings, paintings, chastened brass, and woodcarvings that adorn the walls of this restaurant, a network of dark rooms that evokes an antique house in Rajasthan. Food is flavorful, exotic, and extremely good, with a wide array of dishes to choose from. Many of the recipes, such as the lamb tikka marinated in yogurt and spices, were passed on by the chef's grandmother. Those with a carnivorous streak will opt for the Lahore-style lamb marinated in a tantalizing chili sauce or the spicy Punjabi chicken. Delectable shrimp come flavored with either paprika or garlic, and the house specialty, for those who want a taste of everything, is the "village grill" with a three-way marriage of shrimp, chicken, and lamb.

Bygdøy Allé 65. ✆ **22-56-10-25.** Reservations recommended Fri–Sat nights. Main courses NOK135–NOK245. AE, DC, MC, V. June–Aug daily 5–11pm; Sept–May daily 3–10pm. Tram: 10, 12, or 15.

Bygdøy

EXPENSIVE

Lanternen ★ CONTINENTAL Norwegian yachties and their refined palates adore this place. So do we. Set close to the arrivals point for the Bygdøy ferry from the quays near Rådhuset (City Hall), within a low-slung white-painted clapboard-covered house from the 19th century, this restaurant is charming, welcoming, and sophisticated. From the windows of its newly renovated woodsy, modern interior, you'll see a thousand odd privately-owned sailboats and small yachts bobbing in the nearby marina, giving the entire venue a distinctly nautical appeal. Appetizers and main courses are wisely limited but well chosen and intriguing to the tastebuds. To begin your meal, try the homemade creamy fish soup or the chili-flavored steamed mussels flavored with fresh garlic and white wine. Fresh, seasonal, and high-quality ingredients characterize the main courses, which range from poached sole with lobster sauce and shrimp to herb-marinated filet of lamb. I recommend the baked chicken breast, enlivened with the additions of cured ham and mozzarella, and bound with a Madeira-laced sauce.

Huk Aveny 2. ✆ **22-43-78-38.** www.restaurantlanternen.no. Reservations recommended. Main courses NOK165–NOK245. AE, DC, MC, V. Mon–Sat 11:30am–10:30pm; Sun 1–8pm. Closed 1st 2 weeks of Jan. Bus: 30 or the Bygdøy ferry from the quays near Rådhuset (City Hall).

Frogner

VERY EXPENSIVE

Restaurant Le Canard ★ FRENCH/CONTINENTAL This deluxe restaurant is located in the suburb of Frogner, about 1km (⅔ mile) west of the center. But if you haul yourself here, you'll encounter a smart, stylish restaurant in one of Oslo's more fashionable neighborhoods. The classically oriented cooking demonstrates first-class workmanship without being showy. The mansion that contains this prestigious restaurant is almost as intriguing as the cuisine. Religious symbols are scattered throughout the building, which was designed in the 1880s by a noted Jewish architect named Lowzow. Look for the Star of David in some of the stained-glass windows, and representations of the Lion of Judah here and there. The always impeccable menu might include scallops in risotto with pumpkin and truffle, or grilled wild turbot from Trøndelag in pied de cochon and celery root. One enduringly popular dish is a perfectly roasted duck—that is, with most of the fat cooked off—set off to perfection with a blend of mango and olive *jus*.

President Harbitzgate 4. ✆ **22-54-34-00.** www.lecanard.no. Reservations recommended. Main courses NOK240–NOK395; fixed-price menus NOK695–NOK1,095. AE, DC, MC, V. Mon–Sat 6–11pm. T-banen: Nationaltheatret.

EXPENSIVE

Palace Grill ★★ 🎁 INTERNATIONAL Don't be misled by the word *grill:* This is not a fast-food hamburger joint, but a chic rendezvous. Hip, sophisticated, and unwaveringly upscale, this is a posh but artfully battered neighborhood restaurant, near the Royal Palace, whose clients just happen to have included the crown prince of Norway. Begin with a drink in the high-ceilinged, cowboy rock-'n'-roll bar, which attracts both young-at-heart divorcees and status-conscious young singles. The restaurant, which lies across from the bar within a building that functioned long ago as an elementary school, contains only eight tables and a tiny kitchen, which bustles with a barely controlled creative frenzy. Everything is made fresh for the day of your arrival—the menu actually changes every single day of the year—and dishes range from scallops with burnt butter sauce and fresh ginger, to rare-cooked tuna with glazed beets, to breast of duck with red-wine-and-duck-stock sauce.

Solligaten 2, off Drammensveien. ✆ **23-13-11-40.** www.palacegrill.no. Reservations not accepted. In Palace Grill, all main courses NOK120 each. In Palace Reserva, 10-course set-price menu NOK1,085. AE, DC, MC, V. Restaurant Mon–Sat 5–10:30pm. Bar daily 3pm–1am. Tram: 11, 12, or 13.

Holmenkollen

EXPENSIVE

De Fem Stuer (Five Small Rooms) ★★ NORWEGIAN/CONTINENTAL Its turn-of-the-20th-century "national romantic" architecture has firmly established this restaurant as something of a historic monument for the diners who trek, ski, or ride uphill on tram no. 1 from Oslo to reach it. On the lobby level of one of the recommended hotels (Holmenkollen Park Hotel Rica, p. 108), the restaurant is in a section that retains its original Viking revival (or "dragon-style") construction. You'll find faded country-Norwegian colors, carved timbers and logs, and a general sense of 19th-century rusticity. As its name implies, the restaurant contains five separate dining areas, four of them small and cozy to the point of being cramped and intimate, the other being high-ceilinged and stately looking. The menu changes twice a month, but some of the better starters include an excellent marinated whale meat in a saffron-and-chili sauce. You might prefer to try less guilt-inducing dishes such as the guinea hen with foie gras or the pesto-griddled ocean crayfish with tiny peas. Expect such delightful main dishes as a ginger- and chicken-stuffed quail with morels and shiitake mushrooms in a port-wine sauce, or filet of reindeer with parsnips.

In the Holmenkollen Park Hotel Rica, Kongeveien 26. ✆ **22-92-20-00.** Reservations recommended. Main courses NOK285–NOK350; fixed-price menus NOK565–NOK855. AE, DC, MC, V. Mon–Sat noon–2:30pm & 6–11pm. Tram: 1 (to its terminus).

Frognerseteren ★ NORWEGIAN Frognerseteren strikes me as the most Norwegian of all Oslo's Norwegian restaurants. Set within a short hike (or cross-country-ski trek) from the end of Oslo's tram no. 1, the Frognerseteren rests in a century-old mountain lodge in the Viking revival style. (Richly embellished with dragon and Viking-ship symbolism, the building helped define the Viking revival style that became the architectural symbol of independent Norway.) There's a self-service section and a more formal sit-down area within several small, cozy dining rooms. The chef specializes in succulent game dishes, including breast of guinea fowl with Madeira sauce, whole roasted filet of reindeer, and venison tenderloin and game sausage garnished with root vegetables, baked in puffed pastry, and served with a cherry sauce. You can also order poached, marinated, or smoked Norwegian salmon.

Holmenkollveien 200. ✆ **22-92-40-40.** www.frognerseteren.no. Reservations recommended. Cafe platters NOK52–NOK185; restaurant main courses NOK285–NOK355. DC, MC, V. Mon–Sat 11am–10pm; Sun 11am–9pm. Tram: 1.

MODERATE

Holmenkollen Restaurant NORWEGIAN/CONTINENTAL Partially built from logs and local stone, and perched near the summit of a hill outside Oslo, close to the city's world-renowned ski jump, this restaurant evokes a mountain chalet. The entire place was completely refurbished in 2010, giving it a well-tuned modern look and feel but with definite references to its past glory: Gorgeous exposed wood, large rough-hewn stone fittings, and ornate, Art Deco-meets-driftwood lighting fixtures. Originally built in the 1930s, it is a frequent target for bus tours whose participants are hauled up to admire the high-altitude view over Oslo and to get a good meal. Main courses in the self-service restaurant include rib-sticking fare that's substantial and unpretentious, including platters of roast meats or fish, but also salads and pastas. Meals in the upstairs dining room might begin with a Caesar salad with herb-roasted chicken and a Parmesan crust or a chilled gazpacho served with pan-fried shrimp. Take delight in the pan-fried trout with spring-fresh asparagus and a chive sauce, or the roasted filet of veal with baby summer vegetables in a wine sauce. Steamed halibut is another delectable treat, with leeks, fresh dill, and a butter sauce. A great time to come is on Sunday between noon and 4pm for the sprawling lunch buffet (NOK395).

Holmenkollveien 119. ✆ **22-13-92-00.** www.holmenkollenrestaurant.no. Reservations recommended. Main courses in restaurant NOK195–NOK295; platters in the self-service restaurant NOK90–NOK280. AE, DC, MC, V. Cafeteria daily 11:30am–4pm; restaurant Mon–Sat 10:30am–10pm; Sun 10:30am–8pm. Tram: 1.

Grünerløkka

MODERATE

Markveien Mat og Vinhus ★ 🎁 NORWEGIAN/FRENCH/ITALIAN In the heart of the always trendy Grünerløkka area, this restaurant evokes the Oslovian version of the Left Bank bohemian life. The walls are covered with the art of a local painter, Jo Stang, and the waiters welcome diners—in their terms—"as we would in our own home." This is an excellent choice for dining on well-prepared cuisine. The ambitious menu includes such delights as artic trout with chanterelles and vermouth sauce, and rack of lamb with baked garlic and squash. Many dishes are flavored with a sauce made of fresh herbs. For something more truly Norwegian, try the reindeer in a green peppercorn sauce, with bacon and Brussels sprouts, which appears on the menu occasionally.

Torvbakkgate 12. ✆ **22-37-22-97.** www.markveien.no. Reservations recommended. Main courses NOK258–NOK278; fixed-price menus NOK465–NOK735. AE, DC, MC, V. Mon–Sat 5–11pm. Closed July 15–Aug 7. Tram: 12.

Südøst NORWEGIAN/INTERNATIONAL In a former bank building in the trendy Grünerløkka district, this place is casual chic, drawing young Oslovian sophisticates to its precincts, especially at night. In summer, Südøst boasts a terrace, filled mainly with people who come here both to eat and drink and to take in the view. The people-watching is among the best in town. Food is prepared with a certain zest, including grilled swordfish with a risotto, or grilled tuna fish. The best recommendation, at least for us, is always the fresh catch of the day. The vegetables are often market-fresh. You can also order one of the set menus, which are rewarding and most filling.

5 Trondheimsveien. ✆ **23-35-30-70.** www.sydost.no. Main courses NOK239–NOK269; fixed-price menus NOK495–NOK565. AE, MC, V. Mon–Thurs 11am–10pm; Fri–Sat 11am–11pm; Sun noon–5pm. Tram: 17.

Oslofjord

MODERATE

Ekeberg ★ NORWEGIAN/INTERNATIONAL The view from here of the Oslofjord was said to have inspired Edvard Munch in the creation of his masterpiece, *The Scream.* When the all-white building, designed by Oslovian Lars Backer, was completed in 1929, it was said to be one of the foremost Functionalist buildings in Europe. By the end of the 1990s, the restaurant was closed and left to decay until its new owners took it over and completely renovated it. Today it is a modern building with the classic features retained from 1929.

This complex contains several places to eat, including a bar/lounge, but Ekeberg is clearly the best place for dining. Most foreigners visit just for lunch, enjoying the fish soup, the mussels steamed in wine, or the open sandwiches (one made with smoked trout). At night you can dine more festively, enjoying main dishes such as reindeer sirloin with mushrooms, chestnuts, and spinach; or Hardanger trout with bacon and asparagus.

Kongsveien 15. ✆ **23-24-23-00.** Reservations recommended. Lunch main courses NOK130–NOK160; 3-course fixed-price lunch NOK375–NOK475. Dinner main courses NOK150–NOK285; fixed-price dinner menus NOK220–NOK580. AE, DC, MC, V. Mon–Sat 11am–midnight; Sun noon–10pm. Tram: 18 or 19.

EXPLORING OSLO

6

Oslo is most often viewed as a summer destination. Because Oslovians are starved of sunlight, everyone takes to the outdoors in summer, and many of them stay up virtually around the clock this time of year. If you come in winter, you'll find short days, with darkness descending around 3pm.

But Oslovians counter the climate by becoming the candlelit center of the world, and the flickering lights make bar-hopping a warm, cozy experience. To compensate for those long, dark nights, the nightlife of Oslo becomes even more frenetic in the winter months. From rock clubs to Mozart concerts, after-dark activity in Oslo is more amped up than ever before. The city's cultural events and special art exhibitions also pick up during the winter.

Seasons aside, some travelers would be happy to come to Oslo anytime just for the views of the harborfront city and the Oslofjord. Panoramas are a major attraction, especially the one from Tryvannstårnet, a 117-m (384-ft.) observation tower atop 570-m (1,870-ft.) Tryvann Hill in the outlying area. Many other attractions are worthy of your time and exploration, too. The beautiful surroundings make these sights even more appealing.

Try to allocate at least 2 or 3 days to exploring Norway's capital. After a stay here, most visitors head west to Bergen and the fjord district or continue east by train or plane to Stockholm, the capital of Sweden.

THE BIG SIX

If you've budgeted only a day or two for Oslo, make the most of your time and see only the "platinum" attractions, saving the "gold" and "silver" rated sights for your return visit. I've narrowed the major attractions down to "The Big Six."

Henie-Onstad Kunstsenter (Henie-Onstad Art Center) ★★★ Norway's largest collection of modern art is worth the trip to the museum's beautiful setting beside Oslofjord, 11km (6¾ miles) west of Oslo. It was inaugurated in 1968 to house a gift of some 300 works of art from Sonja Henie, former figure skating champion and movie star, and her husband, shipping tycoon Niels Onstad.

Oslo Attractions

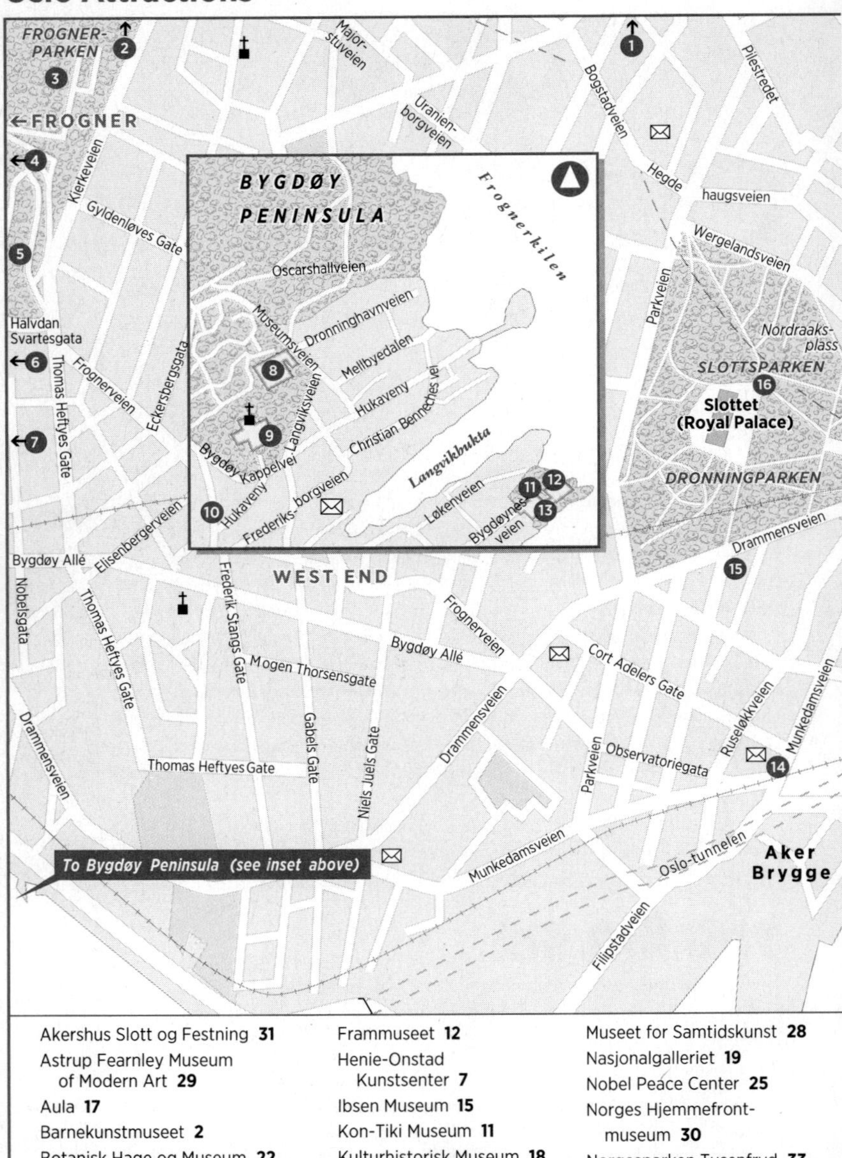

Akershus Slott og Festning **31**
Astrup Fearnley Museum of Modern Art **29**
Aula **17**
Barnekunstmuseet **2**
Botanisk Hage og Museum **22**
Emanuel Vigeland Museum **2**
Forsvarsmuseet **32**
Frammuseet **12**
Henie-Onstad Kunstsenter **7**
Ibsen Museum **15**
Kon-Tiki Museum **11**
Kulturhistorisk Museum **18**
Kunstindustrimuseet **20**
Munch Museet **22**
Museet for Samtidskunst **28**
Nasjonalgalleriet **19**
Nobel Peace Center **25**
Norges Hjemmefront-museum **30**
Norgesparken Tusenfryd **33**
Norsk Folkemuseum **8**

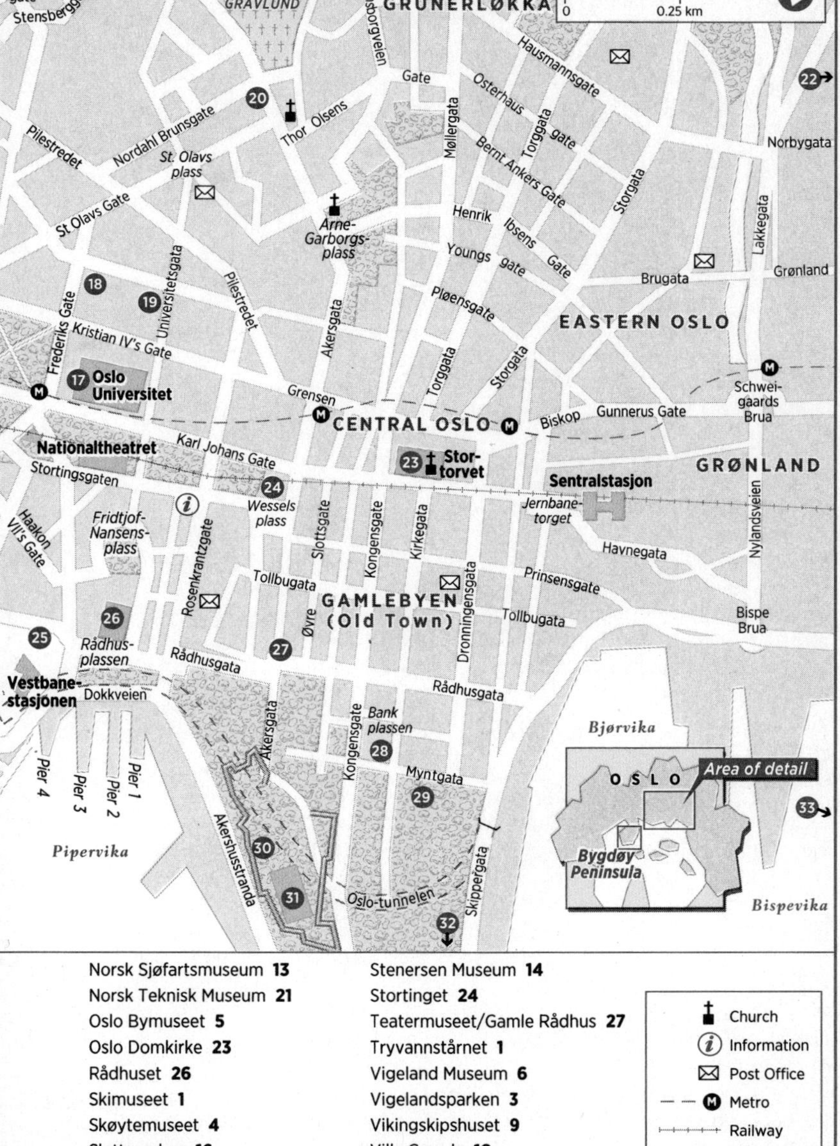
Sofies-gate
Stensberggata
VÅR FRELSERS GRAVLUND
Fredensborgveien
GRÜNERLØKKA
21
0 1/4 mi
0 0.25 km
Hausmannsgate
22
Gate
Osterhaus gate
Thor Olsens
20
Nordahl Brunsgate
Pilestredet
St. Olavs plass
St Olavs Gate
Møllergata
Torggata
Bernt Ankers Gate
Norbygata
Storgata
Arne-Garborgs-plass
Henrik Ibsens Gate
Youngs gate
Lakkegata
Grønland
Brugata
18
19
Universitetsgata
Pilestredet
Pløensgate
Frederiks Gate
Kristian IV's Gate
Akersgata
EASTERN OSLO
Torggata
Storgata
17 Oslo Universitet
Grensen
Schwei-gaards Brua
CENTRAL OSLO
Biskop Gunnerus Gate
Nationaltheatret
Karl Johans Gate
23 Stor-torvet
GRØNLAND
Stortingsgaten
24
Sentralstasjon
Wessels plass
Jernbane-torget
Haakon VII's Gate
Fridtjof-Nansens-plass
Rosenkrantzgate
Slottsgate
Kongensgate
Kirkegata
Nylandsveien
Havnegata
Tollbugata
Prinsensgate
GAMLEBYEN (Old Town)
Dronningensgata
Tollbugata
Øvre
Bispe Brua
26
25
Rådhus-plassen
27
Rådhusgata
Vestbane-stasjonen
Dokkveien
Rådhusgata
Akersgata
Bank plassen
Kongensgate
Bjørvika
28
Pier 4
Pier 3
Pier 2
Pier 1
Myntgata
29
OSLO
Area of detail
33
Akershusstranda
Pipervika
30
Skippergata
Bygdøy Peninsula
31
Oslo-tunnelen
Bispevika
32
Norsk Sjøfartsmuseum 13
Norsk Teknisk Museum 21
Oslo Bymuseet 5
Oslo Domkirke 23
Rådhuset 26
Skimuseet 1
Skøytemuseet 4
Slottsparken 16
Stenersen Museum 14
Stortinget 24
Teatermuseet/Gamle Rådhus 27
Tryvannstårnet 1
Vigeland Museum 6
Vigelandsparken 3
Vikingskipshuset 9
Villa Grande 10
Church
Information
Post Office
Metro
Railway

SO, WHO WAS THIS sonja henie, ANYWAY?

Norwegians young and old know the story of one of their most legendary public figures, Sonja Henie (1912–69). In America, however, only the older generation might be able to identify this former figure skater and movie actress who won gold medals for figure skating at the 1928, 1932, and 1936 Winter Olympics.

Henie was born in Oslo, the daughter of a furrier. Having learned skating and dancing as a child, she became the youngest Olympic skating champion when she won her first gold medal at age 15. She became a professional in 1936 with a tour of the United States, performing in ice shows as late as the 1950s. The bright-eyed, bubbly blonde managed to parlay her championships into an effervescent but short motion-picture career.

Twentieth Century Fox ordered writers to tailor film properties for her, to keep the comedy and romance light, and to get her on those skates as much as possible. Often she was teamed with top-rate stars, such as Ray Milland and Robert Cummings in *Everything Happens at Night* in 1939, and Don Ameche, Ethel Merman, and Cesar Romero in the 1938 film *Happy Landing.* The year 1939 also saw her teamed opposite Rudy Vallee and Tyrone Power in *Second Fiddle.* Only Shirley Temple and Clark Gable outranked her at the box office that year.

In 1940, when Hitler invaded Norway, she published her autobiography, *Wings on My Feet,* which included a picture of her receiving congratulations from Hitler, surrounded by Nazi officials at the 1936 Olympics. The association with the Nazis tarnished her reputation during the war, but the outcry against her died down after the war.

In 1960, Henie retired with her third husband, Niels Onstad, a wealthy Norwegian businessman and art patron. In 1968, they founded the Henie-Onstad Kunstsenter (p. 125), near Oslo, as a showcase for Henie's extensive collection of modern art. The next year, at the relatively early age of 57, Norway's most famous daughter died. She was aboard an aircraft carrying her from Paris to Oslo for medical treatment. At the time of her death, she was one of the 10 wealthiest women on Earth.

Henie's bequest, beefed up by later additions, virtually spans modern art in the 20th century, from Cubism with Braque to Surrealism with Ernst. In fact, the collection is so vast that it frequently has to be rotated. I'm always particularly drawn to the CoBrA Group, with works by its founder, Asger Jorn, and by Karel Appel. You can head downstairs to Henie's trophy room to see her three Olympic gold medals—she was the star at the 1936 skating competition—and 10 world championship prizes. Henie garnered 600 trophies and medals, all of which are on display.

Besides the permanent collection, plays, concerts, films, and special exhibits take place. An open-air theater-in-the-round is used in the summer for folklore programs, jazz concerts, and song recitals. A top-notch, partly self-service restaurant, the Piruetten, is also on the premises. Plan to spend about 2 hours here.

Høkvikodden, Sonja Henlesvie 31. ✆ **67-80-48-80.** www.hok.no. Admission NOK80 adults, NOK30 children 6–16, free for children 6 & under. Free for all Wed. Tues–Fri 11am–7pm; Sat–Sun 11am–5pm. Bus: 151, 161, 252, or 261.

Munch Museet (Edvard Munch Museum) ★★★ Edvard Munch (1863–1944) was Scandinavia's greatest painter and, in an act of incredible generosity, donated this collection to his beloved Oslo. The treasure trove is so vast—1,100 paintings, 4,500 drawings, and 18,000 prints—that it can be shown only in rotation. The curators keep a representative sampling of his works on display at all times, so you can trace his development from Impressionism to symbolism.

Love, death, darkness, and anxiety were his overarching themes. The latter was best expressed in his most famous painting, *The Scream,* which is actually a series composed of four versions. This museum's version of the Munch masterpiece is valued at $75 million. Unsurprisingly, its August 2004 theft caused a huge international uproar, especially within art communities. Fans of Munch's *The Scream* and his *Madonna* (also nicked by the robbers) can once again gaze upon these paintings, which were recovered in the summer of 2006. Police were cagey at a news conference about how the paintings were recovered. *The Scream* and *Madonna* were part of the artist's "Frieze of Life" series, focusing on the artist's usual themes: Sickness, death, anxiety, and love, many of which the museum's curator probably experienced during the paintings' disappearance.

We are especially moved by Munch's early works, such as *At the Coffee Table* (1883), where you can see the preliminary vision that would grow into a future masterpiece. By the 1890s, Munch's paintings had matured into virtual masterpieces. I stand in awe of the *Red Virginia Creeper,* in which the house is being devoured by a plant. *Dagnyi Juel* is his portrait of Ducha Przybyszewska, the Berlin socialite with whom he'd fallen in love (unfortunately, Strindberg was also infatuated with this femme fatale, who would, incidentally, go on to marry a third lover altogether). Most fascinating is a series of self-portraits, which explore his mental state at peak moments of his life, such as *The Night Wanderer* (1923) and *Self-Portrait by the Window* (1940).

Impressions

People shall be made to understand the greatness of my art; when facing it, they shall learn to remove their hats, as if in a cathedral.

—Edvard Munch

Plan to devote at least an hour and a half to Munch.

Tøyengata 53. ✆ **23-49-35-00.** www.munch.museum.no. Admission NOK75 adults, NOK40 children. Free for all Oct–Mar. June–Aug daily 10am–6pm; Sept–May Tues–Fri 10am–4pm, Sat–Sun 11am–5pm. T-banen: Tøyen. Bus: 60.

Nasjonalgalleriet (National Gallery) ★★★ This museum houses Norway's greatest and largest collection of art. Most visitors flock here to see Edvard Munch's *The Scream,* one of four versions, this one painted in 1893. This painting was stolen in 1994 and, like the version taken from the Edvard Munch Museum in 2004 (see above), was subsequently recovered. *The Scream,* which is reproduced in countless posters around the world, still inspires artists today and continues to work its way into popular culture. For example, in a 2006 episode of *The Simpsons,* Bart and his friends steal a copy of *The Scream* in a parody of the real thefts.

Munch has paintings here in addition to *The Scream,* a total of 58 of his works, some of them among his most celebrated, including *The Dance of Life, Moonlight,* and *Ashes.* Most of Munch's works on show were painted in the closing years of the

19th century. There are also several self-portraits—the reason he was called "the handsomest man in Norway."

The leading Norwegian Romantic landscape painter Johan Christian Dahl (1788–1857) is in fine form here, but some find his paintings a little too sentimental. A favorite is Christian Krohg, who painted it like it was, drawing inspiration from sailors to prostitutes. Scandinavian painting in general is also showcased, with one salon containing works from the Golden Age of Danish painting.

Although not extensive compared to some national collections, European painting in general is well displayed, with old masters represented from Van Dyck to Rubens, from El Greco (a remarkable *St. Peter Repentant*) to Cézanne and Matisse. Van Gogh weighs in with a self-portrait, Picasso with his *Guitar*. Look for the works of Gustav Vigeland, although you'll get better acquainted with him at Vigelandsparken (see below).

All the art displayed was created before 1945, the year Norwegians freed themselves from the Nazi yoke. Allow 2 hours for a visit.

Universitetsgaten 13. ✆ **21-98-20-00.** www.nationalmuseum.no. Free admission. Tues–Wed & Fri 10am–6pm; Thurs 10am–7pm; Sat & Sun 11am–5pm. Tram: 10 or 12.

Norsk Folkemuseum (Norwegian Folk Museum) ★★★ ☺ Take a tour of Norway in just 1 day. From all over the country, museum curators moved 155 buildings from their original sites and, with great difficulty, transported and reassembled them on 14 hectares (35 acres) on the Bygdøy Peninsula.

Among the old buildings is the **Gol Stave Church ★★★**, moved here a century ago. Dating from 1200—still with no windows—it came from the town of Gol, 224km (139 miles) northwest of Oslo. One of the oldest such museums in the world, the Folk Museum contains many buildings from the medieval era, including the Raulandstua, one of the oldest wooden dwellings still standing in Norway.

Wander the streets of **Gamlebyen** or **Old Town ★**, a reproduction of an early 20th-century Norwegian town. The rural buildings are grouped together by region of origin, and the urban houses are laid out in the form of an old town.

Eventually, the curators decided to make this open-air folk museum a living, breathing entity. They feature a variety of activities, including horse-and-buggy rides, folk music, dancing by men and women in native dress, traditional arts and crafts, and even "Norwegian evenings," a summer food tasting of regional specialties and folk dancing. Artisans demonstrate age-old crafts such as pottery, weaving, silversmithing, and the making of candles, which you can purchase in their workshops. At the Christmas fair, some 120 old-fashioned stands also sell handmade products.

Inside, the museum's 225,000 exhibits capture every imaginable facet of Norwegian life, past and present. Furniture, household utensils, clothing, woven fabrics, and tapestries are on display, along with fine examples of Norwegian rose-painting and woodcarving. Farming implements and logging gear pay tribute to the development of agriculture and forestry. Also look for the outstanding exhibit on Norway's Sami population. You can easily spend 3 hours here.

After the millennium, the museum incorporated the **Bygdø Royal Farm,** with its cultivated fields and grazing lands offering hikes along the trails.

All together, the museum is a living textbook of Norwegian culture that is not to be missed.

THE MAN behind THE SCREAM

Scandinavia's greatest artist, Edvard Munch (1863–1944), was a pioneer in the expressionist movement. *The Scream,* painted in 1893, is his best-known painting. There are four known versions of this painting, one of which was stolen from the Edvard Munch Museum in August 2004. This painting, along with another Munch masterpiece, *Madonna,* were recovered by Norwegian police in August 2006 and returned to the museum. Munch grew up in Oslo (then called Christiania) and was often ill. Early memories of illness, death, and grief in his family had a tremendous impact on his later works. His father's death may have contributed to the loneliness and melancholy of one of his most famous works, *Night* (1890).

By the early 1890s, Munch had achieved fame (though slight in comparison with his renown today). He was at the center of a *succès de scandale* in Munich in 1892 when his art was interpreted as "anarchistic provocation."

Munch went to Berlin to escape, entering a world of literati, artists, and intellectuals. He met August Strindberg and they discussed the philosophy of Nietzsche, symbolism, psychology, and occultism. The discussions clearly influenced his work. His growing outlook was revealed to the world in an 1893 show in Berlin, where several paintings had death as their theme. His *Death in a Sickroom*, in particular, created quite a stir.

In 1896, Munch moved to Paris, where he made exquisite color lithographs and his first woodcuts. By the turn of the 20th century, he was painting in a larger format and incorporating some of the Art Nouveau aesthetics of the time. *Red Virginia Creeper* and *Melancholy* reflect the new influences. Prominent people also asked Munch to paint their portraits, and he obliged. His 1904 group portrait of Dr. Linde's sons is a masterpiece of modern portraiture.

A nervous disorder soon sent him to a sanitarium, and he had a turbulent love affair with a wealthy bohemian nicknamed "Tulla." The affair ended in 1902 when a revolver permanently injured a finger on Munch's left hand. He became obsessed with the shooting incident and poured out his contempt for Tulla in such works as *Death of Murat* (1907). Munch also became increasingly alcoholic, and, in 1906, he painted *Self-Portrait with a Bottle of Wine.*

From 1909 until his death, Munch lived in Norway. In his later years, he retreated into isolation, surrounded only by his paintings, which he called "my children." The older Munch placed more emphasis on the monumental and the picturesque, as in landscapes or people in harmony with nature.

In 1940, he decided to leave his huge collection of paintings to the city of Oslo upon his death. Today the Edvard Munch Museum provides the best introduction to this strange and enigmatic artist.

Museumsveien 10. ✆ **22-12-37-00.** www.norskfolke.museum.no. Admission NOK100 adults, NOK25 children 16 & under. Jan 2–May 14 & Sept 15–Dec 30 Mon–Fri 11am–3pm, Sat–Sun 11am–4pm; May 15–Sept 14 daily 10am–6pm. Ferry: From Pier 3 facing the Rådhuset (summer only). Bus: 30 from the Nationaltheatret.

Vigelandsparken ★★★ The sculptures of Gustav Vigeland, the most prominent among Norwegian sculptors of the 20th century, are at once some of the most beloved and disdained in Europe. Wherever you stand, it's well worth exploring this park, which holds 227 of Vigeland's monumental sculptures, mostly devoted to the theme of mankind's destiny. The artist worked for a total of 4 decades on this 30-hectare (74-acre) park but, sadly, died 1 year before his lifetime achievement could be completed.

The chief treasure here is the **Vigeland Monolith ★★★**, a 16-m (52-ft.) sculpture composed of 121 colossal figures, all, amazingly, carved from one piece of stone. The monolith is easy to spot, as it rises on top of the highest hill in the park. Summer lovers often visit it at night, as it's floodlit and somehow seems even more dramatic at that time. A set of circular steps envelops the statue. On the steps leading up to the monolith are 36 groups of other figures carved in stone by the great artist. The column itself, with its writhing figures, is said to symbolize the struggle of life and the transcendence of everyday life, which is one of the main themes running through Vigeland's work.

Impressions

I am anchored to my work so that I cannot move. If I walk down the street one day a thousand hands from work hold on to me. I am tied to the studio and the road is never long.

—Gustav Vigeland, 1912

The "best of the rest" of the sculptures lie along a paved axis stretching for 1km (⅔ mile). These sculptures depict Vigeland's interpretation of life beginning at birth and ending in death. The most famous of these statues, which you'll quickly recognize because it is one of the most reproduced pieces of art in Oslo, is ***The Angry Boy (Sinnataggen)* ★★**. Based on a sketch Vigeland made in London in 1901, it shows a kid stamping his feet and scrunching his face in anger.

Frogner Park, Nobelsgate 32. ✆ **23-49-37-00.** www.vigeland.museum.no/en/vigeland-park. Free admission to park; museum NOK50 adults, NOK25 children. Museum free to all Oct–Mar. Park open daily 24 hr. Museum June–Aug Tues–Sun 10am–5pm; Sept–May Tues–Sun noon–4pm. Tram: 12.

Vikingskipshuset (Viking Ship Museum, University Museum of Cultural Heritage) ★★★ ☺ A fascinating chapter in Viking history came alive when three Viking funereal ships were discovered in the Oslofjord between 1867 and 1904. The vessels, all dating from the 9th century, had each been buried in a blue clay that preserved them. The ***Oseberg* ★★**, which required 30 oarsmen to move it through the water, is the most impressive, with its dragon and serpent carvings. Apparently, the ship was the resting place of a noblewoman; though plundered for much of its booty, many of her burial furnishings are on display.

The finest remaining example of a Viking longship, the ***Gokstad* ★**, when unearthed in 1880 from its burial site dating back to the 9th century A.D., had also been sacked by ancient grave-robbers, although a skeleton, believed to be a petty king of Vestfold was found nearby. Among the few artifacts uncovered were bedposts with animal-head ornamentation, fragments of a sledge, and even a gaming board (think early Las Vegas). The largest ship of the lot, the *Gokstad* could accommodate 32 oarsmen and travel at a speed of 12 knots.

Built around the same time as the *Gokstad,* the ***Tune,*** built around A.D. 900, is less impressive, though it was the tomb of a powerful chieftain. The badly damaged ship was intentionally not restored so that visitors could see the details of shipbuilding in the Viking era.

The *Gokstad* & the New World

In 1893, Norwegians built a replica of the *Gokstad* and sailed it to New York harbor, proving how seaworthy Viking ships were. From New York, it was transported overland to the World's Fair that year in Chicago. The ship needs restoring and remains in storage in Illinois.

For kids, the ships here conjure up the legend and lore of the Viking era that flourished in the Middle Ages. I've seen kids looking up in awe at the excavated ships long after their parents have taken in the exhibitions. Give or take some time for gawking, you'll spend about an hour here. ***Tip:*** If you go between 11:30am and 1pm, you'll tend to avoid the summer mobs who descend on this building, where the rounded white walls give the feeling of a burial tomb.

Huk Aveny 35, Bygdøy. ✆ **22-85-19-00.** www.khm.uio.no. Admission NOK60 adults, NOK30 children. Oct–Apr daily 10am–4pm; May–Sept daily 9am–6pm. Ferry: From Pier 3 facing the Rådhuset (summer only). Bus: 30 from the Nationaltheatret.

OTHER TOP ATTRACTIONS

Museums

Astrup Fearnley Museum of Modern Art ★ This is one of those special spots art lovers stumble across in their travels, wondering why such a place isn't better known. Actually, this privately funded museum has been around since 1993, when Norway's leading architects and designers constructed the stunningly designed building to showcase both Norwegian and international post–World War II art. Works by '60s icon Yoko Ono can be seen here. The equally controversial British artist Damien Hirst is also on view, with his installation of *Mother and Child Divided.* The changing exhibitions are often drawn from the museum's permanent collection, much of which is kept in storage. On my last visit, I feasted on another British blood-and-gore type, Francis Bacon, along with the gentler Lucian Freud and Gerhard Richter. Introduce yourself to some locally known Norwegian artists of great stature, especially Knut Rose, Bjørn Carlsen, and Arne Ekeland. If you prefer your sculptures oversize, wander through the garden, with such works as Niki de St. Phalle's sparrow. Allow at least 40 minutes.

Dronningensgatan 4. ✆ **22-93-60-60.** http://afmuseet.no. Admission NOK60 adults, free for children 18 & under. Wed–Sun noon–5pm. T-banen: Stortinget. Tram: 1, 2, 10, or 12. Bus: 27, 29, 38, 51, or 56.

Aula (Great Hall) Admirers of the work of Edvard Munch, like us, will want to see the Great Hall of the university, where Scandinavia's greatest artist painted murals. I've gone here repeatedly over the years just to look at Munch's depiction of *The Sun,* the mural showing rays gently falling over a secluded Norwegian fjord. Until it moved to larger headquarters at the City Hall, this used to be the site of the Nobel Prize award ceremony. Plan on spending 20 minutes here.

University of Oslo, Karl Johans Gate 47. ✆ **22-85-95-55.** Free admission. June 20–Aug 20 daily 10am–4pm. T-banen: Stortinget.

Emanuel Vigeland Museum ★ We'll let you in on something if you promise not to tell. This museum has been accurately dubbed "Oslo's best-kept secret," and sometimes the work of Emanuel Vigeland (1875–1948), the younger brother of

Gustav, rivals that of his more celebrated sibling. The main attraction here—besides the fact that Emanuel was the architect of his own museum—is a barrel-vaulted room covered with frescoes that depict human life from conception to death. Some of the scenes are explicitly erotic, and his works have been simultaneously acclaimed and denounced as "decadent." The most curious of the motifs I discovered is on the short wall by the entrance. Still embraced in copulation, a dead couple yields a mighty pillar of smoke and infants: Creation, death, and birth inseparably linked. To further a theme, Emanuel decided to turn the museum into his mausoleum. His ashes were laid to rest in an urn above the entrance.

Grimelundsveien 8. ✆ **22-14-57-88.** www.emanuelvigeland.museum.no. Admission NOK40. Mid-May to mid-Sept Sun noon–5pm; mid-Sept to mid-May Sun noon–4pm. T-banen: No. 1 Frognerseteren to Slemdal station, then a 7-min. walk.

Forsvarsmuseet (Armed Forces Museum) In the heart of Oslo at the ancient Akershus Fortress (p. 138), this museum traces the history of Norway from the Viking era up to the occupation of Norway by the Nazis in World War II. Enough artifacts are on view to satisfy any fan of military history, and the history of the Nordic wars is depicted. The best part of the museum is the World War II exhibition, which includes guns, tanks, bombs, and fighter planes. Especially moving is a depiction of how the resistance contributed to the final victory for the Allies. It seems a bit ironic that this museum occupies Akershus, which was used by the Germans as their headquarters during the occupation (1940–45). Give yourself around an hour to explore this museum in a fortress, then head to the on-site cafeteria for some fortification of your own.

Akershus Fortress, Bygning 62. ✆ **23-09-35-82.** www.fmu.mil.no. Free admission. May–Aug Mon–Fri 10am–5pm, Sat–Sun 11am–5pm; Sept–Apr Tues–Fri 11am–3pm, Sat–Sun 11am–4pm. Tram: 1, 2, or 10.

Kulturhistorisk Museum (University Museum of Cultural Heritage) From the cold Arctic wastelands to the hot, sunny islands of Asia, this museum—owned by the University of Oslo—is a vast treasure trove, containing everything from a carved *stavkirke* (stave church) to a 1,000-year history of the coins of Norway. Viking artifacts and a **display of gold and silver** ★ from the 2nd through the 13th centuries are in the Treasure House. In the medieval hall, keep an eye out for the reddish Ringerike Alstad Stone, which was carved in relief, and the **Dynna Stone** ★, an 11th-century runic stone honoring the handsomest maiden in Hadeland. There's also a rich collection of ecclesiastical art in a series of portals from stave churches. Grant this museum at least 45 minutes.

Frederiksgate 2 (near Karl Johans Gate). ✆ **22-85-99-64.** Free admission. May 15–Sept 14 Tues–Sun 10am–4pm; Sept 15–May 14 Tues–Sun 11am–4pm. Tram: 11, 17, or 18.

Kunstindustrimuseet (Museum of Decorative Arts & Design) ★ Founded in 1876, this is one of the oldest museums in Norway and among the oldest applied-arts museums in Europe. Since 1876 it has owned the bold, imaginative **Baldishol tapestries** ★ from the early part of the 12th century. Few Draculas could resist furnishing their home with the antique dragon-style furniture. A royal wardrobe is also on display, including the wedding gown Queen Sonja wore in 1968 (Lady Di had no competition here). The collection of **18th-century Norwegian silver** ★, glass, and faience (a type of glazed pottery) is stunning, and there is also an impressive selection of contemporary furniture and crafts. Allow yourself an hour here.

FROMMER'S favorite OSLO EXPERIENCES

Enjoying Fresh Shrimp off the Boats In the morning, head for the harbor in front of the Rådhuset and buy a bag of freshly caught and cooked shrimp from a fisherman. Although this may not be everyone's idea of a good breakfast—sales begin around 7 or 8am and may end in late morning—shrimp lovers will find Valhalla here.

Experiencing Life on the Fjords In the summer, head for the harbor, where boats wait to take you sightseeing, fishing, or to the beach.

Hanging Out in the Students' Grove Summer is short in Oslo, and it's savored. Late-night drinkers sit in open-air beer gardens along Karl Johans Gate, enjoying the endless nights. A favorite spot for a beer and to watch the passing parade is Studenten, on the corner of Karl Johans Gate and Universitesgata.

Listening to Street Musicians Hundreds of musicians flock to Oslo in the summer to play in bars and outside on the street. You can enjoy their music along Karl Johans Gate and at the Stortorvet marketplace.

Taking the Ferry to Bygdøy The Bygdøy Peninsula offers a treasure trove of attractions, including Viking ships, Thor Heyerdahl's *Kon-Tiki,* seafood buffets, a sailboat harbor, and bathing beaches. At the folk museum are old farmsteads, houses, and often folk-dancing.

Café Solliløkken and the museum shop on the ground floor are in rooms from the 1830s that originally were in a small country house. The cafe offers homemade pastries and light meals, mostly sandwiches and salads, but also some hot Norwegian specialties every day (most often fish).

St. Olavs Gate 1. ✆ **22-03-65-40.** www.nationalmuseum.no. Free admission. Tues–Wed & Fri 11am–5pm; Thurs 11am–7pm; Sat–Sun noon–4pm. T-banen: Stortinget. Bus: 37.

Museet for Samtidskunst (National Museum of Contemporary Art) Opened in 1990, this collection of works acquired by the state after World War II presents an array of international and Norwegian contemporary art. Previously grouped together in the National Gallery, the works have more room to breathe here, in what was once the central bank of Norway. I once saw a painting here of a three-headed woman with 14 breasts, but don't worry—exhibits change frequently. Allot 30 minutes to explore the collection.

Bankplassen 4. ✆ **22-86-22-10.** www.nationalmuseum.no. Free admission. Tues–Wed & Fri 11am–5pm; Thurs 10am–7pm; Sat–Sun noon–5pm. Tram: 10 or 12. Bus: 60.

Nobel Peace Center One of Oslo's newest attractions, the ultramodern center presents the history of the founding father of the prize, Alfred Nobel, "the dynamite king," and the biographies and careers of Nobel Peace Prize laureates such as Nelson Mandela. In addition to changing exhibits, a permanent exhibition illustrates the careers of the laureates through film, including recordings of actual Peace Prize ceremonies. If you're lucky, you might catch a glimpse of one of the winners of the Peace Prize who sometimes come to the renovated train station to give lectures.

Rådhusplassen. ✆ **48-30-10-00.** www.nobelpeacecenter.org. Admission NOK80 16 & over; NOK55 seniors/students, free 15 & under. June–Sept 15 daily 10am–7pm; off-season Tues–Sun 10am–8pm. Tram: 10 or 12.

Norges Hjemmefrontmuseum (Norwegian Resistance Museum) ★ From underground printing presses to radio transmitters, from the German attack in 1940 to the liberation in 1945, the museum documents Norway's World War II resistance activities. Photographs documenting the Nazi attack on Norway have been printed on black iron sheets, and a cluster of German rifles is arranged to form the dreaded swastika that Norwegians grew to hate. The war-time traitor and so-called "minister president," Quisling, is deservedly vilified in the exhibits. I am especially moved by the daring underground newspapers, which appeared as early as the summer of 1940 and continued to publish throughout the dark years of the war. The artifacts here can usually be absorbed in about an hour. Outside is a monument dedicated to Norwegian patriots, many of whom were executed by the Nazis at this spot.

Akershus Fortress. ✆ **23-09-31-38.** www.mil.no. Admission NOK30 adults, NOK15 children. Sept–May Mon–Fri 10am–4pm, Sat–Sun 11am–4pm; June–Aug Mon–Sat 10am–5pm. Tram: 10, 12, 15, or 19.

Norsk Teknisk Museum (Norwegian Technological Museum) You don't really have to be an engineer to enjoy this museum, which showcases Norway's major developments in industry, technology, transport, medicine, and science. The first aircraft, royal automobiles, a Model-T, the first car and tram in Norway, a paddle steamer, even a robot center where you can program your very own robot—all of these exhibits and more are on display here on the outskirts of the city, with views along the banks of the Akerselva River. One intriguing exhibit documents the flight of the *Leiv Eiriksson,* a small plane that was the first ever to travel between America and Norway, flying from New York to Bergen in 1935 in 57 hours.

Kjelsåsvn 143. ✆ **22-79-60-00.** www.tekniskmuseum.no. Admission NOK90 adults, NOK50 students & children, family ticket NOK220. Tues–Fri 9am–4pm, Sat–Sun 11am–6pm. Bus: 54.

Skimuseet (Ski Museum) ★ ☺ Founded in 1923, this is the oldest ski museum in the world—as such, even the royal family of Norway has added their skis to the collection. At Holmenkollen, an elevator takes visitors up the ski-jump tower for a **panoramic view ★★★** of Oslo and the fjord, one of the greatest vistas you are likely to experience in Norway. At the base of the ski jump, the Skimuseet displays a wide range of exhibits, including a 4,000-year-old pictograph from Rødøy in Nordland that documents skiing's 1,000-year history. The museum also has skis and historical items from various parts of Norway—from the first "modern" skis, dating from about 1870, to a ski dating from around A.D. 600. Artifacts from the Antarctic expeditions of Amundsen are on display, as well as the Scott expeditions into the snowy wastelands. You can even see relics of Fridtjof Nansen's slog across the Greenland icecap: A historical version of Survivorman, he built a boat from his sled and canvas tent to row the final 100km (62 miles) to "the end of the world." Allow 45 minutes. The museum will remain closed during most of 2011 due to renovation at the Holmenkollen complex.

Kongeveien 5, Holmenkollen. ✆ **22-92-32-00.** www.holmenkollen.com. Admission (museum & ski jump) NOK90 adults, NOK45 children. May & Sept daily 10am–5pm; June–Aug daily 9am–10pm; Oct–Apr daily 10am–4pm. T-banen: Holmenkollen SST Line 15 from near the Nationaltheatret to Voksenkollen (30-min. ride), then an uphill 15-min. walk.

Skøytemuseet (Ice-Skating Museum) ☺ In the land of skaters and skiers, it seems appropriate to have a museum devoted entirely to ice skating. This museum tells the story of many fascinating competitions on ice. You'll learn about the heroes of the speed-skating world, including Axel Paulsen (1855–1938) and Oscar Mathisen (1888–1954), along with their participation in world championships. Kids and adults alike should delight in seeing the first skates ever made in Norway—made with real bone—as well as examples of the most advanced high-tech skates of today. Opened in 1914, this museum displays artifacts illustrating "major moments" in speed and figure skating. Allot about 30 minutes here.

At the Frogner Stadium, Middelthunsgate 26. ✆ **22-43-49-20.** www.skoytemuseet.no. Admission NOK20 adults, NOK10 children. Tues & Thurs 10am–2pm; Sun 11am–3pm. Tram: 12.

Stenersen Museum ★ Part of the City of Oslo Art Collections, the most avant-garde temporary exhibitions in Oslo are presented here on a regular basis alongside three of the greatest private collections in Norway. Rolf E. Stenersen, a financier, author, and collector (1899–1978), donated some 300 paintings, even watercolors and prints by Edvard Munch, though you can see better Munch works at the National Gallery and at Munch's namesake museum. What you get here are the best examples of flourishing interwar Norwegian modernism, including some 300 paintings and 100 drawings from Amaldus Nielsen, "the painter of the south," whose best works were set in southern Norway. Finally, the widow of Ludvig O. Ravensburg donated some 160 works by her artist husband (1871–1958). Known for his burlesque humor, he was a relative of Munch. Allow 45 minutes to see this museum.

Munkedamsveien 15. ✆ **23-49-36-00.** www.stenersen.museum.no. Admission NOK45 adults, NOK25 students & children. Free to all Oct–Mar. Tues & Thurs 11am–7pm; Wed, Fri, & Sat–Sun 11am–5pm. Tram: 10 or 12. T-banen: Nationaltheatret.

Teatermuseet/Gamle Rådhus (Oslo Theater Museum) In the hometown of Bjørnson and Ibsen, theater buffs flock to this recently renovated and updated museum mainly to view its theatrical memorabilia. A century and a half of Oslovian theatrical history unfolds here, going through the golden years of the Christiania Theater, where many of Ibsen's plays were performed for the first time. The mementos include pictures and costumes, and exhibitions relive the era of the circus, vaudeville, and marionette theater. The museum has recordings of some of the great highlights in Norwegian theatrical history, with some of the country's most celebrated artists. There's also a rich collection of ballet costumes and portraits of the actors. Plan on an hour's visit.

Christiania Torv 1. ✆ **22-42-65-09.** www.oslomuseum.no. Free admission. June–Aug Tues–Sun 11am–4pm. Tram: 10 or 12.

Vigeland Museum ★ This museum is for connoisseurs who didn't get enough of the monumental artist Gustav Vigeland in Vigelandsparken (p. 131). Opposite the southern entrance to Frogner Park, this was the 1920s' former home of the great sculptor and also served as his studio. When he died in 1943, his ashes were placed in the tower of the museum. On the ground floor, nine rooms show a wide medley of his sculptures and drawings, while two rooms upstairs display plastic sketches, drawings, and woodcuts. His apartment upstairs is comprised of two sitting rooms, a library, and a bedroom—not exactly monastic, but not luxurious at all. Of a certain historical interest, Vigeland also sculpted busts of two of the most famous of all Norwegians, Edvard Grieg and Henrik Ibsen. The museum was closed at press time but is due to reopen by spring 2011.

Nobels Gate. ✆ **23-49-37-00.** www.vigeland.museum.no. Admission NOK50 adults, NOK25 seniors, students, & children 7-16, free for children 6 & under. Free to all Oct–Mar. June–Aug Tues–Sun 10am–5pm; off-season Tues–Sun noon–4pm. T-banen: Majorstuen.

Historic Buildings

Akershus Slott og Festning (Akershus Castle & Fortress) ★★ ☺ It has withstood fierce battles, drawn-out sieges, and a few fires, and changed shape architecturally since King Haakon V ordered it built in 1299, when Oslo was named capital of Norway. A fortress, or *festning,* with thick earth-and-stone walls surrounds the castle, with protruding bastions designed to resist artillery bombardment. The moats and reinforced ramparts were added in the mid-1700s. For several centuries it was not only a fortress, but also the abode of the rulers of Norway. Now the government uses it for state occasions. From the well-manicured lawns there are **panoramic views ★** of Oslo and the Oslofjorden. In summer, concerts, dances, and even theatrical productions are staged here. Forty-minute English-language guided tours are offered Monday to Saturday at 11am and 1 and 3pm, and on Sunday at 1 and 3pm.

Festnings-Plassen. ✆ **23-09-39-17.** www.nasjonalefestningsverk.no/akershus/. Admission NOK65 adults, NOK25 children. Sept–May Sat–Sun noon–5pm; June–Aug Mon–Sat 10am–4pm, Sunday 12:30–5pm. Tram: 10 or 12.

Oslo Domkirke (Oslo Cathedral) ★ Oslo's restored 1697 cathedral at Stortorvet (the marketplace) contains works by 20th-century Norwegian artists, including bronze doors by Dagfin Werenskiold and a 1950 tempera ceiling by Hugo Louis Mohr. The choir features stained-glass windows crafted by Emanuel Vigeland (not to be confused with the sculptor, Gustav), and in the transepts are those by Borgar Hauglid. The **pulpit and altarpiece ★**, carved in the late 17th century with lovely motifs of acanthus leaves, also remain to delight. The five-story-tall organ dates from the 18th century and would challenge even a budding Norwegian Liberace. Most visits here take half an hour. A bilingual service (in Norwegian and English) is conducted on Wednesday at noon, and an organ recital is presented on summer Saturdays at 1pm. ***Tip:*** For a great panoramic view of Oslo, go to the nightwatchman's room in the steeple, which was added in 1850.

Stortorvet 1. ✆ **23-31-46-00.** www.oslodomkirke.no. Free admission. Daily 10am–4pm. T-banen: Stortinget. Bus: 17.

Rådhuset (City Hall) Inaugurated in 1950, the City Hall, whose architecture combines romanticism, classicism, and functionalism, has been called everything from "aggressively ugly" to the pride of Norway. Aesthetics aside, the whole world looks toward this simple red-brick building with its iconic double towers every December when the Nobel Peace Prize is awarded. Luminaries such as Yasser Arafat (1994), Martin Luther King, Jr. (1964), Nelson Mandela (1993), and Jimmy Carter (2002) have claimed their prizes under this roof. It houses, among other things, a stunning 25×13-m (82×43-ft.) wall painted by Henrik Sørensen, and the mural *Life* by Edvard Munch. Tapestries, frescoes, sculpture, and woodcarvings by Dagfin Werenskiold are also on display. Guided tours in English are available, though far from necessary. Be sure to check out the astronomical clock and Dyre Vaa's swan fountain in the courtyard. Allow about 20 minutes.

Rådhusplassen. ✆ **23-46-16-00.** www.radhusets-forvaltningstjeneste.oslo.kommune.no. Free admission. Daily 9am–6pm. 45-min. guided tours Mon–Fri 10am, noon, & 2pm. Tram: 10 or 12.

Stortinget (Parliament) This yellow-brick building sounds a grace note amidst the urban landscape. The original neo-Romanesque exterior, constructed from 1861 to 1866, has been preserved, and the finest artists decorated the interior, with works depicting scenes from the country's history or daily life. You're shown through on a guided tour and can see where some of the world's most progressive and socially conscious politicians meet. The tours, which last 20 minutes, are open to the public. (There's no need to book ahead, but try to arrive 15 minutes before the tours begin.)

Karl Johans Gate 22. ✆ **23-31-35-96.** www.stortinget.no. Free admission. Guided tours in English July 1–Aug 15 Mon–Fri 10 & 11:30am & 1pm; Sept 15–June 15 Sat 10 & 11:30am & 1pm. Closed Aug 16–Sept 14 & June 16–30. T-banen: Stortinget. Tram: 13, 15, or 19.

On Bygdøy

Located south of the city, the peninsula is reached by commuter ferry (summer only) leaving from Pier 3, facing the Rådhuset (City Hall). Departures during the day are every 40 minutes before 11am and every 20 minutes after 11am, and a one-way fare costs NOK40 (an Oslo Pass also works here). The no. 30 bus from the Nationaltheatret also runs to Bygdøy. The museums lie only a short walk from the bus stops on Bygdøy.

For reviews of Bygdøy's **Vikingskipshuset** (p. 132) and the **Norsk Folkemuseum** (p. 130), see "The Big Six," earlier in this chapter.

Frammuseet ★ Go here to see the world's most famous polar ship, *Fram,* dating from 1892. The brave little ship that Fridtjof Nansen sailed across the Arctic from 1893 to 1896 is perfectly preserved in its original condition. The trip made the handsome, fur-coated Viking one of the most renowned of all polar explorers. The noble *Fram* set out on a second expedition, this one headed by Otto Sverdrup, who sailed around southern Greenland to Canada's Ellesmere Island between 1898 and 1902. For its third and most famous journey, from 1910 to 1912, the *Fram* ventured to the Antarctic under the command of Roald Amundsen, who subsequently became the first explorer to reach the South Pole. Plan on spending half an hour here.

Bygdøynesveien 36. ✆ **23-28-29-50.** www.fram.museum.no. Admission NOK60 adults, NOK25 children, NOK120 family ticket. June–Aug daily 9am–6pm; Sept & May daily 9am–5:45pm; Nov–Feb daily 10am–3pm. Ferry: From Pier 3 facing the Rådhuset (summer only). Bus: 30 from the Nationaltheatret.

Kon-Tiki Museum ★ ☺ *Kon-Tiki* is a world-famous balsa-log raft. In 1947, the young Norwegian scientist Thor Heyerdahl and five comrades sailed it from Callao, Peru, to Raroia, Polynesia (6,880km/4,270 miles). It was not Heyderdahl's aim to discover new lands. He wanted to prove that the people of Polynesia originally came from South America, and showed how ancient civilizations could have done so by using a raft such as *Kon-Tiki.* Besides the raft, there are other exhibits from Heyerdahl's subsequent visits to Easter Island. They include casts of stone giants and small originals, a facsimile of a whale shark, and an Easter Island family cave, with a collection of sacred lava figurines hoarded in secret underground passages by the island's inhabitants. The museum also houses the original papyrus *Ra II,* in which

Heyerdahl crossed the Atlantic in 1970. Although kids like to be taken here, adults will find it fascinating as well. Those who get really interested can read Heyerdahl's account of his adventures in his book, *Kon-Tiki,* published in countless editions around the world (available in the museum shop, of course). Most visits to this museum take about 45 minutes.

Bygdøynesveien 36. ✆ **23-08-67-67.** www.kon-tiki.no. Admission NOK60 adults, NOK25 children. Apr–May & Sept daily 10am–5pm; June–Aug daily 9:30am–5:30pm; Oct & Mar daily 10:30am–4pm; Nov–Feb 10:30am–3:30pm. Ferry: From Pier 3 facing the Rådhuset (summer only). Bus: 30 from the Nationaltheatret.

Norsk Sjøfartsmuseum (Norwegian Maritime Museum) ★ ☺ Norway is extremely proud of its seafaring past, a glorious tradition that lives on at this museum that chronicles the maritime history and culture of the rugged country, complete with a ship's deck with helm and chart house. One somewhat gruesome section focuses on shipwrecks. Many boats speak of adventure, including the Gibraltar Boat, a fragile craft in which Norwegian sailors fled Morocco to the safety of British Gibraltar in World War II. There's also a three-deck section of the passenger steamer *Sandnaes,* and a carved-out tree trunk is said to be the oldest surviving Norwegian boat. The Boat Hall features a fine collection of original small craft. The fully restored polar vessel *Gjoa,* used by Roald Amundsen in his search for the Northwest Passage, is also on display. The three-masted schooner *Svanen* (Swan) is moored at the museum. Built in Svendborg, Denmark, in 1916, *Svanen* sailed under the Norwegian and Swedish flags. The ship now belongs to the museum and is used as a training vessel for young people. Visits require about 45 minutes.

Bygdøynesveien 37. ✆ **24-11-41-50.** www.norsk-sjofartsmuseum.no. Admission to museum & boat hall NOK60 adults, free for children. Mid-May to Aug daily 10am–6pm; Sept to mid-May Mon–Wed & Fri–Sun 10am–4pm; Thurs 10am–6pm. Ferry: From Pier 3 facing the Rådhuset (summer only). Bus: 30 from the Nationaltheatret.

Villa Grande ★ This was once the most notorious address in Norway, the home of Vidkun Quisling, the Norwegian collaborator and Nazi leader who presided over his conquered country during World War II. In Norway, Quisling and the word *traitor* are virtually the same. With historical irony, the government opened Villa Grande, once known as "Gimie," to the public in 2006, turning it into a Holocaust exhibition. Exhibitions focus on the Nazi-led genocide of millions of Jews and the

The Loftiest Lookout Tower in Scandinavia

Tryvannstårnet (✆ 22-14-67-11), at Voksenkollen, dazzles you with its panoramic sweep of Oslofjord and Sweden to its east. The gallery is approximately 570m (1,870 ft.) above sea level. A 20-minute walk down the hill returns you to Frognerseteren, and another 20-minute walk down the hill takes you to the Holmenkollen ski jump, where the 1952 Olympic competitions took place. It's also the site of Norway's Holmenkollen Ski Festival (p. 40).

Admission is NOK40 for adults or NOK25 for children. It's open May to September daily 10am to 5pm, off-season daily 10am to 4pm. Take the T-banen to Frognerseteren (SST Line 1) from near the Nationaltheatret in the direction of Voksenkollen (a 30-min. ride). From here, it's a 15-minute walk uphill.

SUGGESTED itineraries FOR OSLO

If You Have 1 Day

Arm yourself with a bag of freshly cooked shrimp—purchased right off the shrimp boats at the harbor in front of the Rådhuset (City Hall)—and take a ferry over to the Bygdøy Peninsula. Visit some of Oslo's major attractions—they're within walking distance of each other. Explore the Viking ships, the polar ship *Fram,* the Kon-Tiki Museum, the Norwegian Maritime Museum, and the Norwegian Folk Museum. In the late afternoon, go to Frogner Park to admire the Vigeland sculptures.

If You Have 2 Days

On your first day, follow the itinerary above. On your second day, take the Frommer's walking tour (p. 144) and have lunch in a Norwegian restaurant. In the afternoon, explore the Edvard Munch Museum. In summer, during clement weather, visit the Studenter Lunden (Students' Grove), near the National Theater, for some beer and fresh air.

If You Have 3 Days

For your first 2 days, follow the itinerary "If You Have 2 Days" (see above). On the morning of Day 3, take another Frommer's walking tour (p. 148), eating lunch along the way. In the afternoon, explore Akershus Castle and the adjoining Norwegian Resistance Museum. By late afternoon, visit the lofty lookout tower at Tryvannstårnet and see the Skimuseet at Holmenkollen, taking in the sweeping view of the Oslo environs. Have dinner at Holmenkollen.

If You Have 4 or 5 Days

For the first 3 days, follow the itinerary "If You Have 3 Days," above. On Day 4, head south from Oslo for a 1-day excursion to the Oslofjord country, with stopovers at the Old Town at Fredrikstad; Tønsberg, Norway's oldest town; and Sandefjørd, an old whaling town. Head back to Oslo for the night. On Day 5, see the rest of Oslo's major sights, such as the National Gallery, the Historical Museum, and the Henie-Onstad Art Center, 11km (7 miles) from Oslo—a major museum of modern art.

persecution of other minorities. The exhibition begins ominously as you enter and see a picture of the German ship SS *Donau,* shown on November 26, 1942, at a snowy wharf in Oslo.

Huk aveny 56, Bygdøy. ✆ **22-84-21-00.** www.hlsenteret.no. Admission NOK50 adults, NOK25 children 11 & under, NOK100 family ticket. Daily 11am–4pm.

PARKS & GARDENS

Botanisk Hage og Museum (Botanical Gardens) ★ I visit here just to see the more than 1,000 alpine plants gathered from around the world. Complete with waterfalls, the rock garden is an oasis in the heart of Oslo. It's home to many exotic plants, including cacti, orchids, palms, and a "living fossil" from Japan: The Maidenhair Tree, which was planted in 1870. The tree produces lots of seeds, but they remain unfertilized because the nearest male Maidenhair Tree grows in Copenhagen. There's a museum in the park with a botanical art exhibit. Plan on spending 45 minutes here.

Sars Gate 1. ✆ **22-85-16-30.** www.nhm.uio.no. Free admission. Apr–Sept Mon–Fri 7am–8pm, Sat–Sun 10am–8pm; Oct–Mar Mon–Fri 7am–5pm, Sat–Sun 10am–5pm. Bus: 31.

A ROYAL PAIR: THE un-fairy tale ROMANCE

Prince Haakon of Norway may be a direct descendant of Queen Victoria, but he shares little in common with that staunch monarch. Instead of going to Balliol College, Oxford, as did his father, King Garald V, Haakon was a fun-loving young man on campus at the University of California at Berkeley.

When it came to taking a bride, as he did in Oslo on August 25, 2001, he shocked conservative Norway, challenging one of the world's most tolerant and enlightened societies. Crown Prince Haakon married Mette-Marit Tjessem Hoiby (whom he called "the love of my life"), an unconventional royal pairing. The prince had never been married before, but the princess and future queen of Norway was a divorcée and mother. The couple lived together before marriage in the palace with her 3-year-old son by a previous marriage to a convicted cocaine supplier.

Before marrying the prince, Mette-Marit had a "well-known past in Oslo's dance-and-drugs house-party scene," as the Oslo press so delicately phrased it. It was rumored that pressure was brought on the young prince by conservative elements to give up a claim to the throne, eerily evocative of Edward VII's decision to marry the twice-divorced Wallis Warfield Simpson in the 1930s. It is said that Haakon considered renouncing the throne but decided to maintain his status as the heir apparent. "I think this is where I'm supposed to be," he finally said to the press, ending months of speculation.

King Harald was supportive of his son's decision. As the future king himself, he had spent a decade trying to persuade his own father, Olav V, to sanction his marriage to his commoner childhood sweetheart (the present Queen Sonja was born a shopkeeper's daughter). Olav himself had also intervened when his daughter, Princess Märtha Louise, was cited as a correspondent in a divorce proceeding in London.

The wedding has come and gone, and there is no more talk of revolution over this "scandal." As Ine Marie Eriksen, a law student from Tromsø, explained, "Why should Prince Haakon and Mette-Marit live by rules of the 18th century? That would take away the very thing that the Norwegian people like about our monarchy."

Since their marriage, the royal couple have had two children—Princess Ingrid, born January 21, 2004, and Prince Sverre Magnus, born December 3, 2005. In 1990, the Norwegian constitution was altered, meaning that the eldest child, regardless of gender, takes precedence in the line of succession. The law is not retroactive, however. That means that Crown Prince Haakon is in line for the Norwegian throne, not his sister, Princess Märtha Louise (born 1971). Haakon was born on July 20, 1973.

Marka ★★, the thick forest that surrounds Oslo, is just one of the giant pleasure parks in the area. You can also take a tram marked HOLMENKOLLEN from the city center to Oslomarka, a forested area where locals go for summer hikes and for winter skiing. The ride to the stop at Oslomarka takes only 20 minutes, and there are trains every 30 minutes or so, depending on the season. The area is dotted with about two dozen *hytter* (mountain huts) where you can seek refuge from the weather, if needed. **Norske Turistforening,** Youngstorget 1, (✆ **40-00-18-68;** www.turistforeningen.no), sells maps with the hiking paths and roads of the Oslomarka clearly delineated. It's open Monday to Friday 9am to 4pm. A favorite trail—and you should have this pinpointed on a map—is a signposted walk to **Sognsvannet ★**, a beautiful loch (lake) flanked by forested hills and encircled by an easy hiking trail stretching for 4km (2½ miles). In winter, the loch is iced over; but, in summer, those with polar-bear blood can take a dip. Even in summer, swimming here is like taking a bath in ice water. In lieu of swimming, then, you might find the banks of this lake better suited for a picnic.

Slottsparken The park surrounding the Royal Palace (Slottet) is open to the public year-round. The changing of the guard, albeit a weak imitation of the changing of the guard at London's Buckingham Palace, takes place daily at 1:30pm. When the king is in residence, the Royal Guard band plays Monday to Friday during the ceremony. The palace was constructed from 1825 to 1848. Some first-time visitors are surprised at how relatively unguarded it is, without walls or rails. You can walk through the grounds but can't go inside unless you have managed to swing an invitation from the king. The statue at the front of the castle (at the end of Karl Johans Gate) is of Karl XIV Johan himself, who ruled Norway and Sweden. He ordered the construction of this palace but died before it was finished. Allot about 20 minutes.

Drammensveien 1. Free admission. Daily dawn–dusk. T-banen: Nationaltheatret.

LITERARY LANDMARKS

See also "Walking Tour 2: In the Footsteps of Ibsen & Munch," below.

Ibsen Museum Now theatergoers from around the world can pay tribute to Ibsen by visiting his former apartment. In 1994, Oslo opened this museum to honor its most famous writer, Ibsen, who lived here from 1895 until his death in 1906. The apartment, within walking distance of the Nationaltheatret, was where Ibsen wrote two of his most famous plays, *John Gabriel Borkman* and *When We Dead Awaken*. The museum curators have attempted to re-create what the apartment was like during Ibsen's day as much as possible, with the author's original furniture. The attraction has been called "a living museum," and regularly scheduled talks on playwriting and the theater, recitations, and theatrical performances take place here. Allow 25 minutes.

Henrik Ibsens Gate 26. ✆ **22-12-35-50.** www.ibsen.net. Admission NOK85 adults, NOK25 children. Mid-May to mid-Sept daily 11am–6pm; mid-Sept to mid-May Mon–Wed & Fri–Sun 11am–4pm, Thurs 11am–6pm. Guided tours in English at noon, 1, & 2pm. Tram: 13, 15, or 19.

Oslo Bymuseet (City Museum) Housed in the 1790 Frogner Manor at Frogner Park, site of the Vigeland sculptures (see the earlier listing for Vigelandsparken, p. 131), this museum surveys the history of Oslo over the past 1,000 years—the red coats that the city's first policemen wore, the first fire wagon, relics of the great fire of 1624, the exhibits of the Black Death in 1348–50. It also contains mementos of Henrik Ibsen, from the chair and marble-topped table where he sat at the Grand Café to the glasses from which he drank. Frogner Park, with its streams, shade trees, and lawns, is an ideal spot for a picnic. If not that, then go for the delicious ice cream or pastries served at the on-site Café Mathia. It takes about an hour to view the highlights of the museum.

Frognerveien 67. ✆ **23-28-41-70.** www.oslobymuseum.no. Free admission. Tues–Sun 11am–4pm (June–Aug closes at 5pm). Tram: 12.

ESPECIALLY FOR KIDS

Oslo offers numerous attractions suitable for children and grown-ups alike. Two that can equal the thrill of a fjord trip are seeing the excavated Viking burial ships at the **Vikingskipshuset** (p. 132) and the Boat Hall at the **Norwegian Maritime Museum** (p. 140), both on the Bygdøy Peninsula.

Other sights of special interest to children include the polar exploration ship *Fram* at the **Frammuseet** (p. 139); the balsa-log raft *Kon-Tiki* at the **Kon-Tiki Museum** (p. 139); the **Ski Museum** (p. 136), **Lookout Tower** (p. 140), and ski jump at Holmenkollen; the **Norwegian Folk Museum** (p. 130), depicting life in Norway since the Middle Ages; and the ancient **Akershus Castle & Fortress** (p. 138) on the Oslofjord.

Barnekunstmuseet (International Museum of Children's Art) ☺ Here you can see the world through the eyes of a child. The collection in this unique museum consists of children's drawings, paintings, ceramics, sculpture, tapestries, and handicrafts from more than 30 countries, some of which would have pleased Picasso. There's also a children's workshop devoted to painting, drawing, music, and dance.

Lille Frøens vei 4. ✆ **22-46-85-73.** www.barnekunst.no. Admission NOK60 adults, NOK40 children. Mid-Jan to late June & Sept to early Dec Tues–Thurs 9:30am–2pm, Sun 11am–4pm; June 24–Aug 15 Tues–Thurs & Sun 11am–4pm. Closed Mon, Fri, & Sat year-round & Aug 15–31; closed early Jan. T-banen: Frøen.

Norgesparken Tusenfryd ☺ This is the largest amusement park in Norway, conceived as a smaller version of Copenhagen's Tivoli Gardens. It includes a number of simple restaurants, a roller coaster with a loop and corkscrew, an amphitheater with all-day entertainment by musicians, clowns, and other performers, and many games of skill or chance. In the summer, there is also a water park. The park is 19km (12 miles) south of Oslo Central railway station.

Vinterbro by E6/E18/Mossevelen. ✆ **64-97-64-97.** www.tusenfryd.no. All-day ticket NOK240–NOK360 depending on time of year. Free children under 95cm (37½ in.) high. Late Apr–Sept daily 10:30am–8pm. Closed Oct–late Apr. Bus: Shuttle service from Oslo Central station daily 9:30am–4pm; final return shortly after park closes. Fare NOK40 adults, NOK25 children.

OSLO ON FOOT: WALKING TOURS

WALKING TOUR 1: HISTORIC OSLO

START:	**Aker Brygge.**
FINISH:	**Royal Palace.**
TIME:	**2½ hours.**
BEST TIMES:	**Any day when it's not raining.**
WORST TIMES:	**Rush hours (weekdays 7–9am and 5–7pm).**

Start at the harbor to the west of the Rådhuset at:

1 Aker Brygge

This steel-and-glass complex is a rebuilt district of shops and restaurants that was developed from Oslo's old shipbuilding grounds. It has a fine view of Akershus Castle.

Walking Tour 1: Historic Oslo

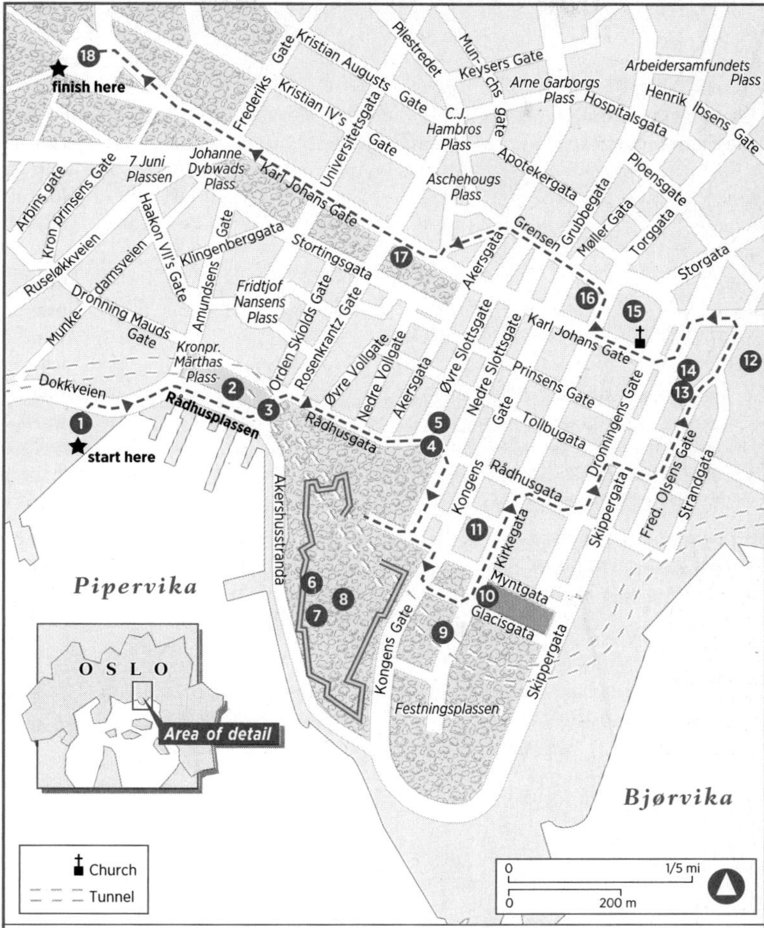

1 Aker Brygge
2 Rådhuset
3 Statue of Franklin D. Roosevelt
4 Christiania Torv
5 Kafé Celsius
6 Norges Hjemmefrontmuseum
7 Akershus Slott og Festning
8 Execution Site
9 National Monument to the German Occupation
10 Grev Wedels Plass
11 Bankplassen
12 Oslo Sentralstasjon
13 Karl Johans Gate
14 Basarhallene
15 Oslo Domkirke
16 Stortorvets Gjæstgiveri
17 Stortinget
18 Slottet

Head east along Rådhusplassen, looking to your left at the:

2 Rådhuset (City Hall)

The Oslo City Hall, built in 1950, is decorated with artwork by Norwegian artists.

Climb the steps at the east end of the square and a small hill to see the:

3 Statue of Franklin D. Roosevelt

Eleanor Roosevelt flew to Oslo to dedicate this statue.

This area is the heart of the 17th-century Renaissance city. Take Rådhusgata east to the traffic hub of:

4 Christiania Torv

The yellow house on your left, the Young Artists Association, was once the home of the dreaded royal executioner. His fee depended on the type of execution performed.

5 Kafé Celsius

To the right of the Young Artists Association is Kafé Celsius, Rådhusgatan 19 (✆ 22-42-45-39), Oslo's oldest residential house. Today it's a charming arts-oriented cafe that serves tasty food. Sandwich prices start at NOK118. You can also order pasta salads and such dishes as ratatouille or tortellini. On cold days, there's a fire in the fireplace. It's open Monday to Saturday 11am to midnight, Sunday 11:30am to 7:30pm.

Continue along Rådhusgata, turning right onto Nedre Slottsgate. Walk to the end of the street. At Myntgata, turn right and pass through a gate. You are now on the external grounds of Akershus Castle. The first building on the right is the:

6 Norges Hjemmefrontmuseum (Norwegian Resistance Museum)

The museum has displays on events related to the Nazi occupation of Norway from 1940 to 1945.

Also at the site is:

7 Akershus Slott of Festning (Akershus Castle & Fortress)

The structure dates from 1300 but was rebuilt in the 17th century. Take a guided tour and walk the ramparts.

In front of the Norwegian Resistance Museum, pause on the grounds to look at the:

8 Execution Site

Here Nazi soldiers shot prisoners, often Norwegian freedom fighters. There's a memorial to the resistance movement, and you'll have a good view of the harbor in the distance.

Cross the drawbridge to the east, right before Kongensgate, and continue through the castle grounds to the:

9 National Monument to the German Occupation

This commemorates Norway's suffering at the hands of the Nazis.

After seeing the monument, turn left (north) into:

10 Grev Wedels Plass

This is the site of Den Gamle Logen (Freemasons' Lodge). In 1850, Ibsen wrote poems here. At no. 9 and Dronningensgatan 4 is the Astrup Fearnley Museum of Modern Art, with changing exhibits of Norwegian and foreign art from the postwar period.

Head north along Kirkegata until you reach:

11 Bankplassen

This former site of the old Bank of Norway is now the Museum of Contemporary Art (Bankplassen 4), with the state collection of international and Norwegian modern art acquired since World War II. This square was once Oslo's social center. Ibsen staged his first play here in 1851 (at a theater that burned down in 1877).

From Bankplassen, turn right onto Revierstredet and left onto Dronningensgatan. At one time the waterfront came up to this point. Go right at the Central Post Office onto Tollbugata. At the intersection with Fred Olsens Gate, turn left and walk to the:

12 Oslo Sentralstasjon (Oslo Central Railway Station)

Trains arrive at Oslo's rail hub from the Continent here and depart for all points linked by train in Norway.

Turn left onto the main pedestrian-only street:

13 Karl Johans Gate

The street stretches from Oslo Central railway station in the east to the Royal Palace at its west end.

On your right you'll pass the:

14 Basarhallene

Boutiques and shops, hawking everything from food to clothing to crafts, fill this huge complex.

Turn right at Kirkegata, heading for the:

15 Oslo Domkirke (Oslo Cathedral)

This 17th-century cathedral resides at Stortorvet, Oslo's old marketplace. Like the City Hall, the cathedral is decorated with outstanding works by Norwegian artists.

16 Stortorvets Gjæstgiveri

Old Oslo atmosphere lives on at the Stortorvets Gjæstgiveri, Grensen 1 (✆ 23-35-63-60), on a busy commercial street. This drinking and dining emporium, dating from the 1600s, is often filled with spirited beer drinkers. A beer costs NOK63. It's open Monday to Saturday from 11am to 11pm, Sunday (Sept–Apr only) 3 to 9pm.

From Stortorvet, walk west on Grensen until you reach Lille Grensen. Cut left onto this street, returning to Karl Johans Gate. On your left at Karl Johans Gate 22 will be the:

17 Stortinget (Parliament)

Constructed from 1861 to 1866, this evocative structure is richly decorated with works by contemporary Norwegian artists.

Continue west along Karl Johans Gate, passing many of the monuments covered on "Walking Tour 2: In the Footsteps of Ibsen & Munch" (see below). Eventually you'll reach Drammensveien 1, the:

18 Slottet (Royal Palace)

This is the residence of the king of Norway and his family. The public is permitted access only to the park.

WALKING TOUR 2: IN THE FOOTSTEPS OF IBSEN & MUNCH

START:	**National Theater.**
FINISH:	**National Gallery.**
TIME:	**2 hours.**
BEST TIMES:	**Any day when it's not raining.**
WORST TIMES:	**Rush hours (weekdays 7–9am and 5–7pm).**

The tour begins at Stortingsgaten 15, just off Karl Johans Gate near the Students' Grove in Oslo's center, site of the:

1 Nationaltheatret (National Theater)

Study your map in front of the Henrik Ibsen statue at the theater, where many of his plays were first performed and are still presented. The Norwegian Nationaltheatret (© **81-50-08-11**), inaugurated in 1899, is Norway's largest and one of the most beautiful in Europe.

Facing the statue of Ibsen, continue up Stortingsgaten toward the Royal Palace (Slottet). Cut left at the next intersection and walk along Ruselokkveien. On the right, the **Vika Shopping Terraces,** an unattractive row of modern storefronts tacked onto an elegant 1880 Victorian terrace, used to be among Oslo's grandest apartments. During World War II it was the Nazi headquarters.

Continue along this complex to the end, turning right onto Dronnings Mauds Gate, which quickly becomes Lokkeveien. At the first building on the right, you come to:

2 Ibsen's private apartment

Look for the blue plaque marking the building. The playwright lived here from 1891 to 1895. When his wife complained that she didn't like the address, even though it was one of Oslo's most elegant, they moved. Ibsen wrote two plays while living here.

Turn right onto Arbinsgate and walk to the end of the street until you reach Drammensveien. At Arbinsgate 1 is the:

3 Ibsen Museum

In the first building on the left, at the corner of Arbinsgate and Drammensveien, you'll see an Omega store, but look for the blue plaque on the building. Ibsen lived here from 1895 until his death in 1906. He often sat in the window, with a light casting a glow over his white hair. People lined up in the street below to look at him. The great Italian actress Eleanora Duse came

Walking Tour 2: In the Footsteps of Ibsen & Munch

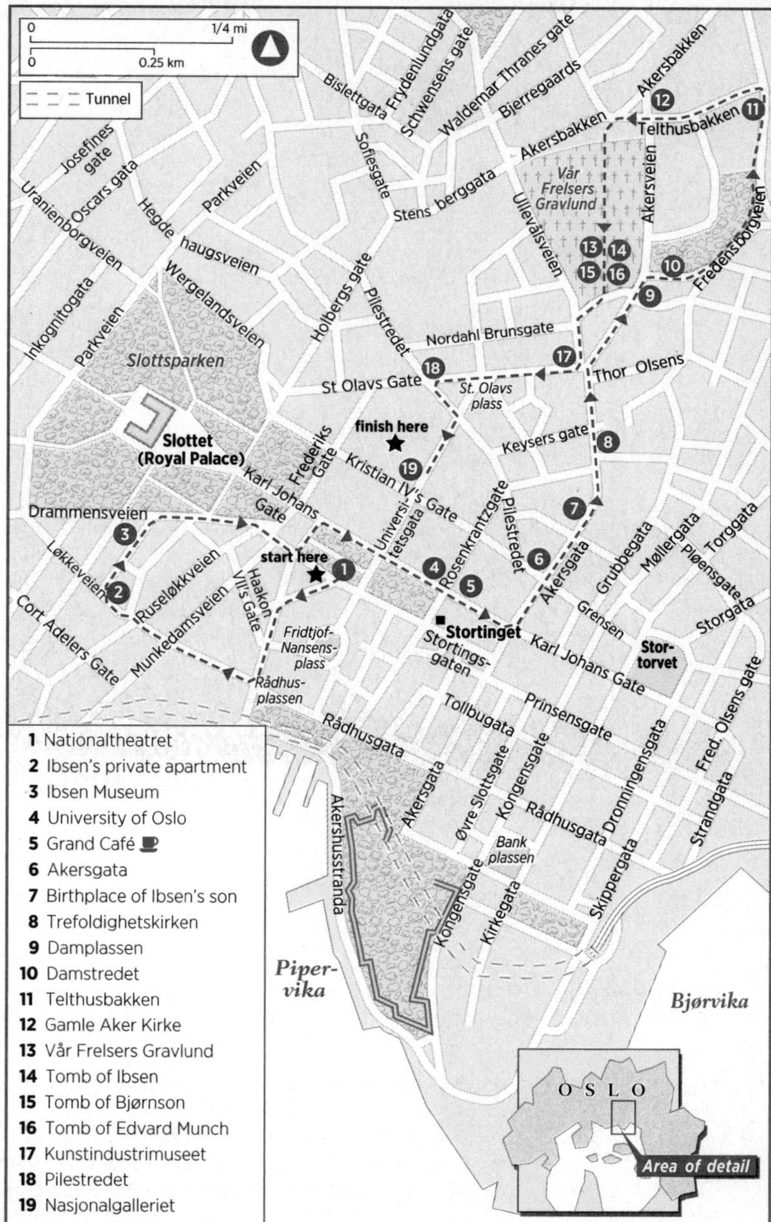

here to bid him a final *adieu,* but he was too ill to see her. She stood outside in the snow and blew him kisses.

The king of Norway used to give Ibsen a key to enter the private gardens surrounding the Royal Palace. Today, everyone has this privilege.

Turn right on Drammensveien and continue back to the Nationaltheatret. Take Karl Johans Gate, on the left side of the theater, and walk east. On your left at Karl Johans Gate 47, you'll pass the:

4 University of Oslo

Aula, the Great Hall of the university, is decorated with murals by Edvard Munch. The hall is open to the public only from June 20 to August 20, daily from 10am to 3pm. For information, call ✆ **22-85-95-55.**

Twice a day Ibsen followed this route to the Grand Café. Admirers often threw rose petals in his path, but he pretended not to see. He was called "the Sphinx" because he wouldn't talk to anybody.

5 Grand Café

(Karl Johans Gate 31 (✆ 23-21-20-00), was the center of social life for the literati and the artistic elite, including Munch. Today a favorite with many visitors, but also with hundreds of Oslovians who appreciate tradition, it is the most famous cafe in all of Scandinavia (see p. 112 for a complete review). On the far wall of the cafe, you can see Per Krogh's famous mural, painted in 1928. Ibsen, with a top hat and gray beard, is at the far left, and Munch—called the handsomest man in Norway—is seated at the second window from the right, at the far right of the window. The poet and playwright Bjørnstjerne Bjørnson can be spotted on the street outside (second window from the left, wearing a top hat), because he wouldn't deign to come into the cafe. You can order snacks, drinks, and big meals here.

Returning to the street, note the Norwegian Parliament building (Stortinget) on your right. Proceed left and turn left onto Lille Grensen. Cross the major boulevard, Grensen, and walk straight to:

6 Akersgata

This street was used for Ibsen's funeral procession. Services were conducted at the Holy Trinity Church on June 1, 1906.

Veer left to see the:

7 Birthplace of Ibsen's son

On your left, at the corner of Teatergata and Akersgata, is the site of the famous Strømberg Theater, which burned down in 1835. It was also a residence, and Ibsen's son was born here in 1859.

Also on Akersgata is:

8 Trefoldighetskirken (Holy Trinity Church)

This church was the site of Ibsen's funeral.

A little farther along Akersgata is St. Olav's Church. Turn on the right side of this imposing house of worship onto Akersveien and go to:

9 Damplassen

This small square—one of the most charming in Oslo—doesn't appear on most maps. Norway's greatest poet, Henrik Wergeland, lived in the pink house on the square from 1839 to 1841.

Take a right at the square and head down:

10 Damstredet

The antique wooden houses along this typical old Oslo street are mainly occupied by artists.

Damstredet meanders downhill to Fredensborgveien. Here, a left turn and a short walk will take you to Maridalsveien, a busy but uneventful thoroughfare. As you walk north along this street, on the west side look for a large, unmarked gateway with wide stone steps inside. Climb to the top, follow a little pathway, and go past gardens and flower beds. Pass a set of brick apartment buildings on the left, and proceed to:

11 Telthusbakken

Along this little street, you'll see a whole row of early Oslo wooden houses. Look towards the right in the far distance at the green building where Munch used to live.

Telthusbakken leads to Akersveien. On your left you can see the:

12 Gamle Aker Kirke (Old Aker Church)

Enter at Akersbakken, where Akersveien and Akersbakken intersect. Built in 1100, this is the oldest stone parish church in Scandinavia that's still in use. It stands on a green hill surrounded by an old graveyard and a stone wall.

A short block from the church along Akersbakken (veer left outside the front of the church and go around a corner), you'll come to the north entrance of the city's expansive burial ground:

13 Vår Frelsers Gravlund (Our Savior's Cemetery)

In a section designated the "Ground of Honor" are the graves of famous Norwegians, including Munch, Ibsen, and Bjørnson.

Signs don't point the way, but it's easy to see a tall obelisk. This is the:

14 Tomb of Ibsen

His wife, Susanna, whom he called "the cat," is buried to the playwright's left. She died in 1914. The hammer on the obelisk symbolizes his work *The Miner,* indicating how he "dug deep" into the soul of Norway.

To the right of Ibsen's tomb is the:

15 Tomb of Bjørnson

The literary figure Bjørnstjerne Bjørnson (1832–1910) once raised money to send Ibsen to Italy. Before the birth of their children, Ibsen and Bjørnson agreed that one would have a son and the other a daughter, and that these children would marry each other. Miraculously, Ibsen had a son, Bjørnson a daughter, and they did just that. Bjørnson wrote the national anthem, and his tomb is draped in a stone representation of a Norwegian flag.

To the far right of Bjørnson's tomb is the:

16 Tomb of Edvard Munch

Scandinavia's greatest painter has a surprisingly unadorned tomb. If you're visiting on a snowy day, it will be buried because the marker lies close to the ground. Munch died during the darkest days of the Nazi occupation. His sister turned down a request from the German command to give Munch a state funeral, feeling that it would be inappropriate.

On the west side of the cemetery, you'll come to Ullevålsveien. Turn left on this busy street and head south toward the center of Oslo. You'll soon see St. Olav's Church, now on your left. Stay on the right (west) side of the street. At St. Olavs Gate 1, where Ullevålsveien intersects with St. Olavs Gate, is the:

17 Kunstindustrimuseet (Museum of Applied Art)

Even if you don't have time to visit the museum, you may want to stop inside for a snack at Café Solliløkken (p. 135).

After visiting the museum, continue along St. Olavs Gate to:

18 Pilestredet

Look to the immediate right at no. 30. A wall plaque on the decaying building commemorates the fact that Munch lived here from 1868 to 1875. In this building he painted, among other masterpieces, *The Sick Child.* He moved here when he was 5, and many of his "memory paintings" were of the interior. When demolition teams began razing the building in the early 1990s, a counterculture group of activists known as "The Blitz Group" illegally took over the premises to prevent its destruction. On its brick-wall side, his masterpiece *The Scream* was re-created in spray paint. The protesters are still in control of the city-owned building, and they are viewed as squatters on very valuable land. There is some fear that if a more conservative government comes into power, officials will toss out the case, throw out the activists, and demolish the building. For the moment, however, they remain in control.

At Pilestredet, turn left. One block later, turn right onto Universitesgata, heading south toward Karl Johans Gate. You'll pass a number of architecturally interesting buildings and will eventually arrive at Universitesgata 13, the:

19 Nasjonalgalleriet (National Gallery)

The state museum has a large collection of Norwegian as well as international art. Two rooms are devoted to masterpieces by Munch.

ORGANIZED TOURS

Norway Yacht Charter **Båtservice Sightseeing,** Rådhusbrygge 3, Rådhusplassen (✆ **23-35-68-90;** www.boatsightseeing.com), offers a 90-minute boat tour. You'll see the harbor and the city, including the ancient fortress of Akershus and the islands in the inner part of the Oslofjord. Cruises depart from Pier 3 in front of the Oslo Rådhuset (City Hall). They run from mid-May to late August daily every half-hour from 9:45am to 3:45pm during the high season, less frequently at the beginning and end of the season. Tickets are NOK170 for adults, NOK85 for children.

If you have more time, take a 2-hour summer cruise through the maze of islands and narrow sounds in the Oslofjord. From May to September, they leave daily at 10:30am and 1, 3:30, and 5:45pm (slightly more often in July and Aug); the cost is NOK240 for adults, NOK120 for children. Refreshments are available onboard.

See the "Summer Evenings on the Oslofjord" box below for information on the outfitter's 3-hour evening fjord cruise, which includes a seafood buffet.

SUMMER evenings ON THE OSLOFJORD

Summer evenings aboard a boat on the Oslofjord can be restful and exhilarating, but if you happen to be without a private yacht of your own, there are several outfitters who can help. The best of these is **Båtservice Sightseeing AS ★**, Rådhusbrygge 3 (City Hall Pier no. 3; ✆ **23-35-68-90;** www.boatsightseeing.com), which operates from a low-slung concrete building directly atop one of the piers adjacent to Oslo's City Hall. Between late June and the end of August, weather permitting, they operate nightly cruises that showcase, better than any other means of transportation, the intricate cays, skerries, sandbars, and rocks of the Oslofjord.

You'll travel aboard one of three historic sloops, each of which retains some real maritime charm, with pinewood masts and complicated 19th-century rigging. During these excursions, you'll be moving by diesel-powered engines, not by wind power. The oldest and most oft-used of the three ships is the *Johanna,* a wood-sided sloop originally built in 1892. Passengers sit at plank-built tables on an open deck, retreating to a glassed-in cabin, or even below deck, if the weather turns foul.

Included in the price are heaping buckets of Norwegian shrimp—served buffet-style from a central table on deck—which you'll peel yourself, then eat with bread, butter, and mayonnaise. Beverages come from a cash bar (beer only), and entertainment derives from the vistas and panoramas that unfold on all sides. They include views of the hundreds of private summer homes, often inhabitable only 4 months a year, built alongside the Oslofjord. Departures are nightly at 7pm (late June–Aug only), with a return scheduled for 10pm. The price is NOK395 per person. Significantly, most of the participants aboard these cruises are likely to be Norwegians, some of them from Oslo, who appreciate the chance for a first-hand view of the midsummer sea and its banks. There are other tours, too, which range in price from NOK170 to NOK620.

City Tours **H. M. Kristiansens Automobilbyrå,** Hegdehaugsveien 4 (✆ **23-15-73-00;** http://hmk.no/), has been showing visitors around Oslo for more than a century. Both of their bus tours are offered daily year-round. The 4-hour "Oslo Highlights" tour is offered at 10:15am. It costs NOK320 for adults, NOK160 for children. The 2-hour "Oslo Panorama" tour costs NOK215 for adults, NOK105 for children. It departs at 10:15am. The starting point is in front of the Nationaltheatret. Arrive 15 minutes before departure; tours are conducted in English by trained guides.

ACTIVE SPORTS

From spring to fall, the Oslofjord is a center for swimming, sailing, windsurfing, and angling. Daily excursions are arranged by motor launch at the harbor. Suburban forest areas await hikers, bicyclists, and anglers in the summer. In the winter, the area is ideal for cross-country skiing (on marked trails that are illuminated at night), downhill or slalom skiing, tobogganing, skating, and more. Safaris by Land Rover are arranged year-round.

BATHS The most central municipal bath is **Vestkantbadet,** Sommerrogate 1 (✆ **22-56-05-66;** www.vkbspa.no), which offers a Finnish sauna and Roman baths.

This municipal bath is near the American embassy, just 1km (⅔ mile) north of Oslo's center. It's primarily a winter destination and is closed in July. Admission is NOK130. The baths are open Monday, Tuesday, and Wednesday 9am to 8pm, Tuesday and Thursday to Friday 9am to 7pm, and Saturday 10am to 4pm. Mondays and Wednesdays are reserved for men; the other days are reserved for women. Prices for massages start at NOK400 for 25 minutes. If you book a massage (✆ **22-44-07-26**), you can use the baths free.

The much larger **Frognerbadet,** Middelthunsgate 28 (✆ **23-27-54-50**), in Frogner Park, is an open-air pool near the Vigeland sculptures. The entrance fee is NOK78 for adults and NOK37 for children. It's open mid-May to early September Monday to Friday 7am to 7:30pm, Saturday and Sunday 10am to 6pm. Take tram no. 2 from the Nationaltheatret.

BEACHES You most likely didn't come to Oslo to go to the beach. Even if you did, you'll find that you often have to swim from a rocky shore. Sun-loving Oslovians, desperate to absorb whatever sun they can get on a summer day, often take to whatever remotely resembles a beach. Their few short weeks of summer last until around mid-August, when snow flurries start appearing in the Oslo sky.

Our favorite beach, and the most easily accessible from the center of Oslo, is **Huk,** on the Bygdøy Peninsula. To reach Huk, take bus no. 30 A—marked BYGDØY—to its final stop. Should you arrive by boat on Bygdøy, follow the signs along Juk Aveny to the beach. My recommendation is to go over for the day; view the Viking Ship museum, the Folk Museum, and other attractions in the morning; then head for the beach—preferably with the makings of a picnic—for the early afternoon. In case there are any prudes in your party, be duly warned: Half of the beach (the northwestern side) is reserved for nudists. That same warning should go for all beaches in Norway; many Scandinavians enjoy stripping down for the beach.

Once you get here, don't expect a traditional Hawaiian beach. The beach is mostly grass lawns and some smooth rocks that you can lie on to sun yourself like a lizard. If the beach at Huk is overcrowded, as it's likely to be on a summer day, take a 10-minute walk through the forest a bit north of where the bus stops. This leads to the more secluded beach at **Paradisbukta.**

These beaches are my favorites primarily because of their proximity to the center, not because they rival anywhere in the Mediterranean. But my secret reason to go there is to people-watch. After a day at the beach, you'll soon agree with a common assessment: Norwegians are among the healthiest-looking people in the world.

Our second-favorite beach is at **Hovedøya,** on the southwestern shore of the rocky island of Hovedøya. To get here, board boat 92 or 93 leaving Oslo from the pier called Vippetangen. From late May to mid-August, these boats depart daily from around 6am to midnight.

This is the closest island to the mainland, and it's wildly popular in summer, as ideal for a picnic as it is for walks. The island is filled with walking paths, most of which lead to the ruins of a 12th-century Cistercian monastery. My main reason for liking this beach is its fun-loving atmosphere. It's a wonderful break from too much museum-hopping, and it'll give you a good chance to meet with the English-speaking Oslovians (whose initially icy reserve can melt quickly).

You can also reach a number of beaches on the east side of the fjord by taking bus no. 75B from Jernbanetorget in East Oslo. Buses leave about every hour on weekends. It's a 12-minute ride to **Ulvøya,** the closest beach to the fjord and one of the best and safest for children. Nudists prefer a section here called **Standskogen.**

FISHING Good fishing is to be found in the Oslofjord and in the lakes that envelop Oslo. An especially popular "fishing hole" is the vast area of Marka (see "Skiing," below). You can rent canoes from **Tomm Murstad** at Tryvannsvn 2 at Holmenkollen (✆ **22-49-67-07** or 22-13-95-00; www.sjoleir.no) to use for fishing. For information on the nearest place to buy a fishing license, or for more information, contact **Oslomarkas Fiskeadministrasjon** at Sørkeldalen 914, Holmenkollen (✆ **40-00-67-68;** www.ofa.no).

GYMS Male and female weight lifters call **Harald's Gym,** Hausmannsgate 6 (✆ **22-20-34-96**), the most professional gym in Oslo. Many champion bodybuilders have trained here, and its facilities are the most comprehensive in Norway. Nonmembers pay NOK100 for a day pass. It's open Monday to Friday from 9am to 9pm, and on Saturday and Sunday from noon to 6pm.

JOGGING Marka, the forest that surrounds Oslo, has hundreds of trails. The easiest and most accessible are at Frogner Park. A great adventure is to take the Sognasvann train to the end of the line, where you can jog along the fast-flowing Sognasvann stream for an hour or so. **Norske Turistforening,** Youngstorget 1 (✆ **40-00-18-68;** www.turistforeningen.no), sells maps outlining hiking trails around the capital, and the staff can give you advice about routes.

SKATING Oslo is home to numerous skating rinks. One of the best is the **Narvisen Skating Rink,** Skikersuppa, Karl Johans Gate (✆ **22-33-30-33**), open daily 11am to 9pm, charging adults NOK55 for skate rentals, children NOK30. The rink is closed from April to November.

SKIING A 15-minute tram or bus ride from central Oslo to Holmenkollen will take you to Oslo's winter wonderland, **Marka,** a 2,579-km (1,599-mile) ski-track network. Many ski schools and instructors are available in the winter. You can even take a sleigh ride. Other activities include dogsled rides, snowshoe trekking, and Marka forest safaris. There are 14 slalom slopes to choose from, along with ski jumps in all shapes and sizes, including the famous one at Holmenkollen. For information and updates on ski conditions, you can call Skiforeningen, Kongeveien 5 (✆ **22-92-32-00**). The tourist office can give you details about the venues for many of these activities.

TENNIS The municipal courts at **Frogner Park** are usually fully booked for the season by the locals, but ask at the kiosk about cancellations. **Njårdhallen,** Sørkedalsceien 106 (✆ **23-22-22-50**), offers indoor tennis Monday to Thursday from 7am to 10pm, Friday to Sunday 7am to 8pm. Book your court well in advance. During good weather, you might prefer outdoor tennis at **Njårds Tennis,** Jenns Messveien 1 (✆ **23-22-22-50**), a cluster of courts that are generally open whenever weather and daylight permit.

SHOPPING

The Shopping Scene

Those who are "born to shop" will like Oslo, as it's one of the most shopper-friendly cities in Scandinavia, with traffic-free streets set aside for prospective buyers. The heart of this district is the **Stortorvet,** where more than two dozen shops sell everything from handicrafts to enameled silver jewelry. At the marketplace on Strøget, you can stop for a glass of beer at an open-air restaurant in fair weather. Many stores are clustered along **Karl Johans Gate** and the streets branching off it.

BEST BUYS Look for bargains on sportswear, silver and enamelware, traditional handicrafts, pewter, glass by Hadeland Glassverk (founded in 1762), teak furniture, and stainless steel.

SHIPPING GOODS & RECOVERING VAT Norway imposes a 20% to 25% value-added tax (VAT), but there are ways to avoid paying it (see "Taxes," in chapter 16). Special tax-free exports are possible; many stores will mail goods home to you, which makes paying and recovering tax unnecessary.

SHOPPING HOURS Most stores are open Monday to Friday from 9am to 5pm, Saturday 9am to 3pm. Department stores and shopping malls keep different hours—in general, Monday to Friday 9am to 8pm and Saturday 9am to 6pm. Many shops stay open late on Thursday and on the first Saturday of the month, which is called *super lørdag* ("super Saturday"). During the holiday season, stores are also open on Sunday.

Shopping Malls

Mall shopping is a firmly entrenched tradition in Oslo, thanks to the uncertain weather—and North American influences. When it rains or snows, discerning shoppers have several malls from which to choose.

Our favorite place for wandering and shopping in Oslo is **Aker Brygge ★★** (**© 22-83-26-80;** www.akerbrygge.no), a former shipbuilding yard that has been recycled as a postmodern complex of steel-and-glass buildings. In all, there are nearly 65 shops here, most of them upmarket fashion boutiques. There are also 40 restaurants, along with pubs, movie houses, and theaters. When it's raining, duck into the indoor shopping mall. Even if you don't buy anything, Aker Brygge makes for a great people-watching experience. The location is right on the harborfront, across from the Tourist Information Center at Vestbanen.

Eger Karl Johan ★★★, Egertorget (www.egerkarljohan.no), is located at the center of Karl Johans Gate. It is a brand-new shopping center with a large number of upscale shops offering both men's and women's clothing and accessories. It holds Norway's largest collection of exclusive brands under one roof.

Paléet ★★, Karl Johans Gate 37–43 (**© 22-41-26-30;** www.paleet.no), is set on Oslo's most central and most opulent shopping street. The weatherproof complex consists of 45 different shops and boutiques, all of them relatively upscale and flooded with light from skylights. You can purchase candles, incense, sweaters, art, housewares, cosmetics—you name it. Thirteen different restaurants, including burger and beer joints and one serving Indian food, refuel weary shoppers. You can also stop to admire a bronze statue of skating great (and former movie star) Sonja Henie.

Oslo City ★, Stenersgate 1 (**© 81-54-40-33;** www.oslocity.no), opposite Oslo Central station, is the biggest shopping center in Norway—loaded with shops and restaurants, though they are not quite as upscale as those in the previous two malls. Also near Oslo Central station, **Galleri Oslo,** at Vaterland, has been called Europe's longest indoor shopping street. Businesses are open daily, including Sunday, until midnight. A walkway connects Galleri Oslo to Oslo Central station.

Shopping A to Z

ANTIQUES

Blomqvist Kunsthandel ★★ Built as an auction house by its original owners in 1870, this place is full of history and style. Its two large rooms have glass ceilings, creating tons of natural light. Inside you'll find either one of their six annual auctions or one of their many Norwegian art exhibitions. In 1918, a gallery show released the full collection of an artist by the name of Edvard Munch. His prints and canvasses can still be seen here during temporary exhibitions. While this venue acts as an auction house, items up for bid include antiques ranging from fine jewelry and paintings to furniture and sculpture. Tordenskiolds 5. ✆ **22-70-87-70.** www.blomqvist.no. T-banen: Nationaltheatret.

ARTS & CRAFTS

Bærums Verk ★ 🎁 For a unique adventure, head out of town to a restored ironworks site dating from 1610. Here you'll find some 55 different shops selling handicrafts and other items including jewelry and woolens, plus exhibitions and six restaurants. If time remains, visit the ironworks museum on-site and see a smelting production dating from the 17th century. Verksgata 15, Bærum Verk. ✆ **67-13-00-18.** www.baerumsverk.no. Bus: 143 or 153.

Kunstnernes Hus ★★ This is the best place to see and to purchase the latest in cutting-edge Norwegian art. This is an artist-run exhibition hall for contemporary art that first opened in 1930 and since that time has been one of the country's major showcases for avant-garde national art. On the ground floor are two well-lit galleries and a reception area, and on the floor above are two more sky-lit galleries. Admission is NOK50 for adults and NOK25 for students and for children ages 7 to 17. Children 6 and under go in free. Hours are Tuesday and Wednesday 11am to 4pm, Thursday and Friday 11am to 6pm, and Saturday and Sunday noon to 6pm. Wergelandsveien 17. ✆ **22-85-34-10.** www.kunstnerneshus.no. T-banen: Sentrum.

Norway Designs ★★★ This is the only store in Norway that came into being as the result of a crafts exhibit. Shortly before it was established in 1957, an exposition of Norwegian crafts went to Chicago and New York, and it attracted a lot of attention. The upscale merchandise here—crystal, pewter, jewelry, and knitwear—emerged from the innovative designs of that exposition. Stortingsgaten 28. ✆ **23-11-45-10.** www.norwaydesigns.no. Tram: 2, 8, or 9.

Pur Norsk ★★ Since the minds behind cutting-edge design house Norway Says parted ways last summer, the downtown boutique of Pur Norsk is now the best place in the country to get your Nordic design fix. They sell innovative Norwegian-designed housewares, including tumblers, wine glasses, kitchenware, and furniture items—little of which you're likely to have encountered before. You can also pick up many Norway Says classics here—they're soon to become collectors' items. Thereses-gate 14. ✆ **22-46-40-45.** www.purnorsk.no. Tram: 18 or 19 to Stensgaten.

BOOKS

Bjorn Ringstrøms Antikvariat ★ One of the largest bookstores in Oslo houses a wide selection of Norwegian and Norwegian-American authors. They are also deeply rooted in books pertaining to Norwegian history and politics. A wide range of collectibles can also be found, ranging from antique books and color plates to records and maps. This century-old structure lies directly across the street from the Museum of Applied Art. Sad to report, those days when you could walk in and buy an original edition of Ibsen's plays for $10 have gone with the wind. Ullevalsvn 1. ✆ **22-20-78-05.** T-banen: Stortinget.

Damms Antikvariat ★★ This is the oldest antiquarian bookstore in all of Norway, in business since 1843. This warm and friendly place is full of history and intrigue, offering a wonderful selection of fiction and travel books. Although they focus mainly on Norwegian titles, you may come across a first edition of a Hemingway or Steinbeck novel. Among some of the rarer treasures, you'll find a page from the *Catholicon*, the first book ever printed with nonreligious subject matter—though this is not for sale. Akersg 2. ✆ **22-41-04-02.** www.damms.no. T-banen: Stortinget.

Tanum Karl Johan ★ This fine bookstore in the center of town is the largest and most comprehensive in Oslo. It offers a vast selection, including many English titles. Karl Johans Gate 37–41. ✆ **22-41-11-00.** www.tanumbokhandel.no. T-banen: Stortinget.

DELI

Fenaknoken ★ This is the most famous deli in Oslo. Quality, not quantity, is their self-described motto, and they do live up to their words. You'll find everything you need to create the perfect outdoor meal. Cured and smoked meats from all over Europe hang on its walls, along with homemade jams and jellies on their shelves, a wide array of sharp and mild cheeses, and, as they claim, the best **smoked salmon ★★★** in the world, although I don't agree with Sean Lennon, who claimed that it is "better than world peace." A specialty of the house is *fenalnlaar,* cured and seasoned sheep's meat. The only beverage is beer, which is supplied by a local brewery. For your actual picnic, I suggest you take your food to one of the beaches, either **Huk** on the Bygdøy Peninsula (p. 154) or **Hovedøya** (p. 154). Tordenskiolds 7. ✆ **22-42-34-57.** www.fenaknoken.no. T-banen: Nationaltheatret.

DEPARTMENT STORES

GlasMagasinet ★ Claiming that smaller boutiques tend to charge more, locals usually head for this big department store, which specializes in unusual home and kitchen accessories. Since 1739, this has been a leading outlet for knitwear, pewter, traditional rose-painting, and crystal. Today there are more than two dozen fashion shops alone, and **Hadeland Glassverk ★★★** is the largest outlet in Norway for glass goods. You can also find a moderately priced coffee shop and a fairly decent restaurant. Stortorvet 9. ✆ **22-42-53-05.** www.glasmagasinet.no. T-banen: Stortinget. Tram: 11 or 17.

Steen & Strøm ★★ The largest department store in Norway, Steen & Strøm specializes in Nordic items, especially for the outdoors. Look for hand-knit sweaters and caps, hand-painted wooden dishes reflecting traditional Norwegian art, and pewter dinner plates made from old molds. There's a souvenir shop on the ground floor. Kongensgate 23. ✆ **22-00-40-00.** www.steenstrom.com. T-banen: Stortinget.

FASHION

For Everyone

H&M This large worldwide chain of stores is very well known for selling fashionable goods at reasonable prices. They carry everything from children's apparel to trendy clothing for men and women. Also on the menu are accessories, including a large selection of handbags and belts. Stenersgate 1 (Oslo City Shopping Center). ✆ **23-15-99-00.** T-banen: Jernbanetorget.

For Men

Peak Performance ★★ This store is the number one choice for the outdoorsman who seeks the most stylish performance clothing. There is a tremendous selection of jackets, shirts, and accessories—their numerous styles and colors of Gore-Tex and fleece items are a real draw. Bogstadsvn 13. ✆ **22-96-00-91.** www.peakperformance.com. T-banen: Majorstuen.

For Women

MA Heavy on Norwegian designers, this fashion boutique also offers some of the best in Italian, Australian, and Belgian designs. Shoes and other accessories are plentiful, too. Prices range from obscene to reasonable. Hegdehaugsvn 27. ✆ **22-60-72-90.** Tram: 15.

Oleana ★ This shop carries the award-winning designs of Solveig Hisdahl. Clothing items are made mainly of wool and silk and include elegant knitwear, skirts, cardigans, and shawls. Other items feature jewelry and silk scarves from some of the top Norwegian designers. Michelle Obama purchased four shift dresses while here in 2009. Stortingsgaten 8. ✆ **22-33-31-63.** www.oleana.no. T-banen: Nationaltheatret.

Ove Harder Finseth ★★ This unique clothing store stars the painstaking and laborious productions of designer Ove Finseth. Each one-of-a-kind dress or gown is full of color (no black or gray), intricately detailed, and wonderfully ornate. The client list is quite impressive. Even the princess of Norway had her wedding gown designed here. Custom-made jewelry, bags, and hats are also sold. Pilius Plass 3. ✆ **22-37-76-20.** T-banen: Girneanetorgen.

Soul From Milan to Paris, this store keeps on top of the ever-changing fashion industry. The selection will meet all of your high-fashion needs, from bags by Prada to shoes by D&G. Bygdøy Allé 28. ✆ **22-55-00-13.** Bus: 30, 31, or 32.

FOLK COSTUMES

Heimen Husflid ★★ This leading purveyor of modern and traditional Norwegian handicrafts and apparel carries antique, reproduction, and original regional and national folk costumes, known in Norwegian as *bunads*. More than three dozen different styles of *bunad* come from many different counties of Norway, both north and south. Cozy, hand-knit sweaters in traditional Norwegian patterns are a special item. Pewter and brass goods are first-rate. It's about a block from Karl Johans Gate. Rosenkrantzgate 8. ✆ **23-21-42-00.** www.heimen.net. T-banen: Stortinget. Tram: 7, 8, or 11.

FURNITURE

Rom for Ide ★★ This is one of those stores that never seems to follow trends but always ends up looking trendy. This furniture outlet, hidden away from the city's shopping streets, specializes in modern yet classic designs. The contemporary and sleek look is the product of Norway's best and brightest new designers. Aside from the furniture, the Norwegian arts and crafts here are also a great buy. Jacob Aallsgate 54. ✆ **22-59-81-17.** www.romforide.com. T-banen: Majorstuen.

Tannum ★ 🎁 The furniture sold here is contemporary and stylish. The outlet, which has been in business for 60 years, still purveys the latest in modern furnishings. Tons of glass-and-steel accents on clean and good-looking pieces are imported from Italy, Germany, Sweden, Denmark, Holland—basically everywhere but Norway. Karl Johans Gate 37. ✆ **22-41-11-00.** www.tannum.no. T-banen: Stortinget.

JEWELRY, ENAMELWARE, PEWTER & SILVER

David-Andersen ★★★ Founded in 1876, this outstanding jeweler sells **enameled demitasse spoons** ★ and sterling silver bracelets with enamel. They're available in many stunning colors, such as turquoise and dark blue. Multicolored butterfly pins are also popular in gold-plated sterling silver with enamel. David-Andersen's collection of **Saga silver** ★★ was inspired by Norwegian folklore and Viking designs, combined with the pristine beauty of today's design. The store also offers an exquisite collection of pewter items. Other branches are located in Aker Brygge and on Bogstadveien. Karl Johans Gate 20. ✆ **24-14-88-00.** www.david-andersen.no. T-banen: Stortinget.

Esaias Solberg ★ 🎁 Opened in 1849 and long beloved by Oslovians, this is the largest and oldest venue for antique and second-hand gold and silver in Oslo. Brands of watches sold here include Rolex and Patek Philippe, as well as countless others. They also sell diamond-studded gold and silver necklaces, brooches, and earrings. Outside of jewelry, they also offer some wonderful antique coffee sets, trays, and goblets. The owner of this place has a simple motto: "Antique jewelry is no more expensive than modern jewelry, and any second-hand jewelry sells at half of what it originally cost." Kirkeresten. ✆ **22-86-24-80.** www.esaias.no. T-banen: Jernbanetorget.

Heyerdahl ★ Want to outfit yourself like a Viking chieftain or bejewel yourself like an ancient queen? Between the City Hall and Karl Johans Gate, this store offers an intriguing selection of silver and gold Viking jewelry. There are articles in pewter and other materials, including Viking vessels, drinking horns, and cheese slicers. The store also has an array of woodcarvings depicting trolls, as well as one of Oslo's largest collections of gold and silver jewelry. Roald Amundsens Gate 6. ✆ **22-41-59-18.** www.heyerdahl.no. T-banen: Nationaltheatret.

MUSIC

Los Lobos Straight out of 1950s' Hawaii, this independent music store caters to all genres and styles of music outside of the mainstream. Aside from music ranging from blues to techno, you'll find cigarette cases, Hawaiian and bowling shirts, tons of denim, belt buckles, snakeskin boots, and much more. Don't expect to find the Top 40 here; this place is for the more alternative music listener. Thorvald Meyers Gate 30. ✆ **22-38-24-40.** www.loslobos.no. Tram: 11 or 12 (to Olaf Ryes).

Norsk Musikforlag This centrally located store's selection of CDs, records, and cassette tapes is the best in Oslo. Kirkergata 30. ✆ **23-60-20-10.** www.norskmusikkforlag.no. T-banen: Stortinget.

PERFUME

Gimle Parfymeri This spacious perfumery is filled with the best in perfume and skin-care items. All employees are trained makeup artists who offer skilled applications and skin-care consultations. They also carry an array of clothing and accessories that are sold exclusively at this store. Bygdøy Allé 39. ✆ **22-44-61-42.** www.parfymeri.no. T-banen: Majorstuen.

SWEATERS

Oslo Sweater Shop Some 5,000 handcrafted sweaters are in stock here, close to the Royal Palace. Try them on before you buy. In theory, at least, you can tell the origin of a Norwegian sweater by its pattern and design, but with the growth in machine-made sweaters and the increased sophistication of Norwegian knitwear, the distinction is becoming blurred. Here, as in virtually every other sweater shop in Oslo, only about 10% of the sweaters are handmade—the remainder are high-quality and first-rate but most likely were crafted on an electric knitting machine. Sweaters start at around NOK1,000, rising to several thousands of kroner. Other items include necklaces, pewterware, souvenirs, and Norway-inspired trinkets. Next to the Clarion Hotel Royal Christiania, Biskop Gunnerus Gate 3. ✆ **22-42-42-25.** www.oslosweatershop.com. Bus: 30, 31, or 41.

OSLO AFTER DARK

Oslo has a bustling nightlife that thrives past midnight. The city boasts more than 100 night cafes, clubs, and restaurants, several dozen of which stay open until 4am.

Oslo is also a favorite destination for international performing artists in classical, pop, rock, and jazz music. Fall and winter are the seasons for cabaret, theater, and concerts. There are four cabarets and nine theater stages throughout the city.

For movie lovers, Oslo has a fair amount to offer as well. The city has one of the most extensive selections in Europe, with 30 screens and five large film complexes. Films are shown in their original languages, with subtitles.

The Entertainment Scene

The best way to find out what's happening is to pick up a copy of ***What's On in Oslo,*** from the tourist office detailing concerts and theaters and other useful information. Oslo doesn't have agents who specialize in discount tickets, but it does have an exceptional number of free events. *What's On in Oslo* lists free happenings as well as the latest exhibits at art galleries, which make for good early evening destinations.

The world-famous **Oslo Philharmonic** performs regularly under the leadership of Mariss Janson at the Oslo Konserthus. There are no Oslo performances between June 20 and the middle of August.

If you visit Oslo in the winter season, you might be able to see its thriving opera and ballet company, **Den Norske Opera.** Plays given at the **Nationaltheatret** (where plays by Ibsen are regularly featured) are in Norwegian, so those who know the language should enjoy hearing the original versions of his plays.

The Performing Arts

CLASSICAL MUSIC

Oslo Konserthus ★★★ Two blocks from the Nationaltheatret, this is the home of the widely acclaimed Oslo Philharmonic. Performances are given fall to spring, on Thursday and Friday. Guest companies from around the world often appear on other nights. The hall is closed from June 20 until mid-August, except for occasional performances by folkloric groups. The box office is open Monday through Friday 11am to 5pm and Saturday 11am to 2pm. Munkedamsveien 14. ✆ **23-11-31-11.** www.oslokonserthus.no. Tickets NOK200–NOK800. T-banen: Stortinget.

OPERA & DANCE

Den Norske Opera & Ballet ★★★ One of the greatest cultural advancements in Norway occurred in the spring of 2008 when this long-awaited opera house opened. Set smack on the Oslofjord waterfront, this graceful Italian marble building, which resembles a glacier slipping its way into the fjord, won the 2009 Mies van der Rohe award for contemporary architecture. It's the new home of the finest opera and ballet troupes in Norway. The stunning, very modern structure cost $840 million. The horseshoe-shaped main auditorium seats 1,369, and stage and theater technology are state-of-the-art. Den Norske plans 300 performances a year. The "Song of Norway" never was better. The box office is open Monday to Friday from 10am to 8pm, Saturday from 11am to 6pm. Kirsten Flagstads Plass 1, in Bjørvika. © **21-42-21-00.** www.operaen.no. Tickets NOK180–NOK450 except for galas. Take any tram heading toward the Central Station.

THEATER

Nationaltheatret (National Theater) ★★★ This theater at the upper end of the Students' Grove opens in August, so it may be of interest to off-season drama lovers who want to hear original versions of Ibsen and Bjørnson. Avant-garde productions go up at the **Amfiscenen,** in the same building. There are no performances in July and August. Guest companies often perform plays in English. The box office is open Monday through Friday from 9:30am to 6pm and Saturday 11am to 6pm. Johanne Dybwads Plass 1. © **81-50-08-11.** www.nationaltheatret.no. Tickets NOK150–NOK400 adults, NOK85–NOK170 students and seniors. T-banen: Nationaltheatret. Tram: 12, 13, or 19.

Summer Cultural Entertainment

Det Norske Folkloreshowet (Norwegian Evening) performs from July to August at the Norwegian Folk Museum, Museumsveien 10 (© **22-12-37-00** for reservations). The performances are on Tuesday, Wednesday, Friday, and Saturday at 5:30pm. Tickets cost NOK250 for adults, NOK50 for children (T-banen: Stortinget).

The ensemble at the **Norwegian Folk Museum,** on Bygdøy, often presents folk-dance performances at the open-air theater in the summer. See *What's On in Oslo* for details. Most shows are given on Sunday afternoon. Admission to the museum includes admission to the dance performance. Take the ferry from Pier 3 near the Rådhuset (City Hall).

Special & Free Events

Oslo has many free events, including summer jazz concerts at the Nationaltheatret. In front of the theater, along the Students' Grove, you'll see street entertainers, including singers, clowns, musicians, and jugglers.

Concerts are presented in the chapel of **Akershus Castle & Fortress** (p. 138)**,** Akershus Command, on Sunday at 2pm. During the summer, promenade music, parades, drill marches, exhibits, and theatrical performances are also presented in the castle grounds.

In August, the **Oslo Kammermusikfestival** (**Chamber Music Festival**) presents concerts by Norwegian and foreign musicians at Akershus Castle & Fortress. For more information, visit www.oslokammermusikkfestival.no.

The **Oslo Jazz Festival** (www.oslojazz.no), also in August, includes not only old-time jazz but also classical concerts, opera, and ballet performances.

Films

American and British films are shown in English with Norwegian subtitles. Tickets are sold for specific performances only, and often for specific seats. Many theaters have showings nightly at 5, 7, and 9pm, but really big films are usually shown only once an evening, generally at 7:30pm.

Because of the city's long winter nights, filmgoing is big business in Oslo. Two of the city's biggest theaters are the **Saga kino,** Stortingsgata 28 (✆ **82-05-00-01;** www.oslokino.no/kinofakta/saga/; T-banen: Nationaltheatret), and the **Klingenberg kino,** Olav V's Gate 4 (✆ **82-05-00-01;** www.oslokino.no/kinofakta/klingenberg/; T-banen: Nationaltheatret). Most tickets cost between NOK90 and NOK130 for adults and are half-price for children. For matinees (usually on Mon and Thurs) the cost is reduced to NOK70 for adults and half-price for children.

The Club & Music Scene

DANCE CLUBS & DISCOS

There are standard age requirements to enter clubs and bars in Oslo and throughout Norway. For those taverns or other places holding a liquor license only for beer and wine, a visitor must be 18 years old or older. For establishments serving hard liquor, the minimum age is 20. In some reviews, varying age requirements are cited where appropriate.

Smuget ★ This is the most talked-about nightlife emporium in Oslo, with long lines of the best and brightest, especially on weekends. It's behind the Grand Hotel in a 19th-century building that was once a district post office. There's an active dance floor with disco music and a stage where live bands (sometimes two a night on weekends) perform. The clientele—mostly ages 20 to 30—includes artists, writers, rock stars, and a cross-section of the capital's night owls. The complex is open Monday through Saturday nights. A restaurant serves a range of international cuisines from 11am to 3am, live music plays from 10pm to 3am, and there's disco music from 10pm till very late. Half-liters of beer cost NOK45; main courses run from NOK135 to NOK249. Rosenkrantzgate 22. ✆ **22-42-52-62.** www.smuget.no (in Norwegian). Cover NOK80–NOK120. T-banen: Stortinget.

JAZZ & ROCK

Blå ★ This is the leading jazz club in Oslo. Dark and industrial, with lots of wrought iron and mellow lighting, this place books some of the best jazz acts in the world. The crowd is a mix of young and old, dressed in casual but sophisticated attire. The weeknights focus strictly on jazz, with the weekend providing more of a disco atmosphere, recruiting DJs from all over the world to spin the best in techno and house. It's open nightly 11am to midnight. Brenneriveien 9C. ✆ **98-25-63-86.** www.blaaoslo.no (in Norwegian). Cover NOK30–NOK110, depending on the act. Tram: 11, 12, or 13.

Café Mono If you're looking for a relatively underfinanced punk-rock nightclub with beer-stained walls and a decor that could withstand, undisturbed, an invasion from a foreign army, this is it. It's a haven for the alternative, boozy, and occasionally alienated youth culture of Oslo. There's recorded music virtually all the time, a changing roster of live bands (many of them from the U.S.) appearing every Sunday to Thursday beginning around 10:30pm, and recorded house and garage-style dance music every Friday and Saturday. Whenever there's live music, the cover varies from NOK10 to NOK800, with better-known groups charging a good deal more; otherwise, it's free. It's open Monday to Saturday 3pm to 3:30am. Pløensgate 4. ✆ **22-41-41-66.** www.cafemono.no (in Norwegian). T-banen: Stortinget.

Herr Nilsen ★ This is one of the most congenial spots in Oslo and a personal favorite, in that it hosts some of the top jazz artists in Europe—and America, too. Overlooking the courthouse square, it's the perfect place to while away a snowy

Oslo After Dark

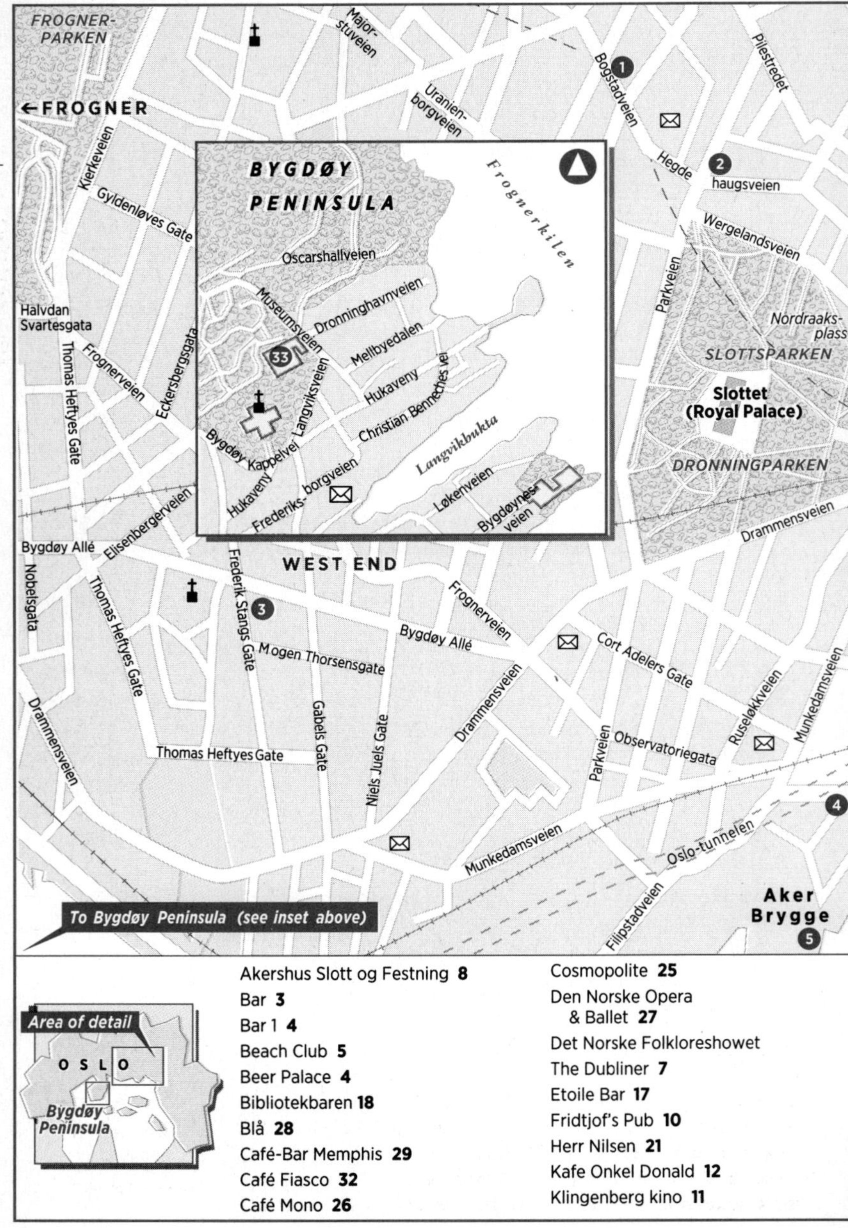

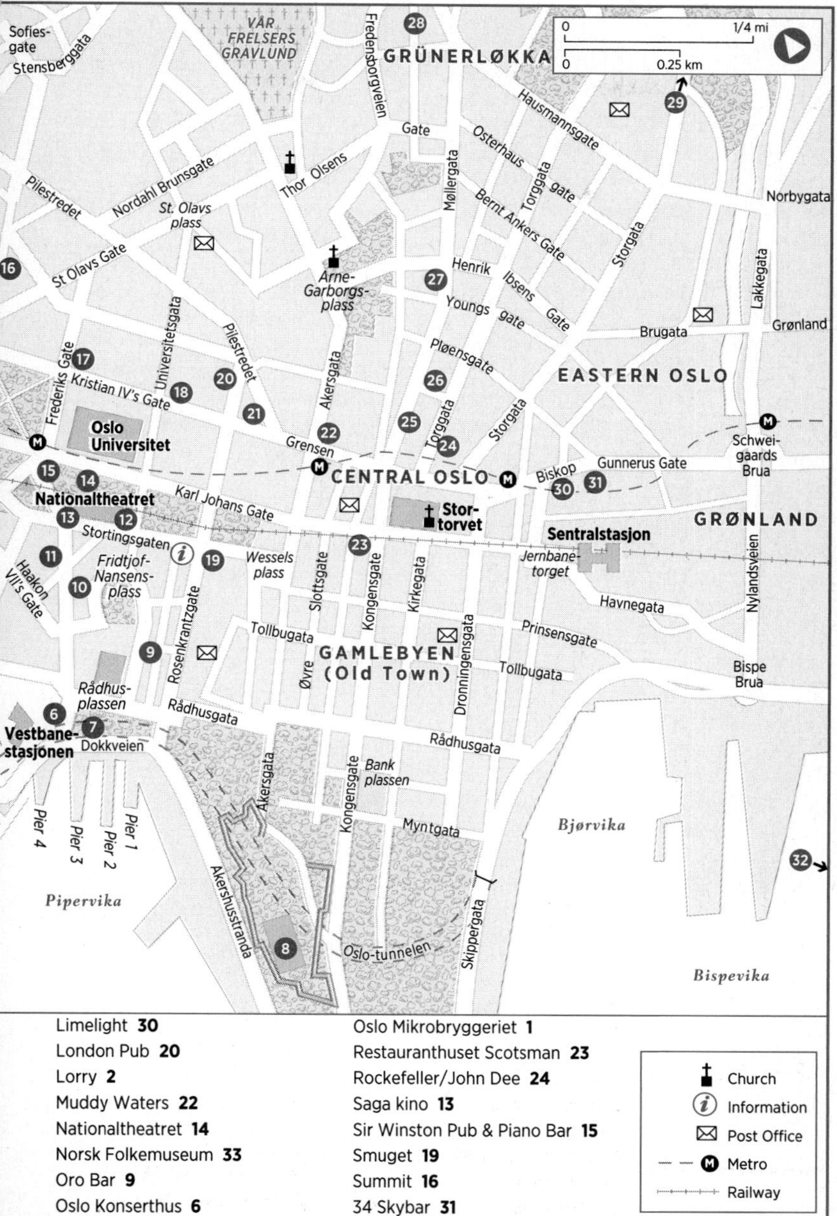

Limelight **30**
London Pub **20**
Lorry **2**
Muddy Waters **22**
Nationaltheatret **14**
Norsk Folkemuseum **33**
Oro Bar **9**
Oslo Konserthus **6**
Oslo Mikrobryggeriet **1**
Restauranthuset Scotsman **23**
Rockefeller/John Dee **24**
Saga kino **13**
Sir Winston Pub & Piano Bar **15**
Smuget **19**
Summit **16**
34 Skybar **31**

evening. The Dixieland music played here evokes New Orleans. It's open Monday to Saturday 2pm to 3am, Sunday 3pm to 3am. C. J. Hambros Place 5. ✆ **22-33-54-05.** www.herrnilsen.no (in Norwegian). Cover NOK100–NOK200. T-banen: Stortinget.

Muddy Waters ★ If you long for blues music, make your way to this club, with its two fully equipped stages. At least one live band plays almost every night, often with big names, both local and international. This is not necessarily a club for moppets, as a slightly older crowd (at least those over 30) flocks here. Beer costs NOK55. It's open daily 2pm to 3am. Grensen 13. ✆ **22-40-33-70.** www.muddywaters.no. Cover Fri–Sat only, usually NOK90. T-banen: Sentrum.

Rockefeller/John Dee With a capacity of 1,200 patrons, this concert hall and club is one of the largest establishments of its kind in Oslo. It's one floor above street level in a 1910 building, formerly a public bath. Live concerts feature everything from reggae to rock to jazz. When no concert is scheduled, films are shown on a wide screen. Simple foods, such as pasta and sandwiches, are available in the cafe. Most of the crowd is in the 18-to-40 age bracket. It's usually open Sunday to Thursday from 8pm to 2:30am, and Friday and Saturday from 9pm to 3:30am. Showtime is about an hour after the doors open. Torggata 16. ✆ **22-20-32-32.** www.rockefeller.no/english.html. Most tickets NOK100–NOK250, though some can be as much as double this price, depending on the act. T-banen: Stortinget.

NIGHTCLUBS

Cosmopolite This lively international club plays music from all over the world, from Lapland to Africa. A young crowd in their 20s and early 30s flocks here to hear folk music, tango from Argentina, jazz, funk, or whatever. Latin American salsa is often featured, and there's a big dance floor. It's open nightly 8pm to 3am. Møllergata 26. ✆ **22-11-33-08.** www.cosmopolite.no (in Norwegian). Cover generally NOK150. T-banen: Jernbanetorget.

The Dubliner ★ This cozy and rustic bar is one of the oldest Irish pubs in Oslo. Housed in a building dating from 1666, the Dubliner holds true to its traditional Irish ancestry once you're inside. The crowd here does vary in age from 20 to 50 but consists mostly of Oslo's Irish and English communities. It offers a typical pub-grub type of menu and plenty of Irish beers on tap. On Friday and Saturday nights, traditional and contemporary Irish music can always be heard. On Tuesday, they hold "jam sessions," where local musicians can bring their instruments and play at being rock stars for the night. It's open Sunday and Monday noon to 1am, Tuesday to Thursday noon to 2am, and Friday and Saturday noon to 3am. Rådhusgata 28. ✆ **22-33-70-05.** www.dubliner.no. Cover Fri–Sat only, NOK80. T-banen: Stortinget.

Restauranthuset Scotsman The huge, chaotic Scotsman offers several floors of entertainment. For a la carte dining, with an emphasis on beef, head to the cellar restaurant. For nightly live music and a colorful clientele, check out the English-style pub on the first floor. If dancing is your thing, you'll want to stop in the second-floor disco. For gamblers, the third floor features pool tables and off-track horse betting. The fourth floor is strictly for private parties. The fifth and sixth floors have a fully equipped fitness center to help you burn off your trip to the cellar. It's open daily 10am to 3am. Karl Johans Gate 17. ✆ **22-47-44-77.** T-banen: Nationaltheatret.

The Bar Scene

PUBS & BARS

Bar For a late afternoon drink, try this simply-named spot. Actually a slight misnomer, it comprises three intimate bars, as well as an Asian-inspired restaurant. It has become Oslo's hippest place for a drink since it opened in late 2009. Gregarious, gorgeous clientele come for both *vorspiel* (a pre-party drink) and *nachspiel* (a late-night after-party). Bygdøy Allé 18. ✆ **40-00-38-34.** www.baroslo.com. Tram: 12.

Bar 1 For the connoisseur of brandy, this small cognac-and-cigar bar is the ultimate. You'll find close to 300 different varieties of cognac, plus a selection of the finest whiskeys. Accompany your libation with one of their wide selection of Cuban and Dominican cigars. As you could imagine, you'll find a subdued yet sophisticated post-40 crowd here. It's open daily 4pm to 3:30am. Holmensgate 3. ✆ **22-83-00-02.** www.bar1.no. Tram: 22.

Beach Club This place embodies (and is actually modelled after) a classic American diner, adding plenty of Norwegian flair. Its large booths and tables are welcoming—and the burgers are great. There is a bar but not much of a social scene, mostly businessmen having drinks. Mellow, loungy music plays every night. It's open Tuesday to Friday 11am to midnight, Saturday noon to midnight. Aker Brygge. ✆ **22-83-83-82.** www.beachclub.no. T-banen: Nationaltheatret.

Beer Palace As you might guess from the name, beer is the main draw at this English-style pub attracting people aged 20 to 30 who consider themselves *ølkjennere* (beer aficionados). The atmosphere is intimate and cozy, with exposed brick walls and couches in the upstairs lounge. A dartboard and pool table provide excitement and entertainment on the first floor. Softly played rock 'n' roll completes the mood. It's open Monday to Thursday 1pm to 1:30am, Friday 1pm to 3am, and Saturday noon to 3am. Holmensgate 3. ✆ **22-83-71-55.** www.beerpalace.no (in Norwegian). Tram: 10 or 12.

Bibliotekbaren (Library Bar) In a lobby that evokes the Edwardian era, this is a perfect spot for people-watching—that is, middle-aged-people-watching. Sheltered behind racks of leather-bound books, which you can remove and read, you'll feel like you're in a well-furnished private club. There's live piano music at lunchtime, when you can choose from a selection of open-faced sandwiches for NOK60 to NOK100. It's open daily from 10am to 11:30pm; alcohol service starts at 1:30pm. A beer will cost you NOK59; mixed drinks begin at NOK98. In the Bristol Hotel, Kristian IV's Gate 7. ✆ **22-82-60-22.** T-banen: Stortinget.

Etoile Bar This elegant bar with a Far Eastern motif is attached to Norway's most famous hotel, the Grand. You might see members of Parliament from across the street. The "Star Bar" has views of historic Oslo. Business people from out of town mingle at night with a young, spirited Oslo crowd. To reach the bar, you take a special elevator at the right of the hotel entrance. Beers cost NOK67; stronger drinks run from NOK107. It's open Monday to Thursday 3pm to 1am, Friday and Saturday 3pm to 2am, Sunday 6pm to 2am. In the Grand Hotel, Karl Johans Gate 31. ✆ **23-21-20-00.** www.grand.no/en/. T-banen: Stortinget.

Fridtjof's Pub This Norwegian pub offers a cozy retreat for a late-night drink. It consists of a ground floor with deep red walls, comfortable sofas, and some tables and chairs. The mezzanine has much of the same, providing an unobstructed view of the crowd below whose ages range from 20 to 50. Both floors have interesting photos of polar expeditions, mainly because it's named after Fridtjof Nansen, the first Norwegian to successfully explore the North Pole. In summer, the party usually moves outside, where you can enjoy views of the harbor and City Hall directly across the street. It's open daily noon to 1am. Fridtjof Nansens Plass 7. ✆ **93-25-22-30.** www.fridtjof-pub.no (in Norwegian). T-banen: Nationaltheatret.

Limelight Steeped in the atmosphere of the theater, this fashionable bar is a favorite rendezvous for drinks before or after a show. It draws mainly a middle-aged crowd and is open Tuesday to Saturday 6pm to 1am (closed June 21 to Aug 11). Beer costs from NOK54 and mixed drinks cost NOK94 and up. In the Grand Hotel, Karl Johans Gate 31. ✆ **23-21-20-00.** www.grand.no/en/. T-banen: Stortinget.

Oro Bar This glamorous tapas bar, associated with the restaurant Oro, evokes the stylish and hip locales of warmer climates. An intensely fashionable crowd in their 30s and 40s—and in intensely expensive clothing—drops in for meals and people-watching. You can eat or just have a drink. Small sandwich plates start at NOK129. It's open Monday to Saturday 6pm to 2am. Tordenskiolds 6A (entrance on Kjeld Stubs Gate). ✆ **23-01-02-40.** www.ororestaurant.no. T-banen: Stortinget.

Oslo Mikrobryggeriet This small, English-style pub/micro-brewery attracts a mixed, 30-something crowd. Aside from some cognacs and whiskeys, offerings include six in-house beers, the most popular being Oslo Pils. With its cozy and warm atmosphere and good music, this brewery is sure to please. It's open daily 3pm to 1am. Bogstadvn 6. ✆ **22-56-97-76.** www.mikrobryggeriet.no (in Norwegian). T-banen: Majotsstuem.

Sir Winston Pub & Piano Bar In the style of a traditional English pub, this place has a cozy, friendly atmosphere with comfortable couches and laid-back lounge music. You'll find anyone here from slick businessmen sipping martinis to neighborhood college kids putting back a few pints while watching the game. Books and pictures of Sir Winston Churchill crowd the wall. An open fireplace provides warmth on cold Nordic nights. It's open Monday to Wednesday 11am to 1am, Thursday 11am to 2am, Friday and Saturday 11am to 3am, and Sunday noon to 1am. Karl Johans Gate 10. ✆ **22-41-14-41.** www.sir-winston.no (in Norwegian). T-banen: Jernbanetorget.

Summit ★ On the 21st floor of the Radisson BLU Scandinavia Hotel, this bar boasts one of the best crowds and one of the best views in town. However, it's mainly known for serving Oslo's best strawberry daiquiris and for its view of the city from the men's-room window. Frequented by businesspeople, and almost everyone else between the ages of 30 and 60, the lively bar is also popular with out-of-towners. It's open Monday to Thursday 4pm to 1am, Friday and Saturday 4pm to 2am. Holbergsgate 30. ✆ **23-29-30-00.** www.radissonblu.com/scandinaviahotel-oslo/. T-banen: Nationaltheatret.

34 Skybar ★ On the top floor (34th floor) of the Radisson BLU Plaza Hotel, this bar is known as the most vertigo-inducing and panoramic in Oslo. And at 100m (330 ft.) above the ground, it's also Northern Europe's highest. In the ultramodern interior, surrounded by a glass ceiling and walls, you'll find Oslo's young, professional elite in their 20s, 30s, and 40s sipping on sophisticated cocktails. The view and people-watching are worth the trip. It's open Monday to Thursday 4pm to 1am, Friday and Saturday 4pm to 1:30am. Sonja Henie Plass 3. ✆ **22-05-80-00.** www.radissonblu.com/plazahotel-oslo. T-banen: Sentralstasjon.

CAFES

Café-Bar Memphis This is a hip, industrial-looking bar with a fondness for such U.S.-derived kitsch as Elvis memorabilia and late, late drunken nights that feature Jack Daniel's and beer. There's a limited roster of menu items (seafood pastas, scrambled eggs with ham or bacon and toast), but most of the clients come to sip well-priced cocktails with friends and colleagues. It's open Monday to Thursday 11am to 1am, and Friday and Saturday 11am to 3am. Thorvald Meyers Gate 63. © **22-04-12-75.** Tram: 11, 12, 13, or 30.

Café Fiasco Although the owners established this cafe to cater to commuters, the business goes way beyond just serving a fast glass of beer to travelers waiting for their trains. It's oddly located on a sloping, pedestrian ramp that interconnects the bus and railway stations, with views of the surrounding skyscrapers. Inside you'll find a welcome jolt of humanity and a sense of multiculturalism. Reggae, Soca, and hip-hop music blare at a sometimes scruffily dressed crowd that's far from bourgeois. Coffee, depending on what's in it, costs from NOK18 to NOK76; cocktails begin at NOK80. Late at night, long after the commuter trade has ended, the place and surrounding pedestrian passageways become an aggressive singles scene. It's open Monday to Thursday 9am to 1am, Friday 9am to 3am, Saturday 11am to 3am, and Sunday noon to 1am. Schweigaardsgate 4. © **21-66-69-57.** www.fiasco.no (in Norwegian). T-banen: Jernbanetorget.

Kafe Onkel Donald Of the many bars and pubs that flourish after dark in Oslo, this is the most artfully designed (in this case, by well-known Norwegian architect Petter Abrahamsen in 2001). Its soaring interior spaces evoke the entranceway to a postmodern opera house, and a network of short staircases will take you from the surging energy of the glossy-looking main bar to a series of more intimate mezzanines. The house special cocktail is an Onkel Donald, a head-spinner combining vodka, peach liqueur, cranberry juice, and sour mash. It's open Monday to Wednesday 11am to midnight, Thursday to Saturday 11am to 3am, and Sunday noon to 2am. Universitesgata 26. © **23-35-63-10.** www.onkeldonald.no (in Norwegian). T-banen: Nationaltheatret.

Lorry This busy, suds-drenched cafe was established 120 years ago as a working-class bar. Since then, the surrounding neighborhood (virtually across the street from the park that flanks the Royal Palace) has zoomed upward in prestige and price. Now the cafe's low-slung, wood-sided building is tucked among villas. There's an outdoor terrace for warm-weather dining, but the heart and soul of the place is its Victorian, black-stained interior. Offerings include 130 kinds of beer (from NOK71), 12 of which are on tap. The menu consists of salads, sandwiches, and burgers, as well as larger dishes, priced at NOK98 to NOK189, but from around 10:30pm to closing, all everybody seems to do here is drink. It's open Monday to Saturday 11am to 3:30am, and Sunday noon to 1:30am. Parkveien 12. © **22-69-69-04.** www.lorry;no. Tram: 11.

GAY & LESBIAN BARS

This city of slightly under 600,000 residents has few gay bars. Pick up a copy of *Blick*, available at most newsstands within the central city. Otherwise, call the **Norwegian LGBT Association,** Valkyriegaten 15A (© **23-10-39-39,** Mon–Fri 9am–4pm). Alternatively, explore the website www.VisitGayOslo.no.

London Pub This is the most consistent and reliable gay pub in Oslo, with a relatively mature crowd of unpretentious gay men and—to a much lesser extent—women.

Set within the cellar of a building a few steps from the prestigious Bristol Hotel, it contains a battered-looking, beer hall–style trio of underground rooms with two bar areas and a pool table. During busy periods, usually late in the week, this place can be fun, convivial, and genuinely welcoming to newcomers from faraway places, though it's fairly quiet early in the week. It's open daily from 3pm to 3:30am. The attached disco, **London Club,** is upstairs and is a bit more animated and festive than its downstairs cousin. It's open daily 8pm to 3:30am, and occasionally has a cover charge of NOK40. C. J. Hambros Plass 5 (entrance on Rosenkrantzgate). ✆ **22-70-87-00.** www.londonpub.no. T-banen: Stortinget.

SIDE TRIPS FROM OSLO

7

The fjord towns within easy striking distance of Oslo are filled with history and rich in the lore of the Viking past of southern Norway. You can explore the east or west side of the Oslofjord. With time for only one, I suggest the historic east side, centering around Fredrikstad and Halden.

Stretching for 100km (about 60 miles), Oslofjord is Oslo's link to the open sea. Touring the fjord's western and eastern banks is richly rewarding. The eastern shore also has many beaches with fine sands frequented by Oslovians in summer, especially in July. Even then, however, the waters may be too cold for you if you come from hotter climes than Norway. The western side of the fjord was the site of several Viking settlements, and some of their remains or ruins can be seen today.

FREDRIKSTAD: NORWAY'S OLDEST FORTIFIED TOWN ★

96km (60 miles) S of Oslo; 34km (21 miles) S of Moss

If your busy schedule allows you to visit only one mellow old town along the Oslofjord, make it this one. Lying at the mouth of the Glomma River, Fredrikstad is Norway's oldest fortified town. Visitors come here mainly to see **Gamlebyen** (the Old Town)**,** one of the best preserved in eastern Norway.

King Fredrik II founded the town in 1567 as a trading post between the mainland of Europe and western Scandinavia. Its characteristic landmarks are the 1880 cathedral and the delicate, silver-arched Glomma Bridge, which stretches 824m (2,700 ft.) from end to end and rises 40m (130 ft.) over the water.

Essentials

GETTING THERE **Trains** from Oslo Central railway station depart for Fredrikstad about every 2 hours. The trip takes about 1 hour from central Oslo. Call ✆ **81-50-08-88** or visit www.nsb.no for rail information.

A frequent **bus** service operates daily from Oslo to Fredrikstad, the trip taking 1½ hours. Visit www.nor-way.no for information.

Motorists should take the E6 highway south from Oslo, toward Moss. Continue past Moss to the junction at Route 110, and follow the signs south to Fredrikstad.

VISITOR INFORMATION The **Fredrikstad Turistkontor** is at Torvgaten 59 (✆ **69-30-46-00;** www.opplevfredrikstad.com). It's open June 10 to September 4 Monday to Friday 9am to 5pm, Saturday to Sunday 11am to 4pm. The rest of the year, it's open Monday to Friday from 9am to 4:30pm. You can also rent bikes here.

SPECIAL EVENTS During the second week of July, the **Glomma Festival,** named for the town's river, takes place in Fredrikstad. Many Oslovians drive south to attend this 1-week program of events, highlighted by musical performances. Ritual "duels" are staged, along with sailing-ship exhibitions and regattas.

GETTING AROUND Across the river on the west is the modern industrial part of town; although a bridge links the areas, the best way to reach the Old Town is by ferry, which costs NOK10. The departure point is about four blocks from the Fredrikstad railway station, at Strandpromenaden. Follow the crowd out the main door of the station, turn left, and continue down to the bank of the river. The ferry operates every 15 minutes Monday to Friday 7am to 11pm, Saturday 7am to 1am, and Sunday 7:30am to midnight. You can also travel between the two areas by bus (no. 360 or 362).

To call a **taxi,** dial ✆ **02600** or 69-36-26-00. If the weather is fair, I recommend renting a **bicycle.** They're available at the tourist office (see above).

What to See & Do

Fredrikstad was founded as a marketplace at the mouth of the River Glomma. **Gamlebyen** (the **Old Town**) ★ became a fortress in 1663 and continued in that role until 1903, boasting some 200 guns in its heyday. It still serves as a military camp and is the best-preserved fortress town in Scandinavia, but the moats and embankments make for an evocative walk.

The main guardroom and the old prison contain part of the **Fredrikstad Museum,** Tøihusgata 41 (✆ **69-11-56-50**). At the southwestern end of Gamlebyen is a section of the museum in a former guardhouse from 1731 (it was militarily active until 2002). Inside is a model of the Old Town and a collection of artifacts, both civilian and military, collected by city fathers over a span of 300 years. It's open Tuesday to Friday from noon to 3:30pm, Saturday and Sunday 11am to 4pm (closed Oct to Apr). Admission is NOK50 for adults, NOK20 for children.

Isegran: Famous in Norse Sagas

If you like to read Norse sagas, visit the ruins of the 13th-century fortress Isegran on an island directly west of Gamlebyen. This once-mighty fortress stood as a fortification against the advancing Swedish armies in the mid-1600s. There are various exhibitions here in the summer. Isegran is only 400m (¼ mile) west of the Old Town, but there is no ferry link. You have to drive south on Route 108 until you see the signposted turnoff. You can also take bus no. 365 (NOK25) from the bus station, or take a no. 15. Alternatively, you can take the red city ferry (NOK10) from Blomstertorvet by the river.

Side Trips from Oslo

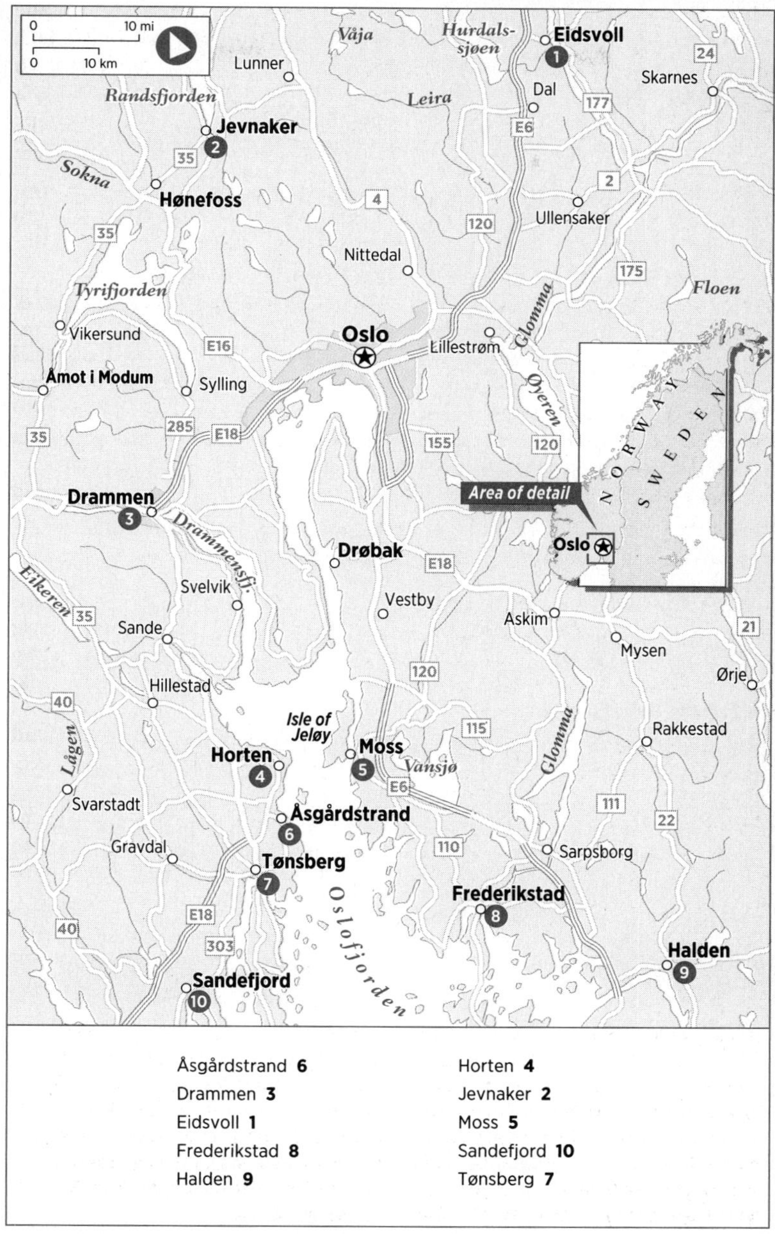

The cathedral of Fredrikstad, **Fredrikstad Domskirke,** Ferjestedsveien (✆ **69-30-02-80**), was constructed in 1860 in a Flamboyant Gothic revival style. Its most notable features are its stained-glass windows by Emanuel Vigeland, the younger and lesser-known brother of Norway's most famous sculptor, Gustav Vigeland. The church was also decorated by other leading Norwegian artists. The Domkirke lies on the western bank of the Glomma and opens onto a small park. It is open Tuesday to Friday 11am to 3pm, and admission is free.

Outside the gates of the Old Town stands what remains of **Kongsten Festning,** the fortress of Fredrikstad, which was constructed on Galgeberget Gallows Hill and used by the townspeople as an execution site for criminals. When the Swedes took over the site in 1677, they fortified the stronghold with 20 cannons, underground chambers, passages, and a strong arsenal. Today you can amble among the embankments, walls, stockades, and turrets. It is always open and charges no admission. To reach it, walk 15 minutes beyond the Gamlebyen drawbridge, turning off Tornesveien at the Fredrikstad Motell & Camping.

Shopping

Since Fredrikstad's heyday as a trading port and merchant base, the Old Town has attracted craftspeople and artisans, many of whom create their wares in historic houses and barns. Many of these glassblowers, ceramic artists, and silversmiths sell their products at local shops.

Glasshytta This rustic shop acts as a retail store and glassblowing studio and its merchandise is sold all over the country. The artisans specialize in everything glass, including stemware and carafes, plates, bowls, and paperweights. You can also specify what you need and watch your custom creation come to life in the skilled hands of a local craftsperson. The glass comes in a wide array of colors. They blow glass until 3pm; shop hours are daily 11am to 4pm. Torsnesvn 1. ✆ **69-32-28-12.** Bus: 541.

Where to Stay

Rica City Hotel ★ This is no mere hotel, but rather the lifeblood of town entertainment. Situated in the town center near the railway station, this stylish and modern hotel offers well-appointed accommodations. All rooms are well-furnished, with a good number of amenities and tidy bathrooms. The hotel also has two good restaurants, one serving an a la carte international menu, the other offering lighter pizza-and-burger fare.

Nygard 44-46, N-1600 Fredrikstad. ✆ **69-38-56-00.** www.ricacityhotel.no. 110 units. NOK1,095–NOK1,495 double. AE, DC, MC, V. Parking NOK150. Bus: 31. **Amenities:** 3 restaurants; 4 bars; nightclub; sauna; rooms for those with limited mobility. *In room:* TV, Wi-Fi (in most), minibar (in some), hair dryer (in some).

Victoria Hotel ★ Established in 1883 near the cathedral park, this Art Nouveau structure is the town's oldest hotel. I prefer its antique style and homey comfort over the Rica City Hotel (see above). Like its competitor, the Victoria lies in the heart of town and affords wonderful views of the grounds of the Fredrikstad cathedral. Many renovations have resulted in the welcoming, cozy hotel you'll find today. Each comfortable guest room is well furnished in classic English style, and all of them contain neatly kept bathrooms.

Turngaten 3, N-1600 Fredrikstad. ✆ **69-38-58-00.** www.hotelvictoria.no. 65 units. NOK950–NOK1,320 double. Rates include buffet breakfast. AE, DC, MC, V. Parking NOK150. Bus: 31. **Amenities:** Restaurant; bar. *In room:* TV, Wi-Fi, hair dryer.

Where to Dine

Engelsviken Brygge ★ 🎁 SEAFOOD This hideaway restaurant is set at the edge of the crescent-shaped bay that's dominated by the fishing hamlet of Engelsviken, population about 400 hardy souls. Despite its remote locale, it's sought out for its atmosphere by diners from as far away as Oslo. It originated a century ago as a simple fisherman's cottage, but in the mid-1990s its owners added sprawling windows overlooking the sea, enlarged its premises to include a modern kitchen, repainted the place in bright red, and came up with a number of cracking fish dishes that have since become legendary. One good example is the creamy fish soup loaded with chunks of fish and shellfish; you can order this excellent dish as a starter or main course. Other offerings include grilled Atlantic halibut with a Béarnaise sauce; a risotto-inspired shrimp and oyster rice; a "symphony" platter loaded high with filet of salmon, catfish, and sea devil; and grilled, poached, or fried versions of most of the fresh local fish. For anyone not particularly interested in seafood, there's also a juicy version of fried beefsteak studded with chunks of garlic and served with a creamy peppercorn sauce.

Engelsvikveien 6, in the hamlet of Engelsviken, 15km (9¼ miles) northwest of Fredrikstad. ✆ **69-35-18-40.** www.engelsvikenbrygge.no. Reservations recommended. Main courses NOK125–NOK295. AE, DC, MC, V. Mon–Thurs 5–9pm; Fri 5–9:30pm; Sat 1–9:30pm; Sun 1–8pm. From Fredrikstad, follow the signs to Oslo for 4.8km (3 miles), & then turn left onto the road signposted ENGELSVIKEN.

Major-Stuen ☺ INTERNATIONAL Sizzling pizzas and fresh fish platters draw both locals and visitors to this 18th-century house at the edge of the Old Town. Its warm-weather outdoor terrace is one of the most popular places in town. Inside is both a pub and a large dining room that attracts a lot of families with small children for its unpretentious but plentiful food. Among the most popular dishes are pizzas, filet of beef served with vegetables and salad, Wiener schnitzel, and marinated whale steak in black peppercorn sauce (eco-unfriendly as it may be). Also known as Majoren, this is the only restaurant in the region that offers fjord-caught whale steak (NOK255) year-round.

Voldportsgate 73. ✆ **69-32-15-55.** www.majoren.no. Reservations recommended. Main courses NOK185–NOK295. AE, DC, MC, V. Sun–Thurs noon–9pm; Fri–Sat noon–10pm.

Prestegaarden ★ NORWEGIAN/INTERNATIONAL For tradition and atmosphere, this restaurant has zero competition in the Old Town (although Engelsviken Brygge, outside of town, is even more atmospheric; see above). It was built in 1803 as the home of the village priest, in a style known in North America as "carpenter Gothic." Set within the Gamlebyen Gjestegaarder inn, the simple but flavorful meals are served near a massive fireplace in the cellar or, weather permitting, in the outdoor courtyard. The well-prepared fare includes baked salmon with dill sauce, filet of sole with lemon-butter sauce, and fish-and-clam casserole with herbs. An assortment of fresh game dishes is served in the fall.

Færgeportgaten 78. ✆ **69-32-30-40.** Reservations recommended. Most main dishes around NOK250. AE, DC, MC, V. Mon–Fri 3pm–midnight; Sat–Sun noon–2am.

Side Trips from Fredrikstad

Fredrikstad is most often visited on a day trip from Oslo. However, if you'd like to stay at one of the few hotels in Fredrikstad (p. 174), you can enjoy a day or two exploring some intriguing nearby sights.

The most concentrated collection of archaeological monuments in Norway lies along Route 110 between Fredrikstad and Sarpsborg to the east. Norwegians have dubbed the highway **Oldtidsveien,** or **"Old Times Way"** ★. Along this historic sunken road between the two towns, many ancient stoneworks and rock paintings have been found. Look for the signposts as you drive along.

The most idyllic way to tour the Oldtidsveien is by bike if the weather is fair. (If it's not, you really shouldn't even make this trip.) Bike rental is available at the Fredrikstad tourist office (see above).

If you take Route 110, you will approach all the clearly marked attractions detailed below. Along the trail you'll come first to **Solberg,** a hamlet with a trio of panels featuring nearly 100 carved figures, thought to be 3,000 years old. In the village of **Gunnarstorp,** you can see several standing stones, including a few dating from the Iron Age as well as a Bronze Age burial ground. Other ancient attractions are found at the village of **Begby,** which has some depictions of ancient people, including boats and wild animals. Rock paintings at **Hornes** depict nearly two dozen ancient boats with oarsmen.

The hamlet of **Hunn** contains the largest archaeological site in Norway, with 4,000-year-old remains of Stone Age civilization, Viking grave mounds and stone circles, and even signs of ancient cultivation methods. At a nearby hill, you can look at the ruins of the Ravneberget fortification, with walls dating from the 4th century A.D.

Along this road you can also visit some more modern attractions. Midway between Fredrikstad and Sarpsborg in Hvidsten is the **Roald Amundsen Centre** at Framveien 9 (✆ **69-34-83-26;** www.roaldamundsen.no), the 1872 birthplace of Amundsen, who, in 1911, was the first explorer to reach the South Pole. A monument is dedicated to him, and the house is filled with memorabilia of his exploits. You'll approach Hvidsten 7km (4½ miles) east of Fredrikstad along Route 110. The center is open from April to September, Saturday and Sunday from 10am to 8pm, but these hours have been known to change. Admission is NOK40 for adults, NOK20 for children.

If you end your exploration in Sarpsborg, you can visit the **Borgarsyssel Museum,** Gamlebygata 8 (✆ **69-11-56-50;** www.ostfoldmuseene.no), 14km (8½ miles) east of Fredrikstad. It's open from June to August, Tuesday to Friday 10am to 4pm, Saturday and Sunday noon to 5pm. In the off-season, it's open Tuesday to Saturday 11am to 3:30pm. This museum of the province of Østfold is an open-air exhibit filled with 30 period structures moved here from various parts of southern Norway. Many cultural artifacts are exhibited, and you can also walk through an herbal garden. Kids should also enjoy the petting zoo. On-site are the ruins of King Øystein's St. Nikolaus Church, built in 1115 but torched by the advancing Swedish army in 1567. There is no admission charge to the museum grounds; however, viewing the exhibits and going on a guided tour costs NOK40, for which you must call ahead if you visit outside of the summer months.

En route back to Fredrikstad, you can stop off at the **Storedal Kultursentet (Cultural Centre),** at Storedal (✆ **69-16-92-67;** www.storedal.no), 8km (5 miles) east of Fredrikstad. This was the birthplace of King Magnus in 1117. He became

BRIDGE by LEONARDO DA VINCI

In Tuscany, Leonardo da Vinci drew the plans for a bridge in 1502. It was never built in his day. However, in 2001, da Vinci's stunningly modern pedestrian bridge opened in Norway, of all places.

The 99-m (325-ft.) laminated timber bridge links Norway with its eastern neighbor, Sweden, at the town of **Aas,** a 26-km (16-mile) drive south of Oslo. Many Oslovians, who have no real intention of going to Sweden, drive down to walk across this remarkable piece of Renaissance engineering.

Of course, da Vinci had a 216-m (708-ft.) stone span in mind to cross the Golden Horn inlet at the mouth of the Bosporus, between Peta and Istanbul. Sultan Bejazet II, at that time a patron of da Vinci, feared that it was impractical to build such a bridge. The plan died until the original da Vinci drawings were uncovered among some documents in the late 1950s.

Although only a scaled-down version of what da Vinci designed, it's a stunning bit of engineering, standing 8m (26 ft.) high at its pinnacle.

king of Norway at the age of 13; 5 years later he was blinded and has since then been called King Magnus the Blind. The center is dedicated to blind people as well as those suffering from other disabilities. On-site is a beautiful botanical garden; it costs NOK30 to enter. Two artists, Arne Nordheim and Arnold Haukeland, designed *Ode to the Light,* a "sound sculpture" that translates the fluctuations of natural light into music. The center is signposted from Route 110. It's open late May to August daily 10am to 5pm, charging no admission.

HALDEN: THE BURNING CITY ★

30km (19 miles) S of Fredrikstad; 144km (89 miles) S of Oslo; 2km (1¼ miles) W of Swedish border

Halden lies at the Iddefjord in the far southeasterly corner of Østfold province, bisected by the Tista River and hemmed in by forested hills. The town of 27,000 makes an idyllic stopover for those touring the eastern bank of the Oslofjord or heading across the border to Sweden. If you have time to see more than Fredrikstad, head for Halden, especially on a summer day when yachties from Oslo fill its pretty little picture-postcard harbor.

Historically, Halden was a frontier outpost that was heavily fortified to fend off attacks by the Swedes. It was—and still is—known for Fredriksten fortress, where Norwegian patriots successfully held off Sweden's frequent attacks from the east. These regional fighters made a bold decision in 1659. To drive out the attacking Swedes, they set fire to their own town. The Swedes retreated, although the fortress withstood the siege and the town fire. Attacked by the Swedes again in 1716, the townspeople of Halden once again torched their city to halt the Swedish advance into Norway. These incidents, along with numerous fires set by Mother Nature, gave the town its nickname: "The Burning City."

Today a prosperous little border town, Halden has the dubious distinction of being the site of the country's oldest nuclear power station. In 1959, nuclear energy was introduced here to fuel regional wood-based industries. It is now used for research purposes only.

Essentials

GETTING THERE

BY RAIL Halden is a stopover on the main rail links between Oslo and Gothenburg, Sweden, on that country's western coast. Depending on the time of day, trains depart Oslo once every hour or once every 2 hours. The trip takes 1¾ hours, a one-way ticket costing NOK231. Call © **81-50-08-88** or visit www.nsb.no for rail schedules. The train is quicker than, and much preferred to, the bus.

BY BUS **Nor-Way Bussekspress** (© **81-54-44-44;** www.nor-way.no) in Oslo runs buses every 3 hours during the day to the town of Svinedsun. Once in Svinedsun, you must take a local bus—or a taxi if you arrive later in the evening—for the final approach to Halden.

BY CAR Motorists from Oslo can follow the E6 south to reach Halden. Driving time is about 1½ hours.

BY FERRY From the middle of May until the middle of August, you can enjoy a day's adventure by taking a ferry, **MS *Sagasund*** (© **90-99-81-11;** www.mssagasund.no), departing from Halden and sailing over to Strömstad on the west coast of Sweden. Strömstad belonged to Norway until 1658. Today it's a colorful seaside resort and an embarkation point for the remote Kloster Islands, Sweden's most westerly isles, where cars are prohibited. The warming waters of the Gulf Stream give these islands their luxuriant vegetation. During the summer, the ferry runs daily except Sunday; in the fall and spring it runs Tuesday, Thursday, and Saturday only at 11am and takes 2 hours; a round-trip fare costs NOK150 in the summer, NOK100 in other months. Call the tourist office (see below) for details.

VISITOR INFORMATION

The **Halden tourist office,** at Torget 2 (© **69-19-09-80**), is open June to August Monday to Friday 9am to 4:30pm, and from September to May Monday to Friday 9am to 3:30pm.

What to See & Do

The most idyllic place when the sun is shining is **Busterudpark** at Busterudgaten in the center of town. This century-old park serves as a reminder of how life used to be in this town, and is complete with a bandstand from 1879. In the summer, a military band often holds concerts here. The sculptor, Dyre Vaa, erected a monument in the park in 1939 to honor F. A. Reissiger and Oscar Borg for their efforts to promote music in Halden. The park is hardly memorable or filled with attractions, but I like to come here with the makings of a picnic just like the townspeople did back in the 19th century.

Keep Your Eye on Your Kid

One thing prevents the Fredriksten Fortress from being truly kid-friendly: The towering bastions are not fenced in and can be dangerous. If you visit with children, be sure to watch them carefully.

Fredriksten Festning (Fredriksten Fortress) ★ Dominating a forested hill, this crowning citadel of Halden was built in 1661 by King Frederick III to protect the Danish-Norwegian kingdom against sieges from Sweden, which had already

THE mysterious DEATH OF KING KARL XII

You can see a monument within Fredriksten Fortress marking the spot where the Swedish King Karl XII was shot during a 1718 siege. Many Norwegian guides tell you that it wasn't their countrymen who killed the king, but one of his own. A warmongering monarch, Karl had exhausted his troops and tested their loyalty on the battlefield. Many soldiers were tired of him and his endless battles. It has never been proven where the fatal bullet came from. Swedes maintain that a soldier within the fortress killed Karl. There is strong speculation, however, that he was assassinated by a Swedish soldier eager to return to home and hearth.

unsuccessfully attempted attacks on Oslo and Copenhagen. The king called in engineers from the Netherlands to build what he hoped—successfully so—would become an impregnable fortress. It took 10 years for the Dutch to create this network of labyrinthine passages and perimeter walls so thick they could withstand cannonballs. The gates were also heavily fortified, as were the bastions. They designed the complex of buildings in the shape of a star, at the highest point in the sprawling town, along two ridges.

In a former prison in the eastern curtain wall, you'll find the **Krigshistorisk Utstilling (War History Museum).** Exhibits depict the history of battle in Halden from the 1600s through the Nazi takeover in 1940. Another museum, **Byen Brenner** ("The Town is on Fire"), explores the history behind the town's unfortunate nickname.

An **apothecary** has been installed in the former Commandant's Residence, which dates from 1754. Modern exhibits trace the history of pharmacology from early folk remedies that relied on bird claws to 20th-century advances in medicine. **Bakery** and **brewery** exhibits are also housed within the complex. The bakery could turn out bread for some 5,000 men, and the brewery could produce 3,000 liters of beer a day.

There is no more idyllic place for lunch in Halden than at the fort's own **Fredriksten Kro,** a mellow old pub with outdoor seating in fair weather.

To reach the fortress, take the steep footpath beginning at Peder Colbjørnsens Gate, going up to the principal gatehouse. The stronghold is still in use by the Norwegian army, so not all of the complex can be visited. You can easily spend 2 hours here, although most visitors absorb it in less than an hour.

Peder Colbjørnsens Gate. ✆ **69-18-31-49.** www.nasjonalefestningsverk.no/fredriksten Admission NOK50 adults, NOK25 children. Guided tours NOK50 adults, NOK25 children. May 18–Aug 22 daily 10am–5pm.

Rød Manor ★ 🎁 This is one of the most impressive and best-preserved manor houses in southeastern Norway, and its gardens, at least to us, are the most impressive in southern Norway. The exact age of the historic core of this building is unknown, although the east wing was added in 1733. Today much of the place looks as it did in 1750, when the Tank and Ankers families resided here. Still elegant, it has lovely interiors filled with objets d'art, hunting trophies, and one of the largest private collections of weapons in Scandinavia. You can see the house only by guided tour. On your own, you can stroll the beautiful **English-style gardens ★★** with their towering deciduous trees or walk a pathway bordered by hazelnut trees. The symmetrical, baroque-style walkways evoke the gracious living of a grander era (assuming you were rich). The location is signposted 1.5km (1 mile) west of the town center. Plan to spend about 45 minutes here.

Rød Herregård. ✆ **69-18-54-11.** http://www.halden.museum.no/herregard.html (in Norwegian). Admission NOK60 adults, NOK30 children. Tours June 22 to mid-Aug Tues–Sun noon, 1, & 2pm (additional Sun tour at 3pm); May 2–June 20 & mid-Aug to late Sept Sun noon, 1 & 2pm. Closed Oct–April.

Where to Stay

Grand Hotell The Grand isn't all that grand anymore, but since 1898 it's been putting up rail passengers who arrived at the terminus across the street. It's still well maintained and tries to stay up-to-date, although the Park (see below) is now the hotel of choice. The rooms are simple and clean, with modern furnishings and well-kept bathrooms with shower units. The cheapest ones are those that have not been renovated yet. Dinner is not served here, but the standby Dickens restaurant (see below) is nearby. The hotel seems to make up for this lack by serving one of the best breakfast buffets in town.

Jernbanetorget 1, N-1776 Halden. ✆ **69-18-72-00.** www.grandhotell.net. 33 units. NOK850–NOK1,400 double. Rates include buffet breakfast. AE, MC, V. **Amenities:** Breakfast room; bar; lounge. *In room:* TV, Wi-Fi.

Park Hotel ★ This is the more comfortable and up-to-date of Halden's two hotels, with a location in a pleasant garden at the center of town. It was originally built in the 1970s; about half of the rooms lie within a newer wing that was added in 2000. The four-story weatherproof building offers increased amenities and more diversions than its only other competitor. There is an exceptionally helpful and well-informed staff. Each of the spacious rooms has wooden floors and pastel color schemes.

Marcus Thranes Gate 30, N-1776 Halden. ✆ **69-21-15-00.** www.park-hotel.no. 64 units. NOK1,090–NOK1,430 double; NOK1,990 suite. Rates include buffet breakfast. AE, DC, MC, V. **Amenities:** Restaurant; bar; babysitting; exercise room; sauna. *In room:* TV, Wi-Fi, minibar, hair dryer.

Where to Dine

Dickens INTERNATIONAL You won't find grand cuisine here, but those dependable favorites often consumed by Norwegians with a mug of beer: A Dickens burger with bacon, nachos with jalapeños, or a chicken salad with crispy bacon. More substantial fare includes grilled cod with broccoli and white wine sauce. Lamb steak is another tasty choice, flavored with garlic, thyme, and rosemary. In winter, diners retreat into the 17th-century cellar to enjoy well-prepared and affordable meals. In summer, an outdoor table is preferred on a barge floating in the harbor. Visitors predominate in the summer months, with regulars returning when the wind blows cold.

Storgata 9. ✆ **69-18-36-91.** www.dickens.no (in Norwegian). Reservations recommended Sat–Sun. Main courses NOK196–NOK237. AE, DC, MC, V. Mon–Thurs 11am–10pm; Fri–Sat 11am–11pm; Sun 1–9pm. Closed Christmas.

Munch's Little Summer Cottage

In one lazy afternoon, you can explore the little coastal town of Åsgårdstrand, located just outside the doorway of its larger neighbor, Horten. The town achieved fame in the 17th century when shipping and sailing companies were based here. In time, it was discovered by artists, one of whom was Edvard Munch, Scandinavia's most famous painter, who found inspiration along the coast for some of his best-known works.

Today you can still visit Munchs hus (Edvard Munch's House), at Edvard Munchs Gate 25 (© 33-08-21-31). Once a summer house and studio where Munch spent seven seasons, it's been turned into a museum of Munch memorabilia. It was here that he painted his masterful *Girls on the Bridge, Dance of Life,* and *Melancholy.* When Munch died in 1944, the house remained as it was—basically a primitive fisherman's cabin that the artist had purchased in 1897. Called "the handsomest man in Norway" at the time, the artist is said to have taken advantage of his good looks to romance the local girls during his summer sojourns here.

The house is open from June to August Tuesday to Sunday 11am to 6pm, and from September to May Saturday and Sunday 11am to 6pm. Admission is NOK40. Little Åsgårdstrand lies 10km (6¼ miles) south of Horten. Horten itself lies 35km (22 miles) south of Oslo's "bedroom community" of Drammen, which is 40km (25 miles) southwest of Oslo. Take the E18 south from Oslo via Drammen. From Tønsberg city center, take bus no. 1 to Åsgårdstrand.

Halden After Dark

Siste Reis Pub Next to the Grand Hotel building, this is a small, cozy, and friendly Irish-style pub decorated with pictures of local musicians along with classic advertising posters. Close to the train depot, the pub offers many different brews on tap, from Irish Guinness to Danish Tuborg, and especially the local favorite, Borg, a new taste sensation for many first-time visitors to Norway. Most of the patrons, ranging in age from 18 to 40, come here to talk but also to listen to Irish folk music on weekdays, or recorded rock 'n' roll on Friday and Saturday. Snacks are served along with the brew. It's open Monday to Friday 3pm to 2am, Sat 11am to 2am and Sunday 1pm to 2am. Jernbanetorget 1. © **69-17-53-07.**

TØNSBERG: THE FIRST SETTLEMENT ★

102km (63 miles) S of Oslo

Tønsberg is Norway's oldest town. And just how old is it? No one is certain. But documentation—including the *Saga of Harald Hårfagre,* by Snorre Sturluson—puts the date around 871, when King Harald Fairhair united parts of the country and the Viking town became a royal coronation site.

The renowned Viking ships *Gokstad* and *Oseberg,* on display in Oslo's Bygdøy Peninsula, were discovered at a site near Tønsberg on the western bank of the Oslofjord. King Olav of Vestfold and King Sigrød of Trøndelag, both killed in battle, have their tombs at Haugar.

In the Middle Ages, Tønsberg became a major Hanseatic trading post for eastern Norway, with links to Rostock along the Baltic. In the 1600s, it was known as a major port in eastern Norway, worthy of Bergen in the west. By the mid-1800s, Tønsberg was a port for whalers in the Arctic and Antarctic seas, rivaling Sandefjord (see below). It was also the headquarters of Svend Foyn, known as the "father of Norwegian sealing and whaling."

However, don't be completely misled by the town. Tønsberg is also quite up-to-date with the 21st century and not mired in antiquity. Modern Tønsberg is a 104-sq.-km (41-sq.-mile) town with some 32,000 residents. It consists of a historic area filled with old clapboard-sided houses and a commercial center with a marketplace. Foodies around the world seek out the Jarlsberg cheese that is made here.

In 3 hours, you can see it all.

Essentials

GETTING THERE

BY TRAIN Trains depart for Tønsberg from Oslo Central railway station at intervals of 60 to 90 minutes from 6am to 11:30pm every day, requiring a travel time of about 90 minutes and a fare of NOK201 each way. The railway station is in the town center. For information and schedules, call ✆ **81-50-08-88** or visit www.nsb.no.

BY BUS There is no NOR-WAY bus service from Oslo.

BY CAR Take Route 18 south from Oslo via Drammen.

VISITOR INFORMATION

Tønsberg Tourist Information is at Storgaten 38 (✆ **48-06-33-33;** www.visittonsberg.com). It's open Monday to Friday 9am to 4pm. A little tourist kiosk on the island of Tjøme provides information in July daily from 11am to 5pm. Also visit www.visittonsberg.com for information.

What to See & Do

Slottsfjellet, a huge hill fortress near the train station, is loftily touted as "the Acropolis of Norway." In its heyday, these 13th-century ruins blossomed as the largest medieval fortifications in Norway, attracting the Swedes who came to destroy it in 1503. It has only meager ruins today, and most people visit for the view from the 1888 lookout tower, **Slottsfjelltårnet** (✆ **33-31-18-72**), rising 17m (56 ft.) tall. Its tower with the walls of the fortress ruin open May 15 to June 25 Monday to Friday from 10am to 3pm, June 26 to August 20 daily from 11am to 6pm, rest of the year Sunday from noon to 4pm. Admission is NOK40 for adults, NOK20 for children.

Nordbyen is the old, scenic part of town, with well-preserved houses. **Haugar Cemetery,** at Møllebakken, in the center of town, holds the Viking graves of King Harald's sons, Olav and Sigrød.

Sem Kirke (Sem Church), Hageveien 32 (✆ **33-36-93-99**), the oldest church in Vestfold province, was built of stone in the Romanesque style around 1100. It's open Thursday and Friday 10am to noon, but inquire at the vestry if it's not open during these hours. Admission is free.

Another attraction is **Fjerdingen,** a street of charming restored houses near the mountain farmstead at the **Vestfold Fylkesmuseum** (see below). Tønsberg was also a Hanseatic town during the Middle Ages, and some houses have been redone in typical Hanseatic style—wooden buildings constructed along the wharfs as warehouses to receive goods from fellow Hanseatic League members.

Haugar Vestfold Kunstmuseum This museum is good for a rainy day. The main reason to visit is to introduce yourself to "Odd Nerdrum," a strangely named, internationally known figurative painter hailed as "the Rembrandt of Norway." The museum displays two of his best-known works, *Man Imitating Cloud* and *Woman with Doorknob*. One of his most curious works is called *Hermaphrodite*. One wing of the museum is devoted entirely to Odd Nerdrum, but there are also 160 works by other artists. Tønsberg's art museum lies in the center of town in a building from 1918. Nearby are two Viking gravesites, said to hold the bodies of Olav and Sigrød, sons of the king, Harald Hårfagre (Fairhair).

Gråbrødragate 17. ✆ **33-30-76-70.** www.haugar.com. Admission NOK70. June–Aug Mon–Fri 11am–5pm; Sept–May Tues–Fri 11am–4pm, Sat–Sun noon–5pm year-round.

Vestfold Fylkesmuseum ★ The relics on display at this museum honor Tønsberg's once glorious past. Lying at the foot of Slottsfjellet, it features many Viking and whaling treasures. One of the chief sights is the skeleton of a blue whale, the world's largest mammal. The weight of this particular whale can't be determined, but some whales caught off the coast of Norway have weighed in at 150 tons. There's also a Viking ship, the *Klastad* from Tjolling, built about A.D. 800.

In the rural section of the museum, visit the **Vestfold Farm,** which includes a 1690 house from Hynne, a timbered barn from Bøen, and a storehouse from Fadum (with its characteristic apron, or platform). The Heierstadloft (ca. 1350) is the oldest preserved timbered building in Vestfold, and there's a smithy with a charcoal shed, a grain-drying house, and a mountain farmstead.

You can have lunch here at the farmstead. A typical meal includes *rumgraut* (porridge made with sour cream)—definitely an acquired taste—and other farm foods. The area is perfect for a picnic on a summer day.

Frammannsveien 30. ✆ **33-31-29-19.** www.vfm.no. Admission NOK60 adults, NOK10 children. Mid-May to mid-Sept Tues–Fri 10am–5pm, Sat & Sun noon–4pm. Closed mid-Sept to mid-May.

Going to the End of the World

In just a half-hour drive, you can leave Tønsberg and travel to what locals call Verdens Ende ★, or "World's End." It lies at the southernmost tip of Tjøme, the southernmost island among the low-lying islands and skerries, or rocky islets, jutting out into the Oslofjord, where it empties into the sea. This is a particularly dramatic spot. Usually the wind is blowing rather strongly, stirring up the blue-black waters. Old fishing jetties can be seen in the distance. You'll also see an array of rocky islets and big rocks worn smooth by the turbulent waves. This is romantic Viking country and the setting for many summer homes. No one comes here for the excitement: It's just a scenic hideaway. If you don't have a car, take bus no. 101 from Tønsberg; the ride takes 45 minutes and costs NOK65 one-way. Once here, you'll see a "17th-century" lighthouse. Actually, the original is gone and this is a copy from 1932.

Where to Stay

Hotel Maritim This hotel has long been a local favorite—since 1955, in fact—but the opening of the Quality Hotel Tønsberg (see below) has put it in second place. Located on a square beside the ruins of the Church of St. Olav, the hotel occupies a five-story building that's a 10-minute walk east of the railway station on the main pedestrian street. The rooms, which are kept in good condition, are well furnished and have a color scheme to rival the spring flowers of Norway. Some of the units are quite large, and each comes with a small bathroom with shower. Fregatten, a good restaurant offering a Norwegian, Japanese, and Chinese cuisine, is on the ground floor. The helpful staff can arrange boat trips or bikes for guests.

Storgata 17, N-3126 Tønsberg. ✆ **33-00-27-00.** www.maritimhotell.com. 34 units. NOK990–NOK1,190 double; NOK1,590–NOK1,690 suite. Rates include continental breakfast. AE, DC, MC, V. Closed Dec 22–Jan 5 & 4 days at Easter. **Amenities:** Restaurant; bar. *In room:* TV, minibar.

Quality Hotel Tønsberg ★ This hotel—the best in the area—is a member of the Quality chain in Norway, meaning a stylish hotel in Nordic minimalist fashion. This Quality is scenically located along the waterfront at the southern end of town. In spite of its location, it is rather tranquil at night. Launched in 2002, the five-story structure is the latest hotel to grace the cityscape of Tønsberg. Its bedrooms are large, and most of them open onto views of the fjord. All are decorated in pastels, and most have carpeting, except for the two dozen units that are set aside for those suffering from allergies. Traditional Norwegian food is served at the on-site restaurant.

Ollebukta 3, N-3126 Tønsberg. ✆ **800/228-5151** or 33-00-41-00. www.choicehotels.no. 292 units. NOK980–NOK2,795 double. Children 4 & under stay free in parents' room. Rates include continental breakfast. AE, DC, MC, V. **Amenities:** Restaurant; bar; babysitting; outdoor heated pool; fitness center; sauna. *In room:* TV, Wi-Fi, minibar, hair dryer.

Where to Dine

Brygga CONTINENTAL/NORWEGIAN This rustic-looking restaurant with an outdoor terrace that opens onto a harbor view is your best choice in town. The Norwegian-style decor includes light gray tones, light-colored woods, and walls covered with modern paintings by local artists. But be warned, Tønsberg is not a hot address for discerning foodies. During the week, Brygga feels like a pub, especially when soccer matches are shown on a big TV screen. The chefs try to please most palates, offering everything from the town's best pizza's to the notable filet of reindeer and moose. If you like meat, the chefs will prepare you an excellent beefsteak with béarnaise sausce and a salad. We prefer their shellfish dishes, especially their seafood salad studded with shrimp, among other delectable items.

Nedre Langgate 32. ✆ **33-31-12-70.** www.brygga.net. Reservations recommended. Main courses NOK195–NOK270. DC, MC, V. Mid-May–end Aug daily 10am–2am; Sept–May daily 5pm–11pm.

Himmel & Hav NORWEGIAN/INTERNATIONAL This minimalist-style cafe decorated in bright colors features house specialties that would probably never make the menu of a Greenpeace luncheon: Reindeer, for example, or even whale steak. Less controversial dishes include a surf-and-turf of filet of beef, sautéed with bacon and served with scampi in a Madagascar pepper sauce. On my last visit, I was impressed with the chef's handling of a freshly caught grilled halibut. During the day, classical or jazz music plays in the adjoining Café del Mar.

Nedre Langgata 32. ✆ **92-84-33-78.** www.himmeloghav.net (in Norwegian). Reservations recommended. Main courses NOK98–NOK199 lunch, NOK198–NOK229 dinner. AE, DC, MC, V. Cafe daily 11am–2am; kitchen service until 10:30pm.

SANDEFJORD ★

125km (78 miles) S of Oslo; 24km (15 miles) S of Tønsberg

Although a modern town today, Sandefjord was one of the most famous stamping grounds of the Vikings in the Middle Ages. Its natural harbor along a 9.8-km (6-mile) fjord made it the whaling capital of the world at one time. A monument remains at the harbor to the once prosperous whaling industry, which made Sandefjord the richest city in Norway. Today it has built up the third-largest merchant fleet in Norway.

This old port still has a bit of 19th-century charm and character, though much of the old was torn down to make way for modern developments.

You can afford to skip most of the town and concentrate on the waterfront, a breezy section of green parks and beautifully maintained gardens. If the day is sunny, what I like to do is rent a bike (inquire at the tourist office), make a picnic basket with some seafood from the "fishtraders" who hang out by the harbor, and set off along the coast for an adventure. You might also poke about in the little stores and shops, ducking into one of the cozy harborfront cafes for a warming coffee, and stroll along, admiring the many sculptures that dot the waterfront.

Sandefjord attracts summer visitors seeking boating fun in its archipelago and on its many beaches. The archipelago is studded with 115 so-called "islands," most of which are rocky outcroppings inhospitable to the day-tripper. I asked a longtime local boatman which island was his favorite among dozens of possibilities. "The one that gets the most sun on any given day," he said. "After a long cold winter, we in Norway want sun. So we stop our boats off at the hottest rock and sunbathe a little, often in just our underwear, if that."

Locals refer to the town as the "Bathing City" (*Badebyen* in Norwegian). Yachties from Oslo also fill up the harbor in summer after having sailed through the skerries, or rocky islets.

On a summer day, I always like to stroll along its waterfront, enjoying the fresh salt air and the beautiful parks and gardens. You'll see a magnificent compound of buildings constructed in 1899 in the dragon motif so popular in Norway. The baths were closed in 1940, at the beginning of the Nazi occupation, and the site today is the civic center.

Essentials

GETTING THERE The country's second-busiest international airport is **Sandefjord Airport Torp** (✆ **33-42-70-00**). Some budget airlines such as Ryanair use this smaller airport rather than the one in Oslo. In addition to its air link, there is one daily **ferry** connection to Strömstad, Sweden, taking 2½ hours. For schedules and information, call **Color Line,** Tollbugata 5 (✆ **81-00-08-11;** www.colorline.no).

From Oslo there are several **express trains** reaching Sandefjord in just under 2 hours, for NOK243 one-way. For information and schedules, call ✆ **81-50-08-88** or visit www.nsb.no. Frequent **buses** also run between Oslo and Sandefjord daily, and there are also good bus connections between Tønsberg and Sandefjord. Visit www.nor-way.no for information. To reach there by car, follow Route E18 from Oslo. The airport is located 10km (6¼ miles) from the city center.

VISITOR INFORMATION The **Sandefjord tourist information office** is at Torvet (✆ **33-46-05-90;** www.visitsandefjord.com). From early July to late August it's open Monday to Friday 9am to 5:30pm, Saturday 10am to 5pm, and Sunday 12:30 to 5pm. Off-season it's open only Monday to Friday 9am to 4pm.

What to See & Do

Lying off Storgata, **Hvalfangstmuseet (Commander Christensen's Whaling Museum,** Museumsgaten 39; ✆ **33-48-46-50**), has a life-size replica of a mighty **blue whale ★**, its tongue alone weighing 3½ tons. The museum chronicles the controversial whaling industry that nearly drove this mammoth sea beast to extinction. In the heyday of whaling, Sandefjord sent out vast "floating factories" to process the whale meat and its by-products. Admission is NOK55 for adults, NOK30 for ages 7 to 17, and free for those 6 and under; a family ticket costs NOK135. Hours from May to August are daily 10am to 5pm; in September daily 10am to 4pm; from October to April Monday to Saturday 11am to 3pm, Sunday noon to 4pm.

Sandefjord preserves a slice of its past at **Øvre Myra Cotter's Farm,** Solvangveien 8 at Nyphen. In use since 1770, this is the last cotter's farm in the area. (A cotter was a hired hand who occupied a cottage in return for services on the farm.) Inquire at the tourist office (see above) about joining one of the guided tours in summer to this homestead.

Outdoor Pursuits

After all this maritime history, you, too, can head for the water if the day is fair. The best beach, **Langeby,** lies 7km (4⅓ miles) from the center, and buses from Sandefjord go there hourly. You'll find dozens of other beaches along the 146-km (91-mile) coastline. My favorite public beach—arm yourself with a map from the tourist office—is at **Søllokka,** reached along Route 303 by following the directions north to Tønsberg. I also like **Granholmen,** reached along RV 303 following the directions south to Larvik, the latter the hometown of Thor Heyerdahl, of *Kon-Tiki* fame.

The area is a popular site for scuba divers. The best outfitter is **Neptun Dykkersenter,** Hegnasletta 13 (✆ **33-46-14-90**), which will rent all the necessary equipment to qualified divers. There is no regular place to rent boats, but you might inquire here about rentals, or check with the tourist office to see what might be available. Outdoor activities are a casual thing at Sandefjord, a sort of do-it-yourself operation that changes from season to season.

Where to Stay

Clarion Collection Hotel Atlantic ★★ ☺ This is the town's most atmospheric hotel thanks to its reverence for the city's maritime tradition. Built on the site of an older structure, this hotel respected its 1914 origins in its brand-new design. The tasteful interior takes a whaling theme as its motif. Bedrooms have sleek, modern styling, and each comes with a private bathroom with shower (six units also have a tub). Suites have their own fireplaces and Jacuzzis. Children under 12 stay free, but a rollaway bed is an additional fee. The on-site dining room serves a light supper in the evening that is free to guests.

Jernbanealleen 33, N-3200 Sandefjord. ✆ **33-42-80-00.** www.clarionhotel.com. 109 units. NOK1,045–NOK1,945 double; NOK2,750 suite. Rates include continental breakfast & light supper. AE, DC, MC, V. **Amenities:** Dining room; sauna; rooms for those with limited mobility. *In room:* TV, Wi-Fi, minibar, hair dryer.

Hotel Kong Carl ★ This is a longtime favorite of previous Frommer's writers, who have memories of staying here when fishermen were (practically) still harpooning whales. Near the town center and marketplace, this white clapboard-sided house dates from 1690 and has been an inn since 1721. Bedrooms come in a wide range of sizes, and most of the accommodations are at least partially furnished with antiques. Lunch and dinner are served Monday to Saturday in a regional restaurant; you can also enjoy a beer on the summer terrace.

Torvgaten 9, N-3201 Sandefjord. ✆ **33-46-31-17.** www.kongcarl.no. 25 units. NOK990–NOK1,490 double. Rates include continental breakfast. AE, DC, MC, V. Closed Dec 22–Jan 2 & 1 week at Easter. **Amenities:** Restaurant. *In room:* TV, minibar, hair dryer.

Rica Park Hotel Although a chain, this hotel still manages to offer personalized service. Idyllically positioned overlooking the harbor and a city meadow, the hotel still has the lingering aura of its birthday in 1958. Dark woods contrast with the pastel-colored walls, and each bedroom is furnished with rich fabrics, thick carpeting, and comfortable furnishings. Bathrooms are up-to-date and well equipped, with three-quarters of them having a tub as well as a shower. Many locals patronize the hotel's gourmet restaurant, Park Garden, for special occasions. Even if you're not a guest, consider dropping in here for entertainment. During the summer, live shows are staged with local bands, international artists, and Norwegian cabaret acts.

Strand Promenaden 9, N-3201 Sandefjord. ✆ **33-44-74-00.** www.rica-hotels.com. 233 units. NOK1,295–NOK1,895 double; NOK2,700 suite. AE, DC, MC, V. **Amenities:** 2 restaurants; bar; piano bar; babysitting; saltwater indoor pool; fitness center; sauna; rooms for those with limited mobility. *In room:* A/C (in some), TV, minibar, hair dryer.

Where to Dine

Smak ★★★ FRENCH/ASIAN FUSION This is the best restaurant along Oslofjord. The chef, Odd Ivar Solvold, has won three national culinary championships, and he certainly deserves his acclaim. For this new building, the chef chose Sven Lund as his architect, the same man who also designs for the king of Norway.

The dining is quite formal, and the wine cellar (*vinbar*) is on the same floor as the dining area. Foodies celebrate Solvold for his seafood, and he secures the finest catches. His lemon-baked turbot with carrot and coriander cream is a prize-winning dish indeed, as is his pan-fried seawater crayfish with a crustacean emulsion. Savor his filet of tuna, or opt for a meat course, none better than the rack of venison in a tangerine sauce. For dessert, I was enthralled by his pickled peach with vanilla and apricot-mascarpone ice cream. Attached is a less formal cafe that has been completely redone, featuring international dishes such as carpaccio, paella, and sushi.

Thor Dalsgate 9. ✆ **33-46-27-41.** www.smak.no. Reservations required. Main courses NOK225–NOK285. AE, DC, MC, V. Tues–Sat 6–11pm.

EIDSVOLL: CRADLE OF INDEPENDENCE

80km (50 miles) N of Oslo

To appreciate this site, you might well need to have some true Norwegian blood flowing through your veins, as many Americans do. Reached from Oslo via the E6, motorists arrive at **Eidsvoll,** Carsten Ankers vei (✆ **63-92-22-10;** www.eidsvoll1814.no), where, on May 17, 1814, the country's constitution was signed after 6 intense weeks of negotiation and rewriting. It was the most liberal constitution the world had ever known and today is the oldest existing constitutional charter in Europe.

Even if you're not interested in the political implications of Norway, a visit to the manor house **Eidsvoll-bygningen** is worthwhile for its insiderish view of the lifestyles of the upper crust of the early 1800s.

The two-floor house with 30 rooms is constructed entirely of timber. Portraits of the members of the 1814 Norwegian Parliament are on display here, but far more intriguing is the collection of objects used to furnish the house, including a well-stocked library, elegant dining rooms, lavish bedrooms, English antiques, and murals depicting figures from Greek mythology.

The cast-iron stoves are works of art. The Ankers family, who lived in the house, also owned the local ironworks, and they insisted on only the best for themselves.

You can also visit the Room of the Constitutional Committee, where the original wooden benches are still in place, along with a series of paintings of Norwegian landscapes.

The house is open May to August daily from 10am to 5pm; admission is NOK70.

If you're not driving, you can reach the manor house by taking train no. 450 from Oslo Central railway station to Eidsvoll. Trains run every 1 to 2 hours for the 50-minute journey. From here you can take a local bus to the nearby town of Eidsvoll Verk. The manor house lies 4km (2½ miles) east of the E6 on the edge of Eidsvoll Verk.

JEVNAKER: NORWAY'S OLDEST GLASSWORKS

70km (42 miles) NW of Oslo

With the glories of the banks of the Oslofjord behind you, head northwest from Oslo along the scenic banks of yet another fjord, **Tyrifjord,** enjoying some of the best land- and seascapes in eastern Norway before arriving at **Hadeland Glassverk ★**, Route 241, Jevnaker (✆ **61-31-66-00;** www.hadeland-glassverk.no).

In operation since 1762, this is one of the oldest glassworks in Scandinavia. To launch the company, most of the workers were brought in from Germany. Until 1814, the company was owned by the king of Denmark and Norway.

This place is a real family attraction, and many activities are specifically designed for children. Kids and adults alike will be fascinated watching some of Norway's most skilled glass-blowers practice their art at the Glass Hut. Kids can blow their own glass or dye their own candles here. ***Note:*** The pre-Christmas scene is particularly active here, so plan on crowds at that time of year.

Other highlights include a visit to "Honey House" to enjoy a freshly baked confection, or a trip to the factory shop to browse for bargains. Children can also play in a house designed for them, watch a tinsmith at work in the pewter workshop, or take rides on the gentle horses in the park out back during the summer.

On the main square of the glassworks is the **Hadeland Glassworks Art Gallery,** opened in 1997, with an exhibition of the works of 50 internationally known artists.

Admission is free, and the glassworks can be visited Monday to Saturday 10am to 4pm, and Sunday 11am to 5pm. To reach Jevnaker, motorists can follow the E16 toward Hønefoss, then Route 241 into Jevnaker.

LILLEHAMMER & THE PEER GYNT ROAD

8

One of the premier areas of wilderness in Europe, this is the perfect region to visit if you love the great outdoors. From Olympic ski conditions on snow-capped mountains to glaciers in national parks, expect high-adrenaline thrills in both winter and summer.

Visitors arrive at the likes of Jotunheimen Nasjonalpark specifically seeking a close encounter with Nordic nature. When touring the area, you might even meet up with the rare musk ox. But keep your distance and admire these beasts from afar. If threatened, the shaggy creature can charge at 60kmph (over 35 mph).

This chapter will guide you through some of Norway's highest mountain peaks, which are a hiker's paradise in summer and a ski mecca in winter. In addition to its many resorts and enchanting wooden villages, this section of Norway is filled with hidden gems such as the town of Røros, an evocative former copper-mining site that is now preserved as a UNESCO World Heritage Site.

Lying to the east of the western fjord district, eastern central Norway is the virtual playground of Scandinavia, embracing the greatest national parks, the fabled ski resort at Lillehammer, and some of the nation's most panoramic scenery. At times it may seem remote and distant, but much of it is within an easy 1- to 2-hour drive from Oslo.

HAMAR: GATEWAY TO LAKE MJØSA

134km (83 miles) N of Oslo; 58km (36 miles) SE of Lillehammer

As a town, Hamar is no particular beauty, but it's at the center of a beautiful region of central Norway. If it's a choice between Lillehammer and Hamar, make it Lillehammer. But if you have that extra day to spare, journey to Hamar, if for no other reason than to enjoy Lake Mjøsa.

Located on the large and scenic Lake Mjøsa, Hamar is the capital of Hedmark County and one of Lillehammer's rivals for the winter-sports enthusiast. It makes a good stopover en route from Oslo to Lillehammer,

Lillehammer & the Peer Gynt Road

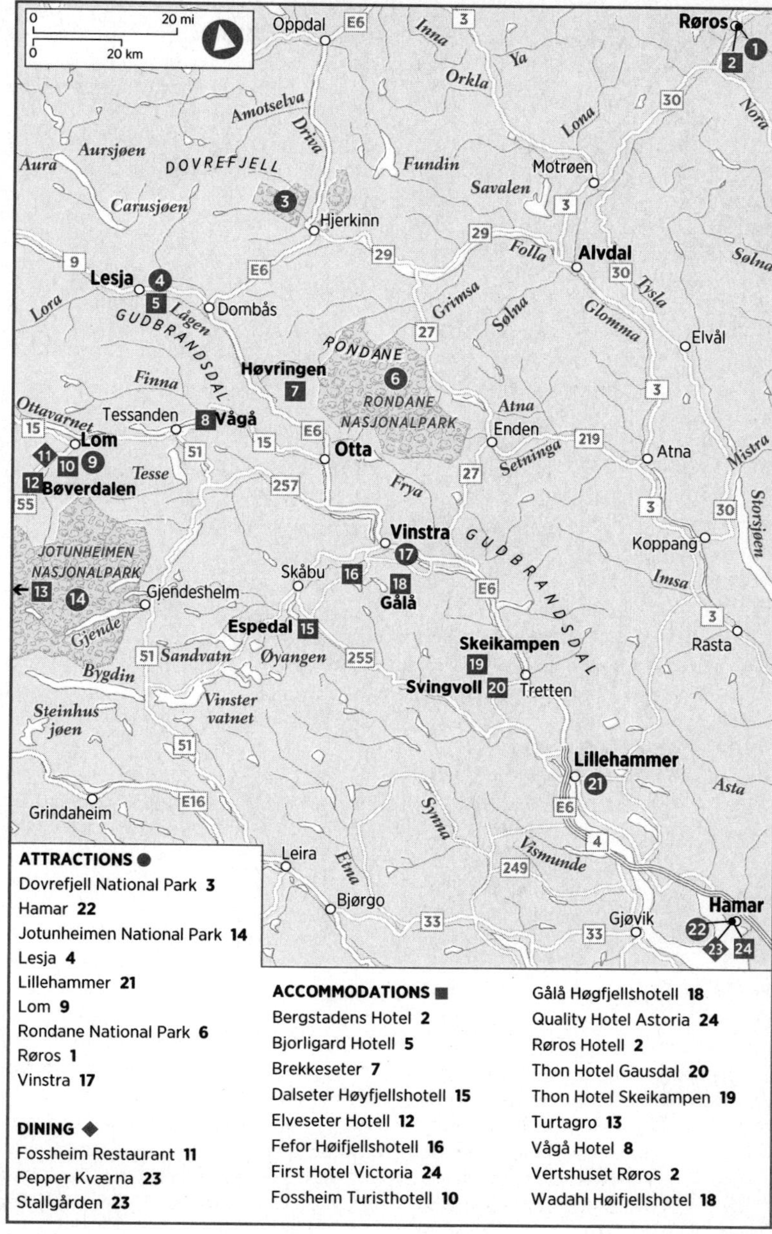

but it also has many attractions in its own right if you'd like to base yourself here and drive up to the more crowded Lillehammer.

In the Middle Ages, Hamar was the seat of a bishop, and a handful of ecclesiastical ruins remain from those glory days. Hamar was also the home of Kirsten Flagstad, one of the world's most famous operatic sopranos.

Hamar's Viking ship–shaped ice-skating hall was the site of skating events during the 1994 Winter Olympics.

Hamar is a good spot not because of any great architecture, but because of its natural setting. Its most charming assets are its marinas and waterside cafes, which, at least in summer, capture some of the charm of Norway. If you want to see old Norway, explore the ruins at the Hedmarksmuseet (see below).

More alluring than the rather dull modern buildings of Hamar itself is the surrounding fertile farmland, full of forests and pastures. In such a bucolic setting, it is easy to understand why many Oslo residents build summer homes here and use Lake Mjøsa as their playground during the few short weeks of sun they have. Many towns such as Hamar are mere refueling stops for their visits to the nearby national parks and lakes.

Essentials

GETTING THERE Frequent **trains** run between Oslo and Hamar, costing NOK238 one-way and taking 1¼ hours; visit www.nsb.no for schedules. Nor-Way Bussekspress runs daily **buses** from Oslo; visit www.nor-way.no for schedules. **Motorists** should take the E6 north from Oslo until they see the signposted turnoff for Hamar.

VISITOR INFORMATION The local tourist office is at Vikingskipet (✆ **62-51-75-03;** www.hoa.no), open Monday to Saturday 8am to 4pm. From mid-May to mid-August, hours are Monday to Friday 9am to 7pm, Saturday to Sunday 10am to 4pm. Or visit www.norway.com/hamar for information.

What to See & Do

Hedmarksmuseet & Domkirkeodden About 1.5km (1 mile) west of the town center, the ruins of the nearly 1,000-year-old Hamar Cathedral jut out into Lake Mjøsa. The site can be reached by a scenic walk, or you can take bus no. 6 from the Hamar library, costing NOK60 one-way. These ruins are evocative and call attention to Hamar's once-important role in Norway's ecclesiastical world. The church was constructed of locally quarried limestone, with Romanesque architecture, although later additions were Gothic.

The ruins are protected by a steel-and-glass cover provided in 1998. This protective umbrella is the largest glass construction in Europe, fanning out for 2,600m (8,500 ft.). Adjoining this is an archaeological museum displaying artifacts found in the area, and an open-air folk museum featuring 18th- and 19th-century houses. In an organic garden you can see nearly 400 different types of herbs. The best time to visit these ruins is in summer when concerts or plays are also presented.

Strandveien 100. ✆ **62-54-27-00.** www.hedmarksmuseet.no. Admission NOK80 adults, NOK35 children, NOK200 family ticket (off-season prices slightly cheaper). May 23–June 20 Tues–Sun 10am–4pm; June 21–Aug 15 daily 10am–5pm; Aug 16–Sept 9 Tues–Sun 10am–4pm. Closed Sept–May, check website for occasional events.

Sailing on Norway's Oldest Paddle Steamer

The best way to travel to Hamar is aboard the world's oldest paddle steamer, *Skibladner* ★★ (✆ 61-14-40-80; www.skibladner.no), which calls not only at Hamar but at Eidsvoll and Lillehammer, among other points, once daily. The ship was built in 1854 and is still in good shape, stretching 50m (160 ft.) long and measuring 5m (16 ft.) wide. It has a cruising speed of 12 knots and sails from the middle of June to the middle of August. Onboard is a luxurious 70-seat restaurant that's fully licensed and serves regional specialties. The most popular route is between Hamar and Lillehammer, taking 4 hours and costing NOK220 per person one-way or NOK320 return.

Kirsten Flagstad Museum If you've never heard the music of Norway's greatest opera diva, Kirsten Flagstad (1895–1962), it's worth coming here to listen to her operatic recording in a special room. This museum of Flagstad memorabilia lies about 50m (160 ft.) from the marketplace and a 10-minute walk from the railway station. On the ground floor you can purchase records, books about the star, and souvenirs. A special costume room is of particular interest because the Metropolitan Opera contributed some of the gowns that Kirsten wore in her most famous performances. Memorabilia and photographs, including the star's private albums, letters, contracts, and magazine and newspaper publicity, round out the exhibit. The collection of recordings here is the largest Flagstad trove in the world, covering her entire career from her first recordings in 1914 to her last memorable recordings in San Francisco.

Kirkegata 11. ✆ **62-53-32-77.** www.kirsten-flagstad.no. Admission NOK50 adults, NOK50 children, family pass NOK110. June–Aug Tues–Sun 11am–6pm; Sept–May Tues–Fri noon–3:30pm.

Kunstbanken Hedmark Kunstnersenter (Hedmark Artists' Center) This restored center for the arts offers changing exhibitions featuring regional artists, mainly painters and sculptors. Check with the tourist office to see what's currently showing. The center is beautifully situated by Lake Mjøsa, west of town, which makes for an idyllic walk along the lake.

Parkgate 21. ✆ **62-54-22-60.** www.kunstbanken.no. Admission free. Tues–Fri 11am–4pm, Sat–Sun noon–5pm.

NSB Jernbanemuseet (National Railway Museum) About the last profession I'd want to follow is that of a Norwegian railroad engineer, blasting through mountains and rugged terrain to lay track or carve out tunnels; but for the railroad buff, this museum is pure bliss. Established in 1896 on the shores of Lake Mjøsa, it collects and displays bits of Norwegian rail history dating from its beginnings in the 1850s. Vehicles include models from 1861 to 1950, among them three royal coaches and several steam locomotives weighing up to 150 tons. There is a museum park with several station buildings, railway tracks, and other exhibits, as well as a "dining car" serving snacks and refreshments. A small train travels through the grounds of an adjacent amusement park.

Strandveien 163. ✆ **62-51-31-60.** www.norsk-jernbanemuseum.no. Admission NOK75 adults, NOK40 children. July to mid-Aug daily 10am–5pm; off-season Mon–Sat 11am–3pm, Sun 11am–4pm. Take bus 1 from the railway station or walk 30 min. from the town center, north along the shore of Lake Mjøsa.

THE VOICE OF THE CENTURY

Kirsten Flagstad (1895–1962), to whom a museum of memorabilia is dedicated in Hamar, remains one of the all-time legends of opera. Interpreting the operas of Henry Purcell or Richard Wagner, among other composers, Flagstad had no equal in her day. At the age of 40, she was planning to retire but was invited to perform at New York's Metropolitan Opera on February 2, 1935. The rest is history. Her performance was broadcast across Canada and the United States, and it created a sensation, with music critics labeling her "The Voice of the Century." Her Brunhilde in San Francisco ensured her lasting fame in America. Along with Lauritz Melchior, Flagstad is credited with keeping the Metropolitan Opera alive in New York during the difficult days of the Depression on the eve of World War II.

Her popularity waned when she returned to Nazi-occupied Norway to be with her husband, Henry Johansen. It was a naive decision that would harm her incredible popularity in the United States for the rest of her life. During the war she never sang for the Germans. But her husband, Johansen, in ill health, was arrested by the Norwegians at the end of the war and labeled a war profiteer, even though he'd aided the Allied resistance. He died a year later.

On Flagstad's return to postwar America, a political campaign, labeled in the press as one of "extreme vituperation," was waged against her. Demonstrations marred each one of her performances in New York and San Francisco. Nevertheless, her devoted fans still clung to her. At age 54, when most divas are in retirement, Flagstad continued to perform with the San Francisco Opera, scoring some of her greatest successes with *Tristan und Isolde* and *Die Walküre.* During the tragic years of the war, her voice had "darkened" and lost some of its brilliant upper register. But all of her concerts were still sold out to die-hard fans.

Fortunately, her recorded voice remains to win new generations of fans among opera lovers. Many music critics now hail her as "the diva of the 20th century." Flagstad's recorded voice has become "immortal," glowing with richness, power, and an expressiveness that is not only beautiful, but also intensely dramatic.

Viking Ship Olympic Arena This modern sports arena hosted events during the 1994 Winter Olympics. While that seems like a long time ago, folks around here will be talking about it for years to come. The arena, lying within walking distance of the town center, is built in the shape of a Viking ship. Today it is the site of numerous sports events, performances, and exhibitions, and can hold some 10,000 spectators. It's been called a "sports cathedral without equal." Visits are possible when events aren't being staged.

Åkersvikaveien. ✆ **62-51-75-00.** www.hoa.no**.** Admission NOK30; ice-skating (late July to mid-Aug) NOK50. June 30 to mid-Aug daily 8am–8pm; off-season Mon–Fri 8am–3pm.

Where to Stay

First Hotel Victoria Set between the edge of the lake and the town's main pedestrian shopping street, this hotel originated in the 1850s as a small inn and grew over the years into the seven-story, modern-looking, gray-sided chain hotel you'll see today. The well-known Norwegian "Skagen painter," Christian Krohg, would regularly stay at the Victoria when visiting the region. From his regular table he gazed out over Lake Mjøsa for inspiration. Parts of the hotel are rather grand, especially some of the paneled, large-windowed public rooms whose deep sofas evoke the ethos of a private estate or social club. Most of the rooms are soothing, contemporary, monochromatic, and popular with business travelers from all over Scandinavia.

The hotel restaurant—large, contemporary, attractively formal, and outfitted with large windows—is open daily for lunch and dinner.

Strandgata 21, N-2317 Hamar. ✆ **62-02-55-00.** www.firsthotels.com. 115 units. NOK900–NOK1,100 double. Rates include buffet breakfast. AE, DC, MC, V. Free parking. **Amenities:** Restaurant; bar; room service; rooms for those with limited mobility. *In room:* TV, Wi-Fi, minibar.

Quality Hotel Astoria ★ Stay at the Victoria (see above) if you want tradition, but choose the Astoria if you prefer your hotels sleek and modern. Built in the early 1970s in the commercial center of town, this hotel was radically renovated in the late 1990s into a well-managed, middle-bracket enclave of efficiency and warmth. Because of its renovations, it promotes itself as "the newest hotel in town." Each room has a writing table; comfortable, contemporary-looking furniture; and a pastel color scheme. The in-house restaurant is separately recommended in "Where to Dine," below.

Torggata 23, N-2317 Hamar. ✆ **62-70-70-00.** Fax 62-70-70-01. www.choicehotels.no. 78 units. NOK1,100–NOK1,400 double. Rates include buffet breakfast. AE, DC, MC, V. Nearby parking NOK50. **Amenities:** 2 restaurants; cocktail bar; the "Dirty Nelly" pub; nightclub; rooms for those with limited mobility. *In room:* TV, Wi-Fi, minibar.

Where to Dine

Pepper Kværna NORWEGIAN This restaurant is quite a step above standard hotel dining. The entire place was renovated several years ago, though it still retains some of the dark woods from earlier incarnations. The menu offers savory preparations of such local ingredients as steak, pork filet, lamb schnitzel, and several fish dishes. The seasonal menu changes regularly.

In the Quality Hotel Astoria, Torggata 23. ✆ **62-70-70-00.** Main courses NOK230–NOK290. AE, DC, MC, V. Mon–Thurs 5–11pm; Fri–Sat 6–11pm

Stallgården NORWEGIAN/INTERNATIONAL This is the largest and most imaginative dining, drinking, and disco venue in Hamar. It was built in 1849 as an inn, and the high-ceilinged interior was transformed into its present incarnation in 2010. The street-level pub, with thick beams and rustic artifacts, has been transformed into a delicate cafe/restaurant with a local-meets-global menu based on regional ingredients and culinary traditions. During the summer, a beer garden sprawls out into a disused stable yard out back. Meanwhile, the stone-vaulted cellar, originally conceived as a coal cellar, is today artfully illuminated with a mixture of candles and electric lights. The food here is typified by the Brazilian barbecue concept of *churrascaria*.

The top floor of the restaurant features a nightclub with DJs as well as live music.

Torggata 82. ✆ **62-54-31-00.** www.stallgarden.no. Reservations recommended Fri–Sat. Main courses NOK179–NOK375. AE, DC, MC, V. Street-level pub daily 11am–10:30pm. Dinner in cellar-level restaurant daily 6–10:30pm. Disco Thurs–Sat 10pm–3am.

Hamar After Dark

For the largest drinking and dining venue in town, refer to Stallgården under "Where to Dine," above.

Also popular is the **Irishman Pub,** Strandgata 31 (✆ **62-52-33-92;** www.irishman.no), which draws a lively crowd, usually in the 30- to 50-year-old bracket, to its 1930s-era precincts. The decor? Classic Irish pub, down to the pictures of famous Irishmen lining the walls. On Friday evening, live bands play a range of classic rock and Celtic tunes. Of course, Guinness and Irish whiskeys rule the night. Open Sunday and Monday noon to 8pm, Tuesday to Thursday noon to 12:30am, and Friday and Saturday noon to 2:30am.

LILLEHAMMER OF OLYMPIC GLORY ★★

169km (105 miles) N of Oslo; 363km (225 miles) S of Trondheim

Surrounded by mountains, Lillehammer is one of Europe's favorite resorts and my own choice for many a vacation. The town, at the head (northern end) of Lake Mjøsa, became internationally famous when it hosted the 1994 Winter Olympics. Today the sports sites and infrastructure benefit greatly from the two-billion-kroner investment that the government put into Lillehammer to make it worthy of the games. Skiers in winter can take advantage of many of these improvements.

Though Lillehammer's luxury and skiing appeal may lag behind that of chic alpine resorts such as St. Moritz in Switzerland or St. Anton in Austria, Lillehammer's charm is in the fact that it is just a simple country town. "Winter City"—as Lillehammer is sometimes called—does, for its part, have excellent natural ski conditions, even if it doesn't get much of that famous alpine sunshine.

However, even if you're not considering it for a ski holiday, Lillehammer is an attractive venue for summer vacationers, as it has a number of attractions (see below) and a broad appeal for families.

With a population of 23,000, Lillehammer is surrounded by forests, farms, and small settlements. Its main pedestrian street, **Storgata ★**, is known for its well-preserved wooden buildings.

At the southern end of the Gudbrandsdal Valley, Lillehammer was founded as a trading post back in 1827. Over the years, it has attracted many artists who have been drawn to its beautiful landscapes and special Nordic light. The most famous artist who lived here was Sigrid Undset, who won the Nobel Prize for literature in 1928.

If you're driving into Lillehammer, the convoluted traffic patterns, one-way streets, and tunnels may confuse you. It's better to park as soon as you can and explore Lillehammer on foot. It's easy to navigate, and, frankly, there isn't that much to see in the very center once you've walked the Storgata. Lillehammer's greatest attractions, such as its ski slopes and the Maihaugen Museum, lie on the outskirts.

At the peak of summer, the streets, which contain both attractive wooden structures and a lot of ugly modern buildings, are full of people shopping, eating, or drinking. In winter, skiers take over. Considering the fame of Lillehammer, many visitors expect a far more beautiful town than they discover here.

Lillehammer

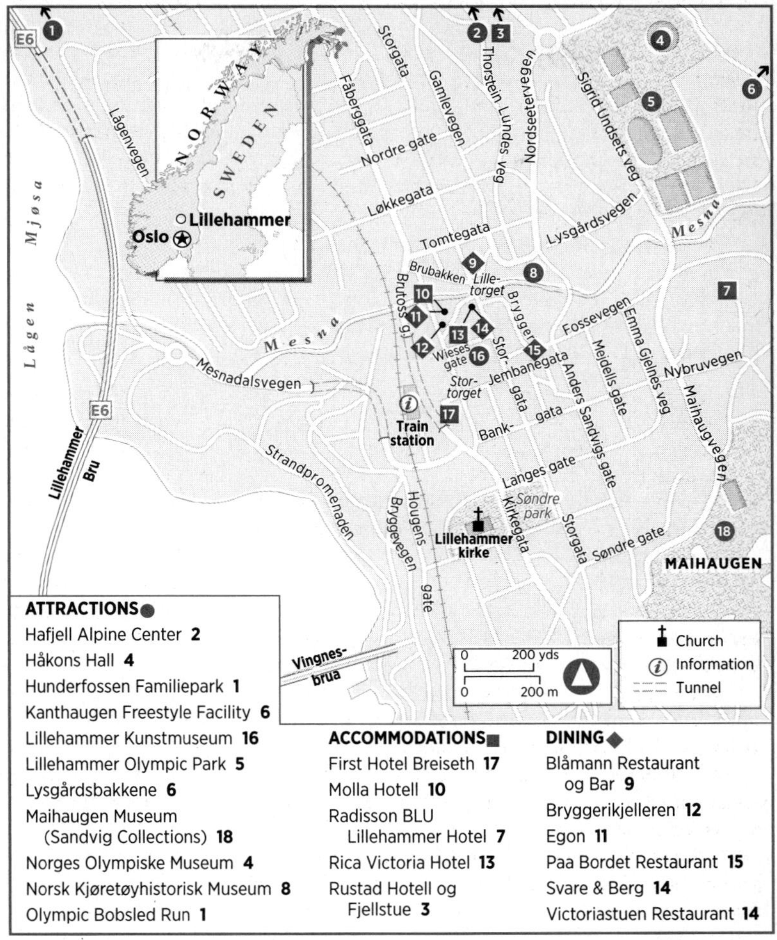

What you'll see in Lillehammer is shop after shop—some 250 in all—crowding the Storgata and streets branching off from it. Some of these stores, such as those selling crafts, will be of interest to visitors. Others (hardware stores and the like) mainly serve the population living in the province.

Essentials

GETTING THERE

BY TRAIN From Oslo, express trains take about 2 hours 20 minutes, and local trains take about 3 hours. Depending on the time of year, there are five to eight trains per day. Call ✆ **81-50-08-88** or visit www.nsb.no for information.

BY BUS Bus trips between Oslo and Lillehammer take about 2½ hours and depart two or three times a day. Visit www.nor-way.no for information.

BY CAR Head north from Oslo along the E6.

VISITOR INFORMATION

The **Lillehammer Tourist Office** is adjacent to the railway station at Jernbanetorget 2 (© **61-28-98-00;** www.lillehammer.com). From mid-June to mid-August, it is open Monday to Friday 8am to 6pm, and Saturday and Sunday 10am to 5pm. Off-season hours are Monday to Friday 8am to 4pm and Saturday 10am to 2pm.

What to See & Do

Hunderfossen Familiepark (Hunderfossen Family Park) ☺ At this kiddie fun park, you'll find a presentation of the most popular Norwegian fairy tales, more than 50 activities for children and adults, and lots of space to roam around. There are a merry-go-round and a Ferris wheel, as well as carnival booths, a cafeteria, and a swimming pool. A 12-m (39-ft.)-tall troll at the gate welcomes visitors. The park is 12km (7½ miles) north of Lillehammer on the E6.

Fåberg. © **61-27-72-22.** www.hunderfossen.no. Admission NOK285 adults, NOK180 seniors, NOK230 children 3–13, free for children under 90cm (35½ in.) tall. May–Sept daily 10am–6pm. Closed Oct–Apr. Bus: Hunderfossen from Lillehammer.

Lillehammer Kunstmuseum (Lillehammer Art Museum) This museum of art is better than most provincial museums in Norway because so many great artists, including Edvard Munch, were inspired by the area. In 2008, it was voted Norwegian Museum of the Year. In 1963, it opened as a contemporary museum but later expanded into an annex designed by the Norwegian architecture firm Snøhetta. To bridge the gap between the two buildings, sculptor Bard Breivik created a sculpture garden using the elements of water and stone. In the center of town, the museum displays one of Norway's largest collections of national art, with pieces dating from the 1830s to the present. Some of Norway's major artists are represented, including Axel Revold, Erik Werenskjold, and Christian Krogh. But most international visitors seek out works by Edvard Munch. The collection includes four of his paintings, including *Portrait of Ida Roede*. This gallery also possesses one of the biggest collections of paintings from the so-called Norwegian Romantic period. Opened in the winter of 1992, it was one of the major cultural venues during the 1994 Olympics.

Stortorget 2. © **61-05-44-60.** www.lillehammerartmuseum.com. Admission NOK90 adults, NOK60 students & seniors, free for children 18 & under. June 28 to mid-Aug daily 11am–5pm; mid-Aug to June 27 Tues–Sun 11am–4pm.

Maihaugen Museum (Sandvig Collections) ★★ Many Norwegian towns have open-air museums featuring old buildings that have been moved and put on display. This is one of the best of them. This museum consists of 180 buildings, from manor houses to the cottage of a poor yeoman worker, and there are more than 40,000 exhibits. The houses reassembled here and furnished in 17th- to 18th-century style came from all over the Gudbrandsdal (Gudbrands Valley). Of particular interest is the Garmo stave church, built in 1200.

You can also visit 37 old workshops, displaying activities ranging from gunsmithing to wood engraving, and a large exhibit covering Norwegian history from 10,000 B.C. to the present. The museum lies about 10 minutes on foot from the town center or a 20-minute walk from the train station. Head up Jernbanegata, turn right onto Anders Sandvigs Gate, and then go left up Maihaugvegen, following the signposts. The city's concert hall is also at the museum, and two on-site cafeterias serve Norwegian food.

Maihaugvegen 1. ✆ **61-28-89-00.** www.maihaugen.no. Admission NOK140 adults, NOK70 children 6–15, free for children 5 & under. June–Sept daily 10am–5pm; Oct–May (indoor museum only) Tues–Sun 11am–4pm. Bus: 6.

Norsk Kjøretøyhistorisk Museum The Norwegian Museum of Historic Vehicles illustrates the development of transportation from the first sledges and wagons to modern-day cars. The most intriguing, and perhaps saddest, exhibitions are the cars left over from Norway's attempt to build up an automobile-manufacturing industry. The most famous of these is the strange "Troll Car," a kissing cousin of Sweden's Saab. The last ones were made in the 1950s and are viewed as collectors' vehicles today. The museum is two blocks east of the railway station.

Lilletorget 1. ✆ **61-25-61-65.** Admission NOK40 adults, NOK20 children 7–14, free for children 6 & under. June 15–Aug 20 daily 10am–6pm; Aug 21–June 14 Mon–Fri 11am–3pm, Sat–Sun 11am–4pm.

Olympic Sites

The **Lillehammer Olympic Park ★★** was the site of the 1994 games and is today one of the major centers for sports in Norway. In **Håkons Hall,** there are facilities for fitness training, squash, badminton, soccer, handball, volleyball, and other pursuits. Visitors can attend various sporting events here, especially hockey matches, but also indoor golfing events. Check with the tourist office to see what might be in the offing at the time of your visit.

Also in the hall is the **Norges Olympiske Museum (Norwegian Olympic Museum),** Olympiaparken (✆ **61-05-76-50;** www.ol.museum.no), the only such museum in Scandinavia, with exhibitions not only about Lillehammer's role as host of the games in 1994, but also on the entire history of the Olympics up to the present day. In all, there are some 6,000 individual exhibits, as well as documentaries of the games. Admission is NOK100 for adults and NOK50 for children. It's open June to August daily from 10am to 5pm; off-season hours are Tuesday to Sunday 11am to 4pm.

Lysgårdsbakkene, the ski jump tower (✆ **61-05-42-00;** www.olympiaparken.no), is open daily from mid-June to mid-August from 9am to 8pm, charging NOK20 for admission. You can take a chairlift to the top of the big ski jump for a **panoramic view ★★** of the Olympic Park and the surrounding area. The chairlift costs NOK50 for adults and NOK45 for children. Although you can also take the chairlift back down, it makes a lovely stroll to walk down instead.

In the upper part of the park, the **Lillehammer Skiklub** (✆ **61-27-58-00;** www.lillehammer-skiklub.no) has areas for cross-country skiing, plus a ski lodge and a cafeteria. The **Kanthaugen Freestyle Facility** (✆ **61-05-42-00**) is one of the most compact facilities of its type in the world, with hills for aerials, moguls, and "ballet." Skiing instruction is offered on the ballet hill.

The **Olympic Bobsled Run** (contact Lillehammer's Olympic Park, ✆ **61-05-42-00**) is not in the park but at Hunderfossen, 15km (9¼ miles) north of the town. This is northern Europe's only artificially refrigerated bobsled and luge track. It's 1,365m (4,477 ft.) long, and the height difference from start to finish is 114m

(374 ft.). The track has 16 curves. From October to March, visitors can try bobsledding or "bobrafting." The bobraft is a rubber sled that to us looks like a big bathtub. Even in the warmer months, from April to September, you can still try the wheelbob (a bobsled on wheels), which takes four passengers per trip at a speed of 100kmph (60 mph). Rates for the bobraft facility (winter only), bobsled run (winter only), and wheeled bobsled (summer only) are the same: NOK220 per person.

Outdoor Activities

BIKING & HIKING The best mountain-biking and hiking possibilities are from the **Nordseter Hyttegrend (Nordseter Activity Center; ✆ 61-26-40-12;** www.nordseter.no**)**, lying 15km (9¼ miles) northeast of the town center of Lillehammer. Follow the signs to Nordseter on the approach roads to Lillehammer.

Once at this lakefront sporting complex, you'll find many options for biking, hiking, climbing, boating, and canoeing. From here you can hike up to Mount Neverfjell at 1,089m (3,572 ft.). In summer, a 21-gear mountain bike rents for NOK180 per day; a rowboat or canoe for excursions on the waters of Lake Nevelvatnet rents for NOK300.

Free maps (and advice) are available for anyone who wants to ramble along the well-marked hiking trails radiating outward and into the surrounding hills. Likewise, the best biking routes in the area can be plotted for you.

SKIING Lillehammer has a 94-m (308-ft.) slope for professionals and a smaller jump for the less experienced. The lifts take skiers some 450m (1,500 ft.) above sea level up the slalom slope, and more than 400km (250 miles) of marked skiing trails are packed by machines. The Lillehammer Ski School offers daily classes, and several cross-country tours are held weekly. Ask at the tourist office (see "Visitor Information," p. 198) for details.

Hafjell Alpine Center (**✆ 61-27-47-00;** www.hafjell.no) was the main venue for Olympic alpine competitions in 1994. It has seven lifts and 20km (12 miles) of alpine slopes. The location is 15km (9¼ miles) north of town. A "Vinterbuss," costing NOK40 one-way and taking 20 minutes, runs here from the center of Lillehammer about six times per day. Lillehammer is also the starting point for some 400km (250 miles) of prepared cross-country tracks, 5.8km (3⅔ miles) of which are illuminated.

Lillehammer gears up in December for its winter sports season. In addition to the ski center, there's an admission-free **skating rink** where you have to bring your own skates. It's open in the winter Monday to Friday from 11am to 9pm, and Sunday 11am to 5pm. In the winter, you'll also discover festivals, folklore nights, and ski races.

In winter, **Nordseter** is the focal point of two separate slopes—for both the beginner and the intermediate-level downhill skier. It also has a vast network of cross-country ski trails. A lift pass, valid for a full day, costs NOK355 per person, and ski equipment (either downhill or cross-country) rents for NOK305 per day. It's located 12km (7½ miles) northeast of Lillehammer. Take bus 260 from the city center.

Shopping

In the center of Lillehammer is **Husfliden ★★**, Storgata 47 (**✆ 61-26-70-70;** www.norskflid.no), a respected name in Norwegian handicrafts, presenting a vast array of Norwegian products, ideal as gifts or souvenirs. The location is near Sigrid

Undsets Plass. One of Norway's oldest established jewelers, in business since 1868, is **Gullsmed Frisenberg ★★**, Storgata 74 (✆ **61-25-03-36;** www.frisenberg.no), now run by the fourth generation of the founding family. Merchandise includes some of the best jewelry selections from Scandinavia's leading designers.

Sport 1, Kirkegata 55 (✆ **61-24-70-70;** www.sport1lillehammer.no), opposite the Lillehammer Art Museum, offers a huge selection of winter and summer attire. Whatever you need in the realm of sports gear, you are likely to find here. **Belsvik Match,** Storgata 72 (✆ **61-25-47-09;** www.belsvik.no), is Lillehammer's oldest and biggest clothing outlet. Merchandise comes in a wide range of price categories. Most visitors prefer to come here to pick up some traditional Norwegian knitwear.

Where to Stay

First Hotel Breiseth ★ At the time of its opening in 1898, this was the most fashionable hotel in Lillehammer, and it became known as a summer gathering place for artists. Within an easy walk of the Olympic Park, and close to the bus and train terminals, its convenient location makes the Breiseth a winning choice. After several renovations, there are still a number of traditional touches, as evidenced by the turn-of-the-20th-century public rooms, with artwork on the walls and marble pillars holding up ceilings. During the winter, the blazing fireplace in the parlor is a popular hangout. Guest rooms tend to be on the small side, but are completely fresh and tastefully furnished in natural woods. One wing caters specifically to those with allergies, with natural-fiber linens and a strict no-smoking-or-pets policy.

1–5 Jernbanegata 1, N-2609 Lillehammer. ✆ **61-24-77-77.** www.firsthotels.no/breiseth. 89 units. NOK1,100–NOK1,600. Rates include buffet breakfast. AE, DC, MC, V. **Amenities:** Restaurant; bar; sauna; room service; rooms for those with limited mobility. *In room:* TV, Wi-Fi, minibar, hair dryer.

Molla Hotell ★★ Though not on quite the same level as the Radisson BLU (see below), this is one of the most modern and desirable hotels in this vast area, rising 11 floors from its location in the town center. It was originally constructed to host visitors to the 1994 Winter Olympics. The hotel is the second-tallest building in town and the site of one of Lillehammer's most sought-after restaurants, Egon, which is recommended separately (p. 203). Pastel-decorated bedrooms are comfortably decorated with pine furnishings, quilted bedspreads, and regional art. The location is easily the most romantic in town, a converted mill dating from 1863, set right by a rushing stream and small waterfall. Another winning feature is the panoramic rooftop bar.

Elvegata 12, N-2609 Lillehammer. ✆ **61-05-70-80.** www.mollahotell.no. 58 units. NOK1,250 double. Rates include buffet breakfast. AE, DC, MC, V. **Amenities:** Restaurant; bar; sauna; room service; rooms for those with limited mobility. *In room:* TV, minibar, hair dryer.

Radisson BLU Lillehammer Hotel ★★★ ☺ Set at the halfway point between the open-air museum at Maihaugen and the Olympic Park, this is the best hotel in Lillehammer, opening onto a 3.5-hectare (8½-acre) park. Lying 600m (⅓ mile) from the main street, it is Lillehammer's most traditional hotel, a smoothly running and efficient operation with the best facilities in town. A small midrise, it greets you with a fountain at the entrance, with good taste in paintings, paneling, artifacts, and carpeting that add to the style of the hotel. Bedrooms are well organized and feature bright fabrics and homelike touches throughout. The drinking and dining facilities are top-rate.

Turisthotelveien 6, N-2609 Lillehammer. ✆ **61-28-60-00.** www.radisson.com. 303 units. Sun–Thurs NOK795–NOK1,335; Fri–Sat NOK1,020–NOK1,635. AE, DC, MC, V. **Amenities:** 2 restaurants; 4 bars; 2 heated pools (1 heated indoor); fitness room; sauna; children's programs; room service; rooms for those with limited mobility. *In room:* TV, Wi-Fi, minibar, hair dryer.

Rica Victoria Hotel ★ Established in 1872, this is a traditional choice for vacationers, but it has kept up with the times. The complex consists of an older concrete building along with a more modern six-floor structure, typified by heavy beams, brown-leather sofas, and brass chandeliers, as well as paintings. Guests gather near the fireplace in the lounge when it's cold outside, and there is a pub-style steakhouse and a disco (both are occasionally used by nonguests and locals). I prefer the bedrooms in the original house to the more sterile newer units, but all rooms are comfortable enough. The Victoriastuen Restaurant, reviewed separately below, offers guests excellent on-site dining.

Storgata 84B, N-2615 Lillehammer. ✆ **61-27-17-00.** www.rica.no. 109 units. NOK1,045–NOK1,295 double. Rates include buffet breakfast. AE, DC, MC, V. **Amenities:** Restaurant; bar; disco; room service; rooms for those with limited mobility. *In room:* TV, minibar, hair dryer.

Rustad Hotell og Fjellstue ★ This has more of a Klondike feeling than the sleek first-class hotels previously recommended, and I actually prefer it for that reason. You can settle into the wilderness at this favorite spot 18km (11 miles) north of Lillehammer. The log-and-timber chalet is on the edge of a lake, with a dock for swimming and boats. The property is surrounded by private grounds with views of the water or the mountains. Hiking trails are available in many directions, and there are some 300km (190 miles) of well-prepared cross-country tracks in winter. The staff can arrange swimming, canoe and boat trips, fishing, and a winter ski school. Skis can be rented on-site. The bedrooms are small to midsize, each comfortably furnished.

Sjusjøen, N-2612 Lillehammer. ✆ **62-33-64-64.** www.rustadhotel.com. 46 units. Mid-June to mid-Sept NOK695–NOK1,230 double; mid-Sept to mid-June NOK720–NOK1,380. Rates include buffet breakfast. AE, DC, MC, V. **Amenities:** Restaurant; bar; sauna. *In room:* TV, minibar (in some).

Where to Dine

Blåmann Restaurant og Bar MEXICAN/NORWEGIAN Quesadillas with chicken and fried reindeer may seem like an odd juxtaposition of culinary traditions, but this long-standing favorite more or less succeeds in its offerings. Housed in an old-fashioned building but done up with modern, sleek black tables and chairs, it offers views of the Mesna River on one side of the restaurant. In summer, there is outdoor seating over the river. A delicious hunter's soup is made with mushrooms, beef (or reindeer), and spices, and served with sour cream and a baguette. My favorite dish is the mountain trout served in a sour-cream sauce with cucumber salad and potatoes. Some of the more exotic main dishes include *bacalhau* and Cajun burgers, and you can also order succulent Norwegian lamb. For dessert, they offer banana splits, chocolate fondant, or crème brulée.

Lilletorvet 1. ✆ **61-26-22-03.** www.blaamann.com. Reservations recommended. Main courses NOK229–NOK345. AE, DC, MC, V. Mon–Sat noon–11pm; Sun 1–10pm.

Bryggerikjelleren NORWEGIAN This 1814 brewery, a 7-minute walk east of the train station, was transformed in 1969 into a pub-restaurant, offering beer, steaks, and tasty main dishes. It's done a roaring trade ever since and is especially popular in winter with people who've just come off the ski tracks. In fact, when the weather's bad and no one can ski or climb in the hills, this is one of the most popular watering holes in town. The joint especially attracts a good share of the hardcore drinking crowd. The Norwegian fare is rather typical, though there are some interesting Scandinavian dishes such as garlic gratinated crayfish tails and a salad of chorizo and scampi marinated in chilis. They'll feed you well with generous portions, and most dishes are priced at the lower end of the scale.

Brenneriet Nattklub (The Distillery) is linked to the restaurant. It's open Wednesday, Friday, and Saturday from 11pm to 3am. On Friday there's a NOK70 cover charge, going up to NOK80 on Saturday.

Elvagata 19. ✆ **61-27-06-60.** www.bryggerikjellerenrestaurant.no. Reservations not accepted. Main courses NOK180–NOK410. AE, DC, MC, V. Daily 6–11pm.

Egon ★ ☺ NORWEGIAN/INTERNATIONAL Housed in a grinding mill from 1863 and connected by a covered passageway to the Molla Hotel next door, this restaurant offers three floors of seating, lots of cozy nooks and crannies, and big-windowed views of the river. There's outdoor seating in summer, and a worthy collection of rustic country antiques and mill implements hanging from the ceiling beams and rafters. Menu options include an a la carte menu, access to a set-price salad and pizza buffet, and a children's menu comprised of simple burgers, frankfurters, and pastas. Specialties include a "black and white" platter of filets of veal and filet mignon, served with pepper sauce; rack of Norwegian lamb; and some rather banal, diet-conscious fish dishes such as baked salmon with mushrooms, paprika, and mashed potatoes.

In the Molla Hotel, Elvegata 12. ✆ **61-25-23-40.** Reservations recommended. Main courses NOK144–NOK267. AE, DC, MC, V. Mon–Sat 11am–11pm; Sun noon–11pm.

Paa Bordet Restaurant ★ NORWEGIAN/INTERNATIONAL Now run by a local catering company, this restaurant is housed in a rustic timbered building dating from 1880. It's long been known locally for its excellent cuisine, prepared with quality ingredients—and its multiple-course menus. (This means that even if you want something a la carte, you're probably going to have to select it from the prix-fixe menu.) The menu rotates seasonally and per the chefs' fancy but all the dishes are made with consummate skill. Regular appearances are made by marinated wild salmon, linguini with mushroom sauce, and crispy breast of duck with parsley. For dessert, try the Norwegian standby of Gudbrandsdalen cheese.

Bryggerigata 70. ✆ **61-25-30-00.** www.bordet.no. Reservations recommended. Main courses NOK275; 3-course fixed-price menu NOK475; 4-course fixed-price menu NOK525. AE, DC, MC, V. Fri & Sat 6–10pm. Closed late June to late Aug.

Victoriastuen Restaurant ★ NORWEGIAN/INTERNATIONAL Located in the Rica Victoria Hotel (p. 202), a few minutes' walk north of the railway station, this lively restaurant offers some of Lillehammer's finest dining year after year, its windows opening onto the town center. The restaurant is nostalgically outfitted in what Norwegians refer to as "farmer's colors"—strong blues and reds with an antiquelike patina. The kitchen provides quality local dishes; fresh mountain trout or catfish, served in a butter sauce with a cucumber salad, is particularly good.

Charging less, Dolly Dimple's, one floor above, is a pub, pizzeria, and steakhouse. It provides good food in far less formal surroundings.

In the Rica Victoria Hotel, Storgata 84B. ✆ **61-27-17-00.** Main courses NOK250–NOK330. AE, DC, MC, V. Daily 11am–2pm & 3–11pm.

Lillehammer After Dark

Felix Pub & Scene A pub since 1984, this major venue for the alternative rock scene is housed in a historic building from 1832. Visited by musicians, students, and others, it often stages live concerts on the ground floor of its two floors. Patrons range in age from 18 to 30, and they listen to recorded music—rock, punk rock, whatever—if there aren't any live groups playing. Storgata 31. ✆ **61-25-01-02.** www.felixpub.no. Cover from NOK50 for live music concerts. Daily 10pm–2am.

Marcello Nightclub This is the region's major nightclub, holding at capacity anywhere from 250 to 300 patrons on its dance floor, set down in the basement of this market-square building. The dancers, ranging in age from 30 to 45, move to recorded music, which runs the gamut from pop to country. Only beer and wine are sold, and the doorman assured us, "It's easy to get in unless you're too drunk." On the whole, you'll find oldies and R&B on Fridays, and club music and Europop on Saturdays. Storgata 86. ✆ **61-25-90-90.** Thurs–Sat 10pm–3am.

Svare & Berg This popular bar features red velvet chairs, a massive bar, and even a fireplace for evening drinkers. There is room for 120 people, and the place is generally populated by 20- and 30-somethings. It is one of the more upscale places to come drinking in town—and a last-ditch place to meet someone in the wee hours. Strandgata 71. ✆ **62-53-40-68.** www.svareberg.no. Thurs–Sat 8pm–2am.

Toppen Bar This bar offers panoramic views, with vistas of Lillehammer, the Olympic areas, and Lake Mjøsa. It's known locally as Lillehammer's highest *vannpost,* or watering hole, located on the top floor of the Molla Hotel. Go easy, though: The suds can go to your head fast at this elevation. In the Molla Hotel, Elvegata 12. ✆ **61-05-70-80.** www.mollahotell.no/toppen-bar/. Mon–Sat 8pm–2am.

VINSTRA: THE PEER GYNT ROAD

220km (136 miles) NW of Oslo; 61km (38 miles) NW of Lillehammer

As much as I enjoy Lillehammer, my heart has been equally won over by the wildness of the Peer Gynt country, where you'll encounter nature somewhat more raw. Although this is primarily known as a ski area, the summertime—when you can cruise along mountain roads, past old farmsteads and fish-filled lakes, enjoying the alpine flowers and the wild birds—is equally delightful.

The Peer Gynt Road ★★★, between Lillehammer and the little town of Vinstra, takes you right into the heart of Peer Gynt country. Henrik Ibsen came this way when he was researching his masterpiece, *Peer Gynt,* published in 1867 and later set to music by Edvard Grieg. Ibsen based his tale in part on the exploits of one Per (spelled with only one "e") Gynt Haga, a real-life Norwegian folk hero noted for such exploits as riding on the backs of reindeer at breakneck speed.

As you drive through the Gudbrandsdal (Gudbrands Valley), you can travel the same route that bewitched the original hero, and outside Vinstra you can visit a monument to Per Gynt Haga himself, in the cemetery adjoining the Sødorp Church, 1.5km (1 mile) south of town. The road passes two large resorts, **Skeikampen** (in

Gausdal) and **Gålå** (in Wadahl), before rejoining the E6 at Vinstra. Visit www.peergyntvegen.no for more information on the road.

The Peer Gynt country is an unspoiled mountain region with peaks that range from 769m to 1,499m (2,522 ft.–4,917 ft.). This is one of Norway's oldest and best-known sports districts. The skiing center at Fefor was opened in 1904, and it was here that the adventurous Capt. Robert Falcon Scott tested the equipment for his expedition to the South Pole.

Essentials

GETTING THERE

BY TRAIN Following more or less the same route as the buses but taking a bit less time, trains travel from Oslo Central station via Gardermoen airport and Lillehammer to Vinstra, taking 3 to 3¼ hours, for NOK482 one-way. The price includes a seat reservation, which, in light of the many weekenders who go to Peer Gynt country from Oslo, is a good idea. For railway information call ✆ **81-50-08-88** or visit www.nsb.no.

BY BUS Buses depart from Oslo's central bus station, immediately adjacent to Oslo Central railway station. They make a stop at the bus station at Gardermoen airport, then continue on to Lillehammer and Vinstra. There are three to four of these per day. The one-way fare for the 4½-hour trip is NOK415. Call **Nor-Way Bussekspress** (✆ **81-54-44-44;** www.nor-way.no) for reservations and information. You could also try **Gausdal Tourist Information,** Segalstad Bru, N-2651 Gausdal (✆ 61-22-45-34, www.gausdal.com), who can give information on schedules.

BY CAR From Lillehammer, continue northwest on the E6 into Vinstra.

BY TAXI Passengers arriving at the bus or railway station (they're adjacent to each other) usually have to migrate by taxi to their hotel, as most hotels are in isolated spots up in the mountains. A taxi from Vinstra to Gålå, for example, costs from NOK350 for up to four passengers (two or three if they have a lot of luggage). Usually a hotel will send a van down to meet its passengers as part of the cost of the hotel package. Alternatively, ring ✆ **61-29-04-40** to order a taxi.

VISITOR INFORMATION

The best source of information about touring in the area is the Lillehammer Tourist Office (p. 198).

Outdoor Activities

The **Peer Gynt Trail ★★★** is ideal for those who'd like to combine cross-country skiing with alpine skiing. All the facilities in the ski region are within easy reach of all the hotels in the area. A ski bus links the resorts of Espedalen, Fefor, and Gålå with two other ski areas—Lauvåsen and Skeikampen—further on. In all, there are 24 slopes totaling 28km (17 miles), eight lifts and one chairlift. In the entire area there are some 460km (290 miles) of well-prepared trails and 170km (110 miles) of stick-marked trails in beautiful surroundings. Skiers rate the Peer Gynt Trail among Norway's best cross-country skiing areas, and floodlit trails in Espedalen and in Gålå make it possible to ski even after dinner.

You can purchase a 1-day Troll Pass, costing NOK320 for adults and NOK265 for children. The pass entitles you to all the lifts in the area. Check with the local resorts for further information. You can pick up maps and other data at the tourist center at Vinstra (see above). Cross-country skis can be rented for around NOK210 per day; slalom (alpine) skis tend to cost a little bit more.

In summer, **Norske Bygdeopplevelser** (✆ **61-28-99-70;** www.norske-bygdeopplevelser.no) offers cycling trips and mountain hikes through Peer Gynt land. They also offer extended ski tours, for example an 8-day, 170-km (106-mile) trip through Rondane Nasjonalpark to Lillehammer.

What to See & Do

Much revered by the Norwegians, Bjørnstjerne Bjørnson, author of the national anthem of Norway, lived with his wife Karoline at an old farmstead, **Aulestad** (✆ **61-22-41-10**), in Gausdal, 18km (11 miles) northwest of Lillehammer, from 1875 until his death in 1910. His first novel, *Synnøve Solbakken,* published in 1857, narrated the lives of ordinary folk in a vernacular language based on regional dialects—something fairly uncommon in Norwegian literature at the time. He won the Nobel Prize for literature in 1903. In 1934, the house was opened as a national museum, and today it is filled with Bjørnson memorabilia. It's signposted near the hamlet of Follebu. Aulestad is open from late May to August daily 11am to 5pm, and in September Tuesday to Sunday 11am to 4pm. There are regularly scheduled guided tours. Admission is NOK100 for adults, NOK50 for children under 16.

Where to Stay & Dine

Most people travel the Peer Gynt Road as an excursion from Lillehammer. But if you'd like to stay around for a few days, here are several recommended accommodations, scattered throughout the area at various hamlets and resorts.

Dalseter Høyfjellshotell ☺ There are far grander hotels in the area than this entrancing wilderness oasis, but the staff here really do their best to sort out outdoor activities. Ski trails begin just outside the entrance to the hotel, and during the summer you can buy a fishing permit and try your luck at catching trout, char, and perch. Mountain biking expeditions can also be arranged, with information on marked trails where you can hop off and hike—or just sit and breathe the fresh mountain air. This family-run hotel, built in 1963 but kept well up to date, is set on a hillside overlooking a panorama of forests and mountains. The bedrooms are outfitted in a cozy, comfortable Norwegian regional style, with no shortage of heat during the Arctic winters. In winter, evening dance music contributes to a festive ski-lodge atmosphere, and meals of well-prepared country fare are served in a warm, inviting room. The hotel is entirely nonsmoking.

Gudbrandsdalen, N-2658 Espedalen. ✆ **61-29-99-10.** www.dalseter.no. 88 units. NOK1,430–NOK1,900 double. Rates include buffet breakfast. Children 4 & under stay free in parents' room; 3-night minimum stay. DC, MC, V. Closed Oct–Dec 21. **Amenities:** Restaurant; bar; heated indoor pool; 2 tennis courts; exercise room; 2 saunas; large kids' playroom; rooms for those with limited mobility. *In room:* TV.

Fefor Høifjellshotell ★ ☺ The core of this hotel dates from 1891, when it was a modest-size, plank-sided mountain inn, sheltering summer hikers and winter skiers beside the Fefor Innsjø (Lake Fefor), 13km (8 miles) east of Vinstra. Today, greatly expanded with a series of modern wings, it's an upper-middle-bracket refuge with the most charming old hotel cores in the region. Designed in Norwegian national style, it features red Nordic dragons on the roof, blazing fireplaces, and

BJØRNSTJERNE BJØRNSON: YES, WE love THIS LAND

Ranking along with author Henrik Ibsen, Bjørnstjerne Bjørnson (1832–1910), winner of the 1903 Nobel Prize for literature, left part of his world behind at this old farmstead at Aulestad (see above), which the public can now visit in Gausdal. He was a towering figure in the history of Norway, having achieved fame as a poet, dramatist, novelist, journalist, editor, public speaker, and theater director.

His immortality was ensured when his poem "Ja, vi elsker dette landet" ("Yes, We Love This Land") was selected as the Norwegian national anthem.

The son of a pastor, Bjørnson grew up in a farming community, later the setting for several of his novels. From 1857 to 1859 he was Ibsen's successor as artistic director of the Bergen Theater, where he married actress Karoline Reimers in 1858.

From 1866 to 1871 he was director of the Christiania Theater in Oslo. While in self-imposed exile between 1860 and 1863, he wrote some of his most enduring works. Some of his best-remembered works are *The Heritage of the Kurts* (1884) and *In God's Way* (1889).

Later in life, he became an ardent socialist, working for peace and international understanding. Although he enjoyed worldwide fame in his life and his plays helped to bring "social realism" to Europe, his international reputation today pales when compared to his sometimes friend and always rival, Ibsen.

heavy iron chandeliers. Bedrooms are cosy with wood trimming, and contemporary, with views over the lake and the mountains. Access to the ski lifts requires a 12-minute hike across flat ground from the hotel. On the grounds of this hotel are 20 wood-sided, bare-bones cabins for 6 to 12 people. Each has cooking facilities, and they are available year-round. If you enjoy rustic, outdoorsy surroundings, these just might be perfect for you. Cabins are rented only by the week, costing roughly NOK10,000.

N-2640 Vinstra. ✆ **61-29-33-00.** www.fefor.no. 114 units. Mon–Thurs NOK2,250 double; Fri–Sun NOK2,650 double. Rates include half-board. AE, DC, MC, V. **Amenities:** Restaurant; bar; indoor heated pool; 2 saunas; children's programs. *In room:* TV.

Gålå Høgfjellshotell ★★★ ☺ This resort is the preferred choice in the area, a supremely luxurious hotel combined with a historic core, making for some old-fashioned nostalgia wedded to elegance and modern amenities. There's a real sense of 19th-century Norwegian national style scattered around this hotel, since its architectural style derives from its origins around 1870 as a high-altitude sanatorium. More allure comes from its location—within a short walk of the ski lifts, and easily accessible from the slopes on skis. Accommodations are rustic and old-fashioned, calling to mind something of a skier's and hiker's boutique hotel. Its Mor Aases Kjøkken restaurant is the best in the area, with freshly caught organic trout from Lake Gålå, seasonal game, and fresh berries and herbs.

Despite its intimate size, the hotel also functions as manager and rental agent for about 130 self-catering cabins, suitable for 6 to 10 occupants, scattered throughout the district. Each has a kitchen, and amenities range from bare-bones to relatively plush. They're favored by families and extended groups of friends traveling together.

Depending on the season and their size, they cost NOK3,540 to NOK12,280 per week without meals or services during the winter—and at least half that during the summer.

N-2646 Gålå. ✆ **61-29-76-65.** www.gala-resort.com. 42 units. NOK1,220–NOK2,230 double in summer; rates include buffet breakfast. NOK2,000–NOK2,310 double in winter; rates include half-board. AE, DC, MC, V. **Amenities:** Restaurant; bar; outdoor heated pool; tennis court; sauna; children's programs. *In room:* TV, hair dryer.

Thon Hotel Gausdal ★★ There are now two Thons in the area, though Gausdal is the market leader. Lying 8km (5 miles) northwest of the town of Svingvoll, it is one of the most traditional lodges in the area. Its original core is from 1876 but was burned to the ground by the Nazis. The hotel lies in the center of the small but popular mountain resort of Gausdal, 16km (10 miles) west of Tretten, the nearest railway station (pick-ups available). Bedrooms are in a style that approximates modern Scandinavian, with views of the mountains and both shower and bathtub. Kilometers of hiking or ski trails surround the hotel, and provisions can be made for downhill or cross-country skiing in winter and horseback riding or trekking in summer. There is immediate access to ski lifts, a sports center with a ski school, and ski-rental facilities. Even if you're passing through just for the day, you might want to stop in to sample the hotel's *smörgåsbord.*

Skeikampen, N-2652 Svingvoll. ✆ **61-05-51-50.** www.thonhotels.com/gausdal. 129 units. NOK790–NOK1,040 double. Rates include buffet breakfast. AE, DC, MC, V. **Amenities:** Restaurant; bar; indoor heated pool; 18-hole golf course; 3 tennis courts; sauna; 1 room for those with limited mobility. *In room:* TV, Wi-Fi, minibar (in some), hair dryer.

Thon Hotel Skeikampen ★ ☺ This is the more affordable of the two Thons in the area, and is one of the finest places to lodge in the ski region—though it's open year-round. It offers attractive public rooms filled with antique and modern furniture, and acres of woodland grounds. Most of the cozy bedrooms, decorated in light pastels, open onto scenic views. Ski aficionados will enjoy the nearby (300m/1,000 ft. away) lift and smaller rope tow, as well as a ski school with child-care facilities. The hotel is set right at the timberline, with forested and rocky paths well marked for climbers. There are wine-tasting events and dinners held in the on-site Spanish-themed restaurant. The hotel lies 38km (24 miles) from the railway station at Tretten, and arrangements can be made for transportation from there to the hotel.

N-2652 Svingvoll. ✆ **61-28-50-00.** www.thonhotels.com/skeikampen. 115 units. NOK790–NOK1,090 double. Children 4 & under stay free in parents' room. Rates include buffet breakfast. AE, DC, MC, V. **Amenities:** Restaurant; bar; fitness room; spa; sauna; rooms for those with limited mobility. *In room:* TV, minibar (in some), Wi-Fi, hair dryer.

Wadahl Høifjellshotel ★★ This is one of the more luxurious of the several hotels positioned on the ski slopes around Lillehammer, with an isolated hillside location that allows residents to ski from the hotel's front door to the ski lifts, and then ski back to the hotel from the upper reaches of the surrounding slopes. The hotel is only a few minutes away from the Gålå Høgfjellshotell, with identical access to hiking and cross-country trails. If faced with a choice between the two, I'd choose the Gålå for its superior cuisine, but the Wadahl is not far behind.

Cozy and rustic, with a sports-conscious clientele that often drives from as far away as Oslo for weekend getaways, the Wadahl was originally established in 1900 as a survival station for the high mountains around it. It was transformed into a resort hotel in 1930 and has been expanded several times. Rooms are comfortably furnished and modern-looking, with Ikea-esque furnishings. Midwinter and midsummer are equally desirable high seasons here, and weekend stays are more expensive than weekdays.

N-2646 Gålå. ✆ **61-29-75-00.** www.wadahl.no. 100 units. Mon–Thurs NOK700–NOK825 per person including half-board; Fri–Sun NOK1,750–NOK2,600 for 2 persons. AE, DC, MC, V. Closed Nov–Dec & May Mon–Thurs. **Amenities:** Restaurant; bar; large outdoor heated pool; indoor heated pool; outdoor lighted tennis courts; sauna; rooms for those with limited mobility. *In room:* TV, minibar.

LOM ★ & JOTUNHEIMEN NASJONALPARK ★★★

62km (38 miles) NW of Otta; 180km (112 miles) NW of Lillehammer

With its towering peaks and foreboding glaciers, **Jotunheimen Nasjonalpark,** one of the greatest parks in Norway, lies in Lom municipality. The village of **Lom** can also be your gateway to the fjord country, as two of the grandest fjords in Norway, **Geiranger** and **Sognefjord** (see chapter 12), are a short drive to the west. Lom also lies near the Reinheimen, and Breheimen Nasjonalparks, only established in 2009 (www.visitjotunheimen.com).

In one of the most colorful settings of any rustic little village in Norway, Lom straddles the Prestfossen Waterfall and the Bøvra River. A village of great and traditional charm, despite heavy tourist traffic, Lom has retained much of its log-cabin architecture and boasts a stave church from 1158.

Some 900km (560 miles) of Lom's municipal border are covered by glaciers and mountains, the most important and dramatic of which are **Glittertind,** at 2,452m (8,043 ft.), and **Galdhøpiggen,** at 2,469m (8,098 ft.).

Essentials

GETTING THERE **Nor-Way Bussekspress** (✆ **81-54-44-44;** www.nor-way.no) **buses** pass through Lom from Oslo at the rate of four per day, costing NOK500 one-way and taking 6½ hours. By **car,** continue northwest from Lillehammer or Vinstra on the E6 to Route 15, at which point you head west into Lom.

VISITOR INFORMATION For information about the area, including hiking, head for the **Jotunheimen Reiseliv** (✆ **61-21-29-90;** www.visitjotunheimen.com), in the Norsk Fjellmuseum (see below). You can also purchase hiking maps here, which are necessary if you plan to tour Jotunheimen Nasjonalpark.

What to See & Do

In the center of Lom, the **Stavkyrke** (stave church) (✆ **61-21-73-39**) dates from 1158 but was enlarged in 1635 when it was restyled in a cruciform shape. In 1667, two naves were added. The church is admired for its early-18th-century paintings and Jakob Saeterdalen's pulpit and chancel from 1793. Charging NOK50 for adults, but free for children 14 and under, it is open late May to August 15 daily 9am to 8pm, August 16 to September 30 daily 10am to 4pm.

An even more impressive sight is the **Fossheim Steinsenter** (mineral museum) ★ (✆ **61-21-14-60;** www.fossheimsteinsenter.no), with Europe's biggest and most varied exhibition of rare and stunningly beautiful rocks, along with gems, minerals, and fossils, plus jewelry on sale. Part of the museum is devoted to exotic geological specimens gathered from all over the world, while one section, the "Time Axis," features a kilometer-long walk through Lom, with displays and sections covering nearly five million years of the Earth's history. The owners take pride in the national stone of Norway, thulite, which was first discovered in Lom in 1820 and is now quarried. (Manganese gives thulite its reddish color.) Admission is free, and the center is open mid-June to mid-August daily 9am to 8pm. In the off-season, hours are Monday to Friday 10am to 3pm.

The **Norsk Fjellmuseum** (**✆ 61-21-16-00;** www.fjell.museum.no) in Lom is the visitor center for Jotunheimen Nasjonalpark (see below). The center has a dual role as a museum filled with intriguing exhibits about mountaineering and an information center for hikers in the park. Exhibits feature both the culture of the mountain people and the park's natural history. A 10-minute mountain slide show is also presented. Admission is NOK50 for adults and NOK30 for children 12–16. It is open late June to mid-August daily 9am to 7pm; mid-May to late June and late August to mid-September Monday to Friday 9am to 6pm and Saturday 10am to 4pm. Off-season hours are Monday to Friday 10am to 3pm, Saturday and Sunday by appointment only.

Jotunheimen Nasjonalpark: "Home of the Giants"

Norway's greatest national park is dominated by the **towering peaks ★★** of **Galdhopiggen** and **Glittertind.** It is a land of glaciers, mountains, lakes, and waterfalls. It has more than 60 glaciers and is crisscrossed by valleys that split it up into ridges and high plateaus.

Heavily visited since 1813, it has become one of the best-developed wilderness tour areas in northern Europe, with its efficient "linkage" of hotels, tourist huts, and private cabins that lie along well-marked trails. It attracts both beginning and advanced mountain hikers, along with the glacier and rock climbers who descend upon the park in summer.

The beauty of the park, and especially its wildflowers in spring, has inspired some of Norway's most famous composers and writers, including Edvard Grieg and Henrik Ibsen. Although its wild reindeer have departed, flocks of tame reindeer are kept on farmsteads by farmers in Vågå and Lom. Fishermen come to the park to catch red char and mountain trout.

First-timers often take the high and panoramic **Sognefjellet ★★**, a road linking Lom with Lustrafjorden. Built in 1939 by unemployed youth, this is the best access to the northern tier of the park. The road peaks at 1,434m (4,704 ft.), making it the highest mountain road in the north of Europe. In fact, the elevation here is so high that for the most part the snow doesn't melt until early July. It can even snow here during the hottest period of the summer.

Impressions

It [Besseggen Ridge] cuts along with an edge like a scythe for miles and miles . . . and scars and glaciers sheer down the precipice to the glassy lakes, 1,600 feet below on either side.

—Henrik Ibsen

In all, the park encompasses 3,900 sq. km (1,500 sq. miles), with an amazing number of towering peaks, some 200 of which rise above 1,900m (6,200 ft.). Norway's highest waterfall, **Vettisfossen ★★**, with its 275-m (900-ft.) drop, is also found in the park. The waterfall lies a short walk from the Vetti Lodge on the western frontier of the park.

The most popular hike in Norway is along the **Besseggen Ridge ★★** towering over Lake Gjende. The trail links the mountain lodges of Memurubu and Gjendesheim. One of the most famous lakes in Norway, Gjende appears in the writings of Henrik Ibsen. The author had his Peer Gynt tumble from the ridge into the lake on the back of a speeding reindeer. The lake is 18km (11 miles) long and 146m (479 ft.) deep. Its emerald-green waters are fed by glaciers. In summer, you can travel by boat on the lake (NOK130 return), with several departures daily between mid-June and early September. Check www.gjende.no for schedule and/or price changes.

Obtain complete and detailed maps from the tourist office before setting out into the park, and know that the weather can change at a moment's notice. You can also arrange with the tourist office to hire a guide, which is highly recommended.

Where to Stay

Elveseter Hotell ★★ In one of the untouched wilderness areas of Jotunheimen Nasjonalpark, this is one of the most exceptional hotels in central Norway. It accepted its first overnight guest in 1870, while it simultaneously functioned as a farmstead whose workers and overseers were completely snowbound for at least 6 months of the year. Today you'll find a compound of 19 Tolkienesque buildings, many antique, all of them plank-sided and some of them with sod roofs. They are nestled beside a river on a valley floor that's flanked on both sides by some of the most jagged and snow-covered mountains in Norway. Two of the buildings boast foundations from 1579 and 1640, respectively. Others are newer structures fancifully trimmed in the Norwegian national style, with Viking-inspired motifs. A wide range of outdoor activities is available here, including midsummer cross-country skiing, every kind of trekking and climbing, and river rafting. Frequent folkloric shows are presented in an on-site theater.

Elveseter, N-2687 Bøverdalen. ✆ **61-21-99-00.** www.elveseter.no. 88 units. NOK1,150 double; NOK1,600–NOK2,100 apartment. Rates do not include breakfast (NOK100 extra). Evening 5-course meal NOK595 per person. AE, DC, MC, V. Closed Nov to mid-May. From the hamlet of Bøverdalen, 24km (15 miles) from Lom, drive 3.3km (2 miles) southwest & follow the signs to Elveseter. **Amenities:** Buffet-style restaurant; bar; indoor heated pool; sports facilities. *In room:* (no phone).

Fossheim Turisthotell ★★ Owned over the years by multiple generations of the Garmo family, things haven't changed much in this great old hotel, first established in 1897. The site was once run as both a farm and a hotel, but has seen dramatic improvements and expansion over the years. A new addition called "Amerika" was designed to attract post–World War II American visitors, who demanded rooms with private bathrooms, and many rooms were renovated at the end of 2008. The main building is still accented with stout ceiling beams and Norwegian antiques, and there are also nearby log cabins built in the old style. All the rooms are very comfortable and decorated in a cozy, rustic fashion. One of the reasons to stay here is to enjoy the cuisine; see "Where to Dine," below.

N-2688 Lom. ✆ **61-21-95-00.** www.fossheimhotel.no. 46 units. NOK1,200–NOK1,500 double. Rates include buffet breakfast. AE, DC, MC, V. Closed mid-Dec to mid-Feb. **Amenities:** Restaurant; 2 bars. *In room:* TV (no phone).

Turtagro This area was in the vanguard of mountain sports in Norway. In 1876, one William Cecil Slingsby came here from Britain to climb Store Skagastølstind, which put the area on the tourist maps. For nature lovers who want a Norwegian alpine setting against a backdrop of snow-covered peaks and glaciers, one of the most isolated hotels in Norway occupies a forested, mountainside site 9.5km (6 miles) northeast of the hamlet of Fortun and 59km (37 miles) northeast of the village of Sogndal. It opened its doors in 1887 as an emergency station for mountaineers and trekkers. Today, this trio of red-painted, wood-sided buildings features wood paneling and a minimalist rustic decor. There are rock-bottom budget accommodations in the dorm-style chalet, with 66 beds and shared bathrooms. The dining room serves hearty food, flavorful and plentiful.

N-6877 Fortun. ✆ **57-68-08-00.** www.turtagro.no. 19 units, plus 66 dormitory-style beds in an outbuilding. NOK950–NOK1,175 per person double, including buffet breakfast; NOK370 per dorm bed. AE, DC, MC, V. Closed Oct–Mar. **Amenities:** Restaurant; bar; babysitting. *In room:* (no phone).

Vågå Hotel Country comfortable, big-windowed, and well respected, this is the only hotel, and one of the most oft-recommended restaurants, in the hamlet of Vågå, where about half of the county's population of 4,000 people live. Substantial-looking and solid, it was originally built in the 1950s, enlarged and radically reconfigured in the 1960s and again in the 1970s. Its interior is cozy and richly paneled, in ways that make it seem older than it actually is, with local pine. A fireplace sheathed in heat-conductive ceramic tile throws off a welcome midwinter heat. The comfortably furnished but rather minimalist bedrooms are small to midsize. There's an indoor swimming pool, big enough to swim laps in. Because the local downhill ski lifts are about 32km (20 miles) away, this hotel attracts fewer downhill skiers than cross-country skiers.

N-2680 Vågå. ✆ **61-23-95-50.** www.vagahotel.no. 56 units. NOK1,080 double. Rates include buffet breakfast. AE, DC, MC, V. From Lom, drive 32km (20 miles) east, following Rte. 15 & signs to Otta. **Amenities:** Restaurant; 2 bars; indoor heated pool. *In room:* TV.

Where to Dine

Fossheim Restaurant ★★★ NORWEGIAN An enticing aroma originating in the kitchen spreads across the hills, luring visitors here. Set within the cozy, old-fashioned dining room of the Fossheim Turisthotell (see above), amid a scattering of 19th-century Danish and Norwegian antiques, this is the most famous and recommended restaurant in the region. It's well known for the imaginative use of local fish and game, as well as for its various multi-course menus—from three to eight. All menu items contain the freshest local ingredients, and the selection changes with the season. The best examples include baked wild salmon served with fresh vegetables and a creamy sauce; whole fried mountain trout served with herbs and a sour-cream sauce; and award-winning versions of reindeer filet and breast of wild ptarmigan served pinky-rare, each with a creamy game sauce enriched with wild mushrooms. Some of the building's original late-19th-century character remains, including lavish use of pinewood paneling and big-windowed views of the mountains and the local stave church.

In the Fossheim Turisthotell. N-2688 Lom. ✆ **61-21-95-00.** www.fossheimhotel.no. Reservations recommended. Fixed-price menus NOK375–NOK1,600. AE, DC, MC, V. Daily 1–4pm & 7–10pm.

RONDANE ★★ & DOVREFJELL ★ NASJONALPARKS

Lesja: 159km (99 miles) N of Lom

The last ice age carved out one of Norway's most dramatic landscapes in the Rondane and Dovrefjell Nasjonalparks. With their barren mountains, narrow canyons, and deep cirques, they bring out the adventurer in us. If you have time for more than Jotunheimen (see above), you're in for more scenic glory here. While Rondane is favored by hikers and gets more visitors, bird watchers flock to Dovrefjell.

Allow about 2 days for Rondane and at least 1 day for Dovrefjell, to scratch the surface of the great outdoors here.

Essentials

GETTING THERE During the summer, there are two **buses** a day (9:45am and 3:15pm) from the little town of Otta, on the E6 northwest of Lillehammer, to the Spranghaugen parking area near the town of Mysusaeter; the parking area is the start of the most frequented routes through Rondane. The trip takes 45 minutes and costs NOK50 one-way; outside summer the buses only run on weekends. There is also one bus a day (1:35pm) from Lillehammer to the gateway town of Dombås. There is no public transportation to Dovrefjell. For bus information, call © **81-54-44-44** or visit www.nor-way.no. Alternatively, try the Otta tourist information office at © **61-23-66-70.**

Motorists can reach gateway towns such as Lesja or Dombås by taking the E6 northwest from Lillehammer.

VISITOR INFORMATION For details on exploring both Rondane and Dovrefjell, go to the **Nasjonalparksenter,** Sentralplassen, in Dombås (© **61-24-14-44**). It's open mid-June to mid-August Monday to Saturday 9am to 8pm, Sunday 9am to 4pm; mid-August to mid-June Monday to Friday 9am to 4pm.

Exploring Rondane

Rondane Nasjonalpark is vastly impressive with its towering peaks, waterfalls, and deep valleys. The little town of Lesja can be your gateway to the park, which lies to its southwest. Henrik Ibsen called Rondane "palace piled upon palace." Created in 1962, the 572-sq.-km (221-sq.-mile) park was the first to open in Norway.

The area has been inhabited for thousands of years, as ancient Viking burial mounds and centuries-old reindeer traps reveal. More than two dozen species of animal, including reindeer, and some 125 species of birds, populate the park.

The park is divided into a trio of mountain areas, all above 2,000m (6,600 ft.). To the east of the Rondane massif rises **Rondeslotteet** (2,178m/7,144 ft.). To the west are **Veslesmeden** (2,016m/6,612 ft.), **Storsmeden** (2,017m/6,617 ft.), and **Sagtinden** (2,018m/6,619 ft.), all linked by narrow "saddles." The third group is split by the deep valley of Lungglupdalen and crowned by **Midtronden** (2,114m/6,934 ft.).

One of Norway's great areas for hikers, Rondane has poor soil, and the ground is often covered with lichens instead of more luxuriant flora. The park is peppered with little lakes and rivers, the landscape broken in part by dwarf birch trees.

Most visitors begin their hikes at the Spranghaugen parking area. From this point, the most popular hike in the park is the 6km (3¾-mile) jaunt to **Rondvassbu,** followed by a 5-hour return climb to the summit of **Storronden** (2,138m/7,013 ft.).

The **Sjoa,** Europe's best river for rafting, cuts through the park with its rushing white waters. The rafting season starts in mid-May and lasts until the end of September. **Sjoa Rafting** in Heidal (✆ **61-23-60-37;** www.heidalrafting.no) offers trips through the gorge, and other activities in the park. Afternoon rafting trips along an 11-km (6¾-mile) stretch of the Sjoa run 3½ hours and cost from NOK890.

Exploring Dovrefjell

Dovrefjell (full name Dovrefjell-Sunndalsfjella) **Nasjonalpark** was enlarged in 2002 to take in more of the surrounding area, including the **Fokstumyra marshes ★★**, home to around 75 resident bird species; some 50 other species, such as the loon bird, the lapwing, the great snipe, and the ruff, have also been spotted. The park now includes territory in three counties, making it the largest continuous protected area in Norway.

The center of the park was set aside for protection in 1974. The aim was to safeguard the highlands around Snøhetta, which soars to a height of 2,286m (7,498 ft.). Hikers can ascend Snøhetta in about 6 hours.

The park is now home to wolverines, arctic foxes, and reindeer, as well as the rare musk ox, a thick-coated animal which can survive at amazingly cold temperatures, and also lives in parts of Greenland and Alaska. It can weigh up to 446 kilograms (983 lb.). In 1931, 10 musk oxen were introduced to Dovrefjell, having been shipped over from Greenland. Because these animals once inhabited Dovrefjell, they bred successfully. The herd is now estimated to number about 80. It is highly unlikely you'll come across the elusive wolverine or the arctic fox, however.

In another section of the park, the Knutshøene mountains, lying to the east of the E6, rise to 1,690m (5,543 ft.). This section of the park includes Europe's most diverse intact alpine ecosystem.

Before setting out to explore the park, arm yourself with a good map from the visitor center (see above). One of the most intimate ways to explore the park—and my favorite way of doing it—is in one of the 5-hour guided tours offered by **Moskus Safari Dovrefjell (Dovrefjell Park Musk Ox Safari Company),** N-2660 Dombås (✆ **46-42-01-02;** www.moskus-safari.no). Between mid-June and mid-August they depart daily at 9am, usually from the Spranghaugen parking area, near Mysusaeter, or—with prior reservations—from one of the area's hotels. After a 40-km (25-mile) bus or van ride, participants get out for short hiking treks across the tundra (sturdy shoes and protective raingear are recommended) for close-up observation of musk oxen and their habitat. The cost is NOK325 per person (lunch not included), and participants are usually returned either to the Spranghaugen parking area or to their hotels between 1 and 2pm.

For information on other sporting or sightseeing options within the park, contact the Dombås tourist information office at ✆ **61-24-14-44.**

Other Attractions

In the center of the historic town of Lesja, you can visit **Lesja Bygdatun** (✆ **61-24-41-43**), consisting of a dozen houses moved to this site and revealing how life was lived in the 18th and 19th centuries. You can explore farm dwellings,

SIGRID UNDSET country

Winner of the Nobel Prize for literature in 1928, Sigrid Undset (1882–1949) still enjoys an international audience. She lived and wrote about this area in central Norway and was known for her novels about Scandinavia in the Middle Ages. Her *Kristin Lavransdatter* became an international bestseller. Her books have been translated into all major languages. Undset wrote 36 books and was a great storyteller who was particularly adept at exploring human psychology.

Born in Denmark in the same year as James Joyce and Virginia Woolf, Undset came to Norway at age 2, where in time she devoured Norse sagas, finding inspiration for her later work.

In 1919, she moved to Lillehammer, after a life in Oslo, the subject of many of her novels. An outspoken critic of Nazi Germany, she fled to neutral Sweden in April 1940 when the Germans invaded her country. In the 1940s she came to the United States to plead her occupied country's cause. Upon her return to Norway in 1945, she lived for another 4 years but never wrote another word.

You can recapture some of the atmosphere of Undset's prize-winning trilogy, *Kristin Lavransdatter,* by visiting the **Jørundgard Middelalder Senter** at Sel (✆ **61-23-37-00;** www.jorundgard.no). This medieval farm was re-created in 1995 for the Liv Ullmann film *Kristin Lavransdatter.* The film helped put Undset back on the Norwegian cultural map, especially among young people.

The farm lies in Sel, 15km (9¼ miles) north of Otta, which is reached along the E6. The center consists of 16 buildings and a consecrated stave church. You can join in a guided tour and taste foods of the Middle Ages. The center is open for guided tours, costing NOK90, daily from 10am to 4pm from mid-June to mid-August.

cookhouses, barns, storehouses, and a forge hammering out wrought-iron products. Archaeological finds unearthed in the region are also displayed here. An association of farm women bakes and cooks daily at the coffeehouse and restaurant, which serves waffles and other traditional baked goods. On Saturday, they serve the famous *rumgraut* (porridge made with sour cream). There is also a craft shop selling embroideries, painted china and glass, wooden bowls, and other items made in Lesja. From June 20 to August 18, it is open daily from 10am to 5pm, charging NOK40 to enter. Children 15 and under enter free.

Where to Stay & Dine

In addition to the choices below, the **Rondane Spa** (✆ **61-20-90-90;** www.rondane.no), at the gateway to Rondane Nasjonalpark, is the only spa-hotel in this region of central Norway.

Bjorligard Hotell ★ This is the area's most appealing hotel. I liken it to a large, contemporary chalet, thanks to exposed wood, weathered siding, and a design that might have been inspired by a mountainside lodge in Switzerland. Redecorated and renovated, it lies within a 7-minute walk of the village ski lifts, attracting a sports-oriented and, in many cases, rather youthful clientele. Public areas contain paneling, a blazing fireplace, rustic artifacts, and cozy, comfortable seating nooks. Bedrooms range from midsize to spacious, and include a number with four-poster or king-size double beds; all come with views over the surrounding landscapes.

N-2669 Bjorli. ✆ **61-24-44-00.** www.bjorligard.no. 49 units. NOK750–NOK850 per person double. Price includes breakfast. AE, DC, MC, V. Bjorli lies northwest of Lesja along the E6. **Amenities:** Restaurant; bar; indoor heated pool; sauna; fitness room; Jacuzzi. *In room:* TV, kitchenette.

Brekkeseter ★ ☺ This hotel, set directly at the tree line (where the forest ends and the rocky uplands begin), dates from 1772, when its central core functioned as a farm for the midsummer production of hay, and the spring and fall gathering of moss (used as cattle feed) from the surrounding mountains. Today the site comprises several dozen separate buildings, each an old-fashioned plank-sided testimonial to the building techniques of yesteryear. The largest of these, built in stages between 1772 and 1995, functions as a small-scale, conventional hotel. None of the rooms in this part of the hotel has a TV or phone, but the simple but cozy decor reflects the barren but beautiful landscape outside. The cabins contain a full kitchen, ideal for families.

N-2673 Høvrigen. ✆ **61-23-37-11.** www.brekkeseter.no. 12 units, 20 cabins. NOK850 per person double including half-board; NOK300–NOK5,000 cabin (2–10 occupants). AE, MC, V. Hotel closed Easter to mid-June & mid-Oct to Jan, but cabins are available. **Amenities:** Restaurant; babysitting. *In room:* (no phone).

RØROS: NORWAY'S GREAT MINING TOWN ★★

159km (99 miles) SE of Trondheim; 399km (247 miles) N of Oslo

Exploring a mining town might sound like a put-off, but this relic of another day is the finest of its kind in Scandinavia and beloved by Norwegians. As you strolled through the National Gallery in Oslo, you may have been struck by the arresting paintings crafted by the Norwegian artist Harald Sohlberg. His paintings made Røros famous internationally, and a statue of him stands at Harald Sohlberg Plass.

Tucked away in the mountains of eastern Norway at the northern end of the Osterdal Valley, Røros is famous because of its rich copper mines, which were launched in 1644 and ran until going bankrupt in 1977. Now this old mining town is on UNESCO's list of World Heritage Sites. It is the most famous and evocative of Norway's mining towns.

More than 3 centuries old, it is known for its collection of 100 well-preserved buildings from the 17th and 18th centuries. Many of Norway's old wooden towns have long since burned to the ground, but the Old Town of Røros is still so authentic that film companies regularly use it as an authentic backdrop. One such film was *An-Magritt,* starring Liv Ullmann, adapted from the work of Røros's best-known author, Johan Falkberget, who lived in the town until his death in 1967. Some of Astrid Lindgren's *Pippi Longstocking* classics were filmed in Røros as well, and it was used as a setting for Siberia in the film adaptation of Solzhenitsyn's *A Day in the Life of Ivan Denisovich.*

In recent years, Røros has become the country's premier region for local, small-scale, and organic food products; the town has been featured in several episodes of the popular show "New Scandinavian Cooking." The town is also very accessible to nature, with hiking and cross-country ski trails that begin right in the center of town. Winter here presents an almost certain "snow guarantee," although the town is popularly known as the coldest inhabited spot in Norway, with the lowest recorded temperature having descended to –50.4°C (-58.72°F).

Essentials

GETTING THERE

BY AIR Røros airport (✆ **72-41-39-00**) is a 4-minute drive from the center of town. **Widerøe Airlines,** a partner of SAS, flies to and from Oslo daily.

BY TRAIN Three trains per day arrive Monday through Saturday from Trondheim, taking 2½ hours, and three trains come from Oslo, taking 5 hours. For train information and schedules, call ✆ **81-50-08-88** or visit www.nsb.no.

BY BUS Three buses per day connect Trondheim and Røros Monday through Saturday, taking 3¼ hours. Visit www.nor-way.no for information.

BY CAR From Trondheim, take the E6/Route 30 south for 2½ hours.

VISITOR INFORMATION

For information, go to the **Røros Reiseliv Turistkontoret,** Peder Hiortsgata 2 (✆ **72-41-00-00**), a block from the train station. From June 20 to August 15, hours are Monday to Saturday 9am to 6pm, Sunday 10am to 4pm. The rest of the year, hours are Monday to Friday 9am to 3:30pm and Saturday 10:30am to 12:30pm. Also visit www.roros.no for information.

What to See & Do

The best way to see Røros is to take a guided walk through the Old Town, starting at the tourist office (see above). In summer, tours leave several times daily, costing NOK60 (free for children). In the off-season, only Saturday tours are conducted.

In town you can also visit **Røros Kirke,** Kjerkgata, which dates from 1650. The church was established to cater to workers in the smelting works. More than a century later, it was substantially rebuilt in baroque style, seating 1,600 worshippers, an amazingly large congregation for a town of this size. It is an eight-sided stone structure with a pulpit sitting over the altarpiece. Admission is free, and it is open from mid-June to mid-August. The church was undergoing extensive renovation at press time, so check with the tourist office regarding specific opening hours.

Røros offers several other attractions, including the **Røros Museum-Smelthytta,** Malmplassen (✆ **72-40-61-70;** www.verdensarvenroros.no), site of the first smelting works in the area, dating from 1646. A model exhibition here illustrates old mining and smelting technology, including ore hoists, waterwheels, horse-drawn winches, and furnaces. One section displays regional costumes from the 1800s. The building is a reconstruction of the original structure, which burned in a fire in 1953. Admission is NOK60 for adults or NOK30 for children under 15. It's open mid-June to August daily 10am to 6pm; in other months, it's open Monday to Friday 11am to 3pm and Saturday and Sunday 11am to 2pm.

To get a sense of what Rørøs was like as a historical mining town, pay a visit to **Sleggveien** (street) (✆ **72-40-61-70;** www.verdensarvenroros.no), where five reconstructed homes show how manual workers—a cobbler, a watch repairman, and an engraver among them—once lived. During the summer months some of the houses are open daily from 11am to 4pm. There is no admission fee.

A highlight of a visit to Røros is a side trip to **Olavsgruva,** or Olav's Mine (✆ **72-40-61-70;** www.verdensarvenroros.no), lying 13km (8 miles) northeast of Røros in Kojedalen. A guided walking tour will take you through 3 centuries of mining. The system here consists of two mines, Nyberget and Crown Prince Olav's mine. Nyberget is by far the oldest, as the Prince Olav mine was begun only in 1936. The tour takes you 50m (160 ft.) below the surface and 500m (1,600 ft.) into the cavern, where miners of yore toiled in miserable conditions. The temperature is about 5°C (41°F) all year. Sound-and-light effects help re-create the mood of the old mines. Tours are conducted five times daily from June to mid-August, twice daily from mid-August to September, and Saturday only in the off-season, and cost NOK90 for adults (free for children under 15). If you're driving, follow signs along Route 31 northeast from the center of Røros. A round-trip by taxi will cost NOK500.

The **Johan Falkberget Museum** (✆ **95-90-63-19**) honors the area's favorite son. The author Johan Falkberget (1879–1967) was reared at Trondalen Farm in the Rugel Valley outside Røros. He became a famous author around the world, translated into 20 languages. His most celebrated book was *An-Magritt,* made into a 1969 film starring Liv Ullmann, about a peasant girl who transported copper ore in the Røros mines. Falkberget's early poverty and toil in the mines colored all his works. The trilogies *Christianus Sextus* (1927–35) and *Bread of Night* (1940–59) concern mining life in the 17th and 18th centuries. They emphasize the virtues of hard work and Christian love. The Falkberget museum lies beside Lake Rugelsjø. Admission is NOK65 for adults and NOK30 for children. Tours are offered from July to August 5 Tuesday to Sunday at 1pm. Local trains from Røros will take you to Rugeldalen station, lying 20km (12 miles) north of Røros. From the station you can take the gorgeous signposted walk leading up to the museum.

Except for the Røros Museum-Smelthytta, all tours must be arranged through the tourist office.

Shopping

Silversmiths, woodcarvers, painters, potters, and glassblowers abound in greater Røros, which has the second-highest density of artists and craftsmen anywhere in Norway, and also holds a good number of non-chain stores selling sportswear and outdoor gear. Pottery, sculpture, and wall decorations, all of high quality, are sold at **Per Sverre Dahl Keramikk,** Mørkstug 5 (✆ **72-41-19-89**).

Where to Stay & Dine

Bergstadens Hotel This heavily renovated hotel is the center of social life in Røros. In the center of town near the train station, this landmark hotel was built before World War II but was brought up to date during extensive renovations. A cozy, well-run choice, it is furnished in a modern Nordic style, and half of the bedrooms open onto views of the mountains; some even have balconies. The staff is helpful in arranging outdoor activities such as horseback riding. The hotel houses the largest concentration of eating and drinking establishments in town. There are two on-site bars, Nilsenhjørnet Bar & Møtested and the Hiort Pub. The hotel's main restaurant, Bodegaen Mat & Vin, serves classic and bountiful Norwegian cuisine, while a second restaurant, Lauritsen og Bruse, is similar in menu but decorated in a rough, rustic style, with walls adorned with old photos and rusty, disused tools.

Oslovein 2, N-7374 Røros. ✆ **72-40-60-80.** Fax 72-40-60-81. www.bergstaden.no. 90 units. June–Aug NOK1,200 double; Sept–May NOK1,400 double. Children 3 & under stay free in parents' room. Rates include continental breakfast. AE, DC, MC, V. **Amenities:** 2 restaurants; 3 bars; indoor heated pool; sauna; room service. *In room:* TV, minibar, hair dryer.

Røros Hotell ★ Luxury may not be the right word for this well-established hotel, but its accommodations are the finest in the area. Most of this hotel's 166 rooms enjoy good views, given the establishment's high-altitude position over the town, north of the railway station. It was built in the mid-1950s but has recently been renovated and expanded. The bedrooms are decorated in light pastels, opening onto a view of the Old Town. Furnishings are comfortable and tasteful, each unit coming with a small bathroom. Run by a local chef, the hotel puts a strong focus on local food. It is the only hotel in town with a pool, and perfect for outdoor types as the hiking trails and skiing tracks begin literally right outside the front door. They offer cross-country ski hire, and kick-sleds are free for use by guests.

An-Magrittsvei, N-7361 Røros. ✆ **72-40-80-00.** Fax 72-40-80-01. www.roroshotell.no. 166 units. May–Aug NOK1,000 double, NOK1,900 suite; Sept–Apr NOK1,250 double, NOK2,150 suite. Children 3 & under stay free in parents' room. Rates include buffet breakfast. AE, DC, MC, V. **Amenities:** 2 restaurants; 2 bars; indoor heated pool; sauna; rooms for those with limited mobility. *In room:* TV, hair dryer (in some), minibar, Wi-Fi (free).

Vertshuset Røros NORWEGIAN If you're seeking the most authentic Norwegian experience for dining or lodging, this is your most atmospheric choice. Vertshuset Røros offers well-prepared food and comfortable lodgings within one of the oldest and most nostalgically decorated dining and overnight venues in town. The restaurant directly fronts the street and features attentive service, lots of early-20th-century decorative objects, and a menu that focuses on fish and game caught, trapped, or shot within the region. Stellar examples include filets of reindeer or elk in juniper-berry sauce; grilled trout and salmon caught in local waters, sometimes served meunière style; and succulent preparations of lamb. Beefsteak is always a good bet, and the selection of wines comes from throughout Europe. The attached hotel is set within a separate red clapboard building. It features 31 double rooms and seven apartments, some of which have kitchenettes. They rent for NOK1,050 to NOK1,250, double occupancy, with breakfast included. In-room amenities include TV with cable connection.

Kjerkgata 34, N-7374 Røros. ✆ **72-41-93-50.** www.vertshusetroros.no. Reservations recommended. Main courses NOK289–NOK345. AE, DC, MC, V. Daily 7am–11pm.

Easy Excursions

Norway's second-largest lake is part of **Femundsmarka Nasjonalpark ★** (✆ 62-45-88-96), lying in the southwest of Norway bordering Sweden. It became a national park in 1971 and, as part of the largest continuous stretch of wilderness in Scandinavia, it is great for hiking, fishing, and canoeing and has long been a retreat for falconry. In the park's upper elevations, I've seen wild reindeer grazing. In summer, nearly three dozen musk oxen call the park home before migrating during the winter months.

From June 13 to August 24, a limited number of buses go between Røros and Synnervika, a hamlet that is the gateway to the park. Once at the park, you can take the ferry, **MS *Foemund II*** (✆ **72-41-37-14;** www.femund.no), a diesel-engine boat that sails from the northern shore of Lake Femunden. The boat sails daily from June 13 to August 15, allowing you to take in the shores of this beautiful lake. Fares start at NOK125, with children under 15 sailing for half-price. The cost of a ticket depends on how far you ride. Other day excursions include trips to the summer farming areas around Vingelen, Sweden, less than an hour away by car.

SOUTHERN NORWAY

9

The Norwegians themselves go to the south in summer for their vacations—largely because this part of the country gets more sunshine than any other. Norwegians refer to this area as "Sørlandet," a landscape of valleys, mountains, rivers, and lakes. Gulf Stream temperatures make taking a dip possible in summer.

Although there is much for the foreign visitor to see and do here, the sheer drama of other regions, including the western fjord district and the region north of the Arctic Circle, far outweighs the more modest attractions of southern Norway. But if you've got an extra week, you're in for a great time, especially in Rogaland, the southwestern part of the country, which has been termed "Norway in a nutshell" thanks to its wide variety of attractions. Bathed in a mild climate (at least, for Norway), southern Norway is a land of fjords, mountains, green valleys, beaches, old towns, and villages—and is also a great place to go fishing.

The coastal lands of southern Norway, shaped geographically like a half-moon, are studded with beaches, bays, and sailing opportunities. Within this area, the Telemark region is known for its lakes and canals, which are used for summer boating and canoeing. A port city, Larvik, is the hometown of one of Norway's most famous sons, Thor Heyerdahl, the explorer famous for the *Kon-Tiki* expedition, among other voyages. From Skien, visitors can explore the water network. Arendal is a charming old town with a harbor near some of the best beaches. Kristiansand S is a link between Norway and the rest of Europe. The Christiansholm Fortress has stood here since 1674, and the town is near Haresanden, a 10-km (6¼-mile)-long beach.

The region lives today in the technological future, thanks to its oil industry, but it also harks back to the country's oldest inhabitants. Here, the Viking king Harald Hårfagre (Fairhair) gathered most of Norway into one kingdom in A.D. 872. The locals say that it was from here that the Vikings sailed to discover America.

Southern Norway

LARVIK: HOME OF A GREAT EXPLORER

15km (9¼ miles) S of Sandefjord; 130km (81 miles) SW of Oslo

As you head south, consider stopping over for a few hours to take in the charm of the old port of Larvik. This is a main port for ferries sailing for Frederikshavn, Denmark, and it's also famously associated with its favorite homegrown boy, Thor Heyerdahl (1914–2002), whose *Kon-Tiki* you may have already seen on the Bygdøy Peninsula in Oslo. Heyerdahl organized and led the expedition on this balsa raft from Peru to Polynesia in 1947 to show that aboriginal South Americans could have voyaged to the Oceanic Islands.

In addition to Heyerdahl, Larvik's largest export is a mineral known as larvikite, some 270 million years old. The quarry here is the town's largest industry.

Larvik is a major transportation hub and communications center for southeastern Norway. It also makes a good center for exploring such small but colorful ports as Stavern to its immediate south.

Essentials

GETTING THERE If you're coming from outside Norway, you're most likely to arrive from Hirtshals in Denmark, as **Color Line** (✆ **22-94-42-00;** www.colorline.com) offers **ferry** service between the two cities. The line runs one or two daily ferries, taking 3 hours 45 minutes and costing NOK310.

Trains from Oslo, often 20 a day, pull into the terminus on Storgata, also the site of the bus station. The trip takes 2 hours and costs NOK277 one-way; visit www.nsb.no for further information.

Motorists heading south from Oslo along the E18 should pull into Larvik some 2 hours later.

VISITOR INFORMATION The **Larvik Tourist Office,** Storgata 48 (✆ **33-69-71-00;** www.visitlarvik.no), opposite the ferry terminal, is open Monday to Friday from 8:30am to 4pm.

GETTING AROUND Do as many of the locals do in summer and rent a bike from the tourist office (see above). The Vestfold region is riddled with well-mapped trails for biking, stretching from one end of the province to the other. Before setting out, purchase the map *Sykkelkart Vestfold,* available for NOK90 from the tourist office.

What to See & Do

The major attraction is the **Larvik Museum ★** (✆ **98-23-12-90;** www.larvikmuseum.no), a three-in-one cultural attraction. The classic, baroque-timbered **Herregården Manor House,** Herregårdssletta 6, was built between 1674 and 1677 as the home of Ulrik Frederik Gyldenløve, the Norwegian governor-general. As the illegitimate son of King Fredrik IV of Denmark, he became the Duke of Larvik and was shipped off to Norway to escape the intrigue of the Danish court. The house is filled with 17th- and 18th-century antiques.

The **Larvik Sjøfartsmuseum (Maritime Museum),** Kirkestredet 5, is housed in Larvik's oldest brick building, from 1730. On the idyllic little island of Tollerodden, east of the harbor, this museum displays ship models, paintings of sailing vessels, and other nautical artifacts to bring the port's maritime history alive. One section of the museum is devoted to the daring exploits of Larvik-born Thor Heyerdahl. Finally, the **Fritzøe Museum** on Langestrand Island displays tools, equipment, drawings, and models illustrating the iron-production era in Larvik from 1670 to 1870.

The three museums charge a combined ticket of NOK50 for adults or NOK10 for children under 16. The Herregården and Maritime Museums are open June 6 through September 12 daily from noon to 4pm; the Fritzøe collection is open only by prior arrangement.

If time remains, consider a visit to **Larvik Kirke,** Kirkestredet (✆ **33-17-30-00;** www.larvik.kirken.no (in Norwegian)), the port's Trinity Church. Commissioned in 1677, it was finished in 1763 when a tower was added. Inside its chief treasure is *Suffer the Little Children to Come Unto Me,* an altarpiece painting by Lucas Cranagh that was commissioned by Duke Gyldenløve. A monument outside was the creation of Arne Vigeland, commissioned to erect a memorial to Norwegians who died in World War II. Admission to the church is free, and it's open June 25 to August 10 daily from 11am to 1pm and 6 to 8pm.

Where to Stay & Dine

Hotell Greven ★ One hotel here can serve all your needs for lodging, drinking, and dining. Still going strong after 2 centuries, Hotell Greven is not only the most traditional choice, but also the best in the area, as it has kept abreast of the times. In spite of countless renovations, its lounges and rooms still retain an old-fashioned aura—and that's how the locals prefer it. There is style and grace here, and the prices are very reasonable for this part of the country. Each good-size bedroom is tastefully furnished. The chefs have abandoned those old-time Mother Norway recipes; in both of their restaurants, they feature a savory Continental cuisine, Dolce Vita serving Italian specialties and Kreta offering food from the Greek islands, where many Norwegians now vacation. The piano bar on-site makes this the liveliest venue in Larvik.

Storgata 26, N-3256 Larvik. ✆ **33-18-25-26.** www.hotell-greven.no. 24 units. NOK900 double; NOK1,100 suite. Rates include continental breakfast. AE, DC, MC, V. **Amenities:** Bistro; piano bar; dance bar; room service. *In room:* TV.

KONGSBERG: WHERE SILVER WAS KING

84km (52 miles) SW of Oslo; 40km (25 miles) W of Drammen

For more than 3 centuries, Kongsberg was the silver-mining town of Norway. Back in 1623, two children here spotted a big ox butting a cliff with his horns, uncovering a silver vein. Their father hoped to profit from the windfall, but the king heard the news and promptly dispatched his soldiers to force the man to reveal the location of the mother lode.

Suddenly, Kongsberg was overrun. Between the 1623 discovery and 1957, some 1.35 million kilograms (1,490 tons) of pure silver filled the king's purse. Even today, though the mines are closed, Kongsberg is still home to the Royal Norwegian Mint, which has been operating in the town since 1686.

Today some 6,000 workers are employed in high-tech companies located here, and instead of silver you'll find industries such as aerospace and car-part production.

The falls of the Lågen River divide the town into two parts. The oldest district, lying west of the river, is the site of the major attractions, while the newer part in the east encompasses the visitor information center, the traffic hubs, and the best shops.

Essentials

GETTING THERE From Oslo Central railway station, **trains** leave hourly during the day, taking 1½ hours to reach Kongsberg at a cost of NOK169 for a one-way ticket. For more information, call ✆ **81-50-08-88** or visit www.nsb.no. There is also a 24-hour **bus** service from Oslo with **Nettbuss Telemark** (✆ **35-02-60-00;** www.nettbuss.no/telemark), taking 1½ hours and costing NOK150 per one-way ticket. **Motorists** can take the E18 southwest from Oslo to Drammen, from where they should continue southwest on Route 11.

VISITOR INFORMATION The **Kongsberg Tourist Office,** Schwabesgate 2 (✆ **32-29-90-50;** www.visitkongsberg.no), is open from May 1 to June 21 and August 15 to September 30 Monday to Friday 9am to 4pm, Saturday 10am to 2pm; from June 22 to August 14 Monday to Friday 9am to 6pm and Saturday and Sunday 10am to 2pm. During the rest of the year, it's open Monday to Friday 9am to 4pm.

GETTING AROUND You can walk around the Old Town or rent a bike from the tourist office (see above) at a cost of NOK100 per day.

SPECIAL EVENTS Now beginning its 4th decade, the **Kongsberg International Jazz Festival** is attended by some of the most important jazz artists in Europe. The King's Mine and the baroque church are among the choice concert venues for this major musical event. The festival takes place during the first week of July. Call ✆ **32-73-31-66** for details, or visit www.kongsberg-jazzfestival.no.

What to See & Do

Kongsberg Kirke ★★, Kirketorget (✆ **32-29-90-50**), an elaborate baroque and rococo church, evokes something you might find in Bavaria, hardly in a more minimalist Norway. But this church is one of the sightseeing wonders of the south, and I recommend a stopover here even if you don't have time to check out the rest of town. The largest baroque church in Norway lies in the old town on the west bank of the Lågen River. Seating a 2,400-member congregation, this 1761 church bears witness to the silver-mining prosperity of Kongsberg. The beautiful interior is all the more stunning for three huge, glittering glass chandeliers created at the Nøstetangen glassworks.

As a curiosity, note that the rococo altar joins the large pulpit, altarpiece, and organ pipes on a single wall. Constructed in the shape of a cross, the church has a tower surmounting one of its transepts. You can still see the royal box, reserved for visits from the king, and the smaller boxes meant for the top mining officials. Naturally, the church owns many valuable pieces of silver. In olden days, it took six strong men to ring the church's mammoth bell, which was cast in Denmark.

Admission to the church costs NOK30 for adults and NOK10 for children under 16. There's usually an informed English-speaking guide on the premises. From mid-May to late August, it's open Monday to Friday 10am to 4pm, Saturday and Sunday 2 to 4pm. The rest of the year, it's open Tuesday to Thursday 10am to noon. If your visit doesn't correspond to any of these hours, the tourist office might be able to open the church for you if you phone them in advance.

At the **Norsk Bergverksmuseum (Norwegian Mining Museum) ★**, Hyttegata 3 (✆ **91-91-32-00;** www.norsk-bergverksmuseum.no), you'll find four museums housed in a single converted building that once belonged to the Silver Mining Company.

The Norsk Bergverksmuseum traces 3 centuries of silver mining. You might think only specialists would be interested, but hundreds of visitors wander about, learning about mining. One 18th-century working model illustrates the entire process of mining the precious silver ore. The machinery used in the smelting process can still be seen in the basement. Some of the specimens on exhibit are made of pure silver.

Also on-site is **Den Kongelige Mynts Museum,** devoted to the Royal Mint, which was relocated here in 1685. The museum contains a rare collection of coins minted in town. A third museum, the **Kongsberg Våpenfabrikks Museum (Kongsberg Arms Factory Museum),** traces the city's industrial history from 1814 onward.

Finally, the **Kongsberg Skimuseum** honors local skiers such as Birger Ruud and Petter Hugsted, who went on to Olympic glory and world championships. A historic collection of skis and equipment is on view. The most recent exhibition details the daring exploits of Børge Ousland and Erling Kagge on their ski expeditions to the North and South Poles, which attracted world attention.

Admission to all four museums costs NOK80 for adults and NOK30 for children under 16. From mid-May until the end of August, hours are 10am to 5pm daily; off-season hours are noon to 4pm daily.

Lågdalsmuseet (Lågdal Folk Museum), Tillischbakken 8–10 (✆ **32-73-34-68;** www.laagdalsmuseet.gratisnettside.no (in Norwegian). You might also want to explore **Lågdalsmuseet** a 12-minute stroll southeast from the rail depot. Nearly three dozen antique farmhouses and miners' cottages were moved to this site. It is now the most history-rich exhibit of how life used to be lived in the scenic Numedal Valley, which was mainly home to the families of miners and farmers. The 19th-century workshops you'd expect (most open-air museums in Norway have these), but the optics museum and the World War II Resistance Museum came as a surprise to us. Admission is NOK40 for adults and NOK10 for children. From June 23 to August 14, the museum is open daily from 11am to 5pm. From mid-May to June 22 and August 15 to August 31, it is open Saturday and Sunday 11am to 5pm. In the off-season, hours are Monday to Friday 11am to 3:30pm.

Other than the church, the town's raison d'être is still **Kongsberg Sølvgruvene ★★** (✆ **91-91-32-00**), the old silver mines that put Kongsberg on the map in the first place. To reach these mines, you can take a Buss Ekspress from Kongsberg to the hamlet of Saggrenda, a distance of 8km (5 miles), taking 10 minutes and costing NOK65. Departures are hourly from Kongsberg. Once at Saggrenda, it is a 10- to 15-minute walk to the entrance to the mines, where you can take a guided tour lasting 90 minutes. You can also drive from Kongsberg to Saggrenda, 8km (5 miles) southwest on Route 11.

The tour of the mines begins with a ride on a little train that goes 2.3km (1½ miles) inside the mountain to the King's Mine, a journey back in time. The train stops at a depth of 342m (1,122 ft.), at the entrance to the King's Mine, which reaches a depth of 1,070m (3,510 ft.). You can still see the *fahrkunst,* invented by

German miners. Dating from 1880, it was the first "elevator" to carry miners up and down. You'll also see the old mining equipment on display.

Regardless of the time of year, wear warm clothing before descending into the mines. You visit the mines by conducted tour, but the hours are a bit irregular: May 18 to June 30 daily 11am and 1 and 3pm; July 1 to August 14 daily 11am, noon, and 1, 2, 3, and 4pm; August 15 to 31 daily 11am and 1 and 3pm; September Saturday and Sunday noon and 2pm; October Sunday noon and 2pm. The rest of the year, the mines are closed. Tours, including the ride aboard the underground train, cost NOK150 for adults and NOK110 for children under 16.

Where to Stay

Best Western Gyldenløve Hotell This long-standing favorite, hardly an exciting choice, is in the town center, still evoking the 1950s' era in which it was built. However, it's been remodeled over the years and is a fine and serviceable choice if your expectations aren't too high. Bedrooms are medium in size and furnished like standard motel rooms—not stylish but comfortable, each equipped with a midsize bathroom with a tub or shower. The hotel also has a small pharmacy on-site, a whirlpool, and a sauna where guests can meet fellow guests while turning lobster-red. The on-site, full-service restaurant serves respectable international cuisine.

Hermann Fossgate 1, N-3600 Kongsberg. ✆ **32-86-58-00.** www.gyldenlove.no. 62 units. NOK950–NOK1,575 double. Rates include buffet breakfast. AE, DC, MC, V. **Amenities:** Restaurant; exercise room; sauna; rooms for those with limited mobility. *In room:* TV, Wi-Fi, minibar, hair dryer.

Quality Hotel Grand ★ This chain hotel is the best in the area, with more style, comfort, and facilities than Gyldenløve, and the prices are rather similar. All bedrooms are small but have been renovated over the past few years; some of them open onto views of a waterfall, the others onto views of the mountains. Less than half of the units have bathrooms with tub and shower; the rest have only showers. The hotel also offers the best drinking, dining, and entertainment facilities in town. Its piano bar is a nightly attraction, and on Friday and Saturday nights from 9pm to 3am there is disco action. You also have a choice of light dining in a lounge or more formal Norwegian and international cuisine in the hotel's main restaurant.

Christian August Gate 2, N-3611 Kongsberg. ✆ **32-77-28-00.** www.grandkongsberg.no. 176 units. NOK782–NOK1,420 double. Children 11 & under stay free in parents' room. Rates include continental breakfast. AE, DC, MC, V. **Amenities:** 2 restaurants; 2 bars; indoor heated pool; sauna; rooms for those with limited mobility. *In room:* TV, minibar, hair dryer.

Where to Dine

Big Horn Steak House ★ STEAKHOUSE/INTERNATIONAL A large chain-run restaurant, Big Horn serves the best steaks in the area, in a setting inspired by an American steakhouse. The chefs have access to the best-quality beef in Norway, though non-beef options are just as excellent. Try the marinated pork ribs with barbecue sauce, or the grilled scampi served with chili sweetcorn. Starters include American-style "buffalo wings" with blue cheese, or French-ified vineyard snails with garlic and Gorgonzola. For dessert, the house favorite is ice cream Grand Canyon or a chocolate mousse with blackberries.

Thomesvn. 4. ✆ **32-72-30-60.** www.bighorn.no. Reservations recommended. Main courses NOK169–NOK286. AE, DC, MC, V. Daily 4–10pm.

Easy Excursions: Heddal Stavkirke ★★★

Even if you have to skip the mines, head for the greatest manmade attraction in southern Norway. The **Heddal Stavkirke (Heddal Stave Church)** lies 33km (20 miles) west of Kongsberg, reached on Route 134 toward Notodden. This medieval architectural masterpiece is still in use today. Heddal, 25m (82 ft.) high and 19m (62 ft.) long, is the largest of the 28 stave churches remaining in Norway.

The oldest part of the church, the chancel, was built of wood in 1147. About a century later, the structure was enlarged to its present form. Runic inscriptions reveal that the church was consecrated in 1242 and dedicated to the Virgin Mary. Inside are a beautiful wooden carved chair from 1200, a baptismal font from 1850, and two of the original pillars from the church. The altarpiece is the work of an unknown artist in 1667, and the wall painting, also by an unknown artist, is from 1668. Dragons and serpents, along with grotesque human heads, decorate the portals.

The church (✆ **35-02-00-93;** www.heddalstavkirke.no) charges admission of NOK60 for adults, NOK25 for children. From June 20 to August 20, it is open daily 9am to 7pm. From May 20 to June 19 and August 21 to September 10, hours are daily 10am to 5pm.

SKIEN: MEMORIES OF HENRIK IBSEN

138km (86 miles) S of Oslo; 30km (19 miles) W of the Larvik–Frederikshavn (Denmark) ferry connection

Long proud of its association with playwright Henrik Ibsen (1828–1906), who was a Skien native, this bustling industrial town and government center is visited not only for its literary associations, but because it is the principal gateway to the **Telemark Canal** (p. 229) and the starting point for many trips.

Skien is an old town, dating from 1100, although it wasn't until 1358 that it received its royal charter. Fire and floods ravaged Skien over the centuries, destroying the entire town at times. The last disastrous fire occurred in 1886, and a new town had to be created out of the debris. Skien covers an area of 786 sq. km (303 sq. miles), with nearly 50,000 inhabitants.

Essentials

GETTING THERE **Trains** run every hour or two from Oslo to Skien, taking 2¾ hours and costing NOK300 one-way. Call ✆ **81-50-08-88** for schedules, or visit www.nsb.no.

Motorists can take the E18 south from Oslo toward Larvik to the signposted turnoff to Route 36, heading northwest into Skien.

You can also **fly** to the small Torp airport (✆ **33-42-70-00**) near Skien. Even though it's small, it is the country's second-busiest international airport. From the airport, buses run to the center of Skien.

VISITOR INFORMATION For information, go to the **Skien Tourist Office,** Nedre Hjellegate 18 (✆ **35-90-55-20;** www.grenland.no), which is open during July and August daily 9am to 5pm, and the rest of the year from Monday to Friday 8:30am to 4pm.

What to See & Do

Henrik Ibsen left Skien in 1843 when he was 15 years old, returning only briefly as part of an unsuccessful attempt to borrow some money to enter prep school in Oslo.

He lived at several addresses in Skien, including a small house in an old neighborhood, Snipetorp 27, near the town center. The house on Snipetorp is one of several in the neighborhood that have been proclaimed protected monuments. Ibsen's former home is now a cultural center and an art gallery.

Bø Sommarland ☺ This is the country's largest water park, drawing families from all over Norway during the summer. More than 100 different activities await you here, including a kids' water park (ideal for small children) and Bøverstranda ("the Beach"), along with water slides and Sommarlandelva, a 250-m (820-ft.)-long artificial river. Near the entrance is a scenic lake, Steinjønn, where you can borrow a canoe for a ride. The Flow Rider is for those who love skateboarding, snowboarding, or surfing. Of course, the waves here are artificial, but they are said to be the best of their kind in the world. You can also experience Europe's first roller-coaster flume.

The latest draw is the Space Ball, a centrifugal slide that creates the illusion of being in a whirlpool. The attraction begins as visitors enter a dark tunnel before being thrown into the Space Ball, which spirals down toward the center and drops visitors into a deep pool. There's also a big amusement area, Las Bøgas, with a Ferris wheel, an amusement arcade, merry-go-rounds, and lots of games. Family-friendly entertainment, from clown shows to band performances, is also presented daily. The park lies 50km (31 miles) from Skien and 25km (16 miles) from Notodden.

Bø. ✆ **35-06-16-00.** www.sommarland.no. Admission NOK310 adults, NOK265 children 15 & under. June–Aug daily 8am–dusk.

Henrik Ibsen Museum ★ This is a must for all Ibsen fans. Ibsen's childhood home, Venstøp Farm, lies 5km (3 miles) northwest of Skien. The house is furnished with objects actually used by the Ibsen family when they lived here from 1835 to 1843, when Henrik was 7 until the age of 15. The building itself dates from the early 19th century, and the dark attic was the inspiration for the playwright's *The Wild Duck*. Two paintings are by Ibsen—he had originally wanted to become an artist, but his wife ("the cat") insisted that he become a playwright. In her words, she "gave" the world a great dramatic talent but spared it a mediocre artist. The now-modern museum offers visitors a multimedia exhibition on Ibsen's life and works, and even includes a tour of the workings of Ibsen's brain.The museum was given to the Telemark Museum in 1958, and is one of three Ibsen museums in Norway.

Venstøp. ✆ **35-54-45-00.** www.telemarkmuseum.no/museum/henrik-ibsen-museum. Admission NOK70 adults, NOK30 children 15 & under. May Sat–Sun 11am–5pm; June–Aug Mon–Fri noon–5pm, Sat–Sun 11am–5pm. Open Sept–Apr on request.

Telemark Museum ★ This 1780 manor house, **Brekkeparken,** attracts everybody from fans of Ibsen's *A Doll's House* to botanists and devotees of Norwegian folk art. Luring theater buffs from around the world, it allows you to visit Ibsen's reconstructed study and the bedrooms from his Oslo apartment, as well as his "blue salon." In addition, there's a remarkable collection of **folk art ★** from the 1700s and 1800s, including many authentic pieces such as national costumes, textiles, handicrafts, and woodcarvings. As you wander the park in late spring, especially in May, you can take in the largest **tulip park ★★** in Scandinavia. In addition to the main building, there are some 20 old structures that have been moved here from different districts in Telemark.

Øvregate 41. ✆ **35-54-45-00.** www.telemarkmuseum.no. Admission NOK70 adults, NOK30 children 15 & under. Mid-May to Aug Mon–Fri noon–9pm, Sat–Sun 11am–10pm.

Where to Stay

Clarion Collection Hotel Bryggeparken Because it's constructed in a traditional style, this hotel near the harbor and river looks much older than it is. In actuality, the five-story brick structure was only completed and opened in 2001. Offering the freshest rooms in town, it is furnished in a contemporary style; some rooms feature balconies with water views. From 6 to 9pm nightly, guests can enjoy a light evening meal, which is included in the rate. If you want older and more traditional accommodations, check into the Thon Hotel Høyers (see below).

Langbryggen 7, N-3724 Skien. ✆ **35-91-21-00.** www.choicehotels.no. 103 units. NOK1,110–NOK2,260 double. Rates include continental breakfast. AE, DC, MC, V. Closed Dec 20–Jan 2. **Amenities:** Restaurant; bar; indoor heated pool; sauna; rooms for those with limited mobility. *In room:* TV, Wi-Fi, minibar, hair dryer.

Thon Hotel Hoyers ★ In a structure dating from 1853, this much renovated and improved hotel is the leading choice in town, and my personal favorite. It stands in the center of gardens stretching to the water and lies a 3-minute taxi ride from the rail station. Its tidy bedrooms are fairly sleek, with modern Scandinavian furnishings in beiges and grays, as well as comfortable beds. The hotel's restaurant, Madame Blom (see "Where to Dine"), boasts some of the finest dining and drinking in Skien. It lies almost 1km (about ½ mile) south of the railroad station.

Kongensgate 6, N-3701 Skien. ✆ **35-90-58-00.** www.thonhotels.com/hoyers. 73 units. NOK833–NOK1,233 double. Rates include continental breakfast. AE, DC, MC, V. Closed Dec 22–Jan 2. **Amenities:** Restaurant; bar; 1 room for those with limited mobility. *In room:* TV, Wi-Fi (in some), minibar, hair dryer.

Where to Dine

Brasseriet Madameblom ★ NORWEGIAN This restaurant at the oldest hotel in Telemark, the Thon Hotel Hoyers (see above), is your best option for moderately priced food. During the day many locals drop in for a feast of *smørbrød*—open-faced sandwiches. The kitchen also turns out more substantial and rib-sticking fare. I was enticed by the appetizer of smoked trout, served with a creamy apple-and-celery salad. The main courses are well prepared and concentrate on ingredients from Norway's fields and streams. Try the steamed mussels in white-wine sauce or the breast of duck with sherry sauce, fresh asparagus, and mustard-marinated potatoes. There is an especially good wine collection.

Kongensgate 6. ✆ **35-90-58-00.** www.thonhotels.com/hoyers. Reservations recommended. Main courses NOK198–NOK265. AE, DC, MC, V. Mon–Fri noon–2pm; Mon–Sat 4–10pm.

Easy Excursions: The Telemark Canal ★★

Skien is the gateway to the Telemark Canal, which was completed in 1892. Some 500 men labored for 5 years on this canal, blasting their way through mountains. Today it contains a total of 28 lock chambers, and the route runs from Skien in the east to the ancient Norwegian town of Dalen in the west. The canal affords a sailing route of 105km (65 miles) with an elevation difference of 72m (236 ft.), via eight locks. Vrangfoss, the biggest staircase-lock, has five lock-chambers and a lifting height of 23m (75 ft.).

At the turn of the 20th century, the canal became known as the "fast route" between eastern and western Norway. Nostalgic canal boats, the MS *Victoria,* the MS *Henrik Ibsen,* and the MS *Telemarken,* will take you from Skien to Dalen, a 10-hour trip on this historic waterway, costing around NOK600 round-trip. Although hardly a Panama Canal journey, I highly recommend this trip, as it's a comfortable, easy way to penetrate some of the lakes and rivers of inland Norway.

As you sail along, you'll pass wild pastures and private farmland so manicured it appears deliberately landscaped, and a countryside dotted with scenic summer homes (many owned by residents of Oslo) and churches. Along the way you'll also encounter panoramic vistas in many directions, with views of deep, dark forests, which some Norwegians claim are still inhabited by trolls. Swift-flowing streams add to the landscape drama, as do forested hillsides and deep valleys, some of which draw skiers in winter. The engineer in you may also be fascinated by the original stone walls of the canal, as well as the closing mechanisms.

For information and bookings, contact **Telemarkreiser,** Handelstorget (✆ **35-90-00-20;** www.visittelemark.com) in Skien.

WHERE TO STAY & DINE IN DALEN

Dalen Hotel ★★ At the terminus of the Telemark Canal, with "dragon heads" and Viking-inspired gingerbread dripping from its eaves, this historic hotel bears some architectural similarities with Norway's medieval stave churches. It is often cited as a fine example of the Norwegian national style. Built in 1894, it was a lodging for prominent guests interested in seeing the natural beauty of a region that had just opened thanks to the completion of the canal. Today, the ocher-brown woods here still evoke the fantasy and whimsy of the late Victorian age. It is graced with symmetrical towers, soaring turrets, wide verandas, and high ceilings. Rooms come in various shapes and sizes, all decidedly old-fashioned but well maintained.

The on-site Dalen Restaurant is the area's best place to eat, with market-fresh Norwegian and international cuisine. On warm summer days I prefer meals under a willow in the garden, with a terrace that opens toward a swan-filled lake. The cooking is not fancy, but it's affordable and tasty. Set meals, which are changed daily, cost from NOK200 to NOK400.

N-3880 Dalen I Telemark. ✆ **35-07-90-00.** www.dalenhotel.no. 38 units. NOK1,800–NOK2,200 double; NOK2,700–NOK3,200 suite. Rates include buffet breakfast. AE, DC, MC, V. Closed Nov–Mar. **Amenities:** Restaurant; bar. *In room:* Hair dryer.

ARENDAL

239km (148 miles) SW of Oslo; 69km (43 miles) E of Kristiansand S

"I have found heaven on earth," Harald Hagerup, a local painter, has said of Arendal. After spending some time here, I concur that it is a worthwhile little stopover.

Arendal, the government center of the Aust-Agder district, was once known as "the Venice of Scandinavia." At the time it was riddled with canals, but following a disastrous fire, these were filled in and turned into wide streets. That took away a lot of the charm, but much remains to enchant.

For the best look at old Arendal, visit **Tyholmen ★★**, in the center, with its handsomely preserved 18th-century wooden houses. Many artists and craftspeople have moved here from Oslo, taking over the wood-framed structures and restoring them. In summer, the harbor, **Pollen,** is filled with boats and people, as this is one of the most popular centers for domestic tourism in Norway. Many Norwegians come here to take boat trips among the neighboring rocks and traverse the delta of the Nidelva River.

After Ibsen, the region's second-most-famous son was Knut Hamsun, called the "Balzac of Norway," who won the Nobel Prize for literature in 1918. His novels give a vivid portrait of 19th-century Norwegian values, and his works are still very popular in Germany, almost more so than they are in Norway.

Essentials

GETTING THERE

BY TRAIN Four trains a day arrive from Oslo, requiring a change of trains at Nelaug. Trip time, including the transfer, is 4½ hours. For schedules and more information, call ✆ **81-50-08-88** or visit www.nsb.no.

BY BUS Nor-Way Bussekspress (✆ **81-54-44-44;** www.nor-way.no) buses travel between Oslo and Arendal, taking 4 hours and costing NOK350 for one-way passage.

BY CAR From Skien, the E18 continues south to Arendal.

VISITOR INFORMATION

For helpful advice about Arendal and the surrounding area, go to the **Region Arendal Turistkontor,** Peder Thomassons Gate 1 (✆ **37-00-55-44;** www.arendal.com). It's open mid-June to mid-August Monday to Friday 9am to 6pm, Saturday 11am to 6pm and Sunday noon to 6pm. Otherwise, hours are Monday to Friday 8:30am to 4pm.

What to See & Do

Arendal Rådhus In the center of town, the Rådhus, or Town Hall, is better known as the second-largest timber building in Norway and the country's single tallest timber structure. It was originally built in 1815 by a rich shipowner, but became the Town Hall in 1844. Regrettably, the city fathers of the late 1800s made some unfortunate decisions, such as flattening the dramatic domed ceiling. The elegant original staircase remains, and the hall also contains about 300 antique portraits, many from the 19th century—and some of them quite amusing. If you're Norwegian, look for some of your ancestors. The tourist office (see above) can organize guided tours upon request.

Rådhusgata 19. ✆ **37-01-30-00.** Mon–Fri 9am–3pm.

Aust-Agder Kulturhistoriske Senter ★ 🎁 This is an unusual museum, a result of the fact that the town's sailors were asked to bring home curios from their global sailing that might interest those left behind. These seafarers succeeded so admirably that this museum was opened in 1932. In addition to finds from around the world, the museum showcases the folk art of the region and is filled with memorabilia of the history of the town, mainly artifacts from its seafaring heyday. One exhibit is dedicated to the ill-fated slave ship *Fredensborg,* which sank off

Tromøy in 1768. The museum lies about 1.5km (1 mile) north of the center; to reach it, follow the signs in the direction of Oslo.

Parkveien 16. ✆ **37-07-35-00.** www.aaks.no. Admission NOK20 adults, NOK10 children. June 22–Aug 17 Mon–Fri 9am–5pm, Sun noon–5pm; Aug 18–June 21 Mon–Fri 9am–3pm, Sun noon–3pm.

Where to Stay

Clarion Hotel Tyholmen ★ Two highly regarded chain hotels compete for your patronage here. I give the nod to the Clarion. Enjoying panoramic views of one of Norway's loveliest harbors, this hotel is the best in the area for an overnight stopover. Architecturally, the main section of the hotel was inspired by the 1800s, the heyday of the sailing vessels that put Arendal on the map. The decor of each bedroom reflects the history of a different ship constructed in Norway, and each unit is named after a particular vessel. All of the accommodations are decorated in soothing pastels with modern furnishings. A new addition, meanwhile, offers a more modern style in furnishings. The hotel's restaurant, Tre Seil (see below), is popular in the area during the summer, and you may want to come for food and drink even if you're not a guest. It's a 2-minute walk south of the bus station.

Teaterplassen 2, N-4800 Arendal. ✆ **37-07-68-00.** Fax 37-07-68-01. www.clariontyholmen.com. 96 units. NOK995 double. Rates include buffet breakfast. AE, DC, MC, V. **Amenities:** Restaurant; bar; sauna; rooms for those with limited mobility. *In room:* A/C, TV, Wi-Fi, minibar, hair dryer.

Thon Hotel Arendal Under new Thon management, this hotel has been improved and expanded, though the exterior continues to evoke the decade of its creation—the 1960s (no great compliment). Bedrooms come in gentle, monochromatic tones of cream, gray, and white. Each of the tiled bathrooms has its own shower, and 10 have bathtubs as well. The breakfast room is modern and minimalist, and free Wi-Fi is available throughout the hotel. The hotel's restaurant, Serdinand, is separately recommended below.

Fiergangen 1, N-4800 Arendal. ✆ **37-05-21-50.** Fax 37-05-21-51. www.thonhotels.com/arendal. 120 units. NOK790–NOK1,745 double. AE, DC, MC, V. **Amenities:** Restaurant; 1 room for those with limited mobility. *In room:* TV, Wi-Fi, minibar, hair dryer.

Where to Dine

Tre Seil ★ NORWEGIAN "Three Sails," located in the Clarion Hotel Tyholmen (see above), is an excellent restaurant with large windows looking out over the moored yachts and boats bobbing in the harbor. The well-to-do clientele comes for the nautical decor and seasonal menu. For a recommended main course, I suggest the baked halibut with potato cream, chorizo, sweet beans, and shellfish sauce. You might also try the pan-fried tusk with steamed vegetables, orange, and coriander butter. For an interesting taste of new Norway, opt for the scallops marinated in lime with pickled cucumber, avocado, and roe.

In the Clarion Tyholmen Hotel, Teaterplassen 2. ✆ **37-07-68-00.** www.clariontyholmen.com. Reservations recommended. Main courses NOK125–NOK145. AE, DC, MC, V. Mon–Sat noon–10pm.

Easy Excursions: Merdø Island

In the bay of Arendal, **Merdø Island ★** is like a time capsule. Virtually intact architecturally from its days as a prosperous 19th-century town, the island's clapboard-sided houses retain their allure today.

There are no restaurants, only a small summer cafe, and there's a lovely bathing beach nearby where you can picnic.

The **Merdøgaård Museum** (© **37-07-35-00**) on the island is run by the Aust-Agder Kulturhistoriske Senter (see above). The museum is the perfectly preserved early-19th-century house of a long-departed sea captain, with the furnishings still intact. The Senter can book guided tours in the off-season. It's open mid-June to mid-August daily from noon to 4pm. Admission is NOK20 adults, NOK10 children.

To reach the island, take a **Skisøferga ferry** (© **90-97-43-61;** www.skilsoferga.no) departing from Arendal's harborfront. Departures are every 30 minutes from 9am to 6pm from late June to mid-August, and the boat makes stops at two or three other islands before reaching Merdø. The ferry costs NOK45 each way, and the trip takes 20 minutes. For schedules and more information, contact the tourist office.

Lying 20km (12 miles) west of Arendal in the center of Grimstad is the **Grimstad Bymuseum–Ibsen Museet,** Henrik Ibsensgate 14 (© **37-04-04-90**). Henrik Ibsen worked in this town at a pharmacy while pursuing the pharmacist's daughter. Ibsen also wrote his first play, *Catalina,* here. The Grimstad museum includes the old pharmacy where Ibsen lived as an apprentice. Admission is NOK50 for adults, NOK20 for children. It's open June 26 to August 15 Monday to Saturday 11am to 5pm, Sunday noon to 5pm; June 5 to June 25 and August 16 to September 12 Saturday 11am to 5pm and Sunday noon to 5pm. There are guided tours every hour.

The nearby island of **Tromøy** offers a fabulous network of walking paths in the woods and along the shore. The pebble-and-boulder beach is popular during the summer, and there are easier hikes inland.

KRISTIANSAND S: THE SUMMER CITY ★

526km (326 miles) SE of Bergen; 342km (212 miles) SW of Oslo

The fifth-largest town in Norway, with some 80,000 inhabitants, is called *Sommerbyen,* or "the Summer City." Indeed, it is an excellent place to spend the summer months, especially since many of its attractions are closed during the winter season.

Visitors heading to Bergen and the fjord country often arrive in Norway at Kristiansand S (not to be confused with Kristiansund N in the north). The biggest town and an important port of Sørtlandet (the south coast), and Norway's largest ferry port, Kristiansand S offers the most attractions, the largest number of hotels and restaurants, and the most activities of any town along the southern coast.

Founded by King Christian in 1641, Kristiansand S is a busy port and industrial center, yet it has many charming old streets and antique houses clustered cozily together. **Kvadraturen,** "the quadrant," is known for its right-angled street plan that was influenced by the Renaissance period's strict adherence to form. **Markens** is the town's pedestrian precinct and meeting place.

Essentials

GETTING THERE

BY AIR Kristiansand airport lies at Kjevik, 16km (10 miles) east of the town center. SAS (© **05400;** calls from within Norway only) flies from Oslo to Kristiansand. An airport bus runs between here and central Kristiansand.

BY TRAIN Anywhere from three to six trains link Oslo and Kristiansand daily, taking 4½ hours, with a one-way ticket costing from NOK199 if you book online in advance. Call ✆ **81-50-08-88** for more information, or visit www.nsb.no.

BY BUS Nor-Way Bussekspress (✆ **81-54-44-44;** www.nor-way.no) buses travel down from Oslo in 5½ hours, with a one-way ticket costing NOK320. Buses run two to four times daily. Two other bus companies, **Konkurrenten** (✆ **67-98-04-80;** www.konkurrenten.no) and **Lavprisexpressen** (✆ **37-93-15-15;** www.lavprisekspressen.no), also operate on this route.

BY FERRY International ferries link Kristiansand to Hirtshals in the northern reaches of Denmark's Jutland peninsula—the shortest ferry link between Norway and Denmark. Ferries run three to four times daily, depending on the time of year, with the sea voyage taking 4 hours. Both **Color Line** (✆ **22-94-44-00;** www.colorline.com) and **Fjord Line** (✆ **81-53-35-00;** www.fjordline.no) operate ferries. Depending on the time of year, fares range from NOK69 to NOK1,040. The highest fares are charged on weekends from mid-June to mid-August.

BY CAR From Arendal, the E18 continues southwest to Kristiansand.

VISITOR INFORMATION

Go to **Inspirasjon Sørlandet,** Rådhusgata 6 (✆ **38-12-13-14;** www.regionkristiansand.no), which also distributes bus, train, and ferry schedules. From June 14 to August 15 it's open Monday to Friday 9am to 6pm, Saturday 10am to 6pm, and Sunday noon to 6pm. The rest of the year hours are Monday to Friday 9am to 4pm.

GETTING AROUND

Municipal buses through the town center cost NOK20 per ride. Contact the tourist office (see above) for information.

Sights & Outdoor Activities

Although Kristiansand S has plenty of museums, churches, and other sights, many visitors come here for outdoorsy activities in summer. My favorite sport here is biking, thanks to some 70km (43 miles) of bike trails. You can pick up maps of the area at the tourist office (see above), and bikes can be rented at **Kristiansand Sykkelsenter,** Grims Torv 2 (✆ **38-02-68-35**). Many head toward the hills with their bikes, but I always prefer to take the coastal route.

If you're a fisherman, you can obtain a permit at the post office, which will allow you to fish at **Vestre Grievann,** a lake north of the town that is known for perch, trout, and eel.

Another pleasurable experience is horseback riding at **Islandshestsenteret** at Søgne (✆ **38-16-98-82;** www.islandshestsenteret.no). Stables here hold the rare Icelandic horse, which is smaller than most breeds.

Agder Naturmuseum og Botaniske Hage (Agder Museum of Natural History & Botanical Garden) The present exhibitions, which opened in 1990, show part of the natural history of southern Norway. Colorful minerals are on display, and the museum includes a beautiful botanical garden. The complex contains the largest collection of cacti in Norway. As part of the package, you can visit the neighboring **Gimle Estate** ★, a 19th-century manor house with elegant, antiques-heavy interiors and a historic **rose garden** ★★ planted in 1850. From the center of town, motorists can take the E18 east, crossing a bridge. After the bridge, turn right and follow the signs. Bus no. 22 also runs there.

Gimleveien 23. ✆ **38-05-86-20.** www.naturmuseum.no. Admission to museum NOK40 adults, NOK15 children; admission to house & garden NOK55 adults, NOK20 children. June 20–Aug 19 daily 11am–5pm; Aug 20–June 19 Tues–Fri 10am–3pm, Sun noon–4pm. Closed Dec 16–Jan 7.

Christiansholm Festning (Christiansholm Fortress) The present "defenders" of this fortress, with its 5-m (16-ft.)-thick walls, are a lot friendlier than they were in the early 1940s, during the darkest days of the Nazi occupation. At that time, the Germans took over this fortress and trained their guns out to sea, expecting an Allied invasion that never came. A landmark along the Strandepromenaden, this fortress dates from 1674. The installation was ordered by King Christian IV of Denmark, to protect the Skagerrak Straits from invasion, not only from pirates but from the roving Swedes, who came only once, in 1807 during the Napoleonic Wars. The local citizenry paid for the fortress with their labor and with heavy taxes.

Festningsgata. ✆ **38-00-74-65.** Free admission. May 15–Sept 15 daily 9am–9pm.

Kristiansand Domkirke Constructed in neo-Gothic style in 1884, this is the third-largest church in Norway, seating 1,800 worshippers. You may want to check it out, especially when there is organ practice (weekdays at 11am). You can climb the tower for NOK20 for a **panoramic view** ★ of the area. Summer concerts are also presented here, especially at the weeklong International Church Music Festival in mid-May, with organ, chamber, and gospel music on tap.

Gyldenløvesgate 9. ✆ **38-19-69-00.** www.kirkefestspill.no**.** Free admission. June–Aug daily 11am–2pm.

Kristiansand Dyrepark (Kristiansand Zoo & Amusement Park) ★ ☺ Today the major family attraction in the south of Norway, Kristiansand Dyrepark has been billed by some as "Norway's Disneyland." Although it doesn't quite hold up to all that Disney has to offer, it does provide summer amusements for the area. The park is comprises five parks: The highlight is **Nordisk Vilmark,** a simulated wilderness area where you can walk on boardwalks over the habitats of wolverines, lynx, wolves, and moose. The zoo itself contains many exotic specimens, including some Arctic species, and diverse animals roam in large enclosures. The park covers an area of 60

Walking the Streets of the Old Town

The best-preserved district is Posebyen ★, along the river in the northeastern part of town. It survived a disastrous fire in 1892 that swept over Kristiansand. The streets are filled with the original one- and two-story houses that accommodated workers in the 19th century. You'll see small-paned windows, iron fences, benches, and flower boxes. The kitchens and bedrooms were built in the rear, with separate doorways leading to little gardens. The most interesting parts of the area lie between Festningsgaten and Elvegata and between Rådhusgaten and Tordenskiolds. The best time to visit is on a Saturday from mid-June to August, when a market is held with street stalls and all kinds of produce for sale. Pick up the small guide, *A Stroll Through Posebyen,* in the tourist office.

Heading for the Fish Market

On a lovely summer evening, stroll down to the fish market at Grovane, where you can purchase fresh shrimp from one of the vendors and enjoy them on the pier as you people-watch and breathe the fresh air of Norway's all-too-fleeting summer. Small bridges lead to wooden, maritime-inspired structures painted in red and yellow, housing a series of restaurants by the canal. There's no better way to spend an evening in Kristiansand.

hectares (148 acres). Children should delight in **Kardemomme by** (Cardamom town), a re-created "town" suggesting a hamlet in Africa. The town is based on a well-known children's story by Thorbjørn Egner, and famous characters from Egner's story stroll about, greeting visitors. A pirate ship, a circus, a play area, giraffes, a farm, and other amusements, including a bobsled track and a water slide, also await you here.

Along the E18. ✆ **38-04-97-00.** www.dyreparken.no. Admission, including all activities, NOK150–NOK370 adults, NOK130–NOK290 children. Mid-May to Aug daily 10am–7pm; Sept to mid-May daily 10am–3pm. Take the Dyreparkbussen (bus) from the center. The park is signposted off the E18 9km (5½ miles) east of the town center.

Kristiansand Kanonmuseum (Cannon Museum) Lying 8km (5 miles) south of town, the Cannon Museum recalls the dark days of World War II when Nazi forces were installed here and at Christiansholm Festning (see above). The museum preserves the Germans' heavy Vara Battery cannons, which gave them control over the strategic Skagerrak Straits. The 337-ton cannons had a range of 55km (34 miles). You can visit the bunkers where 600 German soldiers and 1,400 laborers lived, and even see their scribbling, in German, on the walls.

Møvik. ✆ **38-08-50-90.** www.kanonmuseet.no. Admission NOK80 adults, NOK40 children. June 6–Aug 15 daily 11am–6pm; Aug 16–Sept 26 Mon–Wed 11am–3pm, Thurs–Sun 11am–5pm; Oct–June 16 Sun noon–4pm.

Oddernes Kirke ★ It may not be bigger than the Domkirke (see above), but it's a lot prettier. One of the oldest parish churches of Norway lies 1.5km (1 mile) east of the town center, reached by bus no. 22. The church, whose nave and choir were built around 1040, was dedicated to St. Olav, patron saint of Norway. After viewing the church's interior, be sure to wander the grounds, particularly the ancient cemetery with its impressive rune stones.

Jegersbergveien 6. ✆ **38-19-68-60.** Free admission. Early July to mid-Aug Mon–Fri 11am–2pm.

Vest Agder Fylkes-Museum ★★ If you are growing a bit jaded with open-air museums, note that this one, 4km (2½ miles) east of town on the E18, is one of the largest and best in Norway. From all over the Setesdalen region, nearly 50 antique farm and town dwellings were moved to this site, some with provincial furnishings. Traditional costumes of the region are also displayed, along with other artifacts from the past. Folk dancing is staged Wednesday at 6pm from mid-June to mid-August. Once a year the main building houses thematic exhibitions devoted to 18th- and 19th-century Norwegian life.

Vigeveien 22B. ✆ **38-10-26-80.** www.vestagdermuseet.no. Admission NOK50 adults, NOK25 children, NOK120 family ticket. June 20–Aug 20 Mon–Fri 11am–5pm, Sat & Sun noon–5pm; off-season Sun noon–5pm.

Nearby Attractions

The **Setesdalsbanen** (✆ **38-15-64-82;** www.setesdalsbanen.no) runs a steam train along 4.8km (3 miles) of narrow-gauge track. The locomotive, built in 1894, starts its run at Grovane, 20km (12 miles) from Kristiansand, from where it traveled for 78km (48 miles) between Kristiansand and Byglandsfjord, providing a vital link between Setesdalen (the Setesdal Valley) and the southern coast. At one time it transported nickel from the mines along with other exports such as timber. Today, the train runs only to Røyknes, 8km away, with departures from Grovane from June 13 to August 29 on Sunday at 11:30am, and 1:20 and 3:10pm. A round-trip fare is NOK100 for adults and NOK50 for children.

The countryside around Kristiansand is rich with rolling meadows, birch-clad hills, deep valleys, and mountain moors. My favorite spot for a hike is in the **Baneheia Skog** (Baneheia Forest). The trail begins only a 15-minute walk north of the town center. Trails are cut through the forest, which is studded with evergreens and graced with small lakes. You can make this walk easy or lazy, or a challenge if you head up some of the steeper hills. It's best to pick up the makings of a picnic before heading here.

Another favorite place for hikers is **Ravnedalen** (Raven Valley), which is signposted just northwest of Kristiansand. This is a lush park that bursts into wildflower bloom in spring. You can wander its narrow, winding trails for hours. The climax comes when you climb 200 steps to a 93-m (305-ft.) lookout point. You're rewarded with one of the most **panoramic vistas ★★** along the southern coast.

You can also drive along the E18 to **Mandal,** Norway's southernmost town, 42km (26 miles) southwest of Kristiansand. Here you can walk the streets of its historic center, with its old wooden houses, and stroll its long sandy beach, Sjøsanden.

At the southernmost point in Norway is **Lindesnes Fyr** (✆ **38-25-54-20;** www.lindesnesfyr.no), Norway's first lighthouse, dating from 1656. Inside is an exhibition of lighthouse artifacts. Admission is NOK50 for adults (free for children under 12). It's open late June to early August daily 10am to 8pm, May to early June and early August to early October daily 11am to 5pm, and off-season Tuesday and Sunday 11am to 5pm.

In summer, boat trips are offered to the archipelago of offshore skerries (isolated rock islands). Visits are possible to Lillesand to the east and to the island of Bragdøya (www.bragdoya.no), which lies right off the coast at Kristiansand and offers many scenic strolls and places for sunbathing. You can sail aboard the M/S *Maarten* from pier 6 in Kristiansand, daily in summer at 11am. The trip costs NOK220 for adults or NOK115 for children. This is the best bet for visitors who'd like to absorb some of the scenery of the rugged southern coast of Norway.

Shopping

The largest shopping center in southern Norway lies 12km (7½ miles) east of Kristiansand toward the zoo. **Steen & Strøm Sørlandssenteret** (✆ **38-04-91-00**) offers more than 100 stores plus a dozen restaurants and cafes.

Closer to the center of town is **SlottsQuartalet,** Tordenskiolds 9 (✆ **38-02-79-99;** www.slottsquartalet.no), at the top end of the Markens pedestrian street, near **Sandens** (www.sandens.no), Markensgate 10, another good mall. You'll find various shops and cafes at both of these spots.

Where to Stay

Clarion Hotel Ernst ★★ Kings, diplomats, politicians (Nelson Rockefeller, Hubert Humphrey), and even Nazi officers during World War II have chosen this hotel as their favorite. The only hotel in town with a doorman, the Ernst first opened its doors in 1859. The classic look and feel of the place has been preserved, and it stands somewhat in opposition to the more sleekly modern look of the Caledonien (see below). Bedrooms come in different sizes with individual color schemes, but each contains a fairly well-sized bathroom. The location is ideal: about 200m (600ft.) from the central bus terminal, railway station, and ferry dock. It is the only area hotel with a restaurant and drinking spots to rival the Caledonien.

Rådhusgaten 2, N-4611 Kristiansand S. ✆ **38-12-86-00.** Fax 38-02-03-07. www.ernst.no. 135 units. Sun–Thurs NOK870–NOK1,680 double. Rates include buffet breakfast. AE, DC, MC, V. Parking NOK125. **Amenities:** Restaurant; 2 bars; nightclub; babysitting; room service; rooms for those with limited mobility. *In room:* A/C, TV, Wi-Fi, minibar, hair dryer.

Quality Hotel Kristiansand ★ ☺ There is no better address for families with small children in all of southern Norway, although the managers of the Rica Dyreparken, reviewed below, might claim the same. The hotel is one of Sørlandet's biggest, lying 11km (6¾ miles) east of the town center. The building is modern, and the bedrooms are freshly and comfortably furnished with cheerful pastels and wooden furnishings. Everything is geared to families with children, including a large playroom, organized kiddie activities, and even a special buffet for youngsters in the dining room. Visitors can also take advantage of toys around the grounds, provided by the hotel.

Sorlandsparken, N-4696 Kristiansand S. ✆ **38-17-77-77.** www.quality-kristiansand.no. 210 units. NOK843–NOK2,125 double. AE, DC, MC, V. Free parking. **Amenities:** Restaurant; bar; babysitting; outdoor heated pool; sauna; children's center & programs; rooms for those with limited mobility. *In room:* TV, Wi-Fi, minibar, hair dryer.

Radisson BLU Caledonien Hotel ★★ Located in the town center, the largest hotel in the area is the best hotel in southern Norway, although my heart still belongs to the Clarion Hotel Ernst. Built in 1968 near the fish market, it remains smart and stylish because of frequent renovations. A stay here is very convenient, as the hotel is within walking distance of the train and bus stations, as well as the ferry terminal, theaters, cinemas, and the best shopping. The good-size bedrooms are furnished with contemporary pieces and midsize bathrooms, though the decor isn't particularly memorable. The hotel's restaurant is far superior to a typical hotel dining room, and the drinking facilities, including pub, disco, and piano bar, are among the best in town.

Vestre Strandgate 7, N-4601 Kristiansand S. ✆ **38-11-21-00.** www.radissonblu.com/hotel-kristiansand. 205 units. NOK1,095–NOK1,795 double; NOK2,500 suite. AE, DC, MC, V. Parking NOK120. **Amenities:** Restaurant; 2 bars; babysitting; room service; rooms for those with limited mobility. *In room:* A/C, TV, Wi-Fi, minibar, hair dryer.

Rica Dyreparken Hotel ★ ☺ This novelty hotel is sure to delight as many as it will alienate. Lying right in one of the most popular holiday parks in Norway, it was architecturally inspired by Noah's Ark. Staying here should delight animal lovers of all ages. All the public lounges and bedrooms have motifs relating to the animal kingdom—you might opt to stay in a monkey room or a horse room, relax on an African safari bed, or recline in a tiger-striped chair in one of the Jungle Jim bedrooms.

The hotel even has its own bridge, as well as a large bar terrace where you can sit out on a summer night enjoying the fresh air. The in-house Norwegian restaurant is named—you guessed it—Noah's Ark.

Dyreparken, N-4609 Kristiansand S. ✆ **38-14-64-00.** www.ricadyreparkenhotel.no. 160 units. NOK920–NOK1,270 double. Rates include buffet breakfast. AE, DC, MC, V. Free parking. **Amenities:** 2 restaurants; bar; children's center; babysitting; laundry service/dry cleaning; rooms for those with limited mobility. *In room:* TV, minibar, hair dryer.

Where to Dine

Bakgården ★ FRENCH/INTERNATIONAL The interior of this well-established restaurant is accented with oil lamps, creating a mellow atmosphere. The cuisine is an unending festival celebrating southern Europe, and the chefs frequently add flair, borrowing recipes from around the world, although dishes are tailored to local palates. The chefs continue to come up with intriguing flavor combinations, though they are very well known for their pan-fried cod, served with celeriac purée, broccoli, cauliflower, and butter. One of the spicier menu items is the marinated fillet of chicken served with ratatouille, corn on the cob, and Caribbean sauce. Don't overlook the starters, especially the scampi marinated in chili, garlic, ginger, and rum! The pricey wine list may elicit a gasp from you—in Norway, wine is priced like liquid gold.

Tollbodgate 5. ✆ **38-02-79-55.** Reservations required. Main courses NOK197–NOK330. AE, DC, MC, V. Daily 3–11pm.

Bølgen & Moi ★★ CONTINENTAL When champagne soup arrives as a starter, you know you're in a special place. This is a member of a chain of fine-dining restaurants that now stretches across Norway. It occupies a big-windowed replica of a 19th-century warehouse, set within the "tourist zone" of Kristiansand, on the docks, almost immediately adjacent to the waterfront. Inside, within a color scheme of white, dark wooden paneling, and touches of apple green, a uniformed and cheerfully hard-working waitstaff manages to be simultaneously informal, unpretentious, and chic. Menu items derive from the culinary canon of two of Norway's pre-eminent chefs and restaurant entrepreneurs, Trond Moi and Toralf Bølgen, and change each month according to the season. Worthy specialties include gratinated langoustines with tarragon and garlic, amandine potatoes, and lettuce; or pork loin ribs with sweet potato purée, apples, and soy-based barbecue sauce. For dessert, try the chocolate mousse with ginger sabayonne and fresh berries.

Sjølystveien 1A. ✆ **38-17-83-00.** www.bolgenogmoi.no (in Norwegian). Reservations recommended. Main courses NOK195–NOK325. AE, DC, MC, V. Mon–Sat 4–10pm.

Sjøhuset (Sea House) ★ NORWEGIAN Set directly on the harborfront in the center of town, this restaurant is housed in a century-old former salt warehouse whose oxblood-red walls are very distinctive. Inside you'll see the massive structural beams of the restaurant's original construction, and a stone-sided fireplace. In summer, I prefer the waterfront terrace. Specialties include filet of halibut with sautéed oyster mushroom, asparagus, and fresh tomatoes, served with chive and passion-fruit *beurre blanc*. Another delight is reindeer filet served with fresh asparagus, broccoli, and cauliflower, red onion compote, and creamy wild mushroom sauce.

Østre Strangate 12. ✆ **38-02-62-60.** www.sjohuset.no (in Norwegian). Reservations required in summer. Main courses NOK280–NOK390. AE, DC, MC, V. Mon–Sat 3pm–11pm.

Kristiansand S After Dark

There is cultural life here—the acclaimed **Kristiansand Symfoniorkester (Kristiansand Symphony Orchestra)** performs year-round at Kongensgate 6 (✆ **38-07-70-00;** www.kso.no). Concerts are also presented year-round at **Musikkens Hus,** Kongensgate 54 (✆ **38-14-87-30**). Check with the tourism office (p. 234) to see if any performances are scheduled at the time of your visit. **Telfords Pub,** in the Radisson BLU Caledonien Hotel (see "Where to Stay"), is a watering hole with an authentic Scottish interior and atmosphere, attracting a heavy-drinking crowd (20s to 40s). It's open late (until 3:30am) on Fridays and Saturdays. The best piano bar is the **Lobbybaren,** also in the Radisson BLU Caledonien Hotel, attracting an older crowd.

STAVANGER

Who would have thought that the once-sleepy provincial city of Stavanger, fourth-largest in Norway, would ever be named European Capital of Culture (for 2008)? The old Stavanger is gone forever. Today it's a bright, cosmopolitan city and one of my favorites in Norway. What brought about this miraculous change? "Black gold" (oil, that is) from the North Sea. Packing riches and economic clout, Stavanger has become the oil capital of Norway.

The good news is that the place still retains a bit of its old charm as a famous seaport set in some of the most beautiful fjord and mountain country in Norway. Since the 9th century, fresh fish and vegetables have been sold at the old marketplace. Many of its low wooden houses, some of which have been around for nearly a millennium, still remain.

Stavanger has also burst out with some of the most engaging museums in the southwest, although not quite on the level of Bergen when it comes to cultural offerings. Still, nowhere is finer in Stavanger than its historic harbor, where you can see ships both new and old.

Long before the North Sea oil boom, it was the herring fishermen who put Stavanger harbor on the map. In the 19th century, this harbor simmered, its wharves teaming with net-makers and net-menders, coopers, and smiths. The port today not only constructs the rigs for those offshore oilfields, but refines the oil as well.

You can wander the narrow streets of Stavanger for hours, visiting its shops, bars, restaurants, cafes, and art galleries. Budget at least 1 busy day for this bustling old seaport on the Ryfylkefjord.

ORIENTATION

Arriving

BY AIR Flights land at **Stavanger International Airport** at Sola, 14km (8¾ miles) south of the city center. **SAS** (✆ **91-50-54-00**) flies between Oslo, Bergen, Kristiansand S, and Stavanger. **Widerøe** (✆ **81-00-12-00;** www.wideroe.no) flies from Bergen to Stavanger. **Norwegian** (✆ **81-52-18-15;** www.norwegian.no) travels between Stavanger, Trondheim, and Oslo. These airlines also serve Stavanger from a number of European cities, including London. A taxi from the airport to the city center goes for NOK200 to NOK250.

BY TRAIN Direct trains from Oslo require seat reservations and take 8 hours, via Kristiansand S. A one-way fare costs NOK886. About three trains per day arrive in Stavanger from Oslo, and there is one overnight service. For rail information, call ✆ **81-50-08-88** or visit www.nsb.no.

BY BUS There is no direct bus link between Oslo and Stavanger. However, **Nor-Way Bussekspress** (✆ **81-54-44-44;** www.nor-way.no) runs a service between Oslo and Kristiansand S, taking 5 hours and costing NOK350 one-way. From Kristiansand S, you can continue on another bus to Stavanger, taking 4 hours and costing NOK380. The bus station is adjacent to the train station.

BY BOAT From Bergen, **Flaggruten** (✆ **05505** or **55-23-87-00;** www.flaggruten.no) runs an express catamaran to Stavanger, taking 4½ hours and costing NOK750 for a one-way trip. Ferries depart from the eastern part of town across a body of water known as **Byfjorden.**

BY CAR Because of the jagged coastline of western Norway, access by car from Bergen to Stavanger requires a 149-km (93-mile) detour, incorporating high-speed motorways and three different ferry crossings. It usually takes 6½ to 7 hours to drive to Stavanger from Bergen. Access from Kristiansand S is much easier: Continue west from Kristiansand S until you reach the end of the E18.

Essentials

VISITOR INFORMATION You can find all relevant visitor information at the **Stavanger tourist office,** Domkirkeplassen 3 (✆ **51-85-92-00;** www.destinasjon-stavanger.no). From June to August it is open daily 7am to 8pm; from September to May Monday to Friday 9am to 4pm, Saturday 9am to 2pm.

CITY LAYOUT Most of Stavanger's attractions lie within an easy walk of the historic harbor. **Vågen Gamle Stavanger,** the Old Town, is on the western side of Vågen. This historic harbor is now a colorful marina with several sailing ships usually at anchor and a fish market held daily until 4pm.

In the center of Stavanger, immediately north of the train and bus stations and about a 10-minute walk from the main harbor, is a large pond called **Breiavann.**

GETTING AROUND Most of the historic core of Stavanger is walkable, which is about the only way to get around unless you take a taxi. The historic town is filled with narrow streets and pedestrian walkways. Local buses fan out to the suburbs, including Sola, site of the airport. Fares start at NOK30. For more information, call ✆ **51-51-65-30.**

If the weather is fair, you can rent a bike at the tourist office for NOK200 per day. Be sure to request a free *sykkelkart* (cycling map) of the area.

For a taxi, call **Norgestaxi Stavanger** at ✆ **91-00-80-00** or **Stavanger Taxi-central** at ✆ **51-90-90-90.**

SPECIAL EVENTS Stavanger is called *Festivallbyen* ("Festival City"), and celebrations take place all year. For complete listings while you're in town, ask at the tourist office (see above). Spring's best festival is **MaiJazz** (www.maijazz.no), beginning in the second week of May, when internationally known musicians come to Stavanger to perform top-quality jazz.

Around mid-June the **Den Store Norsk Humorfestivalen (Great Norwegian Humor Festival)** takes place, with well-known artists performing. There are revues, street entertainers, and shows for children. For more information, visit www.humorfestivalen.no.

The **International Chamber Music Festival** (www.icmf.no) occurs in mid-August, an event that attracts some of the world's most acclaimed classical artists to Stavanger. Some 20 concerts are staged within the course of a week. The **Stavanger Vinfest (Stavanger Wine Festival),** beginning in mid-March and lasting 10 days, celebrates all things enological. See www.stavangervinfest.no.

[Fast FACTS] STAVANGER

Banks One of the most central banks for exchanging money is **SpareBank,** Domkirkeplassen (✆ **02002**). You can also exchange money from June to August at the tourist office (see above).

Car Towing Call ✆ **51-53-88-88,** a 24-hour hotline.

Consulates There is no U.S. representative. Brits can go to the **U.K. Consulate** at Prinsens Gate 12 (✆ **51-52-97-13**).

Dental Service There is a dentist open every day to handle emergencies. The name of the dentist is published in the Saturday newspapers. Otherwise, call for an appointment at the office of Hans Kristian Ognedal, Kongsgate 44 (✆ **51-52-03-17**).

Doctor In an emergency, call ✆ **51-51-02-02.** Otherwise, ask your hotel staff to recommend a doctor, any of whom will speak English.

Emergencies Call ✆ **110** for fire, ✆ **112** for the police, or ✆ **113** for an ambulance.

Laundry If your hotel doesn't have facilities, go to **Renseriet,** Kongsgate 40 (✆ **51-89-56-53**).

Left Luggage Go to **Byterminalen** (no phone), the city bus station, located adjacent to the train station, Monday to Friday 7am to 8pm, Saturday 8am to 10pm.

Pharmacy Your best bet is **Vitusapotek Løven,** Olav V's Gate 11 (✆ **51-91-08-81**), open daily 9am to 11pm (to 8pm on public holidays).

Post Office The main post office is at Haakon VII's Gate 9, open Monday to Wednesday and Friday 8am to 5pm, Thursday 8am to 6pm, and Saturday 9am to 1pm.

WHERE TO STAY

Because Stavanger is an oil boomtown and full of businesspeople for most of the year, you'll find expensive hotels and a dearth of good, moderately priced choices. But the good news is that in the summer months and on weekends, the first-class and better-rated hotels slash their prices, so nearly all of them fall into the "moderate" category during peak tourism season.

Expensive

Clarion Hotel Stavanger ★★ This is Stavanger's second-tallest building at 14 stories, and better than the Radisson BLU sisters listed below (it's midway between these two hotels). It's a smoothly contemporary blockbuster that's on every corporate list as a well-managed hotel. (About 70% of its clients work in the oil or oil services industries.) Set 2½ blocks uphill from the harbor, it lies within a 7-minute walk of every attraction in the Old Town. It's a tall, elegant, contemporary hotel with decor accented with lots of polished stone, burnished copper, and Nordic birch. Pahr

Iversen, a locally well-known artist, crafted the paintings in the lobby and the tile work in most of the bathrooms.

Ny Olavskleiv 8, N-4004 Stavanger. ✆ **51-50-25-00.** www.clarionstavanger.com. 250 units. Mon–Thurs NOK1,380–NOK2,895 double, NOK2,580–NOK3,995 suite; Fri–Sun NOK980–NOK1,580 double, NOK1,980–NOK2,180 suite. Rates include buffet breakfast. AE, MC, V. Parking NOK70. **Amenities:** 2 restaurants; bar; health club w/saunas & a view over the town; rooms for those with limited mobility. *In room:* A/C, TV, Wi-Fi, minibar, hair dryer.

Radisson BLU Atlantic Hotel ★ The largest and most traditional luxury hotel in Stavanger is this behemoth, though I gravitate more to its sibling, the Royal (see below). Until its height was surpassed around the turn of the millennium by a taller contender in the suburbs, its 13 stories made it the tallest building in town. Everything about it evokes the artfully spare minimalism of the heyday of Scandinavian modern design, thanks to lots of carefully finished hardwood and stone, plus glass and stainless steel. Bedrooms here are well conceived and very comfortable. Suites are large and supremely comfortable refuges, replete with leather upholstery, deep hardwoods, and, in many cases, big-windowed views over the town. Restaurant Antique serves seasonal specialties with panoramic views of Lake Brelavannet. The King Oscar Bar & Salon and the Alexander Pub are glamorous places to meet for a drink.

Olav V's Gate 3, P.O. Box 307, N-4002 Stavanger. ✆ **51-76-10-00.** www.radissonblu.com/atlantichotel-stavanger. 354 units. Mon–Thurs NOK1,795–NOK1,995 double; Fri–Sun & mid-June to mid-Aug daily NOK995–NOK1,295 double; year-round NOK2,000–NOK5,000 suite. AE, DC, MC, V. Parking NOK100 per night. **Amenities:** Restaurant; cafe; pub; reduced rates at a nearby health & exercise club; sauna; room service. *In room:* TV, Wi-Fi, minibar, hair dryer.

Radisson BLU Royal Hotel ★★★ Built in 1987 and since radically renovated, this is the smaller and plusher of Stavanger's Radisson BLU hotels. Its rooms rise around an atrium-style lobby that's outfitted with pale oak paneling and pale blue carpets and upholsteries. Bedrooms are outfitted in four different decorative styles: A warm but minimalist version of Scandinavian modern, a generic Asian style, a high-tech design, and one the hotel refers to as "ecological," featuring lots of handcrafted ceramics and weavings made from nonsynthetic materials. The eight suites here, with separate sitting areas and business-class amenities, are the best in the city.

Løkkeveien 26, P.O. Box 307, N-4002 Stavanger. ✆ **51-76-60-00.** www.radissonblu.com/royalhotel-stavanger. 204 units. Mid-Aug to mid-June Mon–Thurs NOK1,795–NOK2,195 double; year-round Fri–Sun & mid-June to mid-Aug daily NOK1,045–NOK1,345 double; year-round NOK2,700–NOK4,200 suite. Rates include buffet breakfast. Parking NOK120. AE, DC, MC, V. **Amenities:** 2 restaurants; bar; indoor heated pool; fitness room; sauna; Jacuzzi; room service. *In room:* TV, Wi-Fi, minibar.

Skagen Brygge Hotell ★★★ No hotel in Stavanger offers the charm and character of this favorite, modern in comforts but in the past architecturally (even if its white wooden "wharfhouses" are merely replicas). This is the most architecturally distinctive and the most visible hotel in town, thanks to its prime harborfront location in the center of Stavanger's historic core. About 10 of its rooms occupy a 19th-century brick building that's partially concealed at back. But the genuinely dramatic part of this hotel fronts the harbor. As a replacement for warehouses that, over the decades, burned to the ground, architects duplicated the look of an interconnected series of steep-gabled, tall, narrow town houses, modernized with oversize windows

Where to Stay & Dine in Stavanger

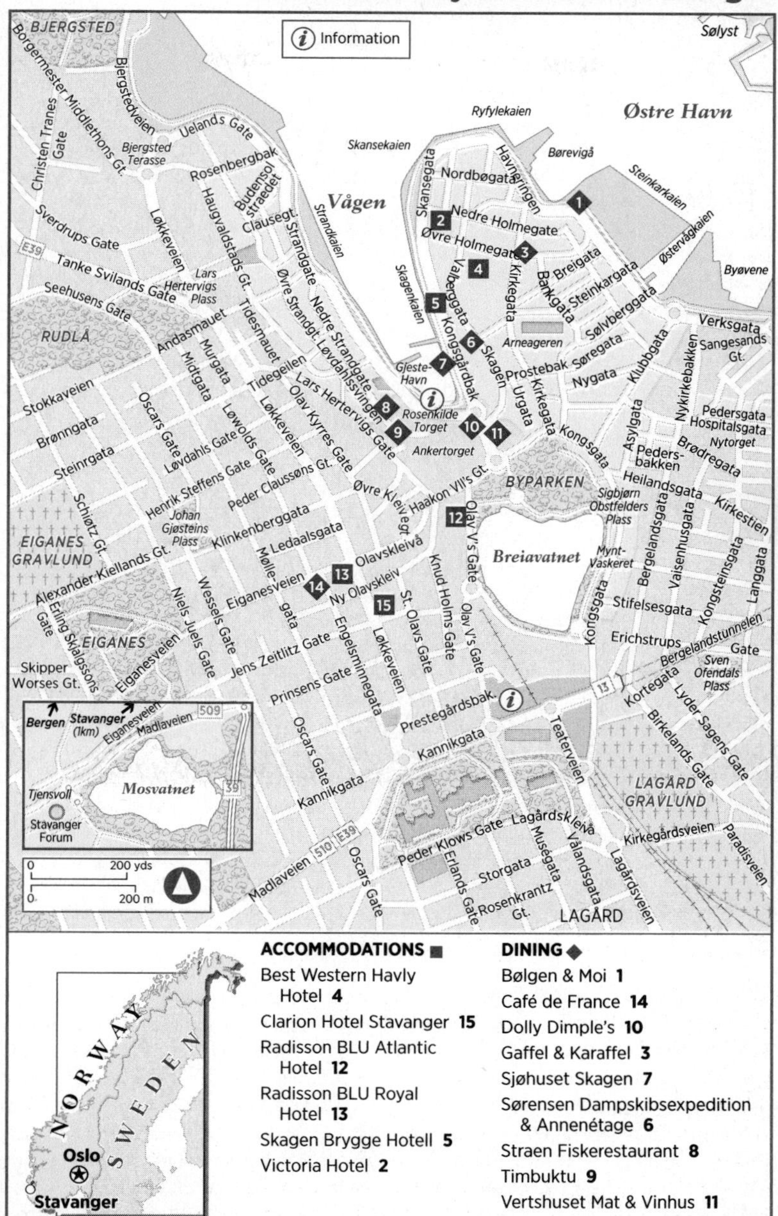

and a sense of postmodern flair. Older rooms are cozy and warm, with exposed masonry and flowered Laura Ashley fabrics. Sunnier, more dramatic, and more panoramic are the big-windowed accommodations in the newer section, some of which might evoke greenhouses if it weren't for their leather-upholstered furniture, hardwood floors, Oriental carpets, and sense of high-tech flair.

Skagenkaien 30, N-4004 Stavanger. ✆ **51-85-00-00.** www.skagenbryggehotell.no. 110 units. NOK1,645 double; NOK3,650 suite. Rates include buffet breakfast. AE, DC, MC, V. No on-site parking. **Amenities:** Exercise area w/sauna & Turkish bath. *In room:* A/C, TV, minibar.

Moderate

Best Western Havly Hotell This comfortable hotel is hardly the best, but it's the most affordable in an otherwise very pricey city. Best Western's only hotel in town is positioned on a street that runs parallel to the wharf. Small-scale, boxy, and modern, it was built in the 1960s in a low-rise design that doesn't interfere (too much) with the antique buildings around it. There's no bar, no restaurant, and few amenities, but considering the well-maintained accommodations and its great location, no one seems to care. It attracts business travelers from other parts of Scandinavia.

Valberggate 1, N-4006 Stavanger. ✆ **51-93-90-00.** www.havly-hotell.no. 42 units. Mid-Aug to June Mon–Thurs NOK1,260 double, Fri–Sun NOK990 double; July to mid-Aug NOK990 double. Rates include buffet breakfast. AE, DC, MC, V. No on-site parking. *In room:* TV, Wi-Fi, hair dryer.

Victoria Hotel ★ Stavanger's oldest hotel is now an acceptable place to hole up for the night. It was inaugurated in 1900 in a red-brick-with-stone-trim building that's now carefully preserved as a town landmark. It's set prominently at the edge of the harbor, but in a less-touristed waterfront area used by fishing boats and oil-supply ships. Over the years, the hotel's role in Stavanger has changed: Its clientele was once concerned with the herring and canning industries; now about 85% of its clients are middle-bracket employees in oil-service industries. Expect a thoroughly decent, muted hotel with a helpful staff, and a lobby that's outfitted in a paneled style you might expect from a 19th-century hotel in England. Rooms are well maintained and not overly large, each with conservative traditional furniture. Each room has a floor plan that, thanks to the hotel's U-shaped layout and antique shell, is different from its neighbors.

Skansekaien 1, N-4001 Stavanger. ✆ **51-86-70-00.** www.victoria-hotel.no. 107 units. Mon–Thurs NOK1,085–NOK1,985 double, NOK2,990 suite; Fri–Sun NOK860–NOK1,095 double, NOK2,210 suite. Rates include buffet breakfast. AE, DC, MC, V. Parking NOK50. **Amenities:** Restaurant; bar. *In room:* TV, Wi-Fi, minibar.

WHERE TO DINE

Expensive

Bølgen & Moi ★★ CONTINENTAL It might be a member of a chain, but it's hardly McDonald's—in fact, it serves the finest cuisine in Stavanger's increasingly competitive culinary market. The restaurant is on the ground floor of the avant-garde premises of Stavanger's oil museum. Its interior is as spare, angular, metallic, and minimalist as the museum itself. Some of its drama derives from its position, straddling a pier and a rocky headland jutting out into Stavanger's harbor. Illuminated mostly by candles, the menu offers such innovative dishes as smoked breast of duck and foie gras terrine with cognac-marinated plums; or nori-baked salmon with mango chutney, pickled ginger, wasabi mayo, and corn chips. To see the heights that the chef can reach, order the venison sirloin with apple-and-red-onion compote, chanterelles, almond potato purée, and port-wine sauce: Out of this world.

In the Norsk Oljemuseum (Norwegian Petroleum Museum), harborfront, Kjeringholmen. ✆ **51-93-93-51.** www.bolgenogmoi.no. Reservations recommended. Small platters NOK139–NOK175; main courses NOK195–NOK255; fixed-price menus NOK495–NOK695. AE, DC, MC, V. Daily 11am–5pm; Tues–Sat 6pm–midnight. Bar until midnight.

Café de France ★ NORWEGIAN/INTERNATIONAL Set in a pink-sided building immediately uphill from the Radisson BLU Royal Hotel, this restaurant is elegant, upscale, and committed to presenting French food with flair and sensitivity. "Trude" supervises the dining room, and her husband, Steinar, is the hard-working chef. From the kitchens emerge dishes that change with the season but that could grace some of the grandest tables. Some fine examples include king crab from the North Atlantic and freshly caught fish from the Stavanger region. The owners buy their lamb, beef, chicken, and vegetables (in season) from the best farmers in Rogaland.

Eiganesveien 8. ✆ **51-52-86-26.** www.cafedefrance.no. Reservations recommended. Main courses NOK340; fixed-price menus NOK650–NOK795. AE, DC, MC, V. Mon–Sat 6–10pm.

Gaffel & Karaffel ★ NORWEGIAN/INTERNATIONAL The "Fork & Carafe" is one of the hippest restaurants in Stavanger. The wooden tables have no tablecloths, the red halls are hung with knives and forks, and there's a popular bar downstairs. The historic building, from 1871, was originally the private home of a fisherman and his family. The dishes are made from high-quality ingredients; you'll be tempted by the pan-fried scallops with petit pois purée and bacon, or the breast of duck, fondant potatoes, fried mushrooms, and applesauce. Also try the popular tapas menu (NOK249). One indulgent dessert specialty is blackcurrant sherbet.

Øvre Holmegate 20. ✆ **51-86-41-58.** www.gaffelogkaraffel.no, Reservations recommended. Main courses NOK189–NOK315; fixed-price menu NOK495. AE, DC, MC, V. Mon–Sat 6–11pm. Closed Dec 22–Jan 8 & 1 week at Easter.

Sørensen Dampskibsexpedition & Annenétage ★ NORWEGIAN When the wood-sided warehouse that contains these restaurants was built in 1876, the waters of Stavanger's harbor literally lapped at its foundations, and goods were unloaded directly from ships moored beside it. Today a road separates its front entrance from the harbor. The heavy timbers and all-wood interior evoke a rich sense of nostalgia for the 19th-century mercantile days.

The street-level brasserie (Dampskipsexpedition, or "Steamship Expedition") is the more convivial and animated (and cheaper) of the two venues—a warren of varnished pine planks, polished brass, nautical-nostalgic memorabilia, and beer suds. Menu items served in the street-level brasserie include sirloin of beef with gnocchi and a Madeira sauce, and grilled salmon with *beurre blanc* and salmon roe. Upstairs, an interconnected series of late-19th-century Victorian parlors is the setting for Annenétage, a much more rigid and pretentious gourmet restaurant. Food items here are innovative: An example is monkfish with cauliflower and scallops flavored with pumpkin and served with avocado. You can also order smoked trout with slices of apple and celeriac; and a dessert specialty of chocolate marquise with espresso sauce.

Skagen 26. ✆ **51-84-38-20.** Reservations recommended. In street-level brasserie, main courses NOK264–NOK295; in upstairs restaurant, fixed-price menu NOK755. AE, DC, MC, V. Street-level brasserie daily 11am–midnight; upstairs restaurant Mon–Sat 6–11pm.

Straen Fiskerestaurant ★ SEAFOOD This is the best seafood restaurant in Stavanger, its windows opening onto a view of the harbor. It amusingly bills itself as "world famous throughout Norway." The old-fashioned interior is straight out of the 1950s, with homelike decor and grandmotherly touches. Once you've settled in, begin with the grilled scallops and mushrooms with a tantalizing Jerusalem artichoke purée. You might proceed to the finest item on the menu: Norwegian grilled lobster with a peppery butter. Other main courses maintain a balance between simplicity and elegance, as exemplified by the crab legs with homemade saffron pasta, fresh garlic, and tomato oil, or the poached halibut with pea lentils and a bacon cassoulet with beets—everything served with orange butter. The food is perfectly cooked and appears in generous portions. There is a nightclub upstairs and a sushi restaurant downstairs that's served by the same kitchen.

Nedre Strandgate 15. ✆ **51-84-37-00.** Reservations recommended. Main courses NOK195–NOK265; 3-course fixed-price menu NOK495; 4-course fixed-price menu NOK585. AE, DC, MC, V. Mon–Sat 6pm–1:30am. Closed Dec 22–Jan 7.

Timbuktu ★ INTERNATIONAL The fixed-price menus here are arguably the best in town. Stylish and popular, this restaurant is set beside a cobbled square that opens directly onto Stavanger's Vågen (harborfront). Inside, within a decor of pale birch with ebonized trim, there's a busy bar area (Mon–Sat until between midnight and 1:30am) and somewhat crowded tables. Try the masterly salad of lime- and olive-marinated skate or a platter of very fresh sushi as a main course. Chefs cook up an excellent catch of the day, such as trout with mung bean purée and mint juice. Carnivores will enjoy the poached chicken with celery root purée, romanesco, and blood orange foam.

Nedre Strandgate 15. ✆ **51-84-37-40.** www.herlige-restauranter.no/timbuktu/. Reservations recommended. Main courses NOK225–NOK259. Fixed-price menus NOK425–NOK590. AE, DC, MC, V. Mon–Tues 6pm–midnight; Wed–Sat 6pm–2am.

Vertshuset Mat & Vinhus ★★ CONTINENTAL One of the Old Town's most appealing restaurants, this "food and wine house" is set on a street running parallel to the old port, within an early-19th-century wooden house. Its interior is both high-tech and woodsy-looking. Lunches tend to feature *husmanskost* (grandmother-style) dishes such as Nordic meatballs, filet of reindeer, grilled salmon steaks, pizzas, and fish and chips. Dinners are more elaborate and, at least in terms of cuisine, more stylish, with memorable dishes that include filet of pork served with a creamy mushroom sauce and vegetables, and garlic salmon with creamy herb sauce; or perhaps a "symphony" of different kinds of fish—fried, steamed, grilled, or broiled. On-site is the cozy XO Bar.

Skagen 10. ✆ **51-89-51-12.** Reservations recommended. Lunch pizzas & platters NOK125–NOK230; dinner main courses NOK250–NOK310. AE, DC, MC, V. Daily 11am–10pm. Bar until midnight or 1am, depending on business.

Moderate

Dolly Dimple's ☺ PIZZERIA This is the Stavanger branch of an enormously popular nationwide chain of pizzerias whose Greek-born owner lives in—wait for it—Stavanger. It was established in honor of "the world's most beautiful fat girl," in this case, Celesta Geyer, whom the owner had seen as a sideshow attraction at an American circus in the 1970s. Today her pen-and-ink likeness (seriously zaftig thanks to the many pizzas she has consumed since becoming Norway's official representative of the pizza-loving world) is displayed in about 60 locations throughout Norway. Pizzas here are delicious, coming in 25 already defined versions, in various degrees of spiciness, plus any number of custom-designed options. Standards include "Los Banditos," made from strips of marinated beef, chicken, Mexican-style tomato salsa, jalapeño peppers, and cheese; Nordic versions can be built with, among other ingredients, smoked salmon, crème fraîche, and shrimp.

Kongsgårdsbakken 1. ✆ **04440** (within Norway only). www.dolly.no. Pizzas NOK110–NOK248. AE, DC, MC, V. Mon–Fri 10am–10pm; Sat 10am–6pm.

Sjøhuset Skagen INTERNATIONAL Thanks to the folksy-looking, heavily timbered premises that date from the mid-19th century, this place is more atmospheric and cozier than the many other pub/restaurants that compete with it nearby. Inside you'll find a warren of congenially cramped cubicles and mezzanines that hint at its origins as a warehouse for marine supplies and fish. Frankly, I prefer this place as a drinking-with-snacks venue more than as a restaurant, even though a roster of salads, burgers, and pastas is available, as well as such North Atlantic staples as fish and chips. You can also order an entrecôte served with baked beetroot, fennel, and mushroom braised potatoes and a creamy rosemary sauce; or confit of clip fish served with chili-and-garlic baked potatoes, fried bacon, and herb *aioli.* For something really risqué, though, try the tenderloin of whale served with oven-baked chili potatoes, grilled vegetables, and a creamy port-wine sauce. The place has a lot of charm and historical authenticity.

Skagenkaien 16. ✆ **51-89-51-80.** www.sjohusetskagen.no. Lunch main courses NOK139–NOK189; dinner main courses NOK229–NOK295. AE, DC, MC, V. Mon–Sat 11:30am–midnight; Sun 1–10pm.

OUTDOOR ACTIVITIES

Stavanger has some of the best museums of any port city in western Norway. But if you want to skip all of them, you can spend your time in the great outdoors, as locals often do during Norway's all-too-short summer.

Even if you have to miss some of the town's attractions, try to spend some time along the banks of **Lysefjord** (see "Norway's Most Beautiful Fjord," below). What I like to do is spend a day along Lysefjord and view **Preikestolen.** After arriving back in Stavanger in the late afternoon, you can walk the cobblestone streets of **Gamle Stavanger** (p. 252) and have dinner in one of the city's many good restaurants.

In summer Stavanger is made for walking. The best hiking jaunt is the 4km (2½-mile) walk to **Pulpit Rock** (see "Side Trips from Stavanger," below).

If you want to combine sports with your sightseeing, you can pick up any number of specialized books and maps at the tourist office that will guide you through a vast area, including the rolling hills of the **Setesdalsheiene** and hundreds of little islands and skerries (rocky islets) of the **Ryfylke archipelago.** The tourist office can even arrange for you to stay at one of three dozen cabins in the area, costing from NOK400 for a one-room unit with a hot plate and refrigerator.

Fishermen flock to the **Suldalslågen,** the longest salmon river in western Norway, north of Stavanger. Salmon season lasts from July to September. The best fishing lodge is **Lakseslottet Lindum,** N-4240 Suldalsosen (✆ **52-79-91-61;** www.lakseslottet.no). Call for information if you're interested in renting a cabin or camping facilities.

The best golf is found at the **Stavanger Golf Klubb,** Longebakke 45, Hafsfjord (✆ **51-93-91-00;** www.sgk.no), a lush woodland and landscaped park with an 18-hole international championship course.

Finally, call **Fossanmoen,** N-4110 Forsand (✆ **51-70-37-61;** www.fossanmoen.no), if you'd like to go on a horseback-riding jaunt on an Iceland pony. These trips take you through some of the scenic wonders of this vast fjord country. Depending on your interest, rides can last from 1 hour to all day. Prices range from NOK500 to NOK1,000.

WHAT TO SEE & DO

Arkeologisk Museum (Museum of Archaeology) ☺ The Vikings will live on forever here, where 15,000 years of southwestern Norway's culture and natural history is on parade. Models of prehistoric life attract a lot of attention, as do the changing natural-history exhibitions. Educational films are shown periodically; call ahead to check the schedule. This museum is also home to the public archive of antiquities for Rogaland. It's very family-friendly, offering treasure-hunt games and other activities for kids.

Peder Klowsgate 30A. ✆ **51-83-26-10.** www.ark.museum.no. Admission NOK50 adults; NOK20 seniors, students, & children. June–Aug Mon–Fri 10am–5pm, Sat–Sun 11am–5pm; Sept–May Tues 11am–8pm, Wed–Sat 11am–3pm, Sun 11am–4pm.

Domkirke (Cathedral) ★★★ It's not up there in the celestial ranks with the cathedral of Trondheim, but this is the other great Norwegian church left from the Middle Ages—and it stands proud and relatively intact. Constructed over a decade beginning in 1125, the cathedral is dedicated to St. Swithun. It is said that Bishop Reinald sailed here from Winchester, England, to dedicate the cathedral, carrying with him what was said to be the arm of Swithun.

A fire in 1272 swept over the Romanesque structure, destroying most of it. During the church's reconstruction, a Gothic chancel was added. In the new structure, twin square towers and a mammoth porch were also added at the west end. With the onset of the Reformation, the Domkirke lost its precious relics of the saint along with its bells and several altars. A major restoration from 1938 to 1942 was carried out that, for the most part, returned the church to a Middle Ages look.

Think about timing your visit here to coincide with the organ recital at 11:15am on Thursday. In such an atmosphere, you'll feel as if you've gone back 8 centuries.

The church is 65m (213 ft.) long, with a chancel measuring 22m (72 ft.). The original nave is striking in its simplicity, but other parts are more elaborate, including the large round columns and square capitals. Some capitals are carved with Norse figures such as dragons and griffins. See, in particular, the fine memorial tablets and

What to See & Do in Stavanger

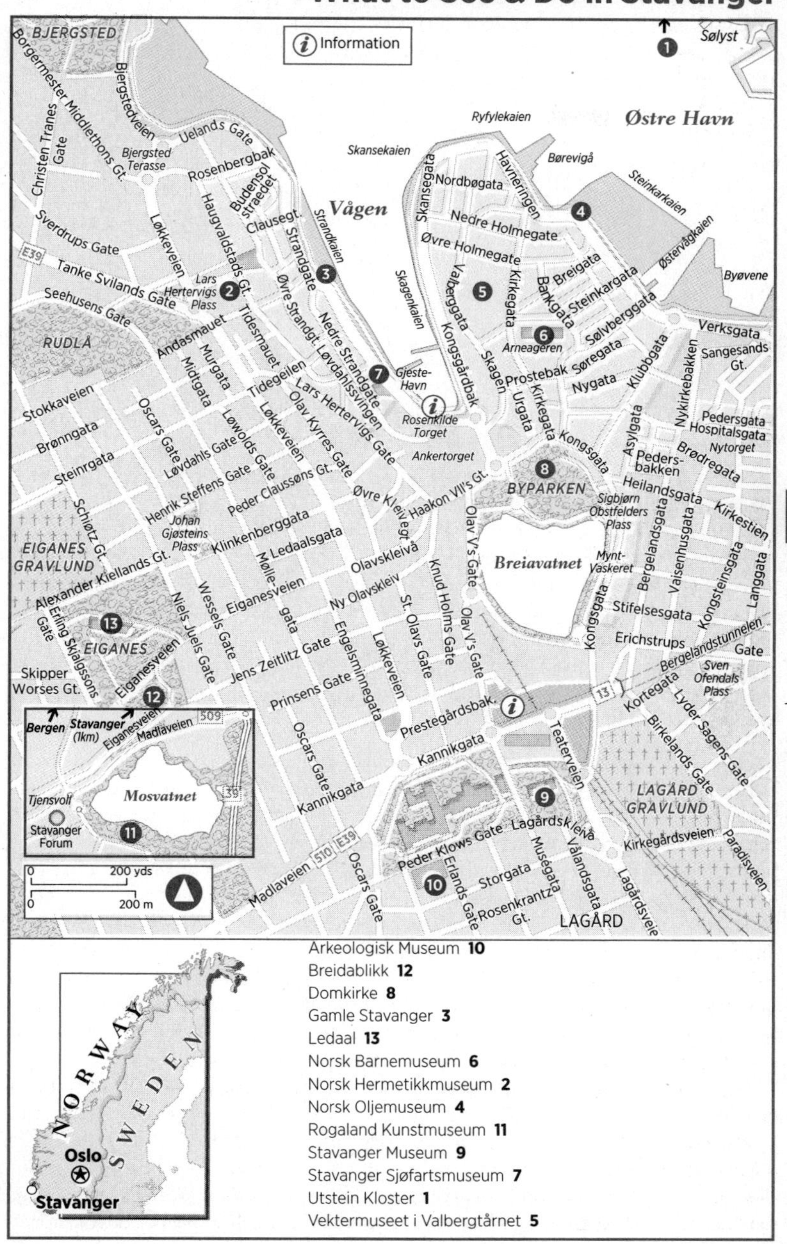

Arkeologisk Museum **10**
Breidablikk **12**
Domkirke **8**
Gamle Stavanger **3**
Ledaal **13**
Norsk Barnemuseum **6**
Norsk Hermetikkmuseum **2**
Norsk Oljemuseum **4**
Rogaland Kunstmuseum **11**
Stavanger Museum **9**
Stavanger Sjøfartsmuseum **7**
Utstein Kloster **1**
Vektermuseet i Valbergtårnet **5**

the famous **pulpit** ★, outstanding examples of baroque art in Norway. The pulpit remains a masterpiece of woodcarving, depicting scenes from the Old Testament and crowned by a baldachin honoring the victories of Christ.

Domkirkeplassen. ✆ **51-84-04-00.** Free admission. June–Aug daily 11am–7pm; Sept–May Tues–Thurs & Sat 11am–4pm.

Gamle Stavanger ★★★ "Old Stavanger" is northern Europe's largest and most impressive—and best preserved—settlement of old-fashioned wooden houses. More than 170 buildings from the late 18th and early 19th centuries are not only preserved but fully renovated. The houses were built with money brought back to Stavanger by seafarers who roamed the world. A walk through the narrow streets of Gamle Stavanger is one of the most memorable city experiences in southern Norway. The houses are owned partly by private residents and partly by the city.

To reach the Old Town, go to the west side of Vågen (the harbor) and climb the steep slope overlooking Strandkaien. Once a district for the working class, the area is now gentrified and rather exclusive, and much attention is focused on these whitewashed wooden houses, often with creepers or geraniums growing in flower boxes. The dollhouse homes are separated by small terraced gardens. In the evening, lampposts from the 1890s light your way through the fog.

Norsk Barnemuseum (Norwegian Children's Museum) ★ ☺ This is the greatest playpen in Norway for children ages 5 to 12. In fact, it is one of the best children's museums in all of Europe. There are loads of kid-specific exhibitions, performances, and storytelling sessions, of course, but the hands-on museum also satisfies a kid's desire to play with toys—it has the largest collection in the country. Activities include climbing up to the "Scary Attic" or visiting a secret treehouse; kids can even embark on a journey in a toy box or whisper into a "Bag of Secrets." The museum also has more pedagogic exhibits dealing with children's rights around the world.

Sølvberggata 2. ✆ **51-91-23-93.** www.norskbarne.museum.no. Admission NOK80 adults, NOK40 children. Tues–Sat 11am–4pm, Sun noon–5pm; mid-June to mid-Aug also Mon 11am–5pm.

Norsk Oljemuseum (Norwegian Petroleum Museum) ★ 🎁 Opened in 1999, this is one of the most unusual museums in Scandinavia and already a much-photographed landmark in the port. It documents how oil was discovered off the coast of Norway in 1969, forever changing the country. The oil industry's celebration of itself, this is a spectacularly dramatic museum that rises directly from the harbor waters. This avant-garde amalgam of stainless steel, granite, and glass resembles a space-age jumble of tin cans. The best parts of the museum are those that convey the huge shock and drama associated with Norway's entrance into the oil industry, which had otherwise been dominated by Arabs and Americans, and Norway's struggle to catch up with the various legalities and international agreements.

The museum is not particularly adept at explaining the technicalities of the drilling rituals, and there's something superficial about the science associated with the construction of oil platforms, even though you can wander through a replica oil platform attached to the main museum.

One of the city's finest restaurants, Bølgen & Moi (p. 246), is within the premises of this museum.

Kjeringholmen. ✆ **51-93-93-00.** www.norskolje.museum.no. Admission NOK80 adults, NOK40 children, students, & seniors. June–Aug daily 10am–7pm; Sept–May Mon–Sat 10am–4pm, Sun 10am–6pm.

Rogaland Kunstmuseum (Rogaland Art Museum) ★ This is Stavanger's museum of fine arts, with temporary exhibitions as well as an impressive permanent collection, consisting of some 2,000 paintings, drawings, and sculptures. Most of these are by Norwegian artists from the beginning of the 19th century to the present. Donated to the museum, the **Halvdan Haftsten Collection ★** includes some 200 paintings and drawings created by eight Norwegian artists between the two world wars. The museum displays the largest and most impressive collection of the works of **Lars Hertervig ★** (1830–1902), one of the greatest Romantic painters of Norwegian landscapes, along with an impressive array of the works of Kitty Kielland. It's 3km (1¾ miles) from the city center, at the northern end of the Old Town and close to Mosvannet, off the E18.

Henrik Ibsen Weg 55, Mosvannsparken. ✆ **51-53-09-00.** www.rogalandkunstsenter.no. Admission NOK50 adults & students, free for children 15 & under. Tues–Fri noon–3pm, Sat–Sun noon–4pm. Bus: 3, 5A, 5B, 7, or 9.

Stavanger Museum ★★ This is a five-part museum that you can visit with just one ticket. If you want to see the entire museum, expect to spend the better part of a day scampering from one point to another across the city. At the main museum, you'll be given a map with the locations of all the museums. All the museums (except as noted below) are open June 15 to August 15 daily from 11am to 4pm; June 1 to June 14 and August 16 to August 31 Monday to Thursday 11am to 3pm and Sunday 11am to 4pm; and during other months only Sunday 11am to 4pm. A ticket for all five museums costs NOK60 for adults, NOK30 for students and seniors, NOK10 for ages 4 to 6 (free for 3 and under).

The main museum, called simply the **Stavanger Museum,** is at Muségata 16 (✆ **51-84-27-00**). Here you can see a permanent collection of stuffed birds and animals from all over the world. The centuries-old history of Stavanger, dating from the Viking era, is also presented, along with dramatized sound recordings about Stavanger in the 1800s.

The **Stavanger Sjøfartsmuseum (Maritime Museum),** Nedre Strandgate 17–19, is set within a converted warehouse dating from 1770. Its permanent exhibition traces the maritime history of Stavanger for the past 2 centuries, from the days of the herring fleets to the booming oil industry of today.

The facade is a trim, white, clapboard-sided building directly on the harborfront. Inside there's a battered post-and-beam construction showing how artfully timbers were used by 19th-century craftsmen; a sense of the dust, dirt, and economic mayhem of the Industrial Revolution; and the pervasive scent of tar and turpentine. Expect a claustrophobic, dark-toned interior; hundreds of ship models and 19th-century maritime accessories; and a horrendous sense of how hard life was in 19th- and early-20th-century coastal Norway.

You can visit a general store from the turn of the 20th century, a reconstructed merchant's apartment from the early 1900s, a reconstructed shipowner's home, and a sailmaker's loft, along with a memorial room to the philosopher Henrik Steffens. There is also a children's shop. This museum is closed in December.

The **Norsk Hermetikkmuseum (Norwegian Canning Museum),** Øvre Strandgate 88A, lies in an old canning factory, with exhibitions tracing the fishing industry, Stavanger's main industry before oil came to town, from the 1890s to the 1960s. Some of the machinery is still working, and on the first Sunday of every month the smoking ovens are stoked up for visitors to taste freshly smoked brisling.

A bike ride TO THE "THREE SWORDS"

On a summer day it's nice to have a picnic out at **Sverd I Fjell,** the Three Swords monument, at Hafrsfjord. This is the spot where King Harald Hårfagre (Fairhair) united Norway into one kingdom in 872. In 1983 Fritz Røed created this monument, and it was unveiled by King Olav. The monument, standing as a symbol of unification, depicts Viking sword sheaths modeled on actual swords found in various parts of the country. The crowns on the tops of the swords represent the Norwegian districts that took part in the epic battle for unification. From the center of Stavanger, bike along Mosvannet and continue along Route 510 toward Sola. Allow about half an hour to reach this monument. Møllebukta, where the monument lies, is a lovely and popular area for a day trip.

This is perhaps the oddest and quirkiest of Stavanger's museums, as well as the city's least polished, but it also evocatively portrays the harsh and boring circumstances of factory work during the Industrial Revolution. It's set within a low-slung clapboard building in a neighborhood of increasingly gentrified antique cottages. Inside, about 50 antique machines are displayed, with sepia-toned photographs of how scores of weary workers crammed sardines, herring, and brislings into galvanized steel tins to be shipped all over Europe. Expect a strong sense of the soot, grime, grease, and fish guts that once permeated this place with odors that stretched for several blocks in all directions. Overall, this museum is one of the city's most effective tributes to the industrial heroism of 19th- and early-20th-century Norway.

The fourth museum, **Ledaal ★**, Eiganesveien 45, was built by Gabriel Schanche Kielland, a shipowner and merchant, between 1799 and 1803. The mansion is a fine example of the neoclassical style as interpreted in western Norway, with interior furnishings that are largely rococo, Empire, and Biedermeier. This is the official—but rarely used—residence of the Norwegian royal family during their visits to Stavanger and Rogaland counties, of which Stavanger is the capital. It's painted a shade of Pompeian red and set adjacent to one of Stavanger's most evocative cemeteries. It's separated from a road leading into Stavanger, about a 15-minute walk uphill from the harbor, by a wall of very large boulders. The look is baron-rustic, permeated with a sense of genteel 18th-century aristocracy and all-wood construction. This museum is closed in December and January.

The fifth museum is **Breidablikk ★**, Eiganesveien 40A. Set across the road from Ledaal (see above), it was built by another merchant and shipowner, Lars Berensten, in 1881–82. The exterior and interior of the house are preserved in their original condition. It's somewhat kitschy, thanks to an exaggerated alpine-*gemütlich* style, a coat of almost-too-bright ocher paint (with dark brown trim), and yard after yard of elaborate gingerbread along the eaves and verandas. It's Victoriana/Carpenter gone wild and an amusing diversion. It's also closed in December and January.

Utstein Kloster ★ This is Norway's only preserved medieval abbey. In the 9th century, Utstein was one of the royal residences of Harald Hårfagre (Fairhair), Norway's first monarch. In 1250 it belonged to Magnus Lagabøter ("the Lawmender") who as king would draft Norway's first constitution, then the most democratic in the world. Magnus gave Utstein to the canons of an Augustinian order, who constructed their abbey around his fortress at the end of the 1200s. With the coming of the Reformation, Utstein became one of the largest private estates in western Norway. In summer, sporadic concerts featuring leading jazz and classical musicians are staged in its chapel.

Mosterøy. ✆ **51-72-00-50.** www.utstein-kloster.no (in Norwegian). Admission NOK60 adults, NOK30 children, free for children 6 & under. May to mid-Sept Tues–Sat 10am–4pm, Sun noon–5pm. Mid-Sept–Nov & Mar to mid-May Sun noon–5pm. Closed Mon (except in July) and closed Dec–Mar.

Vektermuseet i Valbergtårnet Inhabiting a wooden city, the residents of Stavanger lived in constant fear of fire. In 1850–53 they constructed Valbergtårnet, a mock-medieval tower with a panoramic view over Stavanger and its harbor. A guard was stationed here 24 hours a day to be on the lookout for fires. Today the site is visited mainly for the **view ★★**, one of the most memorable cityscape vistas in southwestern Norway. The small Vektermuseet (Watchman's Museum) has been installed here as well, focusing on the guard's duties and on the watchman as a symbol of safety.

Valbergjet 2. ✆ **51-89-55-01.** Admission NOK50 adults, NOK20 children. Tues–Sat 10am–4pm, Sun noon–5pm. Closed Dec–Mar.

SHOPPING

Locals head for the area's major shopping center, **Kvadrat Kjøpesenter** (✆ **51-96-00-00;** www.kvadrat.no (in Norwegian)), at Lura, between Stavanger and Sandnes. There are nearly 160 shops here, selling everything from reindeer hides, sheepskin jackets, and pewter souvenirs to Norwegian handicrafts such as wooden trolls. Other outlets include restaurants, a state-run wine store, a pharmacy, and even a post office, if you want to mail back some of the cards you can purchase.

Most shops are open Monday to Wednesday and Friday from 9am to 5pm, Thursday 9am to 7pm, and Saturday 9am to 3pm.

Gjestal Spinneri ★ 🎁 Motorists and serious shoppers might want to check out this spinning mill, lying 30km (19 miles) southeast of Stavanger in the little village of Oltedal. Established in 1937, it has since become one of Scandinavia's leading producers of hand-knitting yarn and plaids. The mill uses mostly Norwegian lamb's wool, but also English and New Zealand wool, to create high-quality wool garments. The outlet sells all types of yarn and ready-made sweaters and other woolen products at 30% to 40% below the prices you'll find in most city stores. On-site is a cafeteria, so you can also make this a luncheon stopover. 4333 Oltedal. ✆ **51-61-22-00.**

Helger Myhre Marine Supplies This shop would never be considered a staple on Stavanger's tourist circuit, and many non-Norwegian shoppers might bypass it immediately in favor of a more luxurious venue. But if you've ever sailed a boat, or if you happen to own a boat, or if you are merely fascinated with the thousands of articles you could stockpile *if* you owned a boat, this place is well worth a visit. Nautical hardware (everything you'd need to winch, ratchet, hoist, or belay on a sailing craft) is stocked on the street level. Clothing for men, women, and children is upstairs, and a collection of sometimes kitschy-looking "Ahoy, Mate!" souvenirs, many in brass, is scattered around the store. Skagenkaien 22. ✆ **51-89-07-20.**

Helgi Joensen ★ Sculptural pewter—modern decorative art—reaches its peak in Stavanger at the working studio of this renowned artist who grew up on the North Atlantic coast and found inspiration for his work here. Each piece is constructed individually, its texture formed freehand with no casting or molds. One of Joensen's pewter sculptures makes for a good heirloom gift. A visit here is also a chance to explore the working studio of a Norwegian artist. Rosenberggate 21B. ✆ **51-52-98-99.** www.helgijoensen.no.

STAVANGER AFTER DARK

Café Sting ★ Stavanger is not known for its counterculture or bohemian undercurrents, but the little that exists is most visible here. Set atop the highest hill within the town center, a 10-minute walk from the harbor via a flight of winding concrete steps, this cafe lies adjacent to Valbergtårnet, the city's 19th-century stone firewatch station (p. 255). The low-slung, white-sided clapboard house that contains the cafe was built in 1850. Inside are five rooms, most lined with strikingly modern paintings. The cafe serves pastries, beer, wine, and coffee, mostly to liberal-minded members of Stavanger's arts community. The cellar is home to a disco, usually frequented by straights and (to a much lesser extent) gays in their 20s and 30s, that operates Thursday to Saturday 11pm to 3:30am. The cafe is open Monday to Thursday noon to midnight, Friday and Saturday noon to 1:30am, and Sunday 3pm to midnight. Sometimes there's a cover of NOK50 to NOK70. Valberget 3. ✆ **51-89-32-84.** www.cafe-sting.no.

Checkpoint Charlie Mainly a dance place, this club can hold 200 people on a good night. Drawing a crowd in their 20s, it attracts those who like alternative music and hard rock. Live music, often rock 'n' roll, is presented once or twice a week, at which time a small cover, up to around NOK30, might be imposed. It's open daily 8pm to 2am. Nedre Strandgatan 5. ✆ **51-53-22-45.** www.checkpoint.no.

The Irishman This pub, attracting those from their 20s to their 60s, is the expat favorite, drawing a lot of patrons from Ireland, Scotland, and England who are lured by the recorded music they play from those countries—that and the large selection of different whiskeys as well as Scotch single malts; they also sell American bourbon. A house band plays on Thursday evening and Saturday afternoon. It's open Monday to Saturday 5pm to 1:30am, Sunday 1pm to midnight. Holebergatan 9. ✆ **51-89-41-81.**

Newsman Pub ★ This is an earthy, British-style pub that its fans have defined as the most literate in Norway. Its decor was inspired by an old-fashioned newspaper office, the kind where lead type was supervised by stooped men with green eyeshades. You can sit around the woodsy-looking bar, within sight of the framed front pages of newspapers from around the English-speaking world, including banner headlines announcing the deaths of Winston Churchill and JFK and the resignation of Richard Nixon. It's all very adult, and charming in its re-creation of a 1920s-era kind of aesthetic. Rest your pint of beer on an old-fashioned lectern, and perhaps flip through one of the English-language papers displayed, library-style, on rods. There's even an in-house paper, *The Newsman,* that focuses on local politics, personalities, and gossip. The only food is snack items such as muffins and sandwiches. It's open Monday to Saturday noon to 1:30am and Sunday 3pm to 1:30am. Skagen 14. ✆ **51-84-38-80.**

NORWAY'S most beautiful FJORD ★★★

Poets have been inspired by the 42-km (26-mile) **Lysefjord** ("Light Fjord"), the country's most scenic. Its blue waters seem to glow even on a gray day as a luminous mist hovers over the fjord. "Time passes at a sedate pace at Lysefjord," or so wrote Olav Pedersen in 1883. "Your thoughts can wander in peace." That statement is still true today. Other writers have claimed that spending time on the majestic fjord allows them to tune in to nature's harmonious symphony. Sunsets here are often a dramatic mauve color tinged with royal purple.

You can take a day trip to the fjord, combining a traditional ferry ride with an express boat. Of course, weather could be a factor in your decision to go or not to go. For information about schedules and tickets, contact the Stavanger tourist office or **Kolumbus (Rogaland Kollektivtrafikk),** the area's regional transport center at ✆ **51-51-65-30.** In summer, 3- to 6-hour boat trips are organized to the fjord, which is accessible only by boat. A typical excursion offered by **Rødne Fjord Cruise** (✆ **51-89-52-70;** www.rodne.no) costs NOK380 for adults, NOK280 for seniors, and NOK200 for children ages 4 to 15.

SIDE TRIPS FROM STAVANGER

The region surrounding Stavanger, both north and south, is one of the most beautiful in southwestern Norway, with some spectacular natural attractions. Fjord and mountain landscapes meet in a majestic explosion of beauty that you can only find in the Norwegian fjords. There are some manmade attractions as well, but Mother Nature wins out over those.

PREIKESTOLEN ★★★ "Pulpit Rock" is a mammoth cube of rock with a vertical drop of 609m (1,998 ft.) over Lysefjord. It can be visited on either a boat or bus trip, or by a car-ferry trip and short drive, taking about 45 minutes from the center of Stavanger. If you want to climb the rock, you can take a boat-and-bus hiking jaunt. A pathway leads to the top. Jimmy Stewart, in the Hitchcock film *Vertigo,* would have had a tough time of it here, but if you like panoramic vistas, this rock is for you.

The walk from the parking lot to Pulpit Rock is 4km (2½ miles) but can take 2 hours each way. The walk has an elevation rise of 350m (1,148 ft.) and requires both you and your footwear to be in good shape. The last part of the walk passes dizzying drops high above Lysefjord. The weather can change quickly, so remember to bring raingear.

A bus, costing NOK55 one-way, leaves several times daily from the station in Stavanger from late May to early September. The bus is timed to meet ferry departures, which will take you on the initial lap of the journey from Stavanger.

You can also sail by the rock on a fjord cruise, but it's not as impressive from down below. **Rødine Fjord Cruise** (✆ **51 89 52 70;** www.rodne.no) offers a cruise from Stavanger to Pulpit Rock for NOK380 adults, NOK280 seniors, and NOK200 ages 4 to 15. Call for bookings.

11 BERGEN

Bergen—one of Europe's most underrated cities—is enveloped by majestic mountains, the world's most spectacular fjords, and one of Europe's largest glaciers. On even the most rushed of itineraries, try to spare at least 2 days for Bergen to experience the natural beauty that is still preserved here.

In summer, when most visitors arrive, a youthful energy prevails before the deep freeze of winter settles in. Moreover, the July sun shines all night long—and it's party time, often until morning. But there is plenty of life in the wintertime as well; it just moves in from the streets to the taverns and music clubs.

In western Norway, the landscape takes on an indescribable beauty, with iridescent glaciers; deep fjords that slash into rugged, snowcapped mountains; roaring waterfalls; and secluded valleys that lie at the end of twisting roads. From Bergen, the most beautiful fjords to visit are the **Hardangerfjord** (best at blossom time—May and early June), to the south; the **Sognefjord,** Norway's longest fjord, immediately to the north; and the **Nordfjord,** north of that. A popular excursion on the Nordfjord takes visitors from Loen to Olden along rivers and lakes to the **Brixdal Glacier.**

On the Hardangerfjord, you can stay over at a resort such as **Ulvik** or **Lofthus.** From many vantage points, it's possible to see the **Folgefonn Glacier,** Norway's second-largest ice field, spanning more than 260 sq. km (100 sq. miles). Other stopover suggestions include the summer resorts (and winter ski centers) of Voss and **Geilo.** For resorts in the fjord district, see chapter 12, "The West Coast Fjord Country."

Bergen, with its many attractions and excellent transportation, makes the best hub for exploring the fjord district. It's an ancient city that looms large in Viking sagas. Until the 14th century, it was the seat of the medieval kingdom of Norway. Hanseatic merchants established a major trading post here until the 18th century. Seafaring Bergen has given the world two quintessential Norwegian cultural icons—the composer Edvard Grieg and the playwright Henrik Ibsen. A great time to visit the city is during June, when you can catch the many concerts put on at the Bergen International Festival and up at Edvard Grieg's Troldhaugen.

Bergen has survived many disasters, including several fires and the explosion of a Nazi ship during World War II. It's a city with important traditions in shipping, banking, insurance, and industry, and its university is one of the most respected in the Nordic countries.

ORIENTATION

Arriving

BY AIR Flights to and from larger cities such as Copenhagen and London land at the **Bergen airport** in Flesland, 19km (12 miles) south of the city. Dozens of direct or non-stop flights go to just about every medium-size city in Norway with such airlines as **SAS** (✆ **91-50-54-00;** www.sas.no), **Widerøe** (✆ **81-00-12-00;** www.wideroe.no), and **Norwegian** (✆ **81-52-18-15;** www.norwegian.no).

Frequent **airport bus** services connect the airport to the Radisson BLU Royal Hotel and the city bus station. Departures are every 15 minutes Monday to Friday and every 30 minutes Saturday and Sunday. The one-way fare is NOK90.

BY TRAIN Day and night trains arrive from Oslo and stations en route. For information, call ✆ **81-50-08-88** or visit www.nsb.no. Travel time from Oslo to Bergen is roughly 8½ hours. The Jernbanestasjonen (railway station) is at Strømgaten 1.

BY BUS Express buses travel to Bergen from Oslo, Trondheim, Ålesund, and the Nordfjord area. The trip from Oslo takes 11 hours. Visit www.nor-way.no for information.

BY CAR The trip from Oslo to Bergen is a mountain drive filled with dramatic scenery. Because mountains split the country, there's no direct road. The southern route, the E76, goes through mountain passes to the junction with Route 47, heads north to Kinsarvik, and makes the ferry crossing to the E16, leading west to Bergen. The northern Route 7, through the resort of Geilo, heads to the junction with Route 47, then south to Kinsarvik and the ferry.

Visitors with a lot of time may spend 2 or 3 days driving from Oslo to Bergen. Fjords and snowcapped peaks line the way, and you can photograph waterfalls, fjord villages, and ancient stave churches. Visitors without spare time can use an 11-km (6¾-mile) tunnel between Flåm (see "Flåm: Stopover on Europe's Most Scenic Train Ride," in chapter 12) and Gudvangen. From Gudvangen, follow the E16 southwest to Bergen.

A toll is charged on any vehicle driven into the Bergen city center at any time. A single ticket costs NOK15 and is valid until you leave the city.

Visitor Information

The **Bergen tourist office,** Vågsallmenningen 1 (✆ **55-55-20-00;** www.VisitBergen.com), provides information, maps, and brochures about Bergen and the rest of the region. It's open June to August daily 8:30am to 10pm, May and September daily 9am to 8pm, and October to April Monday to Saturday 9am to 5pm. The tourist office can also help you find a place to stay, exchange foreign currency, and cash traveler's checks when banks are closed. You can also buy tickets for city sightseeing or for tours of the fjords.

City Layout

Bergen is squeezed between mountain ranges and water. The city center lies between the harbor, **Bryggen** (check out "Seeing the Sights," later in this chapter), the railway station, and the main square, **Torgallmenningen.**

THE WORLD'S longest ROAD TUNNEL

Thanks to a tunnel, you can now drive from Oslo to Bergen without having to take a ferry across water. Opened in 2001, the **Lærdal Tunnel ★★★**, stretching for 24.5km (15¼ miles) is the longest road tunnel in the world (the longest tunnel is the Gothard railway tunnel in Switzerland, due for completion in 2017, which is over double the length of Lærdal). It lies on the E16, the main road between Bergen and Oslo. The entrance is 296km (184 miles) northwest of Oslo along the E16 highway. Costing over NOK1 billion, it is said to be the safest road tunnel on the globe.

Along with high-tech monitoring, fire safety, and air treatment, the tunnel features a trio of large turning caverns (in case you change your mind and want to go back), 16 other turning points, and nearly 50 emergency lay-bys. Some 400 vehicles per hour can go through the tunnel, the ride taking just 20 minutes.

The area up above gets severe weather in winter, but all is calm in the tunnel. The high mountain passes, at around 1,800m (5,900 ft.), are closed in winter. The panoramic, high-mountain road between Aurland and Lærdal, the so-called "Snow Road," is open only between June and mid-October.

Like Rome, Bergen is said to have grown up around **seven hills.** For the best overall view, take the funicular to **Fløien.** The northern section of the city, **Sandviken,** is filled with old warehouses. The area south of central Bergen is being developed at an incredible rate.

In the center of Bergen, walk on cobblestone streets as you explore the quayside with its medieval houses and the open-air Fish Market. The center has colonnaded shops and cafes, and in **Gamle Bergen,** the old town, you get a taste of the early 19th century.

GETTING AROUND

The good-value **Bergen Card** entitles you to free bus transportation and free entrance to most museums throughout Bergen, plus discounts on car rentals, parking, and some cultural and leisure activities. You can buy it at the tourist office (see above). A 24-hour card costs NOK190 for adults and NOK75 for children 3 to 15; a 48-hour card is NOK250 for adults and NOK100 for children 3 to 15. Children under 3 travel or enter free.

By Bus

The **central bus station (Bystasjonen),** Strømgaten 8 (✆ **55-55-90-70**), is the terminal for all buses serving the Bergen and Hardanger areas, as well as for the airport bus. The station has luggage storage, shops, and a restaurant. City buses are marked with their destination and route number. A network of variously colored city buses serves the city center only. For information, call ✆ **55-59-32-00.** For **bus information** in the Bergen area, call ✆ **177.**

By Taxi

Taxis are readily available at the airport. A ride from the airport to the city center costs around NOK340. To request a taxi, call ✆ **55-99-70-10.**

By Car

PARKING Visitors can park on most streets in the city center after 11pm. For convenient indoor parking, try the **Bygarasjen Busstation** (✆ **55-56-88-70**), a large garage near the bus and train stations, about a 5-minute walk from the city center. It's open 24 hours a day and charges NOK20 per hour or NOK100 for 24 hours.

RENTAL CARS You might want to rent a car to explore the area for a day or two. **Budget** (✆ **800/527-0700** in the U.S.; www.budget.com) maintains offices at the airport (✆ **55-22-75-27**) and downtown at Vestre Strømkaien 5 (✆ **55-32-60-00**). Its least expensive car is NOK661 per day. **Hertz** (✆ **800/654-3001** in the U.S.; www.hertz.com) has locations at the airport (✆ **55-22-60-75**) and downtown at Nygårdsgaten 89 (✆ **55-96-40-70**). For a 2-day rental, the smallest car, a Volkswagen Polo, costs NOK2,099. **Avis** (✆ **800/331-1212** in the U.S.; www.avis.com) has branches at the airport (✆ **55-11-64-30**) and downtown at Lars Hillesgate 20 (✆ **67-25-56-50**). For a 1-day rental, its smallest car, a Fiat 500, costs NOK1,210.

Prices include 23% government tax, collision-damage waiver, and unlimited mileage. Rates per day are lower for rentals of a week or more. Of course, rates are subject to change. The lowest rates are almost always offered to those who reserve their cars from their home country before they leave.

By Ferry

You can take the Beffen ferry across the harbor Monday to Friday from 7am to 4:15pm; they don't run on Saturday or Sunday. One-way fares are NOK20 for adults and NOK10 for children. Ferries arrive and depart from either side of the harbor at Dreggekaien and Munkebryggen. For information, call ✆ **56-14-07-02.**

By Coastal Steamer

Bergen is the cruise capital of Norway, home to a flotilla of well-engineered ships (the Hurtigruten) that carries passengers, cars, and vast amounts of freight up and down the coast. At least 10 boats depart from Bergen, making numerous stops en route before landing 5 to 6 days later at Kirkenes, far north of the Arctic Circle, near the Russian border. You can book a berth on any of these ships for short- or long-haul transits and do a quick bit of sightseeing while the ship docks in various ports.

The most popular tour is a 12-day unescorted northbound cruise—Oslo–Bergen–Kirkenes–Oslo—visiting 34 ports and starting at $1,482 per person (early booking rate), based on double occupancy. You can book tickets on this journey with Hurtigruten (✆ **+47 81-00-30-30,** ✆ +1 866 552 0371 (in U.S.), ✆ +44 845 225 6640 (in U.K.); www.hurtigruten.com). If you're already in Norway, talk to any travel agent. You can make arrangements through Bergen-based **Cruise Spesialisten,** Ulriksdahl 7 (✆ **55-59-68-40;** www.cruisespesialisten.com), or **Kystopplevelser,** Strandkaien 4 (✆ **55-31-59-10;** www.kystopplevelser.no). Both companies have brochures and lots of information about these stalwart Norwegian cruise ships.

Other routes head south from Bergen to Stavanger and other ports, and tours go to some of the fjords to the south. For information and reservations, contact Cruise Spesialisten (see above), or a local operator. The best operator is **Fjord 1** (✆ **55-90-70-70;** www.fjord1.no), which runs fast ferries from Bergen to Sognefjord, the world's longest fjord.

[FastFACTS] BERGEN

Banking Bergen has dozens of banks. The most visible is **DnB Norske Bank,** Lars Hilles Gate 30 (✆ **55-21-10-00**). Branches of many of its competitors can be found near the Radisson BLU Hotel Norge, on Nedre Ole Bulls Plass.

Bookstores One of the best, with a wide range of books in English, is **Norli,** in the Galleriet, Torgallmenningen 8 (✆ **55-21-42-80**). It's open Monday to Friday 9am to 8pm, Saturday 9am to 6pm.

Business Hours Most **banks** are open Monday to Friday from 9am to 3pm, and Thursday until 6pm. Most **businesses** are open Monday to Friday 9am to 4pm. **Shops** are generally open Monday to Wednesday and Friday 9am to 4:30pm, Thursday (and sometimes Fri) 9am to 7pm, Saturday 9am to 3pm.

Currency Exchange You can exchange currency at Bergen airport. In Bergen you can exchange money at several banks or, when the banks are closed, at the tourist office (see above).

Dentists Emergency care outside normal working hours is available at **Bergen Legevakt,** Vestre Stromkaien 19 (✆ **55-56-87-00** or 55-56-87-17), Monday to Friday 6 to 8:30pm, Saturday and Sunday 3:30 to 8:30pm.

Doctors For medical assistance, call **Bergen Legevakt,** Vestre Strømkaien 19 (✆ **55-56-87-00** or 55-56-87-60), 24 hours a day. If it's not an emergency, your hotel can make an appointment with an English-speaking doctor.

Drugstores One convenient pharmacy is **Apoteket Nordstjernen** (✆ **55-21-83-84**), in the Tilbords Interiør Bergen Storsenter shopping mall. It's open Monday to Saturday 8am to 11pm and Sunday 10am to 11pm.

Embassies & Consulates Most foreign nationals, including citizens of the United States, will have to contact their embassies in Oslo (see "Embassies & Consulates" in chapter 16) if they have a problem. Exceptions to this rule include the **United Kingdom,** which maintains a consulate in Bergen, at Øvre Ole Bulls Plass 1 (✆ **55-36-78-10**); and Canada, which keeps a consular address at P.O. Box 2439, Solheimsviken, N-5824 Bergen (✆ **55-29-71-30**).

Emergencies For the **police,** dial ✆ **112;** to report a **fire,** call ✆ **110;** for an **ambulance,** dial ✆ **113.**

Eyeglass Repair A good optician is **Optiker Svabø,** Strandgaten 18 (✆ **55-31-69-51**). It's open Monday to Friday 9am to 4:30pm (Thurs to 7pm) and Saturday 10am to 2pm.

Hairdressers & Barbers One of the best in Bergen is **Prikken Frisørsalong,** Strandkaien 2B (✆ **55-32-31-51**). It's open Monday, Tuesday, Thursday, and Friday 9am to 4pm; Wednesday 10am to 7pm; and Saturday 9am to 2pm.

Hospitals A medical center, **Accident Clinic (Bergen Legevakt),** is open around the clock. It's at Vestre Stromkaien 19 (✆ **55-56-87-00**).

Internet Access Your best bet is **BT Mediabarin,** Torgallmenningen 8 (✆ **55-31-11-60**), in the Galleriet shopping mall.

Laundry Try **Jarlens Vaskoteque,** Lille Øvregate 17 (✆ **55-32-55-04**). It's near the Hotel Victoria in a little alley about 45m (148 ft.) northeast of the 17th-century Korskirken, off Oscarsgate. It's open Monday, Tuesday, and Friday 10am to 6pm; Wednesday and Thursday 10am to 8pm; and Saturday 10am to 3pm.

Libraries The **Bergen Public Library,** Strømgaten (✆ **55-56-85-00**), is open in July and August on Tuesday, Wednesday, and Friday 10am to 3pm, Monday and Thursday 9am to 7pm, and Saturday 9am to 1pm; the rest of the year, it's open Monday to Friday 10am to 8pm and Saturday 10am to 5pm. The library has free wireless Internet, as well as computers available for checking e-mail (it is necessary to sign up for the latter).

Lost Property Various agencies recover lost objects. For assistance, contact the local police station or the **tourist office** (✆ **55-55-20-00**).

Luggage Storage & Lockers Rental lockers and luggage storage are available at the **railway station,** Strømgaten 1. The lockers are open daily 7am to 11pm, and the cost ranges from NOK20 to NOK40 per day, depending on the locker's size.

Police Call ✆ **112.**

Post Office The main post office is at Småstrandgaten 3 (✆ **55-54-15-00**), one block from Torget. It's open Monday to Friday 8am to 5pm (Thurs until 6pm), and Saturday 9am to 2:30pm. If you want to receive your mail c/o General Delivery, the address is Poste Restante, N-5002 Bergen. You'll need your passport to pick it up.

Telephone Most locals have cellphones. As a result there are only a few public phone booths left. Phone cards are available in various denominations at newspaper kiosks and pharmacies. To call abroad, dial ✆ **00;** to call collect, dial ✆ **115.**

WHERE TO STAY

The Bergen tourist office (see "Visitor Information," p. 259) can book hotels as well as accommodations in **private homes.** More than 30 families take in guests during the summer. The booking service costs NOK50, and prospective guests also pay a deposit that's deducted from the final bill. A double room in a private home usually costs NOK600 to NOK1,000, with no service charge. Breakfast is not served.

The hotel rates quoted below include service and tax. Many expensive accommodations lower their rates considerably on weekends and in midsummer. I've mentioned it when these reductions are available, but the situation is fluid, and it's best to check on the spot. All of the recommended accommodations come with private bathrooms unless otherwise indicated.

Expensive

Clarion Collection Hotel Havnekontoret ★★★ This is still the most sought-after place to stay in Bergen. Right on the scenic Bryggen harborfront, the hotel was created from the historic home of the Bergen Port Authority. Architects recycled the building into a first-class hotel of grace and charm, respecting the past style, keeping many early 20th-century neoclassical and baronic features. Book into one of the tower rooms, as the views over the harbor and the cityscape are spectacular. The six-floor property features rooms with a contemporary, colorful decor, each with a state-of-the-art bathroom. Bedrooms have all the most up-to-date amenities. The hotel also maintains the best fitness equipment in the city, and its buffet restaurant

Where to Stay & Dine in Bergen

ACCOMMODATIONS ■

Augustin Hotel **7**
Bergen Travel Hotel **26**
Best Western Hotell Hordaheimen **9**
Clarion Collection Hotel Havnekontoret **1**
Clarion Hotel Admiral **8**
Comfort Hotel Holberg **6**
First Hotel Marin **13**
Hotel Park **32**
Neptun Hotell **17**
P Hotel Bergen **27**
Quality Edvard Grieg Hotel & Suites **34**
Radisson BLU Hotel Norge **22**
Radisson BLU Royal Hotel **2**
Rica Travel Hotel **29**
Scandic Hotel Bergen City **28**
Solstrand Hotel & Bad **34**
Steens Hotel—Bed & Breakfast **33**
Strand Hotel **24**

DINING ◆

Bølgen & Moi **30**
Bryggeloftet & Stuene **3**
Egon **14**
Enhjørningen **4**
Escalón Tapas Restaurant **12**
Finnegaardsstuene **11**
Hanne På Høyden **31**
Holbergstuen **16**
Kaffistova **10**
Lucullus **18**
Naboen **23**
Restaurant Potetkjelleren **15**
Ristorante Stragiotti **25**
Smauet Mat & Vinhus **21**
Spisekroken **19**
To Kokker **5**
Wesselstuen **20**

ⓘ Information

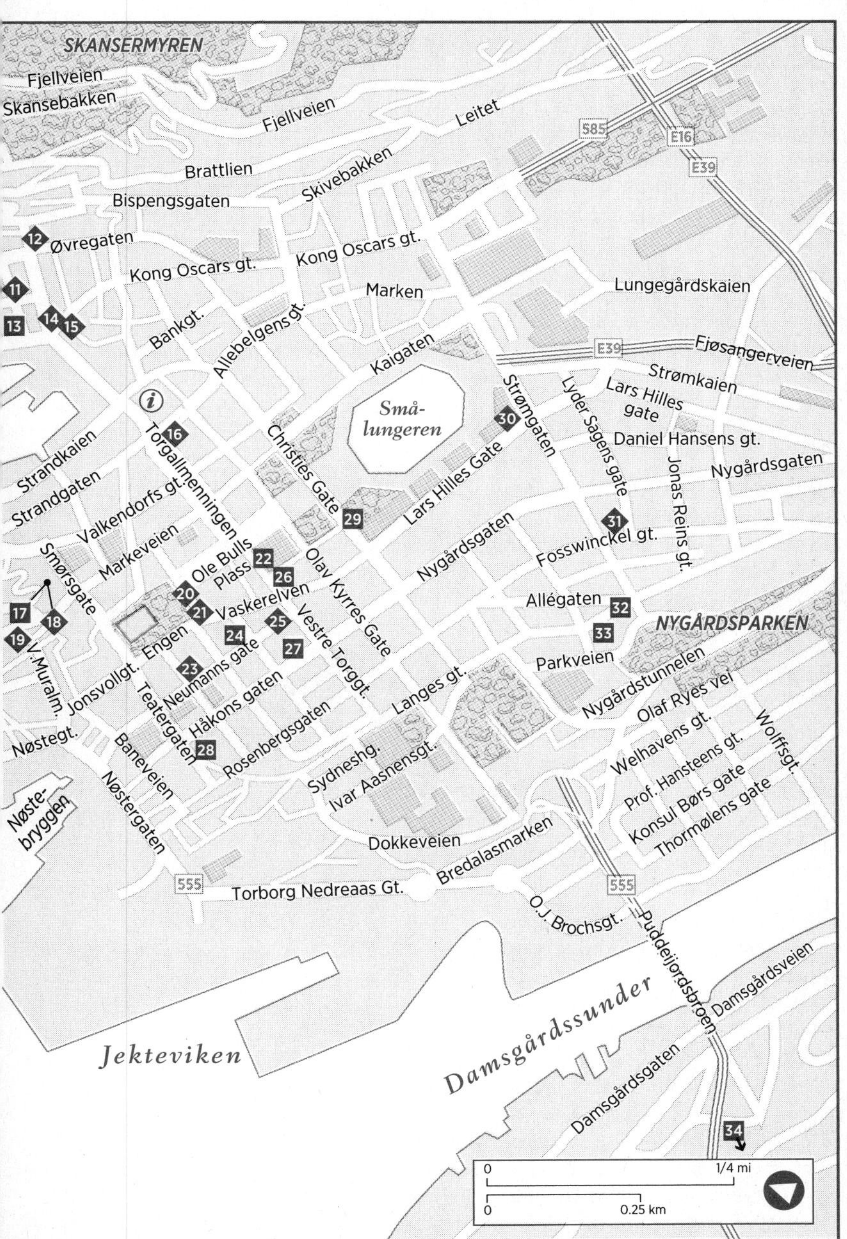
SKANSERMYREN
Fjellveien
Skansebakken
Fjellveien
Leitet
Brattlien
Bispengsgaten
Skivebakken
Øvregaten
Kong Oscars gt.
Kong Oscars gt.
Marken
Lungegårdskaien
Bankgt.
Allebelgens gt.
Kaigaten
Fjøsangerveien
Strømkaien
Lars Hilles gate
Små-lungeren
Strømgaten
Lyder Sagens gate
Daniel Hansens gt.
Nygårdsgaten
Jonas Reins gt.
Strandkaien
Strandgaten
Torgallmenningen
Christies Gate
Lars Hilles Gate
Valkendorfs gt.
Markeveien
Ole Bulls Plass
Olav Kyrres Gate
Nygårdsgaten
Fosswinckel gt.
Smørsgate
Vaskerelven
Vestre Torggt.
Allégaten
NYGÅRDSPARKEN
V. Muralm.
Engen
Neumanns gate
Parkveien
Jonsvollgt.
Teatergaten
Håkons gaten
Langes gt.
Nygårdstunnelen
Olaf Ryes vei
Nøstegt.
Baneveien
Rosenbergsgaten
Sydneshg.
Ivar Aasnensgt.
Welhavens gt.
Wolffsgt.
Prof. Hansteens gt.
Konsul Børs gate
Thormølens gate
Nøste-bryggen
Nøstergaten
Dokkeveien
Bredalasmarken
555
Torborg Nedreaas Gt.
555
O.J. Brochsgt.
Puddefjordsbroen
Damsgårdsveien
Damsgårdssunder
Jekteviken
Damsgårdsgaten
585
E16
E39
E39
11 12 13 14 15 16 17 18 19 20 21 22 23 24 25 26 27 28 29 30 31 32 33 34
0 1/4 mi
0 0.25 km

(serving breakfast and dinner) is even patronized by locals looking for a good start to their day.

Slottsgaten 1, N-5835 Bergen. ✆ **55-60-11-00.** www.choicehotels.no. 116 units. NOK995–NOK2,395 double; NOK2,295–NOK2,795 suite. Rates include buffet breakfast. AE, DC, MC, V. Parking NOK100. Bus: 1, 5, or 9. **Amenities:** Restaurant; bar; fitness room; sauna; room service; rooms for those with limited mobility. *In room:* TV, Wi-Fi, minibar, hair dryer.

First Hotel Marin ★★ ☺ This hotel in a brown-brick building is imbued with a strong maritime theme as befits its location at the Bryggen waterfront, with several of its bedrooms opening onto views of the harbor and the famous Fish Market. This is one of the better first-class hotels in the city, rising seven floors in a streamlined format on a steep hillside. Standard doubles are available, but if you're willing to pay more, you'll get a superior double with more space and upgraded amenities. Each room is tastefully furnished in Nordic modern style with spic-and-span tiled bathrooms. Families often book one of the suites (the Princess Room or the Pirate Room) that come with a separate bedroom with a large double bed and a living room.

Rosenkrantzgaten 8, N-5003 Bergen. ✆ **53-05-15-00.** www.firsthotels.com. 152 units. NOK1,295–NOK1,945 double; NOK2,295–NOK3,295 suite. AE, DC, MC, V. Free parking. Bus: 1, 5, or 9. **Amenities:** 2 restaurants; bar; fitness center; sauna; Turkish bath; Jacuzzi; room service. *In room:* TV, Wi-Fi, minibar, hair dryer (in some).

Radisson BLU Hotel Norge ★★★ This Radisson BLU is the traditional prestige hotel and an even better address than the Radisson BLU Royal (see below). In the city center, near Torgallmenningen, the Norge has been a Bergen tradition since 1885. Built in 1962 and renovated in 2007, it continues to be a favorite of local celebrities. Rooms feature double-glazed windows, bedside controls, and ample bathrooms with showers and, in some cases, bathtubs big enough for two. The ninth-floor units open onto private balconies overlooking a nearby park. The hotel's Ole Bull restaurant serves international food, while Søtt + Salt offers up some of the city's freshest seafood. There's also an on-site piano bar, the American Bar. The Contra Bar, on street level near reception, is a leading nightlife venue, and the Metro disco lies in the cellar; both have separate entrances.

Nedre Ole Bulls Plass 4, N-5807 Bergen. ✆ **55-57-30-00** or 800/333-3333 in the U.S.. www.radissonblu.com/hotelnorge-bergen. 347 units. NOK2,195–NOK2,595 double; NOK3,695–6,195 suite. Rates include breakfast. Children 17 & under stay free in parents' room. AE, DC, MC, V. Parking NOK240; reserve with room. Bus: 2, 3, or 4. **Amenities:** 2 restaurants; 2 bars; dance club; babysitting; heated indoor pool; fitness center; spa; sauna; room service; rooms for those with limited mobility. *In room:* TV, minibar, hair dryer.

Radisson BLU Royal Hotel ★★ Opened in 1982, this hotel was built on the fire-ravaged site of an old warehouse at Bryggen that had stood here since 1702. The hotel offers a choice of standard rooms, business-class rooms, and suites, the latter decorated with locally made arts and crafts, creating one of the coziest ambiences in Bergen. The guest rooms are beautifully maintained, with lithographs and comfortable, upholstered furniture. The hotel has a pub, Madame Felle, named after a lusty matron who ran a sailors' tavern on these premises during the 19th century. The pub's outdoor terrace does a thriving business in summer, and there is also a separate nightclub, the Bryggen Piano Bar, just next door.

Bryggen, N-5835 Bergen. ✆ **55-54-30-00** or 800/333-3333 in the U.S. www.radissonblu.com. 273 units. NOK1,275–NOK2,895 double; NOK4,600 suite. Rates include breakfast. AE, DC, MC, V. Parking

NOK200. Bus: 1, 5, or 9. **Amenities:** 2 restaurants; 2 bars; nightclub; heated indoor pool; fitness center; sauna; room service; babysitting; rooms for those with limited mobility. *In room:* TV, Wi-Fi, minibar, hair dryer.

Scandic Hotel Bergen City ★ This makes a fine stopover assuming there isn't a convention on in town. In the summer months, the hotel fills up with vacationers, attracting mainly commercial travelers in winter. The hotel is convenient for those interested in the Bergen cultural scene, as it lies near the National Theater and the Grieghallen (p. 294). The hotel is stylish and inviting, with midsize bedrooms that are well furnished and kept sparkling clean. The lobby bar is a popular rendezvous area where guests mingle and chat.

Håkonsgate 2-7, N-5051 Bergen. ✆ **55-30-90-80.** www.scandic-hotels.com. 254 units. NOK1,190–NOK2,090 double; NOK1,990–NOK2,290 suite. Rates include breakfast. AE, DC, MC, V. No on-site parking. Bus: 2, 3, or 4. **Amenities:** Restaurant; bar. *In room:* TV, Wi-Fi, minibar.

Moderate

Augustin Hotel ★ The clear winner in the moderately priced category is the oldest family-run hotel in Bergen. The Augustin has one of the best locations in Bergen—right in the harborfront shopping district—with front rooms that have harbor views. Constructed in 1909 in the *Jugendstil* or Art Nouveau style, the Augustin rises six floors. In 1995, it more than doubled in size by adding a new wing, with modern rooms (equipped with larger showers and tubs) designed by award-winning Bergen architect Aud Hunskår. Less up-to-date and somewhat less desirable rooms remain in the old section. The hotel is decorated with lots of art, much of it by well-known contemporary Norwegian artists. The Altona Tavern, once the haunt of Bergen artists and concertmasters in the 17th century, has been creatively integrated into the hotel. The hotel was built on the Altona's foundation, and its nostalgic memory is evoked in the hotel's wine cellar, which is open to the public. Even if you're not a guest, I'd recommend a visit to the on-site Brasserie No. 22, with some of the best shellfish and meat grills in the city.

C. Sundts Gate 22–24, N-5004 Bergen. ✆ **55-30-40-00.** www.augustin.no. 109 units. NOK1,150–NOK2,050 double. AE, DC, MC, V. Parking NOK100. Bus: 2 or 4. **Amenities:** Restaurant; bar; rooms for those with limited mobility. *In room:* A/C, TV, minibar, hair dryer.

Best Western Hotell Hordaheimen This hotel is somewhat staid and certainly not for the party crowd, but it's an enduring favorite. Located near the harbor, it has long been a base for young people from nearby districts. It's operated by the Bondeungdomslaget i Bergen, an association that sponsors cultural and folklore programs, and school and civic groups sometimes reserve nearly all the rooms. The five-story hotel was built at the turn of the 19th century and renovated in stages, with additional rooms completed in 2007. Ongoing refurbishments have kept the hotel looking young. Lars Kinsarvik, an internationally known designer in the late 19th century, created some of the furniture displayed in the public areas. The small, simple guest rooms are immaculate, with good beds and tiny bathrooms.

C. Sundts Gate 18, N-5004 Bergen. ✆ **55-33-50-00.** www.hordaheimen.no. 88 units. Mon–Thurs NOK1,150–NOK1,350 double; Fri–Sun NOK895–NOK1,960 double. Rates include buffet breakfast. AE, DC, MC, V. No on-site parking. Bus: 1, 5, or 9. **Amenities:** Restaurant; lounge; room service; rooms for those with limited mobility. *In room:* TV, minibar, hair dryer.

Clarion Hotel Admiral ★ Set just minutes from such attractions as the Bergen Fish Market, right on the harbor, with panoramic views of Bryggen and the old wharf, location alone is this place's major selling point. In 1906, this was one of the largest warehouses in Bergen, with six sprawling floors peppered with massive trusses and beams. It was miraculously transformed into this modern bastion in 1987. Some rooms are small, but others are midsize to spacious, with shiny, modern bathrooms. Many rooms lack water views, but the ones that do open onto flower-bedecked balconies. This member of the Clarion chain is not as luxurious and well appointed as the Clarion Collection Hotel Havnekontoret (see above).

C. Sundts Gate 9, N-5004 Bergen. ✆ **55-23-64-00.** www.clarionadmiral.com. 211 units. Mon–Thurs NOK1,480–NOK2,495 double, NOK3,000 suite; Fri–Sun NOK1,080–NOK1,780 double, NOK1,510–NOK2,550 suite. Rates include buffet breakfast. AE, DC, MC, V. Parking NOK150; reserve with room. Bus: 2, 4, or 11. **Amenities:** 2 restaurants; bar; room service; rooms for those with limited mobility. *In room:* TV, minibar, hair dryer.

Neptun Hotell ★ The Neptun offers a far livelier ambience and decor than the more run-of-the-mill Hordaheimen (see above). It was built in 1952 long before many of its more streamlined and trend-conscious competitors. Its eight-story premises attract lots of business, especially from Norwegians riding the Hurtigruten coastal steamers (p. 261), who consider it a worthwhile and solid choice in the upper-middle bracket. Each of the bedrooms has a decorative theme related to its name. For example, rooms named after Ole Bull, Nordahl Grieg, Ludvig Holberg, Salvador Dalí, and Joan Miró have photos or artworks commemorating their namesakes' lives and achievements. The hotel's premier restaurant, Lucullus, is one of Bergen's best (see "Where to Dine," below); there's also a likable, bustling brasserie, Pascal.

Valkendorfsgate 8, N-5012 Bergen. ✆ **55-30-68-00.** www.neptunhotell.no. 124 units. NOK1,395–NOK2,145 double; NOK4,995 suite. AE, DC, MC, V. Parking NOK180. Bus: 20, 21, or 22. **Amenities:** 2 restaurants; bar; room service. *In room:* A/C, TV, minibar, hair dryer.

Quality Edvard Grieg Hotel & Suites ★ I'm surprised that this hotel isn't better known, considering the quality of its accommodations. Savvy businesspeople know of its charm, but its location away from the center might be daunting for the casual sightseer. Opened in 1987, this modern, all-suite hotel—Norway's first—lies 19km (12 miles) south of Bergen and 4.8km (3 miles) from the airport. Luxuriously appointed suites are amply sized, with comfortable beds in the rather small sleeping quarters, and a separate lounge. Free airport transfers are arranged for arriving and departing guests Monday to Friday from 7am to 8:45pm.

Sandsliåsen 50, N-5245 Sandsli. ✆ **55-98-00-00.** www.choicehotels.no. 153 units. NOK945–NOK2,180 double. Rates include breakfast. AE, DC, MC, V. Free parking. Bus: 30 from the Bergen bus station. **Amenities:** Restaurant; bar; heated indoor pool; fitness center; sauna; bike rentals; rooms for those with limited mobility. *In room:* TV, minibar, hair dryer.

Rica Travel Hotel This is hardly a glamorous hotel, but it attracts business travelers—those not on generous expense accounts—and summer vacationers trying to survive in high-priced Bergen. The location near Torgallmenningen is ideal, as it's close to attractions, shops, bars, and restaurants. Bedrooms are fairly standard, rather comfortable, and maintained well, but there aren't a lot of extras or facilities. One plus: It has been regularly praised for serving one of the best breakfasts in Bergen.

Christiesgate 5–7, N-5808 Bergen. ✆ **55-36-29-00.** www.rica.no. 159 units. NOK895–NOK2,000 double. AE, DC, MC, V. Parking NOK170. Bus: 2, 3, or 4. **Amenities:** Restaurant; bar. *In room:* TV, Wi-Fi, minibar, hair dryer.

Inexpensive

Bergen Travel Hotel ☺ This recently refurbished place is fine for a good night's sleep—but not a lot more—at an affordable price. In the center of Bergen, the five-story building has been a hotel since the 1970s, although it absorbed a building across the street in 2005. Bedrooms come in various sizes, and each has pale colors and contemporary furniture crafted from dark-grained hardwoods. Some of the accommodations used to be small private apartments, so they can generously accommodate four or more people, which makes them a family favorite. Bedrooms have wooden floors and comfortable but simple furnishings, and four of the units come with small kitchens.

Vestre Torgate 20A, N-5015 Bergen. ✆ **55-59-90-90.** www.hotelbergen.com. 61 units. NOK990–NOK1,320 double. Rates include continental breakfast. AE, DC, MC, V. Closed Dec 22–Jan 4. No on-site parking. Bus: 2, 3, or 4. **Amenities:** Pub. *In room:* TV.

Comfort Hotel Holberg ★ Set near the Nykirken, a 15-minute walk from Bergen's Fish Market, this seven-story hotel built around 1995 (and refurbished in 2009) commemorates the life of the late-18th-century writer and dramatist Ludvig Holberg, "the Molière of the North," one of the most famous writers in Danish and Norwegian letters (who was born in a since-demolished house on the site of this hotel's parking garage). The hotel's lobby is a testimonial to the author's life, with an informative biography, memorabilia, and photographs of stage productions based on his works. Bedrooms are a modernized reinterpretation of the Norwegian "farmhouse" style, with wooden floors, rough-textured half-paneling stained in tones of forest green, and big windows, some of them floor-to-ceiling, that swing open directly onto a view of the quiet residential street below.

Strandgaten 190, 1949 Nordnes, N-5817 Bergen. ✆ **55-30-42-00.** www.choicehotels.no. 149 units. NOK780–NOK2,200 double. Rates include buffet breakfast. AE, DC, MC, V. Parking NOK160. Bus: 1, 5, or 9. **Amenities:** Restaurant; bar. *In room:* TV, Wi-Fi, minibar, hair dryer.

Hotel Park ★ This 1890s' hotel lies on the fringe of Bergen in an area that is rapidly gentrifying. You can often find rooms here when the hotels in the city center are fully booked. The location isn't that far out—it's a 10-minute walk to the train or bus station. The converted four-story town house is in an attractive university area near the Grieghall and Nygårdparken. The rooms are traditionally furnished, often with antiques. Accommodations vary in size, but all have good beds and adequate bathrooms. A neighboring building (furnished in the same style) accommodates overflow guests. Breakfast is served in the dining room; later in the day, sandwiches, small hot dishes, and wine and beer are available there.

Harald Hårfagresgaten 35 & Allegaten 20, N-5007 Bergen. ✆ **55-54-44-00.** www.hotelpark.no. 33 units. NOK1,350 double. Rates include buffet breakfast. AE, DC, MC, V. Parking NOK100. Bus: 11. **Amenities:** Breakfast room; lounge. *In room:* TV, hair dryer, iron.

P Hotel Bergen This cost-conscious, unpretentious, centrally located hotel occupies the premises of what functioned for many years as a turn-of-the-20th-century lodging known as the Ambassadeur. In 2006, it was taken over by the P Hotel chain, which performed a few minor upgrades but then left the venue basically unchanged. Everything here is adequate and comfortable; bathrooms have showers with floor drains rather than tubs. I prefer rooms on the uppermost (fourth) floor beneath the mansard-style roof because of the views over Bergen. Access to these rooms is for the young at heart as it involves climbing an additional flight of stairs beyond where the elevator ends.

Vestre Torgate 9, N-5015 Bergen. ✆ **80-04-68-35.** www.p-hotels.com. 48 units. NOK995 double. Rates include Norwegian breakfast. AE, DC, MC, V. No on-site parking. Bus: 1 or 9. **Amenities:** Breakfast room. *In room:* TV.

Steens Hotel—Bed & Breakfast ★ Among the more established B&Bs, the Steens is the best Bergen has to offer. This is a stylish 1890 house that has been successfully converted to receive guests. Owned and operated by the same family since 1950, Steens offers great accommodations at reasonable prices. The bedrooms are moderate in size and comfortable, and the bathrooms, though small, are well maintained. The best rooms are in front and open onto a park; each unit comes with a neatly maintained private bathroom equipped with a shower. Thoughtful, personal touches include hot coffee served throughout the day in public rooms that evoke a historic aura. The B&B is within a short walk of the bus or rail station.

22 Parkveien, N-5007 Bergen. ✆ **55-30-88-88.** www.steenshotel.no. 18 units. NOK1,340 double. Extra bed NOK250. Rates include Norwegian breakfast. AE, MC, V. Free parking. Bus: 1 or 5. **Amenities:** Breakfast room; lounge. *In room:* TV.

Strand Hotel ★ From the rooftop of this first-rate hotel, all of Bergen is laid out before you. This hotel was once a decaying 1920s' hulk with a rowdy clientele. After the millennium, the rooms were radically upgraded and the second-floor bar became a stylish watering hole. Bedrooms are cozy, efficiently decorated, and comfortable; some have the added advantage of having views directly over the southern flank of Bergen's famous harbor.

Strandkaien 2, N-5013 Bergen. ✆ **55-59-33-00.** www.strandhotel.no. 98 units. NOK1,240–NOK2,240 double; NOK6,000 suite. Rates include buffet breakfast. AE, DC, MC, V. Parking NOK180. Bus: 1, 5, or 9. **Amenities:** Breakfast room; bar; gym; sauna. *In room:* TV, minibar.

On the Outskirts

Solstrand Hotel & Bad ★★★ This is the most prestigious resort in the region around Bergen. Discerning travelers appreciate its isolated location beside the fjord, as well as its history, which dates to 1896. The setting evokes a romantic getaway to the countryside. Colors used throughout the hotel are rich and jewel-toned. Bedrooms are cheerfully painted, high-ceilinged affairs, with a sophisticated mixture of antique and modern furniture. The in-house restaurant serves lunch buffets (from NOK390 per person) and dinners (three courses NOK460). Advance reservations are recommended for meals that—especially on Sunday afternoons—are a magnet for extended families from the surrounding region. The hotel's many amenities include free use of rowboats and putt-putt motorboats, as well as access to a nearby nine-hole golf course.

N-5200 Os. ✆ **56-57-11-00.** www.solstrand.com. 135 units. Mon–Thurs NOK2,480 double, Fri–Sun NOK2,280 double. Rates include buffet breakfast. AE, DC, MC, V. Closed Dec 22–Jan 3 & 1 week at Easter. 24km (15 miles) south of Bergen: drive south on the E39, following signs to Stavanger, turning off at markers to either Os (the region) or Osøyro (the hamlet that functions as the centerpiece of the Os region). Free parking. **Amenities:** Restaurant; bar; indoor heated pool; tennis court; exercise room; spa; saunas; watersports program. *In room:* TV, minibar, hair dryer.

WHERE TO DINE

Very Expensive

Lucullus ★★★ CONTINENTAL Modern art and a grandmotherly decor incongruously meet in this posh, conservative restaurant in the Neptun Hotell (p. 268), a gourmet citadel named after the most famous gastronome of ancient Rome, Lucullus. Tasteful artwork lines the walls of the mostly blue-and-white room, with touches of dark red. The starters continue the elegant tone, with flavor-filled combinations such as reindeer carpaccio with chutney sauce or Russian king crabmeat with monkfish lasagna. Such classic main dishes as breast of duck with a creamy foie gras sauce would be welcome at a top-rated Parisian bistro. The chef is justifiably proud of his tender and flavorful filet of beef Lucullus, the house specialty, although you might opt for a duo of pheasant with a morel-studded butter sauce or quail with a *foie gras* risotto. For dessert, it doesn't get much better than a warm cloudberry soufflé with house-made white chocolate ice cream. The carefully chosen wine list is the best in Bergen.

In the Neptun Hotell, Valkendorfsgate 8. ✆ **55-30-68-00.** www.neptunhotell.no. Reservations recommended. Main courses NOK330–NOK360; fixed-price menus NOK630–NOK850. AE, DC, MC, V. Mon–Fri 5–10:30pm; Sat 7–10:30pm. Closed July. Bus: 20, 21, or 22.

Expensive

Enhjørningen (the Unicorn) ★★ SEAFOOD Part of the charm of this restaurant on the Hanseatic wharf derives from the unlevel floors, the low doorways, and the inconvenient access via narrow staircases to its second-floor dining room. Set within one of the old wooden buildings of the Bryggen complex, adjacent to the harbor, it boasts a history and a name that were recorded as early as 1304. After several fires and the removal of lots of rotted timbers, the inn has been restored to its 1700s' condition. You'll sit in one of several old-fashioned dining rooms set railway-style (end to end) and outfitted like an early-19th-century parlor with framed oil paintings, usually landscapes. It's usually mobbed, especially in midsummer. Choices include savory fresh mussels steamed in white wine with cream, curry, and saffron; oven-baked halibut with saffron *beurre blanc* sauce; herb-fried medallions of monkfish with a morel cream sauce; and *bacalhau* (dried cod) served au gratin with a crusty layer of cheese and boiled potatoes. The star of the restaurant's small selection of meat dishes is grilled filet of beef with a pepper-flavored cream sauce. At Christmas, they serve pungent *lutefisk*, a whitefish that many Norwegians associate with their childhoods.

Bryggen. ✆ **55-32-79-19.** www.enhjorningen.no. Reservations recommended. Main courses NOK295–NOK330; fixed-price menu NOK530. AE, DC, MC, V. Mon–Sat 4–11pm. Closed 2 weeks at Christmas. Bus: 4, 5, 80, or 90.

Finnegaardsstuene ★★★ NORWEGIAN/FRENCH This is one of the leading gourmet restaurants on the west coast of Norway. The foundations of this popular restaurant were laid around 1400, when Hanseatic League merchants used it as a warehouse. Today some of the woodwork dates from the 1700s, and four small-scale dining rooms create a cozy atmosphere. The chefs have created magic in sleepy Bergen with their well-thought-out menu and carefully prepared dishes. The menu changes with the season and the inspiration of the chef. Some of the best dishes might include breast of local duck with wild mushrooms, parsley risotto, and burgundy sauce; or halibut filet, with thyme-flavored, semi-dried tomatoes, and saffron fondant potatoes. Another specialty is slow-roasted French pigeon with foie gras.

Rosenkrantzgate 6. ✆ **55-55-03-00.** www.finnegaarden.no. Reservations recommended. Main courses NOK295–NOK315; fixed-price menus NOK595–NOK825. AE, DC, MC, V. Mon–Sat 6–11pm. Closed 1 week at Easter & Dec 22–Jan 8. Bus: 5 or 21.

Restaurant Potetkjelleren ★★ INTERNATIONAL Set within a few steps of Bergen's Fish Market, this is one of the oldest, most exclusive, and best restaurants in Bergen. Its oldest feature is an antique flagstone floor (the date of construction is unknown) at the base of a cellar whose vaulted ceiling dates from the mid-1400s. (After most of the city's clapboard-sided houses burned to the ground in 1702, the stone-built cellar was used as a dump for the ashes and debris that remained behind. After extensive renovations in the late 1990s, the cellar is now used for additional seating for the restaurant upstairs.) Menu items from the open kitchen change but often include plaice with cauliflower and herb sauce; pan-fried hake with lentils and *beurre noisette*; and a delicious quail served with herb gnocci and a port-wine sauce. There is a different wine for each course, each selected by the chef. The cellar has 300 different vintages.

Kong Oscarsgate 1A. ✆ **55-32-00-70.** www.potetkjelleren.no. Reservations recommended. Main courses NOK280–NOK295; fixed-price menus NOK495–NOK685 without wine, NOK855–NOK1,205 with wine. AE, DC, MC, V. Mon–Sat 4–10pm. Bus: 1, 5, or 9.

Spisekroken ★★ NORWEGIAN/CONTINENTAL Small-scale, charming, and redolent with the scents and aesthetics of early-20th-century Norway, this highly recommended option occupies two floors (street level and cellar) of an antique building in Bergen's historic core. I prefer the cellar, where most of the illumination comes from flickering candles; it seems especially cozy on cold winter nights. Menu items display culinary ambition and flair, and change with the seasons to reflect whatever is local and fresh. This is particularly true of the veal, which is purchased from a local farmer and served with preparations such as Parmesan cheese, chanterelle mushrooms, pesto, and *rösti* potatoes. Other recommendable main courses include roasted sesame trout served with tart lime hollandaise sauce; pasta ribbons and scampi; or filet of reindeer with whipped cream sauce flavored with brown cheese and thyme, served with sautéed spinach, red onions, and potatoes. Imaginative appetizers include king crab with dill butter served with sugar pea sprouts and homemade lemon mayonnaise, or grilled scallops with cream of parsley root and a wild garlic vinaigrette.

Klostergaten 8. ✆ **55-23-01-15.** www.spisekroken.no. Reservations recommended. Main courses NOK139–NOK259; fixed-price 6-course menu NOK625. AE, DC, MC, V. Mon–Sat 4–11pm; Sun 1–10pm. Closed 2 weeks at Christmas. Bus: 1, 5, or 9.

To Kokker ★ FRENCH/NORWEGIAN To Kokker ("Two Cooks"—in this case, Norway-born partners Daniel Olsen and Grete Halland) is a favorite with celebrities ranging from Britain's Prince Andrew to a bevy of French starlets. Savvy local foodies increasingly gravitate here for the chef's well-considered juxtaposition of flavors and textures. Menu items include such time-tested favorites as foie gras with the traditional accompaniments; goose liver terrine with balsamico syrup; filet of venison with chanterelle sauce; and herb-fried monkfish served with mushroom sauce. The

1703 building is adjacent to the oldest piers and wharves in Bergen. The classic dining room, one floor above street level, has a warmly tinted decor of deep red and soft orange, old paintings, and a solidly reliable staff.

Enhjørninggården 3. ✆ **55-30-69-55.** www.tokokker.no. Reservations required. Main courses NOK295-NOK340; 5-course menu NOK675. AE, DC, MC, V. Mon-Sat 5-10pm. Bus: 1, 5, or 9.

Moderate

Bølgen & Moi NORWEGIAN This is a franchise restaurant located in the same building as the Bergen Art Museum. If you're visiting the museum, it makes the ideal choice for lunch, but it's also good and affordable enough to return to for an evening visit. Many workers from the neighborhood patronize the local bar for drinks and conversation. On the lunch menu you can begin with the fish soup, followed by a burger, pizza, or perhaps one of the well-stuffed sandwiches—my favorite being the shellfish with crayfish, shrimp, and crab. At night the menu grows more elaborate, with such main courses as grilled salmon with salmon caviar, or medallions of veal in a morel cream sauce. Braised pork belly might appear with an apple marmalade. Starters include a surprisingly tasty shellfish risotto with scallops, mussels, and pan-fried cod's tongue. Desserts are freshly made, including, for example, a dark chocolate soufflé with homemade raspberry sorbet. Sunday features only a lunch buffet (NOK295).

Rasmus Meyers Allé 9. ✆ **55-59-77-00.** www.bolgenogmoi.no (in Norwegian). Main courses NOK229-NOK320 dinner; fixed-price menus NOK495-NOK645. AE, DC, MC, V. Tues-Sat 11am-10pm; Sun noon-5pm. Bus: 1, 5, or 9.

Bryggeloftet & Stuene ★ NORWEGIAN Charming and well managed, this is the best-established restaurant along the harborfront, a two-level affair originally built in 1910 as a warehouse. The street-level dining room (known as the Stuene) has low-beamed ceilings, carved banquettes, 19th-century murals of old Bergen, and dozens of clipper-ship models. The Bryggeloftet, upstairs, showcases high ceilings, wood paneling, and a venue that's a bit more formal and less animated. Come to this traditional place if you're seeking authentic Norwegian flavors. Dinner in either section might include filet of wolffish, peppered steak, or grilled reindeer filet with a creamy wild game sauce. Several different preparations of salmon and herring are featured, along with roast pork with Norwegian sour cabbage and various preparations of reindeer, grouse, and elk, depending on the season. Between September and February, the menu offers *lutefisk,* an old-fashioned and strong-flavored Norwegian delicacy that is not for the weak-stomached.

Bryggen 11-13. ✆ **55-30-20-70.** www.bryggeloftet.no. Reservations recommended. Main courses NOK220-NOK360; lunch *smørbrød* NOK110-NOK140. AE, DC, MC, V. Mon-Sat 11am-11:30pm; Sun 1-11:30pm. Bus: 1, 5, or 9.

Egon NORWEGIAN/INTERNATIONAL The 1876 building that contains this member of a well-respected nationwide restaurant chain is one of the most distinctive, with some of the most elaborate carved masonry, along the quays. True to its origins as the city's *kjøttbasaren* (meat market), the upstairs of the building contains a half-dozen boutique-style butcher shops and fishmongers. During a 20th-century restoration, archaeologists discovered the rotted keel of a 14th-century wooden ship beneath its foundations. Today the building's ground floor contains a restaurant that's either appealing in its coziness and historicity or daunting because of its ever-present mobs. Menu items include grilled poultry and a grilled tenderloin steak, fresh fish, soups, salads, and pastas, all served in generous portions by a staff that often seems more than a bit harassed. Some food items have just a hint of American flair, especially a "party platter" piled high with nachos, chicken fingers, and onion rings. There's also a bacon-wrapped tenderloin of beef and Cajun-blackened chicken cutlets.

Vetrlidsalmenning 2. ✆ **55-55-22-22.** www.egon.no. Reservations recommended. Main courses NOK165–NOK299. AE, DC, MC, V. Daily 11am–midnight; bar nightly till 1am. Bus: 5 or 21.

Escalón Tapas Restaurant ★ SPANISH Set immediately adjacent to the lowest stage of the Fløibanen cable car, this is a charming, convivial, and unpretentious bar and tapas joint that has consistently won awards as one of the best restaurants of its type in Bergen. It's a few steps down from street level, allowing diners a pavement-level view out over the neighborhood outside or, if they progress into the back of the place, a cavelike interior that's cozy, warm, and dotted with mostly Iberian paintings. Two or—more often—three tapas platters comprise a full meal, depending on your hunger level. The best examples include grilled mushrooms filled with Manchego cheese, Spanish-style potato omelets, meatballs in salsa, scampi in a garlic wine sauce, tuna marinated in olive oil and capers, and shellfish crepes. A wide assortment of Spanish wines is also available.

A second branch **(Lilla Escalón)** is at Neumannsgate 5 (✆ **55-32-90-99**), with the same tapas-based food choices and similar prices. Ironically, despite its name (*lilla* means small), it's almost twice the size of its counterpart, sitting over a wine cellar built in the 18th century. Lilla Escalón is open daily from noon to 1am.

Vertrlidsalmenningen 21. ✆ **55-32-90-99.** www.escalon.no. Tapas NOK44–NOK98; set-price meal consisting of 3 tapas dishes NOK198; 5 tapas NOK596 for 2 people. AE, DC, MC, V. Sun–Fri 3pm–1am; Sat noon–1am. Bus: 5 or 21.

Hanne På Høyden NORWEGIAN A short walk up from the UNESCO-listed harbor is one of Norway's most outstanding restaurants. This newly renovated, rustic chic spot is run by award-winning chef Hanne Frosta, who spends her time coming up with organic, exclusively Norwegian-sourced meals. Crowned Norway's Kitchen Chef of the Year in 2006, Hanne has since become one of Norway's most outspoken advocates of the use of organic local products and is on a campaign to revise the definition of Norwegian food. She is also an avowed champion of the Slow Food movement, which in Norway seeks to preserve local and regional products and cuisines, and stresses the importance of food traditions passed down through generations. The atmosphere of Hanne's restaurant feels at once homespun and very cool. Try her pumpkin soup with birch oil and apple-glazed red onions (NOK110), followed by entrecôte of deer—from nearby Odd Ohnstad farm—with gravy served alongside baked root vegetables and wild mushrooms (NOK325). For dessert, go for her seasonal berries and fruit compote with gooseberry sorbet (NOK 120). This place may well get you to rethink the stereotypes of Scandinavian cuisine.

Fosswinckelsgate 18. ✆ **55-32-34-32.** www.spisestedet.no. Main courses from NOK 230. AE, DC, MC, V. Mon–Tues 11:30am–6pm; Wed–Sat 11:30am–10pm. Bus: 2, 3, or 4.

Holbergstuen NORWEGIAN One floor above street level, this restaurant was established in 1927 midway between the harborfront and Ole Bulls Plass. It was named in honor of the 18th-century writer Ludvig Holberg. He divided his time between Bergen and Copenhagen, and both cities ferociously claim him as part of their cultural heritage. The setting is much like a tavern, with beamed ceilings, an open log fire, lots of exposed wood, and a vivid sense of Old Norway. Some of the most intriguing menu items include grilled stockfish with a bacon and cabbage stew, and grilled salmon with new potatoes. Local favorites are the pan-fried filet of cusk with creamed spinach, root vegetables, *rösti* potatoes, and orange-and-beetroot sauce, and pork filet gratinated with Gorgonzola, served with vegetables and mushroom sauce. This place is a longtime favorite; come here for old-fashioned flavors, not trendy experiments.

Torgallmenningen 6. ✆ **55-55-20-55.** www.holbergstuen.no. Reservations recommended. Main courses NOK239–NOK299. AE, DC, MC, V. Mon–Sat 11am–11pm; Sun 2–10pm. Bus: 1, 5, or 9.

Naboen SCANDINAVIAN With so many Swedes moving to Norway, it was inevitable that they would open a restaurant in Bergen. Many classic Scandinavian dishes are served here, along with some specifically Norwegian dishes. But most reflect the secrets of Swedish cuisine, from the *køttbullar* (ping-pong meatballs) to grilled marinated salmon with mustard sauce and dill-stewed potatoes. If you like to eat well but shun flashiness, this is your place. Offerings change with the season, but locals keep coming back, especially for the array of desserts made fresh daily.

Neumannsgate 20. ✆ **55-90-02-90.** www.grannen.no. Reservations recommended. Main courses NOK194–NOK252. AE, DC, MC, V. Daily 4–11pm. Bus 2, 3, or 4.

Smauet Mat & Vinhus ★ CONTINENTAL The romantic, cozy atmosphere and high-quality food continues to lure me here. Tempting smells and lots of energy emanate from the open kitchen of this candle-studded restaurant whose decor emulates the style of a 19th-century Norwegian farmhouse. In a place so authentically Norwegian, you wouldn't expect a cuisine this thoroughly Continental. Subtly intermingled flavors emerge in the monkfish with nut crust and chorizo francese, or the guinea fowl with chanterelles, celery purée, and red whortleberries. Other standouts include ox tenderloin with Jerusalem artichoke, red onion, mushrooms, and red wine sauce, and, as a starter, pan-fried scallops with cabbage and leek purée, pomegranate and grapefruit. The location, in a house built in 1870, lies just a few steps from the Ole Bulls Plass.

Vaskerelvsmauet 1–3. ✆ **90-29-99-00.** www.smauet.no. Reservations recommended, especially on weekends. Main courses NOK225–NOK275; 3-course menu NOK495; 6-course menu NOK645. AE, DC, MC, V. Sun–Thurs 5–10pm; Fri–Sat 5–11pm. Closed Christmas to New Year's. Bus: 2, 3, or 4.

Wesselstuen NORWEGIAN/CONTINENTAL Other and better restaurants have opened to successfully challenge this longtime favorite, but this is one of the city's most beloved and most traditional. Named after the 18th-century Danish-Norwegian humorist Peter Wessel, it has some of its namesake's framed illustrations and all the trappings of an 18th-century wine cellar. It's decorated in old-tavern style with beamed ceilings, and its adjoining pub is a famous meeting place for locals. The chefs can be experimental at times, and the menu has kept up with the times with more modern ingredients and sauces, but they're also soundly grounded in the classics. Some of the more reliable main dishes include baked trout served with cucumber, crème fraiche, and boiled potatoes; and steamed klipfish (cod) served with pea stew, bacon, carrot, and boiled potatoes. Two other specialties are filet of pork marinated in chili, and grilled beef ribs with an herb sauce.

Øvre Ole Bulls Plass 8. ✆ **55-55-49-49.** www.wesselstuen.no. Reservations recommended. Main courses NOK199–NOK289; fixed-price menu NOK435. AE, DC, MC, V. Mon–Sat 11am–11pm; Sun 2pm–midnight. Bus: 2, 3, or 4.

Inexpensive

Kaffistova NORWEGIAN This elegant cafeteria looks more like a full-service restaurant, with its linen tablecloths and upscale cutlery. On the ground floor of the Hotell Hordaheimen, this no-nonsense place offers aggressively unpretentious and relatively quick meals. Lunchtime features open-faced sandwiches *(smørbrød)* and simple platters of the day. Dinner offerings are a bit more elaborate, with carved meats, pepper steak, meatballs, and an excellent version of mushroom soup. Especially Norwegian-style meals include *kjøttkaker* (rissoles) and *vossakorv* (potato dumplings with salted meat, mashed swedes, and traditional sausage), the latter on the menu from Thursday to Sunday.

In the Hotell Hordaheimen, C. Sundts Gate 18. ✆ **55-33-50-00.** www.hordaheimen.no/kaffistova/. Main courses NOK70–NOK140 lunch, NOK145–NOK190 dinner. AE, DC, MC, V. Sun–Fri 11am–7pm. Bus: 21, 22, or 23.

Ristorante Stragiotti ★ ITALIAN This is the best Italian restaurant in Bergen. Michele Stragiotti, an Italian native from Piemonte, owns this eatery, a short walk from the Ole Bulls Plass. Stragiotti's is a trimmed-down, minimalist testimonial to postmodern Italian simplicity. The house specialty is Norwegian beef with your choice of four sauces (mushroom, black peppercorn, tomato, or Béarnaise). Expect Norwegian rack of lamb (tender and full of flavor), homemade pastas, freshly caught fish, and lots of scaloppine choices, including a savory version with Gorgonzola cheese. A *grigliata di pesce,* wherein Italian cooking techniques are applied to very fresh Norwegian fish, is particularly appealing.

Vestre Torgate 3. ✆ **55-90-31-00.** Reservations recommended. Pizzas NOK110–NOK170; main courses NOK150–NOK300; fixed-price 4-course menu NOK525. AE, DC, MC, V. Daily noon–11pm. Bus: 2, 3, or 4.

WHAT TO SEE & DO

The Top Attractions

The best way to begin is to take a stroll around **Bryggen** ★★★. This row of Hanseatic timbered houses, rebuilt along the waterfront after a disastrous fire in 1702, is what remains of medieval Bergen. The northern half burned to the ground in 1955. Bryggen has been added to UNESCO's list of World Heritage Sites as one of the most significant cultural and historical re-creations of a medieval settlement, skillfully blending with the surroundings of modern Bergen. It's a center for arts and crafts, where painters, weavers, and craftspeople have their workshops, some of which are open to the public.

Akvariet (Bergen Aquarium) ★★ ☺ A 15-minute walk from the city center, this aquarium contains the most extensive collection of marine fauna in Europe, lying on the outermost reaches of the Nordnes district, with a panoramic view of the entrance to the port of Bergen. The exceptional marine life includes seals, penguins, lobsters, piranhas, and a "bearded" cod. Nothing is uglier than the Norwegian

Impressions

Reaching Bergen we fail to find it particularly attractive. Everything is fishy. You eat fish and drink fish and smell fish and breathe fish.

—Lilian Leland, *Traveling Alone: A Woman's Journey Round the World,* 1890

catfish, which wins all those most-hideous-looking contests. In the outer hall you can get the feel of the fish—dip your hand into the shallow pool of unpolluted water pumped up from a depth of 120m (390 ft.) in the fjord outside. Nine glass tanks, each containing about 237,000 liters (62,500 gallons) of water, ring the hall. Downstairs, a wide range of marine life in 42 small aquariums presents many colorful forms of sea life and illustrates evolutionary development. Kids should enjoy the shark tunnel, and the daily seal and penguin feeding time, in summer at 11am, 2, and 6pm, and in winter at noon and 4pm. Every hour you can watch the 3D film *SOS Planet,* as well as Ivo Caprino's film about the Bergen Aquarium. Not only that, you can attend concerts and folkloric musical performances.

Nordnesbakken 4. ✆ **55-55-71-71.** www.akvariet.com. Admission NOK150 adults, NOK100 children, NOK400 family ticket (slightly cheaper in off-season). May–Aug daily 9am–7pm; Sept–Apr daily 10am–6pm. Bus: 11 from the Fish Market.

Bergen Kunstmuseum (Bergen Art Museum) ★★★ This ever-expanding art museum exhibits one of the most impressive collections of paintings in Norway. In the tri-level Lysverk Building overlooking Lille Langegard Lake, the collection consists of more than 9,000 works of art.

Bergen Billedgalleri is devoted to Norwegian and international art from the 13th to 20th centuries. The collection is known for its magnificent **Greek and Russian icons ★** from the 1300s and its **Dutch paintings ★** from the 1700s. Seek out, in particular, *Birch in the Storm,* a famous painting by J. C. Dahl, as well as *Vardøhus Fortress,* by Peder Balke. As for the gallery's **modern art** collection, there is a bit of camp, as in their display of poetry and an exhibition by Yoko Ono, as well as Bjørn Carlsen's mixed-media piece, *Mother, I Don't Want to Die in Disneyland.* The photography of Tom Sandberg confirms his reputation as one of Scandinavia's greatest photographers.

The impressive Rasmus Meyer Collection features paintings from the 18th century up to 1915. It's worth the visit here to gaze upon **Edvard Munch's masterpieces ★★**, especially the dark trio *The Woman in Three Stages, Melancholy,* and *Jealousy.* Some of the best paintings of the **Norwegian Romantics** also hang here, including works by J. C. Dahl, Harriet Backer, and Nikolai Astrup, the latter known for depicting dramatic landscapes in western Norway. In addition to the art, note the decorated ceiling and wall painting in the **Blumenthal Room ★** from the 18th century.

The greatest **modern art ★★** in western Norway is found in the Stenersen Collection. Most of the work, by Norwegian and international artists, is from the 20th century and includes northern Europe's most extensive collection of **Paul Klee's works ★★**. Nearly every modern art master you could think of is here: Picasso, Edvard Munch once again, Joan Miró, Vassily Kandinsky, and Max Ernst, as well as many lesser-known artists.

What to See & Do in Bergen

Akvariet **1**
Bergen Kunstmuseum **13**
Bergen Museum **15**
Bergens Sjøfartsmuseum **16**
Bryggen **7**
Bryggens Museum **6**
Damsgård Hovedgård **20**
Det Hanseatiske Museum **8**
Domkirken **11**
Fantoft Stavkirke **19**
Fisketorget **9**
Fløibanen **10**
Gamle Bergen **3**
Gamlehaugen **19**
Håkonshallen **4**
Lepramuseet i Bergen **12**
Mariakirke **5**
Mount Ulriken **17**
Museet Lysøen/Ole Bull's Villa **19**
Norges Fiskerimuseum **2**
Rosenkrantztårnet **4**
Siljustøl **18**
Theta Museum **7**
Troldhaugen **20**
Vestlandske Kunstindustrimuseum **14**

(i) Information

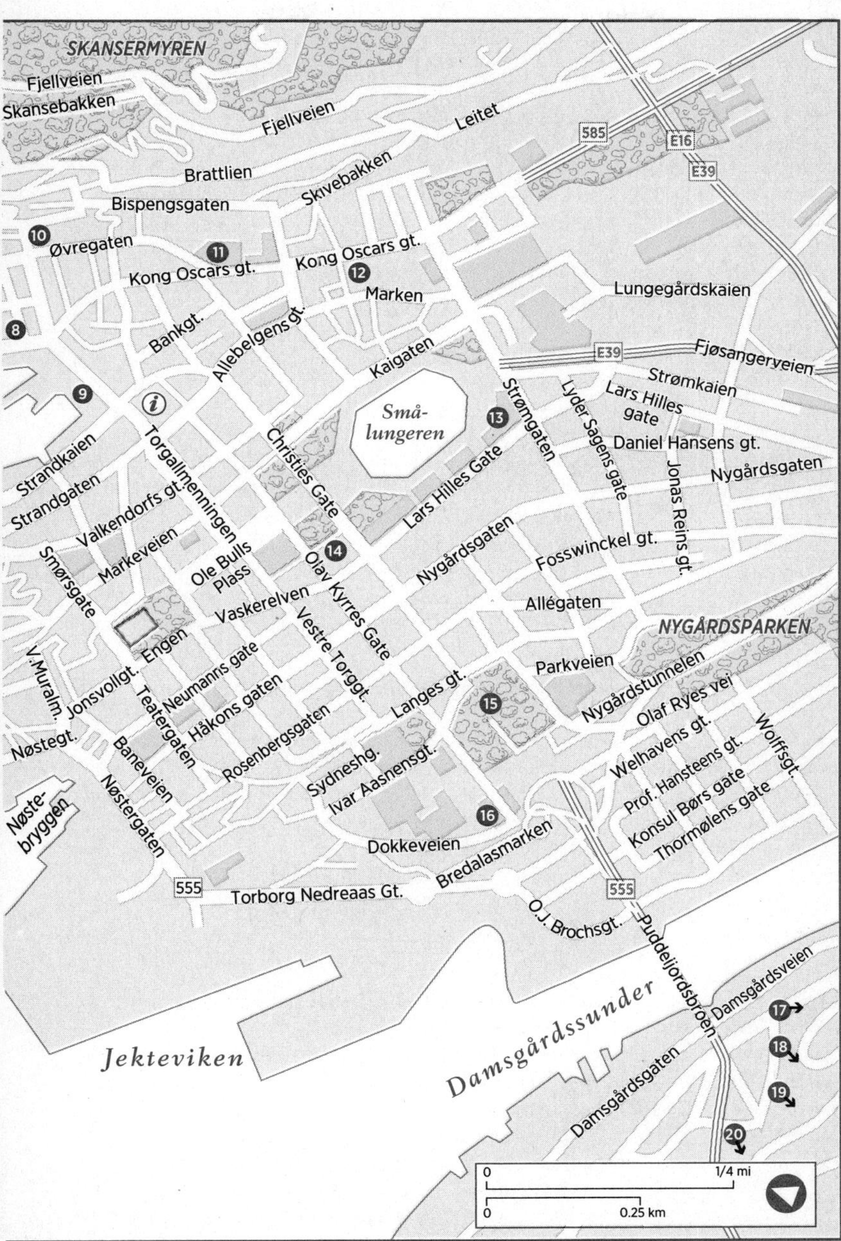
SKANSERMYREN
Fjellveien
Skansebakken
Fjellveien
Leitet
Brattlien
Bispengsgaten
Skivebakken
585
E16
E39
Øvregaten
Kong Oscars gt.
Kong Oscars gt.
Marken
Lungegårdskaien
Bankgt.
Allebelgens gt.
Kaigaten
E39
Fjøsangerveien
Strømkaien
Lars Hilles gate
Små-lungeren
Strømgaten
Lyder Sagens gate
Daniel Hansens gt.
Nygårdsgaten
Jonas Reins gt.
Strandkaien
Strandgaten
Torgallmenningen
Christies Gate
Lars Hilles Gate
Valkendorfs gt.
Markeveien
Ole Bulls Plass
Olav Kyrres Gate
Nygårdsgaten
Fosswinckel gt.
Smørsgate
Vaskerelven
Vestre Torggt.
Allégaten
NYGÅRDSPARKEN
V.Muralm.
Jonsvollgt.
Engen
Neumanns gate
Teatergaten
Håkons gaten
Rosenbergsgaten
Langes gt.
Parkveien
Nygårdstunnelen
Olaf Ryes vei
Nøstegt.
Baneveien
Sydneshg.
Ivar Aasnensgt.
Welhavens gt.
Wolffsgt.
Prof. Hansteens gt.
Konsul Børs gate
Thormølens gate
Nøste-bryggen
Nøstergaten
Dokkeveien
Bredalasmarken
555
Torborg Nedreaas Gt.
555
O.J. Brochsgt.
Puddefjordsbroen
Damsgårdsveien
Damsgårdssunder
Damsgårds gate
Jekteviken
Damsgårdsgaten
0
1/4 mi
0
0.25 km

Rasmus Meyers Allé 3-9. ✆ **55-56-80-00.** www.kunstmuseene.no. Combined ticket to all 3 galleries NOK60 adults, NOK40 students. Mid-May to mid-Sept daily 9am–7pm; mid-Sept to mid-May daily 11am–7pm. Bus: 1, 5, or 9.

Bergen Museum ★ This outstanding collection holds everything from Henrik Ibsen mementos and whale skeletons to beautiful Viking Age objects and Egyptian mummies, along with some of the best church and folk art in Norway. Part of the University of Bergen, this two-in-one museum consists of Cultural History and Natural History departments. Founded in 1825, the museum formed the nucleus of the university, launched in 1946 following the end of the Nazis occupation.

The Naturhistoriske Samlinger is filled with displays and exhibitions from the last ice age, including prehistoric fossils. However, visitors come here mainly to see the **whale collection ★**—northern Europe's largest collection—and the exhibits of snakes, Norwegian birds, and crocodiles (stuffed, fossilized, preserved in jars). The origins of the creatures in the collection range from Greenland to Africa. You can also visit a plant house and a botanical garden.

The Kulturhistoriske Samlinger features exhibitions and displays on art history, archaeology, and anthropology. For many, this is the best collection, covering everything from Egyptian mummies to "Ibsen in Bergen," which traces the writer's growth as a playwright during the 6 years he spent from 1851 to 1857 with the National Theater in Bergen. You'll also find the largest collection of **Norwegian church art ★** in the country, a display of delicate Viking jewelry, and exhibits devoted to such North American cultures as the Aleut and Inuit.

Cultural History Dept., Håkon Sheteligsplass 10; Natural History Dept., Muséplass 3. ✆ **55-58-29-20.** www.uib.no/bergenmuseum. Admission to both museums NOK50adults, NOK25 seniors, free for children & students. June 1–Aug Tues–Fri 10am–4pm, Sat–Sun 11am–4pm; off-season Tues–Fri 10am–3pm, Sat–Sun 11am–4pm. Bus: 2, 3, or 4.

Bergens Sjøfartsmuseum (Bergen Maritime Museum) Set in a scenic location in the middle of the University of Bergen's campus, this museum presents the history of maritime life and seafaring in western Norway. Because the Bergen Museum is so enthralling, this little museum is often overlooked. But if you're already on the campus of the university, it is well worth a look. Exhibits are arranged to offer you a good idea of the shipping industry's importance to port cities and—in a fascinating exhibit—Norway's role in World War II during the Nazi occupation. Displays include artfully arranged and crafted models of the Viking ships that terrorized Europe. Also on display are paintings and marine artifacts rescued from the North Sea.

Haakon Sheteligsplass 15. ✆ **55-54-96-00.** www.bsj.uib.no. Admission NOK30 adults, free for children 15 & under. Daily 11am–3pm. Bus: 2, 3, or 4.

Bryggens Museum This museum was built on the site of Bergen's earliest settlement. While digging into the 800-year-old foundations of the original building, builders uncovered a Pandora's Box of medieval tools, pottery, runic stones, and even ancient skulls. The items they dug up from 1955 to 1972 served to greatly enhance the museum's eventual collection. The museum also illustrates the daily and cultural life of Bergen in the Middle Ages. Call ahead to find out about its regularly changing exhibits, as well as its folk-music and dance performances (p. 294).

Dreggsallmenning 3, Bryggen. ✆ **55-58-80-10.** www.bymuseet.no. Admission NOK60 adults, free for children 15 & under. May–Aug daily 10am–5pm; Sept–Apr Mon–Fri 11am–3pm, Sat noon–3pm, Sun noon–4pm. Bus: 20, 21, 22, 23, 50, 70, 71, 80, or 90.

Damsgård Hovedgård ★ If you have to make choices, visit Edvard Grieg's beloved Troldhaugen. But if you can find the time, Damsgård Hovedgård is an absolute gem. This off-the-beaten-path European palace in miniature from 1770 is the finest example of 18th-century rococo timber architecture in western Norway. The roof is made of black glazed tiles from the Netherlands, a sign of grand extravagance employed in construction back then. In 1983, the municipality of Bergen acquired the house and its furnishings. The interior has been restored to show the original baroque coloring. After a visit inside, wander through the lavish **baroque rose gardens ★★**, with their ponds, Grecian sculpture, and flora in common use 2 centuries ago.

Alleen 29, Laksevåg. ✆ **55-94-08-70.** www.bymuseet.no. Admission NOK50, free for children 15 & under. May–Aug daily 11am–5pm (last tour 4pm). Closed Sept–Apr. Bus: 16 or 17. 3km (1¾ miles) west of Bergen on Rte. 582.

Det Hanseatiske Museum ★ In one of the best-preserved wooden buildings at Bryggen, this museum illustrates Bergen's commercial life on the wharf centuries ago. German merchants, representatives of the Hanseatic League, centered in Lübeck, lived in these medieval houses built in long rows up from the harbor. With dried cod, grain, and salt as articles of exchange, fishermen from northern Norway met German merchants during the busy summer season. Life was cold, dark, and grim for the German stockfish tradesmen who lived here in the remote regions of Norway during long, cold winters. Merchants weren't allowed to build fires for fear of setting all the wood-framed buildings along the wharf ablaze. The Black Death eventually swept through the region, destroying their monopoly on the trade. The museum is furnished with authentic articles dating from 1704.

Finnegårdsgaten 1A, Bryggen. ✆ **55-54-46-90.** www.museumvest.no. Admission May–Sept NOK50; Oct–Apr NOK30; year-round free for children 14 & under. June–Aug daily 9am–5pm; Sept–May Tues–Sat 11am–2pm. Bus: 20, 21, 22, 23, or 24.

Domkirken (Bergen Cathedral) For 9 centuries, this has been a place of worship, but it's amazing that the cathedral is here at all—after all, it's been burned down six times. The first stone church was built in the mid-12th century and dedicated to Olav the Holy, patron saint of Norway. By the 13th century, the Domkirke was in the hands of the Franciscan brothers. The fires that swept Bergen in 1248 and again in 1270 caused massive damage.

Under a grant from King Magnus ("the Lawmender"), the friars rebuilt their church in 1301. Regrettably, the massive fires of 1463 and 1488 again swept over the church. With the coming of the Reformation, the first Lutheran bishop claimed the old Franciscan church and turned it into the cathedral for Norway's oldest diocese. Unfortunately, two more fires destroyed the cathedral in 1623 and 1640. The present building dates from a major restoration in the 1880s, which saw the addition of beautiful stained-glass windows with biblical motifs. All that remains from the 13th century are the Gothic choir stalls and the foundations of the towers. Since the Battle of Bergen in 1665, a cannonball has been embedded in the west wall.

Kong Oscarsgate & Domkirkegate. ✆ **55-59-32-70.** Free admission. Late May to Aug Mon–Sat 11am–5pm, Sun 10am–1pm; off-season Tues–Fri 11am–2pm, Sat 11am–3pm, Sun 10am–2pm. Bus: 1, 5, or 9.

Fantoft Stavkirke ★ This is a rare opportunity to see what a wooden stave church looked like, even if it is just a mocked-up version. In the Middle Ages,

Norway had a total of 750 stave churches, but only 28 are still standing. Architecturally, these churches were unique, with their "dragon heads," carved doorways, and staves or vertical planks. The original stave church, constructed in Fortun in Sogn in 1150, was in 1883 moved to Fantoft, 5km (3 miles) south of Bergen. Regrettably, a self-styled Satanist burned it to the ground on June 6, 1992. Black-metal musician Varg Vikernes served 16 years in prison (he was released in 2009) for arson of the church—and the murder of a bandmate. The present church is an exact duplicate of the original. Adjacent to the church is a large cross from 1050, which was moved here from Sola in Rogaland.

Fantoftveien 46, Paradis. ✆ **55-28-07-10.** Admission NOK40 adults, NOK20 students, NOK15 children. May 15–Sept 15 daily 10:30am–6pm. Bus no. 50 from Bergen bus station, departures every 20 min. for the 10-min. jaunt to Fantoft, plus a 10-min. walk up the hill.

Fisketorget (Fish Market) ★ Always big on social programs, Norway enforced a law at the Fisketorget between 1630 and 1911: Rich Bergen citizens living within a 40-km (25-mile) range of the market were forbidden to purchase fish there. Only the poor were allowed to buy goods, and for daily house use only. Presumably, rich people could afford to go further afield to dine on a seafood meal. Now that it is open to everyone in Bergen, head to this bustling market at lunchtime for freshly opened oysters, a real treat from the sea. Another popular option is freshly boiled shrimp, to eat as you take in views of the waterfront. Some vendors also offer a baguette for your lunch—none better than smoked salmon with some mayonnaise and fresh cucumber. The market is a photographer's delight, with fishermen in their Wellington boots, and weatherbeaten fishmongers (often women) in long, dirty white aprons as the catch of the day is hauled in.

Bergen Harbor. Free admission. June–Aug daily 7am–7pm; Sept–May Mon–Sat 7am–4pm. Bus: 1, 5, or 9.

Fløibanen A short walk from the Fish Market (p. 282) is the station where the funicular heads up to Fløien (Mount Floyen), the most famous of Bergen's seven hills. The nearly century-old funicular was recently upgraded with new cable cars to haul visitors to the 320-m (1,050-ft.) summit. Today two modern carriages featuring glass ceilings and panoramic windows carry visitors to the top to take in the spectacular vista. Once there, you can take one of several paths that provide easy walks through lovely wooded terrain with views of lakes and mountains in the distance. In summer, you can order lunch at the restaurant here, which is open daily and includes a souvenir shop.

Vetrlidsalm 23A. ✆ **55-33-68-00.** www.floibanen.com. Round-trip NOK70, NOK35 children 4–15. April–Aug Mon–Fri 7:30am–midnight, Sat 8am–midnight; Sun 9am–midnight; Sept–Mar Mon–Thurs 7:30am–11pm; Fri 7:30am–11:30pm; Sat 8am–11:30pm, Sun 9am–11pm.

Gamle Bergen ★ This museum offers a rare look at small-town life during the 18th and 19th centuries with various antique dwellings and shops, a bakery, and even the town's local barber and dentist. This collection of more than 40 wooden houses is set in a picture-perfect park. The Old Town is complete with streets, an open square, and narrow alleyways, and some of the interiors are exceptional, including a merchant's living room in the typical style of the 1870s, with padded sofas, heavy curtains, and potted plants. Its old-fashioned, clapboard-sided architecture and renditions of 19th-century domestic life evoke scenes from Ibsen's *A Doll's House.*

Elsesro & Sandviken. ✆ **55-39-43-00.** www.bymuseet.no. Admission NOK50, free for children 15 & under, & students. Houses mid-May to Aug only, guided tours daily on the hour 10am–5pm. Park & restaurant daily noon–5pm. Bus: 20, 23, or 24 from city center (every 10 min.).

Gamlehaugen The king's official Bergen residence was originally occupied in the 19th century by Christian Michelsen, one of the first prime ministers of Norway after it separated from Denmark in 1814. It's open for just a short time each summer, and a visit here will give you a good sense of how the upper class lived at the beginning of the 19th century. The wood-sided villa lies about 10km (6¼ miles) south of the city, overlooking the Nordåsvannet estuary. The interior is a happy marriage of the once-fashionable National Romanticism combined with elegant Art Nouveau. Its gardens are open to the public all year. Don't expect the hoopla you might see at Buckingham Palace—the venue is understated, discreet, and (probably for security reasons) aggressively mysterious. The building was under renovation at press time, but is due to reopen in 2011.

Fjøsanger. ✆ **55-92-51-20.** www.gamlehaugen.no. Admission NOK50, NOK25 children 4–15. June–Aug Tues–Sun noon–3pm; Sept–May Sat–Sun noon–3pm. Guided tours in English June–Aug Tues–Sun at noon. Bus: Fjøsanger-bound bus 60 from the central bus station.

Håkonshallen (Håkon's Hall) Built of local stone, this is the largest secular medieval hall still standing in Norway, though its heyday is long gone. Erected between 1247 and 1261, it took its name from the man who commissioned it, King Håkon Håkonsson, and once served as the political and social center of the 13th-century kingdom of Norway. It was used in 1261 for the wedding and coronation of King Magnus Lagabøter, Håkon's son and co-ruler. By 1520, it had degenerated into a storage depot. Don't expect any great array of artistic treasures here, as the hall has had a rough life. It was damaged in a 1944 fire caused by the explosion of an overloaded Nazi munitions ship, and was later restored. (The explosion damaged nearly every building in Bergen and sent the ship's anchor flying almost to the top of a nearby mountain.) Guided tours are conducted hourly; call in advance to confirm. The Great Hall is also used for concerts and performances.

Bergenhus, Bradbenken. ✆ **55-31-60-67.** www.bymuseet.no. Admission NOK50 adults, NOK25 children. Mid-May to Aug daily 10am–4pm; Sept to mid-May daily noon–3pm (Thurs until 6pm). Closed various days in May. Bus: 5.

Lepramuseet i Bergen (Leprosy Museum) Visiting a former lepers' colony might not be your idea of a hot time, but this museum of early medicine has much to fascinate visitors—and not just those who are doctors. Exhibits focus on the country's contribution to leprosy research, especially the work of Dr. Armauer Hansen, who gave his name to Hansen's disease, the modern name for leprosy. In the Middle Ages, St. Jørgens Hospital here was a hospital for lepers, and many of the oldest buildings date from the beginning of the 1700s. The museum also exhibits the Bergen Collection of the History of Medicine.

Kong Oscarsgate 59. ✆ **55-96-11-55.** www.bymuseet.no. Admission NOK50, free for children & students. May 21–Sept 3 daily 11am–3pm. Closed Sept 4–May 20. Bus: 20, 21, 22, 23, or 24.

Mariakirke (St. Mary's Church) ★★ The oldest building in Bergen, perhaps dating from the first half of the 12th century, is also one of the most outstanding examples of Romanesque architecture in Norway. The oldest ornament in the church is the altar, but the **pulpit ★★** is the richest example of baroque decorative

GRIEG: THE CHOPIN OF THE NORTH

"I am sure my music has the taste of codfish in it," Edvard Grieg, Norway's greatest composer, once wrote. Born in Bergen in 1843, Grieg was the son of a salt-fish merchant. Like Ole Bull (p. 287), Grieg became a towering figure in Norwegian Romanticism.

Sent to the Music Conservatory in Leipzig from 1858 to 1862, Grieg fell under the influence of German Romanticism but returned to Oslo (then known as Christiania) with a determination to create national music for his homeland. Back home he fell heavily under the influence of his country's folk music and "fjord melodies."

When Grieg and the great Norwegian writer Bjørnstjern Bjørnson met, the latter realized he had found someone to compose music for his poems. Their most ambitious project was a national opera based on the history of the Norwegian king Olav Trygvason.

Meeting Henrik Ibsen for the first time in 1866—not in Norway but in Rome—Grieg agreed to compose the music for Ibsen's dramatic poem *Peer Gynt.* In 1868, he finished *Piano Concerto in A Minor,* his first great masterpiece. In 1888 and 1893, Grieg published *Peer Gynt Suite I* and *II,* which remain, around the world, extremely popular orchestral pieces to this day. But Bjørnson was furious that Grieg had teamed up with Ibsen, and the work on their national opera never came to fruition.

During the Nazi occupation, the composer Harald Sæverud (1897–1992) wrote a trio of "war-symphonies" and one called *Ballad of Revolt,* in honor of the Norwegian resistance. After the war, he composed music for Henrik Ibsen's dramatic poem, *Peer Gynt.* Twelve concert pieces extracted from this work are among the most frequently played orchestral works today.

In 1874, Grieg returned to Bergen, where he created such fabled compositions as *Ballad in G Minor, Norwegian Dances for Piano, Mountain Thrall,* and the *Holberg Suite.* He'd married Nina Hagerup, the Norwegian soprano, and together they moved into Troldhaugen, their coastal home, today one of Bergen's major attractions.

It was at Troldhaugen that Grieg created such works as *Piano Sonata for Violin and Piano in C Minor,* the *Haugtussa Songs,* and *Norwegian Peasant Dances.* His last work was *Four Psalms,* based on a series of Norwegian religious melodies.

In spite of poor health and the loss of one lung, Grieg maintained a grueling schedule of appearances on the Continent. But he always came back to Troldhaugen for the summer. Eventually, on September 4, 1907, as he prepared to leave for yet another concert, this time in Leeds, England, he collapsed at the Hotel Norge in Bergen and died in hospital.

art in the country. A gift from Hanseatic merchants, it has carved figures depicting everything from *Chastity* to *Naked Truth.* Unfortunately the church is under extensive renovation and will remain closed until 2015.

Dreggen. ✆ **55-31-59-60.**

Mount Ulriken ★★ For the grandest view in western Norway, visit Bergen's highest mountaintop, at 643m (2,110 ft.). The **Ulriksbanen** (✆ **53-64-36-43;** www.ulriken643.no), the most famous cable car in western Norway, runs up the mountain from Landaas, 5km (3 miles) southeast of the center of Bergen. From the uppermost station of the cable car, you can walk for 4 to 5 hours north along a well-trodden track to the top of the Fløibanen funicular railway (see above), with scenic vistas in all directions. This is my favorite walk in the Bergen area.

Landaas. ✆ **55-55-20-00** for the cable car. www.ulriken643.no/en/, Return fare NOK145, NOK180 children 4–15. Combined cable car & shuttle bus NOK245 adults, half-price children ages 4–15. Sept–Apr shuttle bus departs from Bergen tourist office every half-hour 9am–5pm; May–Aug 9am–9pm. Cable car operates several times an hour in summer, daily 9am–9pm; off-season cable car operates 3–4 times an hour, daily 10am–5pm.

Norges Fiskerimuseum (Norwegian Fisheries Museum) This museum is targeted at fishing aficionados, though it does manage to stir up some controversy, as does Norway itself, with its exhibits on whaling and sealing. (Norway, along with Japan, has been severely criticized by the environmental community for killing endangered whales.) The nature and management of fisheries over the past 150 years are presented in detail, as are exhibits on the sea and its vast, though diminishing, resources. The processing of fish, such as the vital cod, is explained along with exportation methods.

Bontelabo 2. ✆ **55-32-27-10.** www.museumvest.no. Admission NOK40, NOK20 students & seniors, free for children 15 & under. May 15–Sept 15 Mon–Fri 9am–4pm, Sat–Sun 10am–4pm; Sept 16–May 14 Mon–Fri 10am–4pm, Sun 11am–4pm. Bus: 1, 5, or 9.

Rosenkrantztårnet (Rosenkrantz Tower) The Middle Ages live on here, and the aura is rather spooky and foreboding, but the stunning **panorama ★★** of Bergen's seaport is worth the trek. This defense, residential tower, and dungeon were constructed in the 13th century by the governor of Bergenhus (Bergen Castle), Erik Rosenkrantz. Two older structures were incorporated into the tower: King Magnus the Lawmender's keep, from about 1260, and Jørgen Hanssøn's keep, from about 1520. It was rebuilt and enlarged in the 1560s. There are guided tours of the tower and Håkonshallen (see above) about every hour.

Bergenhus, Bradbenken. ✆ **55-31-43-80.** Admission NOK50 adults, NOK25 children. May 15–Aug 31 daily 10am–4pm; Sept 1–May 14 Sun noon–3pm. Bus: 1, 5, or 9.

Siljustøl ★ Although most visitors rightly flock to Edvard Grieg's former home at Troldhaugen, Bergen had an important composer of its own: **Harald Sæverud.** Born here in 1897, the young composer studied first in his hometown before moving to Berlin, where he met and worked with some of the greatest of the 20th-century German composers. Upon returning to Bergen in 1934, he married the wealthy American-born heiress, Marie Hvoslef.

The money for constructing his home, Siljustøl, was a wedding gift to the composer and his new bride. The imposing estate—set on 70 beautiful hectares (173 acres)—was the largest private home in Norway, with 63 rooms, upon its completion in 1939. The house is made of wood and natural stone, and has six toilets, although the composer preferred the more old-fashioned plumbing of Norway—a hole in the floor.

In 1986, Sæverud became the official composer for the Bergen International Festival (p. 40). He lived in Bergen until his death in 1992, at the age of 95. After being given a state funeral, he was buried at Siljustøl, where his gravesite is a pilgrimage destination for fans.

Rådal (near Rte. 582 to the airport), 12km (7½ miles) north of the city center. ✆ **55-92-29-92.** Admission NOK60, free for children 15 & under. Late June–late Sept Sat–Sun noon–4pm. Closed late Sept–late June. Bus: 20 from Bergen bus station.

Theta Museum ★ 🎁 Don't miss this museum if you are fascinated by World War II intrigue, sabotage, and mystery. This little cell was the seat of clandestine Bergen resistance during the darkest days of the Nazi takeover of the city in World War II. It is also Norway's tiniest museum. The one room operated until 1942, when it was discovered by the Germans, who destroyed it. The present room is a reconstruction. The freedom fighters called themselves the "Theta Group," and their aim was to establish contact and communication with the Norwegian government in exile in England. The museum is also the hardest to find in Bergen. Look for a carved depiction of a unicorn placed prominently on the facade of an old building directly fronting the quay of Bryggen. Then make a right, walking away from the water down a narrow alleyway that runs perpendicular to the waterfront, until you see a sign directing you to the museum on the third floor. The building stands at the entrance to Enhjørningsgarden.

Enhjørningsgarden. ✆ **55-55-20-80.** Admission NOK20 adults, NOK5 children. Mid-May to mid-Sept Tues & Sat–Sun 2–4pm. Bus: 1, 5, or 9.

Troldhaugen (Trolls' Hill) ★★★ This can be the most romantic setting in Norway if you arrive as Edvard Grieg's music is drifting up from a summer concert in the 200-seat Troldsalen, a concert hall on the grounds. This Victorian house, in beautiful rural surroundings on Lake Nordås, was Grieg's summer villa and the site where he composed many of his famous works. The house still contains his furniture, paintings, and other mementos. His Steinway grand piano is frequently used at concerts given here during the annual Bergen International Festival (p. 40), and at Troldhaugen's summer concerts. Grieg and his wife, Nina, are buried in a cliffside grotto on the estate.

Troldhaugveien 65, Hop. ✆ **55-92-29-92.** Admission NOK60 adults, free for children 15 & under. May–Sept daily 9am–6pm; Oct–Apr 10am–4pm. Bus 20, 23, 24, or 50. Take the bus south toward Nesttun, get off at the Hopsbraoen exit, turn right & follow a well-marked path to Troldhaugen (15-min. walk).

Vestlandske Kunstindustrimuseum (Western Norway Museum of Applied Art) ★★ 🎁 Stumble into this museum on a rainy day in Bergen to kill some time—you'll come away singing its praises. The various displays span 5 centuries, the most intriguing of which are devoted to the **Art of China ★★★**. This is one of the largest collections of Chinese applied art outside China itself. A feature is a series of huge marble Buddhist temple sculptures. Even an Asian emperor would be impressed by the silk robes embroidered with dragons and the wealth of jade, exquisite porcelain, rare textiles, and delicate paintings. Other treasures include **Ole Bull's violin ★★**, made in 1562 by the Italian master Saló, with the head of an angel carved on it by Benvenuto Cellini. There is also an impressive collection of Bergen silverware. The Bergen silversmiths of the 17th and 18th centuries were celebrated for their heavy but elaborate baroque designs. The collection of tankards, for example, is stunning, most of them embossed with floral motifs, others inlaid with silver coins.

Permanenten, Nordahl Bruns Gate 9. ✆ **55-33-66-33.** Admission NOK50, free for children 15 & under. May 15–Sept 14 daily 11am–5pm; Sept 15–May 14 Tues–Sun noon–4:30pm. Bus: 2, 3, or 4.

OLE BULL: ROMANTIC musician & PATRIOT

One of the most colorful characters in the history of western Norway was Ole Bull (1810–70), the founder of Norway's National Theater and a virtuoso violinist. Leading one of the most remarkable lives of the 19th century, he was not only a celebrated composer but a fervent Utopian socialist and an ambassador for Norwegian culture on his frequent international concerts. He became friends with Liszt, Schumann, Longfellow, Ibsen, and Hans Christian Andersen, among other celebrated men of the day. Bull, noted for both his personal sense of theatrics and his ardent sense of Norwegian nationalism, had a profound influence on Grieg and his music. Bull's best-known musical composition is *Saeterjentens Sondag* for violin and piano.

Born in Bergen, Bull was immediately recognized as a child prodigy. Amazingly, he joined the Bergen Philharmonic Orchestra when he was only 8 years old. One of the great violin virtuosos of all time, a sort of Victorian Mantovani, he won fans in such diverse places as the United States, Cuba, Moscow, and Cairo. He almost single-handedly rekindled an interest in Norwegian folk music, both in Norway and abroad. Over the years, the people of Norway began to regard him as a national symbol.

After his first wife, a French woman, died, Ole Bull married Sara Thorp, of Madison, Wisconsin, and together they built a summer villa at Lysøen in 1872. The strikingly handsome musician let his hyperactive imagination run wild as he created an architectural fantasy he called "Little Alhambra," with its Russian onion dome, pierced-wood Moorish arches, arabesque columns, and elegant trelliswork. It was in Lysøen that he died in 1880. The last of the great Norwegian Romanticists, he was given one of the best-attended funerals in Norway.

Visitors today wander across his "fairytale" 70-hectare (173-acre) property, with its romantic paths studded with gazebos and white shell sand. In the native pine forest, Ole Bull added exotic trees and bushes from all over the world that would grow in Bergen's chilly clime.

You can also see a statue and fountain dedicated to this virtuoso performer on Ole Bulls Plass in the heart of Bergen.

Lysøen

Museet Lysøen/Ole Bull's Villa This villa and concert hall on the nearby island of Lysøen, 26km (16 miles) south of Bergen, were built in 1872–73 for the world-famous violin virtuoso and Norwegian national hero Ole Bull (see box, "Ole Bull: Romantic Musician & Patriot," below). The building, now a national monument, is preserved as it was when the musician died in 1880. It is an architectural fantasy of the 19th century, with a dome, a curved staircase, cutwork trim, and gingerbread gables. Bull built 13km (8 miles) of romantic trails that meander around the island, and, if time remains, you may want to walk some of them, following in Ole Bull's footsteps.

Lysøen. ✆ **56-30-90-77.** Admission NOK30, NOK10 children 4–15. Guided tours mid-May to Aug Mon–Sat noon–4pm, Sun 11am–5pm; Sept Sun noon–4pm. Closed Sept–early May. Drive or take a bus (from platform 20 at the Bergen bus station, marked FANA-OS-MILDE) to Sørestraumen on Rte. 553. Take the Ole Bull ferry from Sørestraumen's Buena quay (round-trip fare NOK50 adults, NOK30 children); there is also a regular ferry from the city center (NOK240). Ferry schedules coincide with opening hours; boats return to the mainland hourly, the last one a few minutes after the museum closes.

Organized Tours

For tour information and tickets, contact the **Bergen tourist office,** Vågsallmenningen 1 (✆ **55-55-20-00**). The most popular (and my most highly recommended) tour is the 3-hour city bus tour. It departs daily at 11am from the tourist office and covers the major attractions, including Troldhaugen and "Old Bergen." It operates May to September and costs NOK300, NOK200 for children 4 to 15.

WALKING TOUR: HISTORIC BERGEN

START: **Fish Market.**

FINISH: **Western Norway Museum of Applied Arts.**

TIME: **1 hour.**

BEST TIME: **Any day between 8am and 5pm (when it's not raining, of course).**

WORST TIME: **When cruise ships anchor.**

1 Fisketorget (Fish Market)

At the turn of the 19th century, this broad esplanade at the innermost reaches of Bergen's harbor teemed with fishermen selling their catch, and reeked of fish blood, guts, and carcasses. Today, in a much-sanitized format, it's a venue for crafts, knitwear, carved Siberian and Sami souvenirs, and, to a lesser degree, fish and seafood.

From here, walk west along the Strandkaien, keeping the harborfront on your right, making a small detour inland at the Strandkaien's end. Within a block, at an angular jut in the avenue known as the Strandgaten, you'll see the solid, partially fortified walls of the:

2 City Wall Gate

This gate was built in 1550 as a checkpoint in a once-contiguous wall that encircled Bergen. Today it stands isolated among the newer buildings and broad avenues that surround it on all sides. There's an inexpensive clothing outlet on its ground floor and an obscure, rarely visited museum (the Buekorps Museum) upstairs.

From here, walk west along Strandgaten, noting the many shops that line the street on either side. Within about 5 minutes you'll reach one of Bergen's most visible houses of worship, the:

3 Nykirken

Noteworthy features of this church are the Danish-inspired mansard roof from around 1761, the copper-capped baroque spire, and its location overlooking the entrance to Bergen's harbor.

From here, walk steeply uphill for a block along the Nykirkeallmenningen, and turn left into the narrow confines of cobbled Ytre Markeveien, noting the antique wood-sided houses on either side. Walk four short blocks to the Kippersmauet and turn left, descending a steep, cobbled alleyway where, at nos. 23 and 24, there was a disastrous fire in 2001. (Two 14-year-old boys are credited with detecting the fire and banging on the doors of neighboring houses, preventing the entire wood-built neighborhood from burning to the ground.)

A Walking Tour of Historic Bergen

4 Café Retro

Klosteret 16 (© 55-31-16-16), is loaded with the kitsch and artful debris of the age of Sputnik, with shelves filled with 1950s-era toasters, fans, and ashtrays (all of which are for sale as art objects in their own right). It sells sandwiches made from "ecological" (organic) breads, priced from NOK45, as well as coffee, tea, soft drinks, and pastries. It's open Monday to Friday 10am to 5pm, Saturday 11am to 5pm, and Sunday noon to 5pm.

Now retrace your steps uphill back to the Ytre Markeveien, and then turn right onto the big square (Holbergsallmenningen), originally conceived as a firebreak. Cross the wide boulevard (Klosteret) and walk east for one short block, turning right (sharply downhill) on the extremely narrow cobbled alleyway identified within a few steps as the:

5 Knøsesmauet

You'll immediately find yourself hemmed in, somewhat claustrophobically, by the antique wooden houses of a district known as the Klosteret. It's composed of compact and, in most cases, impeccably well-maintained wooden houses pressed up against one another. Even today, the risk of fire among the brightly painted historic buildings is a much-feared issue. Especially vulnerable are what local firefighters refer to as "chimney houses"—where cement, stucco, or ornamental masonry facades have been added to otherwise mostly wooden buildings.

Continue descending the Knøsesmauet, bypassing brightly painted wooden houses, some fronted by tiny gardens. Cross the Skottogaten and continue downhill. Turn left onto St. Hansestredet. (St. Hanse is the patron saint of the summer solstice, often invoked in midsummer with bouquets of flowers like those that adorn the houses along this street.) St. Hansestredet, within two short blocks, merges with the busy traffic of the Jonsvollsgaten, a wide commercial boulevard. Walk east for about 3 minutes, cross over the Teatergaten, and continue east along Engen, the eastward extension of the Jonsvollsgaten. On your left rises the stately Art Nouveau bulk of the:

6 National Theater

This arts complex is rich with memories. It was established by violinist Ole Bull, who envisioned it as a showcase for Norwegian-language drama and music. Today performances of Broadway-style musicals alternate with more serious, mostly Norwegian works. Details to look for inside and out include life-size statues of Bjørnstjern Bjørnson, author of Norway's national anthem, and Henrik Ibsen, who served as the theater's director for 5 years. (The stern and magisterial granite sculpture of Ibsen, completed in 1982 and set into the lawns on the theater's eastern side, was considered so ugly that it remained in storage for many years.) On the tree-shaded western side, just outside the entrance, is a flattering likeness, in bronze, of Nordahl Grieg, often referred to as the Norwegian Winston Churchill because he warned of the Nazi menace before many of his colleagues in the Norwegian Parliament.

The theater's lobby survived a disastrous fire in 1916 and a direct hit by a Nazi bomb in 1944. Completely restored in the late 1990s, the lobby has an understated Art Nouveau style and portraits of great Norwegians lining its walls.

Now, with your back to the ornamental eastern side of the theater, walk east along the:

7 Ole Bulls Plass

Descend the gradual slope and note the grand commercial buildings that rise on either side. Broad and flanked by flower beds, restaurants, bars, and shops, it was originally laid out, in an era when virtually everything was made of wood, as a firebreak. Today it's an architectural showcase, named after Norway's first musical superstar.

Descend along the Ole Bulls Plass, past a violin-playing statue of the musical star himself. When the street opens onto the broad esplanade known as Olav Kyrres Gate, note on the right side the fin-de-siècle brick facade of the:

8 Vestlandske Kunstindustrimuseum (Western Norway Museum of Applied Arts)

The statue of a seated male lost in thought, set into a niche on the facade of the Western Norway Museum of Applied Art, commemorates the 19th-century painter J. C. Dahl. It was crafted by one of Norway's first widely celebrated female sculptors, Ambrosia Tønnesen. The abstract sculpture on the lawn in front of the museum, composed of a series of rainbow-colored concentric hoops, honors the early-20th-century Bergen-born composer Harald Sæverud.

OUTDOOR ACTIVITIES

FISHING In the region around Bergen, anyone can fish in the sea without restrictions. If you plan to fish in fresh water (ponds, streams, and most of the best salmon and trout rivers), you'll need a permit, which you can get from the local tourist office closest to where you intend to fish. The tourist office in Bergen does not sell permits. You'll also need the permission of the owner of the land on either side of the stream. The best fjord fishing, where you can angle for cod, mackerel, haddock, and coalfish, is offered by **Reisemål Ryfylke** (© **51-75-95-10;** www.ryfylke.com).

Information and fishing permits, which cost NOK105 to NOK170, are also available from the **Bergen Sportsfiskere (Bergen Angling Association),** Damsgaardsveien 106 (© **55-34-18-08;** www.bergensportsfiskere.no). It's open Monday to Friday 9am to 3pm.

GOLF The best golf course is **Meland Golf Club,** 36km (22 miles) north of Bergen at Frekhaug (© **56-17-46-00;** www.melandgolf.no). This is an 18-hole, par-73 golf course with a pro shop, lockers, and changing facilities. The setting is on 90 hectares (222 acres) in the midst of forests, lakes, and mountains. Greens fees are NOK400 Monday to Friday, NOK500 Saturday and Sunday.

SWIMMING The **Sentralbadet,** Theatergaten 37 (© **55-56-95-70**), has a heated indoor pool. An open-air pool whose season is limited to the fleeting Nordic summer is at **Nordnes Sjøbad,** in Nordnes, out toward the western tip of the southern side of Bergen's harbor. For hours, check with the Bergen tourist office (p. 259). At either pool, adults pay NOK58.

TENNIS **Paradis Sports Senter,** Highway R1, Paradis (© **55-91-26-00**), 6.5km (4 miles) south of Bergen, is the best place to get your game on. The club has five indoor courts, four squash courts, four badminton courts, a health club and gym, and a solarium. It's open Monday and Tuesday 8am to 10pm, Wednesday and Thursday 6:30am to 11pm, Friday 6:30am to 9pm, Saturday 9am to 5pm, and Sunday 11am to 9pm.

WALKING Only 10 minutes away from Bergen by funicular, several roads and footpaths wind around **Mount Fløien,** an unspoiled wood and mountain terrace with lakes and rivers. The **Bergen Touring Club,** Tverrgaten 4 (✆ **55-33-58-10**), arranges walking tours farther afield and supplies information on huts and mountain routes all over Norway. It also provides maps and advice on where to hike. The office is open Monday to Friday 10am to 3pm (Thurs until 5pm).

SHOPPING

Shoppers who live outside Scandinavia and spend more than NOK315 (or NOK285 in the case of food) in any shop bearing the TAX-FREE sign can receive a refund up to 19% of the purchase price when they leave Norway. See "Taxes," in chapter 16, for details.

The Shopping Scene

Bargain hunters head to the **Fisketorget (Fish Market) ★★**. Many local handicrafts from the western fjord district, including rugs and handmade tablecloths, are displayed here. This is one of the few places in Norway where bargaining is welcomed. The market keeps no set hours, but it is best visited June to August daily from 7am to 7pm, and September to May Monday to Saturday from 7am to 4pm. Take bus no. 1, 5, or 9.

HOURS Stores are generally open Monday to Friday from 9am to 4:30pm (until 7pm Thurs and sometimes Fri) and Saturday 9am to 3pm. Shopping centers outside the city are open Monday to Friday 10am to 8pm and Saturday 9am to 6pm. Some food stores stay open Monday to Friday until 8pm and Saturday until 6pm.

Shopping A to Z

ART GALLERIES

Hordaland Art Center & Café ☺ An artistic focal point of its historic neighborhood, this publicly funded art gallery puts on as many as 12 different art exhibitions each year. Originally built in 1742, it served as the local parish school for many years. A children's play area is on-site, and a cafe has pastries, sandwiches, and platters on offer. Klosteret 17, Nordnes. ✆ **55-90-85-90.** Tues–Sun noon–4pm (cafe open Sat–Sun). A 5-min. walk from Torgallmenningen.

FASHION

Kløverhuset ★★ Next to the Fish Market on the harbor, this four-story shopping center has been Bergen's largest and best fashion store since 1923. Bargains include moderately priced and attractively designed knit sweaters, gloves, and Sami jackets. Strandgaten 13–15. ✆ **55-31-37-90.** www.kloverhuset.com. Mon–Fri 9am–8pm, Sat 9am–6pm.

GLASSWARE & CERAMICS

Hjertholm ★★ One of the leading outlets for glassware and ceramics purchases much of its merchandise directly from artisans' studios. The quality goods include glassware, ceramics, pewter, wood, and textiles. Gift articles and souvenirs are also available. Olav Kyrres Gate 7. ✆ **55-31-70-27.** www.hjertholm.no. Mon–Fri 9am–9pm, Sat 9am–6pm.

Shopping Tour

Norway has a centuries-old tradition of crafts, which undoubtedly developed to help people pass the time during the cold, dark winters when farm families were more or less housebound for months. Some of the major crafts were woodcarving, weaving, and embroidery, and these skills live on today at many local artist and craft centers. Some of the best are in Hardanger (around the Hardangerfjord, near Bergen), Sogn (just north of the Sognefjord, also near Bergen), and Telemark (the district around Skien, within a day's drive from Oslo). For a true behind-the-scenes look, Five Stars of Scandinavia, 225A 93rd Avenue S.E., Tumwater, WA 98501 (✆ 800/722-4126; www.5stars-scandinavia.com), will set up a self-guided shopping tour for you, factoring in everything they know about local artisans.

Tilbords Interiør Bergen Storsenter ★★ This outlet has Bergen's best and most extensive collection of glassware, porcelain, and pottery. All the big names are here, including Arabia from Finland and Kosta Boda from Sweden, and even Wedgwood from England. Still, this is a true showcase of Scandinavian design. Much of the merchandise is made by local builders, and the glassware, ceramics, and pottery are of the highest quality. You'll want to pull up a big truck to the store. The price tags will restrain you, however. Torgallmenningen 8. ✆ **55-96-00-10.**

HANDICRAFTS

In and around **Bryggen Brukskunst ★★**, located in the restored Old Town near the wharf, many craftspeople have taken over old houses and ply ancient Norwegian trades. Crafts boutiques often display Bergen souvenirs, many based on designs 300 to 1,500 years old. For example, I purchased a reproduction of a Romanesque-style cruciform pilgrim's badge. Other attractive items are likely to include sheepskin-lined booties and exquisitely styled, hand-woven wool dresses.

Husfliden ★★ Since 1895, Husfliden has been the premier name in Norwegian handicrafts. Top-quality merchandise is sold here, especially hand-woven textiles. The Norwegian sweaters are among the best in town, and there is even a department for national costumes. Many items such as iron bowls and candlesticks are for table settings. Handmade pewter, wooden bowls, hand-woven rugs, and fireplace bellows are other useful items. Well-made, quality wooden toys are also sold here. Vågsallmenningen 3. ✆ **55-54-47-40.**

JEWELRY

Juhls' Silvergallery ★ 🎁 Next to the Radisson BLU Royal Hotel, along the harborfront, Juhls' displays Bergen's most unusual selection of quality jewelry. The designers take for their inspiration the constantly changing weather of the far north and, in their words, provide "a cultural oasis in a desert of snow." Bryggen. ✆ **55-32-47-40.** www.juhls.no. Mon–Fri 9am–8pm, Sat 9am–6pm, Sun 1am–7pm.

SHOPPING MALL

Galleriet ★ This is the most important shopping complex in central Bergen, with 70 stores offering tax-free shopping. Close to the Fish Market, it displays a wide array of merchandise and features summer sales and special exhibitions. It has several fast-food establishments, too. Torgallmenningen 8. ✆ **55-30-05-00.** www.galleriet.com.

SPORTSWEAR

G-Sport Gågaten This store has virtually everything you'd need for every sport available within Norway. The inventory changes radically throughout the seasons, with an emphasis on cycling and hiking in summer and downhill and cross-country skiing in winter. There are special high-energy food supplies (a tablespoon will give you the temporary strength of a gorilla) and high-tech outdoor gear, with a high price tag that reflects the newest trends in sportswear and rough-weather gear. Strandgaten 59. ✆ **55-23-22-22.** www.gsport.no. Mon–Fri 9am–5pm, Thurs 9am–7pm, Sun 10am–4pm.

BERGEN AFTER DARK

The Performing Arts

Grieghallen ★★★ The modern Grieg Hall, which opened in 1978, is Bergen's monumental showcase for music, drama, and a host of other cultural events. The stage is large enough for an entire grand opera production, and the main foyer comfortably seats 1,500 guests for lunch or dinner. Snack bars provide drinks and light snacks throughout the performances.

The Bergen Philharmonic Orchestra, founded in 1765, performs here from August to May, often on Thursday at 7:30pm and Saturday at 12:30pm. Its repertoire consists of classical and contemporary music, as well as visiting opera productions. International conductors and soloists perform periodically. ***Tip:*** Ticket prices on Thursday tend to be at the lower end of the price scale, and prices on Friday and Saturday tend to be at the upper end. Edvard Griegs Plass 1. ✆ **55-21-61-00.** www.grieghallen.no. Tickets NOK120–NOK470. Closed July. Bus: 2, 3, or 4.

National Theater ★★ September to June is the season for Norway's oldest theater, founded in the mid-19th century. It stages classical Norwegian and international drama, contemporary plays, and musical drama, as well as visiting opera and ballet productions. Engen 1. ✆ **55-54-97-00.** www.dns.no. Tickets NOK340. Bus: 2, 3, or 4.

Summer Cultural Entertainment

Bergen Folklore ★ The Bergen Folklore dancing troupe performs at the Bryggens Museum (p. 280) from early June to mid-August on Tuesday at 9pm. The program, which lasts about an hour, consists of traditional folk dances and music from rural Norway. Tickets are on sale at the tourist office and at the door. Bryggens Museum, Bryggen. ✆ **97-52-86-30.** Tickets NOK100 adults, free for children. Bus: 1, 5, or 9.

Films

Konsertpaleet, Neumannsgate 3, and **Magnus Barfot,** Magnus Barfotsgate 12 (**✆ 55-56-90-83**), show all films in their original language with subtitles. The earliest performances at both venues are at 11am, the latest at 11pm. Tickets usually cost NOK85.

The Club & Music Scene

Bryggen Piano Bar ★ This is one of Bergen's more elegant dance clubs, attracting a somewhat conservative crowd in their 40s and 50s. That seems to change a bit on Saturday with the arrival of noisy, fun-seeking 20-somethings who make the place more raucous and animated. Light meals are available, but most people just show up to drink. They also show larger sports matches. Cocktail prices begin at around NOK100, though this drops considerably during the regular happy hour. It's open Thursday to Saturday 10pm to 2:30am. In the Radisson BLU Royal Hotel, Bryggen. ✆ **95-10-22-22.** www.bryggenpianobar.no. Cover NOK75–NOK100, free to hotel guests. Bus: 1, 5, or 9.

Café Opera Built in the 1880s, this large stone-and-timber structure was originally a warehouse; today it functions as both a restaurant and a cafe. After the kitchen closes, it becomes an animated nightclub that's open Tuesday to Saturday 11am to 2:30am. On Tuesday night, there is an open jam session where musicians can entertain or poets can read. On other nights, DJs mix and blend disparate music, depending on their individual tastes. The cafe is host to international DJs and bands on most Fridays and Saturdays. The 20s and 30s crowd finds this to be one of the more entertaining joints after dark for drinking, talking, and flirting—but very few of them actually get up and dance. Engen 18. ✆ **55-23-03-15.** No cover. Bus: 2, 3, or 4.

Madam Felle Dark, woodsy-looking, and cozy, this is an animated and crowded pub with limited food service and live music that packs the place with 20- and 30-somethings 4 nights a week. On those nights (always Fri–Sat, plus 2 weeknights when the schedule changes frequently), live music plays between 9 and 11pm, with a cover charge that might be free or rise to anywhere between NOK80 and NOK280, depending on the season, the mood of the staff, and the reputation of the band that's playing that night. The pub is named after a strong-willed, early-20th-century matriarch who became a noted innkeeper at a spot near here, and who's something of a legend in Bergen. Bryggen. ✆ **55-54-30-58.** www.madamfelle.no. Bus: 20, 21, 22, 70, 80, or 90.

Rick's Café Sprawling and large enough to hold 1,800 raucous and slightly drunken persons at a time, this is a labyrinthine, multi-purpose spot for cabaret and comedy shows (there are two small stages for live performances), some serious drinking (on cold winter nights, things can get rather sudsy), or a friendly pick-up (no doubt encouraged by the bar's potent cocktails). Attracting a crowd of 20- to 40-somethings, it's open daily from 9am, remaining stalwartly open as a cafe throughout the day, then soldiering on as a bar and nightclub from around 5pm to around 2am, depending on business. After 10pm, as many as five separate bar areas dispense alcohol. Veiten 3. ✆ **55-55-31-31.** www.ricks.no. Cover NOK100. Bus: 1, 5, or 9.

Rubinen Rubinen is one of Bergen's most popular dance clubs, attracting an over-35 crowd of mostly married couples who come here to whirl their partners across the floor with great determination. It features all kinds of music, including country-and-western, rock 'n' roll, and occasional bouts of Latin, tango, and formal ballroom dancing. Drinks cost NOK80 to NOK130, depending on what's in them. It's open Wednesday to Saturday 10pm to 3:30am, with live music nightly. Rosenkrantzgate 7. ✆ **55-31-74-70.** Cover NOK90. Bus: 2, 3, or 4.

The Bar Scene

Altona Vinbar ★ This is one of the oldest, most deeply entrenched, and best-known bars in Bergen, boasting an association with the home of literary lion Ludvig Holberg during his years in Bergen. Some of the stone walls and the wooden ceiling are original, dating from the 1600s. Its walls are painted white and the bar is

The Brown Scene

What does a Norwegian mean when he refers to a "brown" nightclub? It's a raucous, boozy, semi-sleazy joint where off-duty prostitutes, bikers, harborfront riffraff, slumming suburbanites, business travelers on short-term leave from their spouses, and all manner of fringe society get together for a rollicking and booze-soaked good time. Don't say you haven't been forewarned.

decorated with modern sculptures. Patrons, ranging from 30 to 60 years old, come here to listen to the recorded classical music and enjoy the elegant drinks, including champagne, cognac, and the best Scotch whisky. It's open Monday to Thursday 6pm to 1am, Friday and Saturday 6pm to 2am. In the basement of the Augustin Hotel, Strandgaten 81. ✆ **55-30-40-72.** www.augustin.no. Bus: 2 or 4.

Baklommen This small and cozy bar, with its old Chesterfield chairs, is a quiet and romantic retreat, downstairs from the To Kokker restaurant. Despite the fact that increasing numbers of 20-somethings have been spotted here recently, a relatively mature crowd, ages 30 to 60, comes here to escape from a lot of the pub rowdiness of Bergen. In the heart of the Hanseatic Wharf, this bar plays recorded jazz music in the background. It has Hansa beer on tap from NOK52 and is open Tuesday to Thursday 6pm to 1am, Friday and Saturday until 2am. Enhjørninggården 3. ✆ **55-32-27-47.** Bus: 1, 5, or 9.

Dyvekes Vinkjeller A sense of spookiness permeates this cozy drinking den. In 1849, a famous Norwegian bandit (Gjest Baardsen, the "Robin Hood of Norway") drank himself to death here. Drinkers have since reported sightings of a young serving wench in 17th-century costume who takes drink orders from patrons and then disappears without bringing the desired quaffs. Come here for wine, priced from NOK65 to NOK220 per glass; beer; colorful patrons (both living and dead) in a wide age range; and a genuine sense of Norwegian history. It's open Sunday to Thursday 3pm to 1am, Friday and Saturday noon to 2am. Hollendergaten 7. ✆ **55-32-30-60.** www.dyvekes.no. Bus: 20, 21, or 22.

Fotballpuben This is the biggest sports pub in Bergen, a rocking and rolling, beer-soaked place with an undeniable affection for soccer and, to a lesser degree, rugby. Feel free to wander through this crowded establishment's labyrinth of inner chambers—joining a 20s-to-50s crowd—whose corners and edges are sometimes upholstered with vinyl padding (to protect inebriated sports fans?). Screens blow up the action whenever there's an intensely contested match. The staff prides itself on serving the cheapest beer in Bergen, from NOK38 to NOK59 per mug, depending on the time of day. It's open daily 9am to 2:30am (Sun from noon). Vestre Torgate 9. ✆ **55-33-66-61.** www.fotballpuben.no. Bus: 1 or 9.

Kontoret (The Office) The most frequented pub in the city center, the Kontoret lies adjacent, through a connecting door, to the Dickens restaurant, where platters of rib-sticking English food cost from NOK149 to NOK169. In the Kontoret, the decor captures the feel of an office from the early 1900s, replete with banged-up manual typewriters and oaken countertops that evoke the green eyeshades and ink-stained printing rituals of an earlier era. The local brew is called Hansa, a half-liter of which costs NOK60. It's open Sunday to Thursday 4pm to 12:30am, Friday and Saturday 4pm to 2am. 4 Kong Olav V Plass. ✆ **55-36-31-33.**

Smakverket Café You wouldn't expect such a hip nightclub and pub to be within an art museum, but in the case of this large, high-ceilinged cube of a room on the museum's rear side, that's exactly the case. Patrons in their 20s and 30s are drawn to the danceable music emerging from a DJ's station on one side; a bar at another end of the room serves beer and sandwiches, and electronic art in kaleidoscopic color is beamed against yet another. The cafe itself is open daily 11am to 5pm; the nightclub is open Saturday 10pm to 2:30am. Windows overlook the large, octagonal reflecting pool on the museum's back side. Pastas and salads cost from NOK90. In the Bergen Art Museum, Rasmus Meyers Allé 3 and 7. ✆ **92-24-91-04.** www.smakverket.no. Bus: 1, 5, or 9.

SIDE TRIPS FROM BERGEN

Sognefjord ★★★

If there's only room for one fjord in your future, make it Norway's longest and deepest fjord, **Sognefjord,** a geologic and panoramic marvel. The terrain soars upward from the watery depths of the North Atlantic, and many waterfalls punctuate its edges with spray. The best way to view the fjord involves a full-day jaunt that's possible only between May 18 and September 15. It combines self-guided travel by boat, bus, and rail. Details on this and other explorations by public transport are available from the Bergen tourist office (see "Visitor Information" in this chapter).

Norway in a Nutshell ★★★

Our most serious recommendation is to go for prolonged experiences in preference for "quickies." That said, no tour I've ever taken in Norway has the drama or excitement of this captivating 12-hour preview of the breadth and diversity of Norway's landscapes, encapsulating the majesty of fjords and of mountains that look like giant trolls.

There are several different transit options. The one most often recommended by Bergen's tourist office, and available year-round, starts at 8:40am at **Bergen**'s railway station. After a 2-hour train ride, you'll disembark at the mountaintop hamlet of **Myrdal,** where you can take in the natural wonders for about 20 minutes before boarding a cog railway for one of the world's most dramatic train rides. The trip down to the village of **Flåm,** a drop of 870m (2,850 ft.), takes an hour and passes roaring streams and seemingly endless waterfalls, at a gradient of roughly 1:18 for almost 80% of the line. It's one of the steepest train lines in the world.

After a 1-hour stopover in Flåm, where you can have lunch or take a brief hike, you'll board a fjord steamer for a ride along the Sognefjord, reaching the fjord-side town of Gudvangen after 2 hours. After 30 minutes in Gudvangen, you'll board a bus for the 75-minute ride to Voss. Here you'll spend 30 minutes before boarding a train for the 75-minute ride back to Bergen. Arrival is scheduled for 8:35pm.

Expect only a rushed overview of each town, as there is more scenery than you can digest in a 12-hour day. The round-trip fare, excluding meals, is NOK975, NOK500 for children 4 to 15, and free for accompanied children under 4. There are discounts for holders of Eurailpasses or Scanrail passes. For more information, contact the Bergen tourist office (p. 259) or **Fjord Tours** (✆ **81-56-82-22;** www.fjordtours.com).

12

THE WEST COAST FJORD COUNTRY

No place in all of Norway holds the enchantment of the fjord country, the single most intriguing region in all of the Scandinavian countries. It's such a superlative spot that *National Geographic* rated the Norwegian fjords as "the world's best travel destination."

Gouged out by glaciers, studded with deep valleys, and characterized by rolling fells and rugged mountain plateaus, the fjord country is a land of farmlands, blossoming orchards, small villages, cascading waterfalls, and Scandinavia's most complex geography. It's a place to slow down and take your time. Just getting from point to point is a bit of an endeavor—but, oh, those views along the way.

Norwegian fjords are narrow arms of the sea, snaking their way inland. It took roughly 3 million years to form the furrows and fissures that give western Norway its distinctive look. At some points the fjords become so narrow that a boat can hardly pass between the mountainsides. Fjords have been of enormous significance to Norwegians through the ages. They served as lifelines to those who settled in the harsh mountain landscape. Instead of building roads to each house and village, they used the easily accessible and navigable fjords. Thus, inland and coastal regions were linked together as the fjords enabled commodities to be transported to the old trading stations. Imagine how centuries ago people would once row across their local fjord in order to attend church on Sunday mornings.

Bergen is the best departure point for trips to the fjords: To the south lies the famous **Hardangerfjord** and to the north the **Sognefjord,** Norway's longest and deepest fjord, some 1,310m (4,290 ft.) deep and cutting 205km (127 miles) inland. Voss, about 1½ hours from Bergen, is a famous ski resort that is also well situated between both the Hardangerfjord and the Sognefjord.

We start in the towns around the Hardangerfjord—**Lofthus, Kinsarvik, Eidfjord,** and **Ulvik**—with a detour to **Voss,** and then move north to the towns around the Sognefjord, including **Balestrand** and **Flåm.**

The West Coast Fjord Country

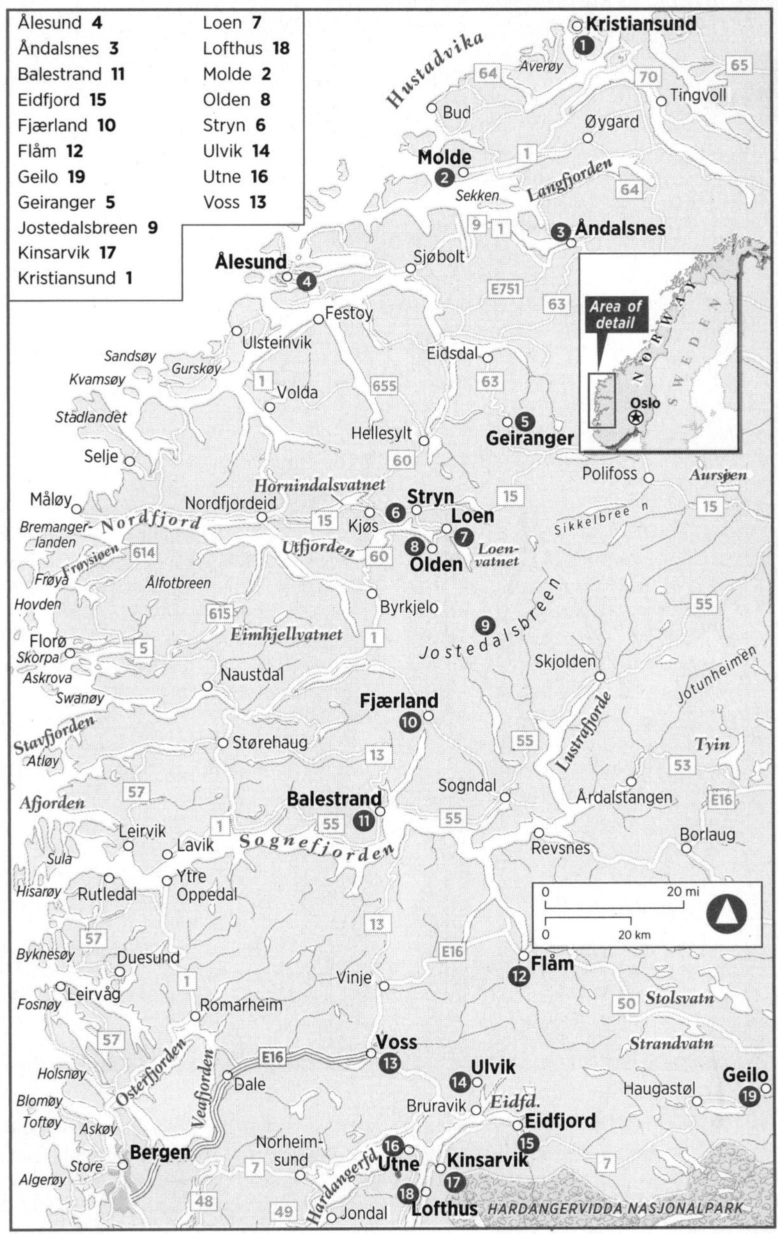

THE FJORDS: mountains & MYTHS

The features of the Earth's landscape have long been tied to folkloric tales; such legends give our world meaning as well as provide explanations for the various anomalies in it. As one of the world's most spectacular natural phenomena, the Norwegian fjords have figured centrally in numerous stories from Nordic mythology. Narrow and deep bodies of water, the fjords lend themselves rather easily to literary interpretation: They may represent anything from a locked-up secret between two people to a symbolic rite of passage from one world to another.

In Norse mythology, the fjord plays a key role in the very creation of the world. One of the seminal Norse gods, the frost giant Ymir, was born of the union of fire and ice. Years later, Ymir's own son, Odin—god of war, magic, wisdom, and poetry—slew his father in order to create the Earth from his remains. Ymir's flesh became soil, his bones mountains and stone, his skull the heavens, and his brains formed the clouds. And from his blood Odin created the rivers, seas, and fjords.

Fjords are also central to the story of Beowulf, one of the best-known heroes of early mythology. At a turning point in the story's plot, Beowulf hops into the fjord waters in order to find Grendel's lair, swimming below the fjord to slay the beast's mother, the evil troll who plans to carry out the destruction begun by her son. In the epic *Saga of the Volsungs*, the fjord plays an obvious symbolic role when father Sigmund allows a ferryman to transport the body of his son Sigurd to the other side of the fjord—and to the other world.

Some of the very fjords that cruise ships travel along while in Norway have specific legends associated with them. In Helgeland county, for example, some 15km (9 miles) from Brønnøysund is Torghatten, a fjord mountain with a 35-m (115-ft.)-wide hole bored right through the middle of it. Norse myth explains the hole with the legend of Hestmannen (the Horseman), a wild and unruly chap who one spring day caught a glimpse of a beautiful nanny, Lekamøya, bathing in fjord waters. Upon realizing she was being watched, the girl fled south. Hestmannen, overcome with rage, followed on his horse. When he realized he was unable to capture Lekamøya, he drew his bow and shot an arrow toward her. The arrow was diverted by a local Brønnøy troll king, who cast his hat into the arrow's path just in front of the mountain. Lekamøya escaped to Nord Trøndelag, but the arrow continued on right through the troll king's hat, creating the large hole in the mountain—which one can visit today.

Modern legends, too, have arisen from the fjords. Many of those marauding mariners known as Vikings ("men of the bay") came from fjordland regions of Norway. Ostensibly, it was their experience out on the fjords—cooped up for long times on cold bodies of water—that led them to want to explore the oceans and the greater world. This geographic repression might have also contributed to the streak of violence they sometimes exhibited.

GETTING THERE Bergen is the traditional gateway to the fjord country. From Bergen, you have a choice of several options for making your way about the district. **Boat** excursions, many of which leave from Bergen, are the traditional way to see the fjords. In summer, dozens of possibilities for these excursions await you. Contact the tourist office in Bergen for details (see "Visitor Information" in chapter 11).

Of the towns recommended in this chapter, Voss, both a winter ski center and a summer mountain resort, has the best **rail** connections with Oslo and Bergen (see www.nsb.no for train schedules).

All of the fjord towns and villages are connected by **buses** that make their way through the mountains and along the fjords, boasting vistas in all directions. Of course, travel by bus can be time-consuming, and often there are only a handful of departures a day, so you'll have to plan your connections in advance. Details on bus routes in the fjord district are available from the central bus station in Bergen, or you can visit www.nor-way.no.

The most expensive option is by private **car.** Most towns and villages have road connections, although you'll have to take several car ferries to cross the fjords.

UTNE: A TRIO OF FJORDS ★

130km (81 miles) E of Bergen; 45km (28 miles) N of Odda

This tiny hamlet is a good place for a first-timer to get acquainted with the unique geography of the fjord country. Utne has a view of the entrances to four fjords: Indre Samlafjord, Granvinsfjord, Eidfjord, and Utnefjord. Across the latter, the formidable bulk of Oksen rises from the headland separating the Granvin and the Eid fjords. A great ravine breaches the steep slope of Oksen. Utnefjorden is almost 3km (2 miles) wide opposite Utne, and nearly 820m (2,700 ft.) deep in places, making it deeper than any other part of the Hardangerfjord.

Utne is at the northern end of the Folgefonn Peninsula, with mountains looming nearby. Two valleys converge on the town, Utnedalen to the east and Fossdalen to the west. The river through Fossdalen forms falls as it drops through the woods toward the end of its course, dividing into two branches as it reaches the fjord.

When fjords were the highways of western Norway, Utne was an important junction. The **Utne Hotel** (see below) opened in 1772.

Getting There

In the west, board the **ferry** at Kvanndal; in the east, at Kinsarvik. From Monday to Friday, ferries leave every hour, and on Saturday and Sunday, every 2 hours. **Train** connections are possible from Voss 38km (24 miles) to the east, on the main Bergen–Oslo line. **Bus** connections are made via Odda in the south and from Bergen in the west. By **car,** head east from Bergen along the E16. At Kvanndal, board the ferry for Utne.

Your Pass to the Fjords

Some 170 hotels and upmarket B&Bs offer discounted overnight rates to holders of the Fjord Pass. The card costs NOK120 and is valid for two adults and all children 14 and under.

The pass is available from Fjord Tours, Strømgaten 4, N-5015 Bergen (✆ 55-55-76-60; www.fjord-tours.com).

A Side Trip to Norway's Only Barony

In 1658, Karen Mowat, a rich Norwegian heiress, wed Ludvig Rosenkrantz, a Danish nobleman. Her wedding present was a farmstead at Hattberg, lying in a valley west of Folgefonna. She and her husband built a castle there, which was granted the status of a barony. That castle and all its side attractions can be visited. It is also a cultural center, B&B, and a luncheon or dinner stopover. The descendants of this noble pair donated the estate to the University of Oslo in 1927. The small castle is enveloped by a rose garden and some of the most dramatic scenery in Norway.

The Baroniet holds many concerts in the summer season, and it's also possible to watch plays by Shakespeare in the courtyard. Lunch (from NOK449), which features freshly grown produce from the baronial estate, is served in a greenhouse. You can also have tea in the Tea Room, where Baroness's rose tea is served with freshly made pastries. Those who are still around in the evening can order dinner at the estate's farm, a three-course meal served beside a 17th-century fireplace. You can also be served more elegantly in the manor itself, with a concert in the Red Room preceding a three- or five-course dinner in the Blue Room.

B&B can be arranged at the home farm. Rooms are well furnished, and most have washing facilities, but you have to share the bathrooms in the hallway. Rates are NOK900 for a double, including breakfast, with an extra bed for children costing NOK150.

The **Baroniet Rosendal,** N-5486 Rosendal (✆ **53-48-29-99;** www.baroniet.no), is open May 13 to July 2 daily 11am to 3pm; July 3 to August 8 daily 10am to 6pm, and August 9 to September 5 daily 11am to 3pm. Admission to the grounds is NOK100 for adults, NOK25 for children 17 and under; concert prices start at NOK150. From Utne, follow Route 550 south in the direction of Odda, taking the Folgefonn Tunnel west and going along Route 48 into Rosendal, where the estate is signposted.

What to See & Do

Founded in 1911, the **Hardanger Folk Museum ★**, lying near the ferry quay at Utne (✆ **53-67-00-40;** www.hardanger.museum.no), celebrates the past of Utne and does so with insight and style. It exhibits old timber buildings, furnished according to their eras, from several of the most inland regions of Hardanger. By the fjord are old boathouses and a general store that once stood on the quayside. In the administrative building are local arts and crafts, national costumes, and data on the fruit-growing industry. The famous Hardanger fiddle, so beloved by Ole Bull and Edvard Grieg, came from this area. The museum owns several of these antique fiddles, and you can also visit a fiddle-maker's workshop here.

The museum charges NOK40 for adults and is free for children. In May, June, and September, it's open daily 10am to 4pm. In July and August, hours are daily 10am to 5pm. The rest of the year, hours are Monday to Friday 10am to 3pm.

Where to Stay & Dine

Utne Hotel ★★★ Dating from 1722, but renovated in 2004, this is Norway's oldest hotel in continual operation. To settle a war debt, King Christian VII granted

Sergeant Børsem permission to operate an inn here, and it's been going strong ever since. Torbjørg Utne (1812–1903)—nicknamed Mother Utne—gave the hotel the romantic character it still possesses. Today a foundation owns the well-preserved hotel. Along with the Hotel Ullensvang (p. 304), this is the best place to stay in the fjord country if you're seeking a genuine Norwegian west-country ambience—you'll certainly not find a radio or TV anywhere here. The hotel is just a few minutes' walk from the ferry quay. The well-maintained, antique-filled bedrooms have the gracious comfort of the 19th century. The hospitable staff can arrange mountain sightseeing tours as well as boat trips on the fjords.

The Utne Hotel restaurant, one of the finest restaurants in the fjord country, is a major reason to stay here. A complete three-course dinner of Norwegian specialties costs a minimum of NOK500, and the dining room is open to nonguests.

N-5779 Utne i Hardanger. ✆ **53-66-64-00.** www.utnehotel.no. 25 units. NOK1,590 double. Children 11 & under stay free in parents' room. Rates include continental breakfast. AE, DC, MC, V. Closed Dec 24 & Easter. **Amenities:** Restaurant; bar.

LOFTHUS ★★: CENTER OF THE HARDANGERFJORD ★★★

379km (235 miles) W of Oslo; 140km (87 miles) E of Bergen

Our favorite spot in the Hardanger district is sleepy Lofthus, once the haunt of Edvard Grieg and other artists. Resting on the fjord, the resort is enveloped by snow-capped mountains, farms, and orchards. Hovering in the background is the Folgefonna Glacier.

Lofthus is actually the collective name for several groups of farms—Helleland, Eidnes, Lofthus, Opedal, Århusm and Ullensvang—extending from north to south along the eastern coastal slopes of Sørfjorden, 6 to 8km (3¾–5 miles) south of Kinsarvik Bay.

The discovery of a runic stone at **Opedal** in the 19th century established that the area has been populated since about A.D. 600. Cistercian monks came to Opedal 7 centuries later and pioneered a fruit-growing industry. Their footpaths are still used, and many visitors have benefited from the 616 steps, the **Monks' Steps** (though there is doubt whether it was actually monks that laid them), that make their way up the steep gradient to the Hardangervidda.

The church and buildings of **Ullensvang** lie around the mouth of the Opo River. The Gothic stone Ullensvang church was probably built at the end of the 13th century, and the builders may have been Scottish or English masons. Although the church has irregular hours, it's usually open during the day from May to mid-September. Ullensvang was the name of the ancient farm where the *prestegård* (church farm) stands facing the church. It is now the name of the church, the hamlet, the parish, and the *kommune* (county), and the site of the Hotel Ullensvang, the most famous hotel in the region (see "Where to Stay").

Essentials

GETTING THERE Board the ferry at Kvanndal for Kinsarvik, where you can make bus connections south to Lofthus. **Train** connections are possible from Voss, 49km (30 miles) to the east, on the main Bergen–Oslo line, and take 1 hour 15 minutes. A **bus** service takes 1 hour from Odda in the south, 15 minutes from Kinsarvik in the north. From Bergen you can go by express bus or **boat** in 2½ hours. **Motorists** can take the E16 east from Bergen to Kvanndal, where you can board a car ferry to Kinsarvik. At Kinsarvik, head south on Route 47 to Lofthus.

VISITOR INFORMATION The summer-only **Lofthus tourist information office,** Strandkaiterminalen (✆ **45-78-58-22**), is open daily June to August noon to 5pm.

What to See & Do

An El Dorado for nature lovers and fjord fanciers, Lofthus is, along with Ulvik (see "Ulvik: Misty Peaks & Fruity Fjord Farms," later in this chapter), one of the best centers for taking in the glories of **Hardangerfjord ★★★**. Your hotel can arrange boat trips, or you can go to the tourist office (see above) and see what excursions might be available at the time of your visit.

Flowing in a northeasterly direction, the Hardangerfjord stretches out for 205km (127 miles). Along the western coast of Norway, the fjord is broad and open, but when its "fingers" dig inland into several branches, it often becomes very narrow. The banks of the fjord are a delight in spring. You'll view not only wildflowers but also lots of blossoming fruit trees along its sloping banks.

The **waterfalls ★★** along both banks are stunning and are reason enough to explore the fjord. When the snows melt in the early spring, the waterfalls that rush down the mountains are at their most powerful.

Motorists can drive along the fjord, taking in its vast panorama. From Skånevik, a small ferry port at the head of Skånevikfjord (a branch of the Hardangerfjord), routes 48, 11, 13, and 7 run for 193km (120 miles) all the way to Norheimsund, the main center on the north side of Hardangerfjord. This road passes by Lofthus, as well as Odda, the principal settlement along Hardangerfjord. Note that if you visit Norheimsund, Ulvik, or Voss, it is necessary to cross by ferry, either from Kinsarvik to Kvanndal or from Brimnes to Bruravik.

You will also be able to take in views of **Folgefonna ★★**, Norway's third-largest glacier, stretching for 37km (23 miles). At its widest point, it measures 16km (10 miles).

Where to Stay

Hotel Ullensvang ★★★ The composer Edvard Grieg, who knew a thing or two about fjord scenery, chose this hotel for his summer vacation in 1878. He came back over many a summer, finding inspiration for music such as *Springtime, The Holberg Suite,* and the *Peer Gynt Suite.* His original piano is still kept in a cottage on the grounds. We like to follow his example, returning every other summer to this 1846 hotel, the single most romantic inn on the edge of the Hardangerfjord—although the Utne Hotel (p. 302) gives it serious competition.

Now a beautifully equipped structure with a garden opening onto the shoreline and with views of the Folgefonna Glacier, the hotel has been run by the Utne family for four generations. It offers rooms ranging from standard to deluxe, handsomely furnished and with well-maintained private bathrooms. Scandinavian kings and plenty of European nobility have patronized the hotel. Tours of the surrounding area, including the best beauty spots along Hardangerfjord, can be arranged with local guides recommended by the hotel. The quality on-site restaurant is reviewed separately below.

N-5787 Lofthus i Hardanger. ✆ **53-67-00-00.** Fax 53-67-00-01. www.hotel-ullensvang.no. 172 units. NOK1,890–NOK2,730 double; NOK3,490 suite. Rates include buffet breakfast & dinner. AE, DC, MC, V. Closed Dec 22–30. **Amenities:** Restaurant; bar; heated indoor pool; tennis court; squash court; gym; spa; sauna; rowboats for fjord cruises; sailboats; room service; rooms for those with limited mobility. *In room:* TV, minibar.

Ullensvang Gjesteheim ★ When we first discovered this place years ago, guests from England were sitting in the garden enjoying food and drink. We figured the inn must be a good place—and so it was. Admittedly, it doesn't match the style and charm of the Hotel Ullensvang, but it's a good runner-up. A cozy, homelike guesthouse in the town center, Ullensvang is run with a personal touch. Bedrooms are comfortably furnished, if a bit old-fashioned, and bathrooms in the corridors are shared and adequate for the job. The dining room serves a Norwegian *koldbord* (cold board) for breakfast and also serves home-cooked Norwegian specialties at lunch and dinner, including such dishes as filet of reindeer, as well as a number of Thai dishes. Lunch and dinner main courses start at NOK115.

N-5774 Lofthus i Hardanger. ✆ **53-66-12-36.** Fax 53-66-15-19. www.ullensvang-gjesteheim.no. 14 units, all w/shared bathroom. NOK710–NOK740 double. Children 4 & under stay free in parents' room. Rates include continental breakfast. AE, DC, MC, V. Closed Sept 13–Apr 26. **Amenities:** Restaurant; bar. *In room:* (no phone).

Where to Dine

Restaurant Ullensvang ★ NORWEGIAN We have found some of the best fjord-country dining at this old inn (p. 304). Norway's most famous composers and writers have sung the praise of places with such settings. The windows of this three-level restaurant open onto dramatic views of the fjord. Guests flock here for the big buffet spread, where you'll find dozens of dishes, many of them locally sourced from the Hardanger region, such as flounder or catfish with steamed fresh vegetables. There are also standard Norwegian dishes such as filet of reindeer, and red deer with a rich game sauce. In summer, expect those delectable cloudberries, like yellow raspberries, served as a soufflé or just fresh with cream.

Lofthus i Hardanger. ✆ **53-67-00-00.** www.ullensvang-gjesteheim.no. Reservations required. Evening buffet NOK495; main courses NOK150–NOK250 a la carte. AE, DC, MC, V. Daily 1–2:30pm & 7–9pm. Closed Dec 22–30.

KINSARVIK: HOLIDAY ON THE KINSO RIVER

119km (74 miles) E of Bergen; 38km (24 miles) S of Voss; 374km (232 miles) W of Oslo

The tiny village of **Kinsarvik** stands on a glacier-formed ridge at the mouth of the Kinso River, which flows into four magnificent waterfalls as it drops from the plateau to Husedalen on its way to the sea.

Since early times, Kinsarvik has been a marketplace hub for the region. It was Hardanger's principal timber port in the 17th and early 18th centuries. When the export of timber was transferred to Bergen in 1750, Kinsarvik developed a shipbuilding industry that continued until 1870, when the village became a center for woodcarving. Today one of its principal manufacturers is a pewter factory.

The plot of grass that slopes to a stony beach near the Kinsarvik ferry terminal is **Skiperstod,** site of a boathouse for naval long ships from about 900 until 1350.

Essentials

GETTING THERE The Bergen–Oslo train stops at Voss, the nearest station to Kinsarvik, with 14 arrivals and departures a day. From Voss, you can journey to Kinsarvik by bus. Trip time from Oslo to Voss is 5½ hours. A **bus** service to Kinsarvik takes 1¼ hours from Odda, 15 minutes from Lofthus. The bus trip from Bergen consumes 2½ hours. **Motorists** can take the E16 east from Bergen to Kvanndal, and then board a car ferry to Kinsarvik. **Boats** leaving from Kvanndal on the northern coast of the Hardangerfjord take about 45 minutes.

VISITOR INFORMATION **Kinsarvik tourist information** (**✆ 53-66-31-12**), in the village center, is open from mid-June to mid-August daily from 10am to 6pm; and January to mid-June and mid-August to December Monday to Friday 9am to 3pm.

What to See & Do

Said to have been constructed by Scottish master builders at the end of the 12th century, **Kinsarvik Church ★** is one of the oldest stone churches in Norway. The interior was restored in 1961 to its pre-Reformation condition. It has a 17th-century pulpit painted by Peter Reimers, a painted and carved altarpiece, and medieval frescoes. The church is constructed in a vaguely Romanesque style, and chalk paintings on the walls show the "weighing of souls" in judgment by Archangel Michael. The church is open mid-June to mid-August daily from 10am to 4pm; admission is free.

Borstova, the building on the fjord side of the green facing the church, was constructed partly from the timbers of St. Olav's Guildhall, the meeting place of the local guild until 1680. It's now a council chamber and social center.

The stone ***minnestein*** **(column)** on the green commemorates local men who fought in the wars that led to the end of Norway's union with Denmark in 1814.

Mikkelparken, Hardanger's only amusement park, located in the middle of Kinsarvik, is open daily mid-June to mid-August. It offers a wide range of activities for children, and is a great place to visit on a summer day. You can pick up supplies and provisions from the town's only grocery store, **SPAR** (**✆ 53-67-11-70**), in the town center, a 2-minute walk from the Best Western Kinsarvik Fjord Hotel (see "Where to Stay & Dine").

On Route 13 to Odda, 6.5km (4 miles) from Kinsarvik, a minor road forks left, providing an alternative route to Lofthus. A short distance from the fork is the **Skredhaugen Museum** (**✆ 53-67-00-40**), a branch of the Hardanger Folk Museum at Utne (p. 302). A collection of 10 timber houses gathered from the Hardanger area and furnished according to the period can be viewed here. There is also a gallery of regional artwork. The museum is open June 10 to August 20 Saturday and Sunday noon to 4pm. Admission is NOK45 for adults and free for children.

Kinsarvik is also an excellent base for exploring all the Hardangerfjord area, including the Hardangervidda mountain plateau (see below). You can rent rowing boats and canoes here to explore the fjord. The tourist office will tell you how to reach the **Nykjesøyfossen** waterfall, or the best viewpoint for taking in the better-known **Søtefossen** waterfall. Many sights in Lotthus, Utne, Eidfjord, and Ulvik can also be easily explored from a base at Kinsarvik.

Where to Stay & Dine

Because of their fjord country charm and isolation, we infinitely prefer to stay at Utne or Lofthus. The downside is that you may not always find accommodations in those places in summer unless you reserve well in advance. A good alternative is Kinsarvik, where rooms may be more readily available.

Best Western Kinsarvik Fjord Hotel ★ ☺ This hotel will not excite you but shouldn't disappoint either. Even though it's a Best Western chain member, this hotel is still family-run, offering personal service and warm fjord hospitality. Set right by the Hardangerfjord, it's rich in historical interest and is a first-class choice for those seeking the experience of combined fjord and mountain landscapes. It's also one of the best-equipped hotels in the area, with modern rooms featuring hardwood floors or carpets. Each comes with a remodeled bathroom with a tub/shower combination. Nonguests exploring the area during the day can enjoy the hotel's lunch menu (main dishes NOK175–NOK245) or the dinner buffet of regional fjord specialties (NOK325). There is live music 7 nights a week in summer.

N-5782 Kinsarvik. ✆ **800/780-7234** in the U.S. & Canada, or 53-66-74-00. www.kinsarvikfjordhotel.com. 70 units. NOK1,450 double; NOK1,650 suite. Children 11 & under stay free in parents' room. Rates include continental breakfast. AE, DC, MC, V. Closed Jan. **Amenities:** Restaurant; bar; fitness center; sauna; room service; babysitting. *In room:* TV, hair dryer.

EIDFJORD: WESTERN GATEWAY TO HARDANGERVIDDA

149km (92 miles) E of Bergen; 336km (208 miles) W of Oslo

North of Kinsarvik, the Eidfjord district, centering around the village of Eidfjord, is one of the oldest settlements in Norway. Stone Age hunters came through here following the migrations of the reindeer to put steaks on their table. Some 950 people still inhabit the northern tip of Hardangerfjord, making their living from agriculture and tourism.

Hikers flock here to go into the hinterlands, where they can encounter Europe's largest herd of wild reindeer. These same hikers may also encounter cascading waterfalls, fjord farms, and mountain lodges in and around Hardangerfjord, which sends "fingers" of deep water into the innermost reaches of the country. Fishermen come here to catch mountain trout that will be cooked for them later that night at their hotel. The town itself enjoys one of the most scenic locations in the district, nestled between a deep fjord and a deep lake, the Eidfjordvatnet.

Essentials

GETTING THERE Take the **train** from Bergen to Voss, where a connecting bus will take you the rest of the way. The train from Bergen to Voss takes 1 hour 15 minutes and costs NOK165 one-way. **Buses** for Eidfjord depart three or four times a day from Voss, taking 1¾ hours. Part of the route requires a 10-minute ferryboat ride across the Eidfjord itself, from Bruravik. In summer the ferry departs every 20 minutes, and in winter every 40 minutes.

From Odda in the south, **motorists** can take Route 47 northward; from Geilo in the east, go west along Route 7. The drive takes an hour.

VISITOR INFORMATION The **Eidfjord tourist office** (✆ **53-67-34-00;** www.visiteidfjord.no) lies right in the town center and is open year-round, daily from 9am to 7pm. The tourist office also rents boats and bicycles. Bikes cost NOK100 per half-day, NOK150 per day. Kayaks cost NOK150 per day; canoes are NOK350 per day.

What to See & Do

Eidfjord county contains nearly one-quarter of the **Hardangervidda Nasjonalpark ★★★**, containing the largest mountain plateau in Europe, rising 1,000 to 1,200m (3,300–3,900 ft.) high and covering about 7,500 sq. km (2,900 sq. miles). The park is home to some 10,000 wild reindeer, supplemented in the summer months by horses, goats, and sheep brought here by local farmers to graze. The park is also home to the habitats of the snowy owl, the arctic fox, the lynx, and other creatures from the frozen tundra of the north, as well as a diverse bird population, ranging from ravens to eagles.

Hiking trails follow footpaths carved centuries ago by early settlers through the mountainous area, leading to more than a dozen tourist huts (log cabins). The tourist office (see above) will provide maps and more information if you want to go hiking.

Before going on a hike, stop in at the **Hardangervidda Natursenter,** Øvre Eidfjord (✆ **53-67-40-00;** www.hardangervidda.org), which has an informative 20-minute movie and exhibits about the park's geology. It's open June to August daily 9am to 8pm; April, May, September, and October daily 10am to 6pm. Admission is NOK120 for adults, NOK60 for children, NOK280 for a family ticket. On-site is a restaurant that makes a good luncheon stopover, plus a souvenir shop.

Several canyons, including the renowned **Måbø Valley ★★**, lead down from the Hardangervidda plateau to the fjords. Part of a 1,000-year-old road across Norway, traversing the Måbø Valley, has been restored for hardy hikers. At a point 18km (11 miles) southeast of Eidfjord, you'll see the dramatic **Voringfoss Waterfall ★**, dropping 145m (476 ft.). It's reached along Route 7.

You can also make an excursion to a small mountain farm at **Kjeåsen Farm ★**, lying 13km (8 miles) northeast of Eidfjord. This is one of the most panoramic sites in all the fjord country. If you climb to the top of the mountain, allow 3 hours there and back; the steep climb makes it somewhat challenging, so bring good shoes. The farm lies about 600m (2,000 ft.) above sea level by the Simafjord.

Sultry, Tropical Norway

Did you know that some half a billion years ago, Norway was situated south of the Equator? You can learn more astonishing facts like this at the Hardangervidda Natursenter in the Eidfjord district.

Numerous lakes and rivers in the county offer good trout fishing. Two rivers, the Eio and the Bjoreio, as well as Eidfjordvatnet (Eidfjord Lake), boast salmon and trout fishing.

Back in Eidfjord, the stone **Eidfjord Kirke** dates from the 14th century. It can be visited with a guide; ask the tourist office (see above) to make arrangements.

Where to Stay & Dine

Eidfjord Hotel This fairly standard choice for overnighting lacks the upmarket appeal of the Quality Hotel (see below), but it does have location going for it. Right next door to the Eidfjord bus station, this hotel was originally built in 1974 to house workers from the Sima Power Station nearby. In 1994, it was converted into this comfortable but uninspired fjord hotel. Bedrooms have wooden floors and solid, comfortable furnishings, with half of the accommodations opening onto views of the fjord. On-site is a well-run dining room serving quite good Norwegian food (meals NOK245 including main course, dessert, and coffee or tea; open daily 6–8pm).

N-5783 Eidfjord. ✆ **53-66-52-64.** www.effh.no. 28 units. NOK1,090 double. Children 5 & under stay free in parents' room. Rates include continental breakfast. DC, MC, V. Closed Jan. **Amenities:** Restaurant; bar; room service. *In room:* TV (no phone).

Quality Hotel & Resort ★★ The architects of this hotel angled the building so that most of its rooms could take advantage of the sun. From the windows you can look out onto some of the most panoramic views in the fjord district. This hotel, completed in 2001 and replacing an older hotel from the 1880s, lies by the fjord in Nedre Eidfjord, close to the bus station. Today, an old-fashioned decor remains, with plentiful antiques. Some 40 of the rooms, most of them carpeted and quite large, open onto views of the fjord. These also have complete tub/shower combinations; the rest come equipped with a shower. The dinner buffet, at NOK345, is the best, and best-value, meal at the resort. There's often evening entertainment at the piano bar Monday to Saturday.

N-5783 Eidfjord. ✆ **53-67-41-00.** www.choicehotels.no. 81 units. NOK1,000–NOK1,795 double. Children 15 & under stay free in parents' room. Rates include continental breakfast. AE, DC, MC, V. Closed Jan. **Amenities:** Restaurant; bar; rooms for those with limited mobility. *In room:* A/C, TV, Wi-Fi, minibar.

ULVIK: MISTY PEAKS & FRUITY FJORD FARMS ★

149km (92 miles) E of Bergen

Ulvik is a rarity—an unspoiled resort. It lies like a fist at the end of an arm of the Hardangerfjord and is surrounded in the summer by misty peaks and fruit farms. It's the beautiful setting, not an array of attractions, that draws visitors. Ulvik's claim to fame? It's where potatoes first grew in Norway. Other than the enchantment of the hamlet itself, the real reason to stay here is for walking and hiking.

Essentials

GETTING THERE If you're not driving, you can reach Ulvik by train or bus from Bergen or Oslo. From either city, take a train to Voss, where you can catch a bus for the 40-km (25-mile), 45-minute ride to Ulvik. Buses run from Voss daily, five times in the summer, three in the winter. In Ulvik the bus stops in front of the church in the town center. There's no formal bus station.

VISITOR INFORMATION Contact the **Ulvik tourist office,** in the town center (© **56-52-62-80;** www.visitulvik.com). It's open June 1 to September 15 Monday to Friday from 9am to 5pm and Sunday 11am to 3pm; September 16 to May 14 Monday to Friday 9am to 2pm. The office can arrange excursions, from trips on fjord steamers to bus tours of the Osa mountains.

What to See & Do

A number of do-it-yourself excursions begin at Ulvik; contact the tourist office (see above) for details. They change seasonally and depend on the weather. Our favorite walk is along the northern tip of the Hardangerfjord, a paradise for hikers. It's home to some 1,000 people and the Continent's largest herd of wild reindeer. Mountain trout attract anglers to the area. I've been through this area in July when the cherries ripen, followed in just 3 weeks or so by the most delicious plums, pears, and apples. It's a great opportunity for a summer picnic, and you can stop to buy fresh fruit and other foodstuffs at one of the roadside farm kiosks.

The Ulvik area offers some of the best walks in the fjord country. These comprise what is known as the **Kulturlandskapsplan** ★—literally "cultural landscape plan"—and include walks to stone-covered grave mounds at Nesheim and Tunheim, a cotter's farm at Ljonakleiv, and a restored country mill in Nordallen in the Osa mountains. The tourist office sells a manual, *Heritage Trails of Ulvik,* outlining details of all these walks, and has information about organized walks, on Tuesday and Thursday in summer, along forest roads and into the mountains.

The village's 1858 **church** (open June–Aug daily 9am–5pm) is attractively decorated in the style of the region. Classical concerts, often by visiting chamber orchestras from other parts of Europe, are offered in summer inside the church. When a concert is to be presented, notices are posted throughout the town.

Shopping

In the center of Ulvik is the summer-only **Husfidsnovae** (no phone), a small crafts shop run by locals who spend their long winter nights concocting arts and handicrafts. For most of them, it's only a hobby; for others it's a full-time job. You'll find woven tablecloths and tapestries, Hardanger embroidery, knitwear, crocheted tablecloths, beadworks for Hardanger folk costumes, ceramics, woodwork, and silver jewelry—all handmade in Ulvik. Hours are irregular, but give it a try to see if it's open.

Where to Stay & Dine

Rica Brakanes Hotel ★★★ There's a famous view of the Hardangerfjord and the surrounding forest from this well-recommended hotel. This is one of the most impressive fjord resorts in the area, although it began modestly enough in 1860 as a five-bedroom inn. It grew over the years, until German warships opened fire on it on April 25, 1940. After the war it was reconstructed, and reopened in 1952. With its custom-designed furniture and textiles, and its very stylish interior, it was hailed as Norway's leading fjord hotel. Soon Princess Juliana of the Netherlands checked in, returning when she was elevated to the throne as queen. Today all that remains of the original building is one small dining room. The new parts of the hotel are airy, sunny, and comfortable. The guest rooms are midsize to spacious and well maintained. In the summer, plane rides over the fjords can be arranged, and windsurfing and boat rentals are available.

N-5730 Ulvik. ✆ **56-52-61-05.** www.brakanes-hotel.no. 143 units. NOK1,155–NOK1,850 double. Rates include buffet breakfast. AE, DC, MC, V. **Amenities:** Restaurant; bar; indoor heated pool; 2 tennis courts; fitness center; sauna; rooms for those with limited mobility. *In room:* TV, Wi-Fi, minibar.

Ulvik Fjord Pensjonat ★ This cozy, family-run hotel in the town center can hardly compete with the Rica Brakanes, but it's not meant to. This is about local Norwegian hospitality and home cooking, and it lures guests back each summer. It is easily one of the finest guesthouses along the Hardangerfjord, with rooms that are spacious and pleasantly furnished in regional Norwegian style. You'll be welcomed by the Hammer family, who won the Norwegian Hospitality Prize in 1989. More than 20 years later, the family is still in charge and still extending the hospitality that brought them acclaim from guests who wander the extensive grounds and take in the panoramic views of the fjord.

N-5730 Ulvik. ✆ **56-52-61-70.** www.ulvikfjordpensjonat.no. 19 units, 17 w/private bathroom. NOK950 double w/private bathroom. Rates include buffet breakfast. MC, V. Closed Oct–Apr. **Amenities:** Restaurant; bar; lounge; free rowing boat; kids' play area. *In room:* Wi-Fi, hair dryer.

VOSS: A WINTER PLAYGROUND ★

38km (24 miles) W of Ulvik; 101km (63 miles) E of Bergen

Set on the main road between eastern and western Norway, there are few better pit stops than Voss. A heavily folkloric site situated between two fjords, Voss is a famous year-round resort and the birthplace of the American football hero Knute Rockne. Even if trolls no longer strike fear into the hearts of farm children, revelers dressed as trolls still appear in costumed folklore programs to spice things up a bit for visitors.

Voss, surrounded by glaciers, mountains, waterfalls, orchards, rivers, and lakes, is a natural base for exploring the two largest fjords in Norway, the **Sognefjord** to the north and the **Hardangerfjord** to the south.

Essentials

GETTING THERE From Ulvik, **motorists** should take Route 20 to Route 13; then follow Route 13 northwest to Voss. There's a frequent **train** service from Bergen (1¼ hr.) and Oslo (5½ hr.). There are six daily **buses** from Bergen (1¾ hr.), though no longer direct buses from Oslo.

VISITOR INFORMATION The **Voss tourist office** (✆ **56-52-08-00;** www.visitvoss.no) is at Evangervegen, on the lakeside opposite the train station. It's open June to August Monday to Friday 8am to 7pm, Saturday 9am to 7pm, Sunday noon to 7pm; September to May Monday to Friday 8:30am to 3:30pm. The **VisitVoss Booking Office,** Vangsgata 20 (✆ **40-71-77-00**), offers an accommodations booking service and also organizes activities in and around Voss; hours are similar to those of the tourist office.

What to See & Do

St. Olav's Cross, Skulegata, near the Voss Cinema, is the oldest relic in Voss, believed to have been raised when the townspeople adopted Christianity in 1023.

A ride on the **Hangursbanen cable car** (✆ **47-00-47-00;** www.vossresort.no) will be a memorable part of your visit. From June to September, it offers panoramic views of Voss and its environs. The mountaintop restaurant serves refreshments and meals. The hardy take the 1126m-long (and 660m-high) cable car up—the trip takes 5 minutes—and then spend the rest of the afternoon strolling down the mountain, which offers excellent views of the Vossevangen area.

This is our personal favorite of all the walks possible in the area (see the tourist office website for a great description of the walk). A round-trip ride costs NOK90 for adults, NOK55 for children 7 to 15, and is free for children 6 and under. Entrance to the cable car is on a hillside a 10-minute walk north of the town center. It's open in summer and winter but closes during the "between season," May to mid-June and September to December.

Vangskyrkja Once an ancient pagan temple stood here. In 1271, a Gothic-style stone-built church was built on the site. This church has suffered, beginning with the 1536 Lutheran Reformation, which destroyed much of its original architecture. What remains is a timbered tower, a Renaissance pulpit, a stone altar, and a triptych, along with fine woodcarvings and a painted ceiling. It's a miracle that anything is left after a Nazi aerial attack destroyed most of Voss—but the church was relatively undamaged. The church lies a 5-minute walk east of the train station.

Vangsgata 3. ✆ **56-52-38-80.** Admission NOK20, free for children 16 & under. Daily 10am–4pm. Closed Sept–May.

Voss Folkemuseum We've seen bigger and better folk museums, but if you have an hour or so in Voss, you might check it out. Almost 1km (⅔ mile) north of Voss on a hillside overlooking the town, this museum consists of more than a dozen farmhouses and other buildings dating from the 1500s to around 1870. They were not moved here but were built on this site by two farm families.

Mølster. ✆ **56-51-15-11.** www.vossfolkemuseum.no. NOK50 adults, free for children. May–Sept daily 10am–5pm; Oct–Apr Mon–Sat 10am–3pm, Sun noon–3pm. Cafe open July noon–4pm.

Skiing

Voss continually adds to its facilities and is definitely in the race to overtake Geilo and Lillehammer as Norway's most popular winter playground. In all, there are 40km (25 miles) of alpine slopes, plus two marked cross-country trails. Eight chairlifts, various ski lifts, and an aerial cableway carry passengers up 788m (2,590 ft.) across two separate ski centers.

A mere 5km (3 miles) from the town center is **Voss Resort,** accessible via the Hangursbanen cable car. One ski lift, some 900m (2,900 ft.) long, goes from Traastolen to the top of Slettafjell, with a wide choice of downhill runs. The Bavallen lift is for the slalom slopes, while the downhill runs are accessed from Lonehorgi.

Lessons at the **Ski School** (✆ **47-00-47-00**), at the end of the cable-car run, are moderately priced. The tourist office and hotels can arrange bookings. Equipment is available for rent. Children 8 and older are allowed on the slopes. A special branch of the Ski School handles these youngsters. Babysitting is available for children 6 and under.

A second ski resort, **Voss Fjellandsby** (✆ **56-53-10-30;** www.vossfjellandsby.no), is set approximately 25km (16 miles) away in Myrkdalen.

Other Outdoor Pursuits

This is Valhalla for **fishermen,** as there are some 500 lakes and rivers in the greater vicinity of Voss. A local fishing license, costing NOK85, is available at the post office or the tourist office (these can also be booked online at the tourist office website). You can catch trout and char using just local tackle. Fishing guides can be booked through the tourist office.

Voss also offers the best **paragliding** in Norway, with flights conducted daily in summer from 11am to 5pm, costing NOK1,500 per person for a tandem flight. The starting point is **Nordic Ventures** (✆ **56-51-00-17;** www.nordicventures.com), in the town center of Voss.

Parasailing and para-bungy are possible at the Vangsvatnet lake, in front of the Park Hotel Vossevangen (see below). The season is from May to October. Parasailing costs NOK550, para-bungy NOK1,800, and water-skiing NOK300 per trip. For information, call **Nordic Ventures** (✆ **56-51-00-17;** www.nordicventures.com).

River sports are big, and a number of outfitters, mainly the **Voss Rafting Center** (✆ **56-51-05-25;** www.vossrafting.no), offer not only rafting but canyoning and river-boarding as well, at prices beginning at NOK770 per person. Their base is at Nedkvitnesvegen 25 in Skulestadmo, roughly 4km (2½ miles) from Voss. There is a pick-up service from Holbergsplass, next to the Park Hotel Vossevangen. The season is from May 1 to October 1. Other outfitters include **Voss Ski & Surf** (✆ **56-51-30-43**), featuring river kayaking for both neophytes and more skilled kayakers; and **Nordic Ventures** (✆ **56-51-00-17;** www.nordicventures.com), offering guided sea kayaking through the Sognefjord, past waterfalls and mountain scenery.

Where to Stay

The best campsite in the area is **Tvinde Camping,** Tvinde, N-5700 Voss (✆ **56-51-69-19;** www.tvinde.no), near the E16. It's one of the most scenic campsites in central Norway, as it lies beside a waterfall, 12km (7½ miles) from the center of Voss. Both tent sites and cabins, the latter in a two-story building with a veranda, are rented here. The cost of the cabins is NOK400 a night, with tent sites costing only NOK160, plus NOK40 for adults and NOK10 for children. The sanitary facilities are rated first-class by Norwegian camping guides, and facilities include a washing machine and dryer, along with an on-site kiosk selling groceries. This camp is reached by public bus no. 950, marked voss-gudvangen, from the center of Voss.

Almost as good is **Voss Camping,** Prestegårdsalléen 40, N-5702 Voss (✆ **56-51-15-97;** www.vosscamping.no), located lakeside and convenient to the attractions and sports of Voss. Its reception area and the campsite itself are open May to September daily 8am to 10pm. The site is well maintained, and the accommodations are reasonably comfortable. Decent cabins are rented for NOK600, with tent sites going for NOK150 to NOK210. There are washing machines and dryers available on-site. To reach the campsite, turn left after leaving the railway station and walk along the rim of the lake, turning right onto a little gravel road (signposted) at the Vangskyrkja Church. Follow this road to the campsite itself.

Both camping sites accept only cash.

Fleischers Hotel ★★★ ☺ In business since the late 1800s, this fjord hotel's peaked, chalet-style roofs and dormers makes it look like something you'd encounter along a lake in Switzerland. Still run by the founding family, the Fleischers, the hotel was modernized and expanded, but much of its original charm remains throughout. The Fleischers can name-drop with the best of them: King Edward of England when he was Prince of Wales in 1885, Emperor Wilhelm II of Germany in 1890 (his private toilet is still displayed in the reception area), and in 1907 the King of Siam. Set on the lakefront beside the Voss train station, the gracious frame hotel has a modern wing with 30 units and terraces overlooking the lake. In the older part of the hotel, the rooms are old-fashioned and more spacious. The restaurant serves an a la carte menu (main courses NOK180–NOK405) and in summer a buffet of local fish and Norwegian specialties (NOK370). This hotel is very kid-friendly, featuring a children's pool with many activities, including a playground and movies.

Evangervegen 13, N-5700 Voss. ✆ **56-52-05-00.** www.fleischers.no. 90 units. NOK1,690 double. Rates include buffet breakfast. AE, DC, MC, V. **Amenities:** Restaurant; bar; lounge; babysitting; indoor heated pool; 2 saunas; children's activities; room service; 1 room for those with limited mobility. *In room:* TV, minibar, hair dryer.

Hotel Jarl Though it doesn't quite hold rank with the Fleischers, the Jarl is a comfortable and reliable option. Placed in the very center of Voss, it has been a durable favorite since its opening in 1972. Maintenance is high here, and all the bedrooms, small to midsize, are tastefully furnished, though it's clear they haven't been updated in a long time. Each features a well-equipped bathroom with a tub/shower combination. The chefs prepare a menu of regional specialties and international dishes using high-quality produce, and after dinner you can do a bit of dancing at the hotel's pub and disco.

Elvegata, N-5700 Voss. ✆ **56-51-99-00.** www.jarlvoss.no. 78 units. NOK1,600 double. Rates include buffet breakfast. AE, DC, MC, V. **Amenities:** Restaurant; bar; pub/disco; indoor heated pool; sauna. *In room:* TV, minibar, safe.

Park Hotel Vossevangen ★ If Fleischers is a bit stuffy for you, Park Hotel Vossevangen offers a livelier venue and a younger crowd. Originally two separate hotels, now joined by a covered passageway, the guest rooms here are attractively furnished and contain well-kept bathrooms, with many offering views onto Lake Vossevangen. The hotel is family-owned and houses the best restaurant in town, the Elysée (see "Where to Dine") as well as Café Stationen, the Pentagon Disco, and the Piano Bar. It's in the town center, a few minutes' walk from the train station.

Utträgate, N-5701 Voss. ✆ **56-53-10-00.** www.parkvoss.no. 131 units. NOK1,550–NOK1,650 double. Rates include buffet breakfast. AE, DC, MC, V. **Amenities:** Restaurant; bar; lounge; babysitting; rooms for those with limited mobility. *In room:* TV, minibar.

On the Outskirts

Stalheim Hotel ★ 🎁 Part of the fun of staying at this old coaching inn on the former postal route between Oslo and Bergen is getting there, traveling on the dramatic but at times harrowing Stalheimskleiva Road, with more than a dozen hairpin turns between Voss and Flåm. The first hotel here opened in 1885, and in time it attracted royalty, including Kaiser Wilhelm II, who visited for 20 summers in a row. In the heart of the fjord district, with views over the Nærøydalen Valley, the present hotel is the fourth in a series on this site. The hotel's own Museum of Norwegian Folk Art is not only one of the largest in the country, but one of the best. The rooms are beautifully furnished and well maintained, and the cuisine is one of the finest in the area.

N-5715 Stalheim. ✆ **56-52-01-22.** www.stalheim.com. 124 units. NOK1,580–NOK2,420 double; NOK1,950 family unit; NOK2,150 triple; NOK3,000 suite. AE, DC, MC, V. 32km (20 miles) N of Voss; follow Rte. E16. **Amenities:** Restaurant; bar; shop. *In room:* Hair dryer.

Where to Dine

MODERATE

Elysée FRENCH/NORWEGIAN At this, the town's best restaurant, the food is more satisfying than at Fleischers and based on the freshest ingredients available locally. Ever had baked sea scorpion? You can here. But if that frightens you away, try the filet of lamb marinated in honey, prepared like cooks did it in the Middle Ages. In season there is always a lusty game dish on the menu, and everything served here is backed up with one of the best wine lists in the area. Nothing satisfies us for a dessert more than the homemade ice cream with fresh berries and a vanilla sauce. The decor of this prestigious restaurant includes *trompe l'oeil* murals based on a modern interpretation of the Pantheon.

In the Park Hotel Vossevangen, Uttrågate. ✆ **56-53-10-00.** www.parkvoss.no. Reservations recommended. Main courses NOK245–NOK300; lunch smörgåsbord NOK335; fixed-price 3-course dinner NOK425. AE, DC, MC, V. Sun–Thurs 1–10:30pm; Fri–Sat 1–11pm.

Fleischers Restaurant ★ NORWEGIAN The dining room of this landmark hotel, a few steps from the Voss train station, hasn't been altered since the hotel opened over a century ago. Long the leading restaurant in the Voss area, the Victorian-style Fleischers remains the traditionalists' favorite. Its lunchtime *smörgåsbord* is a lavish array of all-you-can-eat Norwegian delicacies. Specialties include smoked salmon and filet of beef, lamb, pork, and veal. This is authentic cuisine that would have pleased Ibsen—a real "taste of Norway"—even if it lacks culinary sophistication.

Evangervegen 13. ✆ **56-52-05-00.** www.fleischers.no/en/restaurant. Reservations recommended. Lunch smörgåsbord NOK255; main courses NOK180–NOK420; summer buffet NOK395. AE, DC, MC, V. Mon–Sat 7am–10pm; Sun 7:30am–9:30pm.

BALESTRAND: CENTER FOR SOGNEFJORD ★★

90km (56 miles) N of Voss; 219km (136 miles) NE of Bergen; 204km (126 miles) SW of Fjærland

You might well get fjord fever if you stay here at the junction of Vetlefjord, Esefjord, and the Fjærlandsfjord for too long—that's a lot of fjords to take in. But there's more. Balestrand lies on the northern rim of the Sognefjord.

When the Swedish writer Esaias Tegnér wrote of the snow-covered mountains and the panoramic Sognefjord in the saga of Fridtjof the Brave, the book sold widely and inspired a number of artists to visit the area during the mid-19th century. Soon Hans Gude, Hans Dahl, Johannes Flintoe, and other well-known Scandinavian artists were painting the fjord and mountain landscapes. Their art became so popular that regular visitors were soon flocking to Balestrand to take in the glories of the area for themselves—and so they have continued to this day.

Essentials

GETTING THERE From Voss, **motorists** should continue north on Route 13 to Vangsnes and board a car ferry for the short crossing northwest to Balestrand. You can also take a **train** from Bergen or Oslo to Voss or Flåm, and then make bus and ferry connections north to Balestrand. Bus and ferry schedules are available at the Voss tourist office (✆ **56-52-08-00**) and the Flåm tourist office (✆ **57-63-21-06**). From Bergen there are daily express boats to Balestrand; the trip takes 3½ hours.

VISITOR INFORMATION The **Balestrand tourist office** (✆ **57-69-16-17;** www.visitbalestrand.no) is in the town center. It's open June to August Monday to Saturday 8am to 6pm and Sunday 10am to 5:30pm; May and September daily 10am to 1pm and 3 to 5:30pm; October to April Monday to Saturday 9am to 4pm.

What to See & Do

The staff at the tourist office can help you plan a tour of the area and put you in touch with local craftspeople. You can pick up a list of current excursions and buy tickets for one of the scheduled 1½-day tours.

If it's a summer day, we suggest a leisurely stroll south along the banks of the fjord. You'll pass many 19th- and early-20th-century homes and gardens along the way. Less than 1km (⅔ mile) south along the fjord, you'll come to two **Viking Age burial mounds.** One mound is topped by a statue of the legendary King Bele.

If your appetite's whetted by all the apple trees dotting the landscape, you'll also find several idyllic spots for a picnic.

Want still more walks? Take the small ferry that leaves Balestrand and crosses Esefjord to the Dragsvik side. At this point, you can walk along an old country road that is now abandoned but was in use during the early part of the 20th century. This is a scenic stroll through "forgotten" Norway that goes along for 8km (5 miles).

Kaiser Wilhelm II, a frequent visitor to Balestrand (he was here when World War I broke out, and was politely asked by the Norwegian king to sail peacefully out of town on his yacht), presented the district with statues of two Old Norse heroes, King Bele and Fridtjof the Bold. They stand in the center of town. Another sight is the Anglican church of **St. Olav,** a tiny wooden building that dates from 1897. The church is closed to the public, but its construction can be admired from outside.

You can explore the area by setting out in nearly any direction on scenic country lanes with little traffic, or on a wide choice of marked trails and upland farm tracks. The tourist office sells a touring map for NOK90. There's good sea fishing, as well as lake and river trout fishing. Fishing tackle, rowboats, and bicycles can all be rented in the area.

Back in Balestrand, near the ferry dock, you can visit the **Sognefjord Aquarium** (✆ **57-69-13-03;** www.kringsja.no), with its exhibition of saltwater fish. Especially mysterious is the marine life from the world's deepest fjord. The cast of denizens of the deep include Esefjord herring "lip fish," eels, and sharks. The exhibition consists of a number of large and small aquaria, both indoors and out on the jetty. The marine environments have been authentically re-created, including the tidal belt at Munken

A Boot for the Kaiser

Kaiser Wilhelm II of Germany was on holiday in the village of Balestrand, visiting a friend, when World War I broke out. Norwegian authorities gave the kaiser an ultimatum to leave their territory by 6pm that very day. Not being a man to have his pleasures cut short, Kaiser Wilhelm took his jolly good time drinking his tea and savoring the surrounding landscape before heading full steam out on the fjord aboard his yacht, minutes before the deadline expired.

and the sandy seabed around Staken. A model of Sognefjord shows the currents of the fjord and provides an impression of its depth. There is also an audiovisual presentation. The admission of NOK70 includes an hour of canoeing on the fjord. It's open April to mid-June Monday to Friday 9:30am to 5pm; and mid-June to mid-August daily 9:30am to 5pm.

Excursions on the Sognefjord ★★★

The mighty **Sognefjord,** one of the greatest and most impressive—and one of the deepest—fjords in the world, stretches for a total length of 205km (127 miles). It spreads its powerful "fjord fingers" as far as the **Jostedalsbreen,** the country's largest glacier, and up to Jotunheimen, Norway's tallest mountain range. The widest and most dramatic part of the fjord stretches from the coast to Balestrand. After Balestrand, the fjord grows much narrower.

If you have a choice, opt for a late spring visit when thousands upon thousands of fruit trees can be seen in full bloom along both banks of the Sognefjord. This region is one of the most beautiful on Earth when the blossoms burst forth at that time. The entire district is ideal for skiing, sailing, mountain hiking, and other outdoor activities.

The best way to see the fjord is to take a boat operated by **Fylkesbaatane** (✆ **57-75-70-00;** www.fjord1.no) from Bergen. Balestrand is a stopover on the Bergen–Flåm line, with departures from Bergen once a day, taking 5½ hours and costing NOK470 per person.

Where to Stay & Dine

Dragsvik Fjordhotell ☺ Lying right on a peninsula of natural beauty and opening onto the magnificent Sognefjord, the view from this hotel is like a dream. The hotel itself is more down-to-earth, billing itself as "a home away from home," which it is, to a certain extent. The same family owners—now in the third generation—built this small guesthouse on vacation farmland in 1953. Almost 1km (⅔ mile) from Balestrand and 270m (890 ft.) from the ferry quay at Dragsvik, this hotel is a real bargain. Units are comfortable and well maintained, if small, though the bathrooms are particularly tiny. The large dining room offers a panoramic view of the Fjærlandsfjord. Some accommodations are in what management calls "fjord cabins," complete with kitchen, shower, and toilet. They house anywhere from two to five guests, and are often rented as family units. You can rent bicycles and rowboats from the hotel.

Dragsvik, N-6899 Balestrand. ✆ **57-69-44-00.** www.dragsvik.no. 19 units. NOK550–NOK645 per person double; NOK690–NOK890 cabins. Rates include buffet breakfast. AE, MC, V. Closed Nov–Jan. **Amenities:** Restaurant; bar; room service. *In room:* Hair dryer.

Kviknes Hotel ★★ There was an inn on this site back in 1752, and the present owners, the Kvikne family, who took the inn over in 1877, are still in charge today. The hotel was built in the Swiss style, and its public rooms are now graced with art and antiques. The entire place oozes serious Old-World charm.

Patrons who have enjoyed the family hospitality over the years include movie stars, international artists, royalty, emperors, prime ministers, and presidents. At its core it's an elaborately detailed building with balconies opening onto the edge of the fjord in many of the rooms. The units in the original structure offer old-fashioned Norwegian style, flowery fabrics, and spacious bathrooms with tub/shower combinations. Those in the annex have more of a bland Nordic style. The hotel offers a large dining room (serving lunch and an extensive nightly buffet) with a beautiful fjord view, several lounges, and a dance club. Sports such as water-skiing, windsurfing, and fjord fishing can be arranged, as can helicopter flights to the Jostedal Glacier.

Kviknevegen 8, N-6898 Balestrand. ✆ **57-69-42-00.** www.kviknes.no. 200 units. NOK1,660–NOK2,210 double; NOK2,660 suite. Rates include buffet breakfast. AE, DC, MC, V. Closed Oct–Apr. **Amenities:** Restaurant; bar; babysitting; fitness center; Jacuzzi; sauna; room service; rooms for those with limited mobility. *In room:* TV, hair dryer.

FLÅM: STOPOVER ON EUROPE'S MOST SCENIC TRAIN RIDE ★

96km (60 miles) SE of Balestrand; 165km (102 miles) E of Bergen; 131km (81 miles) E of Voss

Flåm (pronounced "Flawm") lies on the Aurlandsfjord, a tip of the more famous Sognefjord. In the village you can visit the old church (1667), with painted walls done in typical Norwegian country style. But, believe us, the thrill is in the getting there, not in any fantastic attractions once you've arrived.

The best and most exciting way to approach Flåm is aboard the **electric train from Myrdal ★★★**, which connects to trains from Bergen and Oslo. The Flåm mountain railway is the most thrilling train ride in Scandinavia, and possibly the world. The gradient is 1:18 for almost 80% of the line. The twisting tunnels that spiral in and out of the mountain are manifestations of the most daring and skillful engineering in Norwegian railway history. The electric train follows a 19-km (12-mile) route overlooking an 883-m (2,900-ft.) drop, stopping occasionally for passengers to photograph spectacular waterfalls.

The trip takes 50 minutes. In summer, 10 trains a day make the journey to Flåm, beginning at 7:40am and running throughout the day. In winter, about four or five trains a day make the run. Tickets must be purchased in advance. The one-way fare from Myrdal to Flåm is NOK240 (www.flaamsbana.no); try to walk or cycle back as it is a beautiful walk.

Essentials

GETTING THERE By **car** from Balestrand, take Route 55 east along the Sognefjord, crossing the fjord by ferry at Dragsvik and by bridge at Sogndal. At Sogndal, drive east along Route 5 to Mannheller, then take the car ferry to Fodnes. From here, continue to Lærdal, from where you can choose between the Aurlandsfjellet, a national scenic mountain road that is open between June and mid-October, or the world's longest road tunnel (24.5km/15¼ miles) that leads toward Aurland and Flåm.

Bus travel is less convenient. A bus runs several times a day Monday to Saturday between Aurland and Flåm. The trip takes 30 minutes.

From May to September, several **ferries** per day cross the fjord between Aurland and Flåm. The trip takes 30 minutes.

Flåm can also be reached by high-speed **express boat** from Bergen, Balestrand, or Leikanger. The boats carry passengers only. In Bergen, call **Fjord 1** (**© 55-90-70-70;** www.fjord1.no); the one-way trip costs NOK665.

VISITOR INFORMATION The **Flåm tourist office** (**© 57-63-21-06;** www.alr.no), near the railway station, will rent bikes for NOK110. It's open May to September daily 8:30am to 8:30pm. Also see www.visitflam.com for information. The tourist office also rents bicycles for NOK50 per hour or NOK250 per day.

What to See & Do

Flåm is an excellent starting point for car or boat excursions to other well-known centers on the **Sognefjord ★★★**, Europe's longest and deepest fjord. Worth exploring are two of the wildest and most beautiful fingers of the Sognefjord: The **Nærøyfjord** and the **Aurlandsfjord.** Ask at the tourist office about a summer-only cruise from Flåm to both fjords. From Flåm by boat, you can disembark in Gudvangen or Aurland and continue by bus. Alternatively, you can return to Flåm by train.

The Nærøyfjord is the wildest and most beautiful arm of the Sognefjord, and was added to the UNESCO list of World Heritage Sites in 2005. There are sightseeing boats that run between Flåm, Aurland, and Gudvangen daily throughout the year, offering vistas of snow-topped mountains, waterfalls, and idyllic farms splayed about the mountainsides. It's great for spotting seals, eagles, and porpoises. A kayak is another excellent way to experience the fjord.

There are also a number of easy walks in the Flåm district. If time is limited, make that walk along the banks of the **Aurlandsfjord,** leaving the day-trippers and the crass souvenirs in the center of Flåm far behind. The setting along the shoreline supports apple orchards, little hamlets, a fisherman's cottage here and there, and farmland where you can sometimes stop in and buy freshly picked fruit.

A free map with detailed information on the city and surrounding walks is available from the tourist office.

Shopping

One of the biggest gift shops in Norway, attracting mainly train passengers, is **Saga Souvenirs** (**© 57-11-00-11;** www.sagasouvenir.no) at the Flåm Railway Station. Here you'll find all those regional products visitors like to haul away from Norway and take back home. There's an excellent selection of knitwear, along with jewelry and the inevitable trolls. The Flåmsbanamuseum right by the end of the line also has a decent gift shop, though the selection is less impressive.

Where to Stay & Dine

Fretheim Hotel ★★★ A gem of a hotel, this is one of the most charming of all the fjord hotels of western Norway, with a pedigree dating from 1866. A modern annex was added in 2002, although the original and cohesive allure of the place remains. We'd stop over here to patronize the bar, if nothing else, as it opens onto a panoramic vista of the fjord waters. It's just 50m (160 ft.) from the railway station. Long renowned for its hospitality—even King Harald has dropped in—it continues to maintain its high standards.

The staff is most helpful in planning fjord cruises or horseback riding in the area. Rooms are decorated in light colors and range from small to midsize; try, if possible, to get a unit with a balcony opening onto the fjord. All units contain bathrooms with tub/shower combinations. Even if you're a nonguest, consider stopping off to patronize their excellent restaurant, with salmon, of course, being the chef's specialty. Prices for main courses range from NOK120 to NOK290, but the real deal is the NOK340 buffet dinner. Live music will entertain you in the bar.

N-5743 Flåm. ✆ **57-63-63-00.** www.fretheim-hotel.no. 118 units. NOK1,490–NOK1,650 double; NOK2,490–NOK3,890 suite. Children 5 & under stay free in parents' room. Rates include continental breakfast. AE, DC, MC, V. **Amenities:** Restaurant; bar; room service; rooms for those with limited mobility. *In room:* TV, hair dryer, safe.

Heimly Pension This is likely the most affordable choice in town, lying next to Aurlandsfjord, only 400m (1,300 ft.) from the Flåm railway. It is a cozy family-run B&B dating from the 1930s and still carrying the aura of that time. Designed in the style of an A-frame chalet, it offers a ground-floor lounge where international travelers gather. The small to midsize guest rooms are decent enough, though they won't win any design awards. The best views over the fjord are on the two upper floors. A lively pub and a good restaurant serving home-style meals are in an annex across the road.

N-5742 Flåm. ✆ **57-63-23-00.** www.heimly.no. 25 units. NOK995–NOK1,150 double. Rates include buffet breakfast. AE, DC, MC, V. Closed Dec 24–Jan 2. **Amenities:** Restaurant; bar. *In room:* (no phone).

GEILO: A WINTER WONDERLAND

130km (81 miles) SE of Flåm; 239km (148 miles) E of Bergen; 245km (152 miles) W of Oslo

Most motorists driving between Oslo and Bergen in summer have to make a choice—Geilo or Voss? Voss tends to be more popular due to its folkloric activities, while Geilo is the sure winner in the colder months—not least because of its great skiing. A good part of the fun of visiting Geilo in winter, as it is in any alpine retreat, is to enjoy the lavish après-ski life of drinking and dining. In that regard, as a resort this ranks higher than any other ski area in Norway, even compared to the more famous Lillehammer.

Geilo lies 798m (2,620 ft.) above sea level in the Hol mountain district. Although it's not strictly in the fjord country, it's included here because it's a "gateway" there en route from Oslo to Bergen. Together, the Geilo and nearby Ustaoset areas offer some 220km (136 miles) of marked, prepared cross-country ski trails.

Essentials

GETTING THERE From Flåm, motorists return to Aurland to connect with Route 50, which runs southeast through Steine, Storestølen, Hovet, and Hagafoss. In Hagafoss, connect with Route 7 going southwest into Geilo. If you're dependent on public transportation, forget about the meager long-distance bus service and opt for the train connections via Oslo or Bergen. From Oslo, the fare is NOK459 per person one-way, and the trip takes 3½ hours; from Bergen, it's NOK413 one-way and takes 3 hours. If you book in advance online, you can cut this fare by as much as 50%.

VISITOR INFORMATION The **Geilo tourist office** is at Vesleslåtteveien 13 in the town center (✆ **32-09-59-00;** www.visitgeilo.com). It's open June to mid-August Monday to Friday 8:30am to 6pm, Saturday and Sunday 9am to 3pm; mid-August to June Monday to Friday 8:30am to 4pm, Saturday 9am to 2pm. The town doesn't employ street addresses, but everything is laid out easily enough to find.

Outdoor Activities

Geilo is both a summer and a winter destination, although its claim to fame is as a ski resort, the main season lasting from January to March. If you plan on doing a lot of skiing, it's best to purchase the **Vinterlandkoret Ski Pass** at the tourist office. This pass, costing NOK340 per day or NOK1,415 per week, is good for all five ski centers in the area, as well as slopes in nearby resorts such as Ål, Uvdal, and Hemesdal.

Of Geilo's five ski centers, our most preferred is **Geilo Skiheiser** (✆ **32-09-59-20**), with 35km (22 miles) of slopes, many as good as those in the Swiss Alps, 20 lifts, and access to hundreds of kilometers of cross-country trails. Lift tickets cost NOK355 for adults and NOK265 for children.

The favorite areas for families are **Geilolia** (✆ **32-09-55-10**) and **Kikut** (✆ **32-09-60-00**), both west of Ustedalsfjord. Other centers are at **Havsdalsenteret** (✆ **32-09-17-77**), which Norwegian young people have adopted as their favorite, and **Slaatta** (✆ **32-09-02-02**), with its wide range of alpine and cross-country trails (though not as good as those of Geilo Skiheiser). All the ski centers are linked by a free shuttle bus service.

In all, Geilo offers 20 lifts and 40 runs, and plenty of cross-country trails through forests, hills, and moors to **Hardangervidda,** Europe's largest mountain plateau (see "Eidfjord: Western Gateway to Hardangervidda," earlier in this chapter).

In summer, mountain trekking is the passion. Some of the greatest hikes in central Norway are open to you, and the Geilo tourist office is most helpful in offering expert guidance and providing maps. There is a network of marked routes and pathways established since ancient days. The Geilolia Expressen chairlift takes you to the top of the resort at 1,060m (3,478 ft.) above sea level. From that vantage point, marked trails split off in many directions.

If you get tired of hiking, you can always take up rafting, canoeing, cycling, or horseback riding. To go rafting or canoeing, call **Dagaliopplevelser** (✆ **32-09-38-20;** www.dagaliopplevelser.no) or **Serious Fun** (✆ **40-00-57-86**), who organize trips in Dagali and Sjoa. Depending on the day of the week, trips begin at NOK350, going up to NOK810. On your own, you can rent canoes and rowboats at **Fagerli Leirskole,** Skurdalen (✆ **32-09-00-00;** www.fagerli.no).

For horseback riding, call **Geilo Hestesenter** (✆ **32-09-01-81;** www.geilohest.no). You can ride the happy trails from June to October.

To go biking in the area, stop by first at the Geilo tourist office for a cycling map. On your rented bike, you can set out to explore summer roads leading into the surrounding mountains. Bikes can be rented in the center of Geilo at **Sport 1 Geilo**

(✆ **32-09-55-80;** www.sport1geilo.no) for NOK160 to NOK200 per day, or at the **Geilolia** summer park activities area (✆ **32-09-00-00;** www.geilolia.no) from NOK275 per day.

Fishermen flock here to try their luck on the rivers or the region's nearly 100 mountain lakes, which can be fished from June to September. A fishing license (NOK50 per day) is available at the tourist office (see above), and boats and tackle, from NOK160, are available for rent through **Fagerli Leirskole,** Skurdalen (✆ **32-09-47-25;** www.fagerli.no).

What to See & Do

The most exciting possibility is an organized glacier trek on **Hardangerjøkulen,** at 1,860m (6,100 ft.). These take place on Tuesday, Wednesday, and Friday between July and mid-September, depending on whether the snow has melted on the glacier, and can be booked through the tourist office. The tour takes 10 hours and costs NOK650 per person, including a train ride to and from Finse.

A pair of other tours are offered as well: Rafting from NOK350 to NOK800 and a nature and troll safari for NOK400 (NOK250 for children). This latter jaunt is offered Monday, Wednesday, and Friday at 8pm from late June to mid-August, as well as occasionally during the winter months.

Back in the center of town, but only in July, you can visit **Geilojordet,** a 17th-century farm, which is open daily from 11am to 5pm. Some old houses, 2 or 3 centuries old, have been moved to the site and are open for guided tours. You can see how farmers lived at the time and visit such buildings as a storage house or the cattle barn. Cultural activities are also presented at the time, including folk music shows. On-site is a cafe serving coffee, cakes, and drinks.

Where to Stay

Dr. Holms Hotel ★★★ ☺ This is our preferred stopover when driving across Norway between Oslo and Bergen. One of the most famous resort hotels in Norway, it is also the area's finest place to stay. Here, near the railway station, you get elegance, comfort, and traditional styling, as the hotel is filled with original art and antiques. Dr. J. C. Holms, a specialist in respiratory diseases who established the resort so that patients could breathe fresh mountain air, opened the hotel in 1909. Occupied by the Nazis in 1940, it was freed by the Norwegian Resistance in May 1945. There have been many changes since, including the addition of two wings and a swimming complex. The latest major overhaul took place at the time of the millennium. Guest rooms, including 11 family rooms, are beautifully furnished in a romantic English style.

N-3580 Geilo. ✆ **32-09-57-00.** www.drholms.com. 126 units. NOK1,490 double; NOK2,990–NOK3,750 suite. Rates include buffet breakfast. AE, DC, MC, V. **Amenities:** 2 restaurants; cafe; bar; babysitting; indoor heated pool; children's pool; fitness center; 2 Jacuzzis; sauna; room service; rooms for those with limited mobility. *In room:* TV, Wi-Fi, minibar.

Highland Hotel ★ A mere 10 minutes' walk to the downhill ski slopes, this hotel is a good, substantial choice, a viable alternative to the very pricey Dr. Holms or the Vestlia. Bedrooms are small to midsize, each comfortably furnished, though nothing lavish. The standard of maintenance is high, and the staff is one of the more efficient in the area. The on-site restaurant, Café Leo, is a steakhouse offering high-quality beef and stunning views. The hotel also has a piano bar.

Lienvegen 11 N-3580 Geilo. ✆ **32-09-61-00.** Fax 32-09-61-01. www.highland.no. 160 units. NOK1,030 double; NOK1,300 family room. MC, V. **Amenities:** 3 restaurants; bar; nightclub; indoor heated pool; fitness center; sauna; children's playroom. *In room:* TV.

Thon Hotel Vestlia ★★★ ☺ Book into this vastly enlarged and modernized hotel for contemporary comfort, including the best spa between Oslo and Bergen. From a hotel originally built in the 1960s, Helene Hennie, one of Norway's most renowned interior architects, designed and worked on the resort. As part of the complex, there are 34 double and family rooms in small cabins surrounding the main hotel building. Eleven slightly worn-down cabins lie in idyllic locations in the birch forest, with views over Ustedalsfjord and Geilo itself. The restaurant offers solid Scandinavian and Continental meals. Some of the best cross-country skiing in the area begins at the resort's doorstep. This kid-friendly resort also has the best skiing in Norway for children; there's even a ski lift system suitable for kids and a children's ski club. In summer, guests go hiking, boating, horseback riding, or play golf. The best nighttime entertainment is also provided at the hotel, including live dance music year-round, almost every evening except Sunday.

N-3580 Geilo. ✆ **32-08-72-00.** www.vestlia.no. 120 units. NOK1,250–NOK1,750 double, including full board; NOK6,990 penthouse. AE, DC, MC, V. **Amenities:** 3 restaurants; dance bar; babysitting; indoor heated pool; golf course; tennis court; fitness center; exclusive spa; sauna; Jacuzzi; playground; rooms for those with limited mobility. *In room:* TV, minibar.

Ustedalen Hotel Geilo This hotel started out in 1890 renting rooms to engineers working on the Bergen railroad. Later it became a convalescence center. Converted into a holiday hotel in the 1970s, it has been upgraded by the addition of a swimming pool. Bedrooms are small but comfortably furnished, each with modern furniture and a private bathroom with shower. On location is a good restaurant serving tasty, traditional mountain food, its windows opening onto a view of the Ustedalsfjord.

Gamleveien 32, N-3580 Geilo. ✆ **32-09-67-00.** www.ustedalen.no. 86 units. NOK490–NOK590 per person. Rates include breakfast; the higher rates include half-board but require a minimum of 2 nights. MC, V. **Amenities:** Restaurant; dance bar; indoor heated pool; sauna. *In room:* TV.

Where to Dine

Most visitors to Geilo eat in their hotels, but here are a few additional options.

Hallingstuene ★★★ NORWEGIAN/INTERNATIONAL Leading Norwegian food critics have rated this the best cuisine on the cross-country route between Oslo and Bergen. Set across three red-painted antique cottages near the railway station, Hallingstuene is certainly the most elegant restaurant in Geilo. You'll dine surrounded by old wood and several roaring fireplaces in an atmosphere evocative of a mountain cabin in a Norwegian forest. It's the domain of Frode Aga, a well-known TV celebrity chef. Menu items, many of them composed from locally available ingredients, manage to be simultaneously elegant and rustic. Some fine offerings include grilled mountain trout; carpaccio of reindeer; and an old-fashioned starter, *rakafisk,* boiled trout that's been marinated for 3 months in a mixture of salt brine and sugar. Main courses include grilled filets of reindeer, served in a creamy, wine-flavored game sauce, with fresh veggies. Dessert might be a delicacy such as the

"Queen of the Mountain," boiled and sweetened cloudberries with homemade vanilla ice cream.

Geiloveien 56. ✆ **32-09-12-50.** www.hallingstuene.no. Reservations recommended. Main courses NOK255–NOK345. AE, DC, MC, V. Tues–Sat 5–10pm (Fri–Sat until 11pm), Sun 2–9pm.

Ro Kro NORWEGIAN This place doesn't aspire to be more than it is, a mere refueling stop where you can eat through the night—well, at least until 9pm. In a town celebrated for its cuisine, this is no more than a convenience cafeteria. But it's good for what it is, providing succulent pastas and hearty stews, even grills such as reindeer steaks, when you come in out of the cold or stop off after hiking in summer. Many locals come here for the sandwiches or freshly made salads offered throughout the day. Unlike many cafeterias in Norway, this one maintains a full bar and a selection of beers.

In the Ro Hotel, Geilovegen. ✆ **32-09-50-90.** www.rohotel.no. Main courses NOK110–NOK200. AE, DC, MC, V. Daily 9am–7pm or 9pm, depending on business.

FJÆRLAND: ARTISTS & MOUNTAINEERS ★★

62km (39 miles) S of Olden

A town without road connections until 1986, Fjærland lies along the banks of the Fjærlandsfjord, a scenic branch of the greater Sognefjord. Overpopulation is hardly a problem here. Back in the Viking Age, some 300 hearty souls lived here. Amazingly, today's population is about the same. Locals tell us that dozens of stout-hearted citizens emigrated to America at the turn of the 20th century, heading for such places as the Dakotas or Minnesota. Looking around at the stunning beauty of the area makes us wonder why they left in the first place. The landscape, shaped by glaciers through various ice ages over the past 3 million years and characterized by towering mountains, glacier rivers, and U-shaped valleys, has attracted landscape painters from all over the world.

Mountaineers find the terrain here some of the most challenging in Norway, as both the Supphelle Glacier and the Bøya Glacier come down to the floor of the valley in Fjærland. Both of these glaciers are "pups," the term for chunks of ice that fall from a massive glacier—in this case Jostedalsbreen, the largest on the European continent. The lower Supphelle, at an elevation of just 60m (200 ft.), is the lowest-lying glacier in southern Norway.

The center of the Fjærland is a section called Mundal, with a church, school, shops, and accommodations. Fjærland's population, incidentally, is the most well-read in Scandinavia: This is also known as the **Norwegian Booktown** (www.bokbyen.no), and book lovers from all over the world come here to peruse the town's many legendary second-hand bookshops. In June, the town is packed out for its Solstice Bookfair.

Essentials

GETTING THERE From the resort of Balestrand (see "Balestrand: Center for Sognefjord," earlier in this chapter), passenger (and occasional car) **ferries** depart for Fjærland at 8:15am daily. Several **buses** run daily between Fjærland and the transportation hub at Sogndal, taking 30 minutes and costing NOK107 one-way (www.discoversognefjord.com). Daily buses also run to and from Stryn (see below), taking 2 hours and costing NOK200 one-way. **Motorists** can take the E39 from Olden (see below), following signs to Skei, a village at the base of Lake Jølster. There the road goes under tunnels beneath the Supphelle Glacier for more than 6km (3¾ miles) for the final lap into Fjærland. Tunnels on both the Skei and Sogndal roads are free. Ferries are met by the "Glacier Bus," which takes passengers to the glacier and its museum.

VISITOR INFORMATION The **Fjærland tourist office** (✆ **57-69-32-33;** www.fjaerland.org), on the main road in Mundal, is open May to October daily from 10am to 6pm. It doubles as a bookshop and art gallery.

What to See & Do

This is great hiking country in summer, as parts of Fjærland lie within the **Jostedalsbreen Nasjonalpark (Jostedal Glacier National Park) ★★★**, a landscape that ranges from mountains to glaciers, from fjords to low-lying valleys. Our favorite of the scenic routes is in the southern tier of the park, between Lunde and Fjærland, and crossing Marabreen glacier.

At the head of the fjord, 2km (1¼ miles) north of the village, lies the **Bøyaøyri Estuary ★**, a protected nature reserve. In spring and fall migrations, 90 species of birds can be spotted passing through the area. Some 50 species make their nests at Fjærland, so birders from all over Scandinavia flock here.

The best trail for the average visitor in good physical condition is from the Supphelle Valley up to the Flatbrehytta mountain hut. The more adventurous go on from here to explore the glaciers. The local sports association in Fjærland has mapped out 11 other trails, ranging from a relatively easy 1-hour walk to more difficult treks of 5 to 6 hours. At the tourist office you can pick up a map, *Turkart Fjærland,* for NOK90, outlining all these walks in great detail.

It's possible to drive within about 500m (1,600 ft.) of the Supphelle Glacier. While you can stroll over and actually touch the ice, DANGER signs warn of the possibility of sudden, high-speed **avalanches** (this is an unfathomable amount of ice, even if from a distance it doesn't seem like that much). From June 1 to September 10, you can take guided trips on Flatbreen glacier, starting from the parking lot northeast of the Norsk Bremuseum (see below), just 4km (2½ miles) off Route 5. Trips leave daily at 9am, but they must be booked at least a day in advance, and they require a minimum of three persons. The jaunt includes a hike up the Kvanneholtnipa Mountain, at 1,640m (5,381 ft.).

In town, you can visit the recently expanded **Norsk Bremuseum (Norwegian Glacier Museum;** ✆ **57-69-32-88;** www.bre.museum.no). This is very much a hands-on museum. Exhibits inform you about how fjords are formed, and there is a multiscreen audiovisual show on the Jostedal Glacier, as well as an exhibition on climate change. You can perform your own experiments with 1,000-year-old glacier ice, and see a 30,000-year-old mammoth tusk from the largest mammal ever to live in Norway. Exhibits also tell the story of Ötzi, "the man from the ice," whose 5,000-year-old body was found in a glacier in the European Alps in 1991. The museum is open June to August daily 9am to 7pm; April, May, September, and

October daily 10am to 4pm. Admission is NOK110 for adults or NOK50 for children, with a family ticket going for NOK250.

Time permitting, you should also visit **Astruptunet ★**, at Sandal i Jolster (✆ **57-72-67-82;** www.astruptunet.com), lying on the southern shore of Lake Jølster and reached from the center of Fjærland by a 30-minute drive. Celebrated for his landscapes, Nicolai Astrup (1880–1928) was one of the country's best-known and most-reproduced artists. You can visit the studio where he died and wander about a colony of little sod-roofed buildings. Some of his artwork is on view. Guides bring Astrup alive again with their colorful anecdotes. On-site is a cafe serving old-fashioned sour-cream porridge, tasty waffles, and coffee. Admission is NOK60, free for children 15 and under. It's open daily May 20 to June 19 daily from 11am to 4pm; June 20 to August 16 daily 10am to 5pm; and August 17 to September 20 from 11am to 4pm.

Shopping

Den Norske Bokbyen (Norwegian Booktown; ✆ **57-69-22-10;** www.bokbyen.no) offers some 200,000 books for sale in a dozen or so second-hand shops, which remain open from May to September daily from 10am to 6pm. Most of the titles are in Norwegian, but there are many English-language books, including some rare ones.

Where to Stay & Dine

Hotel Mundal ★★ Although up-to-date, this hotel is one of the best examples of the fashionable architecture that characterized the hotels in Norway in the closing years of the 19th century, the era when Norwegians first started heading for scenic resorts for vacations. Beloved of landscape painters and glacier hikers for decades, this hotel dates from 1891 and has been operated by the same family ever since. A bit quirky, with its wooden scrollwork, peaked roofs, cavernous dining room, and round tower, it would be the Addams Family's hotel of choice if they were traveling the fjord country. In the center of Mundal, it lies 3km (1¾ miles) from the glacier museum. Although old-fashioned, it has kept abreast of the times with constant improvements. The helpful staff will offer bikes or rowboats and assist you in your mountain- and glacier-climbing plans.

Bedrooms come in a range of sizes and styles, but all are comfortably and traditionally furnished, with private bathrooms equipped with tub/shower combinations. Even if you're just passing through, consider stopping at the hotel's restaurant for a traditional Norwegian meal of regional specialties. A lavish four-course dinner goes for NOK540.

N-6848 Fjærland. ✆ **57-69-31-01.** Fax 57-69-31-79. www.fjordinfo.no/mundal. 35 units. NOK850–NOK1,200 per person double; NOK1,200 per person suite. Rates include breakfast. DC, MC, V. Closed Oct–Apr. **Amenities:** Restaurant; cafe; bar; lounge. *In room:* TV.

LOEN/OLDEN/STRYN & THE JOSTEDAL GLACIER

50km (31 miles) S of Hellesylt

For a close encounter with nature, little changed over the centuries, come to this incredible land created by the last ice age. No other Scandinavian country can compete with what Mother Nature gloriously presents here. Choose one of the cluster of hamlets and small resorts for your base and set out for trips through the Jostedalsbreen Nasjonalpark and other scenic wonders. It doesn't matter which village you choose as a base because they are all within easy reach of one another, essentially forming the same community.

The largest settlement, with a population of only 1,500, is **Stryn,** the capital of the upper Nordfjord district. **Olden** is one of the best centers for excursions to the Briksdal Glacier. Its population is 800. Even smaller is **Loen,** with only 400 residents. Loen lies at the mouth of the panoramic Lodalen Valley and is used by many as the gateway into the national park. The village itself is touristy and of little interest, but it makes a good refueling stop for some of the most dramatic excursions in Norway.

Essentials

GETTING THERE Stryn is linked by public transportation to major cities in Norway. **Nor-Way Bussekspress** (✆ **81-54-44-44;** www.nor-way.no) **buses** travel west from Oslo three times daily, taking 8 hours and costing NOK 605 one-way. There are also three to five buses daily from Bergen, taking 6 hours and costing NOK489. The buses also stop at Larvik and Førde.

Motorists leaving Geiranger (see below) can continue south to Stryn, taking the ferry across the Geirangerfjord to the town of Hellesylt, the trip taking less than an hour. From Hellesylt, take Route 60 into Stryn. Once at Stryn, you can drive immediately east to Loen or south to Olden. Distances are short—for example, Loen lies only 10km (6¼ miles) from Stryn.

VISITOR INFORMATION **Reisemål Stryn & Nordfjord,** Tinggata 3 in Stryn (✆ **57-87-40-40;** www.nordfjord.no), is most helpful, dispensing information about touring the area, including hiking trips into the national park. They offer a free booklet, *Guide for Stryn,* outlining trips and cycling routes, and they can direct you to places to rent mountain bikes (NOK200 per day, NOK150 per half-day, NOK50 per hour). There are cheaper places to rent in the area, but none as convenient. Take a look, too, at their brochure for the Nordfjord Walking Festival, which takes place every year for a week in early August. They're open in July daily 8:30am to 8pm; June and August daily 8am to 6pm; and September to May Saturday and Sunday 8:30am to 3:30pm.

The **Olden tourist office** (✆ **57-87-31-26**), in the center of the village, is open June 10 to August 15 daily from 10am to 6pm.

What to See & Do

In addition to the wonders of Norway's largest glacier, Jostedal, the little towns and villages of Olden, Loen, and Stryn are good bases for trips on the **Nordfjord ★★★**, the only fjord to rival the scenic wonders of Sognefjord. The panoramic Nordfjord, with its deep-blue waters, penetrates inland from the coast for 100km (62 miles) before it abruptly halts at the glacier itself. If you have a car, you can **drive the length of the north bank ★★** along Route 15 almost to the head of the fjord at Loen. This is one of the grand motor trips of the fjord country. In the distance are snowcapped mountain peaks, and along the way are pastures, fjord farms, and rock-strewn promontories.

JOSTEDALSBREEN NASJONALPARK ★★★

Jostedalsbreen is an ice plateau, spreading across some 490 sq. km (190 sq. miles), dominating the inner Nordfjord district and stretching out in the direction of Sognefjord and the majestic Jotunheimen mountains. Sprawling northeast from Route 5 to Route 15, it plunges a total of two dozen "arms" into the neighboring valleys. For years, until the advent of modern engineering, this formed an almost impenetrable barrier between the east and west of Norway.

In certain parts, the mammoth ice sheet is some 400m (1,300 ft.) thick, reaching up to 1,950m (6,400 ft.) above sea level. Wildlife here includes reed deer, elk, brown bear, and smaller creatures such as hares and elusive squirrels.

In 1991, Norway placed the glacier under the protection of the Jostedalsbreen Nasjonalpark (Jostedalsbreen National Park).

Before setting out, be sure to visit the **Jostedalsbreen Nasjonalparksenter** at Oppstryn (✆ **57-87-72-00;** www.jostedalsbre.no), 15km (9¼ miles) east of Stryn. Exhibits tell you everything you ever wanted to know about glaciers—and a lot more. You're treated to a panoramic history of the glacier, from "attacks" by meteorites to avalanches. We found a highlight to be wandering through the **Arctic Garden ★★**, with 325 species of endemic plant life. The center is open May 12 to September 20 daily 10am to 4pm; June and August daily 10am to 4pm; and July daily 10am to 6pm. Admission is NOK80 for adults, NOK45 for children.

NIGARDSBREEN ★

The Jostedal is noted for its glacial "arms," sometimes called "tongues," which shoot out into valleys, flowing from the plateau glacier. The most famous of these glacial tongues is **Nigardsbreen ★★**. This section is a remnant of the ice sheet that covered Norway 10,000 years ago.

The well-preserved moraine landscape looks much as it did centuries ago, or so scientists believe. Biochemical dating has found that many moraines date from the "Little Ice Age" that culminated only about 250 years ago. At that time, a deterioration in climate made the Jostedal Glacier grow, as its tongues surged forward, damaging farms and vegetation in the valley. The Nigard Valley and the Nigard Glacier are still studied by scientists, who keep an annual watch on it. These days, research is focused on another deterioration in climate: Global warming. However, Nigard is one of the few glaciers in the world that appears to be expanding.

Nigardsbreen is one of the most popular areas for climbing and walking, a virtual ice-blue wonderland of deep crevasses and oddly shaped pinnacles. From May until mid-September, walks are possible. During the other months, weather conditions are too harsh.

At Nigardsbreen you can visit the **Jostedal Breheimsenteret** (Jostedal Glacier Center) (✆ **57-68-32-50;** www.jostedal.com), designed in the shape of twin ice peaks divided by a crevasse, and nicknamed the "Glacier Cathedral." In addition to a film on the glacier, you can see exhibits about the formation and continued movement of this awesome ice block. The center is open daily May to September from 9am to 7pm; June 21 to August 20 from 10am to 5pm. Admission is NOK50, NOK35 for children 10 to 14.

Jostedalen Breførarlag (✆ **57-68-31-11;** www.bfl.no) offers **guided glacier walks ★★**, including a short trip across the Nigardsvatnet lake and a hike along the glacier arm. This walk carries our most enthusiastic endorsement, and it's one of the most dramatic in terms of winter wonderland scenery in the fjord district. Tours take 1 hour, costing NOK200 for adults and NOK100 for children. Three-hour walks on ice are also possible in summer, leaving the center in Oppstryn at 12:15pm daily and costing NOK525 per person. From June to mid-August, there is an additional departure at 10:15am.

BRIKSDALSBREEN ★★

One of the most dramatic natural sights of Norway, the Briksdal Glacier is reached from the large village of Olden by taking a signposted, panoramic road for 24km (15 miles). The route winds its way to the double glacial "arms" of the Briksdalsbreen and Brenndalsbreen ice masses. The Briksdal Glacier is not only the most accessible, but also the most stunning glacier. Nearby residents grew alarmed in the 1990s when it advanced by some 300m (1,000 ft.), but it now seems to be retreating. The water flowing from the glacier forms a trio of lakes in the valley, which have a dramatic emerald-green color.

For a part of the jaunt up the glacier, you can take a two-wheeled cart pulled by a *stolkjerre,* a sturdy-footed fjord horse. Along the way you'll pass by a thundering waterfall. At the end of the track, hikers may wander deeper into the glacier mass to a height of around 1,700m (5,600 ft.), a distance of only 346m (1,140 ft.) above sea level. In summer, the glacier can be seen "pupping"—that is, giving birth to smaller chunks of ice that fall from the mother lode.

Rides are available from **Oldedalen Skysslag** (**© 57-87-68-05;** www.oldedalen-skysslag.com), costing NOK200 for adults or NOK115 for children, for a 15-minute jaunt. They begin outside the souvenir shop in Briksdal.

The best **organized tours ★★** are conducted by **Briksdal Breføring** (**© 57-87-68-00;** www.briksdal-adventure.com) at the Briksdalsbre Fjellstove (see "Where to Stay & Dine," below). A 3-hour hike on the ice costs NOK350. In summer, there are five departures a day, beginning at 10am, with the last one setting out at 4pm.

STRYN

Stryn was put on the map by British fishermen coming to catch salmon in its waters back in the 1860s. Since then it has grown and developed into a major resort in the fjord district. The **Stryn Sommerskisenter** (**Summer Ski Center; © 92-26-61-50;** www.strynsommerski.no) lies on the Tystigen branch of the Jostedalsbreen. This area offers the country's best summer skiing and is a popular setting for photographers capturing beauties skiing in their bikinis. Its longest run stretches for about 2,100m (6,900 ft.), with a drop of 518m (1,700 ft.). In addition, some 10km (6¼ miles) of cross-country ski tracks are offered. Lift tickets cost NOK320 for adults and NOK250 for children 15 and under, and ski equipment is available for rent.

The road to the ski center, **Gamble Strynefjellsvegen ★★**, is one of the most dramatic in central Norway, with hairpin curves. It goes past waterfalls and glacier tongues, and opens onto panoramic vistas at an elevation of 1,139m (3,737 ft.).

OLDEN

This little resort makes a great launch pad for jaunts to the Briksdal Glacier (see above). In town, you can visit **Singersamlinga** (**© 57-87-31-06**), which displays the artwork of William Henry Singer, a famous American millionaire from Pittsburgh. Singer and his wife, Anna Spencer, spent summers in Olden from 1913 until the late 1930s. He was fond of painting landscapes of western Norway. The house can be visited by appointment (✆ **57-87-31-06**). The cost is NOK300 for a group or family, which includes a 90-minute guided tour.

LOEN

A small fjord farming hamlet, this is a summer resort with many outdoor pursuits. It is also the site of some of the best accommodations in the area.

From Loen you can take one of the most scenic trips in the area to the beautiful **Kjenndal Glacier ★**, lying 17km (11 miles) along a glacial lake, the Lovatnet. This is the least visited of the glaciers. Between June and September, you can take a boat, the *Kjenndal,* up the Lovatnet from Sande (NOK220, NOK210 per child under 14, including return bus), from the **Kjenndalstova Kafe** (✆ **91-84-87-67;** www.kjenndalstova.no), a cafe-restaurant with panoramic views. The cafe is close to the Kjenndal Glacier, so you can soak in the backdrop of cascading waterfalls as you enjoy your freshly caught trout. From the cafe, it's a 2-km (1¼-mile) hike to the glacier's face.

Where to Stay & Dine

Alexandra ★★ English tourists used to dominate as the majority guests here. When the guests were allowed to select a name for the hotel, probably in 1892, they dubbed it Alexandra—a label that is still honored to this day. The most luxurious hotel in the area, the Alexandra dates from 1884 and has been run by the Grov family since it opened. The hotel is also the best equipped in the area, making it the town's only real resort hotel, with different-sized bedrooms that all feature up-to-date furnishings. The location makes a good base for touring the attractions of the Nordfjord and the national park, including the Briksdal Glacier. The hotel has been known for decades for its cuisine, and the same high standards still prevail. It is also a fine dining choice for nonguests, serving a lavish buffet dinner daily from 7:30 to 9pm (Fri–Sat from 7pm) for NOK465, or you can select an a la carte meal.

N-6789 Loen. ✆ **57-87-50-00.** www.alexandra.no. 189 units. NOK2,440–NOK3,040 double. Children 4 & under stay free in parents' room. Rates include half-board. AE, DC, MC, V. Closed Dec 15–27 & Jan 1-25. **Amenities:** Restaurant; 3 bars; nightclub; babysitting; outdoor pool; fitness center; jacuzzi; spa; sauna; room service; rooms for those with limited mobility. *In room:* TV, minibar, hair dryer.

Briksdalbre Fjellstove Although primarily a restaurant, Briksdalbre is also a mountain lodge offering you a rare chance to stay near the Briksdal Glacier. The original lodge was constructed in 1890, and bedrooms are still fairly simply furnished, with small bathrooms equipped with showers. Expect little in the way of amenities, as most of the staff is engaged in tending to the restaurant. However, they will advise on glacier walking, and even arrange horse-and-carriage trips. The lodge serves some of the best regional cuisine in the area and is particularly busy at lunchtime. The cuisine is regional, with many dishes featuring cod and salmon caught in local waters (ever had deep-fried cod jaws?). Typically, you can order filet of reindeer in a well-flavored sauce, or sautéed trout. Dinners start at NOK170 and are served daily from 8:30 to 9:30pm, with no reservations needed.

N-6792 Briksdalsbre. ✆ **57-87-68-00.** www.briksdalsbre.no. 6 units. NOK880–1,080 double; NOK600–850 cabins. Rates include continental breakfast. AE, DC, MC, V. Closed Nov–Apr. **Amenities:** *In room:* TV (no phone).

Loen Pensjonat ★ ☺ 🎁 Built in 1910 next to Loen's church, this B&B is so family-friendly that it's almost like staying in someone's home. We've found it among the most personally run of all the accommodations in the area. It resides on a sheep farm, but in summer the owners send the herd to the upper elevations for better grazing in the mountains. The little inn has a large garden with panoramic views of the fjords. The location is only about 400m (1,300 ft.) from the center of Loen, in the middle of great hiking and fishing country, with many opportunities for glacier trekking. The carpeted bedrooms are small to medium in size, and feature either doubles or twins. Five of the units have a bathroom with a shower; the other rooms share the adequate bathrooms in the corridors.

N-6789 Loen. ✆ **57-87-76-24.** www.loen-pensjonat.com. 14 units, 6 w/private bathroom. NOK490 double w/shared bathroom; NOK640 double w/private bathroom. Children stay free in parents' room. No credit cards. Closed Sept–May. **Amenities:** Breakfast lounge. *In room:* (no phone).

Olden Fjordhotel ★ Beautifully located in Nordfjord, with a backdrop of mountains, this first-class hotel is close to the Briksdal Glacier. You can relax here in comfort and do nothing, or use the hotel as a base for glacier excursions, summer glacier skiing, horseback riding in the hills and along the fjord, or fishing for trout and salmon. This is one of the best-maintained hotels in this fjord-and-glacier country, with renovations nearly every winter. Standard rooms are medium in size and are well furnished, offering good comfort. Superior rooms have more style, are larger, and are allergy-free, with a sitting area included, and bathrooms with both tub and shower. The hotel is one of the liveliest in the area at night, with live piano music. The on-site restaurant serves the best and largest buffet dinners in Olden, for NOK380.

N-6788 Olden. ✆ **57-87-04-00.** www.olden-hotel.no. 60 units. NOK1,300–NOK1,670 double. Children 2 & under stay free in parents' room. Rates include continental breakfast. AE, DC, MC, V. Closed mid-Sept to May. **Amenities:** Restaurant; bar; babysitting. *In room:* TV, hair dryer.

Visnes Hotel & Villa Visnes ★ 🎁 If you are a devotee of inns with character and quirky architecture, but want comfort as well, check in here. On our first visit years ago, the smell of home-baked bread lured us inside, where we found a personal atmosphere and good Norwegian food.

Visnes Hotel was built in 1850 by an ancestor of the present owners. Opening originally as both an inn and a farmhouse, it features rooms that open onto a private balcony with a view of the fjord. Units are spacious and still maintain much of their original Norwegian-Swiss style. Of the two classics, we like the Villa Visnes best because it is even more fanciful in its 1898 architecture, offering comforts on a par with its older sister. Either hotel is a good base for climbing the Jostedal Glacier, and both are convenient for excursions to Geiranger (see below) or the Sognefjord.

The on-site restaurant is the best in Stryn, serving a three-course dinner for NOK465, with both Norwegian and French specialties.

Prestegen 1, N-6781 Stryn. ✆ **57-87-10-87.** www.visnes.no. 15 units. NOK1,150–NOK1,495 double; NOK1,750 suite. Rates include continental breakfast. AE, DC, MC, V. Closed Sept–May. **Amenities:** Restaurant. *In room:* (no phone).

GEIRANGERFJORD: NORWAY'S MOST MAJESTIC FJORD ★★★

85km (53 miles) SW of Åndalsnes; 413km (256 miles) NE of Bergen; 455km (282 miles) NW of Oslo

Most Norwegians consider Geirangerfjord, a favorite body of water for cruises, their most majestic—and we agree. The fjord stretches for 16km (10 miles), is 292m (958 ft.) deep, and is hemmed in by mountain walls rising some 1,600m (5,200 ft.). The village of Geiranger, one of the most justifiably famous resorts in the fjord country, is set at the very head of this narrow fjord.

Perched on rocky ledges high above the fjord are a number of small farmsteads. Waterfalls, such as the celebrated **Syr Søstre** (Seven Sisters) ★★, **Friaren (The Suitor),** and the **Brudesløret** (Bridal Veil), send their shimmering veils cascading down the rock face.

Almost daily in summer, large cruise ships anchor in the Geirangerfjord, as they have done since 1869. Occasionally, some of the world's best-known vessels are moored here at the same time. The fjord is so deep that the old behemoth *Queen Elizabeth* 2 once sailed safely this far inland. Such depths were carved out by the last ice age, when mammoth masses of ice widened and deepened existing valleys. When the ice melted, former valleys became fjords.

Essentials

GETTING THERE Geiranger is linked by the regular **Møre og Romsdal Fylkesbåtar ferry** ★★★ (✆ **71-21-95-00;** www.fjord1.no) with the old Viking port of Hellesylt. The is the most magnificent ferry route in all of Norway. Take the 65-minute ride even if you don't need to get to the other side. Depending on the season, ferries run from May to October at the rate of four to eight a day, the latter only in peak season, June to August. The fare is NOK133 per adult or NOK67 per child; bicycles go free.

From April 1 until the end of September, Hurtigruten **coastal steamers** (p. 397) sail into Geiranger, but only en route to the North Cape.

There is a daily **bus** running in summer from Åndalsnes (see below), taking 3 hours and costing NOK235 for adults (NOK118 for children). For the visitor wanting wild fjord scenery, the morning bus from Åndalsnes goes on from Geiranger to Langvatn, and on the way back to Geiranger takes a rather thrilling 10-km (6¼-mile) jaunt ★★ just for visitors, up to the summit of Dalsnibba (1,500m/4,920 ft.) and stopping at the Flydalsjuvet (see "Seeing the Fjord," below). The return fare is NOK160 per person for adults, half that for children.

By **car,** it's also possible to reach Dalsnibba by toll road (NOK55 per vehicle). From Stryn, take Route 15/63 into Geiranger. The mountain road, known as the Strynefjellsvegen, offers gleaming white snow and views of glacier tongues well into the summer months. The final stretch to Geiranger, called the **Geirangervegen** ★★★, takes you through 38 bends, offering fantastic mountain and fjord views at every turn.

The most dramatic road is the famous Trollstigen from Åndalsnes (see below), a 2-hour scenic drive along Route 63.

VISITOR INFORMATION In the post office complex adjacent to the quay, the **Geiranger tourist office** (✆ **70-26-30-99;** www.geiranger.no) is open only from June to mid-September. Hours vary, so call ahead.

Seeing the Fjord

Accurately acclaimed as "the most beautiful fjord in the world," **Geirangerfjord** ★★★ invites exploration. The best and least expensive way to see the majesty of the fjord is to take the regular ferry service between Hellesylt and Geiranger (see above).

An organized tour, however, gives you a greater view, by going closer to the banks. The best jaunts are run by **Geiranger Fjordservice** (**© 70-26-56-00;** www.geirangerfjord.no), offering 1½-hour sightseeing boat tours at a cost of NOK155 per person. Bookings can be made at the tourist office. Departures are from May to September at the rate of two to four daily.

Geiranger is also blessed with some of the finest excursions in the fjord country, notably to **Dalsnibba ★★★**, lying 21km (13 miles) to the south. The dramatic road to the summit, opened in 1889, goes through a valley hemmed in by tall mountains until it reaches a lookout point at approximately 1,500m (4,920 ft.). The last 5km (3 miles) to the top is a toll road. There are many panoramic lookout points along the way, and you're rewarded with a dramatic view at the top. As one local told us, "This is the lookout point where Satan took Jesus to tempt him with the beauty of the world."

A second great excursion is to the **Flydalsjuvet ★★**. This gigantic overhanging rock, lying 4km (2½ miles) south of Geiranger and opening onto the fjord, is the most photographed in Norway, especially by cruise-ship passengers. To reach it, take the signposted road to Stryn until you see the turnoff.

Shopping

E. Merok Turisthandel (**© 70-26-30-14**) has been selling gifts and souvenirs to visitors since 1928 from its location in the center of the village, overlooking the fjord. Their specialty is Norwegian knitwear, including a fine selection from the prestigious manufacturer Dale of Norway. They also sell items in silver and gold, Norwegian enamel, pewter, and crystal, and souvenirs. In summer, they remain open daily from 9am to 10pm. **Audhild Vikens Vevstove** (**© 70-26-32-12;** www.audhild-viken.no) also has a large selection of gifts and souvenirs, as well as clothes, knitted goods, pewter, books, music, and other items.

Where to Stay & Dine

Geiranger Hotel ★★ This hotel opened in 1860 in the center of the village, the year America was launched into Civil War. Despite its ups and downs over the years, it has remained a durable favorite, staying abreast of the times by installing modern facilities while retaining much of its 19th-century aura. It runs a close second to the Hotel Union Geiranger (see below), offering attractively furnished bedrooms with views over the Geirangerfjord, most often from your own private balcony. Overcrowded with summer visitors, the hotel nonetheless manages to offer personalized service. The bedrooms are midsize and comfortably carpeted, some painted in the deep greens and blues of the fjord itself. Nonguests often stop in to patronize the 300-seat Restaurant Skageflå, serving regional specialties. A Norwegian buffet at NOK300 is a special delight.

N-6216 Geiranger. © **70-26-30-05.** www.hotel-geiranger.no. 151 units. NOK1,140–NOK1,520 double. Children 3 & under stay free in parents' room. Rates include buffet breakfast. AE, DC, MC, V. Closed Oct–Apr. **Amenities:** Restaurant; bar. *In room:* TV.

Grande Fjord Hotel ★ This hotel doesn't carry the pedigree, historical baggage, or charm of the Union or the Geiranger, but for service, contemporary comfort, and staff efficiency, it rates high marks. This 1996 inn with a wood interior looks like a Norwegian country lodge. Its magnet is its sixth-floor restaurant with a panoramic view of fjord waters and of some of the world's largest cruise ships coming and going. The bar/lounge on the sixth floor is the best place to begin or end an evening at Geiranger. The midsize bedrooms are tastefully though rather simply furnished and are immaculately maintained. The carpeted rooms open onto views of the fjord; 42 of them have a tub and shower, the rest a shower only. Many cruise-ship passengers can be found in the restaurant in the summer, enjoying the classical Norwegian buffet of regional specialties (NOK250 per person). The staff can arrange boat rentals for tours of the fjord or book tours on sightseeing vessels.

N-6216 Geiranger. ✆ **70-26-94-90.** www.grandefjordhotel.com. 48 units. NOK980–NOK1,150 double. Children 3 & under stay free in parents' room. Rates include continental breakfast. MC, V. Closed Oct–Apr. **Amenities:** Restaurant; bar. *In room:* TV, hair dryer.

Hotel Union Geiranger ★★★ ☺ Over the years, this hotel has entertained more kings, queens, and kaisers than any other in the area. Dating from 1891 and perched along fjord waters with scenic views, the hotel is not lavish or overly decorated, but imbued with a country feel with its *rosemaling* decorated wood furniture, a style very popular in Norway with both farmers and royalty. The bedrooms are beautifully furnished; all come with immaculately kept bathrooms with tub/shower combinations. Try to book into a room with a balcony or one of the 50 or so with views of the fjords; the other units have mountain views. The hotel restaurant is the finest in the area, serving a classic Norwegian buffet for NOK475, although you can dine a la carte as well. In summer, a live band entertains and there is dancing.

N-6216 Geiranger. ✆ **70-26-83-00.** www.hotel-union.no. 197 units. NOK980–NOK1,560 double; NOK2,410–NOK3,370 suite. Children 4 & under stay free in parents' room. Rates include continental breakfast; suite rates include dinner buffet. AE, DC, MC, V. Closed Dec 15–Feb 1. **Amenities:** 2 restaurants; bar; babysitting; sauna; indoor & outdoor pools; room service. *In room:* TV, minibar, hair dryer.

ÅNDALSNES: LAUNCH PAD FOR TROLLSTIGVEIEN ★

124km (79 miles) E of Ålesund; 450km (280 miles) W of Oslo

Situated in one of the most scenic regions in Norway, Åndalsnes was bombed by the Nazis in 1940, reducing it to rubble. Following the German invasion, the king and his family used Åndalsnes as their exit route in a dramatic escape from Norway. The royals made it, but Åndalsnes was left to pay the price. Today, this industrial alpine town has modernized and is all too ready to forget the period when it was used as a military base.

This is the starting point for the grandest drive in Norway, the **Trollstigen** (see below). It is also the last stop on the rail line from Oslo and, as such, is a gateway to the fjord country. Hiking the Romsdalen Alps and boating the scenic Romsdalsfjord are also good reasons to use Åndalsnes as your base.

Essentials

GETTING THERE **Trains** run daily from Oslo to Åndalsnes, taking 6 hours. From June 15 through August 30, daily **buses** link Åndalsnes with Geiranger, taking 3 to 4 hours. Daily buses also run from Ålesund (2½ hr.) and Molde (1½ hr.). **Motorists** should take the E6 northwest from Oslo toward Lillehammer; at Dombås, head west on the E9 to Åndalsnes.

VISITOR INFORMATION At the train station, the **Åndalsnes tourist office** (✆ **71-22-16-22;** www.visitandalsnes.com) dispenses information. It's open mid-June to mid-August Monday to Friday 9am to 7pm, Saturday and Sunday 11am to 6pm; the rest of the year, it's open Monday to Friday 9am to 3pm.

What to See & Do

Åndalsnes is the starting point for one of the great motor drives in Norway: The **Trollstigen ★★★** (www.turistveg.no), a 2-hour drive along Route 63 south to Geiranger. The highway climbs to 858m (2,815 ft.) over a distance of 20km (12 miles). Along the way, you'll encounter 11 hairpin turns. The last one is called **Ørnsvingen ★★★**, or "Eagle's Bend," offering the greatest views in the fjord country—of the Geirangerfjord.

The so-called Ørneveien, or "Eagle's Road," down to Geiranger was a marvel of Norwegian engineering upon its completion in 1952—a road for daredevils, with a 1:12 gradient. To make matters even more exciting, it's single-lane for most of the hair-raising journey. Passing another car could be lethal unless you're careful.

If you're driving or even on a bus, vehicles can stop in front of the thundering **Stigfossen Waterfall ★**, whose waters drop 180m (590 ft.). **Vegmuseum** (✆ **71-22-16-22**) is a little museum at the pass, with exhibitions relating the story of how this incredible road came to be. It's open late June to mid-August daily from 11am to 3:30pm, charging admission of NOK20.

Another grand highlight of the area is en route to **Dombås** (Rte. 9). Both road and train lines follow the **Trollveggen ★** ("Troll Wall"), a major challenge for mountaineers, rising some 1,800m (5,900 ft.). A combined Norwegian and British team "conquered" it in 1965.

The Åndalsnes tourist office (see above) has more than a dozen leaflets outlining the best hiking trails through the **Romsdalen Alps,** a string of mountains enveloping Åndalsnes. One of the favorite walks is a 3-hour jaunt that begins 50m (160 ft.) north of Åndalsnes and climbs to the summit of **Nesaksla ★★**, rising 715m (2,345 ft.) over Åndalsnes. At the top, you're rewarded with dramatic panoramas; on a clear day you can see down to the Romsdalsfjord. From here, the climb continues to the summit of **Høgnosa,** at 991m (3,250 ft.), and on to **Åkesfjellet,** at 1,215m (3,985 ft.).

The **Romsdalsfjord ★** is one of the most scenic in western Norway, cutting a deep gash into the earth and extending west of Åndalsnes. **Rauma Jakt og Fiskesafari** (✆ **71-22-63-54;** www.rauma-jakt-fiskesafari.no) can arrange 4-hour fishing tours of the fjord at a cost of NOK300 per person. There are three daily scheduled trips during the summer. A fishing license can be obtained for NOK270 from the tourist office.

If mountain climbing is your thing, you can drive 2km (1¼ mile) south from Åndalsnes on the E139 to the **Norsk Tindemuseum** (Norwegian Mountain Museum; ✆ **71-22-12-74;** www.tindemuseet.no); it's signposted. This museum dedicated to mountain climbing was founded by Arne Randers Heen (1905–91), one of Norway's most famous mountaineers and the first to scale many of his beloved country's mountains, including Romsdalshorn (1,555m/5,101 ft.). He climbed that mountain an amazing 233 times, the last time at the ripe old age of 85. At press time, the museum was undergoing a complete reconstruction, due to be completed in 2012 (check with the tourist office in Åndalsnes).

Where to Stay & Dine

Grand Hotel Bellevue ★ Judging from the photographs in the lobby, staying at the original 1890 Grand might have been a hoot, at least architecturally. But along came Hermann Göring's Luftwaffe in 1940, firebombing the hotel in its blitz of Norway and its pursuit of the fleeing king. It wasn't until 1954 that the owners got enough money to rebuild the hotel, which, as was typical of Norway in those reconstruction years, is not as inspired looking as its grandpa. Nonetheless, it has its share of comfort and hospitality, and makes a good base for exploring the fjord and mountain country around Åndalsnes. The bedrooms range from midsize to spacious, and the suites open onto balconies with views of the mountains and the fjord waters. The staff can arrange sightseeing, golf, and fishing for salmon in a nearby river or for cod in the ocean. The on-site restaurant (main courses NOK125–NOK195) is the best choice for dining in Åndalsnes, even if you're not a guest.

Andalgata 5, N-6301 Åndalsnes. ✆ **71-22-75-00.** www.grandhotel.no. 84 units. NOK970–NOK1,950 double; NOK1,500 suite. AE, DC, MC, V. **Amenities:** Restaurant; bar. *In room:* TV, minibar.

ÅLESUND: THE GREAT FISHING HARBOR ★★

127km (79 miles) W of Åndalsnes; 131km (81 miles)—plus 2 ferry rides—SW of Kristiansund N; 59km (37 miles)—plus 1 ferry ride—SW of Molde

Smaller and more architecturally unified than Bergen, this town on a fishhook-shaped peninsula might even be more beautiful than Bergen; its builders had a real romance with the past. Ålesund rests at the top of the fjord country, spread over three islands in an archipelago, with the snowcapped Sunnmøre Alps in the background. After a fire destroyed the town in 1904, it was rebuilt in the style of the times, Art Nouveau. To help rebuild, Kaiser Wilhelm II ordered ship after ship of building materials and provisions to be sent north to his favorite vacationland. Towers, turrets, and medieval romantic facades all around town are spot-on Art Nouveau, and the Ålesund version even includes elements from Nordic mythology.

Essentials

GETTING THERE

BY PLANE The easiest way to reach Ålesund is to fly from Oslo, Trondheim, or especially Bergen, arriving at the Ålesund/Vigra airport. There are also daily flights from Bodø, Kristiansand S, Røros, Stavanger, and Tromsø. Flights are with **SAS** (✆ **70-10-49-00;** www.sas.no) or **Norwegian** (✆ **81-52-18-15;** www.norwegian.com). The airport, on the island of Vigra, is a 20-minute ride north of Ålesund.

BY TRAIN A daily train arrives from Oslo at the Åndalsnes railway station, from where you can take a bus to Ålesund (see below).

BY BUS From Åndalsnes, the nearest rail terminal, there are one to three buses daily from Åndalsnes, taking 2½ hours and costing NOK255 one-way. One or two buses a day arrive from Trondheim, taking 7½ hours. One bus a day also arrives from Bergen, taking 11 hours. Additional buses run from June 15 to the end of August.

BY COASTAL STEAMER A coastal steamer (p. 397) departs Bergen daily at 10pm and arrives at Ålesund at noon the following day.

BY CAR Take the A69 west from Åndalsnes all the way to Ålesund. Alternatively, a car ferry operates between Åndalsnes and Ålesund.

VISITOR INFORMATION The **Ålesund tourist office** (© **70-15-76-00;** www.visitalesund.com), in the Rådhuset (town hall), is open June to August Monday to Friday 8:30am to 7pm, Saturday 9am to 3pm, and Sunday noon to 5pm; the rest of the year, it's open Monday to Friday 8:30am to 4pm.

What to See & Do

Even more fun than exploring Ålesund is escaping from it and checking out the wonders of the islands and peninsulas. The mountain guardian of the area is **Aksla,** at 182m (597 ft.), a scenic sanctuary with a terrace restaurant, offering a view of fjord landscape, ancient Viking islands, and the Sunnmøre Alps. From the center you can take 418 steps up Aksla to a lookout point, **Kniven** ("The Knife"). To reach the steps, go along Lihauggata, from the pedestrian shopping street **Kongens Gate ★★**—one of the best streets for viewing Art Nouveau–style architecture. Motorists can reach Aksla by road by heading down Røysegata, east of the core, and following signs for Fjellstua.

Once the only access to many of the surrounding areas was by ferry, with services at times cut off during stormy weather. In 1987, a 15-km (9¼-mile) network of tunnels was built, connecting Ålesund to four nearby islands, including **Giske, Vigra** (site of the airport), and the inhabited islands of **Ellingsøy** and **Valderøy.**

If you have time for only one island, we suggest you make it Giske, which was the historic seat of the Arnungane, a famous Viking family whose feudal control lasted from 990 to 1582. This flat island is believed to be the birthplace of Rollo, 10th-century founder of the Duchy of Normandy and father of William the Conqueror. You can visit the 12th-century **Giske Kirke,** a marble Romanesque church (© **70-18-80-00**) that was restored in 1756. Admission is NOK20, and hours are June 1 to August 20 Monday to Saturday 10am to 5pm and Sunday 1 to 7pm. Bus no. 664 runs from the center of Ålesund, taking half an hour and costing NOK55 one-way. Giske is also the site of many stretches of white-sand beach, and of the Makkevika bird sanctuary.

Several tours that begin in Ålesund are designed for bird-watchers. The most popular and best of these head to the island of **Runde ★★**, 67km (42 miles) southwest of town. This is Norway's southernmost bird rock, where on jagged cliffs half a million seabirds, representing nearly 250 species, breed each year. They are protected from humans by strict government regulations and from natural enemies by the forbidding terrain.

You can see colonies of these birds beginning in May. They stick around until late in July before flying out. The migrating puffins are worth the trek alone, but you'll also see razor-billed auks, guillemots, storm petrels, kittiwakes, gannets, and other seabirds.

The best tour is a 2½-hour boat ride leaving May to August daily from Runde Quay at 11am, and 1 and 4pm. The cost is NOK180 adults, NOK100 children; call © **70-08-59-81** or 95-11-31-54 to make a reservation. For more information, contact the summer-only **Runde Reiselivslag** (© **70-01-37-90**), which keeps irregular hours.

You can take a **bus and catamaran tour** from Ålesund's Skateflukaien Quay, taking 2½ hours and costing NOK200 one-way. Departures are from mid-June to mid-August. You'll leave Ålesund on a catamaran, going to the neighboring island of **Hareid,** where you'll then board a bus for **Fosnavåg,** which will take you into **Runde** for the boat tours (see above). You can go back to Ålesund by bus; the last one leaves at 5pm.

Ålesund Museum ★ The development of hunting and fishing methods, shipbuilding, and life in Ålesund before and after the big fire of 1904 are the subjects of this museum off Korsegata, near the harbor. The museum's focal points include a large-scale model of Ålesund and one of the most famous boats of the Norwegian fjords, the *Brudeegget.* Originally built in 1904 in the difficult-to-capsize shape of an egg, it became the prototype for thousands of covered rescue boats. Its sturdy design has helped save hundreds of lives after mishaps during stormy weather in the Norwegian seas. You can wander into an 1812 barn that was turned into an old-fashioned grocery store or see exhibits about the town's distinctive Art Nouveau architecture. Especially interesting are exhibits on the German occupation from 1940 to 1945.

Rasmus Rønnebergs Gate 16. ✆ **70-12-31-70.** www.aalesundsmuseum.no. Admission NOK50 adults, NOK10 children, NOK90 family ticket. May 1–June 15 Mon–Fri 9am–3pm, Sun noon–3pm; June 16–Aug 31 Mon–Fri 9am–4pm, Sat 11am–3pm, Sun noon–4pm; Sept–Dec Mon–Fri 11am–3pm.

Atlanterhavsparken ★★ ☺ At Norway's most awesome aquarium, and one of the largest in Europe, you'll meet the denizens of the deep, including some pretty strange marine mammals that you may never have seen before, even if you're an avid aquarium-goer. The 4-million-liter (over-1-million-gal.) aquarium is enormous, and the sea park contains exhibits of marine life found only in the deepest of the fjords. The sanctuary for orphaned seals is inspiring.

Many families spend the day here, going for hikes along marked trails nearby and even getting in the chilly waters for some sea bathing. Time your visit to see the 1pm daily feeding, when divers feed some of the fish by hand. On-site is a cafeteria where you can eat or else secure the makings of a picnic. The aquarium lies at Tueneset, 3km (1¾ miles) west of the town, at the western extremity of the Ålesund Peninsula.

Tueneset. ✆ **70-10-70-60.** www.atlanterhavsparken.no. Admission NOK130 adults, NOK65 children. Sept 1–May 31 Mon–Sat 11am–4pm, Sun 11am–6pm; June 1–Aug 31 Sun–Fri 10am–7pm, Sat 10am–4pm. Bus: 18.

Sunnmøre Museum & Borgundkaupangen ★★ ☺ This settlement was the most important ecclesiastical center between Bergen and Trondheim from the end of the Viking period (around 1000) to 1500. The open-air museum contains some 50 original buildings dating from the late Middle Ages to around 1900. Outbuildings include a sawmill, a boat-builder's shed, a fishermen's inn, and a small 1743 boarding school. The boat halls feature 30 special boats—one of Norway's largest collections of fishing boats—as well as an exact replica of the Viking-era *Fjørtoft.* The museum quay is home to the *Heland,* a fishing boat built in 1937, and a "Shetland Bus" dating from World War II. The *Borgundknarren* is an exact replica of a Viking trading vessel from 1000. A replica of the *Kvalsund* (8th c.) drops anchor at the quay in summer. The main building focuses on the cultural history of Sunnmøre and also contains a cafe and a handicrafts shop. The separate Medieval Museum, built over the excavated remains of 12th-century buildings, depicts daily life in a market town back then.

Borgundgavlen. ✆ **70-17-40-00.** www.sunnmore.museum.no. Admission NOK70 adults, NOK20 children. Sept 6–May 17 Mon–Fri 11am–3pm, Sun noon–4pm; May 18–June 20 Mon–Fri 11am–4pm, Sun noon–4pm; June 21–Aug 15 Mon–Sat 11am–5pm, Sun noon–5pm; Aug 16–Sept 5 Mon–Fri 11am–4pm, Sun noon–4pm. 4km (2½ miles) east of town center. Bus: 13, 14, 18, 23, or 24.

Where to Stay

Clarion Collection Hotel Bryggen ★ On a comfort level, most first-class hotels of Ålesund are on a par with each other. But this steeply gabled six-story hotel easily has the most character. It was originally constructed in 1906 as a fish-processing factory, and is now artfully decorated with antique fishmonger's tools and artifacts. This charm, along with the hotel's location right at the waterfront in the old harbor, and the fact that it consistently has excellent staff and service, means it takes the prize for the best hotel in Ålesund. The hotel contains a reading room with a working fireplace, and the interior decor incorporates the thick walls and massive beams of the original structure into an otherwise modern design. The bedrooms are contemporary and tastefully furnished.

Apotekergata 1–3, N-6004 Ålesund. ✆ **70-10-33-00.** www.choicehotels.no. 105 units. NOK1,080–NOK2,450 double; NOK3,500–NOK4,000 suite. Children 11 & under stay free in parents' room. Rates include buffet breakfast & dinner. AE, DC, MC, V. Parking NOK90. **Amenities:** Restaurant; bar; babysitting; sauna; bike rentals; playground; rooms for those with limited mobility. *In room:* TV, Wi-Fi, minibar, hair dryer.

Radisson BLU Hotel ★★ We respect this hotel for its decision to construct a 21st-century building in the Art Nouveau style of the town. Best in modern comfort and convenience, this hotel inhabits the most scenic area of Ålesund, the Skansekaia district (also known as the "top of the fjord"), with panoramic views over the sea and mountains.

Attracting business clients in winter and foreign visitors in summer, the hotel boasts an international restaurant and bar that serves first-rate Norwegian and international cuisine with gorgeous views. Rooms are bright and spacious, and all guests enjoy a sumptuous breakfast buffet at Bulls Brygge, the pub/restaurant, which later in the day weds Norwegian seafood to Mediterranean flavors. The standard rooms are perfectly comfortable, but if you're willing to pay more for business class (usually upwards of NOK300) you'll have amenities such as better bathrobes, slippers, and newspapers delivered to your door. The most modern places to stay in Ålesund are the Radisson's seven luxurious suites.

Sorenskriver Bullsgate 7, N-6002 Ålesund. ✆ **70-16-00-00.** www.radissonblu.com/hotel-alesund. 131 units. NOK1,220–NOK1,595 double; NOK3,700 suite. Children 11 & under stay free in parents' room. Rates include buffet breakfast. AE, DC, MC, V. Parking NOK90. **Amenities:** Restaurant; bar; room service. *In room:* TV, Wi-Fi, minibar, hair dryer.

Rica Hotel Scandinavie ★ This hotel has a lot going for it, mainly the friendly and efficient staff, who are extremely helpful. Set on a gently sloping street in the town's historic core, this hotel was originally built in 1905 after the great fire destroyed its predecessor. Today it's one of the most authentic Art Nouveau buildings in Ålesund, offering midsize and tastefully furnished bedrooms with antiques or reproductions. Bathrooms are freshly restored and immaculately kept, 30 of them with tub and shower, the rest with shower only. The staff can arrange boat rides on the fjords or bird-watching at Runde. The on-site restaurant serves mainly Italian food. The hotel is entirely nonsmoking.

Lovenvoldgate 8, N-6002 Ålesund. ✆ **70-15-78-00.** www.rica-hotels.com. 70 units. NOK1,095–NOK1,345 double; NOK1,345–NOK1,500 suite. Children 4 & under stay free in parents' room. Rates include buffet breakfast. AE, DC, MC, V. Closed Dec 20–Jan 6. Parking NOK100. **Amenities:** Bar; pub (with live music on weekends); room service; rooms for those with limited mobility. *In room:* TV, Wi-Fi, minibar, hair dryer.

Rica Parken ★ At this 1981 hotel, on a par with the Thon (see below), we were won over by the sauna and some of the suites, which are on the uppermost (ninth) floor, offering panoramic views of the Art Nouveau town and the sea. A tasteful but slightly bland modern design prevails throughout, and each room is comfortable, with a small, immaculate private bathroom—half with tub and shower, the rest with shower. Depending on how much you want to pay, you can rent a standard double or a business-class room, the latter with better amenities. The most luxurious way to stay here is in one of the suites, designed to evoke an upscale private home. A little park at the back of the hotel has a path leading right into the mountains for a lovely hike on a summer day.

Storgata 16, N-6002 Ålesund. ✆ **70-13-23-00.** www.rica-hotels.com. 197 units. NOK1,195–NOK1,395 double; NOK3,000–NOK5,500 suite. Rates include continental breakfast. AE, DC, MC, V. Closed Dec 22–27. Free parking. **Amenities:** Restaurant; bar; sauna; rooms for those with limited mobility. *In room:* TV, Wi-Fi, minibar, hair dryer.

Thon Hotel Ålesund ★ Not quite imbued with the same style and character as the other, more glamorous recommendations, this member of the Thon chain is nonetheless one of the most desirable addresses in town. In spite of a post-millennium overhaul, it still lives on architecturally in 1954, the year of its creation. The location is certainly choice, on the main pedestrian shopping street, within a short distance of the airport shuttle bus and the coastal steamer dock, by the bus station. The small-to-midsize bedrooms come with tasteful, comfortable furniture and wooden floors. The most desirable rooms open onto views of the water. On-site is a well-run restaurant, Storm, specializing in high-quality Scandinavian and international cuisine typical of Norway's first-class hotels.

Kongens Gate 27, N-6002 Ålesund. ✆ **70-12-29-38.** www.thonhotels.com. 110 units. NOK1,095–NOK1,745 double. Children 10 & under stay free in parents' room. Rates include continental breakfast. AE, DC, MC, V. Closed Dec 22–Jan 3. Free parking. **Amenities:** Restaurant; 3 bars; nightclub; room service; rooms for those with limited mobility. *In room:* TV, minibar, hair dryer.

Where to Dine

Whether the food is good or bad, the restaurants in Ålesund share a common bond: The prices are high.

Brasserie Normandie ★ INTERNATIONAL/NORWEGIAN One of the top restaurants in town, this great place has always been known for its good food but its recent complete renovation has made it a standout local dining spot. The food presented has strong Norwegian roots as well as international influences. You might try the salmon, which comes marinated in gin with fresh herbs and is served with mustard sauce. Or for something more substantial, try the sprawling fish platter with monkfish, catfish, salmon, mussels, scallops, and shrimp. Or you might choose to order the pepper steak or roasted lamb filet. If you're really hungry, one option is to go for the four-course dinner (NOK500).

Storgata 16, in the Rica Parken Hotel. ✆ **70-12-50-50.** www.rica.no. Reservations required. Main courses NOK310–NOK325. AE, DC, MC, V. Mon–Sat 5:30–11pm. Closed Dec 22–27.

Fjellstua ★ NORWEGIAN The food at this cafeteria-style restaurant is good, but the view is the reason to come. This mountaintop restaurant opens onto one of the most panoramic vistas in the fjord country. The chef specializes in fish, including *bacalhau* (dried cod), monkfish, and freshly caught fjord salmon. At lunch you might want to settle for sandwiches and burgers. At night, if you don't want fish, there is tender beef from a charcoal grill, as well as flavorful lamb cutlets and pork schnitzels. You can drive to the restaurant's mountaintop location via a complicated system of roads, or climb the 418 rock-hewn steps from a parking lot below.

Aksla Mountain. ✆ **70-12-71-00.** www.fjellstua.no. Reservations recommended. Main courses NOK145–NOK209 lunch, NOK209–NOK338 dinner. AE, DC, MC, V. Daily 11am–8pm. Closed Nov–Mar 15.

Sjøbua Fiskerestaurant ★★ SEAFOOD The atmospheric walls of this 1904 former warehouse were kept intact when it was turned into a restaurant, where parts of its foundation piers are sunk into the harbor. If there is a wait, the maritime-style bar can be a good place to bide your time with a drink. In the coldest months, a blazing fireplace may greet you. The chefs here are in top form, as proven by their tangy fish platter with three different types of whitefish, salmon, mussels, and shrimp. The pan-fried monkfish is especially recommendable, coming with a curry cream sauce. Lobster selected from the tank can be steamed or served grilled with a shellfish sauce. If you arrive in summer, you might prefer a seat in Flottman's Bar next door, which is under the same management.

Brunholmgate 1. ✆ **70-12-71-00.** www.sjoebua.no. Reservations recommended. Main courses NOK280–NOK340. AE, DC, MC, V. Mon–Fri 4pm–1am (kitchen closes 11pm).

Ålesund After Dark

Ta Det Piano, Kipervikgata 1B (✆ **70-10-06-99**), is one of Ålesund's longest-running bars and still one of its most popular. This great hole in the wall is popular with everyone from college students to youthful pentagenarians. It has a good and cheap selection of beers, as well as a small outdoor seating area in the back. And if you're not satisfied with the scene there, you'll have no shortage of other bars a few minutes' walk away.

MOLDE: CITY OF ROSES

59km (37 miles) N of Ålesund; 50km (31 miles) NW of Åndalsnes

Lacking the architectural excitement of Art Nouveau Ålesund, Molde isn't quite as interesting architecturally, yet it occupies one of the most scenic locations in the northern fjord country: the Romsdalfjord, in the Møre og Romsdal district. Lying on the Romsdal Peninsula, it is one of Norway's most dramatic coastlines. Molde is an ideal starting point for excursions along the coast and into the surrounding untamed area.

Norway's "town of jazz and roses" is famed for its view of 222 white-capped Romsdal Alps. When the Nazis attacked Norway during World War II, Molde briefly became, in effect, the country's capital, because the king and the gold reserves were here. King Haakon VII hid in a forest outside the town until he and his son, the future King Olav V, could board a boat for England. Some 300 houses were destroyed during the German bombings in 1940.

The name "Molde," from the Molde farm that occupied much of the area, has appeared in records since the Middle Ages. It was officially recognized as a trading place in 1614, and King Christian IV signed a royal decree declaring that Molde was a trading city in 1742. A modern, pleasant town, it boasts nearly 25,000 citizens.

Essentials

GETTING THERE

BY AIR Årø airport (© **71-21-47-80;** www.molde-airport.com), lies on the coast, 4km (2½ miles) east of Molde. **SAS** (© **71-19-16-80;** www.sas.no) offers three to five flights daily to and from Oslo. **Norwegian** (© **81-52-18-15;** www.norwegian.com) also flies here from Oslo. Once here, bus no. 701 goes from the airport into the center, taking 10 minutes and costing NOK25.

BY TRAIN You can go from Oslo as far as Åndalsnes (see above) by train. From there, you must take a connecting bus to Molde. Call © **81-50-08-88** for schedules.

BY BUS Buses run between Ålesund and Molde daily, taking 2 hours and costing NOK161 one-way; the trip requires a ferry crossing at Vestnes. Call © **71-58-78-00** for schedules.

BY CAR Driving should take about 1½ hours from Åndalsnes or Ålesund, 3 hours from Dombås, or 4 hours from Trondheim. From Trondheim, take the E39 via the ferry from Halsa to Kanestraum, then continuing along a toll road. From Ålesund, take the E69 east.

BY FERRY Coming from either Ålesund or Åndalsnes, board one of the frequent car ferries at Åfarnes or at Vestnes for the crossing north to Molde.

BY COASTAL STEAMER The Hurtigruten coastal steamer visits Molde on its way between Bergen and Hammerfest (both directions).

VISITOR INFORMATION

The **Molde tourist office,** Torget 4 (© **71-20-10-00;** www.visitmolde.com), will provide tourist information and assist in arranging excursions. From June 20 to August 20, it's open Monday to Friday 9am to 6pm, Saturday 9am to 3pm, and Sunday noon to 5pm. In the off-season, it's open Monday to Friday 8:30am to 4pm.

SPECIAL EVENTS

The preeminent event on the Molde calendar is its international **jazz festival ★★★**, held around the middle of July and attended by some 100,000 fans. The major open-air concerts are held at the Romsdalsmuseet (see below), although many indoor venues are used as well. For more information, contact the **Molde International Jazz Festival,** Sandvegen 1A (© **71-20-31-50;** www.moldejazz.no). Tickets cost from NOK150 to NOK700, though many of the concerts are free.

What to See & Do

The view of the 222 peaks of the **Romsdal Alps ★★★** is worth the trip to Molde. The most scenic and most dramatic peaks are the **Romsdalshorn,** at 1,559m (5,114 ft.), and the **Troll Tinder,** at 1,905m (6,248 ft.). The best vantage point for

Memories of the Literati

Today the famous Moldegård house, Fannestrandveien 40, 1km (⅔ mile) east of Molde, is privately owned and can be viewed only from the outside. It was the main house of the original Molde farm, built in 1710 by Hans Nobel. Bjørnstjerne Bjørnson, who wrote Norway's national anthem, among other poems, often visited here, taking his last trip to Moldegård in 1907. The cottage's more famous association is with Henrik Ibsen, who lived here in 1885 and used this beautiful rococo building for the setting of one of his best-known plays, *Rosmersholm.*

all of this wonder is the Varden viewpoint, rising 407m (1,335 ft.) over Molde. Visitors can take a taxi up and ask the driver to wait for 20 minutes or so while they absorb the view. An alternative for the more athletic is to walk up a marked trail from the center. We prefer this climb to a taxi, although you must allow about an hour of huffing and puffing to reach the top. Once here, you should be able to take in the island-studded Romsdalfjord as well as the peaks.

Molde Domkirke In the heart of town near Torget (the market square), Molde Cathedral, created by architect Finn Bryn in 1957, is the largest postwar cathedral in Norway and the third church to rise on this site. The old altarpiece, *Resurrection,* by Axel Ender, is from the church that the Nazis bombed in April 1940 when they learned that the king was escaping from Molde. As the bombs were falling, a local patriot ripped out the painting with a knife and managed to save it from the fire.

Kirkebakken 2. ✆ **71-11-14-60.** www.molde.kirken.no (in Norwegian). Free admission. Mon–Fri 9am–3pm.

Rådhuset (Town Hall) The 1966 Town Hall, near Torget, is a well-conceived municipal building of concrete and glass. The *Rose Maiden* fountain celebrates Molde as the "town of roses." Marble floors and stone walls blend harmoniously, and domes and skylights capture the Northern Lights. The roof terrace has a garden with 2,000 roses.

Rådhusplassen. ✆ **71-11-10-00.** Free admission. Mon–Fri 8am–3:45pm.

Romsdalsmuseet (Romsdal Museum) ★★ ☺ This is one of the better open-air museums in the fjord district, and its creators showed a certain cleverness. They not only designed Bygata, an early-20th-century street, but they also used remnants of wooden stave churches that were about to be scrapped to create a single, whole church, a neat feat of architectural design. Some "scavengers" went raiding the Romsdal region, searching for antique buildings, including a 16th-century *aarestue,* or log cabin. In all, they managed to save 50 buildings, which stand here today. In summer, local children in regional costumes may sometimes perform folk dances. The museum is a 10-minute walk northwest of the town center.

Per Amdams vei 4. ✆ **71-20-24-60.** www.romsdalsmuseet.no. Admission NOK70, free for children under 15. Mid-June to June 30 Mon–Sat 11am–3pm, Sun noon–3pm; July Mon–Sat 11am–6pm, Sun noon–6pm; Aug 1 to mid-Aug Mon–Sat 11am–3pm, Sun noon–3pm.

Nearby Attractions

Part of the Romsdal Museum, the **Fiskerimuseet** (**Fisheries Museum;** ✆ **93-42-54-06**) lies on the island of Hjertøya. Its collection consists of more than two dozen buildings moved here from the western coast of Romsdal, including dwellings, boathouses, a mechanic's workshop, and other maritime buildings. There are authentic old fishing boats and gear, and you can see how the Norwegian coastal fishermen, sealers, and whalers lived in olden times. The Fisheries Museum is open mid-June to mid-August daily from noon to 5pm. Tickets cost NOK70. A water taxi (round-trip NOK60 adults, NOK40 children; trip time 10 min.) leaves from the marketplace, Torget, in the center of Molde during the museum's open hours.

Trollkirka (Troll's Church) ★, near Eide, is a natural wonder with seven underground caves and grottoes, and a 14-m (46-ft.) waterfall. Going through these grottoes, with their subterranean streams, is a mystical experience. To reach the gateway to the cave, walk up from the signposted main road, a distance of 2.5km (1½ miles), a scenic and pleasurable walk; allow about an hour, and wear sturdy shoes. A bus run by Eideauto goes to the site two to seven times per day from the center of town (there is no number, but the front of the bus reads "Kristiansund over Eide"). The area is an open site and can be explored at any time.

To wander back into the past, you can visit **Veøy Stone Church,** dating from the 11th century, on **Veøy Island.** The little village of Kaupangen on the island was the center of Romsdal until the 14th century, and has a rich Viking past. If you'd like to visit, ask at the Romsdal Museum (see above). You're taken here by a boatman for a cost of NOK90 per person, although each boat must have at least four people.

Finally, motorists, armed with a map and directions from the tourist office, can drive 2 hours up Langfjorden and along the Eikesdalsvatnet lake to the waterfall at **Mardalsfossen** ★★. This is the world's fourth-highest unbroken waterfall, a two-level cascade dropping 655m (2,148 ft.). Its greatest single drop is 297m (974 ft.). Mardalsfossen flows only between June 20 and August 20.

Where to Stay

EXPENSIVE

Quality Hotel Alexandra Molde ★★ At the Molde Jazz Festival, you'll find us sitting in the Bar Alex, drinking and talking to some of the world's leading jazz artists, who like to stay here. This is the town's choicest traditional hotel, named for Princess Alexandra of Wales, who checked in here in the 1880s. After being destroyed and reconfigured over the years, it consists of three different structures from the 1950s, 1970s, and 1980s, all facing a common grassy area. The entire hotel, which has recently been renovated, is set on the main street of town, overlooking the public gardens and the nearby fjord. The comfortable bedrooms are furnished in a sleek modern style. The hotel is one of the best equipped in town, and its restaurant, Værtshuset (reviewed separately below), and bar are popular with both locals and visitors.

Storgaten 1–7, N-6413 Molde. ✆ **71-20-37-50.** www.choice.no. 163 units. NOK720–NOK1,670 double. Children 11 & under stay free in parents' room. Rates include buffet breakfast. AE, DC, MC, V. Parking NOK90. **Amenities:** 2 restaurants; bar; babysitting. *In room:* TV, minibar, hair dryer.

Rica Seilet Hotel Molde ★★ If you want tradition, hang out at the long-established Alexandra (see above). But if you're seeking avant-garde architectural style and post-millennium amenities and comfort, head here. Jutting out into Romsdalsfjorden, the hotel was designed to evoke a sail. Rising 15 floors, this well-run "ship" is sleek and efficient, and often the venue for conferences. Of all the lodgings in Molde, the rooms here have the most spectacular views. The best way to enjoy the scenery is to treat yourself to a suite, with its own balcony. The most spacious suites have the best-designed interiors in Molde, providing real luxury in this provincial outpost. Some of the junior suites offer a round bed. The Alexandra can't match some of the dramatic features of this hotel, especially the Skybar, with its own terrace suspended 60m (200 ft.) above the water. There is also a lobby bar and a waterfront restaurant serving light fare in summer. The on-site a la carte restaurant features gourmet and international specialties.

Gideonvegen 2, N-6412 Molde. ✆ **71-11-40-00.** www.rica-hotels.com. 224 units. NOK950–NOK1,845 double. Rates include buffet breakfast. AE, DC, MC, V. Free parking. **Amenities:** Restaurant; Sky Bar; Moldebadet spa center; room service; rooms for those with limited mobility. *In room:* TV, minibar, hair dryer.

MODERATE

Comfort Hotel Nobel Originally built in 1920, this is one of the few buildings—and the only hotel in Molde—that was not destroyed by Nazi bombs. Although the reception area retains some of its antique accessories, the hotel has been modernized and enlarged. Today it offers pleasant accommodations in Molde. A few of the better rooms have views of the sea; these get booked up first, of course. The staff can arrange trips to the museums or to the mountains. Under separate management, there is a cafe, Fole Godt, on the same site.

AMTM Kroghsgate 5, N-6413 Molde. ✆ **71-25-15-55.** www.choice.no. 49 units. NOK722–NOK1,352 double. Children 11 & under stay free in parents' room. Rates include continental breakfast. AE, DC, MC, V. Free parking. **Amenities:** *In room:* TV, Wi-Fi, minibar.

Thon Hotel Moldefjord This is hardly the shining star of the Thon chain, but it is a long-standing favorite of budget-minded travelers. Dating from the late 1940s, this building was converted into a hotel in 1998, and right away it became one of the town's most desirable places to stay. Opening onto harbor views, with the mountains as a backdrop, the hotel upholds the traditions of Thon, a leading Norwegian chain. Guests are comfortably housed in carpeted, midsize rooms with a choice of twins or a "honeymoon bed." There is a decent restaurant, Egon, on the ground floor.

Storgata 8, N-6400 Molde. ✆ **71-20-35-00.** www.thonhotels.no/moldefjord. 84 units. NOK707–NOK1,395 double. Children 3 & under stay free in parents' room. Rates include continental breakfast. AE, DC, MC, V. Free parking. **Amenities:** Restaurant; lobby bar; 1 room for those with limited mobility. *In room:* TV, Wi-Fi, minibar, hair dryer.

INEXPENSIVE

Hotell Molde In an expensive town, this hotel still keeps its prices reasonable. In the commercial center near Torget, the market square, this hotel first opened its doors in 1910. Regrettably, the Nazis bombed it in World War II. Today, following renovations, it's one of the more up-to-date choices in town. Painted as gray as a Norwegian November afternoon, it is a privately owned establishment. Rooms are merely functional but well kept and comfortably furnished with wooden floors and small bathrooms (with showers). The on-site restaurant, Rød (see below), is a more popular venue than the hotel itself.

Storgata 19, N-6413 Molde. ✆ **71-20-30-00.** www.hotellmolde.no. 36 units. NOK880–NOK1,395 double. Children 2 & under stay free in parents' room. Rates include continental breakfast. AE, DC, MC. Free parking. **Amenities:** Restaurant; bar. *In room:* TV, minibar.

Where to Dine

Rød SOUTHWESTERN On the street level of the Hotell Molde (see above), this restaurant serves a medley of food that has won it many admirers locally and abroad. Many fjord dwellers like to come here for a change of pace from the usual offerings in the area. The chefs roam the world for inspiration, stopping off, perhaps, in Louisiana before heading on to Mexico. Tempting menu items include fish and scampi cooked in a wok with vegetables, or marinated salmon with a mustard vinaigrette. You can also order a big steak grilled and served with a pepper sauce. Dried codfish comes with potatoes and olives in a spicy tomato sauce. If that doesn't appeal, in the same building is another great a la carte place to dine, Restaurant Gørvel.

In the Hotell Molde, Storgata 19. ✆ **71-20-30-00.** www.hotellmolde.no. Reservations recommended. Main courses NOK150–NOK295. AE, DC, MC, V. Daily 11am–10:30pm.

Værtshuset NORWEGIAN This is the busiest restaurant in town at the time of the Jazz Festival. The well-patronized restaurant, located in the Quality Hotel Alexandra Molde (see above), a short walk from the Town Hall, has known various incarnations. It's decked out in Norwegian-tavern style with antiques and massive ceiling timbers. The menu may be predictable—fish soup or chicken with vegetables and noodles, say—but it's all prepared very well and served in generous proportions. For spicier fare, ask for the garlic shrimp as an appetizer. The marinated salmon is the chef's specialty, and it's invariably good and fresh. That other favorite, cod, is prepared poached, fried, or baked with different sauces.

In the Quality Hotel Alexandra Molde, Storgata 1–7. ✆ **71-20-37-50.** Reservations recommended. Main courses NOK195–NOK265. AE, DC, MC, V. Daily 4–10:30pm.

TRONDHEIM

Founded by the Viking King Olav I Tryggvason in the 10th century, Trondheim is Norway's third-largest city and was the country's capital until the early 1200s. Scenic and pleasant, it's a bustling university center, with expansive avenues created after a fire razed most of the town in 1681. The city lies on the south bay of the Trondheim Fjord, at the mouth of the Nidelva River.

Noted for its timbered architecture, Trondheim retains much of its medieval past, notably the Gothic-style Nidaros Domkirke. Pilgrims came from all over Europe to worship at the shrine of Olav, who was buried in the cathedral and canonized in 1031. The city's fortunes declined during the Reformation. Under the Nazi occupation Trondheim became the base for German naval forces in northern Norway, with U-boats lurking deep in its fjord.

Today Trondheim is a progressive city with a rich cultural life, as well as a high-technology center for research and education. Its center is compact and best explored on foot; most of the historic core lies on a small triangular island surrounded by water but linked via bridges.

Trondheim lies 684km (425 miles) north of Bergen and 552km (343 miles) northwest of Oslo. Oslo and Bergen are more major destinations, but if you have a day or two to spare, make it to Trondheim. I often prefer it during "term time," when 25,000 students bring it to vibrant life, biking around town, drinking in the bars, hanging out in the cafes, and listening to the sounds of jazz, often imported from New Orleans.

If you're heading north from here, take time to appreciate city life before journeying into the northern wilds, which are rarely tamed but for the odd town or large settlement. If you're arriving in Trondheim from the north, you'll view it as a return to civilization and all those pleasures it brings.

ORIENTATION

Essentials

ARRIVAL

BY PLANE Flights to Trondheim land at **Værnes airport** (✆ **74-84-30-00**), 32km (20 miles) east of the city center. Most visitors fly here from either Bergen or Oslo. There are also daily connections with Copenhagen. Service is provided by **SAS** (✆ **74-80-41-00;** www.sas.no),

Widerøe (✆ **81-00-12-00;** www.wideroe.no), and **Norwegian** (✆ **81-52-18-15;** www.norwegian.no).

From the airport you can take the airport bus, **Flybussen** (✆ **73-82-25-00**), costing NOK90 for a one-way trip into the center. The trip takes 40 minutes, ending at the railway station. From the center of Trondheim, buses leave for the airport from Erling Skakkes gate daily from 5am to 9pm. Departures Monday to Friday are every 15 minutes, with fewer departures on Saturday and Sunday.

A taxi from the airport to the center costs a minimum of NOK500 for up to three people.

BY TRAIN Two trains a day arrive from Stockholm (12 hr.) and three from Oslo (7 hr.) into **Trondheim Sentralstasjon** (Trondheim Central railway station). A one-way fare from Oslo to Trondheim is NOK852. If you're heading for the Arctic Circle, Trondheim has links to Bodø (10 hr.; NOK982 one-way). For rail information, call ✆ **81-50-08-88** or visit www.nsb.no.

BY BUS Buses from various parts of Norway arrive at the **Rutebilstasjon,** the city bus terminal, adjacent to the railway station. Trondheim lies at the crossroads of bus travel in Norway, a transportation hub between southern Norway, including Oslo (9½ hr.; NOK860 one-way) and Bergen (over 10 hr.; NOK789 one-way), and northern Norway, including Bodø. For information about long-distance buses, contact **Nor-Way Bussekspress** (✆ **81-54-44-44;** www.nor-way.no). There are also very inexpensive seats available on **Lavprisexpressen** (✆ **67-98-04-80**) buses, with tickets for as little as NOK49. However, to get them this cheap you must purchase at least several days in advance.

BY BOAT Hurtigruten **coastal steamers** (✆ **81-00-30-30**) stop in Trondheim. In addition, ships of **Fosen Teraffikklag Kystekspressen** (✆ **73-89-07-00**) travel between Kristiansund N and Trondheim (3½ hr.; NOK525). Trondheim departures are from Pirterminalen Quay.

BY CAR From Oslo, motorists can take the E6 express highway north, via Lillehammer all the way into Trondheim.

VISITOR INFORMATION

Contact the **Trondheim tourist office,** Munkegate 19 (✆ **73-80-76-60;** www.trondheim.no), near the marketplace. In peak season—mid-June to early Sept—it is open Monday to Friday 8:30am to 6pm, Saturday and Sunday 10am to 6pm; from June 2 to 22, Monday to Friday 8:30am to 6pm, Saturday and Sunday 10am to 4pm; during other months, Monday to Friday 9am to 4pm, Saturday 10am to 2pm.

GETTING AROUND

You can travel all over Trondheim and to outlying areas on city buses operated by **Team Traffikk** (it also goes by the name of AtB), Kongens Gate 34 (✆ **73-87-14-00**). Tickets for **single rides** are sold on buses for NOK30, NOK15 for children 4 to 16; children 3 and under travel free. If you don't have exact change, you'll receive a credit slip from the driver, which can be redeemed at the TT office or on a later trip. A **day card** for 24 hours of unlimited rides costs NOK70 per person or NOK120 for a family. For local bus information on the greater Trondheim area, call ✆ **81-53-52-30.**

For a local **taxi,** TrønderTaxi maintains a special five-digit telephone number (✆ **07373**) that's in service 24 hours a day. The biggest taxi ranks are found at Torvet, the market square, and at the railway station.

Trondheim, known for its allegiance to all things "green" (ecologically speaking), maintains a fleet of several hundred red-painted bicycles at bike racks scattered around the city. To secure one, head for the tourist office (see above) and pay a fee of NOK70, plus a cash or credit card deposit of NOK200, for which you will get a sort of credit card. Inserting this into a slot on the bike rack releases the bike, which you're then free to use for up to 5 days without additional charge. When you're through with the bike, bring it back undamaged and your deposit will be returned. The whole system will make you want to write an ode to the joys of visiting a civilized country.

CITY LAYOUT

From the railway station, walk south across the bridge to the triangular island forming the city's central core, **Midtbyen.** In Norse sagas, it was referred to as Nidarneset (Nidar Headland). A major street, **Kongens Gate,** splits the island into two parts. The best way to explore this area is on foot; you can easily walk to all major attractions, including Nidaros Domkirke and the Archbishop's Palace.

The very center of Trondheim is the **Torvet,** or market square. The **Fish Market (Fisketorvet)** is reached from Torvet by walking north along Munkegate.

At Nidareid, by the narrow isthmus between the river and the fjord, lies ancient **Skansen.** The remnants of the old city fortifications to the west can still be seen here. Today this area is a green park with a panoramic view of the fjord.

The **Bakklandet** district, noted for its antique, slightly off-kilter wooden houses, built in the 17th century for canning-factory workers and fishermen, is most easily accessible from the rest of Trondheim via the Old Town Bridge, an early-20th-century iron structure that is the most-photographed bridge in Trondheim. The area used to stink of rotting fish, and in the 1910s and 1920s it came very close to being demolished. But after the decline of the fishing industry and the end of the canning factories, a greater emphasis was placed on preserving the site as a historical record of days gone by. Today its most famous and most celebrated restaurant is **Bryggen,** and its most famous pub is **Den Gode Nabo ("The Good Neighbor").** The neighborhood also holds a number of students' pubs, one of which is the **Kaktus** (see "Trondheim After Dark," later in this chapter). The neighborhood is quite small—40 buildings or so—and easily toured on foot.

[FastFACTS] TRONDHEIM

Automobile Association Driving in the wilds of central Norway in the vast open stretches around Trondheim might be hazardous if the weather turns bad. For directions and information about road conditions, or even reroutings, call the **Norwegian Automobile Federation** at ✆ **92-60-85-05.**

Consulates There is no U.S. consulate in Trondheim. The consulate for Great Britain is at Beddingen 8 (✆ **73-60-02-00**). For embassies and consulates in Norway, see "Embassies & Consulates," in chapter 16.

Dentists If you need emergency assistance, call ✆ **73-50-55-00.**

Emergencies For fire dial ✆ **110,** for the police ✆ **112,** and for an ambulance ✆ **113.**

Hospitals For a non-emergency, your hotel can put you in contact with an English-speaking doctor. For a medical emergency, call Trondheim Emergency Hospital, Olav Kyrresgate 17 (✆ **73-52-25-00**).

Internet Access Go to the Trondheim Public Library, Peter Egges Plass 1 (✆ **72-54-75-00**), open Monday to Thursday 10am to 7pm, Friday 10am to 4pm, and Saturday 10am to 3pm; from September to April it is also open Sunday noon to 4pm.

Laundry If you don't use the services your hotel provides, you can go to **Elefanten Vaskeri,** Mellomveien 20 (✆ **73-51-29-89**), which is open Monday to Friday 10am to 6pm and Saturday 11am to 4pm. It's one of the most northerly laundromats in Norway.

Parking Garages The major garages are **Bakke P-hus,** Nedre Bakklandet 60 (✆ **72-54-65-33**), and **Midtbyen P-hus,** Sandgata 28 (no phone).

Pharmacies The most central pharmacy is Løveapoteket, Olav Tryggvasons Gate 28 (✆ **73-83-32-83**), a bustling emporium of the health industry, in the Behaven Shopping Complex in the heart of town. Hours are Monday to Friday 9am to 5pm, Saturday 10am to 3pm.

Police The police station is at Gryta 4 (✆ **02800**). For emergencies, dial ✆ **112.**

Post Office The main post office is at Dronningens Gate 10 (✆ **81-00-07-10**), open Monday to Friday 8am to 5pm (Thurs until 6pm), Saturday 9am to 2pm.

WHERE TO STAY

Many hotels offer special summer prices from mid-June to the end of August. The rest of the year, hotels feature weekend discounts if you stay 2 nights.

Expensive

Britannia Hotel ★★ For old-world tradition, the Britannia can't be beat. This grande dame of Trondheim hotels was built in 1897, with a white-stucco facade, a majestic slate-covered dome, and a tower evocative of the grand Victorian monuments of England. The renovated guest rooms have wooden floors, and the most tranquil units front the courtyard but are also the smallest rooms. One unique feature is a series of "Artists' Rooms," decorated with works from nationally famous artists, but for all-out grandeur, try one of the 11 regal suites, half of which are duplexes. If you like boas and gilt-plated "ice," you can check into the Flettfrid Andresen Room (no. 724)—the campest room in Norway.

Dronningens Gate 5, N-7001 Trondheim. ✆ **73-80-08-00.** www.britannia.no. 247 units. Mon–Thurs NOK1,695–NOK2,295 double; Fri–Sun NOK1,295–NOK1,595 double; NOK3,500–NOK6,500 suite. Rates include buffet breakfast. AE, DC, MC, V. Parking NOK225. Bus: 3, 4, 5, or 7. **Amenities:** 3 restaurants; 4 bars; babysitting; indoor heated pool; fitness center; spa; sauna; room service; rooms for those with limited mobility. *In room:* TV, Wi-Fi, minibar, hair dryer.

Clarion Collection Hotel Grand Olav ★★ This six-story hotel was designed in 1989 by the architect of the nearby Radisson BLU Royal Garden Hotel (see below), a close competitor, and radically renovated in a style the hotel refers to as "modernized rococo." The Grand Olav is a bit more stylish than its sibling, the Hotel Bakeriet (see below), and I prefer it for its grace and character. The hotel is adjacent to a building complex that includes elegant boutiques and Trondheim's largest concert hall. The midsize-to-spacious bedrooms are tastefully and comfortably furnished, all with a certain flair.

Kjøpmannsgata 48, N-7010 Trondheim. ✆ **73-80-80-80.** www.choicehotels.no. 106 units. Mon–Thurs NOK1,292–NOK1,945 double; Fri–Sun NOK1,037–NOK1,245 double; NOK1,800–NOK6,000 suite. Rates include buffet breakfast & a light evening meal. AE, DC, MC, V. Parking NOK168. Bus: 6 or 7. **Amenities:** Small lobby bar; rooms for those with limited mobility. *In room:* A/C, TV, minibar, hair dryer.

Radisson BLU Royal Garden Hotel ★★★ This glittering extravaganza on the see-and-be-seen circuit is Trondheim's largest and best hotel. It lacks the tradition of the Britannia (see above) but outdistances the Clarion hotels for pure luxury and amenities. This is the most architecturally dramatic and innovative hotel in Trondheim. Originally built in 1984 to replace a row of waterfront warehouses that had burned down, it rises abruptly on stilts just above the Nidelva River. Inside is an intriguing array of angled glass skylights, stone floors, soaring atriums, and plants. Rooms are comfortable and tastefully contemporary, outfitted in gray, earth tones, and/or blue. The most elegant of the hotel's restaurants, the Prins Olavs Grill, is recommended separately below.

Kjøpmannsgata 73, N-7010 Trondheim. ✆ **73-80-30-00.** www.radissonblu.com/hotel-trondheim. 298 units. Sun–Thurs NOK1,595–NOK1,900 double; Fri–Sat NOK1,095–NOK1,495 double; NOK3,000–NOK5,000 suite. Rates include buffet breakfast. AE, DC, MC, V. Parking NOK195. Bus: 1 or 4. **Amenities:** 2 restaurants; bar; indoor heated pool; health club & exercise center; Jacuzzi; sauna; room service. *In room:* TV, Wi-Fi, minibar, hair dryer.

Moderate

Best Western Chesterfield Hotel ★ 🎁 This small, cozy, centrally located, English-inspired hotel has a lobby that resembles an English pub (they even sell drinks from the reception desk). A collection of leather-upholstered Chesterfield sofas adds to the Anglophile theme. Built in 1947, it originally functioned as a doctor's office and an office building, but in 1992 it was transformed into the charming seven-story hotel you see today. A light evening meal—usually featuring a stew pot of some kind of hearty, rib-sticking soup and fresh bread—is included, buffet-style, as part of the price. Bedrooms are medium size, high-ceilinged, and very pleasant, with full-grained wooden furniture.

Søndregate 26, N-7010 Trondheim. ✆ **800/780-7234** in the U.S., or 73-50-37-50. www.bestwestern.com. 43 units. Sun–Thurs NOK825–NOK1,595 double; Fri–Sat NOK995–NOK1,090 double. Rates include buffet breakfast and light evening meal. AE, DC, MC, V. No on-site parking. Bus: 1 or 4. **Amenities:** Pub-style lobby bar; sauna; rooms for those with limited mobility. *In room:* TV, hair dryer.

Clarion Collection Hotel Bakeriet ★ 🎁 ☺ Although its chain partner Grand Olav (see above) is a bit more cutting-edge, the Bakeriet is also a worthy choice in every way. One of the most atmospheric hotels in Trondheim occupies the premises of what was between 1863 and 1963 the largest bakery in Norway. It calls to mind a museum, thanks to a number of displays that showcase the ovens, cooling racks, and paraphernalia associated with the building during its early days. Kids should eat up these displays, including the elaborate 20th-century bakers' costumes lining the upstairs hallways leading to the large and very comfortable bedrooms. Many of these have carefully finished half-paneling, easy chairs, and settees.

Brattørgata 2, N-7010 Trondheim. ✆ **73-99-10-00.** www.choicehotels.no. 109 units. NOK890–NOK2,390 double; NOK2,540 suite. Rates include breakfast & a light evening supper. AE, DC, MC, V. Parking NOK200. Bus: 1 or 4. **Amenities:** Breakfast room & lounge; babysitting; fitness room; Turkish bath; sauna; bike rental; rooms for those with limited mobility. *In room:* TV, Wi-Fi, minibar, hair dryer.

Where to Stay & Dine in Trondheim

ACCOMMODATIONS ■

- Best Western Chesterfield Hotel **3**
- Britannia Hotel **17**
- Clarion Collection Hotel Bakeriet **5**
- Clarion Collection Hotel Grand Olav **6**
- Comfort Hotel Lipp **11**
- Comfort Hotel Park **22**
- Nova Hotell **13**
- Prinsen Hotell **1**
- Radisson BLU Royal Garden Hotel **7**
- Thon Hotel Gildevangen **4**
- Thon Hotel Trondheim **18**

DINING ◆

- Blåbrygga **2**
- Chablis Brasserie & Bar **21**
- Credo **9**
- Havfruen **19**
- Jonathan's **16**
- Kafe Choco Boco **20**
- Kvilhaugen Gård **15**
- Palm Garden **16**
- Prins Olavs Grill **8**
- Ramp **14**
- Restaurant Egon **12**
- Sushi Bar **10**
- Tavern på Sverresborg **23**
- Vertshuset Grenaderen **23**

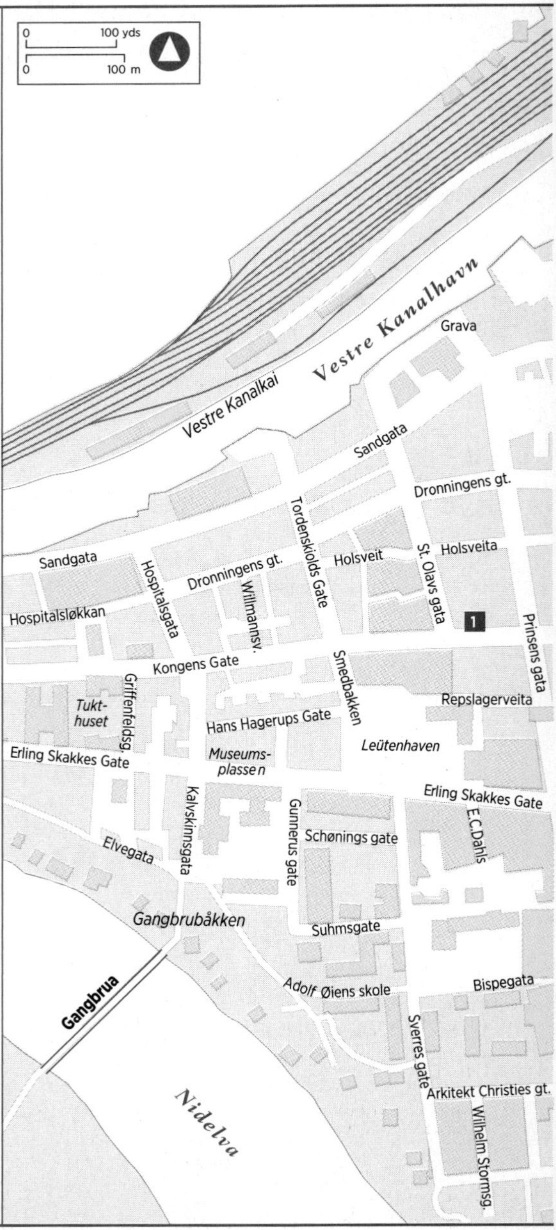

0 100 yds
0 100 m
Vestre Kanalhavn
Grava
Vestre Kanalkai
Sandgata
Dronningens gt.
Tordenskiolds Gate
Holsveit
St. Olavs gata
Holsveita
Sandgata
Hospitalsgata
Dronningens gt.
Willmannsv.
Hospitalsløkkan
1
Prinsens gata
Kongens Gate
Smedbakken
Repslagerveita
Tukt-huset
Griffenfeldsg.
Hans Hagerups Gate
Leütenhaven
Erling Skakkes Gate
Museums-plassen
Erling Skakkes Gate
Kalvskinnsgata
Gunnerus gate
Schønings gate
E.C.Dahls
Elvegata
Gangbrubåkken
Suhmsgate
Adolf Øiens skole
Bispegata
Gangbrua
Sverres gate
Arkitekt Christies gt.
Nidelva
Wilhelm Stormsg.

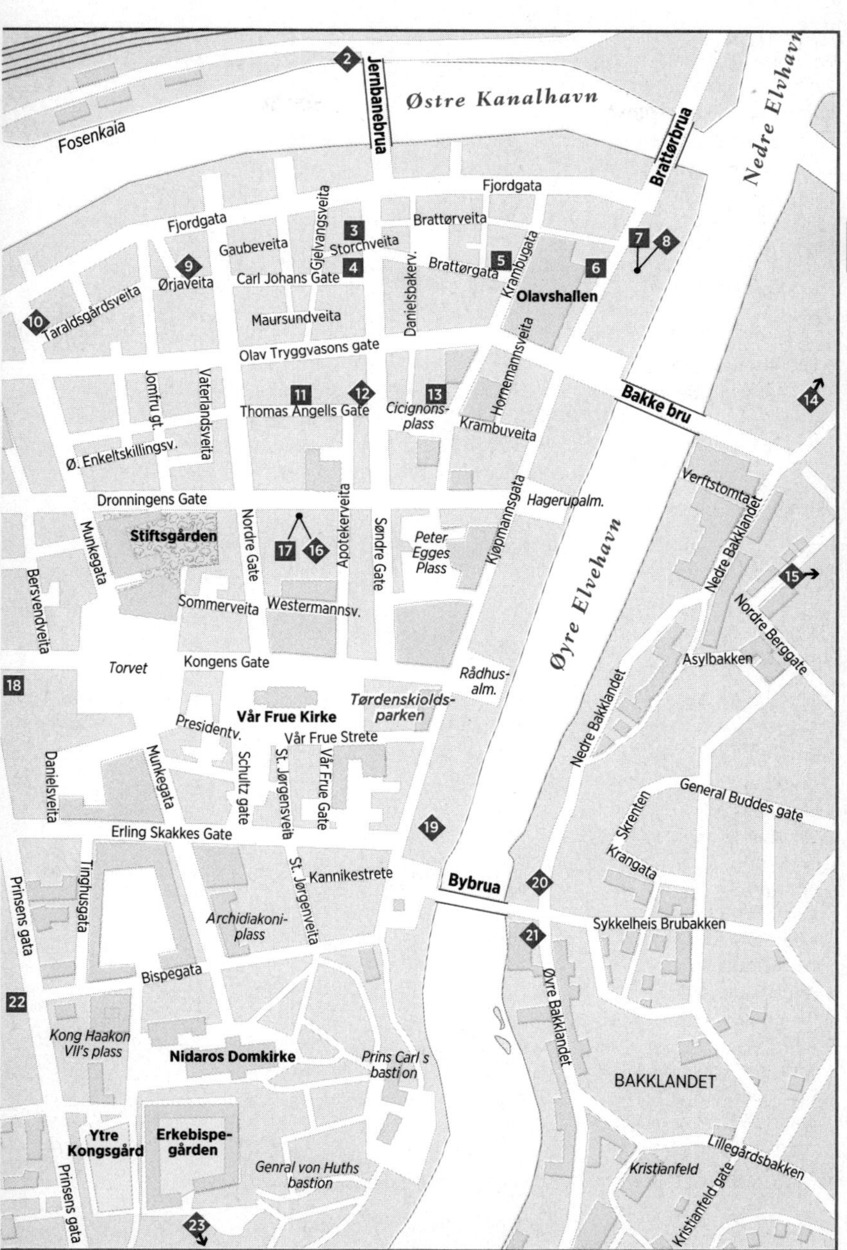

13

TRONDHEIM | Where to Stay

Comfort Hotel Park In the center of Trondheim, near Nidaros Domkirke (Dome) and the river, this well-run, red-brick chain hotel enjoys a prime location. Bedrooms are midsize, sleek, and streamlined, offering good (though not grand) comfort. What makes this hotel different from its competitors are special features such as a top-floor sauna and an outdoor hot tub. In the basement, laundry facilities are available to guests, while rooms have irons. The best accommodations offer free Internet access plus a kitchenette. In addition to the sizeable Norwegian breakfast in the morning, coffee and tea are served to guests in the afternoon.

Prinsensgate 4A, N-7012. ✆ **73-83-39-00.** www.choicehotels.no. 116 units. NOK995–NOK1,895 double; NOK1,295–NOK2,295 suite. AE, DC, MC, V. Parking: NOK110. Bus: 1 or 4. **Amenities:** Bar; sauna; Wi-Fi in lobby. *In room:* TV, minibar.

Prinsen Hotell This six-story building dating from the early 1960s is now one of Trondheim's better hotels. Set in the heart of the historic center, the hotel is a blend of pale pastel colors and solid, substantial furnishings. It caters mainly to business clients in the winter but is frequented by many non-Norwegian tourists in the summer. Most of the bedrooms are midsize and many feature replica Norwegian wooden country furniture. Many of the rooms open onto a view of the fjord waters. On-site is the oldest pub in Trondheim, **Kieglekroa,** whose specialty is a locally famous steak (the "Fairytale Steak"), served in the immediately adjacent Egon restaurant.

Kongens Gate 30, N-7012 Trondheim. ✆ **73-80-70-00.** www.prinsen-hotell.no. 81 units. NOK990–NOK1,390 double. Children 11 & under stay free in parents' room. Rates include buffet breakfast. AE, DC, MC, V. Parking NOK150. Bus: 1 or 4. **Amenities:** Restaurant; bar; pub; coffee shop; room service. *In room:* TV, Wi-Fi, minibar, hair dryer.

Thon Hotel Gildevangen ★ One of Trondheim's most architecturally distinctive antique hotels, the Gildevangen sits behind a dramatic-looking facade of massive, carefully chiseled stone blocks. Originally built in 1910 as an office building and transformed into a hotel in 1930, a recent restoration has provided it with clean, uncomplicated, quiet bedrooms. Breakfast is included in the price, and from Monday to Thursday a light evening meal is included as well. Each unit has big windows, generous dimensions, and a high ceiling.

Søndregate 22B, N-7010 Trondheim. ✆ **73-87-01-30.** www.thonhotels.com/gildevangen. 110 units. NOK1,050–NOK1,652 double. Rates include buffet breakfast, & on Mon–Thurs a light evening meal. AE, DC, MC, V. No on-site parking. Bus: 46. **Amenities:** Bar. *In room:* TV, minibar, hair dryer.

Inexpensive

Comfort Hotel Lipp This decent but lackluster choice offers some of the most affordable rooms in the city—and it's conveniently located in the commercial center. Built in the early 1990s with an unfortunately bland modern, angular facade, this middle-bracket hotel offers rooms that are comfortable and cozy, but without any frills. Accommodations are outfitted in neutral, monochromatic tones, each with hardwood floors and a meticulously tiled bathroom. Immediately adjacent to the hotel, but under separate management, is an unpretentious bar and grill, Graffi's, which serves burgers, steaks, pastas, seafood, and salads.

Thomas Engells Gate 12B, N-7011 Trondheim. ✆ **73-51-21-33.** www.cityliving.no. 35 units. NOK970–NOK1,070 double. AE, DC, MC, V. Bus: 3 or 4. **Amenities:** Restaurant; bar. *In room:* TV, fridge, hair dryer.

Nova Hotell Situated in a public office building, this hotel lies close to the attractions at the historic center. The experienced staff tend to bedrooms outfitted in a modern, if conservative, style and are rather cozy, with cushioned furniture, small bathrooms, and often carpeted floors. The bathrooms in the singles have showers only.

Cicignons Plass, N-7011 Trondheim. ✆ **73-80-63-00.** www.nova-hotell.no. 44 units. NOK1,095 double. Children 3 & under stay free in parents' room. Rates include continental breakfast. AE, DC, MC, V. Closed 2 weeks at Christmas & 1 week at Easter. No on-site parking. Bus: 1 or 4. **Amenities:** Restaurant; rooms for those with limited mobility. *In room:* TV, Wi-Fi, hair dryer.

Thon Hotel Trondheim This six-story hotel near the market square is a deliberately simple, relatively inexpensive B&B with medium-size guest rooms but offering little flair or frill. Outfitted with sun-kissed color schemes, many of the rooms contain an extra foldaway bed. The beds are comfortable, and the bathrooms, while small, are equipped with tub/shower combinations. Constructed in 1913, the hotel was renovated and expanded in 1990, with additional small-scale renovations conducted ever since.

Kongens Gate 15, N-7013 Trondheim. ✆ **73-88-47-88.** www.thonhotels.com/trondheim. 115 units. NOK925–NOK1,570 double. AE, DC, MC, V. Parking NOK160. Airport bus stops here. **Amenities:** Breakfast room; rooms for those with limited mobility. *In room:* TV, minibar, hair dryer.

WHERE TO DINE

Be sure to try the local specialty, ***vafler med øst* (waffle and cheese),** sold at most cafeterias and restaurants. Most restaurants will automatically add around 15% service charge to your bill. If you like the service, it's customary to leave some extra small change as well.

Expensive

Chablis Brasserie & Bar ★ FRENCH This polished but informal brasserie serves excellent food. The elaborate place settings and sparkling crystal make it one of the neighborhood's most appealing dining venues. In summer, many diners prefer an outside table to soak up the fair weather. The best dishes include redfish with mussel ragu, baked leek, and dill oil; and monkfish with spinach, fennel, celery purée, and veal broth. Another specialty is breast of duck *pac choi*, with fondant potato and calvados broth. Always check to see what the catch of the day is, as the fish served here is extremely fresh.

Øvre Bakklandet 66. ✆ **73-87-42-50.** www.chablis-brasseriogbar.com. Reservations required. Main courses NOK255–NOK295; fixed-price 3-course menu NOK475. AE, DC, MC, V. Mon–Sat 5–11pm. Bus: 4, 5, 7, or 52.

Credo ★★ CONTINENTAL This is Trondheim's trendiest restaurant, and includes an art gallery and jazz bar as well. The contemporary setting features modern furniture and white walls that showcase a changing array of paintings (most of which are for sale) on loan from a nearby art gallery. The seasonal cuisine infuses fresh local meats, vegetables, and produce with cooking techniques inspired by France, Italy, and Spain. Menu items change with the inspiration of the chef but especially tasty is the changing array of game dishes featuring duck, elk, pheasant, venison, or grouse. The cellar boasts nearly 2,000 varieties of wine, including a collection of German Rieslings that is among the most comprehensive in Scandinavia. For more about the jazz bar, see "Trondheim After Dark."

Ørjaveita 4. ✆ **73-53-03-88.** www.restaurantcredo.no. Reservations recommended. Set-price menus NOK550–NOK660. AE, DC, MC, V. Restaurant Mon–Sat 6–10pm (last order). Closed July & 1 week each at Christmas & Easter. Bar Mon–Sat 4pm–3am (no annual closings). Bus: 3, 4, or 5.

Havfruen ★★ SEAFOOD The freshness of the seafood served here never fails to impress us. Set amid a cluster of some of the oldest warehouses in town, along the Nidelven River, this is the best fish restaurant in Trondheim. Built around 1800 on the site of an earlier warehouse, it's studded with old beams and trusses and plenty of authentic antique charm. Meals are prepared in the open-to-view kitchen, with a seasonal menu based on fish migration patterns in the frigid waters surrounding Trondheim. The staff is more than knowledgeable to advise you, but you might begin enticingly enough with the creamy fish chowder, the city's best, although a close contender includes lobster bisque with lobster and fresh spinach ravioli. For a main course, you are likely to be won over by the dried, salted cod with risoni, tomato, pancetta, and basil oil; or perhaps the breast of lamb with root vegetables and creme of potato.

Kjøpmannsgata 7. ✆ **73-87-40-70.** www.havfruen.no. Reservations required. Main courses NOK265–NOK310; fixed-price menus NOK550–NOK750. AE, DC, MC, V. Mon–Sat 5pm–midnight. Closed Dec 23–Jan 7. Bus: 5, 6, 7, or 9.

Prins Olavs Grill ★★★ CONTINENTAL In a fierce neck-and-neck race for culinary supremacy over the Britannia's restaurant, the chefs here have devised an entirely new repertoire of dishes with imaginative flavor combinations. Set on the lobby level of the also-recommended hotel, this restaurant is named after a once-majestic British Navy ship, the *Alexandra,* purchased by the Norwegian navy in the 1930s and then sunk by the Nazi air force in 1940. Today many of the ship's gilded architectural embellishments, as well as a photographic history of the vessel, decorate the walls of one dining room. Dishes from the open kitchen include appetizing starters such as a carpaccio of beef with pine kernels and grated Parmesan; citrus-marinated salmon with Szechuan peppers and an endive-flavored cream sauce; roasted rack of lamb with a parsnip-and-garlic-flavored cream sauce; and oven-baked halibut with a nut crust and seasonal mushrooms and a sherry-flavored cream sauce.

In the Radisson BLU Royal Garden Hotel, Kjøpmannsgata 73. ✆ **73-80-30-00.** www.radissonblu.com/hotel-trondheim. Reservations recommended. Main courses NOK250–NOK310; fixed-price 5-course menu NOK650. AE, DC, MC, V. Daily 5–11pm. Closed July. Bus: 1 or 4.

Moderate

Blåbrygga ★ SEAFOOD This is one of the two most popular seafood restaurants in Trondheim. It's not as chic, cutting-edge, and sophisticated as the Havfruen (see above), but it serves an intelligent, imaginative cuisine at somewhat better prices. It's housed in a glass-sided pavilion that overlooks a fleet of fishing vessels moored in a canal a short walk from the railway station. Inside, a navy-blue color scheme, varnished mahogany, and pin lighting work to enhance the nautical decor. I recommend lime-and-chili-marinated scampi served on a salad bed of rucola and fresh tomato as a starter. Drawn from the cold, deep waters of Norway, the braised monkfish is served with fresh veggies, mashed potatoes, and white wine sauce. If you're here on a summer day, try the rhubarb soup with cinnamon ice cream.

Fosenkaia. ✆ **73-51-60-71.** Reservations recommended. Main courses NOK220–NOK245. AE, DC, MC, V. Sun–Thurs 2–11pm, Fri–Sat 2pm–midnight. Bus: 1 or 4.

Jonathan's ★ NORWEGIAN/FRENCH This restaurant, though fine in every way, is far less impressive than the elegant Palm Garden in the same hotel—but it's also far more affordable. Jonathan's is designed in the manner of a Mediterranean wine cellar, with antiques, a big, open fireplace, and waiters colorfully dressed as troubadours. The beautifully prepared food relies on high-quality ingredients. Launch yourself with such tantalizing starters as smoked salmon or "Trondheim caviar" (fish roe). Smoked salmon is also grilled as a main course, especially tasty when garnished with shellfish and accompanied by fresh vegetables. The veal schnitzel is as good as anything this side of Vienna. They are especially known for their *kjellerbiff*, a scrumptious steak served with spiced and fried potatoes and one of three sauces: Mango/peanut, garlic, or chili.

In the Britannia Hotel, Dronningens Gate 5. ✆ **73-80-08-00.** www.britannia.no/restaurant/jonathan/. Reservations required. Main courses NOK230–NOK280. AE, DC, MC, V. Mon–Sat 5–11pm; Sun 4–10pm. Bus: 5, 6, 7, or 9.

Kvilhaugen Gård ★ 🎁 NORWEGIAN Literally meaning "Rest Hill Farm", come here not just for the good food, but also to experience Trondheim as it once was. Surrounded by the trees and lawns of a prosperous residential suburb 4km (2½ miles) east of the city center, this historic restaurant and pub is set in an 1820s-era red-sided manor barn (*fjøset*). Inside are signs indicating which areas were once reserved for cows, sheep, and pigs. Diners and drinkers enjoy themselves below massive antique ceiling beams, lingering over midafternoon snacks or full meals. These might include melon with Parma ham; creamy fish soup; chicken salad; baked trout, arctic char, turbot, or salmon; or roasted filets of beef or reindeer. The food is good, wholesome, regional fare, made with well-chosen ingredients and cooked with local flavor.

Blussuvollsbakken 40. ✆ **73-52-08-70.** www.kvilhaugen.no. Reservations recommended for meals but not for snacks. Snacks NOK110–NOK150; main courses NOK165–NOK298. AE, DC, MC, V. Mon–Wed 4–11pm; Thurs 4pm–midnight; Fri–Sat 4pm–1am; Sun 1–7pm. Bus: 60.

Sushi Bar JAPANESE The best of Trondheim's two sushi places, this is set on the city's main street. It is outfitted in neutral beige tones, with large oil paintings and an open kitchen where a team of experts filet, roll, and prepare artfully simple, fresh raw fish. The best value is *sushi moriawase*, a main-course platter, consisting of 10 pieces of sushi and six pieces of *maki* (fish filet rolled, with rice, into a roulade), well priced at NOK239.

Munkegate 39. ✆ **73-52-10-20.** www.sushibar.as. Main courses NOK195–NOK255. AE, DC, MC, V. Sun–Mon 3–10pm; Tues–Fri 3–11pm; Sat 1–11pm. Bus: 5, 6, 7, or 9.

Vertshuset Grenaderen ★ 🎁 NORWEGIAN For rustic charm and authentic Nordic meals, this longtime favorite is hard to beat. The setting is a rather upscale rendition of the blacksmith shop this space was over a century ago. Today, amid flickering candles and a collection of 19th-century wood- and metal-working tools, there is a strong air of olde worlde Norway. Menu items include some time-tested workhorses such as gin-marinated smoked salmon; cream of fish and shellfish soup; small-scale platters of fish roe; that air-dried standby of *lutefisk*, served with bacon; several kinds of grilled beefsteak, some accompanied with grilled shrimp; barbecued pork ribs; and a dessert specialty: Wild-berry parfait with whiskey sauce. One of the city's best values is the lunchtime buffet, served year-round; in fall, it focuses on fresh game dishes from the surrounding tundras and forests. A more elaborate version of that same buffet is also served throughout the day on Sunday.

Kongsgårdsgata 1. ✆ **73-51-66-80.** Reservations recommended. Main courses NOK165–NOK349; lunchtime buffet (until 4pm) NOK175; 3-course menu NOK204; Sun buffet NOK205. AE, DC, MC, V. Mon–Sat noon–midnight; Sun 1–9pm. Dec–Apr closed Mon. Bus: 5, 6, 7, or 9.

Inexpensive

Ramp VEGETARIAN/FISH A delectable vegetarian cuisine is served at this restaurant, a popular hangout with local university students. Norway traditionally has been a land of carnivores, and it's rare to encounter a vegetarian restaurant in the north. Here the cooks emphasize flavor and borrow freely from an international repertoire of meat-free dishes, including hummus and shrimp salad sandwiches. A delectable Caesar salad is also served, as are veggie and fish burgers. Always count on an array of freshly made pastries.

Strandveien 25A. ✆ **73-51-80-20.** www.lamoramp.net. Main courses NOK75–NOK135. MC, V. Mon–Wed 10am–midnight; Thurs–Fri 1pm–1am; Sat noon–1am; Sun noon–midnight. Bus: 1 or 4.

Restaurant Egon AMERICAN This is one of the friendliest joints in Trondheim and a good place to meet the city's younger set. It's in the center of the city in an early-20th-century stone building that was once a bank. Within a labyrinth of dark, woodsy-looking pub areas and dining rooms, the restaurant serves the Norwegian equivalent of American-style diner food, including pizza cooked in an open brick oven. In summer, the venue spills out onto the terrace outside.

Thomas Angellsgate 8 (entrance on Søndregate). ✆ **73-51-79-75.** Pizzas, burgers, salads, & platters NOK155–NOK298. AE, DC, MC, V. Mon–Sat 11am–midnight; Sun noon–11pm. Bus: 1 or 4.

Tavern på Sverresborg ★ NORWEGIAN No restaurant in town offers more authentic Norwegian cuisine than this historic eatery, 4.8km (3 miles) south of the city, adjacent to the Sverresborg Trøndelag Folk Museum (p. 374). Built as a private merchant's house in 1739 and later transformed into a clapboard-sided tavern with wide-plank flooring and antique rustic accessories, it's one of the few wooden buildings of its age in this area. The most desirable and oft-reserved table is directly in front of a fireplace in a side room. There's an emphasis on 18th- and 19th-century recipes, such as *spekemat,* a collection of thinly sliced ham, salami, and smoked mutton, served with flatbread, scrambled eggs, and sour cream. From the taste-of-Norway menu you can also enjoy homemade fishcakes fried in butter, or lightly cured herring with beets, sour cream, and onion rings. Another good-tasting dish is marinated chicken breast with a sour cream sauce, sprinkled with chervil and parsley.

Sverresborg Allé, at Trøndelag Folk Museum. ✆ **73-87-80-70.** www.tavern.no, Reservations recommended. Main courses NOK75–NOK335. AE, DC, MC, V. Mon–Fri 4pm–midnight; Sat–Sun 2pm–midnight. Bus: 8.

The Leading Cafe

Kafe Choco Boco LIGHT FARE This chocolate lover's cafe is just one of several branches in the city. Popular among local students, it serves *varm chocolade* and other chocolate drinks, including one rather horrifyingly sweet concoction made with marshmallows. Mint and caramel also flavor these chocolate drinks. For the non–chocolate lover, there are plenty of other items on the menu, including ciabatta sandwiches, salads and nachos, small slices of pizza, and freshly made cakes, muffins, and brownies. There is also an on-site art gallery, featuring revolving exhibitions of local talent.

Nedre Bakklandet 5. ✆ **73-50-43-35.** www.choco.no. Sandwiches NOK65–NOK119; cakes NOK25–NOK 119. MC, V. Daily 11am–midnight. Bus: 1 or 4.

WHAT TO SEE & DO

Erkebispegården (Archbishop's Palace) ★★ Visit Scandinavia's oldest secular building in conjunction with Nidaros Domkirke (see below). It was once the center of the Norwegian archdiocese, comprising not only Norway but also the Faroe and Shetland islands, the Isle of Man, Iceland, and even Greenland. Today's museum, which was founded in the late 12th century, lies close to the cathedral precincts. Until the Reformation came in 1537 and the archbishop got the boot, the palace was the home of every reigning ecclesiastical authority in Trondheim. Once the archbishops were gone, it became the official address for the Danish governors, and was later taken over by the Norwegian military. As you stand in the courtyard, you can see buildings that date from the 1160s to the 1990s. In summer, there are daily guided tours of the historic buildings.

If time is short, try at least to visit the **Archbishop's Palace Museum,** displaying artifacts discovered when two large storage buildings on this site burned to the ground in 1983. After 5 years of excavations, many artifacts were discovered, and the museum opened in 1997. Even more intriguing are the **sculptures ★★★** removed from Nidaros Domkirke for safekeeping: Gargoyles, mythological figures, and animals of the Middle Ages live on here. The cathedral and its famous sculptures are also explained in an audiovisual presentation.

Another option here is the **Hjemmefrontmuseet** (Army and Resistance Museum), in the **Rustkammeret** at Kongsgårdsgata (✆ **73-99-52-80**), charging no admission. It is open June to August only, Monday to Friday 9am to 3pm, Saturday and Sunday 11am to 4pm. The history of the military is traced from the days of the Vikings, and includes exhibits on the Norwegian Resistance during the destructive occupation by the Nazis in World War II.

Kongsgårdsgata. ✆ **73-53-91-60.** Admission NOK50 adults, NOK25 children. May to mid-Sept Mon–Sat 10am–3pm, Sun 10am–3pm; mid-Sept to Apr Tues–Fri 11am–2pm, Sat 11am–3pm, Sun noon–4pm. Bus: 5, 6, 7, or 9.

Kristiansen Festnung Though at times a bit grim, this fortress offers wonderful views from its precincts—reason enough to visit. Located about 2km (1¼ miles) east of the city center, this is a stone-sided, thick-walled vestige of the military power of the army that occupied Trondheim during the 17th and 18th centuries. Built by the Danes between 1681 and 1682 as a defense against the Swedes during the reign of Christian IV, it alone is credited with successfully fending off the attacks of the Swedish army in 1718, thereby saving Trondheim from foreign occupation. It was constructed in a nine-sided design that may have been influenced by the French military architect Vauban. Between 1816 and 1901, it functioned as the headquarters of Trondheim's firefighting brigades. Under the Nazi occupation, the fort was used as a site of execution for members of the Norwegian Resistance; a plaque has been erected in their memory. On warm days, expect to see sunbathers

What to See & Do in Trondheim

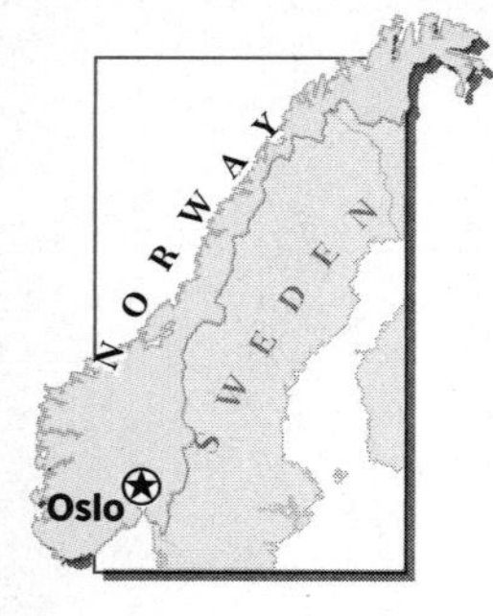

Erkebispegården **8**
Kristiansen Festnung **9**
Nidaros Domkirke **7**
Nordenfjeldske Kunstindustrimuseum **5**
Ringve Museum **2**
Stiftsgården **4**
Sverresborg Trøndelag Folk Museum **1**
Trondheim Kunstmuseum **6**
Trondhjems Sjøfartsmuseum **3**

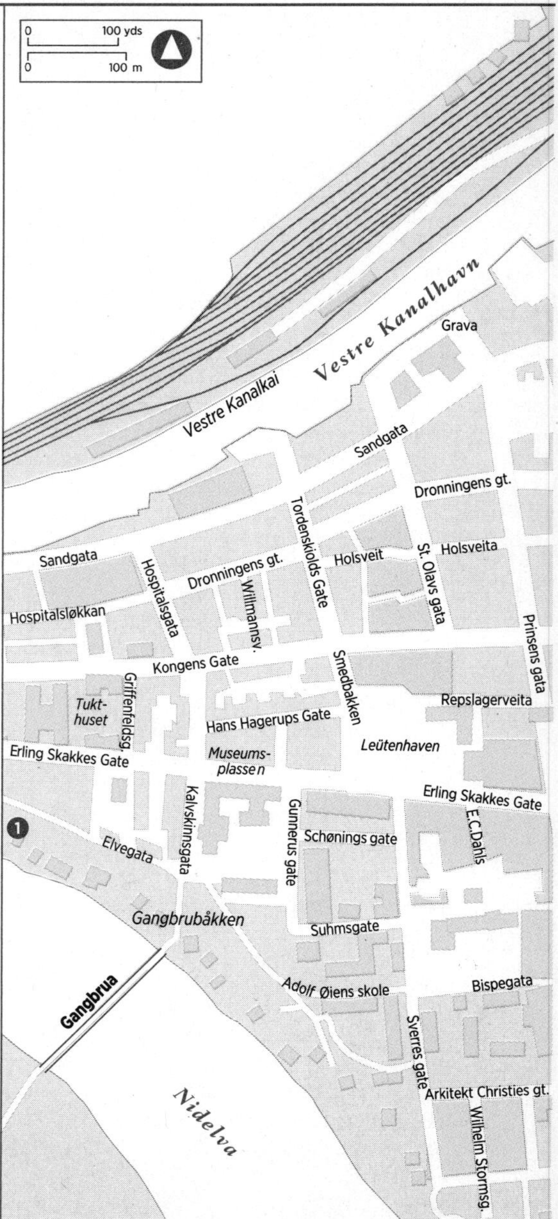

0 100 yds
0 100 m
Vestre Kanalhavn
Grava
Vestre Kanalkai
Sandgata
Dronningens gt.
Tordenskiolds Gate
Holsveit
St. Olavs gata
Holsveita
Sandgata
Hospitalsgata
Dronningens gt.
Willmannsv.
Hospitalsløkkan
Prinsens gata
Kongens Gate
Smedbakken
Repslagerveita
Griffenfeldsg.
Tukt-huset
Hans Hagerups Gate
Leütenhaven
Erling Skakkes Gate
Museums-plassen
Erling Skakkes Gate
Kalvskinnsgata
Gunnerus gate
E.C.Dahls
Schønings gate
Elvegata
Gangbrubåkken
Suhmsgate
Gangbrua
Adolf Øiens skole
Bispegata
Sverres gate
Arkitekt Christies gt.
Nidelva
Wilhelm Stormsg.

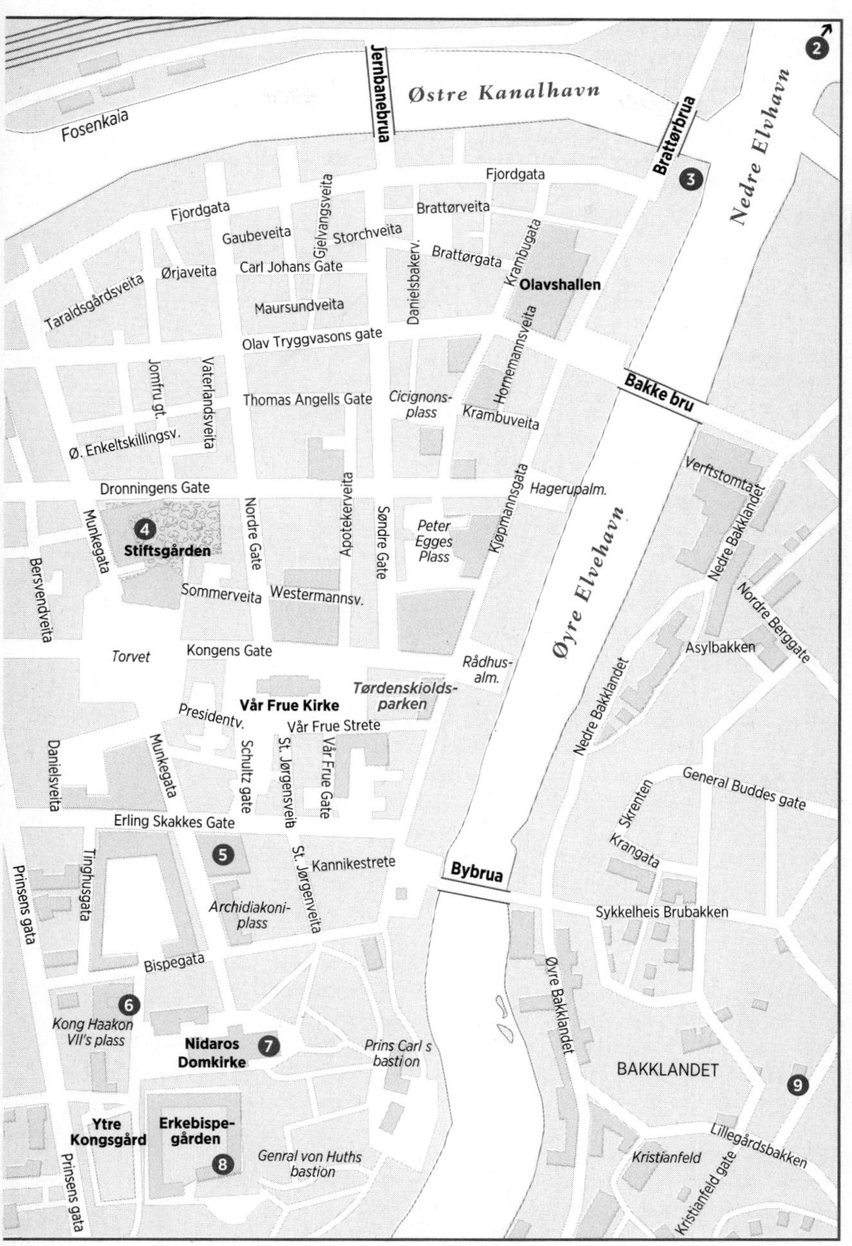
Østre Kanalhavn
Jernbanebrua
Fosenkaia
Brattørbrua
Nedre Elvhavn
Fjordgata
Gjelvangsveita
Brattørveita
Storchveita
Gaubeveita
Brattørgata
Krambugata
Carl Johans Gate
Ørjaveita
Taraldsgårdsveita
Danielsbakerv.
Olavshallen
Maursundveita
Olav Tryggvasons gate
Hornemannsveita
Jomfru gt.
Vaterlandsveita
Thomas Angells Gate
Cicignons-plass
Bakke bru
Krambuveita
Ø. Enkeltskillingsv.
Kjøpmannsgata
Hagerupalm.
Verftstomta
Dronningens Gate
Nordre Gate
Apotekerveita
Søndre Gate
Peter Egges Plass
Nedre Bakklandet
Munkegata
Stiftsgården
Bersvendveita
Sommerveita
Westermannsv.
Øyre Elvehavn
Nordre Berggate
Asylbakken
Torvet
Kongens Gate
Rådhus-alm.
Tørdenskiolds-parken
Vår Frue Kirke
Presidentv.
Vår Frue Strete
Danielsveita
Schultz gate
St. Jørgensveita
Vår Frue Gate
General Buddes gate
Skrenten
Erling Skakkes Gate
Krangata
Tinghusgata
Prinsens gata
Kannikestrete
St. Jørgenveita
Bybrua
Archidiakoni-plass
Sykkelheis Brubakken
Bispegata
Øvre Bakklandet
Kong Haakon VII's plass
Nidaros Domkirke
Prins Carl s basti on
BAKKLANDET
Ytre Kongsgård
Erkebispe-gården
Genral von Huths bastion
Lillegårdsbakken
Kristianfeld
Kristianfeld gate
2
3
4
5
6
7
8
9

An Escapist's Retreat

The Ringve Botaniske Hage (Ringve Botanical Gardens), Lade Allé 58 (© 73-59-22-69), form part of the University of Trondheim's Museum of Natural History and Archaeology. This is one of the finest places to be on a summer day in Norway. You can wander through a historic, Renaissance-style herb garden, enjoying trees of the Northern Hemisphere as well as some 2,000 unique plants. The entire park is laid out in English-garden style. Head for the nearest bench—and the day is yours. The admission-free park is open all year.

and families with children playing on the verdant lawns that have replaced the muddy, pounded-earth floor of the historical fort. From its ramparts, you'll see the best **panorama ★★** in town, encompassing fjords, towers, and the entire city of Trondheim.

Rosenborg. No phone. Free admission. Gates to the compound open year-round Mon–Tues when the Norwegian flag is flying above the fortress; Wed–Sun 8am–midnight. The interior of the compound can be visited between June & mid-Aug daily 11am–4pm. Bus: 63.

Nidaros Domkirke (Trondheim Cathedral) ★★★ Thousands upon thousands of medieval pilgrims have visited this grand cathedral, and it remains an extremely popular stop today. Dating from the 11th century, Nidaros easily dwarfs Oslo Cathedral as the most important, historic, and impressive ecclesiastical building in Scandinavia. It's located in the city center, near the Rådhus. The burial place of the medieval Norwegian kings, it was also the site of the coronation of Haakon VII in 1905, an event that marked the beginning of modern Norway.

Construction actually began on the cathedral in 1070, and some of its oldest parts still remain, primarily from the mid-12th century. Following the battle of Stiklestad, King Olav Haraldson was entombed under the high altar. In time, Olav became St. Olav, and his remains were encased in a gem-studded shrine.

The cathedral has weathered several disastrous fires that swept over Trondheim, though it was reconstructed each time in its original Gothic style. (The section around the transept, however, is Romanesque.) During the Reformation, the cathedral was looted of precious relics. By 1585, Nidaros had been reduced to the status of a parish church. Around 1869 major reconstruction work was begun to return the gray sandstone building to its former glory.

The west facade is particularly impressive, with its carved figures of royalty and saints. It's especially appealing after dark, when the facade is floodlit (the lights usually stay on every evening till midnight—it's worth a stroll even if you have to make a detour to do it). The interior is a maze of mammoth pillars and columns with beautifully carved arches that divide the chancel from the nave. The grandest feature is the stunning **rose window ★**. The cathedral's **stained-glass windows ★**, when caught in the proper light, are reason enough to visit. Gustav Vigeland, the famous sculptor, carved the **gargoyles** and **grotesques ★** for the head tower and northern transept. A small museum inside displays the **crown jewels of Norway ★★**.

Bispegate 5. © **41-79-80-00.** Admission to cathedral & museum NOK50 adults, NOK25 children. Cathedral & museum May 1–June 10 Mon–Fri 9am–3pm, Sat 9am–2pm, Sun 1–4pm; June 11–Aug 19

Mon–Fri 9am–6pm, Sat 9am–2pm, Sun 1–4pm; Aug 20–Sept 14 Mon–Fri 9am–3pm, Sat 9am–2pm, Sun 1–4pm; Sept 15–Apr 30 Mon–Fri noon–2:30pm, Sat 11:30am–2pm, Sun 1–3pm. Bus: 5, 6, 7, or 9.

Nordenfjeldske Kunstindustrimuseum (National Museum of Decorative Arts) ★★★ This is the single greatest museum in central Norway, holding one of Norway's most eclectic collections. Dating from 1893, the museum is devoted to applied art, placing special focus on changing trends in world art, especially in modern design and handicrafts. You'll see both historical and modern collections of furniture, textiles, silver, and a lot more, along with temporary exhibitions.

Displayed on the lower floor, the historical exhibitions span the period from 1500 to 1990; the specialty is furnishings from northern Europe, including Germany and England. The **Arts and Crafts collection** focuses on the creative breakthroughs of British craftsman and designer William Morris and his followers at the end of the 1800s and is rich in metalcraft, avant-garde ceramics, and printed textiles. The **Art Nouveau collection** is heavy on French art; most of it was purchased at the 1900 World Exhibition in Paris. An entire salon on the lower floor is devoted to contributions to Art Nouveau architecture by the Belgian architect and designer Henri Van de Velde.

The **Contemporary collection** concentrates on objects from the postwar era—not only in Europe but also from as far away as Australia and America. Scandinavian design gets the most airplay, of course, and there is an interior entirely designed by Finn Juhl, the Danish architect, in 1952. Of special interest are 200 **wall hangings and tapestries by Hannah Ryggen ★**, clustered in one gallery. This Swedish artist, born in 1894, married Hans Ryggen, the Norwegian painter, and lived outside Trondheim until her death in 1970.

Other collections include a **costume exhibition,** with garments dating from the 17th century, with the 1920s and 1930s most heavily represented. Other exhibitions are devoted to some 300 pieces of **jewelry** in modern design, and a **Japanese collection** showcasing that country's creativity in metalwork, lacquer, textiles, and pottery.

Munkegate 3–7. ✆ **73-80-89-50.** www.nkim.museum.no. Admission NOK60 adults, NOK30 children, students, & seniors. June 1–Aug 20 Mon–Sat 10am–5pm, Sun noon–5pm; off-season Tues–Sat 10am–3pm (Thurs until 5pm), Sun noon–4pm. Bus: 5 or 46.

Ringve Museum ★★ 🎁 This is the only Norwegian museum specializing in musical instruments from all over the world. Set on the Ringve Estate on the Lade Peninsula, the building originated in the 1740s as a prosperous manor house and farmstead. The mansion was the birthplace of Vice-Admiral Peter Tordenskiold, the Norwegian sea hero. The museum today consists of two parts—the manor house and a permanent exhibition in the estate's former barn. In the barn you can hear the unique sounds of Norwegian folk instruments; there's even a hands-on exhibition where you can express your inner folk musician. At specified times, concerts are given on carefully preserved antique instruments, including an impressive collection of spinets, harpsichords, clavichords, pianofortes, and string and wind instruments. Also on the premises is an old *kro* (inn) that serves waffles, light refreshments, and coffee.

Ringve Manor, Lade Allé 60 (3.3km/2 miles east of the city center). ✆ **73-87-02-80.** www.ringve.no. Admission NOK80 adults, NOK30 children 7–15, NOK60 students, NOK160 families. Mid-Apr to mid-May Mon–Fri & Sun 11am–4pm; mid-May to mid-June daily 11am–3pm; mid-June to Aug 5 daily 11am–5pm; Aug 6–Sept 9 daily 11am–3pm; Sept 10 to mid-Apr Sun 11am–4pm. During open hours, multilingual guided tours depart at least once per hour. Bus: 3 or 4.

THE FIRST EUROPEAN TO discover AMERICA

Trondheimers have no doubt who first discovered America—or, put more politically correct, who was the first European to discover an already inhabited continent. Here is the official line as taught in local schools: "Leiv Eiriksson sailed to Nidaros in the year A.D. 999. The visit to Olav Tryggvason's new royal farm must have been a success. Leiv Eiriksson became the king's man and stayed as a guest all winter. Spring came and he was a changed man. He had been baptized as a Christian. He launched his mighty boats at Skipakrok and sailed over the ocean to Greenland and further, far, far to the west. Leiv Eiriksson made the discovery of a lifetime—America."

To honor Leiv Eiriksson, there is an emigrant monument, the **Leiv Eiriksson Statue,** at Pirsenheret, Brattøra (take any bus through downtown Trondheim that runs to Pirterminalen). It was a gift from Americans of Scandinavian heritage to honor Trondheim's millennium celebration in 1997. The statue was erected and dedicated to emigrants who left Norway to seek a new life in America. It's an exact copy of the original, which stands in Seattle.

Stiftsgården (The Royal Residence) When the royal family visits Trondheim, they stay here—and they never run out of bedrooms. With 140 rooms, it is the largest secular wooden building in northern Europe, a massive pile in late baroque style. The buttercup-yellow royal palace, near the marketplace, was built as a private home by a rich merchant's widow in the 1770s, when Trondheim began to regain its prosperity. The exterior walls were notched together, log-cabin–style, then sheathed with wooden exterior panels. The unpretentious furnishings represent an amalgam of design styles.

Munkegate 23. ✆ **73-80-89-50.** www.kongehuset.no. Admission NOK60 adults, NOK30 children, NOK100 family. Guided tours every hour on the hour. June 1–June 19 Mon–Sat 10am–3pm, Sun noon–5pm; June 20–Aug 20 Mon–Sat 10am–5pm, Sun noon–5pm. Closed Aug 21–May 31. Bus: 3, 4, 5, 46, or 52.

Sverresborg Trøndelag Folk Museum ★★★ ☺ This is the best folkloric museum in Norway, and it's chock-full of farmhouses, cottages, churches, and town buildings, representing aspects of everyday life in the region over the past 3 centuries. Kids often find this attraction a sort of "Trondheim Disneyworld," but this educational, entertaining space is more real than Mickey Mouse land. Standing 5km (3 miles) west of the center, the complex is composed of 60 historic wood and stone buildings, all laboriously dismantled and reassembled here. Among the most intriguing buildings are Trondheim's first all-brick building and the 200-year-old barns, many with sod roofs, many painted red, and most built of weathered natural wood. The proudest structure here is Norway's northernmost stave church. There's a cafe on the premises, but if you want a good meal, head next door to the celebrated restaurant **Tavern på Sverresborg** (p. 358), which serves traditional Norwegian dishes.

On the grounds, within an antique building, is a separate museum, the **Sverresborg Ski Museum.** Tracing the history of skiing in Norway, it contains antique skis from the 1600s to today, some carved in patterns inspired by the Vikings, and some with fur or sealskin cladding which prevented them from sliding backwards during cross-country skiing. The museum is surrounded by a nature park with animals. Entrance is included in the price of admission to the Folk Museum, and hours are the same, too.

Sverresborg Allé. ✆ **73-89-01-00.** www.sverresborg.no. Admission NOK85 adults, NOK35 children, NOK210 family ticket, free for children 4 & under. June–Aug daily 11am–6pm; Sept–May daily 11am–3pm. Bus: 8.

Trondheim Kunstmuseum (Trondheim Art Museum) ★ We used to come here just to gaze upon the collection of lithographs by Edvard Munch, on loan from the Edvard Munch Museum in Oslo. In the wake of Munch thefts, however, the art was returned to Oslo. Still, there is an array of Norwegian painters to introduce yourself to here, and none is better known nationally than Christian Krohg (1852–1925). He is one of the leading figures in the transition from romanticism to naturalism. After Munch, he is in the running for one of Norway's most famous artists, celebrated today for his images of prostitutes. But when he published a novel, *Albertine,* on this theme in 1886 he was arrested.

You'll also see works by Theodor Kittelsen (1857–1914), who bridges the gap between neoromantic and naïve painting. He is known for his illustrations of fairy tales and legends, especially of trolls. Black-metal bands such as Burzum have used some of his pictures, including from his book *Svartedauen (The Black Death)*, as album art.

No one painted Norwegian landscapes better than Hans Fredrik Gude (1825–1903), a romantic painter who celebrated nature. His work is displayed along with that of his friend Adolph Tidemand, another leading figure in Norwegian painting. Both drew inspiration from dramatic mountain scenery and idyllic, sunny landscapes.

In all, there are more than 2,750 paintings that go back as early as 1800. Most of the art is Norwegian, although there is a fairly good collection of Danish art as well, along with a limited selection from international artists.

Bispegate 7B. ✆ **73-53-81-80.** www.tkm.museum.no. Admission NOK50 adults, NOK30 children & students, NOK40 seniors. Mid-June to mid-Aug daily 10am–5pm; off-season Tues–Sun 11am–4pm. Bus: 4.

Trondhjems Sjøfartsmuseum (Trondheim Maritime Museum) An old penitentiary from 1725 was turned into this Norwegian maritime showcase, presenting countless models of sailing ships, marine instruments, and prow figureheads. Some unusual exhibits include an 18th-century whaling ship and a harpoon gun. Nautical artifacts rescued from the frigate *The Pearl,* which sank in Norwegian waters in 1781, are on display. Daring divers rescued these artifacts in *Titanic*-cold waters.

Fjordgata 6A. ✆ **73-89-01-00.** Admission NOK55 adults, NOK25 children, students, & seniors. June 15–Aug 15 daily noon–4pm; Aug 16–June 14 Sat & Sun noon–4pm. Bus: 52.

Organized Tours

At the tourist office (p. 348), you can purchase tickets for guided tours of the city between mid-May and early September, lasting 2 hours and taking in the highlights. Departure is from Torvet, the market square, daily at 11am. The cost is NOK235 (accompanied children under 16 go free).

The tourist office also publicizes a 1½-hour sea tour, along the canal harbor, up the Nidelven River, to the fjord, costing NOK150 (NOK60 for children aged 3 to 14). From June 18 to August 13, it leaves Tuesday to Sunday at noon and 2pm; from August 14 to September 17 tours are on Wednesday, Friday, and Sunday at 1:30pm.

ZEALOTS, "PERVERTS" & THE ax man

Munkholmen (Monk's Island) is a small, rocky, inhospitable, and richly historic island a short distance offshore from Trondheim. When weather permits, daily ferries depart for picnicking, bird-watching, and beach excursions on the island, from the northern terminus of Munkegate, hourly between 10am and 7pm. A round-trip ticket for the 10-minute jaunt costs NOK60 (NOK30 for children 14 and under); buy tickets onboard.

But there's more to this sparse island than fun, games, and picnicking sites. For hundreds of years, beginning in 1658, the island functioned as a prison and execution site, with a prominent hangman's scaffold, instruments of torture, and wooden blocks where executioners would hack off the heads of wretches condemned as criminals, "perverts," or enemies of the Church or State. Before that, in the 11th century, the island was developed by Benedictine monks into one of the first two Christian monasteries in Scandinavia, housing zealots who shivered away the winters as winds and snows howled down the fjord. You can take a guided tour of the island's historic **fortress** for NOK30 (NOK20 for children). You can buy picnic supplies at the Ravnkloa fish market, a few steps from the landing. A cafe and snack bar are built into the much-restored fortifications.

The beach is small, gravelly, and relatively narrow. Some locals insist the place is haunted. What you may come away with is a pervasive sense of melancholy and a profound new appreciation for the hardships and severity of life in medieval Norway. Most first-timers to Munkeholmen return to Trondheim and head immediately for the nearest bar for food, drink, and a replenishment of whatever good cheer they might have lost during their excursion.

Incidentally, **Munkegate,** the broad boulevard loftily called by some locals the "Champs-Elysées of Trondheim," is named for the monks who made frequent, sometimes daily, processionals between the landing at the avenue's base and Trondheim's cathedral, a 20-minute walk to the south.

WALKING TOUR: TRONDHEIM'S HISTORIC CENTER

START:	**Torvet, at the junction of Munkegate and Kongens Gate.**
FINISH:	**Torvet.**
TIME:	**2½ hours.**
BEST TIME:	**Mornings after 8:30am when the Fiskehaller is at its most active.**
WORST TIME:	**Any time in midwinter after 4pm when it's dark, or on any of Trondheim's typical rain-soggy days.**

Begin your tour at the:

1 Torvet

This market square is Trondheim's most prominent traffic circle, at the edge of which is the tourist office and in the middle of which rises a soaring granite column with a statue of the world's handsomest Viking—in this case, an idealized

A Walking Tour of Historic Trondheim

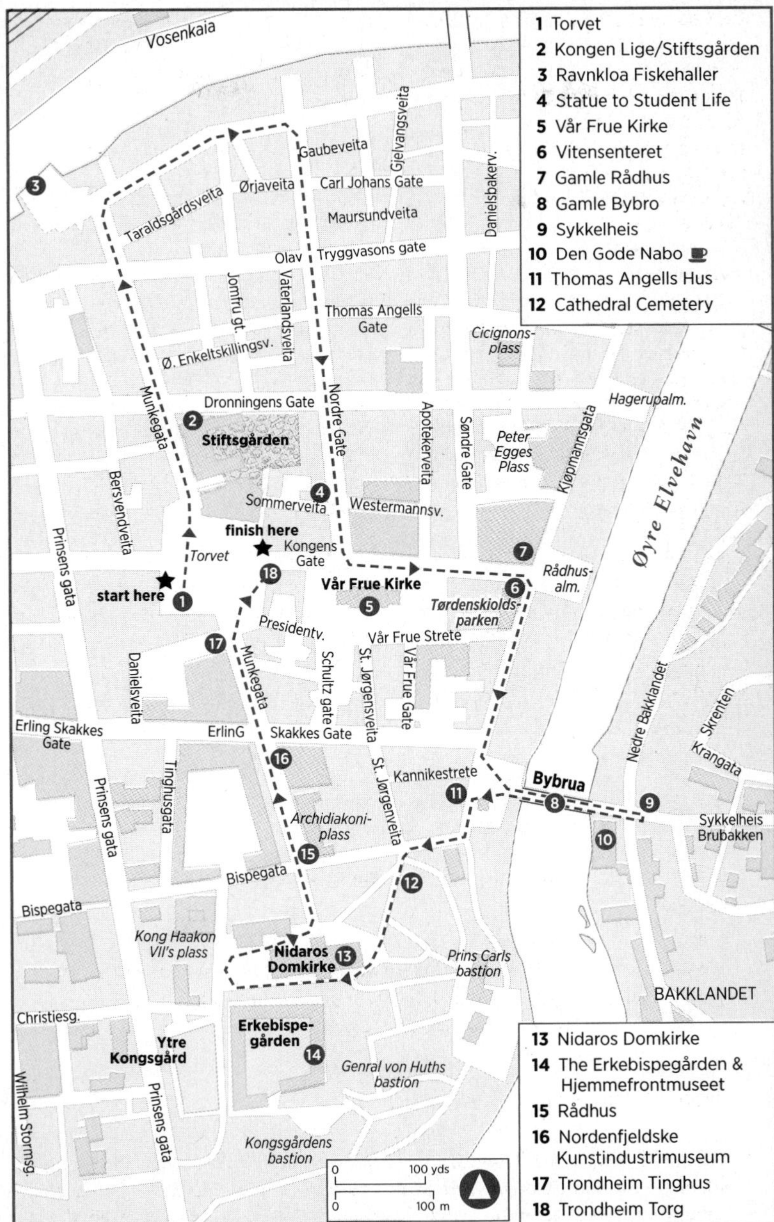

portrait of Olav Tryggvason, founder (in A.D. 997) of Trondheim. Markings on the pavement, tracking the seasonal direction of the sun, define the column on which he stands as the world's largest sundial.

From here, walk north along the Munkegate; its exceptional width was conceived as a firebreak during the rebuilding of Trondheim, after conflagration destroyed many of the city's wooden buildings in 1681. On your right, within a 2-minute walk, is the wood-sided, rustic-looking exterior of Trondheim's most prestigious home, the low-slung 18th-century premises of the:

2 Kongen Lige/Stiftsgården (Royal Residence)

Built in 1778 as the home of the (Danish) king, and with 140 rooms covering almost 4,000 sq. m (43,000 sq. ft.), this is the largest secular all-wooden building in northern Europe. Positioned very close to the street, it's the home of the Norwegian monarch and royal associates whenever they come to Trondheim on official business. If you're interested in visiting its interior as part of a 30-minute tour (only in midsummer), note that the entrance is at the back, near the building's functional and rather unimaginative garden.

Continue walking north along the Munkegate to the:

3 Ravnkloa Fiskehaller

This glass-sided, very clean, and modern fish market is one of the best places in Trondheim for a snack. You can opt for a bagful of freshly peeled (or unpeeled) shrimp or perhaps a salmon sandwich at this cornucopia of seafood and all things fresh. For more details, see "Beauty From the Sea—On Ice," below.

Adjacent to the fish market is the pier for the ferry to Munkeholmen (Monk's Island; p. 366). Fronting this is a contemporary-looking statue, erected in 1990 by artist Nils Aas and dedicated to *Den Siste Viking (The Last Viking)*. Its somber caricature was inspired by a novel of the same name by Johan Bøjer, a former resident of Trondheim who honored the fishermen of Norway for their bravery and fortitude.

From here, walk east along the Fjordgata, then right (south) onto the all-pedestrian Nordre Gate, lined with Trondheim's densest collection of shops. Within a few blocks, rising from the center of the street, you'll see an exuberant testimonial to young love, the:

4 Statue to Student Life

This is a life-size male-female depiction of young people swept away in a frenzy of love, dancing ecstatically on a pile of granite books.

Continue walking south on Nordre Gate to the smaller of the city's two medieval churches:

5 Vår Frue Kirke (Church of Our Lady)

This bulky, boxy, and dignified church was built in 1150, enlarged in 1686, and expanded with a bell tower again in 1739. Regrettably, of the 17 medieval churches that once graced Trondheim's streets, only two (this and the cathedral, visited later in this walking tour) remain. Consider yourself lucky if you happen to arrive during the church's rare opening hours (Wed only, 11am–2pm).

From here, turn left onto Kongens Gate and walk east for about a block to Kongens Gate 1. Here, at the corner of Kjøpmannsgata, behind an impressive-looking 19th-century red-brick facade, is the:

6 Vitensenteret (Children's Technological Museum)

Originally designed in 1833 as the Trondheim branch of the Bank of Norway, it was rebuilt in 1900 into the late-Victorian design you see today. Most visitors come here as part of school groups from the surrounding region, and unless you have small children in tow, I recommend you move on to other venues.

Directly across Kongens Gate, behind a Hanseatic-inspired facade adorned with an eight-pointed star-shaped window and the city's seal, is the:

7 Gamle Rådhus (Old Town Hall)

Originally built in the 1700s, this is now largely a decorative monument: Most of Trondheim's day-to-day administrative duties are handled in the new Town Hall, close to the cathedral and noted later in this walking tour.

Now turn right onto Kjøpmannsgata. In a short distance, on your left, you'll see a row of the oldest warehouses in town, each individual building painted in a cheerful palette of colors. A short distance later, on your left, you'll arrive at the wood planks and iron girders of the:

8 Gamle Bybro (Old Town Bridge)

Originally built of wood in 1861 as a replacement for an all-wood predecessor in 1685, this is the most evocative, beloved, and frequently photographed bridge in Trondheim. Locals refer to it as the "Bridge of Happiness" and claim that your dreams will come true if you wish for them fervently as you walk across it. While you're articulating your dreams, take note of the neo-Gothic mass, atop the ridge on the distant horizon to your right, of the headquarters of Trondheim's university. Also look to your left toward the dozens of carefully preserved 18th- and 19th-century warehouses rising on pilings above the river—proof of how extensive the maritime economy of Trondheim once was.

After you cross the bridge, continue straight across the cobbled intersection (Øvre Bakklandet on one side and Nedre Bakklandet on the other) and walk uphill along the street identified as Sykkelheis. After about 30m (100 ft.), on the right you'll see the local government's contribution to fresh air and exercise, the:

9 Sykkelheis (Municipal Bicycle Lift)

Designed to assist bike riders in their ascent of the steep hill, this mechanized conveyor belt (most of which is concealed beneath a metal-edged groove in the pavement) hauls bicycles, along with their riders, up a steeply inclined, scenic bike path. The cost for 15 minutes of continuous operation is NOK100, which you pay by inserting coins into the machine's coin slot. Frankly, most riders either walk their bikes or cycle in low gear up the relatively short hill, but as a conversation piece, the Sykkelheis is worth a look.

From the Sykkelheis, retrace your steps downhill and turn left onto Øvre Bakklandet. Within a few steps, behind the vine-covered, brown-plank facade of one of the first buildings on your right, you'll find:

10 Den Gode Nabo

(The Good Neighbor), Øvre Bakklandet 66 (✆ 40-61-88-09), is my favorite pub in the city, where you can dine on delectable fish soup. For more about the pub, see "Trondheim After Dark," later in this chapter.

Now retrace your steps back across the Old Town Bridge. When you reach the other side, turn left onto Kjøpmannsgata and walk for about a minute. When you reach a clearing in the bank of trees on the side toward the river, look across the river to the far crest of a stony ridge, for a view of Trondheim's once-strategic 18th-century military stronghold, Kristiansen Festnung (p. 359). During clear weather, a Norwegian flag proudly flies from its summit. Turn right at Bispegate and look on the right side for Trondheim's most elaborate baroque building:

11 Thomas Angells Hus

Originally built in 1770 and extensively restored in 1903 according to its original design, this was conceived as a retirement home for widows. Later it was expanded to allow widows to cohabit with reputable widowers outside the bounds of traditional marriages—a liberal 19th-century trend of which many Trondheimers seem appropriately proud. There's a pleasant garden in the building's interior courtyard, but visiting hours are erratic, and the doors are very likely to be locked at the time of your visit.

Continue walking west along the Bispegate, detouring into the intensely evocative:

12 Cathedral Cemetery

Cemetery walks aren't for everyone, but this one is spiritually evocative and appropriately eerie. For centuries, gravesites here were reserved only for the town's more prominent citizens, and, consequently, many of the grave markers are carefully planned sculptures in their own right. Note the location of this cemetery on your visit in the daylight hours; you may want to make a return visit, perhaps late at night and when it's raining and the wind is howling.

Its majestic trees and undulating walkways lead to the cemetery's centerpiece, the:

13 Nidaros Domkirke (Trondheim Cathedral)

This is in the running for the single most stunning and majestic building in Norway. Spend some quality time here and plan on a return before your departure from Trondheim for a second view of the cathedral's amazing rear (arguably the most spectacular bas-relief in Europe). Plan your second visit after dark, when much of the cathedral's exterior is illuminated (nightly until around midnight). For more about this cathedral, see "Seeing the Sights," earlier in this chapter.

Through a medieval gatehouse that's accessible from the cathedral's back side, wander into the vast and interesting courtyard created by the juxtaposition of two buildings:

BEAUTY FROM THE Sea—ON ICE

Some Norwegians believe that genuine beauty can be found in the fruits of the sea, and even if you don't agree, you should make a point to visit one of Norway's most appealing indoor fish markets, **Ravnkloa Fiskehalle ★** (✆ **73-52-55-21**). Set at the northern terminus of Munkegate, adjacent to the ferry piers serving Munkeholmen Island, this is a glass-and-steel structure of impeccable cleanliness. Inside, independent vendors sell fresh meat on one side and fresh fish, laid out in ordered rows on beds of ice, on the other. Even if you're not prepared to actually cook your purchases, you still might be tempted by the salmon sandwiches, fish salads, and small platters designed as takeout food. A picnic on Munkeholmen Island might be served well by a purchase here. Consider buying a half-kilo (1 lb.) of shrimp per person, along with fresh bread, butter, and mayonnaise (sold here in tubes that you squeeze like toothpaste). Purchase a glass of beer from the on-site beer tap, commandeer one of the indoor or outdoor tables, and dine like Neptune himself. Platters, which include such fare as pan-fried turbot with risotto, or warm fish cakes with salad, cost NOK55 to NOK80 each; sandwiches cost NOK40, and stuffed crab goes for NOK55. The complex is open Monday to Friday 10am to 5pm, Saturday 10am to 4pm.

14 The Erkebispegården & Hjemmefrontmuseet (Archbishop's Palace & Army and Resistance Museum)

The architecture on this square takes you back to the dim, often unrecorded past of Norway in the Middle Ages. The Erkebispegården is the oldest secular building in Scandinavia; work started on the structure in the second half of the 12th century. The Hjemmefrontmuseet is in the Rustkammeret, one of the oldest structures in Norway.

From here, return to the cathedral's front side, and walk north along the Munkgate. The first building you'll see on the right side (on the eastern corner of the Bispegate), is Trondheim's:

15 Rådhus (New Town Hall)

This is not to be confused with the Gamle Rådhus, visited earlier on this tour. This modern, fortress-like brick building is where most of the city's day-to-day administrative functions are carried out. As such, it's not open to the public for casual visits.

Continue walking north along the Munkegate. At the corner of Erling Skakkes Gate, on the street's eastern flank, you'll see Trondheim's homage to the contemporary decorative arts of Norway, the:

16 Nordenfjeldske Kunstindustrimuseum (National Museum of Decorative Arts)

Here exhibits celebrate Norway's contribution to the tenets of modern decor and designs in glass, wood, textiles, and metal.

Continue your northward progression along the Munkegate, admiring the occasional piece of public sculpture along its path. My favorite is the life-size bronze representation of a family of grazing deer. About a block farther along the same street, at Munkegate 20, behind a bas-relief sculpture from the 1940s, is the:

17 Trondheim Tinghus (Trondheim Courthouse)

The courthouse facade bears a post–World War II frieze with symbols and personalities important to the history of Trondheim. Sadly, the interior is not open for casual visits.

From here, a bit to the north, is the Torvet, site of the:

18 Trondheim Torg (Trondheim Market)

You're now back at the point where you began this walking tour.

ACTIVITIES INDOORS & OUT

In summer the people of Trondheim take to their great outdoors. Summer is short, and they aim to make the best of it.

FISHING Fishing aficionados throughout Norway have heard about the waters below the Leirfossen Dam, 8.8km (5½ miles) south of Trondheim's center. When it was built, no provision was made—much to the rage of ecologists—for the migration of salmon to spawning grounds upriver. Consequently, the waters at the dam's base have traditionally teemed with marine life, especially salmon. The largest salmon ever caught at the dam's base weighed 32 kilograms (71 lb.)—an awe-inspiring record. In addition, the Nidelva River is one of the best salmon and trout rivers in Norway. For more information about fishing licenses, contact **TOFA (Trondheim og Omland Jakt- og Fiskeadministrasjon),** Leirfossvegen 76 (✆ **73-96-55-80;** www.tofa.org), the authority controlling fishing in Trondheim and its surroundings.

GOLF Just a 5-minute drive from the Trondheim Airport at Værnes, **Stjørdal Golfklubb** (✆ **74-84-01-50;** www.stjordalgolf.no) is the only 18-hole golf course between Rena in the south and Narvik in the north. For Norway, its season is long, lasting from May until the end of October. Another of the city's golf courses, **Trondheim Golfklubb,** lies at Sommerseter in Bymarka. This 9-hole course opens onto panoramic views of the city. The Midnight Golf Tournament takes place here in June. For play time, call ✆ **73-53-18-85,** or see www.golfklubben.no.

HIKING The greenbelt on the outskirts of Trondheim is called **Bymarka,** and locals use the woodland as a giant park. It offers 60km (37 miles) of gravel paths, plus 80km (50 miles) of ordinary paths. In winter, skiers find 80km (50 miles) of tracks, including six that are floodlit. In summer, my favorite hike is the **Ladestien (Lode Trail)** ★, stretching for 14km (8¾ miles) along the Lade Peninsula and opening onto panoramic views of Trondheimsfjord. A shorter and equally scenic trail, the Nidelvstien, runs along the banks of the Nidelva River from Tempe to the waterfalls at Leirfossen.

SKIING On the eastern flank of the Vassfjellet mountains, the **Vassfjellet Skisenter (ski center)** lies in a sheltered position with good snow conditions. The area begins 8km (5 miles) south of the city limits and offers six tow lifts, including one for kids, plus nine runs in all. The area boasts 4km (2½ miles) of the largest

A MIDSUMMER NIGHT'S DREAM: WARM-WEATHER ski-jumping IN TRONDHEIM

An offbeat adventure that might appeal to those with a high-adrenaline thirst for danger involves the brave athletes who stay well rehearsed in ski-jump techniques throughout the summer. The **Granåsen ski jump** in Trondheim (about 8km/5 miles south of the center), along with the slightly older, Olympic-famous ski jump at Lillehammer, are the only ski jumps in the world that prepare for summer by lining their downhill slopes with high-impact, very slippery plastic. The result is a royally bizarre sport—warm-weather ski-jumping—that's televised throughout Norway, drawing fans from all over. The schedule for these events is highly variable (after all, they're practices, not competitions), and events seem to crop up at erratic moments that may at times correspond to the arrival of cruise ships near the city's harbor. Admission is free. Ask the tourist office for schedule information.

illuminated slopes in Norway. Ski buses run to the area. For more information, call ✆ **72-83-02-00** or visit www.vassfjellet.com.

SWIMMING **Pirbadet** and the **3-T Fitness Center,** Havnegate 12 (✆ **73-83-18-00**), are situated in one of the most avant-garde buildings in Trondheim. Perched beside the sea and the city's commercial piers, and separated from the rest of the city by the sprawling bulk of the railway station, this futuristic-looking, mostly glass, free-form structure houses an astounding collection of pools, water slides, Jacuzzis, and wave-making machines. On the whole, clients tend to be office workers early in the morning, swim students at midday, and recreational swimmers later in the day. On weekends several thousand recreational swimmers cram into its sun-filtered interior. Also on-site is one of the best-equipped gyms in Norway, the 3-T Fitness Center. Entrance to the Pirbadet pool complex costs NOK125 for adults, depending on what time of day they arrive; entrance to the 3-T Fitness Center is NOK185.

TENNIS Trondheim has several courts, both indoor and outdoor. For reservations at a court close to your hotel, call **Trondhjems Tennisklubb** at ✆ **93-63-55-01;** www.trhtk.no.

SHOPPING

Annes Keramik ★ Founded in 1797, this outlet is your best bet for ceramics based on 2-centuries-old Trøndelag-styled designs, mainly in green, yellow, and blue. A number of intriguing household wares are also sold at this small store. It's open Monday, Wednesday, and Friday 9:30am to 5pm, Thursday 9:30am to 8pm, and Saturday 10am to 3pm. Kongesgate 27. ✆ **73-52-53-82.**

Arne Ronning This is the finest outlet for Norwegian knitwear, outfitting the whole family in sweaters and cardigans that can last for a generation. It also offers the largest selection of menswear in Trondheim. It's open Monday, Wednesday, and Friday 9am to 5pm, Thursday 9am to 7pm, and Saturday 9am to 4pm. Nordregate 10. ✆ **73-53-13-30.**

Galleriet, Trondheim Berukunstforening At the Byrhaven Shopping Center, this is a small store on the ground floor of the mall. But it is choice, with an intriguing selection of glasswork, pottery, silver, jewelry, women's clothing, textiles, ceramics, and more. It's a showcase for applied arts from the Trøndelag district. It's open Monday to Friday 10am to 8pm, Saturday 9am to 6pm. Olav Tryggvasonsgate 26. ✆ **73-52-66-71.**

Modern Art Gallery This is the city's largest art gallery. Local artists, including some of the best in the area, are represented here, along with international artists. It presents paintings, watercolors (most often central Norway landscapes), prints, lithographs, and some sculpture. It's open Monday to Friday 10am to 6pm and Saturday noon to 4pm. Olav Tryggvasonsgate 33. ✆ **73-87-36-80.** www.modernartgallery.no.

Sverresborg Trøndelag Folk Museum The museum's gift shop stocks some of the most genuinely charming handmade objects in Trondheim, including handwoven tablecloths and generally endearing hand-knit children's clothing. It's open from June to August daily 11am to 6pm; off-season Monday to Friday 11am to 3pm, Saturday and Sunday noon to 4pm. Sverrsborg Allé. ✆ **73-89-01-00.** www.sverresborg.no/english/.

TRONDHEIM AFTER DARK

If you're here in late July or early August at the time of the week-long **St. Olav Festival,** Dronningens Gate 1B (✆ **73-84-14-50;** www.olavsfestdagene.no), you can enjoy organ recitals, outdoor concerts, and even opera at the Nidaros Domkirke. The internationally acclaimed **Trondheim Symphony Orchestra ★★★**, Olavskvartalet, Kjøpmannsgata 46 (✆ **73-99-40-50;** www.tso.no), presents concerts weekly with some of Europe's most outstanding conductors and soloists. Tickets cost NOK100 to NOK270, and can also be purchased at the main post office.

Bar Credo Upstairs from Credo (p. 374), one of Trondheim's hippest and most charming restaurants, this bar does a flourishing after-dark business in its own right. Come here for a view of the dozens of modern paintings hanging on the walls—the place doubles as an art gallery, and many of the works are for sale. Live music is presented nearly every night by young and ambitious jazz artists from throughout Norway and the rest of Europe. The space is divided into a trio of silver-toned rooms, with lots of flickering candles, making the scene even more intimate. Cocktails start at NOK75, and the venue is cozy enough that you might make some new friends. It's open Monday to Saturday 4pm to 3am. Ørjaveita 4. ✆ **73-53-03-88.** www.restaurantcredo.no.

Bar 3B Sweaty, shadowy, and candlelit, this is the most extreme of the city's counterculture bars, chock-full of clients in their 20s, 30s, and 40s who are defiantly anti-bourgeois. In an environment sheathed in blue and black and the odd mirror, expect a clientele of tattooed bikers, irreverent students, and the anti-establishmentarian. Two bars are set across different floors here, and you might well manage to strike up some conversation with a local or two. It's open Monday to Saturday from 2pm to 2:30 or 3:30am, depending on business, and Sunday from 8pm to 2:30am. Brattørgate 3B. ✆ **73-51-15-50.**

Den Gode Nabo ("The Good Neighbor") Pub ★ This is my favorite pub in Trondheim, occupying the cellar of a 250-year-old warehouse. Within a low-ceilinged labyrinth of rough-hewn timbers and planking are a number of banquettes, behond which is the bar serving 16 kinds of draft beer (NOK62–NOK99 per half-liter). When the weather is pleasant, everyone heads out to the wooden platform floating on the Nidelva River, with great views of Trondheim's antique warehouses, built on pilings sunk deep into the riverbed. The pub food includes the establishment's best-known dish, the "Good Neighbor" fish plate. Priced at NOK125, it contains heaping portions of vegetables, potatoes, and (usually grilled) fish of the day, accompanied by whatever sauce the chef has dreamed up. You can be a good neighbor at this place every day between 4pm and 1am. Øvre Bakklandet 66. ✆ **40-61-88-09.** www.dengodenabo.com.

Kaktus This is one of Trondheim's counterculture bars—the kind of place where bourgeois airs are either ridiculed or simply not tolerated, and where the clients tend to be students in their early 20s. Music ranges from Billie Holiday to Swedish punk, the walls are hung with modern photography, and everyone is drinking at bulky, thick-topped wooden tables crafted in India. The place serves platters of food, some of them vegetarian, others inspired by the traditions of Italy or Mexico. Meals are priced at between NOK100 and NOK230. It's open daily 3 to 11pm. Nedre Bakkland 6. ✆ **73-51-43-03.**

SIDE TRIPS FROM TRONDHEIM

Unlike Oslo or Bergen, Trondheim isn't surrounded by a lot of "must-see" satellite attractions. But all true Norwegians head for Stiklestad.

STIKLESTAD Lying 90km (56 miles) northeast of Trondheim, Stiklestad is the most famous historic site in Norway. It was the site of an epic battle on July 29, 1030, between the forces of King Olav Tryggvason and a better-equipped army of Viking chieftains. The battle marked the twilight of the Viking era and the inauguration of the Middle Ages, a transition that would greatly change the face of Norway—and Europe itself.

Although Olav lost the battle and was killed, in death he triumphed. Word of his death spread, and in time he was viewed as a martyr to Christianity. His followers made him a saint, and within time St. Olav became the very symbol of Norway itself. In the wake of his martyrdom, Christianity quickly spread across the land, with monasteries sprouting up all over the country. As his fame and popularity grew, Olav's gravesite at Nidaros Domkirke in Trondheim would become the destination of nationwide pilgrimages. In time, his death would lead to the unification of Norway under one king.

Every year on the anniversary of his death, a pageant is staged at the open-air theater in Stiklestad, using 350 actors and drawing an audience of thousands. Launched in 1992, the **Stiklestad Nasjonale Kulturhus** (✆ **74-04-42-00;** www.stiklestad.no) is a virtual theme park, with exhibitions on the famous battle, a folk museum, and a church from the 12th century. Some of the artifacts on display here, discovered by archaeologists, are actually relics of the battle.

The open-air **Stiklestad Museum** is a living tableau of regional village life from the 17th century. In summer there are demonstrations of farm life, and a carpenter's cottage, a water mill, and an 18th-century sauna to visit.

Stiklestad Kirke ★ is a Romanesque church from 1150, built over a former wooden church on the exact spot where it is believed King Olav fell in battle. In 1500, the nave of the little church was extended, and a series of 16th-century frescoes decorating the walls of the nave were later uncovered. At one time a stone, said to be the rock on which Olav leaned before he died, was on display here. In medieval times it was said that the stone had miraculous healing powers, but in time it disappeared, never to resurface. A soapstone baptismal font from the 12th century is the only artifact remaining from ancient times. A series of paintings in the chancel, commissioned for the 900th anniversary of the battle, relates the events of that fateful day.

The center can be visited from June to mid-August daily from 9am to 8pm, and in the off-season daily 11am to 5:30pm. In summer, admission is NOK120 for adults, NOK50 for children; in the off-season, it's NOK60 for adults, NOK25 for children. On-site is a restaurant with a museum cafe.

There is no train station at Stiklestad. The nearest is at Verdal, 6km (3¾ miles) away. The train from Trondheim to Verdal takes 1¾ hours, costing NOK147. At Verdal you can take any local bus for Blåmann; all go within 2km (1¼ miles) of the site, for NOK30. The trip takes only 15 minutes. Motorists from Trondheim can reach the center by taking the E6 northeast.

TROMSØ

Tromsø, the gateway to the Arctic, is a North Sea boomtown—both a trade and a financial center. The surrounding snow-topped mountain peaks reach 1,800m (5,900 ft.), and mountain plateaus have good fishing lakes and birch forests.

Tromsø has been the jumping-off point for several Arctic expeditions, including one of the most famous—and doomed. The great explorer Roald Amundsen took off in a plane from Tromsø, to meet his death in 1928 on an Arctic ice cap. Visitors today come here to hike in the summer or go dog-sledding during winters in this Klondike country.

Tromsø is the administrative center of the county of Troms, a trade center, and the site of one of Norway's four universities. It is the capital of northern Norway, and the country's fourth-largest financial center. Tromsø is 1,744km (1,084 miles) north of Oslo, and 566km (352 miles) north of Bodø. Lying some 400km (250 miles) north of the Arctic Circle, Tromsø gets the midnight sun from May 14 to July 21—but not one ray comes through from November 25 to January 21. The climate has a heat record of 31°C (88°F) and a low of -20°C (-4°F).

The title of "Paris of the North" at times feels somewhat overkill, but Tromsø surprised even 19th-century visitors with its sophistication. A church was established here as early as the 1200s, and Tromsø was a thriving community in the Middle Ages. This trading station and fishing port attracted seamen who trafficked in polar bears, seals, and arctic foxes. Its city charter wasn't granted until 1794, however.

The city limits of Tromsø, the largest municipality in Norway, extend for 2,558 sq. km (988 sq. miles), though most of the area is not built up. Tromsø is home to some 63,000 residents, 9,000 of whom are students at the world's northernmost university.

If you should arrive in this polar town in summer, the time of the midnight sun, you'll find Tromsø rocking around the clock, with more pubs per capita than any other town in hard-drinking Norway.

ORIENTATION

Essentials

ARRIVAL

BY PLANE Flights from Oslo, Bergen, and Trondheim arrive at Langnes airport, 13km (8 miles) west of Tromsø. Flights from Oslo take 1 hour 40 minutes; flights from Bergen take 3 hours 10 minutes. Tromsø also has air links with Trondheim in central Norway and such far northern outposts as Alta, Hammerfest, Honningsvåg, and Kirkeness. Tromsø is served by **SAS** (✆ **74-80-41-00;** www.sas.no), **Widerøe** (✆ **81-00-12-00;** www.wideroe.no), and **Norwegian** (✆ **81-52-18-15;** www.norwegian.no). For general information, call the airport at ✆ **77-64-84-00.**

BY TRAIN There is no rail link to Tromsø. The nearest connection is at Narvik (see chapter 15), from where you'll have to go the rest of the way by bus (see below).

BY BUS **Torghatten Trafikkselskap** (✆ **75-01-81-00;** www.tts.no; www.nor-way.no) runs daily express buses to Tromsø from Narvik, taking 4 hours 15 minutes and costing around NOK330 one-way. There are at least three daily buses (departing in the afternoon) Monday to Friday and at least two each on Saturday and Sunday. In summer the same company also operates buses from Tromsø to the North Cape, with a transfer in Alta (see chapter 15); details about this bus change from week to week, so call in advance if you're contemplating such a journey.

BY CAR Take the E6 from Oslo all the way north.

BY COASTAL STEAMER Hurtigruten **coastal steamers** (✆ **866/552-0371** in the U.S.; www.hurtigruten.us) link Tromsø with at least a dozen other cities along the Norwegian coast, including Narvik, Bergen, and Bodø.

VISITOR INFORMATION

For information about Tromsø and the surrounding area, call the **Tromsø tourist office**—also known as Visit Tromsø—at Kirkegate 2 (✆ **77-61-00-00;** www.destinasjontromso.no). From mid-May to August it's open Monday to Friday 9am to 7pm, Saturday and Sunday 10am to 6pm; during other months, it's open Monday to Friday 9am to 4pm, and Saturday 10am to 4pm (Jan–March 11am–3:30pm).

CITY LAYOUT

The center of Tromsø lies on the eastern shore of the island of **Tromsøya.** It is divided by hills from the western shore and the airport at Langnes. A bridge and tunnel link mainland Norway to Tromsøya. Coastal steamers pull into the piers at the foot of Kirkegata, right in the town center.

The heart of town is small enough to make walking around it relatively easy. Running on a north/south axis, the main street is **Storgata.** At the center of this street is **Stortorget,** the main square, opening onto the harbor. Stortorget is the site of a daily open-air market selling flowers and crafts. The busiest part of town lies south of Storgata toward the harbor. Some major streets include **Strandgata, Skippergata,** and **Skansegata.** This area on and just off Storgata is filled with shops, restaurants, bars, and cafes.

Local buses can take you to attractions outside the center.

GETTING AROUND

From the airport, **Flybussen** (✆ **98-23-02-30;** www.flybussen.no/tromso/) will take you into the center in about 15 minutes, for NOK55 one-way. A municipal bus also makes the run for NOK30, or you can take a taxi for around NOK150.

Local buses branch out from the center to serve greater Tromsø. A one-way ride costs NOK30. If you plan to use the buses a lot, you can purchase a 24-hour pass for NOK60 at the tourist office.

The major **taxi stand** is at Strandveien 30 (✆ **77-60-30-00**), outside of Ølhallen, the oldest pub in the city.

In summer consider cycling around town. Bikes can be rented at **Sportshuset,** Storgata 87 (✆ **77-66-11-00;** www.sportshuset.net), for NOK70 to NOK100 per day. My favorite bike ride is to head east from the center in the direction of the Arctic Cathedral (p. 385), crossing the spindly Tromsø Bridge into the suburb of Tromsdal. After a visit here, you can ride for about 10 minutes to the cable car at Fjellheisen (p. 385), lock your bike and ride the cable car to the top for one of the most panoramic views in the north of Norway.

Fast Facts: Tromsø

There are no currency exchanges in the town, however you can change money in any of the banks. The following **banks** have **ATMs: Den Norske Bank** Fr. Langesgt. 14 (✆ **77-62-96-00;** www.dnbnor.no); **Handelsbanken,** Roald A pl. 1 (✆ **77-75-55-20;** www.handelsbanken.no); **Nordea**, Grønnegata 80 (✆ **77-62-27-00;** www.nordea.no); and **Sparebank1,** Storgata 65 (✆ **02244**; www.sparebank1.no). If you need to use the Internet, **Dark Light,** Stortorget 1 (✆ **77-68-74-44;** www.darklight.no), offers Internet access for NOK30 per half-hour to use the computers. Coffee, mineral water, and sandwiches are served, but no alcohol. You can also use the computers at the Tourist Information office for Internet use free of charge. There are several branches of **pharmacies** throughout the town, including Apotek1, Storgata 76 (www.apotek1.no). The main **post office** is at Strandgata 41 (✆ **81-00-07-10**).

WHERE TO STAY

Expensive

Clarion Collection Hotel With ★★ This is the better choice of Clarion's two hotels in Tromsø. I prefer its waterfront location and views to any other hotel in town. Built in a six-story format in 1989, it was named after Richard With, a 19th-century sea captain who contributed to the development of Tromsø and northern Norway. Set behind a modern twin-gabled facade immediately adjacent to the waterfront, it offers good-sized rooms, with hardwood floors; woodsy, well-upholstered decor, sometimes with leather chairs; big weather-tight windows; and tiled bathrooms. One special feature is the skylit top-floor lounge, a nice place to spend a cold winter's evening.

Sjøgata 35–37, N-9291 Tromsø. ✆ **77-66-42-00.** www.choicehotels.no. 76 units. Mon–Thurs NOK1,370 double; Fri–Sun NOK1,120 double. Rates include buffet breakfast & light evening supper (buffet 6–10pm). AE, DC, MC, V. Parking NOK120. **Amenities:** Dining room; health club; sauna; room service; rooms for those with limited mobility. *In room:* TV, minibar, hair dryer.

Radisson BLU Hotel Tromsø ★★★ Reigning today as the grande dame of Tromsø hotels, this well-managed staple from 1965 is the oldest and best established of the town's large-scale hotels, rising 10 stories. The hotel was radically overhauled and expanded in 2008, turning it into the largest such complex in northern Norway. Rooms come in two distinct styles, Arctic or Chili. Rooms in the Arctic style come with soothing white, orange, and green tones, with lots of wood. Those in the Chili style are imbued with hot colors, including red tones, and modern furnishings. It has

Where to Stay & Dine in Tromsø

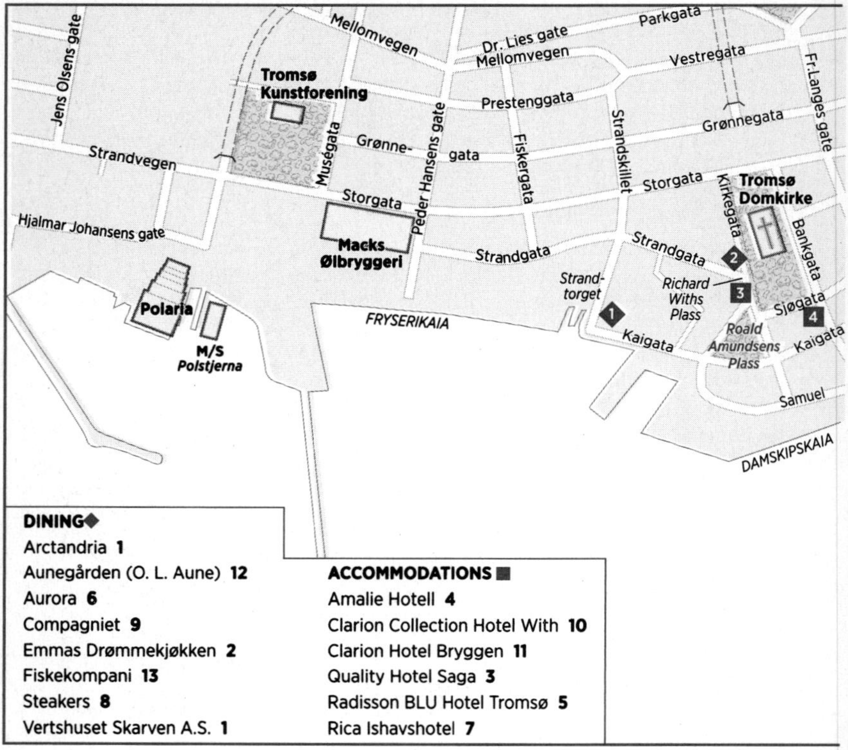

DINING◆

- Arctandria **1**
- Aunegården (O. L. Aune) **12**
- Aurora **6**
- Compagniet **9**
- Emmas Drømmekjøkken **2**
- Fiskekompani **13**
- Steakers **8**
- Vertshuset Skarven A.S. **1**

ACCOMMODATIONS ■

- Amalie Hotell **4**
- Clarion Collection Hotel With **10**
- Clarion Hotel Bryggen **11**
- Quality Hotel Saga **3**
- Radisson BLU Hotel Tromsø **5**
- Rica Ishavshotel **7**

great staff and a more diverse array of food and drinking options than any other hotel in town. Its most upscale restaurant (Aurora) and most famous of its bars (Rorbua) are separately reviewed below.

Sjøgata 7, N-9259 Tromsø. ✆ **77-60-00-00.** www.radissonblu.com/hotel-tromso. 269 units. NOK1,395–NOK1,695 double; NOK3,695–NOK4,700 suite. Rates include buffet breakfast. AE, DC, MC, V. Parking NOK200. **Amenities:** 2 restaurants; 2 bars; health club/sauna on top floor. *In room:* TV, minibar, hair dryer.

Rica Ishavshotel ★★ Although not as lavish or well equipped as the Radisson BLU Hotel Tromsø, this 1995 hotel is the most dramatic-looking in the region, a conversation piece that evokes a metallic space age yacht. Set at the edge of the harbor a few steps from the busiest quay in town, the lobby is cozy and warm. It's big with business travelers, and accordingly roughly half of the rooms are designated as singles. All rooms have a subdued decor, with tiled bathrooms and Nordic modern furniture. The more panoramic of the hotel's two bars is the Skipsbroen, set on the hotel's uppermost floor.

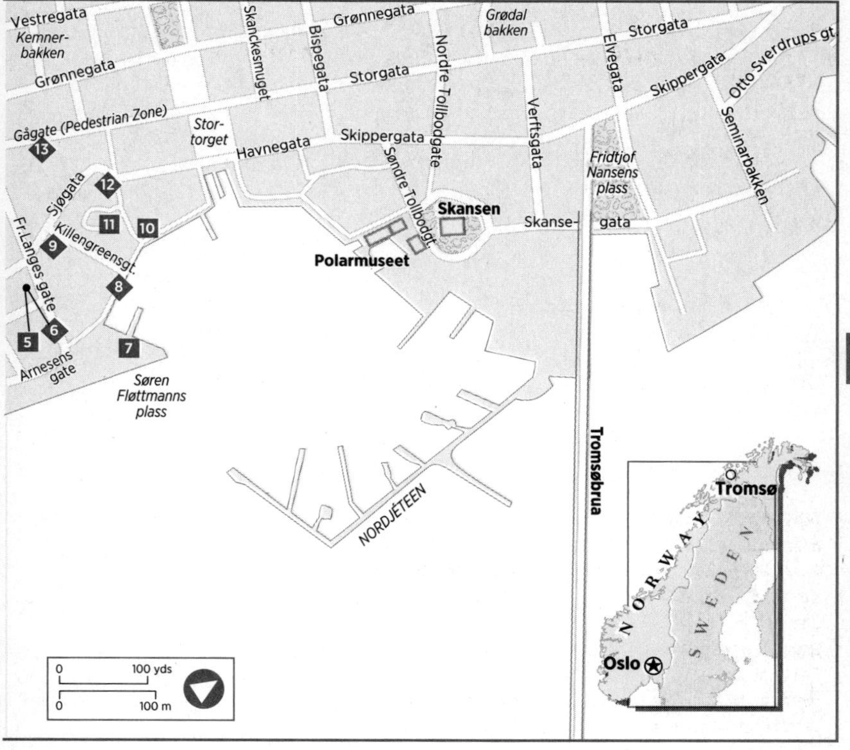

Fr. Langes Gate 2, N-9252 Tromsø. ✆ **77-66-64-00.** www.rica.no/ishavshotel. 180 units. Mon–Thurs NOK2,045 double; Fri–Sun NOK1,295 double. AE, DC, MC, V. **Amenities:** 2 restaurants; 2 bars; babysitting; room service; rooms for those with limited mobility. *In room:* TV, minibar, hair dryer.

Moderate

Amalie Hotell Set in a former office building adjacent to the Radisson BLU Hotel Tromsø (see above), this hotel is known for its affordable rates and well-maintained, comfortable rooms. Bedrooms are simple and cheerful, with few frills but with sturdy, utilitarian wooden furniture and acceptable floral decor.

Sjøgata 5B, N-9008 Tromsø. ✆ **77-66-48-00.** www.amalie-hotell.no/en/. 48 units. NOK995–NOK1,175 double. Rates include buffet breakfast. Light evening supper (nightly 7:30–9:30pm) NOK75 per person. AE, DC, MC, V. **Amenities:** Dining room. *In room:* TV, minibar, hair dryer.

Clarion Hotel Bryggen Clarion is one of the best hotel chains in Norway, and this Tromsø entry is a serviceable and inviting hotel. Built in 2001, this is a large-scale property with a harborfront position that's only a few steps from its main competitor, the Rica Ishavshotel (see above). The hotel has a contemporary lobby, wide hallways, and big-windowed bedrooms that are comfortably laid out. Bathrooms are tiled, brightly lit, and very modern; most have only showers, although 40 units feature tub/showers. My favorite spot here is the outdoor hot tub sheltered on the rooftop terrace near the hotel's sauna, with panoramas over the frigid waters of Tromsø's harbor. On the lobby level are a congenial bar (the Aquarius Bar) and a good restaurant (the Astro) open daily for lunch and dinner.

Sjøgata 19–21, N-9291 Tromsø. ✆ **77-78-11-00.** www.clarionbryggen.com. 121 units. Mon–Thurs NOK1,550 double; Fri–Sat NOK1,395 double; NOK1,900–NOK3,900 suite. AE, DC, MC, V. Parking NOK170. **Amenities:** Restaurant; bar; rooftop sauna w/outdoor hot tub; rooms for those with limited mobility. *In room:* TV, minibar, hair dryer.

Quality Hotel Saga ☺ While not as architecturally exciting as the Rica Ishavshotel (see above), nor as upscale or as plush as the Radisson BLU Hotel Tromsø (see above), this conservative, boxy, banal hotel is set near Tromsø's wood-sided cathedral. Built in 1969, its best rooms are on the uppermost (sixth) floor. Accommodations are warm and comfortable, each sporting contemporary, blond-toned wooden furniture, wooden floors, and off-white walls. Bigger rooms come with a sofa that can be converted to a bed.

Richard Withs Plass 2, N-9008 Tromsø. ✆ **77-60-70-00.** www.choicehotels.no. 103 units. NOK1,445–NOK2,245 double; year-round NOK2,300–NOK3,000 suite. Children 7 & under stay free in parents' room; 50% discount for kids 8–12. Extra beds for children available. Rates include buffet breakfast. Light evening supper (buffet 6–8:30pm) NOK95 per person. AE, DC, MC, V. Parking NOK120. **Amenities:** Dining room; rooms for those with limited mobility. *In room:* TV, alcohol-free minibar, hair dryer.

WHERE TO DINE

Expensive

Arctandria ★★ SEAFOOD Tromso's best fish restaurant is patronized by savvy locals who make their living from the sea and have high standards for seafood. It's set on the top floor of a sprawling antique warehouse immediately adjacent to the water in the town center. The somewhat somber, museum-like interior softens during dining hours, when flickering candles add a sense of romance. The menu comprises almost exclusively fresh fish and shellfish dishes, including some controversial items such as whale meat, seal meat, and shark. The smoked and salted seal meat is a specialty here, served with seaweed remoulade. Their grilled stockfish is also a big hit, served with stewed carrots and bacon.

Strandtorget 1. ✆ **77-60-07-28.** Reservations recommended. Main courses NOK195–NOK385. AE, DC, MC, V. Mon–Sat 4–11pm.

Aurora ★ NORWEGIAN The most upscale of the town's hotel restaurants, this is one of the best places for well-established classics. The interior evokes the Northern Lights, with a minimalist Scandinavian decor. The charming staff members serve food that celebrates the culinary traditions and raw ingredients (shellfish, reindeer, and cold-water fish) of Norway's far north. The best examples include six different preparations of mussels, one with curry. For a true taste of Norway, enjoy such palate-pleasing dishes as poached salt cod with an onion-and-tomato sauté, or pan-fried filet of reindeer with a carrot-and-celery purée spiced with juniper-berry sauce. For dessert, I opt for the delicious lime cheesecake with a coulis of berries.

In the Radisson BLU Hotel Tromsø, Sjøgata 7. ✆ **77-60-00-00.** www.radissonblu.no. Reservations recommended. Fixed-price lunch buffet (Mon–Fri 11:30am–2pm) NOK235; main courses NOK250–NOK300. AE, DC, MC, V. Mon–Sat 11:30am–11:30pm.

Compagniet ★★ NORWEGIAN The movers and shakers of Tromsø call for a table here, especially if they want to impress an out-of-town visitor. Set within an old-fashioned wood-sheathed building, directly across the street from the Clarion Collection Hotel With (see above) and the Clarion Hotel Bryggen (see above), this restaurant is noted as the most charming in town. The cuisine is original and consists of only the freshest ingredients, usually local. All dishes are prepared with a finely honed technique, as exemplified by the arctic sea char flavored with fresh chives and a tantalizing fish roe. From Norwegian meadows comes a tender and flavorful rack of lamb served with raspberry sauce and a potato-and-fresh-vegetable tart, and from the far north, filet of reindeer in a blueberry sauce. Menu specialties vary with the arrival of fresh fish and game from the surrounding waters, tundra, and forests. Fresh fish, including turbot and wolffish, can be ordered breaded and fried; one comes with apricot saffran, *beurre blanc* steamed broccoli, and mashed potatoes, another with root vegetables, sweet potato confit, and creamed chorizo sauce. A particularly good game dish involves filets of wild grouse and reindeer on the same platter, grilled and drizzled with blueberry sauce, and served with root vegetables. The service is the best in Tromsø, and the wine cellar is deep and varied.

Sjøgata 12. ✆ **77-66-42-22.** www.compagniet.no. Reservations required. Main courses NOK269–NOK340. AE, DC, MC, V. Mon–Sat 5–11pm.

Emmas Drømmekjøkken (Emma's Dream Kitchen) ★★★ 🎁 NORWEGIAN If there's such a thing as a culinary personality in Tromsø, it is Emma (also known as Anne Brit), owner of this cozy restaurant across the street from Tromsø's cathedral. Her restaurant, which she runs with her partner Lars, contains only 34 seats, so reservations are important. Before dinner you can descend into the wine cellar, site of an impressive inventory of bottles. If you order champagne, it will be dramatically uncorked by a saber-wielding sommelier. Appetizers include grilled scallops with marinated asparagus, pine nuts, and Parmesan; and pepper-roasted Arctic king crab. Main courses burst with freshness and originality, including stockfish with bacon and creamed cabbage, or breast of Norwegian duck with a raspberry Béarnaise sauce. Another specialty is grilled and marinated rib of lamb with couscous. The best dessert you are likely to encounter in town is the passion-fruit cheesecake with raspberry coulis and a white chocolate mousse.

Kirkegata 8. ✆ **77-63-77-30.** www.emmasdrommekjokken.no. Reservations required. Main courses NOK285–NOK345; fixed-price menus NOK585–NOK950. AE, DC, MC, V. Mon–Sat 6–10pm. Closed 1 week at Christmas.

Fiskekompani ★ NORWEGIAN Not quite up to the high bar raised by Arctandria (see above), this is still a very good addition to Tromsø's dining scene. A visible monument in town, this restaurant is on the town's main shopping street, and features decor that looks older than it is. Menu options, which change with the season, include such starters as tartare of salmon and scallops flavored with coriander and truffle oil, cream of lobster soup with pistachio oil and scallops, and salted redfish with sour cream and onions. Main courses include grilled whale steak with anchovy sauce and *rösti*-style potatoes; fried filet of sea char with spinach, fennel, and almonds; butterflied and batter-fried monkfish served with sun-dried tomatoes, asparagus, and parma ham; and a seafood bouillabaisse made only with fish that thrive in the Arctic waters offshore, served (incongruously) with a garlic-laced *aioli* inspired by the cuisine of Provence.

Storgata 73. ✆ **77-68-76-00.** www.fiskekompani.no. Reservations recommended. NOK285–NOK395. AE, DC, MC, V. Daily noon 4–11pm.

Steakers ☺ STEAKHOUSE This warm, candlelit steakhouse, the most popular in town, is adjacent to the wharves where the coastal steamers dock, midway between the Rica and Clarion hotels (see above). From its oversize windows you can watch the arrivals and departures of fishing and cargo ships. Simple grilled beefsteaks are on the petite side (150g/5 oz.), while boneless tenderloins weigh in at a knockout 400 grams (14 oz.). More elaborate meat dishes are stuffed, basted, or marinated, and might include a "Chicago Gangster" (tenderloin marinated with garlic-flavored butter); a rack of barbecued ribs; or steak marinated in—among other things—tequila and chili peppers. Other specialties include tenderloin of beef in garlic butter, and rack of lamb with potatoes gratinée.

Frederik Langesgate 13. ✆ **77-61-33-30.** www.steakers.no. Reservations recommended. Main courses NOK181–NOK434. AE, DC, MC, V. Mon–Sat 3–11pm; Sun 2–10pm.

Moderate

Aunegården (O. L. Aune) NORWEGIAN/CONTINENTAL Named after a 19th-century butcher shop that stood here for many years, this restaurant is a culinary icon in a town loaded with worthy competitors. The setting includes a Victorian-era tearoom near its entrance and darker, less prim dining rooms lined with slabs of volcanic rock at the back. The main dining room is busy throughout the day, serving salads, sandwiches, and light meals. Lunch brings tuna sandwiches on baguettes, salads, pastas, club sandwiches, and chicken cutlets; dinner offerings move into heartier territory with braised breast of veal and deer, pan-fried sea char, and half-dried cod.

Sjøgata 29. ✆ **77-65-12-34.** www.aunegarden.no. Reservations recommended. Main courses NOK157–NOK305 dinner. AE, DC, MC, V. Mon–Thurs 10:30am–11:30pm; Fri–Sat 10:30am–12:30am; Sun noon–6pm.

Vertshuset Skarven A.S. NORWEGIAN Long a favorite of Tromsø's large student population, this cafeteria is the cheapest of five different restaurants within a 19th-century warehouse adjacent to the waterfront. In the large and high-ceilinged room, you'll be surrounded by lots of nautical memorabilia, antique farm implements, models of 19th-century clipper ships, and an unusual collection of stuffed birds. Good-tasting dishes include hearty stews, baked filet of fish, pork cutlets, soups, and sandwiches—the kind of fare that might be served in the homes of the town's older residents. Overall, this is a cheap and highly atmospheric place for a drink, snack, or meal.

Strandtorget 1. ✆ **77-60-07-20.** www.skarven.no. Reservations not accepted. Sandwiches NOK50–NOK70; platters NOK100. AE, DC, MC, V. Sun–Thurs 11am–12:30am; Fri–Sat 11am–1:30am.

WHAT TO SEE & DO

For the midnight sun or the Northern Lights, the small-scale cable car **Fjellheisen** (✆ **77-61-00-00** for information) hauls sightseers in orange-and-red gondolas from a spot near the Arctic Cathedral (see below), uphill to a small, not-very-exciting cafe and restaurant (Fjellstua Restaurant), 420m (1,380 ft.) above sea level. After this vertiginous trip you are rewarded with a **panoramic view ★★** from the restaurant that extends out over the surrounding countryside. The cable car operates in March Saturday and Sunday 10am to 5pm, April to September daily 10am to 5pm. Round-trip passage costs NOK99, NOK50 for children 6 to 16, and is free for children under 6. Round-trip transport of a bicycle (some bike and hiking trails originate near the cable car's upper station) costs NOK45.

Full meals in the Fjellstua Restaurant cost around NOK260 and include reindeer, dried cod, and fish.

Arctic Cathedral ★★ Northern Norway's most distinctive-looking and controversial church (also known as Tromsdal Church or the Boathouse Church) rose from a location across the harbor from downtown Tromsø in 1965, requiring a transit of the town's longest bridge, completed in 1960, to reach it. Since then, its simple A-frame design has evolved into one of the town's most visible symbols and—thanks to the late-night concerts conducted here for cruise-ship passengers between June and mid-August—one of the most frequently visited sights in the area. The huge stained-glass windows set into the church's triangular front filter light through a gridwork of thin glass strips, creating a magical effect during the brief moments of daylight in the dead of winter. Consistent with Norway's long-established custom of hanging replicas of sailing ships within Norwegian churches as a good luck charm for the vessels' occupants, the organ at the back is shaped like the sails of a ship. Other references to the Arctic's climate and culture abound.

Tromsdal. ✆ **47-68-06-68.** www.ishavskatedralen.no. Free admission during worship services; otherwise, NOK30, free for children 15 & under; admission to concerts NOK100, no discounts available. Mid-Apr to May daily 4–6pm; June to mid-Aug daily 10am–8pm; mid-Aug to Sept daily 4–6pm. Otherwise, the church is closed except for Sun worship services. Concert times coincide with the arrival of cruise ships, but they're usually scheduled for around 10pm every night from June to mid-Aug.

Aurora Borealis ★★★: The Northern Lights

The Northern Lights are one of nature's most spectacular and mysterious phenomena. Under the right conditions, they can be seen in the night sky north of the Arctic Circle in winter. The most practical place to view them in Norway is in Tromsø, but head out in the evening for an area away from town, since city lights can sometimes make the Aurora appear less bright. If seeing these lights is one of your goals, plan to stay around Tromsø for at least 3 days in order to increase your chances of coinciding with the right atmospheric conditions. Anytime from November to March is good, but the lights are generally most visible at the very end of fall and the very beginning of spring.

What to See & Do in Tromsø

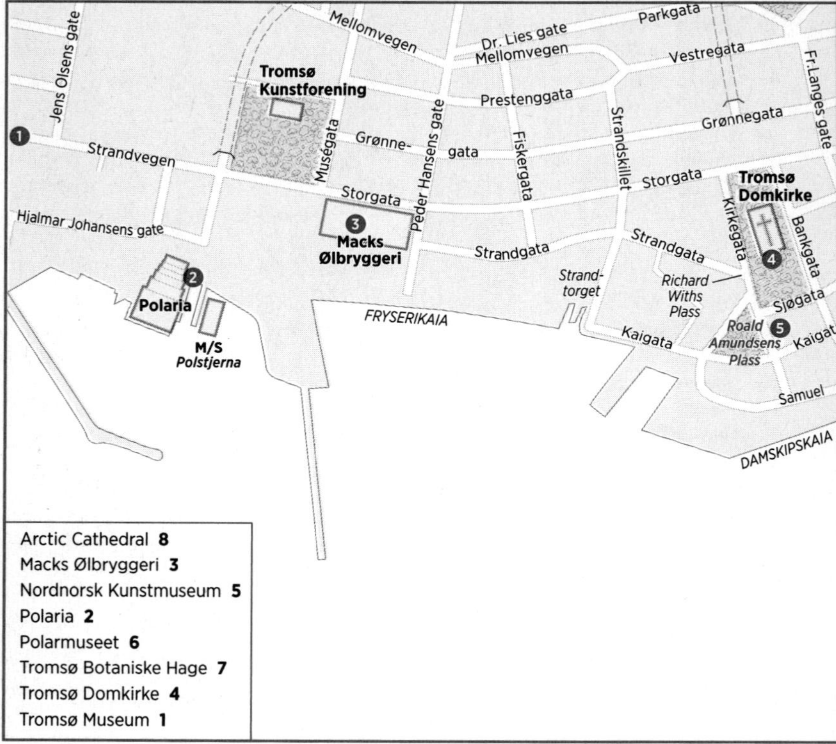

Macks Ølbryggeri (Mack's Brewery) Talk about ice-cold beer. This is the northernmost microbrewery in the world. Launched in 1877, it's been going strong ever since. The brewery currently turns out nearly two dozen brews, including Haakon and Macks Pilsner. Tours are conducted of the brewery, and you're given a shot glass and a sample of beer as a souvenir. You can also sample brews at the on-site Ølhallen Pub.

Storgata 5. ✆ **77-62-45-80.** www.mack.no. Tours NOK130. Oct–May Mon–Thurs 9am–6:30pm, Fri 9am–7pm, Sat 9am–3pm, guided tours are held daily. It's open 1pm; June–Sept Mon–Thurs 9am–5:30pm, Fri 9am–6pm, Sat 9am–3pm, guided tours Mon & Thurs 1pm; or by arrangement. Closed Sun.

Nordnorsk Kunstmuseum The Art Museum of Northern Norway traces art and applied art from 1838 to the present day, with special attention paid to northern Norwegian artists. It features non-Norwegian artists as well, along with sculpture and photography. Anything by Edvard Munch, Scandinavia's best-known artist, attracts the most attention. Lesser-known artists such as Christian Krohg and Axel Revold are displayed, along with the romantic peasant scenes of Adolph Tidemand

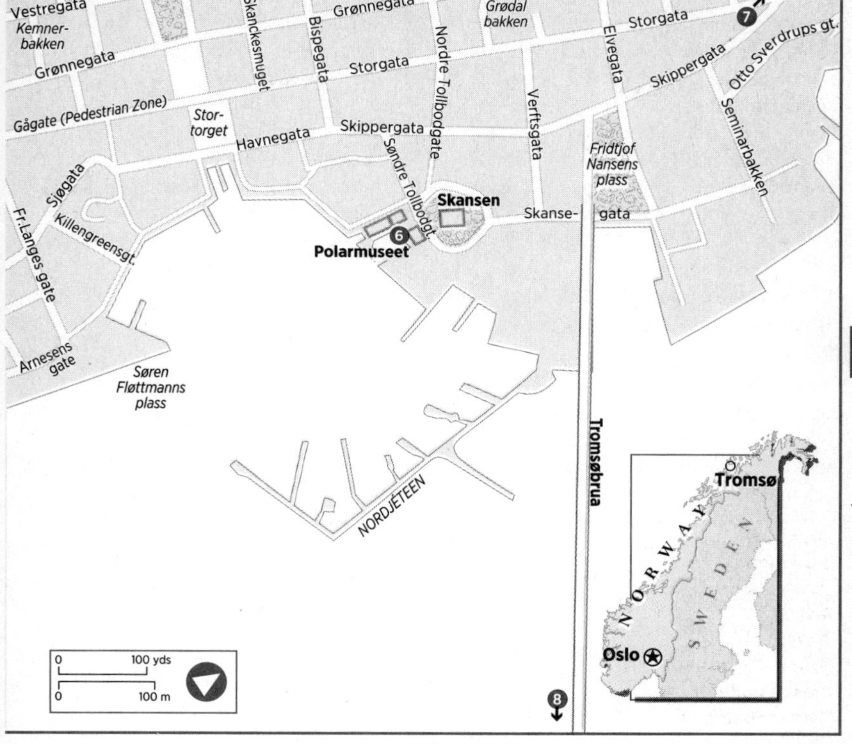

and the beautiful, rugged Norwegian landscapes of Johan Dahl and Thomas Fearnley. The National Gallery in Oslo frequently sends up major works for temporary exhibitions.

Sjøgata 1. ✆ **77-64-70-20.** www.nnkm.no. Free admission. Tues–Fri 10am–5pm, Sat–Sun noon–5pm.

Polaria ★ ☺ Polaria is a Disney-esque scientific homage to the ecologies, climates, and technological potentialities of the Arctic. Viewed from any of the boats out on the harbor, its stainless-steel surfaces resemble a jagged ice floe pressed into fragile but irregular vertical alignments. Inaugurated in 1998 on the waterfront, adjacent to the world headquarters of the Polar Institution of Norway (a respected subdivision of the Norwegian Ministry of the Environment), it's one of the most frequently visited attractions in town. Its design resulted from a competition among 45 noted architects from North America and Europe. The result as viewed from the town evokes a weather-tight factory in wood, glass, and stainless steel that looks like it could survive the harshest Arctic winter.

The dioramas and tableaux—some with artificial snow flurries behind thick sheets of Plexiglas—will leave you with a deeper understanding of the complex and delicate ecosystems of the Arctic. There's an IMAX-size movie theater where an 18-minute film, shot mostly on the Norwegian/Russian island of Svalbard, celebrates the beauty and biodiversity of the Arctic. There's also an aquarium holding what might be the ugliest fish anywhere. Where the signs indicate, you can reach out and touch some of the species—a favorite of children. There is training and feeding of a family of bearded seals daily at 12:30 and 3:30pm.

An indoor pool is for the care, shelter, and feeding of arctic seals, with regular feedings and seal gymnastics. And in the lobby, there's a genuinely wonderful gift shop—one of the best in town—selling souvenirs and some remarkably charming gift items, including hand-painted lacquered boxes hauled in from across Norway's frontier with Russia.

Hjarmar Johansens Gate. ✆ **77-75-01-00.** www.polaria.no. Admission NOK100 adults, NOK85 seniors; NOK50 students, NOK50 children 3–16. Mid-May to Aug daily 10am–7pm; Sept to mid-May daily noon–5pm.

Polarmuseet (Polar Museum) ★ Not to be confused with Polaria (see above), the Polar Museum showcases the bravery and ingenuity of the 19th- and early-20th-century fishermen, hunters, whalers, trappers, and explorers who made the Arctic their home. The museum is set into a complex of interconnected wood-sided, red-painted buildings adjacent to Tromsø's harbor. A bronze statue of explorer Roald Amundsen is positioned directly in front of the museum. Inside, within an antique warehouse whose stout timbers illustrate the construction techniques of the 19th century, you'll find gruesome photographs and dioramas showing how genuinely rough life in the frozen north could be, even as late as the 1960s. On display are antique versions of the hempen ropes, sealskins, sledges, and survival equipment that kept the fishing, hunting, and whaling industries alive. If you ask, a staff member will give you abbreviated pamphlets in English that superficially describe each of the exhibits.

Søndre Tollbugatell. ✆ **77-68-43-73.** www.polarmuseum.no. Admission NOK50 adults, NOK40 students & seniors, NOK10 children 6–18, free for children 5 & under; NOK100 family ticket (2 adults plus any number of children 15 & under). Mid-June to mid-Aug daily 10am–7pm; mid-Aug to Sept 11am–5pm; Oct to Feb 11am–4pm; March–June 15 11am–5pm.

Tromsø Botaniske Hage ★ On the grounds of the University of Tromsø, the world's northernmost botanic garden is one of the most unique I've ever encountered. Arctic tundra and alpine mountain botanicals converge here in a landscape where plants have a shortened growing season and very low temperatures. The season technically lasts from the end of May until mid-October, although the plants experience their real growth only when the midnight sun shines on them day and night. The setting is beautiful, with slopes, a stream, a pond, and terraces. Many of the plants are from the Arctic and Antarctic, as well as various alpine and Himalayan locations. You've seen better botanical gardens, I am certain, but not one growing rare specimens this far north.

Breivika. ✆ **77-64-40-00.** www.uit.no/botanisk. Free admission. May–Sept daily 24 hr.

Tromsø Domkirke One of Norway's largest wooden churches, this is a barn-like, yellow, "carpenter Gothic" monument in the heart of town that's difficult to heat in winter. It is the world's northernmost Protestant cathedral, lying 182m (597 ft.) from the harbor. Consecrated in 1861, it was the creation of architects D. J. Evjen and Heinrich Grosch. Seating some 750 persons, the cathedral shows some classical and Swiss influences. The altarpiece, painted by Christian Brun, is a copy of one within Bragernes church in Drammen outside Oslo. The organ, built by Claus Jensen in 1863, was one of his largest works. In 1944, the church was at the center of history when it was used by evacuees during the Nazi-enforced evacuation of Finnmark and northern Troms. In 1994, the church was restored and returned to its original colors.

Storgata 25. ✆ **77-66-25-80.** Free admission. Tues–Sat 10am–5pm; Sun 10am–2pm.

Tromsø Museum ★ ☺ Affiliated with the University of Tromsø, this museum's collections grew out of artifacts gathered by the oldest scientific institution in northern Norway, established in 1872. It sprawls over three floors and addresses various aspects of natural science (including loads of information on the ecology, botany, geology, and zoology of Norway's far north). There are also exhibits about the Sami people and some about the cultural history of the north. Many of the exhibitions are kid-friendly, especially a life-size dinosaur that children can enter and explore.

My favorite exhibit contains Norwegian church art crafted between the Middle Ages and the 17th century—at least the little bits of it that remain, since so much of it was burned during the Norwegian Reformation. The church artworks on display escaped destruction during the Reformation because, considered less valuable than the works that were actually on display in churches, they were kept in church basements and outbuildings. The museum also contains a device (one of only two in the world, they say) that emulates, planetarium-style, the Northern Lights for which the region is famous. There is also a dazzling video about the Northern Lights. ***Note:*** The gift shop in the lobby contains copies of Viking jewelry that are a lot better than what's sold in some of the town's tourist shops.

Lars Thoringsvei 10. ✆ **77-64-50-00.** www.uit.no. Admission NOK30 adults, free for students & children. Sept to May Mon–Fri 10am–4:30pm, Sat noon–3pm, Sun 11am–4pm; June to Aug daily 9am–6pm.

OUTDOOR ACTIVITIES

In the wilds of northern Norway, walking and especially summer hiking are all the rage, with both locals and visitors. In the environs of Tromsø, more than 100km (62 miles) of trails cut across the mountains. The best one begins at the upper station of the cable car, **Fjellheisen** (p. 385).

For more extensive hiking, including overnight trips, contact **Troms Turlag-DNT** (✆ **77-68-51-75;** www.turistforeningen.no), which organizes tours through the wilderness areas around Tromsø, with stopovers in hotels or mountain shelters maintained by municipalities and conservation groups. Accommodations usually comprise bare-bones mountain cabins, staffed lodges, and self-service huts that come with army-ration-style provisions such as canned goods and freeze-dried staples.

One of the most spectacular trails meanders through the rugged peaks of the **Lyngen Alps** ★, forming the spine of the Lyngen Peninsula, with its glaciated terrain, lying to the east of Tromsø. Arm yourself with a good map from the tourist office before setting out, and don't embark at all unless you're an experienced hill climber. From the eastern banks of the Lyngenfjord, stretching for some 150km (90 miles), you'll enjoy panoramic views in all directions. Mountaineers climb the highest peak, the Jiekkevarre, at 1,833m (6,013 ft.).

Tromsø Villmarkssenter (✆ **77-69-60-02;** www.villmarkssenter.no), 20km (12 miles) west of Tromsø, organizes the best tours in the area, giving you a real close-up experience of nature in the north. Glacier walking, mountain hiking, kayaking, and winter dog-sledding are just some of the activities available. The dog-sledding is pursued November to May, and costs NOK1,350 per person for a daylong journey, including pick-up and drop-off at your hotel.

On one of the less strenuous jaunts, you can get to know some fierce (and fiercely gorgeous) husky dogs. And there can be no better guides than Tove Sorensen and Tore Albrigsten, quite possibly the most experienced dog-sled racers in Norway. This intrepid and inspiring couple reside out here with their three children and several hundred Alaskan huskies, each of whom they know by name. They will regale you with tales from their most challenging and harrowing Arctic adventures and expeditions, after which you'll venture out to meet and greet the sled dogs and their puppies, and if you're gentle and brave, you might even get to pet some of them. The trip takes 2½ hours and is conducted during the summer, at a cost of around NOK650 per person, including transport.

Kayaking is one of the more popular summer sports here, offering the opportunity to paddle along cold, racing waters against a mountain backdrop. Sometimes, if the weather is right, groups take time out to harvest sea mussels. Full-day tours leave daily May to October at 9am (to 4pm), costing NOK1,100 per person, including transport and lunch.

Mountain hikers are taken to **Store Blåmann ★**, at 1,044m (3,425 ft.), the tallest mountain on Kvaløya island, outside Tromsø. This is not like climbing the Matterhorn, and even the somewhat athletic can handle the challenge. The season begins in June and lasts until the first snowfall. Escorted hill-climbing expeditions, each lasting a strenuous 9 hours, go for NOK950 per person, including transportation to and from your hotel, as well as one meal.

In the unlikely event that you're in Tromsø for winter skiing, call the **Tromsø Alpine Ski Center** (✆ **77-60-66-80**), the region's best site for downhill skiing. There is also an array of cross-country skiing trails, some 70km (40 miles) in all. Because of the pitch blackness, nearly three dozen of these trails are floodlit.

Horseback riding across rugged terrain can be arranged by calling **Holmeslet Gård** at ✆ **77-61-99-74.**

SHOPPING

Bianco Footwear This shop is Tromsø's exclusive distributor for one of Scandinavia's most cutting-edge shoe manufacturers, Denmark-based Bianco Footwear. When a bevy of blonde and buxom female beauties failed to stimulate consumer interest in the company's line of footwear, Bianco's art department opted for an all-male lineup of cross-dressing (and not particularly pretty) models, sassily sporting Bianco's line of women's shoes and clothing. Be assured that if you happen to be male and not into cross-dressing, the company markets conventional men's clothing and shoes as well. The store owners call their campaign "extreme art based on solid commercial profits." The Norwegian marketplace seems to agree. Strandgata 26. ✆ **77-65-61-90.** www.bianco.com.

Hekle-Kroken As children, many residents of Norway's far north learn various ways to while away the long winter nights. Many of them turn to arts and crafts. If you're interested in seeing what's available in terms of quilting, embroidery supplies, and knitting patterns, head for this grandmotherly-looking repository of all the ingredients you'll need to engage in some of the most popular hobbies in the region. The setting is a plank-sided antique building in the heart of town. Storgata 91. ✆ **77-68-17-87.** www.heklekroken.no.

Husfliden Winter nights in Tromsø are long, dark, and very cold, and many locals labor, from within their well-heated and weather-tight homes, at arts and crafts. If you're a knitter, a quilter, an embroiderer, or a leatherworker, this shop stocks your raw materials. There's also a small inventory of handmade sweaters knitted by people loosely affiliated with the store. The staff here tends to be elderly, kindhearted, grandmotherly aficionados of the arts-and-crafts scene. Sjøgata 4. ✆ **77-75-88-60.** www.norskflid.no.

Intersport Sports Huset This is the largest sporting-goods store in town, with subdivisions that focus on the equipment you'll need for every conceivable sport, in any season, that's practiced in this severe Arctic climate. Scattered over two separate floors of a showroom in the heart of town, the store stocks bicycles, hiking equipment, white-water rafting and kayaking equipment, all manner of skis, and a state-of-the-art collection of boots, backpacks, and severe-weather clothing. The young staff isn't always the most informed about their stock, but it's still the best bet in town for outdoor gear. Storgata 39. ✆ **77-66-11-00.** www.intersport.com.

TROMSØ AFTER DARK

The bitter cold and an appetite-inducing position immediately adjacent to the blustery fjords of the North Sea seem to unite in a setting that's conducive to hard partying, hard living, and hard drinking in sybaritic Tromsø. This, coupled with a large student population and a passionate interest in all things sports-related, brings about victory and defeat events where joys or sorrows are easily fueled or quaffed with drink.

Evocative of some Alaskan cities, nightlife here mainly consists of massive pub crawls. In Tromsø, the party goes on 24 hours a day, summer or winter: "In winter, you drink all night because of the darkness," said one local pub crawler. "In midsummer, we drink all night because the sun never sets."

Amundsen ★ The leather sofas at this trendy bar are deep, plush, and comfortable, with pale beige and lime walls. Tromsø's most gay-friendly bar, it's named after the famous Norwegian explorer as it is in the building where he used to stay when he lived here. It's open Monday to Thursday noon to 2am, Friday and Saturday 11am to 3:30am, and Sunday 1pm to 2am. Storgata 42. ✆ **77-68-52-34.** No cover charge.

Blå Rock Café You'll be greeted at the entrance to this battered but congenial pub with a sign that screams ROCK AND ROLL RULES, and if you opt to abide by that premise, you might find yourself having a perfectly marvelous, if somewhat grungy, time. The setting is a blue-sided wooden house at the end of the town's main shopping street (Storgata). The staff is friendly, the youthful clientele looks like it was just assigned *Catcher in the Rye*, and the pub's visual and musical references invariably revolve around punk cultural icons from Britain and the U.S. They stock about 50 kinds of beer here, most of it priced at around NOK60 for a foaming half-liter mugful. It's open Monday to Thursday 11:30am to 2am, Friday and Saturday 11:30am to 3am, and Sunday 1pm to 2am. Strandveien 14. ✆ **91-60-34-21.** www.blarock.no. Cover NOK45 Fri–Sat.

Compagniet Nightclub ★ On the premises of a recommended restaurant (see Compagniet in "Where to Dine"), this is one of the more legitimate nightclubs of Tromsø, as opposed to one of the hard-drinking taverns. It is both nightclub and disco, drawing a 20s-to-40s crowd. Live acts might be featured, but only occasionally—definitely don't expect any big names this far north—and there's more often a DJ. It's open Wednesday to Saturday 9pm to 3am (sometimes earlier, depending on business). Sjøgata 12. ✆ **77-66-42-22.** www.compagniet.no. Entrance free until midnight, then NOK60 cover.

Driv Café ★ Set in an antique wood-sided warehouse alongside the harbor in the heart of town, this consummate student hangout was originally built in 1902 as a warehouse for fish. Today, its thick interior beams and aged planking evoke an age when hardworking, hard-drinking fishermen, hunters, trappers, and whalers made their sometimes precarious living from the sea. A simple cafe fills up the seaward side of the place, while a larger, more battered-looking bar area draws the drinking and the drunk, and is lined with bulletin boards listing virtually every cultural activity available within the region. The cafe is open Monday to Thursday from noon till 2am, and Friday and Saturday from noon to 3:30am. Concerts are generally scheduled every Wednesday and Thursday night beginning around 9:30pm, and every Friday and Saturday the place becomes a disco and pick-up bar between 10pm and 2am. Entrance fees to concerts range from NOK30 to NOK160, and admission to the disco costs NOK40. Søndre Tollbodgate 3B. ✆ **77-60-07-76.** www.driv.no.

Emmas Under This is another one of Tromsø's cozy cafes. During the day it serves lunch, mainly light fare such as sandwiches, until 6pm, costing NOK135 to NOK175. Patrons in their 30s and 40s frequent the joint. In the evening, a younger crowd in their 20s and 30s flocks here, listening to recorded jazz and drinking lots of beer, costing NOK55 a mug. It's open Monday to Thursday 7am to midnight, and Friday and Saturday 11am to 2am. Kirkegata 8. ✆ **77-63-77-30.** www.emmasdrommekjokken.no.

G In the center of town, this is a popular, modern all-day cafe and bar. As the night wears on, the patrons get younger as the 40-something crowd turns in for the night. Light food is served; platters cost around NOK70 to NOK100, with large mugs of beer going for NOK70. Paintings exhibited by local artists are for sale. It's open Monday to Thursday 10am to 1:30am, Friday and Saturday 11am to 3am. Storgata 49. ✆ **77-68-25-80.**

Kulturscenen & Studenthuset Driv Lying on Tromsø's inner harbor in a grand building from 1902, this is a cafe, bar, and occasional venue for live concerts. In summer, there's outdoor dining and drinking, as well as dancing on Friday and Saturday nights for a young university crowd. In the dining section, you can order main courses (NOK110–NOK175). It's open Monday to Thursday noon to 1:30am, Friday and Saturday noon to 3:30am. Søndre Tollbodgate 3. ✆ **77-60-07-76.** www.driv.no. Cover NOK50–NOK60.

Rorbua Pub This is Norway's most famous pub, thanks to the fact that one of Norway's most popular weekly TV talk shows, *Du skal høre mye* ("You'll Hear a Lot"), was broadcast from here until 2003. At the height of its popularity, the show attracted a million viewers every Wednesday night. Despite the fact that the hotel that contains the pub was built in 1965, the thick timbers and rough-textured planking evoke a fisherman's cottage *(rorbu)* from the late 19th century. A hard-drinking crowd of all ages turns up here nightly. There's live music Wednesday to Sunday, beginning around 8:30pm. In the cellar of the Radisson BLU Hotel Tromsø, Sjøgata 7. ✆ **77-75-90-05.**

THE ROUTE TO THE NORTH CAPE

The very words "northern Norway" can give one the chills, conjuring up thoughts of polar bears, the summertime midnight sun, and arctic winters of utter darkness. It is an eerie and fascinating land of deep fjords, snowcapped mountains, vast open plains, dramatic island formations, and even fertile farmland (although the growing season is short).

15

Northern Norway is the land of the Sami, where you come face to face with nature under the foreboding sky of the **Finnmark** region. Rushing rivers and lakes teem with fish, and many tiny, weatherbeaten fishing hamlets depend almost entirely on the sea for their livelihood. For most visitors, the ultimate goal is the **Nordkapp** (North Cape), "the end of the world," as the ancient Vikings called it.

Traveling in northern Norway and meeting *nordlendinger* (northerners) is an adventure. However, the deep north may not be as cold as you imagine. Though Finnmark shares the same latitude as Siberia, Greenland, and Alaska, the warming influences of the Gulf Stream give it the longest ice-free coast in the Arctic region.

Of course, flying is the fastest way to get here, but you can also drive toward the Arctic Circle from such cities as Bergen, on one of Europe's most scenic drives. Don't, however, underestimate driving times. From Bergen, allow at least 3 days to reach the Arctic Circle or 5 days to reach the North Cape.

MO I RANA: ARCTIC CIRCLE CITY

450km (280 miles) N of Trondheim

It's not pretty, but "Mo on the Ranafjord" is your gateway to the Arctic, which crosses its municipal boundaries from east to west. With a population of some 25,000 people, it is the third-largest city in the north of Norway.

The Route to the North Cape

Credit for the city's recent rapid population growth goes to the steel and iron industry. In fact, the buildings here are industrial, ugly boxes for the most part, though they are welcoming havens on cold and windy days.

We suggest Mo i Rana as a refueling stop and a gateway to one of the largest wildernesses in Europe. You don't visit it for grand architecture, but for the magnificent setting that it occupies, with adventure travel possible in all directions.

Essentials

GETTING THERE The quickest way to Mo i Rana is on a daily **flight** from Trondheim with **Widerøe** (✆ **81-00-12-00;** www.wideroe.no), arriving at the Røssvoll airport, 14km (8¾ miles) from the center.

You can also arrive by **train** at the **Mo i Rana train station** (✆ **75-13-92-00**). Two or three trains arrive daily from Trondheim, costing NOK795 one-way and taking just over 6 hours. Check www.nsb.no for information.

The **bus** service takes longer, is inconvenient, and saves you neither time nor money, so it's not recommended. **Motorists** can take the E6 north from Trondheim.

VISITOR INFORMATION Near the Sørlandsveien roundabout, **Rana Turistforening,** Ole Tobias Olsensgate 3 (© **75-13-92-00;** www.ranaturistforening.no), offers information about the area and is one of the most helpful tourist bureaus in Norway. It's open mid-June to early August Monday to Friday 9am to 8pm, Saturday 9am to 4pm, and Sunday 1 to 7pm; and in the off-season Monday to Friday 9am to 4pm.

What to See & Do

The city itself has some minor attractions, but if your time is limited, it would be better spent taking a tour of the wilderness.

The **Rana Museum of Natural History,** Moholmen 15 (© **75-11-01-40**), reveals the flora and fauna of the Arctic Circle, with a number of interactive exhibits of particular appeal to families with young kids. The fascinating geology and ecology of the Arctic wilderness come alive here. Admission is NOK50 (free for children 11 and under). It's open Monday to Friday 10am to 5pm, and late June to mid-August daily 11am to 3pm.

About 30km (19 miles) north of Mo lies the grandest natural attraction in this part of Norway, the **Svartisen Glacier ★★★** (*svartisen* means "black ice" in Norwegian). The ice plateau is 1,005m (3,297 ft.) above sea level, covering some 370 sq. km (140 sq. miles) of high mountains and narrow fjords. The Svartisen is second in size in the country only to the Jostedal Glacier (p. 326).

Svartisen (more formally known as Engen Glacier consists of two main glaciers, the Østisen/East Glacier and Vestisen/West Glacier). One arm of the Vestisen is the lowest-lying glacier on the European mainland, continuing all the way down to the Engenbrevannet lake. It continues to grow, advancing by about 40m (130 ft.) a year. Motorists driving along Route 17 by Holandsfjorden can see many arms of the glacier stretching down between mountain peaks.

The Vestisen is one of our favorite sections. To reach the Vestisen, **Engen Skyssbåt** (© **94-86-55-16;** www.rv17.no/engen-skyssbaat) operates two ferries across the Holandsfjorden from Holand and Brasetvik quays (15 min.; NOK50 one-way). They run June to August, Monday to Friday 14 times daily 8am to 9:10pm, and Saturday and Sunday 13 times daily 10am to 9:10pm.

Additional information about the Svartisen and Vestisen glaciers and the ferryboats that access the climbing trails leading up to them are available from the **Meløy tourist office** (© **75-75-48-88,** www.visitmeloy.no), at the port in Holand where the glacier ferry departs.

You can also drive north from Mo i Rana on the E6 for 12km (7½ miles), and after turning off, following signs to the glacier for 23km (14 miles). At the end of the line, you'll find ferries of **Svartisbåten** (© **75-16-23-79**) crossing to within 2.5km (1½ miles) of the Østerdal arm of the glacier. From the disembarkation point, it's still a rigorous 3-km (1¾-mile) hike up to the Austerdalsvatnet lake and the glacier.

If you happen to be in superb physical shape, and if you thrive on high-altitude adventures with just a whiff of primordial danger, there's a local tour operator that might appeal to your cravings: **Rana Special Sports** (© **90-95-11-08;** www.spesialsport.no). Their guides can take you on a full-day climbing excursion on the glacier, with all equipment included (including pitons and special ice cleats for your hiking boots) for NOK750 per person.

COASTAL STEAMER: THE WAY TO GO

Coastal steamers ★★ are elegantly appointed ships that travel along the Norwegian coast from Bergen to Kirkenes, carrying passengers and cargo to 34 ports. A total of 11 ships make the journey year-round. Along the route, the ships sail through Norway's more obscure fjords, revealing breathtaking scenery and numerous opportunities for adventure. At points along the way, passengers have the opportunity to take sightseeing trips to the surrounding mountains and glaciers, and to go on excursions on smaller vessels.

The chief cruise operator is **Hurtigruten** (✆ **866/552-0371** in the U.S. or **0844/448-7654** in the U.K.; www.hurtigruten.com). Various packages are available. Tours may be booked heading north from Bergen, south from Kirkenes, or round-trip. The 12-day round-trip voyage from Bergen to Kirkenes and back is $1,482 per person. For information on these and other trips, including air-cruise packages from the United States, contact Hurtigruten.

The glacier is part of the **Saltfjellet-Svartisen Nasjonalpark** ★★★, stretching over 2,015 sq. km (778 sq. miles). The park takes in the ice field of Svartisen, along with various moorlands that reach as far east as the Swedish border. Information about hiking trails in the park can be obtained from the tourist office in Mo i Rana (see above). The trails can be approached by road from Route 77, which heads east off the E6 to the Swedish frontier.

Norway's best-known "show cave," **Grønligrotta** ★ (✆ **75-13-25-86;** www.gronligrotta.no) lies in the hamlet of Grønli, 26km (16 miles) northwest of Mo. In Scandinavia's only cave with electric lights, your way is illuminated for the half-hour tour into the cave, which has an underground river. As a curiosity, you can see a mammoth granite block ripped off by a glacier and dumped into the cave by the sheer force of the onrushing waters. Visits cost NOK120 for adults, NOK60 for children 15 and under. The cave can be toured hourly, mid-June to mid-August daily from 10am to 6pm.

En Route to Bodø

On the E6 about 80km (50 miles) north of Mo i Rana toward the Arctic Circle, you'll come to the **Polarsirkelsenteret,** N-8242 Polarsirkelen (✆ **91-85-38-33;** www.polarsirkelsenteret.no), offering a multiscreen show depicting the highlights of Norway (NOK50). Many people send cards and letters from here with a special postmark from the Arctic Circle. A cafeteria and gift shop are on the grounds. It's open daily in May 10am to 6pm; and June to August daily 9am to as late as 10pm; admission is free.

Continue north to Fauske and follow Route 80 west along the Skjerstadfjord. Depending on weather conditions, you should reach Bodø in under an hour.

Where to Stay

Comfort Hotel Ole Tobias ★ 🎁 Built in 1993, this is the smallest and coziest hotel in town. The hotel was named after Ole Tobias (1827–1912), a local priest, inventor, and visionary whose well-publicized treks (on foot) between Trondheim and Bodø led to the construction of a railway for the transport of fish from the Arctic waters of the north to canning factories and consumers of the south. Reproductions of many of his photographs hang throughout the hotel. The style feels like something of a private club, with a good bar and restaurant in the basement. Here you'll find a wide-screen TV and a light evening buffet (nightly 6–10pm) that's included in the price of a room. The bedroom decor includes deep-toned "farmer romantic" colors, thick pine furniture, and turn-of-the-20th-century nostalgia, with representations of trains woven into the carpets.

Thora Meyers Gate 2, N-8602 Mo i Rana. ✆ **75-12-05-00.** www.choicehotels.no. 30 units. NOK799–NOK1,420 double. Price includes light evening buffet. AE, DC, MC, V. **Amenities:** Bar; sauna; room service; rooms for those with limited mobility. *In room:* TV.

Where to Dine

Babette's Gjestebud MEDITERRANEAN It may not have complicated food, but this inviting, candlelit tavern has lots of exposed wood and warmth. It was named after the Danish film *Babette's Feast,* in which closed and bitter psyches were released and healed through good food, good wine, and love. The Turkish chef specializes in grilled meats and fresh salads, some garnished with feta cheese, Mediterranean herbs, ham slices, or shrimp. There are pastas with, say, curried chicken, and solid starters such as French onion soup with your choice of garlic-butter or herb-butter bread.

Jernbanegata 22. ✆ **75-15-44-33.** Reservations recommended. Main courses NOK125–NOK280. AE, DC, MC, V. Daily 11am–midnight.

Mo i Rana After Dark

Ramona, Fridtjof Nansensgate 28 (✆ **75-13-40-00**), in the Hotel Meyergården, is the only genuinely viable nightclub and dance club in town; it's actually one of the largest in northern Norway. Set within an ugly commercial building in the heart of the city, the place is subdivided by banquettes and seating areas into three sections painted in tones of pink or yellow. There are bars scattered strategically throughout and a clientele with shifting ages and priorities: Thursday nights are big with students, Saturday is for an older crowd, Friday is the let-down-your-guard crowd. The place is open Friday to Saturday 10pm to 3am, charging an entrance fee of NOK85 per person.

BODØ: GATEWAY TO THE NORTH ★

479km (298 miles) N of Trondheim; 1,430km (889 miles) N of Bergen; 1,305km (811 miles) N of Oslo

This is a great place to spend a day or two—not for the city itself, which is dull architecturally (save for a brand-new cultural center, due to open in 2013), but for the attractions of nature in the wilds that envelop the city. This seaport, the terminus of the Nordland railway, lies just north of the Arctic Circle. Visitors arrive here, the capital of Nordland, for a glimpse of the midnight sun, which shines in the first two weeks of June. But don't expect a clear view of it. What those tourist brochures don't tell you is that many nights are either rainy or hazy, cutting down considerably on your enjoyment of the spectacle. From December 15 to 29, Bodø gets no sunlight at all.

Bodø is Nordland's largest city, with some 47,000 inhabitants living at the northern entrance to Saltfjord. Although burned to the ground by the retreating Nazis at the end of World War II, the city dates back to 1816, when it was founded by merchants from Trondheim seeking a northern trading post. In time it became one of the leading fishing centers of Norway, specializing in the drying of cod, and it has also become known for its ship-repair yards.

Bodø faces an archipelago rich in bird life, and no other city in the world boasts such a large concentration of sea eagles. From Bodø, you can take excursions in many directions to glaciers and bird islands; the most attractive one is to Lofoten (p. 407).

Essentials

GETTING THERE If you're not driving, or traveling by coastal steamer, you can **fly** to Bodø from major cities throughout Norway, usually with connections at Trondheim or Oslo, with **SAS** (✆ **91-50-54-00;** www.sas.no) or **Norwegian** (✆ **81-52-18-15;** www.norwegian.no). The airport lies just over 1km (⅔ mile) southwest of the city center and is accessed by regular bus service (ask at the airport desk for the latest schedule; the cost is NOK90 each way). It is also possible to hire one of the many taxis waiting at the arrivals gate, which charge roughly NOK100 for a trip to the city center. Alternatively, you could simply walk to the city center, which won't take more than 15 minutes (follow Hernesveien from the airport exit).

Two **trains** a day leave Trondheim for Bodø (9 hr. 40 min.). The route, known as the Nordlandsbanen, is one of Europe's most exhilarating overnight train journeys. Visit www.nsb.no for more information.

For **bus** information, contact **SB Nordlandsbuss** in Bodø (✆ **47-88-39-99;** www.177nordland.no) or, for general travel info in Nordland, call ✆ **177.** Fauske is a transportation hub along the E6 to the north and Route 80 due west to Bodø. When asked about Fauske, an employee of the local bus company quipped, "All roads (in and out of Bodø) lead to Fauske." If you're taking public transportation to or from other parts of Norway's far north, you are likely to pass through Fauske. From Fauske there are two buses a day to Bodø (1 hr. 10 min.). If you take the train from Stockholm to Narvik, you can make bus connections via Fauske to Bodø, a total trip of 5 hours.

Motorists can continue north from Mo i Rana to the junction with Route 80 heading west to Bodø.

VISITOR INFORMATION The **Bodø tourist office** is at Sjøgata 3 (✆ **75-54-80-10;** www.visitbodo.com), in the city center. It's open January to May and September to December 19 Monday to Friday 9am to 3:30pm; June to August Monday to Friday 9am to 8pm Saturday 10am to 6pm, Sunday noon to 8pm.

The city is relatively flat, and bikes can be hired at Sirilund Handel on Kjerringøy (www.kjerringoy.info).

Note that high and low tides in Bodø are particularly pronounced. The phenomenon occurs four times within any 24-hour period, twice for incoming tides, twice for outgoing tides, with a brief interlude between high and low tides when the waters are almost eerily still. Many locals within this maritime community, as well as the staff at the Bodø tourist office, will be alert to the schedule of high and low tides on the day of your arrival.

What to See & Do

Bodin Kirke Sitting pretty in clover fields, this intriguing, onion-domed church can be visited along with a trip to the Norwegian Aviation Museum (see below). It lies about 1km (⅔ mile) southeast of the museum. Dating from 1240, the church has seen many changes over the years. The addition of many 17th- and 18th-century baroque adornments jazzes up what was once a severe interior.

Gamle Riksvei 68. ✆ **75-56-54-20.** Free admission. Late June to mid-Aug Mon–Fri 10am–3pm.

Bodø Domkirke As Norwegian cathedrals go, this ranks low on the totem pole. But when the Nazis bombed their previous church on May 27, 1940, locals were eager to open a major place of worship even if they could find no Michelangelo—or money—to build it. What they came up with is fairly respectable. Completed in 1956, this is the most notable building constructed since those German bombers flew over. It features tufted rugs depicting ecclesiastical themes, wall hangings, and a stained-glass window that captures the Northern Lights. A memorial outside honors those killed in the war with the inscription NO ONE MENTIONED, NO ONE FORGOTTEN. There's also an outstanding spire that stands separate from the main building.

Torv Gate 12. ✆ **75-51-95-30.** Free admission. Mid-June to Aug Tues–Fri noon–3pm. Closed Sept to mid-June.

Galleri Bodøgaard Lying 2.5km (1½ miles) from the heart of the city, this museum exhibits the largest private ethnographic collection in northern Norway. Boats, artifacts of daily life, and tools used in hunting and fishing are just some of the items on parade. The site encompasses the German POW camp for Russian prisoners at Bodøgaard.

Skeidalen 2. ✆ **90-72-08-43.** www.bodogaard.no (in Norwegian). Admission NOK50 adults, free for children. Tues–Fri 9am–3pm, Sat–Sun noon–4pm (hours subject to change—check before coming here).

Nordlandmuseet (Nordland Museum) In the city center, the main building of this museum is one of the oldest structures in Bodø. Here you'll find exhibits on, among other things, local fishermen and Sami culture. There's a "dry" aquarium, with stuffed fish, along with silver treasure dating from the Viking era. An open-air section contains more than a dozen historical buildings moved to the site, plus a collection of boats. Part of the exhibit includes *Anna Karoline of Hopen,* the only surviving Nordland cargo vessel.

Prinsengate 116. ✆ **75-50-35-00.** www.saltenmuseum.no. Admission NOK35 adults, children NOK10. May–Aug Mon–Fri 9am–4pm, Sat–Sun 11am–4pm; rest of year Mon–Fri 9am–3pm, Sat 11am–3pm.

Norsk Luftfartsmuseum (Norwegian Aviation Museum) ☺ So this is where that infamous U-2 spy plane finally ended up. On May 1, 1960, the ill-fated plane piloted by Francis Gary Powers was en route from Peshawar in Pakistan to Bodø. It made headlines around the world when it was shot down over Sverdkovsk, creating a major diplomatic incident. Kruschev used the incident to sabotage the summit between the U.S. and the Soviet Union in Paris later that month. This museum, shaped like an airplane propeller, takes you on its own exciting "fly-over" of Norway's civil and military aviation history. Kids and adults alike should soar through the exhibits. You can have a close encounter with large and small aircraft such as the Spitfire and JU52. Hands-on demonstrations reveal the dynamics of flight. In addition, the museum has a collection of photographs of the largest predators in the Nordic countries, including lynx, bears, wolves, wolverines, and, more surprisingly, humans. The museum was built on the site of a World War II German airfield.

Olav V Gata, 2km (1¼ miles) north of Bodø. ✆ **75-50-78-50.** www.luftfart.museum.no. Admission NOK95 adults, NOK40 children 15 & under. Mid-June to mid-Aug Sun–Fri 10am–6pm; Sept to mid-June Mon–Fri 10am–4pm, Sat–Sun 11am–5pm. Bus: 23 or any bus marked CITY NORD.

EAST OF BODØ

Blodveimuseet (Blood Road Museum) ★ About 90km (56 miles) due east of the city is the "Blood Road Museum," re-creating the days from 1942 to 1945 when the Nazis held an iron grip on northern Norway. Thousands of European prisoners of war labored to build roads and railroads in the area, and many lost their lives. In Saltdal alone there were at least 15 POW camps, with nearly 10,000 Russian, Serbian, and Polish prisoners. The "Road of Blood" ran for 2km (1¼ miles) to Saksenvik from the center of Rognan. People still walk this horrible road today, noting the blood-colored cross a prisoner painted on a rock face.

The museum includes a collection of original rural buildings, the oldest dating from 1750. The original, bleak German POW barracks are here as well, revealing the harsh life of the prisoners. The museum was opened in 1995 as part of the 50th anniversary of Norway's liberation from the Nazis.

Bygetunet, Saltnes, about 1km (⅔ mile) east of Rognan. ✆ **75-50-35-35.** www.saltenmuseum.no. Admission NOK35, free for children 15 & under. June 20–Aug 20 daily 11am–5pm. Closed rest of year.

Outdoor Activities

If you'd like to go **horseback riding** under the midnight sun, **Bodø Hestecenter,** Soloya Gård (✆ **75-51-41-48**), about 14km (8¾ miles) southwest of Bodø, rents horses. Buses go there Monday to Friday mornings and evenings, and Saturday mornings. For more information, ask at the Bodø tourist office (see above). The cost is NOK120 for a 45-minute ride.

At the tourist office you can pick up maps detailing **hikes** in the area. The best of these are through the **Bodømarka (Bodø Forest),** with 35km (22 miles) of marked hiking and cross-country skiing trails. For detailed information on tours, including overnighting in the forest, contact **Bodø og Omegn Turist-forening** (**Bodø Trekking Association;** ✆ **75-52-14-13;** www.bot.no), which operates a dozen cabins in the forest.

Bodø is now home to Norway's most modern indoor **water park,** the **Nordlandsbadet** (✆ **75-59-15-00** or 40-60-28-41; www.bodospektrum.no), which offers plenty of waterborne activities for kids as well as a dedicated spa and wellbeing section for adults. In addition to multiple pools—an exercise pool, diving pool, therapy pool, and wave pool, among others—there are chutes, fountains, grottoes, Jacuzzis, saunas, and a "water mushroom." The park is located just opposite the Norwegian Aviation Museum (see above).

THE MAELSTROM From Bodø, you can take a bus to view a mighty maelstrom, the **Saltstraumen Eddy ★**, 33km (20 miles) south of the city. The variation between high and low tides pushes immense volumes of water through the narrow fjords, creating huge whirlpools known as "kettles," which produce an odd yelling sound. Saltstraumen, nearly 3.3km (2 miles) long and only about 170m (550 ft.)

wide, with billions of gallons of water pressing through at speeds of about 10 knots, is the world's strongest maelstrom. Buses run five times a day Monday to Saturday, twice on Sunday. The cost is NOK75 for adults round-trip, half-price for children 11 and under. A round-trip taxi excursion costs in excess of NOK600 for two passengers; check with **Bodø Taxi** (✆ **07550;** www.bodotaxi.no). Bodø Sightseeing (✆ **75-56-30-00;** www.bodosightseeing.no) also has a daily bus departure to Saltstraumen, connecting with the arrival of the Hurtigruten.

VISITING A GLACIER One of Norway's major tourist attractions, **Svartisen Glacier ★★★** (see under Mo i Rana, above), can also be visited from Bodø. The glacier, about 160km (100 miles) south of Bodø, can be reached by car, although a boat across the Svartisenfjord is more exciting. Tours from Bodø on the Helgeland Express, a combined bus-and-ferry excursion, are offered several times in the summer (July and Aug, usually every second Sat, 1–8pm), for NOK800, NOK600 for children 15 and under. **Nordland Turselskap** (✆ **90-63-60-86;** www.nordland turselskap.no) and **Explore Nordland** (✆ **99-23-49-72;** www.explorenordland.no) both arrange glacier tours. You can go ashore to examine the glacier and visit the nearby visitor center (✆ **75-75-10-00**). The Bodø tourist office can provide more information. Depending on conditions, the visitor center may be able to arrange a boat across a narrow, icy channel for a closer look at the glacier.

Where to Stay

The Bodø tourist office can help you book a room in a hotel. It also maintains a list of local B&Bs and will book you a room for a fee of NOK30.

EXPENSIVE

Radisson BLU Hotel ★★ By far the finest and most expensive hotel in the area, this glistening structure is an inviting waterfront oasis that features panoramic views of the water. The well-sized guest rooms are furnished in sleek contemporary style and decorated in a number of motifs, including Japanese, Nordic, Chinese, and British. The hotel is located on the main street at the harborfront and offers some of the best drinking and dining facilities in Bodø, including the Sjøsiden Restaurant. Live music and dancing are offered every Saturday night in the Moloen Bar. The best place for a drink is the Top 13 rooftop bar.

Storgata 2, N-8000 Bodø. ✆ **75-51-90-00** or 800/333-3333 in the U.S. www.radissonblu.com/hotel-bodo. 190 units. NOK895–NOK1,395 double; NOK1,695–NOK2,195 suite. Rates include buffet breakfast. AE, DC, MC, V. Free parking. **Amenities:** 2 restaurants; 2 bars; lounge; babysitting; fitness center; sauna; room service; rooms for those with limited mobility. *In room:* TV, Wi-Fi, minibar, hair dryer.

Rica Hotel ★ Located at the harbor and offering a view of Vestfjorden, this is one of Bodø's best hotels, built in 1986 and enlarged in 1990. It's no match for the Radisson (see above) but is a full-service hotel with plenty of comfort, even though its facade is not the most inviting thing around. Most of the somberly furnished rooms have large writing desks. Only moderate in size, rooms are comfortable and well maintained, with large, comfortable beds. The hotel has two popular restaurants.

Sjøgata 23, N-8001 Bodø. ✆ **75-54-70-00.** www.rica-hotels.com. 113 units. NOK1,100–NOK1,540 double; NOK1,400–NOK1,690 junior suite. Rates include buffet breakfast. AE, DC, MC, V. Parking NOK110. **Amenities:** 2 restaurants; bar; fitness center; sauna; room service; rooms for those with limited mobility. *In room:* TV, minibar, hair dryer.

MODERATE

Bodø Hotell Opened in 1987, this family-run hotel, located in the city center about 2½ blocks from the harbor, is known for its good value. The bedrooms are modern, and although the bathrooms are small, they are well maintained and equipped with shower units. The rooms, also a bit small, are quite cozy, with an attempt at an intimate, homelike feeling. Oriental carpeting, swag draperies, and art on the walls make for a welcoming ambience.

Professor Schyttesgate 5, N-8001 Bodø. ✆ **75-54-77-00.** www.bodohotell.no. 31 units. NOK1,150–NOK1,250 double. Rates include buffet breakfast. AE, DC, MC, V. Free parking. Closed Dec 22–Jan 3. **Amenities:** Lunch restaurant; bar; lounge; sauna; rooms for those with limited mobility. *In room:* TV, Wi-Fi, hair dryer.

Skagen Hotel ★ This discovery offers a lot of charm in a somewhat bleak landscape. Helpful, well-connected staff make this hotel the best in this part of Norway for arranging memorable adventures, including wilderness camping, deep-sea rafting, sea eagle feedings, fishing trips, canoeing, rock climbing, and glacier walks. Bedrooms are of average size, comfortably furnished, and individually decorated, often in attractive cherrywood and with unique, large reading chairs. Thoughtful extras here include breakfast from 6am, and coffee and tea always available in the library. Additionally, there is a free buffet nightly from 7 to 10pm.

Nyholmsgata 11, N-8001 Bodø. ✆ **75-51-91-00.** www.skagen-hotel.no. 72 units. NOK925–NOK1,725 double. AE, DC, MC, V. Free parking. **Amenities:** Bar; gym; sauna; rooms for those with limited mobility. *In room:* TV, Wi-Fi, minibar, hair dryer.

Thon Hotel Nordlys This modern hotel rises six floors to overlook Bodø's harbor. Inside is a collection of valuable contemporary art—some of which is for sale. The guest rooms are contemporary, with yellow pallets, wooden floors, plus tiled bathrooms with tub/shower combinations. Though it's primarily a business hotel, it is fine for a night if you're vacationing. Egon, the hotel's restaurant, specializes in robust American and Norwegian fare.

Moloveien 14, N-8001 Bodø. ✆ **75-53-19-00.** www.thonhotels.no/nordlys. 147 units. NOK791–NOK1,325 double; NOK1,760–NOK1,825 junior suite. AE, DC, MC, V. Free parking. **Amenities:** Restaurant; rooms for those with limited mobility. *In room:* TV, Wi-Fi, minibar.

Where to Dine

Bjørk NORWEGIAN/INTERNATIONAL This award-winning restaurant is regularly ranked as one of the best in northern Norway. The location is a red-brick building a short walk from the Radisson BLU Hotel (where it used to reside). Inside are touches of red, blue, and black; a roaring fireplace; a well-trained staff; and a tempting combination of Norwegian and international cuisine. You might begin with a carpaccio of venison, grilled scallops served with terrine of oxtail, or fried scampi with a sweet-and-sour "Asian" sauce. Main courses include codfish served with shredded beetroot; poached anglerfish in a peanut-based satay sauce; breast of duckling with an herb-based creamy risotto; and stockfish served with tarragon-flavored wine sauce and fresh root vegetables. But they also serve simple, down-home dishes like pizza.

Glashuset Shopping Centre, Storgata 8. ✆ **75-52-52-50.** www.restaurantbjork.no. Reservations recommended. Main courses NOK250–NOK275. AE, DC, MC, V. Daily 10am–10pm.

China Garden CANTONESE Although it doesn't rank with Oslo's Chinese restaurants, this Hong Kong emigré-run eatery is a welcome change of pace this far north. Serving flavorful and spicy Chinese food, the restaurant's two finest dishes are sweet-and-sour shrimp and sweet-and-sour pork laced with garlic and served with black beans. The cooks prepare many other standard dishes competently.

Storgata 60. ✆ **75-52-71-25.** Reservations recommended. Main courses NOK155. AE, MC, V. Tues–Sun 2–11pm.

Bodø After Dark

The largest nightclub in Bodø is the **Rock Café,** Tollbugata 13B (✆ **75-50-46-33;** www.rock-cafe.no), which can hold up to 550 patrons, most in their 20s and 30s. Live bands perform twice a month, while DJs spin on other days. It's open Friday and Saturday 9pm to 3am. Somewhat smaller is **G Nattklubb,** Sjøgata 14 (✆ **75-56-17-00;** www.utibodo.no), open Friday and Saturday 10pm to 3am. There is a live DJ and it tends to be big among 30- and 40-somethings.

Somewhat less frenetic is **Nordlænningen,** Stogata 16 (✆ **75-52-06-00;** www.nordlaenningen.no), a laid-back cellar pub featuring daily live blues, country, or rock, to a crowd ranging in age from 20 to 50. They also serve pub grub, everything from burgers to omelets. Local artists' paintings dominate the decor. A cover charge is imposed on Friday and Saturday nights, from NOK70 to NOK100. It's open Monday to Thursday 1pm to 1:30am, Friday and Saturday 1pm to 2:30am, and Sunday 2pm to 1:30am.

NARVIK: WORLD WAR II BATTLEGROUND

301km (187 miles) NE of Bodø; 1,647km (1,023 miles) NE of Bergen; 1,479km (919 miles) N of Oslo

This ice-free seaport on the Ofotfjord is in Nordland *fylke* (county or province), about 400km (250 miles) north of the Arctic Circle. Narvik, founded in 1903 when the Ofoten (not to be confused with "Lofoten") railway line was completed, boasts Europe's most modern shipping harbor for iron ore.

Narvik played a focal role in World War II. On April 9, 1940, 10 Nazi destroyers entered Narvik waters to sink two Norwegian battleships. The next day five British destroyers arrived to take the German boats on in combat. The tragic battle at sea resulted in the sinking of two destroyers on each side. On April 12, the British sent planes to attack German forces. Allied soldiers reclaimed Narvik by late May, but in early June the Nazis came back to decimate Narvik. The port became a graveyard not only of many men, but also of ships from Germany, Britain, Norway, France, and the Netherlands. On June 8, 1940, Narvik surrendered to the Nazis, who remained in the city until the Allies chased them out on May 8, 1945.

Modern, rebuilt Narvik can be something of an eyesore at times. Still, its setting amid panoramic forests, majestic fjords, and towering mountains makes it an appealing choice. As an added plus, the midnight sun shines here from May 27 to July 19.

Narvik is reached via the northernmost electrified railway line in the world, covering a magnificent scenic route through precipitous mountain terrain and tunnels, over ridges and tall stone embankments. Straumsnes station, 11km (6¾ miles) from Narvik, is the last permanent settlement as you go east. The last Norwegian station,

Bjørnfjell, is well above the timberline, about 3 hours from Kiruna, Sweden and some 140km (87 miles) north of the Arctic Circle.

Essentials

GETTING THERE From Lofoten, **motorists** can catch the car-ferry to Skutvik, operating three times a day. Follow Route 81 northeast to the junction with the E6, and then take the E6 north to Bognes. Cross the Tysfjord by ferry and continue north on the E6 to Narvik.

If you're driving from Kiruna to Narvik, take Route 98 northwest to the E6, then head southwest on the E6 toward Narvik.

The **train** from Stockholm to Narvik runs several times weekly, taking 19 to 23 hours and costing from NOK760 one-way (prices vary with the day). There are two **buses** a day from Fauske/Bodø (5 hr.). Check the websites of Swedish Railways (www.sj.se) or of Veolia transport for bus info (www.bokatag.se).

VISITOR INFORMATION The **Narvik tourist office** is at the railway station, Stasjonsveien 1 (© **46-92-24-66;** www.destinationnarvik.com). It's open Monday to Friday 10am to 3pm; from June to August it's also open Saturday from 9am to 2pm.

What to See & Do

To get a good look at Narvik, take the **Gondolbanen cable car** (© **76-97-72-82;** www.narvikfjellet.com), from directly behind the Norlandia Narvik Hotel, a 10-minute walk from the town center. The car operates from March to October, and the round-trip fare is NOK100, NOK80 for children 6 to 15 (free for 5 and under). In just 13 minutes, it takes you to an elevation of 656m (2,152 ft.), at the top of Fagernesfjell. Here you can soak in the impressive panorama of the town and its surroundings or visit the simple restaurant.

From this peak you can "hike till you drop," as one local advised us. Marked trails branch out in several directions, all equally impressive. A downhill mountain-bike trail also starts near the cable car's final stop. From mid-February to mid-June and in August and September, the cable car operates Monday to Friday from 1 to 9pm, Saturday and Sunday from 10am to 5pm; from mid-June to the end of July, it operates daily from noon to 1am.

Nordland Røde Kors Krigsminnemuseum (War Museum) Near Torghallen in the town center, this museum re-creates the tragic events of the early 1940s, revisiting the epic struggle of the Narvik campaign of 1940 and the years of Nazi occupation from 1940 to 1945. Events from Narvik's destruction by the Germans, who occupied it until the end of World War II, are the focus here. Exhibits detail Germany's battle for Narvik's iron ore and how Nazi forces fought troops from France, Poland, and Norway, and a considerable British flotilla at sea. Experiences of the civilian population and foreign POWs are also highlighted.

Kongensgate. © **76-94-44-26.** www.fred.no. Admission NOK60, NOK35 children. Late April to early June Mon–Sat 10am–4pm, Sunday noon–4pm; early June to late Aug Mon–Sat 10am–9pm, Sunday noon–6pm; late Aug to late April Mon–Fri 11am–3pm.

Ofoten Museum The Ofoten Museum displays artifacts tracing the oldest human settlements in the area, going back to the Stone Age, as revealed in rock carvings. Other exhibits (including a scraper for animal skins and a flint-and-tinder box) show how ancient people lived and worked. Most of the displays are from the 20th century, beginning with the construction of the rail line.

Administrasjonsveien 3. ✆ **76-96-96-50.** www.ofotenmuseum.no. Admission NOK50, free for children 14 & under. Mid-June to mid-Aug Mon–Fri 10am–4:30pm, Sat–Sun 11am–4pm; rest of year Mon–Fri 10am–3pm.

Outdoor Activities

The Narvik tourist office (see above) has a wealth of information about outdoor activities in the city's hinterlands.

One of the great golf courses in northern Norway is the **Narvik Golfklubb,** Skomendalen (✆ **76-95-12-01;** www.narvikgolf.no), lying 18km (11 miles) south of Narvik. In a dramatic setting, surrounded by mountain peaks, this is the world's northernmost 18-hole golf course (par 72). A full round of golf costs NOK350 on weekends and NOK300 during the week, with club rentals going for NOK130. To reach the course from Narvik, follow the signs to Skjomdal, to just before the Skjomen Bridge on the E6.

Narvik has a long skiing season, lasting from November until early June. The cable car (see "Seeing the Sights," above) will deliver you up some 656m (2,152 ft.) where you'll find trail and off-piste skiing. For more information about conditions, call the **Narvik Ski Center** at ✆ **76-94-27-99.**

Divers from all over the world are attracted to Narvik's waters, as it was the scene of a major World War II naval battle. More than 50 planes, both Nazi and Allied, were gunned down here, and three German destroyers are still underwater. **Dive Narvik** (✆ **99-51-22-05;** www.divenarvik.com) can make arrangements for accredited divers for this incredible undersea adventure.

The mountainous landscape around Narvik attracts sports enthusiasts from around Norway and the rest of Europe, some of whom, if they're physically fit and equipped to handle such savage terrain, embark upon hiking excursions on the surrounding tundra. For information about all kinds of adventure sports within dramatically windswept regions around Narvik, including hill climbing, rappelling, fishing on the Ofotfjord, whale-sighting, and dog-sled safaris, contact the tour operator linked to the local tourist office, **Destination Narvik,** Kongensgate 26 (✆ **76-96-56-00;** www.visitnarvik.no). It maintains the same opening hours as the tourist office (see "Visitor Information," above).

Where to Stay

These hotels are located in some of the few buildings that survived World War II.

MODERATE

Quality Hotel Grand Royal ★ The monolithic exterior can be somewhat off-putting, but the Grand Royal is nevertheless the largest and best-equipped lodging in Narvik. It opens onto the main street in the town center, between the train station and the harbor. Built in the 1920s, it was named the Grand Royal because the late King Olav was a frequent visitor; his portraits adorn some public rooms. The comfortable, amply-sized rooms are tastefully and traditionally furnished, and all but a handful have been renovated and upgraded. The artfully contemporary lobby bar is one of the most alluring cocktail bars in northern Norway.

Kongensgate 64, N-8501 Narvik. ✆ **76-97-70-00.** www.choicehotels.no. 119 units. NOK756–NOK1,352 double. Rates include buffet breakfast. AE, DC, MC, V. Bus: 14, 15, 16, or 17. **Amenities:** 2 restaurants; 2 bars; sauna; babysitting; rooms for those with limited mobility. *In room:* TV, Wi-Fi, minibar, hair dryer.

INEXPENSIVE

Nordstjernen Hotel In 1970, the present owner of this hotel opened its doors on the main street of Narvik to offer a viable alternative to the Grand Royal (see above). Much improved over the years, it's still going strong, and keeping its prices within an affordable range, at least for this part of the world. South of the bus station, the hotel has long been known as one of the best values in the area. Guest rooms are decorated in pastels to offset the winter gloom and vary in size, though most are fairly boring.

Kongensgate 26, N-8500 Narvik. ✆ **76-94-41-20.** www.nordstjernen.no. 24 units. NOK975 double. Rates include buffet breakfast. DC, MC, V. Bus: 14 or 16. **Amenities:** Restaurant; lounge. *In room:* TV, hair dryer.

Where to Dine

Pub und Kro INTERNATIONAL Less expensive and less formal than the Grand Royal's main dining room this cozy restaurant is one of the most popular venues for dining and drinking in town. The menu offers an array of fresh Norwegian dishes such as reindeer and cod filet, and a great pepper steak sided with fresh vegetables.

In the Quality Hotel Grand Royal, Kongensgate 64. ✆ **76-97-70-77.** www.choicehotels.no. Reservations recommended. Main courses NOK199–NOK355. AE, DC, MC, V. Mon–Fri 11am–11pm; Sat noon–11pm; Sun 1–9pm.

Narvik After Dark

An animated (and sometimes hard-drinking) bar that attracts lots of younger locals is **Telegrafen,** Dronningensgata 56 (✆ **76-95-43-00;** www.telegrafen.net/narkiv.asp), Narvik's reigning disco, with a good selection of beers and whiskeys. Bands occasionally play, and it's a good spot to catch telecasts of sporting events too.

THE LOFOTEN ISLANDS: THE SOUL OF NORWAY ★★★

Svolvær (southernmost point of the Lofoten Islands): 280km (174 miles) N of Bodø; 1,425km (885 miles) NE of Bergen; 1,250km (777 miles) N of Oslo

The island kingdom of Lofoten, one of the most beautiful regions of Norway, lies about 200km (120 miles) north of the Arctic Circle. Its population of 35,000 is distributed over both large and small islands. Many Norwegian visitors come here to fish, but the area also offers abundant bird life and flora. The midnight sun shines from May 25 to July 7.

Hans Olsen, a local guide, told us, "If you are not already a poet by the time you come here, you will be by the time you leave." He was referring, of course, to the area's beauty, the remoteness of the archipelago, and the mystical Arctic light.

The Lofoten Islands stretch from Vågan in the east to Røst and Skomvær in the southwest. The steep Lofoten mountain peaks—often called the Lofotwall—shelter farmland and deep fjords from the elements.

The major islands are **Austvågøy, Gimsøy, Vestvågøy, Flakstadøy, Moskenesøy, Værøy,** and **Røst.** The southernmost part of Norway's largest island, Hinnøy, is also in Lofoten. The Vestfjorden separates the major islands from the mainland of Norway.

In winter, the Gulf Stream makes possible the world's largest cod-fishing event, called **Lofotfisket,** between January and March. Arctic sea cod spawn beyond the Lofoten Islands, especially in the Vestfjorden, and huge harvesting operations are carried out between January and March, though this has dwindled in importance in recent years.

The first inhabitants of the Lofoten Islands were nomads who hunted and fished, but excavations show that agriculture existed here at least 4,000 years ago. The Vikings pursued farming, fishing, and trading; examples of Viking housing sites can be seen on Vestbågøya, where more than 1,000 burial mounds have also been found.

Impressions

Mirages turn floating mountains topsy-turvy ahead of you and behind your back, while whales are at play and birds are a'shrieking.

—Poet Bjørnstjerne Bjørnson, 1869, describing the Lofoten Islands

From the 14th century on, the people of Lofoten had to pay taxes to Bergen. This was the beginning of an economic dominance lasting for 6 centuries—first by Hanseatic tradesmen and then by their Norwegian heirs.

Harsh treatment of local residents by the Nazis during World War II was key in forging the famous Norwegian Resistance movement. Allied forces, which landed here to harass the German iron-ore boats sailing from Narvik, withdrew in June 1940. They evacuated as many Lofoten residents as they could to Scotland for the duration of the war.

Today the Lofoten Islands have modern towns with shops, hotels, restaurants, and public transportation. In addition to hotels, guesthouses, and campsites, the Lofoten Islands offer lodging in traditional fishing cottages known as *rorbuer.* The larger (often two-story), usually more modern version, is a *sjøhus* (sea house). The traditional *rorbu* was built right at the edge of the water, often on piles, with room for 10 bunks, a kitchen, and an entrance hall used as a work and storage room. Many *rorbuer* today are still simple and unpretentious, but some have electricity, a woodstove, a kitchenette with a sink, and running water. Others have been outfitted with separate bedrooms, private showers, and toilets. The best and most convenient booking agent is **Destination Lofoten** (see "Visitor Information," below).

Essentials

GETTING THERE **Svolvær,** on the east coast of Austvågøy, is the largest town on the archipelago's largest island. From Bodø, **motorists** should drive east on Route 80 to Fauske. Take the E6 north to Ulvsvåg and head southwest on Route 81 toward Skutvik, from where you can take the 1½-hour **ferry** to Svolvær (two to four sailings daily). Passengers without cars pay NOK83 (NOK42 children) each way for passage to Svolvær from Skutvik; one-way transport of a car with its driver costs NOK286, which includes the driver. For ferry information and reservations, contact **Torghatten Nord** (✆ **81-00-30-30;** www.torghattennord.no). In 2007, the Lofast E10 road connected Svolvær to the mainland for the first time in history.

The Lofoten Islands

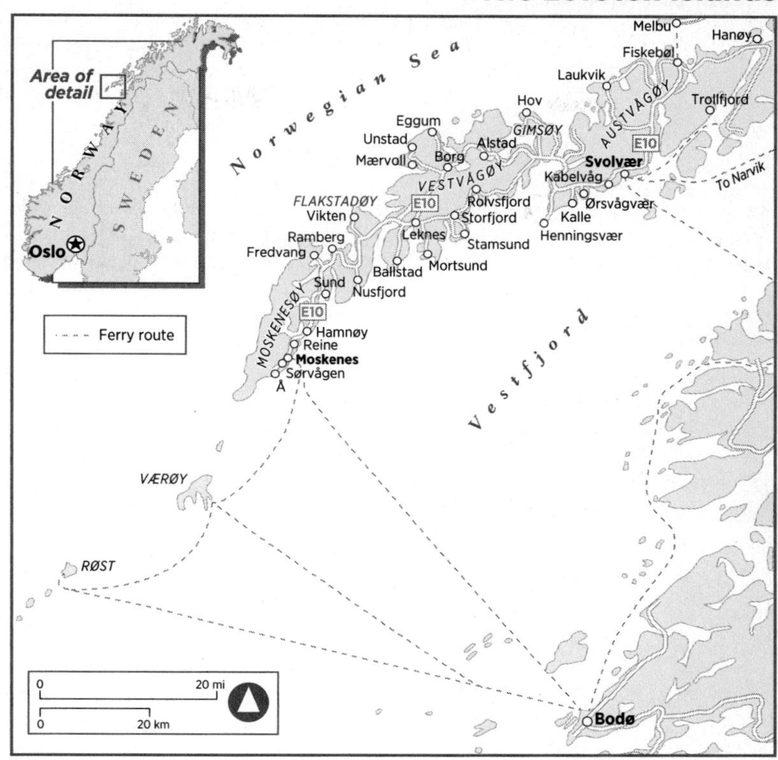

Many visitors take the **train** to Bodø, transferring to a **bus** that crosses to Svolvær on the ferry. Most bus departures from Bodø are timed to coincide with the arrival of trains from Oslo, Bergen, and other points. Buses also go to Ulvsvåg, then on to Skutvik, for the ferry to Svolvær..

Coastal steamers, departing from Bodø at 3pm daily, call at Stamsund and Svolvær.

VISITOR INFORMATION The Svolvær tourist office, **Destination Lofoten,** Box 210, N-8301 Svolvær (✆ **76-06-98-00;** www.lofoten.info) is on the harborfront in a big red building right in the middle of the town square. It's open January 1 to May 16 Monday to Friday 9am to 3:30pm; May 17 to June 6 Monday to Friday 9am to 4pm, Saturday 10am to 2pm; June 7 to June 20 Monday to Friday 9am to 8pm, Saturday 10am to 2pm, Sunday 4 to 8pm; June 21 to August 8 Monday to Friday 9am to 10pm, Saturday 9am to 8pm, Sunday 10am to 8pm; August 9 to August 22 Monday to Friday 9am to 8pm, Saturday 10am to 2pm; August 23 to December 31 Monday to Friday 9am to 3:30pm.

These Boots Are Made for Walking

I recommend specific walks or hikes that I've found enjoyable in the following pages. But be aware that pretty much everywhere in the entire Lofoten archipelago is absolutely perfect for walking or hiking. In places, you'll make your way along lakes dark as peat and past fields of delectable yellow-orange Arctic cloudberries. Or you'll pass bilberries, while taking in fields of reindeer moss and sea eagles flying overhead. Perhaps you'll even come across the second most characteristic animal of the north (after the reindeer): The stately moose.

You can wander field, hill, and dale, even climb a mountain. Also rewarding are walks along the rugged coast, past dwarf willow trees and mountain ash. In some parts of the Lofoten Islands, especially Moskenesøy, you'll discover the ruins of deserted villages. In these cases, the sea proved too harsh a place to make a living, and the inhabitants finally threw in the fishing net and moved on.

GETTING AROUND At the Svolvær tourist office you can pick up a free pamphlet, *Lofoten Info-Guide,* with information about all ferries and buses throughout the archipelago. All inhabited islands are linked by ferry, and buses service the four major islands, including Svolvær. Motorists can drive the E10 from Svolvær to the outer rim of the Lofoten Islands, a distance of 130km (81 miles). One of the **great drives in the north of Norway ★★**, this route will give you a good overall look at the Lofoten Islands.

Our preferred method of getting around the Lofoten Islands is by bike. Cycles can be rented at most of the archipelago's little hotels.

Suggested Itineraries

IF YOU HAVE 1 DAY Arrive at the main port city of **Svolvær,** which will be your gateway to the Lofoten Islands. I suggest you use this as a refueling stop and an arrival and exit port because of its superior transportation links.

Instead of spending the night here, you can head immediately south to the more attractive port of **Kabelvåg** for an overnight stopover. However, while still in Svolvær, you might want to take one of the most dramatic boat trips in the Lofoten Islands, to the famous **Trollfjord** (p. 412).

IF YOU HAVE 2 DAYS Based in the little port of Kabelvåg, you can pay a morning visit to the Lofoten Museum (p. 414), which will provide some useful insight into the people of the islands. You might also visit the **Lofoten Aquarium** (p. 415). For some Lofoten thrills, try to sign up for an adventure trip for the afternoon; see "Seeing the Sights," under Kabelvåg, below.

IF YOU HAVE 3 DAYS Head south to **Henningsvær,** the largest and liveliest of the Lofoten fishing villages. You will find good hotels and restaurants here if you want to spend the night. I suggest a morning visit to the **Lofoten Hus Gallery** (p. 416) to see the largest and best collection of northern Norway art. An even more exciting idea is to take one of the **mountain tours** or **sea eagle safaris** offered in the area (p. 416). The sea eagle jaunt will take only an hour, allowing you time to do some mountain climbing even if it's getting late. If you arrive in midsummer, remember that the sun never sets.

IF YOU HAVE 4 DAYS Continue south to explore **Vestvågøy,** the second-largest island. You can visit the hamlet of **Borg,** where the biggest Viking Age chieftain's homestead in Scandinavia has been excavated. A full-scale replica of the chieftain's house has been reconstructed. **Stamsund,** with its 1,500 inhabitants, makes a good base here, as it is one of the largest fishing villages in western Lofoten.

A mountainous region sprawls both north and south of Stamsund. You can spend most of the afternoon walking and exploring at random, perhaps climbing one of the steep mountains. For my favorite walk in the area, see the "Walking from Fishing Village to Fishing Village" box on p. 422.

IF YOU HAVE 5 DAYS Another day can be spent on the island of **Flakstadøy** visiting fishing hamlets such as **Ramberg,** which lies next to a lovely white beach facing the Arctic Ocean. Drop in at the **Flakstad Kirke,** built in 1780 of wood (p. 419). In 1 day you can visit my favorite island fishing ports, including **Sund,** with its Fiskerimuseum (fishing museum,, p. 420), and **Nusfjord,** which is justifiably the most famous of the little ports because of its agglomeration of fishermen's huts. These are used by fishermen in the winter and visitors in the summer.

IF YOU HAVE 6 DAYS While still based at Flakstadøy, perhaps in the village of Ramberg, you can explore the island to its immediate south, **Moskenesøy** (p. 421). For a true adventure and a chance to capture the spirit of the Lofoten Islands and its people, we consider this the most evocative island. Sculptured by glaciers, the landscape is far more savage than others we have visited.

The most dramatic experience here is a 5-hour tour over often-turbulent waters to the **Moskestraumen,** the treacherous strait separating Moskenesøy from the offshore island of Værøy to the south. These are called "the world's most dangerous waters" and could be the highlight of a trip to the Lofoten Islands. They even inspired Edgar Allan Poe to write a nautical tale. Marine mammals and thousands of seabirds can be seen here.

I'd vote **Reine** (see below) as among the most charming and typical of the Lofoten villages. You can even spend the night here, if you wish, in a rented fisherman's hut. What I recommend is to explore the Moskestraumen one day, then go on a midnight sun cruise the following day.

Svolvær

This bustling (well, bustling for the Lofoten Islands, that is), modern port town lies on the island of **Austvågøy,** the northernmost in the archipelago. It lacks the charm of the island's other fishing communities, and the port is a bit dull, but its crags and sheltered bays form a dramatic Lofoten backdrop. Svolvær attracts the most visitors and has some of the area's best hotels and restaurants. Most Lofoten cultural attractions are within easy reach. The most adventurous travelers will make use of it as a transit point and a place to stock up before heading out to more remote destinations.

WHAT TO SEE & DO

Lofoten Krigsminnemuseum, Fiskergata 12 (© **91-73-03-28;** www.lofotenkrigmus.no), is the finest museum in the north devoted to the tragic World War II era. There's a little-known collection of 1940s' photographs, some of which document the 1941 commando raid on the islands. Also on display is a collection of military uniforms. Admission is NOK40. It's open mid-May to mid-August Monday to Saturday 10am to 10pm, Sunday noon to 3pm and 6 to 10pm; the rest of the year it's open a few hours each day, though when exactly can vary wildly.

Daredevils are lured to Svolvær to conquer the most dangerous climb in Lofoten, the **Svolværgeita** (Svolværur Goat). This 40-m (13-ft.) stone column is perched on a hill behind the port and is known for its two pinnacles, which locals have labeled "the horns of a goat." There's a 1.5-m (5-ft.) jump between the two horns; if you don't make it, you're as good as dead.

One of the most dramatic boat rides in Lofoten is the short trip into the impossibly narrow **Trollfjord ★★**, stretching for 2km (1¼ miles). This is part of the channel that separates the Lofoten island of Austvågøy from the Vesterålen island of Hinnøya. Coastal steamers can barely navigate this narrow passage without scraping the rock walls on either side. One of the most visited sites in Lofoten, this fjord cuts its way westward from the Straits of Raftsundet, opening onto an idyllic Lofoten landscape, famed as the subject of many paintings.

Trollfjord is the easternmost island in Lofoten, and was the scene of the "Battle of the Trollfjord," related by Johan Bojer in his novel *The Last Viking*. The battle, which took place more than a century ago between fishermen in small vessels and those in larger steamships, was first recorded on canvas by one of its witnesses, the artist Gunnar Berg (1863–93). His painting is on view at the Svolvær town hall. Ask at the tourist office about linking up with a boat tour of Trollfjord. Departures are from late April to September, costing NOK350 per adult, NOK150 children.

For the best and most scenic walks in the area, take the ferry over to the islet of **Skrova.** Here you can stroll around and leisurely take in the seascapes. Before heading over, pick up the makings of a picnic at one of the shops in Svolvær and prepare to enjoy it in splendid isolation. You can visit Skrova either via express boats from Svolvær to Bodø/Narvik or on the car ferry between Svolvær and Skutvik. The crossing to Skrova takes half an hour on either boat and costs roughly NOK80 per person.

Another good walk from Svolvær is to the north, heading to the Lille and Store Kongsvatn lakes, on whose banks you might want to have a picnic. You will know you've reached the end of the trail when you come to a power station. If you wish, you can take a path to **Kabelvåg** (p. 414), following the shoreline for most of the way.

SHOPPING

Artists have long been drawn to the archipelago because of the particular quality of its Northern Lights. The leading gallery is **Nordnorsk Kunstnersentrum ★** (**© 76-06-67-70;** www.nnks.no (in Norwegian)), on the island of Svinøya, 1km (⅔ mile) from Svolvær. The Northern Norwegian Artist's Center is run by the artists themselves, offering a wide range of paintings, plus handicrafts, posters, and other items. From June 12 to August 15, it's open daily 10am to 6pm; off-season Tuesday, Wednesday, and Friday 10am to 4pm, Thursday 10am to 7pm, Saturday and Sunday 11am to 4pm. Entrance to the permanent collection costs NOK40, NOK30 for students and seniors, and is free for children 14 and under.

WHERE TO STAY

Anker Brygge ★★ ☺ On a tiny island in the middle of Svolvær harbor, connected by a bridge to the "mainland," this is one of the most atmospheric lodging choices in the area. The quayside structure dates from 1880, when it was a fish-landing station with its own "saltery" and barrel factory. In 1996, it was converted into an inn. Guests can stay in individual red-painted cottages that are rustically adorned with timbers but also have all the modern conveniences. Cabins, called *rorbu* cabin suites, can sleep up to six guests, so they're ideal for families. Each is distinctively furnished; you may feel as if you're staying at some remote lodge in the wilds of a far northern frontier post. Some two dozen of them lie along the quayside or the shore, with views of the harbor and the Lofoten mountains.

Lamholmen, N-8300 Svolvær. ✆ **76-06-64-80.** Fax 76-06-64-70. www.anker-brygge.no. 80 units. NOK1,350 double; NOK2,390 cottages & suites for 2–6 people. Rates include continental breakfast. AE, DC, MC, V. **Amenities:** Restaurant (closed Jan–Feb); bar; sauna. *In room:* TV.

Norlandia Vestfjord Hotel This is a comfortable but unexceptional place. The bright orange building was a former warehouse for marine supplies and fish. After extensive remodeling, it reopened as this well-managed hotel. The guest rooms are all comfortable; but ask for one that overlooks the sea. Facilities include a lobby bar and a pleasant restaurant that specializes in fish and steaks. It serves sustaining fare—nothing remarkable.

Fiskergata 46, N-8300 Svolvær. ✆ **76-07-08-70.** www.vestfjord.norlandia.no. 63 units. NOK695–NOK1,495 double; NOK2,200 suite. Rates include buffet breakfast. AE, DC, MC, V. **Amenities:** Restaurant; bar; room service; rooms for those with limited mobility. *In room:* TV, minibar (in some), hair dryer.

Rica Hotel Svolvær ★ If you book into the right suite here, you can go fishing through a hole in the floor of your room. This is the sleekest, the best, and the most desirable of the chain hotels. Right next to the water, it was opened in 1995, and is renovated and kept in tiptop shape every year. The bedrooms are in separate *rorbu* cabins built of wood, and half of them open onto a private harbor-view terrace. Each room is comfortably furnished, containing immaculate private bathrooms with shower. Norwegian specialties, especially salmon, are served in the first-class restaurant on-site. The restaurant is constructed in the shape of a boat, opening onto panoramic vistas of the ocean.

Lamholmen, N-8301 Svolvær. ✆ **76-07-22-22.** www.rica-lofoten.no. 147 units. NOK745–NOK1,095 double. Rates include continental breakfast & evening buffet. AE, DC, MC, V. Closed Dec 20–Jan 3. **Amenities:** Restaurant; bar; rooms for those with limited mobility. *In room:* TV.

Svinøya Rorbuer ★★ Nothing comes as close to an authentic Lofoten experience as staying in one of these cottages, across a bridge on the island of Svinøya, site of Svolvær's first settlement. You'll be welcomed at the reception area, which was once the general store for the community and the first shop ever to open in Svolvær. Then you'll be shown to one of the red-painted, restored cabins. The main building is from 1820, some of the cabins are from the 19th century, and others are modern but constructed in the old style. All of these fishermen's cabins are furnished to a high standard. Some have well-equipped kitchens. The inn contains the town's best restaurant, the Børson Spiseri (see below).

Gunnar Bergs vei 2, N-8300 Svolvær. ✆ **76-06-99-30.** www.svinoya.no. 30 cabins. NOK1,000–NOK2,970 double. Rates include continental breakfast. AE, DC, MC, V. **Amenities:** Restaurant; bar; Jacuzzi. *In room:* Wi-Fi, kitchen (in some), no phone.

WHERE TO DINE

Børson Spiseri ★ SEAFOOD The town's best restaurant is housed in the Svinøya Rorbuer (see above), across a bridge on the island of Svinøya. I'd come here for the atmosphere alone, but fortunately the food is just as first-rate. The restaurant has been installed in an old quayside building from 1828, the setting for an "arctic menu" that features some of the freshest fish I've ever consumed in the north. The setting is old-fashioned, with antiques from 2 centuries ago, along with maritime artifacts such as fishing equipment and old boats. The chef dishes out specialties such as deep-fried cod tongue with sour cream, traditional Lofoten dried cod with bacon and potatoes, filet of salmon fried in butter and accompanied by mussels, and grilled stockfish with fennel risotto. One dessert specialty is citrus cheesecake with passion-fruit sauce—scrumptious.

Gunnar Bergs vei 2. ✆ **76-06-99-30.** www.svinoya.no. Reservations recommended. Main courses NOK265–NOK309. AE, DC, MC. Daily 5–10pm. Closed Jan & Mon in winter.

Kabelvåg

Much more romantically situated than Svolvær is the port of Kabelvåg, lying 5km (3 miles) to the south. This is also a much better introduction to the quaintness of the Lofoten Islands than Svolvær. The port of wooden buildings encircles the shore of a narrow inlet. In its heyday it was the major village in the Viking era, a position it maintained until the early years of the 20th century. The first *rorbuer* (fishermen's cottages) were erected here in 1120.

One of the best walks in the area, giving you a flavor of the Lofoten Islands, is the road between Svolvær and Kabelvåg. You go from the hustle and bustle of Svolvær, without all that much charm, to a little center of wooden houses hugging the shore of a knobby inlet. Along the way you're treated to seascapes of a certain majesty. Otherwise, frequent buses (every 20 min. in summer) run from Svolvær, taking 15 minutes and costing NOK50 for a one-way fare.

WHAT TO SEE & DO

For NOK140, you can purchase (at any of the sites) a combination ticket, granting admission to the Lofoten Museum, the Lofoten Aquarium, and the Galleri Espolin.

Lofoten Museum, Storvågan (✆ **76-06-97-99;** www.lofotmuseet.no), was constructed over the site of the first town built in the polar world. The regional museum depicts past life in Lofoten, and excavations continue at the site of an old trading post. On the museum grounds, you can visit a boathouse with antique boats, *rorbu* cabins from the 18th and 19th centuries, and cultural artifacts dating from prehistoric and medieval times. Admission is NOK60 for adults, NOK25 for children. It's open June to mid-August daily 10am to 6pm; May and mid-August to end-August Monday to Friday 9am to 3pm, Saturday and Sunday 11am to 3pm; September Monday to Friday 9am–3pm, Sun 11am–3pm; October to December 17 and January 4 to April Monday to Friday 9am to 3pm.

For the adventurous there are **killer whale safaris** in inflatable boats. Day trips to spot whales—the largest group of killer whales in the world come to the Lofoten Islands—are staged from October 29 to January 22. Trips take 4 hours and cost NOK1,050 per passenger. Departure is daily at 9am. To arrange a tour contact Tysfjord Turistsenter, based in Storfjord (✆ **75-77-53-70;** www.tysfjord-turistsenter.no).

Lofoten Kayakk (✆ **76-07-30-00;** www.lofoten-kajakk.no) offers the best **sailing trips** around the Lofoten Islands, in boats built of wood. On these trips, boats cross open water to get from one island to the other. The 3-hour trips cost from NOK500. Departures are daily on request. If you possess the necessary skills, you can also rent a **kayak** to test your luck in the waters of the Lofoten Islands, for NOK420 per day. They also offer guided kayak tours; prices start at NOK850 for a 3-hour tour. This same outfitter also rents bicycles at NOK210 per day.

Close by and opening onto the sea, **Lofoten Aquarium,** Storvågan (✆ **76-07-86-65;** www.lofotakvariet.no), offers nearly two dozen tanks of various sizes filled with fish and other marine animals, including mammals, from the Arctic world. Of special interest are the seal and otter ponds. There's also a salmon-farm exhibit, and much attention is given to the "noble" cod, which has sustained life in these parts for centuries. Admission is NOK110, NOK55 for children ages 5 to 15, and free for children 4 and under. Hours are February to May Sunday to Friday 11am to 3pm (plus Sat in May), June to August daily 10am to 6pm, and September to November Sunday to Friday 11am to 3pm.

The distinctive, contemporary **Galleri Espolin,** Storvågan (✆ **76-07-84-05;** www.galleri-espolin.no), is devoted to the works of artist Kaare Espolin Johnson (1907–94), one of Norway's best-known artists. Espolin was drawn to the archipelago and was fascinated by its life and that of its fishermen. Amazingly, this almost lyrical artist was practically blind for most of his life. He painted not only the fishermen, but also their wives, their boats, and the drama they faced at sea. From June to mid-August, the museum is open daily 10am to 6pm; mid-August to September 10am to 4pm; September to December 11am to 3pm. Admission is NOK60 for adults and NOK25 for children.

On the eastern approach to town, along the E10, stands **Vågan Kirke** (✆ **76-07-82-90**), a church from 1898 that is the second-largest wooden church in Norway, with a seating capacity of 1,200. Also known as the "Lofoten Cathedral," it was constructed for the seasonal population of fishermen who came mostly for the winter catches, swelling the population of little Kabelvåg. Admission is NOK20, but the church keeps no regular hours (it's usually open during the day in summer).

WHERE TO STAY

Kabelvåg Hotell In the center of Kabelvåg, this hotel is a 1995 reconstruction of the original Art Deco villa that once stood here. It is also the site of the best restaurant in town (see "Where to Dine", below). Rising three floors, it's very much an antique wooden structure on the outside, but inside it is modern and completely up-to-date. The small to midsize bedrooms are rather simply but comfortably furnished, with views of the ocean and mountains.

Kong Øysteinsgate 4, N-8310 Kabelvåg. ✆ **76-06-97-00.** www.kabelvaghotell.no. 28 units. NOK900–NOK1,400 double. Children 7 & under stay free in parents' room. Rates include buffet breakfast & dinner. AE, DC, MC, V. Closed early Aug to June 1. **Amenities:** Restaurant; bar. *In room:* TV, hair dryer.

Nyvagar Rorbuhotell ★ This contemporary *rorbu* cabin resort offers gorgeous architecture based on those rustic cabins inhabited by the fishermen who came in winter to harvest cod. The location is convenient, lying only a 3-minute stroll from the area's museums. Each of the well-furnished, fire-engine-red cabins contains two bedrooms and a kitchen, along with a small bathroom with a shower. Expect wood furnishings and wood walls in all units, while about half of the units open right onto the harbor. This hotel also offers one of the most helpful staffs in the area, skilled at arranging such adventures as deep-sea rafting, eagle safaris, or fishing-boat jaunts. Even if you're not a guest, you might visit its lively quayside pub with outdoor table service in summer. In the main building, the Lorchstua Restaurant serves an array of regional dishes from the north.

Storvåganveien 22, N-8310 Kabelvåg. ✆ **76-06-97-00.** www.nyvagar.no. 30 units. NOK1,600 cabin for 2–4 occupants. Rates include continental breakfast. AE, DC, MC, V. Closed Sept–Apr. **Amenities:** Restaurant; bar; sauna. *In room:* TV.

WHERE TO DINE

Krambua SEAFOOD/NORWEGIAN This restaurant in the Kabelvåg Hotell is the best at the port. It has a mellow atmosphere and is decorated with old books, antiques, and animal-skin furnishings. It feels like you're in the far north if you dine here, especially when you're served whale carpaccio. If you're concerned about the politics of eating whale meat, try the great smoked salmon or island cod, served here after a "soft" baking in the oven with white-wine sauce and butter-boiled vegetables. Meat-eaters prefer the filet of reindeer with sautéed potatoes. In summer, wild berries from these Arctic climes will adorn your plate.

In the Kabelvåg Hotell, Kong Øysteinsgate 4. ✆ **76-07-88-00.** www.kabellvaghotell.no. Reservations recommended. Main courses NOK190–NOK275. AE, DC, MC, V. Mon–Sat 11am–11pm; Sun 2–8pm. Closed early Aug to June 1.

Henningsvær ★

The fanciful nickname of "Venice of the North" shouldn't obscure the fact that this is the liveliest and most artistic of Lofoten villages. Lying 20km (12 miles) southwest of Svolvær, this is the largest fishing village in Lofoten. Bus no. 510 runs here from Svolvær, taking 35 minutes and costing NOK60 one-way.

WHAT TO SEE & DO

Based in Henningsvær, the **Nord Norsk Klatreskole (Northern Norwegian School of Mountaineering; ✆ 90-57-42-08;** www.nordnorskklatreskole.no) conducts summer guided tours in the mountains of the Lofoten Islands, following only the most scenic routes, such as to the top of Svolværgeita Peak. Climbing holidays cost from NOK2,500 for a 3-day jaunt. It's always best to stop by to discuss your desires and have the options explained to you. Of course, you can call in advance and have a game plan mapped out before your arrival in town. The mountaineering school also operates a Climber's Café and a store that rents mountaineering gear.

From Henningsvær **sea eagle safaris** are conducted in summer by Lofoten Opplevelser (✆ **76-07-50-01;** www.lofoten-opplevelser.no). Nordland is the land of the sea eagle, and in summer these safaris take you off the coast to see these birds of prey in their natural environment. Near Henningsvær is the world's most compact flock of these majestic birds, which often have a wingspan of some 2m (6½ ft.). Guides include John Stenersen, author of *The Birds of the Lofoten*. From June 20 to August 10, 1-hour safaris cost NOK430 for adults, NOK330 for children.

At the **Lofoten Hus Gallery ★** (✆ **76-07-15-73;** www.galleri-lofoten.no) you can see Norway's largest collection of north-country painters, dramatically installed in a former fish-canning house. The focus is on the well-known artist Karl Erik Harr, plus other notable artists who came to Lofoten at the end of the 19th century. A

20-minute slide show narrates the landscapes of Lofoten and its people, with rare photographs of the white-tailed eagle. It's open daily, March 5 to March 28 11am to 4pm; March 29 to May 19 11am to 6:30pm; May 20 to June 9 10am to 7pm; June 10 to August 14 9am to 7pm; August 15 to August 31 10am to 7pm. Admission is NOK70 for adults, NOK35 for children.

WHERE TO STAY

Henningsvær Bryggehotell ★ This white-painted house is idyllically set at the harbor quay against a backdrop of mountains. Although the setting is old-fashioned and rather picture-postcardy, the interior design is contemporary and stylish. In all, it's a good choice as your base for exploring the northern Lofoten Islands. The mid-size rooms, set over three floors, feature imagery of the Lofoten Islands from the 1900s. On-site is Bluefish, one of the best restaurants on the island (see "Where to Dine", below). The staff will help you arrange sea trips, including rafting and fishing.

Hjellskoeret, N-8312 Henningsvær. ✆ **76-07-47-50.** www.dvgl.no. 30 units. NOK1,500 double & apartments; NOK4,500 suite. Children 11 & under stay free in parents' room. Rates include continental breakfast. AE, DC, MC, V. Closed late Sept to early Mar. **Amenities:** Restaurant; bar; sauna; room service. *In room:* TV.

Henningsvær Rorbuer ★ 🎁 Lying just outside the center of the village, this is an atmospheric choice of over two dozen *rorbuer,* or fishermen's goods stores, standing at the quayside against the backdrop of the "Lofoten Wall" (a string of mountains). You're housed in cabins that simulate a fisherman's cottage from long ago but that offer all the modern amenities. Rooms open onto panoramic views of the Vestfjorden and Mount Vågakallen. These quayside buildings were converted from old fish-landing warehouses. A special feature is a wood-fired sauna and a large wooden bathtub. The hotel's boat, *Kysten,* will take you for trips around the archipelago, and the staff will arrange deep-sea fishing trips in summer. You can also rent boats, and ask to be hooked up with a deep-sea rafting trip. Cabins contain two or three bedrooms, a kitchenette, and a bathroom with shower. All rooms are nonsmoking.

Banhammaren 53, N-8312 Henningsvær. ✆ **76-06-60-00.** www.henningsvar-rorbuer.no. 26 cabins. NOK1,050–NOK2,600 double. MC, V. **Amenities:** Bar; sauna. *In room:* TV, kitchen.

WHERE TO DINE

Bluefish Restaurant NORWEGIAN/SEAFOOD Attached to the Henningsvær Bryggehotel (see above), this is one of the island's best restaurants, often feeding 60 satisfied diners at a time. You'll sit at wooden tables enjoying views of the sea from the restaurant's windows. The chefs try to use whatever fresh ingredients are found in the Arctic so they don't have to import so much. Environmentalists may shun the smoked whale. Fresh salmon is aromatically baked with herbs and served with fresh vegetables. You can also order that staple of the Lofoten Islands, cod, most often fried and served with a lobster sauce or a white-wine sauce. Boiled halibut is another fine choice, appearing in a creamy butter sauce with cucumber salad and boiled potatoes.

In the Henningsvær Bryggehotel, Hjellskoeret. ✆ **76-07-47-50.** www.dvgl.no/en/. Reservations recommended. Main courses NOK175–NOK295. AE, DC, MC, V. June & Aug daily 6–10pm; July daily 4–11pm.

Fiskekrogen ★★ NORWEGIAN/SEAFOOD This quayside restaurant located in a former fish factory is the town's finest, and chef/owner Otto Asheim is justifiably acclaimed in the area. It even enjoys patronage from Queen Sonja, who discovered it during her backpacking days and has returned several times since. The chef is skilled at serving fish almost any way you want it. He cooks with robust flavor and intelligent associations of ingredients, using regional produce whenever possible. His fare is based on the season and what's fresh and good at the market. He does wonders with the famed cod of the area and also serves his own "homemade" caviar. His sautéed salmon or catfish is always tempting. Your best bet might be to order Lofoten lamb with seaweed and a red wine sauce. They even have a few quaintly decorated rooms upstairs if you need something in a pinch.

Dreyersgate 29. ✆ **76-07-46-52.** www.fiskekrogen.net. Reservations required in summer. Main courses NOK175–NOK265. AE, DC, MC, V. Summer daily 4–11pm. Closed in winter.

Vestvågøy

The second-largest island in the archipelago, and relatively flat, Vestvågøy is home to some 11,000 rugged islanders who forge their livelihoods from the sea.

If you base yourself here, I recommend you skip **Leknes** and head instead to **Stamsund** to the immediate east, the best base along the southern coast, with numerous accommodations. Stamsund is the island port where the coastal steamers from Bergen stop.

Buses from Leknes take only 30 minutes to reach Stamsund, costing NOK50 one-way. Leknes can be reached by bus from Svolvær, taking 2 hours and costing NOK120 one-way.

WHAT TO SEE & DO

In the hamlet of Borg, archaeologists uncovered the remains of the biggest Viking Age building ★★ ever found. It's been turned into the **Lofotr Viking Museum** (✆ **76-08-49-00;** www.lofotr.no). The museum has been built up around an impressive full-scale reconstruction of a Viking chieftain's house, 83m (270 ft.) in length. Also on display is the Viking shop *Lofotr,* a replica of the *Gokstad* (p. 132). The remains were discovered in 1981 by a farmer plowing his fields.

The museum setting duplicates the aura of the Iron Age, with light flickering from the hearths or gleaming from cod-liver oil lamps, and the smell of tar wafting through the air. Demonstrations of handicrafts authentic to the Viking era are presented. Artifacts are on display as well, including gold-foil fertility figures, Frankish pottery, and Rhineland glass. Outside you can see domestic animals such as the horses, sheep, and hens that would have been commonplace 1,000 years ago.

Admission is NOK120 for adults, NOK90 for seniors and students, and NOK60 for children, including a guided tour (slightly cheaper in the off-season). It's open daily 10am to 4pm. The Svolvær bus to Leknes passes by the entrance to the museum.

The best walk in the area begins at the road by the local youth hostel. Go for about 300m (1,000 ft.) southeast and then take a right turn onto

Your Own Private Boat for Fishing

As you make your way across the Lofoten Islands, you don't need to make elaborate plans to go fishing. Stop at nearly any fisherman's shack or boathouse at the island ports and ask about renting a small boat for a morning or an afternoon of fishing—preferably one with an outboard motor.

Ringveien for another 400m (1,300 ft.). Here a trail begins that will take about 3 hours to walk, passing the hamlet of Ørntuva and going up to the Heah, a big cairn with a panoramic view toward Henningsvær. This is an easy trail to follow, rising to about 380m (1,200 ft.) above sea level.

WHERE TO STAY & DINE

Skjærbrygga Hotel ★ These old fishermen's cabins still have a rustic flavor but have been renovated with modern comforts and are the most evocative place to stay on Vestvagøy. Located in the middle of Stamsund, these cabins await you with two to six beds each, plus kitchen, living room, and private bathroom with shower. An 1845 klipfish (dried cod) storehouse, the Skjærbrygga, has been turned into a good restaurant. There is also a library, and a lounge with a fireplace.

N-8340 Stamsund. ✆ **76-05-46-00.** www.skjaerbrygga.no. 27 cabins. NOK900–NOK1,050 for 1–2 persons; NOK1,200–NOK1,500 for 3–4 persons. AE, DC, MC, V. **Amenities:** Restaurant; cafe; pub. *In room:* TV.

Stamsund Lofoten Opened in 1974, this brightly painted hostel, made up of old fishermen's cabins in the heart of town and located on the pier, offers a view of the harbor. It's a decent and very affordable place to sleep, with small, simply furnished guest rooms that have good beds.

N-8340 Stamsund. ✆ **76-08-93-34.** 28 units. NOK445 double, NOK550 cabin. Rates include buffet breakfast. AE, DC, MC, V. *In room:* TV.

Flakstadøy

After Austvågøy and Vestvagøy, the E10 continues west to the island of Flakstadøy, with most of its 1,600 well-weathered souls living along the northern tier, around the town of Ramberg (see below), which makes a good base for exploring the island.

Flakstadøy is served by buses running along the main route via Leknes to the end of the line, the curiously named hamlet of Å. If you're motoring, you can take a toll tunnel from Vestvagøy to Flakstadøy for NOK100 per vehicle.

WHAT TO SEE & DO

If you're touring the island, make for the secluded village of **Nusfjord ★**, on the south coast, a setting for some of the island's most dramatic scenery. Both the beauty and the bleakness of this remote village have drawn many artists to the area. UNESCO has added this 19th-century fishermen's village to its list of protected sites.

A favorite walk begins about 300m (1,000 ft.) south of the old school in Nusfjord. Here you will see a cairned path leading to **Nesland,** a trek of about 4 hours round-trip. On this walk, you'll go about 200m (700 ft.) before you reach **Østre Nesland,** where you'll see the only remaining watermill in Lofoten. You'll find a colony of fishermen's huts, some still inhabited during the winter season or rented out to visitors in summer.

Ramberg, with its backdrop of snowcapped Arctic peaks, opens onto a beautiful white beach facing the Arctic Ocean. Just outside the village you can visit **Flakstad Kirke** at Flakstad (✆ **76-09-31-45**), built of wood in 1780 with a distinctive onion-shaped cupola. The altarpiece is older than the church, and the pulpit was painted by Godtfred Ezechiel, a master painter from Bergen. Charging an admission of NOK30, the church is open in summer daily from 10am to 4pm; the rest of the year it's open only during church services.

At Flakstad, another of my favorite walks begins with a drive out to Fredvang, following signposts to Yttersand. At this point, you can park your car and walk for 30 to 40 minutes along the shore to **Mulstøa.** Along the way, you'll find an idyllic spot for a picnic, though you'll need to pack your own provisions as there's nowhere out here to pick up food items.

The old fishing hamlet of **Sund** lies west of Ramberg along the E10. It's visited mainly by those wishing to see the **Sund Fiskerimuseum,** Sund (✆ **76-09-36-29;** www.sundfiskerimuseum.no), near the bridge leading to the island of Moskenesøy. A collection of fishing huts here contains all the paraphernalia needed to capture cod. The fisherman's cabin, or *rorbu,* is the oldest building in Sund, containing a wide range of domestic utensils, tools, and other artifacts used in fishermen's huts of old. On-site is a resident smithy known for his iron sculptures of cormorants. The museum is open June to mid-August daily from 10am to 6pm, charging NOK50 for adult admission and NOK15 for children.

A final attraction is **Glasshytta** at Vikten (✆ **76-09-44-42**). This is the original Lofoten glass-blower's cabin, offering products of high quality and innovative design. It is also the home base of northern Norway's first glassblower, Åsvar Tangrand, who designed Lofoten's seven-pronged logo, which evokes a longboat. The studio, charging an admission of NOK20 for adults (free admission for children), is open from mid-June to mid-August daily 9am to 7pm (curtailed hours off-season). You can purchase some very distinctive and charming pieces here at rather reasonable prices.

WHERE TO STAY

Nusfjord Rorbuer ★ 🎁 Thes "Rorbu" historic, red-sided cabins are secluded and tranquil, offering the most authentic and atmospheric way to stay on the island of Flakstadøy. Many Norwegian families from the south come here for summer holidays, booking a cabin for a week or more, but you can also stay overnight. Outdoor activities such as fishing, boating, and hiking fill one's agenda during the day. Rowboats come with the price of the room, and the helpful staff will also rent you a motorboat if you'd like to fish Lofoten waters. The original fishermen's cabins were built around 1900 but have since been modernized. They are constructed of timbers, and the wooden floors are original, the furnishings a mixture of antique and modern. In summer, there is also a restaurant (see below), serving mainly seafood.

N-8380 Ramberg. ✆ **76-09-30-20.** www.nusfjord.no. 34 cabins. NOK800–NOK2,200 double. Rates include continental breakfast. AE, DC, MC, V. **Amenities:** Summer restaurant. *In room:* Kitchenette, no phone.

WHERE TO DINE

Karoline SEAFOOD/NORWEGIAN Cozy, intimate, and much sought after as a dining enclave during its limited seasonal opening, this place seats only 30 diners at a time within a *rorbu* (fisherman's cottage) that reeks of character and rustic charm. The fish soup is a good choice, followed by the local seafood specialties of the day. As a dining oddity, you might opt to sample the deep-fried cod tongue, one of the islanders' favorite dishes. Meat-eaters can enjoy grilled beef kabobs and a few other dishes. For dessert? Try the old-fashioned apple pie with vanilla ice cream, like your good old mom used to bake.

In the Nusfjord Rorbuer, at the quay. ✆ **76-09-30-20.** www.nusfjord.no. Main courses NOK160–NOK250. AE, DC, MC, V. June–Aug daily 11am–3pm & 5–10:30pm.

Moskenesøy ★

Continuing east on the E10, you'll come to the final road link at the hamlet of Å. This glaciated island extends for 34km (21 miles). Nature has turned this landscape into one of the wildest and most fascinating in Norway. In Moskenesøy you'll reach the highest peak in the western Lofoten Islands at Hermannsdalstind, rising to 1,029m (3,376 ft.).

People live on the eastern side of the island, with its sheltered harbors for the fishing fleet. Even if you're not driving, the island maintains good ferry–bus links with Leknes, Stamsund, and Svolvær. Leknes, for example, lies 55km (34 miles) to the east.

Hurtigruten (**✆ 76-96-76-00,** or reservations 81-03-00-00; www.hurtigruten.com) runs car ferries between Bodø and Moskenes (3 hr.; NOK568 per vehicle and driver, NOK158 per passenger).

The village of Moskenes, with its ferry terminal, is a mere refueling stop. You can stop in for information and guidance at the **Fiskeværsferie Lofoten Turistkontoret** (**✆ 98-01-75-64**), at the harbor. Hours are May Monday to Friday 10am to 5pm; June 1 to June 20 and August 16 to August 31 daily 10am to 5pm; June 21 to August 15 daily 9am to 7pm; March, April, and September Monday to Friday 10am to 2pm.

WHAT TO SEE & DO

Directly east of Moskenes lies the village of **Reine ★**, one of the most scenically located in the Lofoten Islands, its little timber houses set against a panorama of seascapes. **Midnight sun cruises ★★** often set out from here in summer from late May to mid-July. Tours cost NOK725 and last 6 hours. Ask about tickets at the Moskenes tourist office (see above).

There are many *rorbuer* colonies here, because these fishermen's cottages are rented out to summer visitors, many of whom book for a week or two.

Reine's tranquil lagoon, set against a backdrop of mountain pinnacles, has appeared on many a postcard. For the ultimate panorama, you can climb up to the summit of **Reinebringen** at 670m (2,198 ft.), one of my favorite walks in the area.

You can also ask at Moskenes about 5-hour boat tours to the turbulent **Moskenstraumen ★★★**, the strait that separates Moskenesøy from the offshore island of Værøy. They cost from NOK600 and leave Reine twice daily Friday to Sunday in summer. First written about by Pytheas some 2,000 years ago, these wicked straits also inspired nautical tales by Edgar Allan Poe and Jules Verne. Mariners claim that they are the "world's most dangerous waters," yet they attract marine mammals and thousands of seabirds.

Lying 3km (1¾ miles) from Reine is **Sakrisøy,** which is called the "Lilliput of Lofoten fishing villages." If you want to overnight on Moskenesøy, this would make the best base. In what used to be a barn filled with sheep and cows, you will find **Dagmars Dukke- og Legetøymuseum** (**Dagmar's Museum of Dolls and Toys**) (**✆ 76-09-21-43;** www.lofoten-info.no/sakrisoy/), in the center of Sakrisøy. In this "journey back to childhood," a local woman has collected more than 2,500 dolls from all over the world, including antique teddy bears and some historic toys dating from 1860 and beyond. It's open June 16 to August 15 daily from 10am to 8pm; August 16 to 31 and June 1 to 15 daily 10am to 6pm; May and September, Saturday and Sunday noon to 5pm; and off-season by appointment only. Admission is NOK50 for adults and NOK30 for children.

Walking from Fishing Village to Fishing Village

If time allows, I suggest spending a day exploring northern Norway's charming fishing villages. Moskenesøy's landscape is characterized by sheer mountains and a narrow shoreline. As the seas have proved too turbulent, settlements are no longer on the western side of the island. Rather, the rugged inhabitants have moved to the eastern side, where today you can stroll along, taking in the fishing fleets, cargo vessels, and pleasure craft. Along the way you'll find simple cafes for eating local catch of the day.

Begin in the north at little Hamnøy. In rapid order as you stroll south, you'll approach Sakrisøy, Reine, Moskenes, Sørvågen, and Å. Of course, the way to do it, if you have unlimited time, is to rent a fishermen's hut in one of these villages, settle in for the summer, and write a novel.

Once at Sørvågen, a 2-hour hike filled with dramatic scenery will lead you along a signposted and marked rambler's trail to the Lofoten Tour Association's mountain cabin. At Sørvågen you can also break up your trip by taking an hour's walk along the beautiful Sørvagvannet. To extend the walk, you can take a detour into the scenic Studalen Valley.

You'll reach the hamlet of Å at the end of the E10, and from here the only road to take is back to Svolvær. The little fishing village of Å is the setting of the **Norsk Fiskeværmuseum (Norwegian Fishing Village Museum)** (© **76-09-14-88;** www.lofoten-info.no/nfmuseum/), Lofoten's most intriguing fishing museum, founded in 1987. Nothing brings alive the role of a Lofoten fisherman like this museum, which covers a boathouse, Norway's oldest cod-liver oil factory, the homes of fishermen, a *rorbu* cabin, and a 150-year-old bakery, plus exhibits on coastal farming in the Arctic. You can also visit a smithy who still makes cod-liver-oil lamps. Admission is NOK60 for adults and NOK30 for children. Hours are late June to late August daily from 10am to 5:30pm; off-season Monday to Friday 10am to 3:30pm.

Close by is the **Norsk Torrfiskmuseum (Norwegian Stockfish Museum)** (© **76-09-12-11;** www.lofoten-info.no), devoted to stockfish, where you'll learn more than you might ever want to know about Norway's oldest export commodity. You'll see what happens when cod is hauled in from the sea, going through the production processes including drying, grading, and sorting. Admission is NOK50 for adults and NOK40 for children. It's open from June 16 to June 19 Monday to Friday 11am to 4pm; June 20 to August 20 daily 10:30am to 5:30pm.

WHERE TO STAY

Sakrisøy Rorbuer This collection of old-fashioned fishermen's cottages is the best place to stay on this island, as the other overnight possibilities consist of camping, caravan sites, hostels, and restored fishing huts. Facing the water, this is a series of genuine ocher-colored cottages that have been comfortably converted for guests. Under stone roofs, the cottages contain modern conveniences such as private bathrooms with showers. The buildings date from the 1880s but have been much altered and improved over the years.

Sakrisøy, N-8390 Reine. © **76-09-21-43** or 90-03-54-19. www.lofoten-info.no/sakrisoy. 13 cabins. NOK800–NOK1,620 double. MC, V. **Amenities:** Laundry. *In room:* TV, kitchen, no phone.

Værøy

Remote, craggy Værøy, along with the even more remote island of Rost, lies to the far southwest of the Lofoten archipelago and is a bird-watcher's paradise. Værøy's **Mount Mostadfjell ★★** is the nesting place for more than 1.5 million seabirds, including sea eagles, auks, puffins, guillemots, kittiwakes, cormorants, arctic terns, eider petrels, and gulls, that breed from May to August.

Værøy's population is only 750 hearty souls who live on an island of Lilliputian fishing villages; white-sand beaches open onto Arctic-chilled waters, towering ridges, and seabird rookeries.

Torghaten Nord Ferries from Bodø (© **76-96-76-00;** www.torghatten-nord.no) arrive here in 4½ hours and cost NOK525 for a one-way passage with car. For passengers without a car, it's NOK147 each way. There is also a ferry link from Moskenes taking less than 2 hours and costing NOK210 one-way.

If you have the wherewithal, you could also travel quickly and in style from Bodø to Værøy by **helicopter** (© **77-60-83-00;** www.lufttransport.no (in Norwegian)). There are two flights a day going to and from the island, taking just 25 minutes. The timings mean that you could just visit the island for the day, with the first flight leaving Bodo at 9am and the last flight leaving Væroy at 5:15pm.

WHAT TO SEE & DO

The hamlet of **Sørland** lies to the east and south of the mountainous area on the island. At the village of Nordland there is a large pebble beach, **Mollbakken,** right by the road from Sørland. Several burial sites from the Stone Age and the Viking Age have been found here.

The mighty bird cliffs of Mount Mostadfjell are on the southwestern side, facing the ocean. During the summer, trips to these cliffs are organized every day. Contact the tourist office at the ferry dock (© **76-05-15-00**) for more information. If you don't like groups, you can explore on your own, as many hiking trails lead to the bigger rookeries. One jaunt starts 6km (3¾ miles) from Sørland, at the end of the path curving along the north of the island. This is my favorite walk in the remote southern islands because it not only has the best bird-watching in Norway, but it also leads rather eerily over the Isthmus of Eidet to the almost abandoned fishing village of **Mastad,** facing the rugged waters of the eastern shore. At one time, some 150 inhabitants lived here, catching puffins as a source of income, then curing the meat in salt. An unusual puffin dog, the *mastad,* was used to catch the puffins.

Those with a good amount of stamina—and a good set of hamstrings—might venture to make the steep climb from Mastad up **Måhornet peak,** at 435m (1,427 ft.). Allow an arduous hour each way.

The only manmade attraction is the **Værøy Kirke,** a wooden church at Nordland village with an onion-shaped dome. It was taken apart, moved from the village of Kabelvåg, and reassembled at Værøy in 1799. This is the oldest church in the Lofoten Islands. The altarpiece, from around 1400, is a late medieval English alabaster relief depicting the Annunciation, the three Magi (or wise men), the Resurrection, and the Ascension. The church is usually open to visitors in summer but keeps no regular hours.

WHERE TO STAY

Gamle Prestegård (Old Vicarage) ★ Built in 1898, this used to be the residence of a Lutheran priest. The hotel is run and owned by the charming Hege Sørli, who welcomes guests in style. Her rooms have been modernized and are tastefully and comfortably furnished. Five of the units contain a small bathroom with shower; guests in the other accommodations share the adequate public facilities. Sometimes it's possible to arrange dinner here. She doesn't keep a sign out, but it's the house to the left of the church.

N-8063 Værøy. © **76-09-54-11.** www.prestegaarden.no. 11 units. NOK690 double w/shared bathroom; NOK790 double w/private bathroom. Rates include buffet breakfast. No credit cards.

Kornelius Kro Built in 1991, this is a series of cabins furnished to a high standard and offering a snug nest in this remote part of the world. The red-sided cabins are spacious, suite-like rooms, though they have rather small bathrooms with showers. In summer, it becomes quite festive. In the darkest of winter, while things definitely slow down, Kornelius stays open. The cozy bar, one of only two in town, offers a blazing fireplace. It is also known for a pair of wood-fired seawater hot tubs, scene of some memorable local parties. While enjoying the tub, you can be served drinks from the bar.

N-8063 Sørland, Værøy. © **76-09-52-99.** 5 cabins. NOK1,350 for up to 4 people; discounts available for 5 or more. MC, V. **Amenities:** Restaurant; bar. *In room:* TV, kitchen, hair dryer.

WHERE TO DINE

Kornelius Kro Restaurant NORWEGIAN The most popular venue in town is this 110-seat restaurant, installed in a modern building at the Kornelius Kro hotel (see above). It is decorated with antique fish netting and nautical equipment. The lounge bar with its cozy fireplace is appreciated by both locals and visitors. You can eat dinner by firelight or candlelight. Everything is very informal here, and the place is always open in summer (but only for groups in winter). You might begin with a shrimp cocktail, then move on to Norwegian salmon, or cod or steak with vegetables—as wonderfully hearty a meal as you can get up in these parts.

Sørland. © **76-09-50-10.** Meals NOK179–NOK235. MC, V. Daily 7–9am, 5–10pm.

ALTA: CITY OF NORTHERN LIGHTS

809km (503 miles) N of Bodø; 329km (204 miles) N of Tromsø; 1,989km (1,236 miles) N of Oslo

At the turn of the millennium, Alta was rather romantically renamed Nordlysbyen Alta, or "Northern Lights City Alta." For years, this far-northern outpost of 18,000 inhabitants belonged to Finland and was inhabited almost solely by the Sami, who, until the end of the 1960s, held a tremendously popular fair here in spring and fall. On account of fires and the Nazi destruction of the city at the close of World War II, however, almost everything has been rebuilt, resulting in a somewhat dull, soulless look to the place. But people come here for nature, not for town architecture.

Alta is the commercial and mercantile capital of Finnmark; the role of administrative capital falls to Vadsø. The River Altaelva runs through the town. In its 19th-century heyday, Alta enjoyed patronage by British aristocrats who came here to fish the Altafjord, known as the best salmon waters in the world.

At the center of one of Scandinavia's major environmental protests, the Altadammen (dam) was constructed in the 1980s, rising 100m (328 ft.). A former salmon-spawning stream was diverted for hydroelectric power.

Essentials

GETTING THERE The airport at Alta lies 7km (4¼ miles) northeast of the center of town. Three daily direct flights come from Oslo, taking 3 hours, although most passengers change at the northern hub of Tromsø, from where there are four daily flights to Alta. There are no train lines here, but one daily bus runs between Tromsø and Alta, taking 7 hours and costing NOK495 one-way (for information call © **177** from phones within Norway).

VISITOR INFORMATION For information about the area, call or visit **Via Alta Tours,** Sentrums Parken 4, Alta Sentrum, N-9504 Alta (© **78-44-50-50;** www.destinasjonalta.no). From June to August, it's open Monday to Friday 10am to 4pm, Saturday and Sunday 11am to 5pm; the rest of the year it's open Monday to Friday 8:30am to 4:30pm and Saturday 10am to 2pm.

What to See & Do

A series of prehistoric rock carvings at **Hjemmeluft ★★**, about 1km (⅔ mile) southwest of Alta, dates from 2,000 to 5,000 years ago and is the biggest collection of prehistoric rock carvings in the north of Europe. These pictographs, discovered in 1973 and now a UNESCO World Heritage Site, form part of the **Alta Museum** (© **78-45-63-30;** www.alta.museum.no). It is believed that the carvings were originally painted in red ocher, and they have been repainted in the same color to make them stand out better. The carvings, from both the Stone Age and the Iron Age, are linked to the museum by 3km (1¾ miles) of boardwalks, the best place for a walk in Alta. The carvings depict hunting scenes, with clear likenesses of moose, bears, and reindeer. One stunning carving shows an ancient boat carrying a crew of 32 hunters. The paintings aren't visible during snowfalls.

The museum itself shelters an array of exhibitions related to Finnmark and its history, going back 11,000 years. It is open May to late June daily 8am to 5pm; late June to mid-August daily 8am to 8pm; and late August to April Monday to Friday 8am to 3pm, Saturday and Sunday 11am to 4pm. Admission is NOK85, NOK20 for children 16 and under.

From Alta you can take a riverboat excursion along the Alta River up to the **Sautso-Alta Canyon ★★★**, which, at some 400m (1,300 ft.) deep, is the "Grand Canyon" not only of Scandinavia, but of northern Europe. Despite the protests of environmentalists, the canyon has been dammed, but it and the region around it still offer massive scenic beauty. (***Historical note:*** Some claim that the controversy that surrounded the dam's construction between 1979 and 1986 eventually led to some degree of autonomy for the Sami people. At least in theory, they benefited from the many changes that the spotlighting of the dam and the region introduced.) Contact the tourist office (see above) for information on tours.

Shopping

Within Alta's town center, the best inventories of local handicrafts are at the **Håndverkshuset,** Løkkeveien 55 (© **78-44-22-33;** www.haandverkshuset.no), where stacks and stacks of knitted sweaters, hats, gloves, scarves, and Sami (or Sami-inspired) carvings in wood or bone, jewelry, and gift items are presented in abundance. It's open Monday to Friday 10am to 5pm, and Saturday 10am to 4pm; during midsummer it remains open later, depending on the weather, business, and the mood of the shopkeepers.

An equivalent and perhaps more esoteric collection of merchandise is for sale at **Manndalen Husflidslag** (✆ **77-71-62-73;** www.manndalen-husflidslag.no) at Løkvoll in Manndalen, 15km (9¼ miles) west of Alta on the E6. On their vertical looms the Sami make marvelous weavings, some suitable as wall hangings. You can also purchase such clothing as knitwear. It's open Wednesday to Saturday 10am to 3pm.

Where to Stay

Nordlys Hotell Alta ★★ 🎁 Our favorite nest for an overnight stopover in the area is this well-run inn, just off the E6 in Bossekop, a residential suburb about half a kilometer (⅓ mile) south of Alta's center. This is a comfortable hotel whose allure increased greatly after a renovation and upgrading. Bedrooms are attractively and pleasantly furnished, without generating too much excitement. There is a computer with Internet access in the reception area. The hotel enjoys a well-deserved reputation in the area for its food, attracting many locals because its cuisine is based in part on raw materials from Finnmark—that means reindeer and fresh fish.

Bekkefaret 3, N-9512 Alta. ✆ **78-45-72-00.** www.nordlyshotell.no. 32 units. NOK895–NOK995 double. MC, V. Closed Dec–Jan. **Amenities:** Restaurant; bar; sauna; whirlpool; rooms for those with limited mobility. *In room:* TV, minibar (in some), hair dryer.

Park Hotel Alta Sentrum Built in 1987, this is a cozy alternative to the more expensive and expansive Rica Hotel Alta nearby. It's what Norwegians call a *frokosthotellet* or "breakfast hotel." Built to environmentally conscious standards, this hotel is located just off the North Cape Road. It provides a suitable and comfortable overnight that is great as a base for visiting outposts further north. Furnishings are modern, the small to midsize bedrooms have wooden floors, and all rooms have new, firm mattresses. Each has an immaculate bathroom; eight come with a bathtub and shower, the rest with shower only.

E6, N-9501 Alta. ✆ **78-45-74-00.** www.parkhotell.no. 34 units. NOK860–NOK1,235 double. Rates include buffet breakfast & light evening meal. AE, DC, MC, V. **Amenities:** Restaurant; lounge; sauna. *In room:* TV, hair dryer.

Rica Hotel Alta ★ The city's biggest hotel was built in the 1980s in a very contemporary design, but recently renovated and expanded. In an often gray and gloomy climate, the hotel stands out for its brightness, occasionally using white furnishings and artsy photographs of the midnight sun to decorate its midsize bedrooms. Half of the units are carpeted, and the rest offer wooden floors. The Rica has the most dining, drinking, and entertainment facilities in town. Friday and Saturday nights are especially popular here from 10pm to 3am, and there is occasional live music.

Løkkeveien 61, N-9150 Alta. ✆ **78-48-27-00.** www.rica.no. 241 units. NOK1,240 double; 2,100 suite. Children 14 & under stay free in parents' room. Rates include continental breakfast. AE, DC, MC, V. **Amenities:** 2 restaurants; bar; disco; sauna; rooms for those with limited mobility. *In room:* TV, Wi-Fi, minibar.

Thon Hotel Vica Alta Built right after World War II, this was a farmhouse before its conversion to an affordable hotel in 1988. In a town of buildings with no architectural distinction, this timber-built structure has some atmosphere and style. Rooms are decorated in a homelike way and are tastefully furnished with warm colors and small bathrooms with showers. Many locals drop in to the restaurant, Haldde, for their traditional northern Norway fare, a three-course meal in the evening going for NOK550.

Fogdebakken 6, Bossekop, N-9500 Alta. © **78-48-22-22.** www.thonhotels.com. 24 units. NOK791–NOK1,195 double. Rates include buffet breakfast. AE, DC, MC, V. Closed Dec 22–Jan 5 & 1 week at Easter. **Amenities:** Restaurant; bar; babysitting; sauna; room service; 1 room for those with limited mobility. *In room:* TV, minibar (some units).

Where to Dine

Han Steike (Beef House) ★★ STEAKHOUSE The most appealing and popular restaurant in Alta sits in the center of town, behind a drab, gray facade that you'll imagine can withstand virtually any snowstorm. Inside you'll find a warm and cozy steakhouse that's accented with what locals refer to as "Norwegian stone" (gray flagstones) and dark wood paneling. Your waitstaff will ask you what size you prefer for your grilled beefsteak, be it veal, whale steak, lamb chops, spareribs, reindeer, salmon, or cod; know in advance that the "average" appetite might go for the 150- or 200-gram size (about 5–7 oz.). Everything you order comes with a choice of sauces that include mustard, horseradish, peppercorn, mushroom gravy, and hollandaise. Try their reduced-price *dagens* menu, where you can get a fish main for a bargain NOK149.

Løkkeveien 2. © **78-44-08-88.** www.hansteike.no. Reservations recommended. Main courses NOK190–NOK349. AE, DC, MC, V. Tues–Sat 3pm–midnight; Sun 3–9pm.

Alta After Dark

The chief hot spot in town is **Alfa-Omega,** Markedsgata 16 (© **78-44-54-00;** www.alfaomega-alta.no), attracting a solid 30- to 40-something crowd. There is no cover, and the inspiration is all Cuban, with recorded salsa music, pictures of Havana, and Cuban cigars everywhere. There are seats for 40, but often 70 to 80 patrons crowd in here. One section is a very laid-back bar; the other's a contemporary cafe. It's open Monday to Wednesday 8pm to midnight, Thursday 9pm to 1am, Friday 6pm to 2:30am, and Saturday noon to 2:30am. Its only drawback, according to some of the young and restless clients I met here, is its lack of facilities for dancing.

KARASJOK: CAPITAL OF THE SAMI

110km (68 miles) NE of Kautokeino; 11km (7 miles) W of Finnish border

This is the capital of the Sami, with a population of 2,900 inhabitants. Of these, some 90% are of Sami descent, making Karasjok, along with its neighboring town of Kautokeino, a seat of Sami culture.

Karasjok, whose Sami name translates as "river current," thrives in part on reindeer herding. With its many handicrafts and Sami institutions, Karasjok is both the cultural and social hub of Sami-land.

The town is the best place to learn about these once nomadic people who lived on the "roof of Europe." The Sami—historically called Lapps by non-Sami—have inhabited these inhospitable lands since ancient times. Sami settlements stretch along the entire Nordic region, including Finland, Sweden, and Norway. Some Sami maintain links to their ancient culture, whereas others have been assimilated.

The language of the Sami belongs to the Finno-Ugric group, and it is related to both Finnish and Estonian. A large part of Sami literature has been published in the Northern Sami dialect, which is spoken by approximately 75% of Sami. As with all Arctic societies, oral literature has always played a prominent role. Among Sami, this oral tradition takes the form of the *joik,* a type of singing. (Once governments tried to suppress this, but it is now enjoying something of a renaissance—and is listened to even by younger generations.) One of the classic works of Sami literature is Johan Turi's *Tale of the Lapps,* first published in 1910.

Handicrafts are important in the Sami economy. Several designers have developed new forms of decorative art, producing a revival of the Sami handicraft tradition.

Many members of the Sami community agree that the term "Lapp" has negative connotations. It's gradually being replaced by the indigenous minority's own name for itself, *sábme,* or other dialect variations. Sami (or Sámi) seems to be the most favored English term, and the word is being used increasingly.

Essentials

GETTING THERE The town is reached by bus, with most visitors arriving from Hammerfest. This overland trip takes 4 hours and costs NOK360 one-way. Motorists can continue east from Hammerfest along the E6.

VISITOR INFORMATION The **Sapmi Cultural Center,** Porsangerveien 1 (**© 78-46-88-00;** www.sapmi.no) dispenses information for the entire area. It's open June to mid-August daily 9am to 7pm, and the rest of the year Monday to Friday 10am to 4pm.

What to See & Do

Sami Vourká Dávvirat (Sami Museum) ★, Museumsgate 17 (**© 78-46-99-50;** www.rdm.no), is an open-air museum devoted to the Sami people, their history, and their culture. There are other Sami exhibitions, but this is the only one to be called a "national museum" of Sami culture. Most intriguing is the exhibition of old dwellings and artifacts such as an old hunting trap for wild reindeer, showing how people earned their living. Of special interest are the examples of regional dress used in these subfreezing conditions. Also on display are works by local artists. Admission is NOK75. The museum is open the first half of May and the latter half of August daily 9am to 3pm; mid-May to mid-August daily 9am to 6pm; and September to May Tuesday to Friday 9am to 3pm.

Since 2000, the **Sametinget (Sami Parliament),** Sámediggi (**© 78-47-40-00**), has had its headquarters at this impressive piece of modern architecture encased in Siberian larkwood. To carry out this far-north theme, the interior is also filled with native woods such as pine and birch. Unique among parliament buildings, the assembly hall was constructed in the shape of a *gamma* (Sami tent). Tiny bulbs, evoking the Northern Lights, illuminate the 35,000-volume Sami library. Free tours are conducted Monday to Friday, in summer hourly from 9am to 3pm, in winter at 1pm.

Samisk Kunstnersenter (Sami Artists Center), Ivvár Geavli 1 (✆ **78-46-90-02;** www.samiskkunstnersenter.no), is an art gallery devoted to Sami painters, with new exhibitions every month. This is not just about folk art; many Sami painters are as modern as the 21st century. Sami art and handicrafts are also sold here. Admission is free, and it is open Monday to Friday 10am to 4pm, Saturday to Sunday 1 to 4pm.

Karasjok Opplevelser (✆ **95-84-88-55**) organizes adventures in the area, including everything from visits to a Sami camp to gold-panning and riverboat trips. In winter, you can even go reindeer sledding like Santa Claus. Call in advance to see what type of adventure might be offered at the time of your visit.

Many visitors come to hunt and fish. Lake fishing is free, but if you're up for river fishing or wilderness adventure, the guide to call is **Nils Rolf Johnsen,** Svenskebakken 35 (✆ **98-41-04-11**), who makes arrangements for such outings. He can arrange for you to stay in *lavvu* (Sami tents) beside Finnmark's largest lake, Lesjavri, which is excellent for fishing.

SHOPPING

Most visitors who make it this far north like to come back with some souvenirs, particularly handmade Sami knives, a craft and tradition that dates back hundreds of years. The best selection of Sami crafts is available at **Samelandssenteret** (✆ **78-46-72-02** a cooperative crafts store in the town center).

Where to Stay

Engholm Husky Lodge ★ 🎁 Next to the Karasjohka River, 6km (3¾ miles) outside Karasjok, this is a real frontier outpost that connects you with local life more than any other lodging in the area. In addition to cabin rental, you can head out on summer hikes with the huskies or, when the weather turns, join in a dog-sledding tour. Gold-panning, fishing trips, and wilderness tours are also part of the action here. Accommodations are in large, cozy log cabins, each personalized and comfortable. Some of the cabins have private bathrooms; others are shared. Most cabins contain a kitchenette as well. In the *barta,* a special turf-covered log house, guests gather around the open fire sitting on reindeer skins, enjoying good food and drink. Lunch costs NOK200, with dinner going for NOK280.

N-9730 Karasjok. ✆ **91-58-66-25.** www.engholm.no. 5 cabins. NOK400 double, plus NOK300 per person. V. **Amenities:** Restaurant; bar. *In room:* TV, no phone.

Rica Hotel Karasjok ★ This is the best hotel in the area. And with its cozy bar and dining facilities, it's also the major social hub and entertainment venue for the district. The two-story wooden building looks like a ski lodge. It was built in 1983 but has been completely renovated to offer contemporary bedrooms, with comfortable furnishings and wooden floors. All accommodations have strong elements of Sami culture mixed into the interior design, colors, and materials. The bedrooms open onto views of the surrounding forests. The staff is most helpful in arranging tours, regardless of the season—winter dog-sled rides and reindeer races or summer riverboat trips.

Porsangerveien 1, N-9730 Karasjok. ✆ **78-46-88-60.** www.rica.no. 66 units. NOK1,095–NOK1,690 double. Children 3 & under stay free in parents' room. Rates include continental breakfast. AE, DC, MC, V. **Amenities:** 2 restaurants; fitness center; sauna; rooms for those with limited mobility. *In room:* TV.

Where to Dine

Storgammen ★★ 🎁 NORWEGIAN For a unique, exotic experience, head for this restaurant, where you can sit on reindeer skins amidst timber and turf around the fire while you're served a cuisine based on Sami recipes dating back several centuries. You can also dine more elegantly in the regular a la carte restaurant, with formally laid tables and comfortable chairs. A ski lodge restaurant, it is built of timbers and decorated with native Sami costumes. For an appetizer, its smoked reindeer heart is even better than your mother made for you. This might be followed with such regional dishes as filet of reindeer in a game sauce with vegetables. If you've had enough reindeer, you can opt for the delectable grilled arctic char with white-wine sauce and vegetables. The gourmet's favorite summer dessert in Sami-land is a bowl of fresh cloudberries.

In the Rica Hotel Karasjok, Porsangerveien 1. ✆ **78-46-88-60.** Reservations recommended. Main courses NOK220–NOK340. AE, DC, MC, V. Open summertime only, daily 11am–11pm.

Karasjok After Dark

Once again, a cozy wood-paneled room in the **Rica Hotel Karasjok,** Porsangerveien 1 (✆ **78-46-74-00**), is the scene of the after dark "action" in Karasjok.. Patrons range in age from 20s to 50s. There's no cover. It's open Monday to Friday noon to 1am, Friday and Saturday noon to 3am.

HAMMERFEST: WORLD'S NORTHERNMOST TOWN

2,314km (1,438 miles) N of Bergen; 144km (89 miles) N of Alta; 2,195km (1,364 miles) N of Oslo

In his travelogue, *Neither Here Nor There*, author Bill Bryson found Hammerfest to be an "agreeable enough town in a thank-you-God-for-not-making-me-live-here sort of way." However, locals, for their part, are quick to defend how civilized they are, pointing out that they were the first town in Europe to have electric street lighting while Paris and London were still lit by gas.

That Hammerfest is here at all is a sort of miracle. The town was founded because of its natural harbor, a feature that is as important today as it was then. A hurricane flattened the town in 1856, and one of Norway's worst fires leveled it again in 1890, the year it got that street lighting. Hitler ordered that "no building be left standing" during the infamous Nazi retreat of 1945. But Hammerfest bounced back and has been attracting visitors from all over the world who use it as a base for exploring the North Cape in summer. Arctic hunters enjoy their last few drinks in cozy bars here before setting off on expeditions into the wilderness. You just might encounter a polar bear wandering the streets as you stroll back to your hotel.

But it will be oil, not tourism, fueling the economy of Hammerfest, at least for the next 30 years. In 2006, the pumps started sucking oil from offshore wells, estimated to hold 195 billion cubic meters of the black gold. The world's longest undersea pipeline, running for some 145km (90 miles), goes from the mammoth natural gas fields in the Barents Sea to the small island of Melkøya out in the bay off the coast of Hammerfest.

The Hammerfest area stretches from Måsøy, near the North Cape, to Loppa in the south, the wide region including the rugged coasts along the Arctic Sea. The city, at 70° 39' 48" north, achieved its town status on July 7, 1789, making it the oldest town in northern Norway. But is Hammerfest really the world's northernmost town, as often claimed? Other communities exist north of here but locals say that they are villages—not towns.

A ***Meridianstøtta*** (meridian column) stands on the Fuglenes Peninsula, across from the harbor. The monument commemorates the work of scientists from Norway, Sweden, and Russia who conducted surveys at Hammerfest between 1816 and 1852 to establish a meridian arc between Hammerfest and the Danube River at the Black Sea, leading to an accurate calculation of the size of the Earth.

Today Hammerfest is a modern town with an open and unique atmosphere, where the town's square and harbor are natural meeting places.

Essentials

GETTING THERE If you don't take the coastal steamer, you can drive, although it's a long trek. From Oslo, take the E6 north until you reach the junction with Route 94 west. Hammerfest is at the end of Route 94. During the summer there are three buses a week from Oslo, which take 29 hours. SAS has daily flights from Oslo and Bergen to Alta, where you can catch a bus to Hammerfest (Apr–Sept only). For bus information, call **Veolia Transport** (**✆ 78-40-70-00;** www.veolia.no).

VISITOR INFORMATION The **Hammerfest tourist office,** Havnegata 3 (**✆ 78-41-21-85;** www.hammerfest-turist.no), in the town center, is open in summer daily from 9am to 5pm, in winter daily 10am to 2pm. The tourist office organizes hour-long sightseeing tours, departing between 11am and 1pm (call to confirm the time) and costing NOK220.

What to See & Do

This is the world's northernmost town of significant size and a port of call for North Cape coastal steamers. Sami from nearby camps often come into town to shop. Count yourself lucky if they bring their reindeer.

The port is free of ice year-round, and exporting fish is a major industry. The sun doesn't set from May 12 to August 1, and it doesn't rise from November 21 to January 23.

For the best panoramic view of the town, take a zigzag walk up the 72-m (240-ft.) **Salen** "mountain." Atop Salen is a 6-m (20-ft.)-tall square tower, with walls built of gray and blue stone. The old tower was torn down during World War II but was rebuilt in 1984. On a clear day, you can see the offshore islands.

Why not do as 230,000 others have done, and join the **Royal and Ancient Polar Bear Society** (**✆ 78-41-31-00;** english.isbjornklubben.no) here? Apply in person while you're in Hammerfest. Membership costs a one-time fee of NOK180, and proceeds are used to protect endangered Arctic animals through conservation programs. The center is filled with stuffed specimens of Arctic animals, and there is a free exhibition. There's a small museum devoted to the hunting heyday of Hammerfest, which lasted from 1910 to 1950, when eagles, arctic foxes, and polar bears were trapped by the English, and by German officers during World War II. It's in the basement of the Town Hall, on Rådhusplassen, in the same building as the tourist office. Entrance costs NOK40. It's open June to August Monday to Friday 6am to 6pm, and the rest of the year Monday to Friday from 9am to 3pm.

Gjenreisningsmuseet (Museum of Post-War Reconstruction), Söröygatan (© **78-40-29-30**), commemorates the cold, bleak years when local residents, deprived of most of their buildings, livelihoods, and creature comforts, heroically rebuilt Finnmark and northern Norway in the wake of Nazi devastation. Entrance is NOK50 for adults, NOK30 for students, free for children 15 and under. It is open June to September Monday to Friday 9am to 4pm and Saturday to Sunday 10am to 2pm; and off-season daily from 11am to 2pm.

Located a 5-minute walk from the harbor, the **Hammerfest Kirke,** Kirkegate 33 (© **78-40-29-20;** www.kirken.hammerfest.no), was consecrated in 1961 and is known for its avant-garde architecture. Unusually, this *kirke* doesn't have an altarpiece. Instead, you get a large and detailed stained-glass window that is quite beautiful. The altarpiece is in a hall to the right of the main sanctuary. Local carver Knit Arnesen carved the friezes, depicting the history of Hammerfest. Note the chapel across from the church. Dating from 1933, it is the only structure in Hammerfest to survive the Nazi scorched-earth retreat. Admission to the church is free, and it is open in summer from Monday to Friday 9am to 3pm.

Where to Stay

Rica Hotel Hammerfest ★ The town's largest hotel has been kept up fairly well, though parts of it can feel a bit grim and foreboding. It's a mite more comfortable than the Thon, although lacking its character. The best appointed and most spacious accommodations in Hammerfest are here in the form of a junior suite. The largest hotel in town was built in the mid-1970s on steeply sloping land and has been regularly spruced up since then. The standard, midsize guest rooms are decorated with Nordic-inspired pastels, but the look is strictly functional.

Sørøygata 15, N-9600 Hammerfest. © **78-42-57-00.** www.rica.no. 80 units. NOK1,200–NOK1,795 double; NOK1,600–NOK2,295 junior suite. AE, DC, MC, V. **Amenities:** Restaurant; bar; disco; fitness center; sauna; babysitting. *In room:* TV, Wi-Fi, minibar, hair dryer.

Thon Hotel Hammerfest ★ The hotel, built in 1964, is currently under renovation, due to open by early 2011. It opens onto views of the harbor, standing right on the Rådhusplassen (Town Hall Square). The well-sized bedrooms are tastefully and comfortably furnished in modern Scandinavian decor, each with a small bathroom with a shower. The staff can arrange such adventures as rides in a snowmobile or on horseback, and can advise about fishing in local waters. The on-site trio of bars—Banyean, Hans Highness, and the generic hotel bar—is livelier than the watering hole at the Rica.

Strandgata 2-4, N-9600 Hammerfest. © **78-42-96-00.** www.thonhotels.com. 50 units. NOK1,745 double; from NOK1,890 minisuite. Rates include buffet breakfast. AE, DC, MC, V. Closed Dec 20–Jan 2. **Amenities:** Restaurant; 3 bars; sauna; room service; rooms for those with limited mobility. *In room:* TV, Wi-Fi, minibar, hair dryer, iron.

Where to Dine

Hammerfest Mat og Vinhagen ★★ NORTHERN NORWEGIAN A recent change of management has updated this rustic restaurant, which first became famous in the late 1990s when a Trondheim radio station voted it the best restaurant in Norway. It's adjacent to the town's largest pier, overlooking the harbor. Inside, every effort has been made to simulate the wild splendor of northern Norway, with the use of roughly textured wood, stone, and many yards of natural hemp knotted into ropes that form curtains. The kitchen opens to the dining room, adding to the cozy feel. Many recipes and ingredients are derived from northern Norway, with an emphasis on fish and game. You might try reindeer filet carpaccio, or sun-dried carp filet served with mustard sauce.

Strandgata 24. ✆ **78-41-37-66.** Reservations recommended. Main courses from NOK245. AE, DC, MC, V. Mon–Thurs 2:30–11pm; Fri 1–11pm; Sat 6–11pm.

Mikkelgammen ★★ SÁMI This Sámi "turf hut" is available on request and features a traditional three-course Sámi meal, or *bidos*, with guests gathered around a campfire. You'll get reindeer soup as well as reindeer meat for your main course, followed by Arctic cloudberries in whipped cream. Meals are followed by a program of Sámi *joik*, chant-like singing, and stories about life in the far north.

Salen mountain. ✆ **90-04-98-18.** www.mikkelgammen.no (in Norwegian). Reservations essential; book 2 days in advance. NOK245 per person.

Skansen Mat og Vinstue ★ NORWEGIAN/INTERNATIONAL This small, intimate restaurant has an open kitchen with a fireplace at the center. Because it's the north of Norway, you can find fresh catch of the day from the fjord as well as meat dishes such as filet of reindeer and pepper steak (they do prepare the meat exceedingly well). The Rica Bar and Disco, in the cellar, is open Friday and Saturday from 10pm to 3am so you can dance and drink the night away. Admission is NOK75. The minimum age is 20, and beer costs NOK45 to NOK55 per half-liter.

In the Rica Hotel Hammerfest, Sørøygata 15. ✆ **78-41-13-33.** www.rica.no. Main courses NOK200–NOK330. AE, DC, MC, V. Daily 4–11pm.

Hammerfest After Dark

A recently opened club, **Oppe og Nede,** (✆ **90-59-29-30;** www.oppeognede.com), also known as ON, has become the hottest place to be seen in town. Also a restaurant serving decent Scandinavian main courses, it is better known for its dance floor and a bar across two separate floors. The upper floor tends to be strictly for 20-, 30-, and 40-somethings, while the downstairs bar (weekends only) is usually filled with teenagers. It is open Monday 10:30am to 3pm, Tuesday to Thursday 10:30am to 1am, Friday 10:30am to 3am, Saturday 11am to 3am, and Sunday 3 to 10pm. Until renovation of the Thon Hotel Hammerfest is completed, this is your best option in town.

HONNINGSVÅG & THE NORTH CAPE ★★

130km (81 miles) NE of Hammerfest; 2,444km (1,519 miles) NE of Bergen

You have to journey a long way to see the **Nordkapp** (North Cape), the most celebrated attraction in northern Norway. More proximate to the North Pole than to Oslo, the mighty rock stands at a latitude of 71° 10' 21" N. The attraction is generally viewed from mid-May to the end of July, when the midnight sun does not drop below the horizon. As you've come all this way, I'll let you in on a secret. The Nordkapp is touted as the northernmost point of continental Europe, although it actually isn't (see the box, "Europe's Real Northernmost Point," below). To the Sami, the North Cape held great religious significance and was a site for sacrifices. The name "North Cape" came from the British explorer, Richard Chancellor, who drifted here in 1553 when on the hunt for the Northeast Passage.

Considered the world's northernmost fishing village and the gateway to the North Cape, Honningsvåg is a completely modern fishing harbor set in a land of forests, fjord waters, and crashing waterfalls, everything bathed in summer by the eerie light of the midnight sun. Only its chapel withstood the village's destruction by Germans in 1944. Honningsvåg is on the southern side of the island of Magerøy, connected to the North Cape by a 35-km (22-mile) road. It's some 80km (50 miles) nearer to the North Pole than Hammerfest, on the Alta–Hammerfest bus route.

Essentials

GETTING THERE If you don't take the coastal steamer (visit www.hurtigruten.com for information), you can reach Honningsvåg by car. From Oslo (a very long trip—about 30 hours possible only in June–Sept), take the E6 north to the junction with Route 95 north. Since an underwater tunnel was opened in 1999, it is now possible to drive all the way to Honningsvåg and North Cape without use of a ferry.

SAS and Norwegian fly from Oslo and Bergen to Alta; SAS and Widerøe fly from Alta to Honningsvåg.

There are also direct, year-round buses from Alta to both Hammerfest and Honningsvåg. For bus information, call **Veolia Transport** (✆ **78-40-70-00;** www.veolia-transport.no).

VISITOR INFORMATION The **North Cape tourist office,** in the Nordkapphuset (✆ **78-47-70-30;** www.nordkapp.no), can give you information on sightseeing boat trips, museums, walks, and deep-sea fishing. The office is open mid-June to mid-August Monday to Friday 8:30am to 8pm, Saturday noon to 8pm; mid-August to mid-June Monday to Friday 9:30am to 3:30pm.

A SPECIAL EVENT The **North Cape Festival,** held for 1 week in mid-June each year, presents a wide display of local culture. During the festival, participants in the **North Cape March** trek from Honningsvåg to the North Cape and back, a total of around 70km (43 miles).

What to See & Do

Check at the tourist office about organized tours of the area. In the summer, tours visit the splendid bird colony on the little island of **Gjesværstappan ★★**. All sorts of arctic seabirds, including kittiwakes, skuas, razorbills, gannets, puffins, and cormorants, can be seen on the cliffs, and seals by the shore. The details of each tour will vary according to the molting and breeding seasons of the birds. For further information about bird-related tours, contact **Birdsafari** (✆ **78-47-57-73;** www.birdsafari.com). You will need to get to Gjesvær village, either by taxi or local bus (see www.veolia-transport.no for bus transport details).

Nordkapphallen (North Cape Hall) This visitor center has a video presentation and museum exhibits. Downstairs you'll find an excellent video presentation and a cave with a panoramic window facing the Arctic Ocean. On the way to the cave, you'll see several scenes from the history of the North Cape. A monument commemorates the visit of King Oscar of Norway and Sweden to the Cape in 1873, and another exhibit commemorates the arrival of King Chulalongkorn of Siam (now Thailand) who came for a look at the Cape in 1907. There's also a monument marking the terminus of the "Midnight Sun Road." You might be dismayed at the steep entrance price, but the exhibits and the views from within manage to artfully and effectively evoke the drama of the far North. Call before you visit; even in high season, as open hours and days are subject to change without notice.

Nordkapp. © **78-47-68-60.** www.nordkapp.no. Admission NOK215 adults, NOK75 children, NOK505 family. Apr–May 17 daily 11am–5pm; May 18–Aug 17 daily 11am–1am; Aug 18–Aug 31 daily 11am–10pm; Sept daily 11am–3pm; Oct–April 12:30–4pm (access during these months by convoy only). For bus reservations, contact Veolia Transport (© **78-47-58-44;** www.veolia-transport.no) by 3pm the day before travel.

Nordkappmuseet This museum displays the cultural history of the North Cape, including fishery artifacts and an exhibit that details the effects of World War II on the North Cape. The museum lies at the harbor and town center, a 3-minute walk from the coastal steamer and the Rica Hotel Honningsvåg.

In the Nordkapphuset, Fiskeriveien 4. © **78-47-28-33.** www.nordkappmuseet.no. Admission NOK50, NOK20 children 6–16, free for children 5 & under. June 5–Aug 15 Mon–Sat 11am–8pm, Sun noon–7pm; Aug 16–June 4 Mon–Fri noon–4pm.

Where to Stay

Honningsvåg Brygge ★ This hotel in the center of town has plenty of character. The family-run establishment served as a fish factory until the 1970s, when the owners decided to convert it into a hotel. Since then, discerning travelers to the North Cape have been making their way here for quiet nights in contemporary-meets-rustic decor. There is exposed wood everywhere—walls, ceiling, and floors—but the furnishings are modern. Bedrooms are small to midsize, each cozy and comfortably furnished.

Vagen 1A, N-9751 Honningsvåg. © **78-47-64-64.** www.hvg-brygge.no. 27 units. NOK1,100–NOK1,300 double; NOK1,350–NOK1,800 suite. Children 11 & under stay free in parents' room. Rates include continental breakfast (during summer only). AE, DC, MC, V. **Amenities:** Restaurant; bar; rooms for those with limited mobility. *In room:* No phone.

Rica Bryggen Hotel Opened in 1989 and renovated in 2009, this portside hotel is chock-full of facilities and accommodations that lure members of the fishing industry in summer and international visitors in winter. An enduring and reliable choice, the two-floor hotel offers midsize bedrooms, most of them with a view of the harbor. Each unit is carpeted and comfortably furnished; some of the suites contain a private sauna. The on-site restaurant is one of the best dining spots in town (see "Where to Dine", below).

Vagen 1, N-9750 Honningsvåg. © **78-47-72-20.** www.rica.no. 42 units. NOK1,430–NOK1,680 double. Children 11 & under stay free in parents' room. Rates include continental breakfast. AE, DC, MC, V. Closed Dec 21–Jan 2, 2 weeks at Easter, & occasionally at other times depending on demand. **Amenities:** Restaurant; bar; sauna; 1 room for those with limited mobility. *In room:* TV, minibar.

Rica Hotel Honningsvåg The North Cape's northernmost hotel is centrally located near the quay. Advance reservations are strongly advised. This five-story, yellow-fronted building features guest rooms that offer views of the harbor and fairly standard furnishings. The rooms and bathrooms are on the small side (each has its own shower), but the beds are comfortable enough. The on-site Restaurant Bauen

Europe's Real Northernmost Point

It comes as a surprise to some visitors that Europe's actual northernmost point is not the North Cape, but Knivskjelodden, which is west of the cape at 71° 11' 08". You can hike the trail, which is not too difficult if you're in good shape. Wear sturdy boots, of course. Figure on about 5 hours there and back. Once there, you'll have a panoramic sweep ★ of the North Cape plateau. After you've walked the world's northernmost hiking trail, you can sign your name in the hiking association's minute book at Knivskjelodden.

To reach Knivskjelodden, head southwest from the North Cape for 6km (3¾ miles) until you reach a parking lot. Once at the parking lot, you still have 3km (2 miles) to go to the northernmost point from the beginning of the Knivskjelodden track. In all, it's a round-trip of 18km (11 miles) from the North Cape.

(see "Where to Dine") is one of the best in town. The hotel also runs an unpretentious grill and offers disco action on Friday and Saturday nights. The hotel is entirely nonsmoking.

Storgata 4, N-9751 Honningsvåg. © **78-47-72-20.** www.rica.no. 174 units. NOK1,430–NOK1,680 double. Rates include buffet breakfast. AE, DC, MC, V. Closed in winter. **Amenities:** Restaurant; lounge; sauna; rooms for those with limited mobility. *In room:* TV.

Where to Dine

Corner NORWEGIAN Ever tried Arctic pizza? This is the place for it, along with an array of other regional dishes. Many local fishermen as well as international visitors flock here for good, affordable food. The 1960s' building and decor don't necessarily appeal to refined tastes, but the chef will feed you well at a reasonable price. There are no appetizers to speak of, but the main courses are generous. Your best bet is the grilled and locally caught salmon, which comes with fresh vegetables and potatoes. You can also order fresh grilled cod or halibut. Meat-eaters may find the veal schnitzel satisfying. No matter what main course you choose, finish your meal with a slice of apple pie and ice cream. A live band sometimes entertains in the adjoining bar.

Fiskerveien 2A. © **78-47-63-40.** Main courses NOK175–NOK259. AE, DC, MC, V. Summer daily 10am–11:30pm (Fri–Sat until 2am; Sun opens noon).

Restaurant at the Rica Bryggen Hotel ★ NORWEGIAN Looking onto the port, this first-rate restaurant remains committed to opening at least 4 days a week and, if business warrants, it opens on weekends as well. Expect a cozy, weather-tight environment where views of the frigid Arctic night might even stimulate your appetite. Standard Norwegian fare typically includes delicacies from the Arctic Ocean and land-based specialties from the Finnmark plateau—whale or reindeer steaks, perhaps with juniper-berry sauce; at least three types of fish (usually salmon, catfish, or halibut), depending on what arrived from lower latitudes that week; and tender and well-flavored grilled beefsteaks.

Vagen 1. © **78-47-72-20.** Main courses NOK195–NOK225. AE, DC, MC, V. Mon–Thurs noon–2pm & 5–11pm.

Restaurant Bauen NORWEGIAN Located in the cellar of the Rica Hotel Honningsvåg, this place is at its most elegant in the winter, when the tour groups are gone. During the summer, the *smörgåsbord* is in the dining room and a la carte dinners are served in the less formal bistro. The cuisine is competently prepared but never exciting; most of the ingredients are shipped in. In the evening, music begins at 8pm, and the place is very popular with locals. It's decorated with old-fashioned photographs of Honningsvåg.

In the Rica Hotel Honningsvåg, Nordkappgata 2–4. ✆ **78-47-72-20.** Reservations recommended. Buffet NOK210. AE, DC, MC, V. Summer daily 6–10pm.

A Trip to the Nordkapp (North Cape)

The Nordkapp symbolizes the "top of Europe." In prehistoric times, the North Cape Horn was a Sami place of sacrifice. The North Cape's name used to be Knyskanes, but in 1553 it was renamed "North Cape" by the English explorer Richard Chancellor, searching for a sea passage to China. The road to the North Cape is open to traffic from May 1 to October 20.

The first tour ships arrived in 1879. They anchored in Hornvika Bay, and the visitors had to climb 280m (920 ft.) up to the plateau. After the road from Honningsvåg opened in 1956, the flow of tourists turned into a flood. In summer, buses to the North Cape leave daily from outside the tourist office at Fergeveien 4 at Honningsvåg, stop briefly at the ferry terminal across from the North Cape Hostel, and then continue to the visitor center at the North Cape. The one-way passage from Honningsvåg to the North Cape, a travel time of 45 minutes, costs NOK120 adults, NOK80 children. For more bus information, call **Veolia Transport** (✆ **78-47-58-40;** www.veolia-transport.no).

On the road to the Cape is a Sami encampment. It's a bit contrived, but visitors do have an opportunity to go inside one of the tents, and they come away with an idea of how nomadic Sami used to live.

Honningsvåg After Dark

The best place in town for a drink is **Nøden Pub,** Larsfjorda 1 (✆ **78-47-27-11;** www.noden.no), a maritime-styled pub and also the leading soccer pub in town. Patrons range in age from 25 to 50. Music, ranging from regional music to Elvis, is live one night a week during the summer. Pizza is the snack of choice here. It's open Monday to Thursday 6pm to midnight, Friday and Saturday noon to 2am, and Sunday noon to midnight (closed Mon in winter). Later at night, **Z,** in the same building, is the town's most popular disco. Opened in 2007, there is room for some 200 guests and it's where Honningsvåg's younger set hangs out.

16 FAST FACTS: NORWAY

American Express There is an office in Oslo. American Express Reisebyrå, Maribores Gate 13 (✆ **22-98-35-00**), is open Monday to Friday 9am to 6pm, Saturday 10am to 4pm.

ATM Networks See "Money & Costs," in chapter 3.

Babysitters Hotels can often enlist the help of a housekeeper for "child-minding." Give at least a day's notice, two if you can. You can also contact one of the local tourist offices; they often keep a list of available sitters on file.

Business Hours Most **banks** are open Monday through Friday from 8:15am to 3:30pm (Thurs till 5pm), and are closed Saturday and Sunday. The Nordea Bank in the Arrivals terminal at Gardermoen airport in Oslo is open Monday through Friday from 8:30am to 8:30pm, Saturday from 10am to 6pm, and Sunday from 11:30am to 8:30pm. The branch in the Departures terminal is open Monday through Friday from 6am to 6:30pm, Saturday from 6am to 3pm, and Sunday from 6am to 6:30pm. Most **businesses** are open Monday through Friday from 9am to 4pm. **Stores** are generally open Monday through Friday from 9am to 5pm (many stay open on Thurs until 6 or 7pm) and Saturday 9am to 1 or 2pm. Sunday closings are observed.

Car Rental See "Airline, Hotel & Car Rental Websites" below.

Currency See "Money & Costs," in chapter 3.

Doctors Your embassy or consulate, as well as most hotels, keep a list of recommended English-speaking physicians. See "Embassies & Consulates," below.

Drinking Laws Most restaurants, pubs, and bars in Norway are licensed to serve liquor, wine, and beer. The drinking age is 18 for beer and wine, and 20 for liquor.

Driving Rules See "Getting Around," in chapter 3.

Drugstores Drugstores *(apotek)* are open during normal business hours.

Electricity Norway uses 220 volts, 30 to 50 cycles AC, and standard Continental two-pin plugs. Transformers and adapters will be needed with Canadian and American equipment.

Embassies & Consulates If your passport is lost or stolen or you have some other emergency, contact your embassy in Oslo. The embassy of the **United States** is at Henrik Ibsensgate 48, N-0244 Oslo (✆ **21-30-85-40;** norway.usembassy.gov); **United Kingdom,** Thomas Heftyesgate 8, N-0244 Oslo (✆ **23-13-27-00;** ukinnorway.fco.gov.uk); and **Canada,** Wergelandsveien 7, N-0244 Oslo (✆ **22-99-53-00;** www.canadainternational.gc.ca). The **Irish Embassy** is at Haakon VII's Gate 1, N-0244 Oslo (✆ **22-01-72-00;** www.embassyofireland.no). The de facto **Australian Embassy** is the Australian Consulate, Strandveien 20, N-1324 Lysaker

(✆ **67-58-48-48**).The **New Zealand Embassy** is closed in Oslo; contact the **New Zealand Consulate,** Strandveien 50, N-1366 Lysaker (✆ **67-11-00-30**).

There is a British consulate in Bergen, Øvre Ole Bulls Plass 1 (✆ **55-36-78-10**).

Emergencies Throughout Norway, call ✆ **112** for the **police,** ✆ **110** to report a **fire,** or ✆ **113** to request an **ambulance.**

Gasoline (Petrol) See "Getting Around," in chapter 3.

Holidays Norway celebrates the following public holidays: New Year's Day (Jan 1), Maundy Thursday, Good Friday, Easter, Labor Day (May 1), Ascension Day (mid-May), National Day (May 17), Whit Monday (late May), Christmas (Dec 25), and Boxing Day (Dec 26).

Hospitals Nearly all towns throughout Norway have hospitals with English-speaking doctors.

Insurance **Medical Insurance** For travel overseas, most U.S. health plans (including Medicare and Medicaid) do not provide coverage, and the ones that do often require you to pay for services up front, reimbursing you only after you return home.

As a safety net, you may want to buy travel medical insurance, particularly if you're traveling to a remote or high-risk area where emergency evacuation might be necessary. If you require additional medical insurance, try **MEDEX Assistance** (✆ **410/453-6300;** www.medexassist.com) or **Travel Assistance International** (✆ **800/821-2828;** www.travelassistance.com. Another group is **Europassistance Services** (www.europassistance-usa.com).

Canadians should check with their provincial health plan offices or contact **Health Canada** (✆ **866/225-0709;** www.hc-sc.gc.ca) to find out the extent of their coverage and what documentation and receipts they must take home in case they are treated overseas.

Travelers from the U.K. should carry their European Health Insurance Card (EHIC), which has replaced the E111 form as proof of entitlement to free/reduced cost medical treatment abroad (✆ **0845/606-2030;** www.ehic.org.uk). Note, however, that the EHIC only covers "necessary medical treatment." For repatriation costs, lost money, baggage, or cancellation, travel insurance from a reputable company should always be sought (✆ **0870/033-9985;** www.travelinsuranceweb.com).

Travel Insurance The cost of travel insurance varies widely, depending on the destination, the cost and length of your trip, your age and health, and the type of trip you're taking, but expect to pay between 5% and 8% of the cost of your vacation. You can get estimates from various providers in the U.S. through **InsureMyTrip.com** (✆ **800/487-4722**). Enter your trip cost and dates, your age, and other information, for prices from more than a dozen companies.

U.K. citizens and their families who make more than one trip abroad per year may find an annual travel insurance policy works out cheaper. Check out **Moneysupermarket** (✆ **0845/345-5708;** www.moneysupermarket.com), which compares prices across a wide range of providers for single- and multi-trip policies.

Most big travel agencies offer their own insurance policies and will probably try to sell you their package when you book a holiday. Think before you sign. Britain's **Consumers' Association** recommends that you insist on seeing the policy and reading the fine print before buying travel insurance. **The Association of British Insurers** (✆ **020/7600-3333;** www.abi.org.uk) gives advice by phone and publishes *Holiday Insurance,* a free guide to policy provisions and prices. You might also shop around for better deals; try **Columbus Direct** (✆ **0870/033-9988;** www.columbusdirect.net).

Trip Cancellation Insurance Trip-cancellation insurance will help you retrieve your money if you have to back out of a trip before departing, if you have to end your trip abruptly, or if your travel supplier goes bankrupt. Trip cancellation traditionally covers such events as sickness, natural disasters, and State Department advisories. The latest news in trip-cancellation insurance is the availability of **expanded hurricane coverage** and **"any-reason"** cancellation coverage—which costs more but covers cancellations made for any reason. You won't get back 100% of your prepaid trip cost, but you'll be refunded a substantial portion. **TravelSafe** (✆ **888/885-7233;** www.travelsafe.com) offers both types of coverage. Expedia also offers any-reason cancellation coverage for its air-hotel packages. For details, contact one of the following recommended insurers: **Access America** (✆ **800/284-8300;** www.accessamerica.com), **Travel Guard International** (✆ **800/826-4919;** www.travelguard.com), **Travel Insured International** (✆ **800/243-3174;** www.travelinsured.com), or **Travelex Insurance Services** (✆ **800/228-9792;** www.travelex-insurance.com).

Language Norwegians are taught English in grade school. There are two official versions of Norwegian itself, one called *Bokmål,* spoken by about 85% of the population, the other, the lesser known, called *Nynorsk.* Nynorsk is identified as "new Norwegian," but is actually a melding of several older dialects spoken in rural parts of the country. In the north, the Sami have their own language, a distant cousin of Finnish.

Laundry & Dry Cleaning Most hotels provide these services, though they can be pricey. There are coin-operated laundromats and dry cleaners in most Norwegian cities.

Lost & Found Be sure to tell all of your credit card companies the minute you discover that your wallet or purse has been lost or stolen, and then file a report at the nearest police precinct. Your credit card company or insurer may require a police report number or a police record of the loss. Most credit card companies have an emergency toll-free number to call if your card is lost or stolen; they may be able to wire you a cash advance immediately or deliver an emergency credit card in a day or two. **Visa's** emergency number outside the U.S. is ✆ **410/581-9994;** call collect (in Norway, toll-free **80-01-20-52**). **American Express** cardholders should call collect ✆ **905/474-0870. MasterCard** holders should call collect ✆ **636/722-7111.**

If you need emergency cash over the weekend when all banks and American Express offices are closed, you can have money wired to you via **Western Union** (✆ **800/325-6000;** www.westernunion.com).

Mail Airmail letters or postcards to the United States and Canada cost NOK13 for up to 21 grams (7/10 oz.). Airmail letters take 7 to 10 days to reach North America. The principal post office in Norway is the Oslo Central Post Office, at Dronningensgate 15, N-0101 Oslo. Mailboxes are vibrant red and embossed with the trumpet symbol of the postal service. They're found on walls, at chest level, throughout cities and towns. Stamps can be purchased at the post office, at magazine kiosks, and at some stores.

Passports The websites listed below provide downloadable passport applications as well as the current fees for processing applications. For an up-to-date, country-by-country listing of passport requirements around the world, go to the International Travel Web page of the U.S. Department of State at http://travel.state.gov (click on "International Travel for U.S. Citizens"). More information on obtaining a passport for a minor can be found at http://travel.state.gov. Allow plenty of time before your trip to apply for a passport; processing normally takes 4 to 6 weeks (2 to 3 weeks for expedited service) but can take longer during busy periods (especially spring). And keep in mind that if you need a passport in a hurry, you'll pay a higher processing fee; overnight services do exist.

For Residents of Australia You can pick up an application from your local post office or any branch of Passports Australia (✆ **131 232;** www.passports.gov.au), but you must schedule an interview at the passport office to present your application materials. Call the **Australian Passport Information Service** at ✆ **131-232,** or visit the government website at www.passports.gov.au.

For Residents of Canada Passport applications are available at travel agencies throughout Canada or from the central **Passport Office,** Department of Foreign Affairs and International Trade, Ottawa, ON K1A 0G3 (✆ **800/567-6868;** www.ppt.gc.ca). ***Note:*** Canadian children who travel must have their own passport.

For Residents of Ireland You can apply for a 10-year passport at the **Passport Office,** Setanta Centre, Molesworth Street, Dublin 2 (✆ **01/671-1633;** www.irlgov.ie/iveagh). Those under age 18 and over 65 must apply for a 3-year passport. You can also apply at 1A South Mall, Cork (✆ **21/494-4700**), or at most main post offices.

For Residents of New Zealand You can pick up a passport application at any New Zealand Passports Office or download it from their website. Contact the **Passports Office** (✆ **0800/225-050** or 04/474-8100; www.passports.govt.nz).

For Residents of the United Kingdom To pick up an application for a standard 10-year passport (5-year passport for children under 16), visit your nearest passport office, major post office, or travel agency or contact the **United Kingdom Passport Service** (✆ **0300/222-0000;** www.ukpa.gov.uk).

Police Dial ✆ **112** nationwide.

Safety See "Safety," in chapter 3.

Smoking Norway bans smoking in public places. Under the law, Norwegians are allowed to smoke only in private homes and outdoors.

Taxes Norway imposes a 20% value-added tax (VAT) on most goods and services, which is figured into your final bill. If you buy goods in any store bearing the TAX-FREE sign, you're entitled to a cash refund of 12% to 19% on purchases costing over NOK315 (NOK285 in the case of foodstuffs). Ask the shop assistant for a tax-free shopping check. You may not use the articles purchased before leaving Norway, and they must be taken out of the country within 3 months of purchase. Complete the information requested on the back of the check you're given at the store; at your point of departure, report to an area marked by the TAX-FREE sign, not to Customs. Your refund check will be exchanged there in kroner for the amount due you. Refunds are available at airports, ferry and cruise-ship terminals, borders, and train stations.

Telephones The country code for Norway is **47,** but there are no city codes inside Norway. Phone numbers have eight digits. In every case, you dial all eight digits. Toll-free numbers begin with 800 or 810. If a number has a prefix of 815, it costs NOK1 per call. Numbers that start with **82** also cost extra.

Norway is the land of the cellphone; it is estimated that over 90% of all Norwegians have one. If the number you're calling starts with a 4 or a 9, chances are good that you're calling a cellphone number. It is more expensive to call a cellphone than it is to call a regular phone.

For information or operator assistance in Norway, dial ✆ **1881,** or 1882 for international phone numbers.

To place an international call, you can dial directly using the access code of **0,** then the country code and the number: **1** for the United States and Canada, **61** for Australia, **44** for Great Britain, and **64** for New Zealand. For assistance with access codes, call **AT&T Direct** (✆ **800/CALL-ATT**) or **Sprint International Access** (✆ **800/19877**).

Due to Norway's rather quick adoption of cellphones, public phones are being phased out. You can still purchase Telenor's Telekort in many denominations at shops and kiosks. Still, since hotels generally charge exorbitant amounts for ringing from your room, you are best off making a call from your cellphone or laptop. If you plan to make many phone calls while in Norway, it would be wise to invest in a Norwegian SIM card for use in your (unlocked) cellphone. For around NOK200 you can get a Norwegian number plus about 60 minutes of domestic calling time or several hundred domestic text messages. SIMs are available at many 7-Eleven and Narvesen kiosks and newsagents.

Time Norway operates on Central European Time—1 hour ahead of Greenwich Mean Time and 6 hours ahead of Eastern Standard Time. (At noon Eastern Standard Time—say, in New York City—it's 6pm in Norway.) Norway goes on summer time—1 hour earlier—from the end of March until around the end of September.

Tipping Hotels add a 10% to 15% service charge to your bill, which is sufficient unless someone has performed a special service. Most bellhops get at least NOK10 per suitcase. Nearly all restaurants add a service charge of up to 15% to your bill. Barbers and hairdressers usually aren't tipped, but toilet attendants expect at least NOK4. Taxi drivers throughout Norway don't expect tips unless they handle heavy luggage.

Toilets All terminals, big-city squares, and the like have public lavatories. In small towns and villages, head for the marketplace. Hygiene standards are usually adequate. If you patronize the toilets in a privately run establishment (such as a cafe), it's polite to buy something, such as a small pastry or coffee.

Useful Phone Numbers **U.S. Department of State Travel Advisories ✆ 888/407-4747** or 202/501-4444 Monday to Friday 8am to 8pm (http://travel.state.gov); **U.S. Passport Agency ✆ 877/487-2778; U.S. Centers for Disease Control International Traveler's Hotline ✆ 800/232-4636** (www.cdc.gov/travel).

Water Tap water is generally safe to drink throughout Norway. Never drink from a mountain stream, fjord, or river, regardless of how clean it might appear.

AIRLINE, HOTEL & CAR RENTAL WEBSITES

AIRLINES

British Airways
✆ 800/247-9297 (in U.S. and Canada)
✆ 0844/493-0787 (in U.K.)
✆ 08/153-3142 (in Norway)
www.britishairways.com

Continental Airlines
✆ 800/231-0856 (in U.S. and Canada)
✆ 0845/607-6760 (in U.K.)
✆ 08/100-3630 (in Norway)
www.continental.com

Eastern Airways
✆ 0870 366-9100 (in U.K.)
✆ +44-1652/680-600 (outside the U.K.)
www.easternairways.com

Icelandair
✆ 800/223-5500 (in U.S. & Canada)
✆ 22-03-40-50 (in Norway)
www.icelandair.com

KLM
✆ 1-866/434-0320 (in U.S. and Canada)
✆ 0871/231-0000 (in U.K.)
✆ 022/557-557 (in Norway)
www.klm.com

Norwegian
✆ +47/21-49-00-15 (from outside Norway)
✆ 81-52-18-15 (in Norway)
www.norwegian.com

Ryanair
✆ + 353/1-248-0856 (from U.S. and Canada)
✆ 0818/303-030 (in Ireland)
✆ 0871/246-0000 (in U.K.)
✆ 820/00-720 (in Norway)
www.ryanair.com

SAS
✆ 05400 (in Norway)
www.sas.no

SAS Scandinavian Airlines
✆ 800/221-2350 (in U.S. and Canada)
✆ 0871/226-7760 (in U.K.)
www.flysas.com

Widerøe
✆ +47/81-00-12-00
www.wideroe.no

CAR RENTAL AGENCIES

Alamo
✆ 877/222-9075 (in U.S. and Canada)
www.alamo.com

Auto Europe
✆ 888/223-5555 (in U.S. and Canada)
✆ 0800/2235-5555 (in U.K.)
www.autoeurope.com

Avis
✆ 800/331-1212 (in U.S. and Canada)
✆ 0844/581-0147 (in U.K.)
www.avis.com

Budget
✆ 800/527-0700 (in U.S.)
✆ 800/268-8900 (in Canada)
✆ 0844/544-3455 (in U.K.)
www.budget.com

Hertz
✆ 800/654-3001 (in U.S. and Canada)
✆ 0870/844-8844 (in U.K.)
www.hertz.com

National/Europcar
✆ 800/222-9058
www.nationalcar.com

MAJOR HOTEL & MOTEL CHAINS

Best Western International
✆ 800/780-7234 (in U.S. and Canada)
✆ 0800/393-130 (in U.K.)
www.bestwestern.com

Clarion / Comfort / Quality Hotels
✆ 877/424-6423 (in U.S. and Canada)
✆ 0800/444-444 (in U.K.)
www.choicehotels.com

First Hotels
✆ +47/23-11-60-80
www.firsthotels.com

Radisson Hotels & Resorts
✆ 800/395-7046 (in U.S. and Canada)
✆ 0800/374-411 (in U.K.)
www.radisson.com

Rica Hotels
✆ +47/66-85-45-60
www.rica-hotels.com

Scandic Hotels
✆ +46/851-751-720
www.scandichotels.com

Sheraton Hotels & Resorts
✆ 800/625-5144 (in U.S.)
✆ 800/543-4300 (in Canada)
✆ 0800/3253-5353 (in U.K.)
www.starwoodhotels.com

Thon Hotels
✆ +47/81-55-24-41
www.thonhotels.com

17 GLOSSARY OF NORWEGIAN TERMS & PHRASES

The official language of Norway is Norwegian, a Scandinavian tongue related to Danish and, somewhat more distantly, to Swedish. Grammatically speaking, Norwegian is fairly easy for native English speakers to pick up. The structure of the language is very close to that of English, and there are close cognates in English for many Norwegian words. There are only two words of Norwegian origin that have made their way into the English language: "Ski" and "slalom."

Most Norwegians will assume that a foreigner visiting the country does not speak the language. As a result, it is rarely necessary to ask whether someone speaks English; nearly all Norwegians are fluent in English at a very high level. Still, while you don't need to learn Norwegian to get around, picking up at least a few words and phrases can make your travels much more enjoyable.

BASIC NORWEGIAN WORDS & PHRASES

Useful Terms

English	Norwegian	Pronunciation
Yes	Ja	**yaa**
No	Nei	**næi**
Thank you	Takk	**tahk**
Thank you very much	Mange takk	***mahn*-geh tahk**
You're welcome	Ingen årsak	***in*-gehn *aw*-shaak**
Please	Vær så snill	**væh saw snil**
Excuse me	Unnskyld	**ewnshewl**
Hello	Hallo	**hah-*loo***
Goodbye	Ha det bra	**ha-deh-*bra***
Good morning	God morgen	**goo-*maw*-ehn**
Good afternoon	God dag	**goo-*daag***
Good evening	God kveld	***goo kfell***

English	Norwegian	Pronunciation
Good night	God natt	**goo-*naht***
Does anyone here speak English?	Er det noen her som snakker engelsk?	**æh del *noo*-ehn hæh som *snah*-kehr *ehng*-ehlsk**
Do you speak English?	Snakker du engelsk?	***snah*-kehr dew *ehng*-ehlsk**
I don't understand	Jeg forstår ikke	***y'l for-shtor ikka***
I don't speak much Norwegian	Jeg snakker bare litt norsk	***y'l snakka bar-a litt noshk***
How do you pronounce this?	Hvordan uttaler du?	***voo*-rdahn *ew*-tah-lehr dette *deh*-teh**
I'm lost	Jeg hat gått meg bort	**yæh haa got mæi boot**
How are you?	Hvordan star det til?	***voo*-rdahn *stawr deh* til**
Fine, thanks. And you?	Fint, takk. Og deg?	***fint, tukk. oh dy***
My name is	Mitt navn er	**mit nshvn æh**
Pleased to meet you	Hyggelig å treffes	***hew*-gehli aw *treh*-fehss**
I'd like...	Kan jeg få ha...	***kan y'l for haa...***
Excuse me	Unnskyld	***oon-shill***
Just a moment	Et øyeblikk	***et er-yer-blikk***
You're welcome	Vær så god	***vashagoo***
Can you tell me	Kan du si meg	**kahn dew see mæi**
Where are the toilets?	Hvor er toilettene?	**voor æh tooah-*leh*-teh-na**
The bill, please	Regningen takk	***raei*-nin-gehn tahk**
Can I pay with this credit card?	Kan jeg betale med dette kredittkortet?	**kahn yæi beh-*taa*-leh mehd *deh*-teh kreh-*dit*-kor-te**
Which bus goes to	Hvilken buss går til	***Vil*-kehn bewss gawr til**
Help!	Hjelp!	***yelp***
Left	Høyre	***huy-ra***
Right	Venstre	***ven-stra***
Push	Skyv	***sheev***
Pull	Trekk	***trek***
Lower	Nedre	***ned*-ruh**
Upper	Øvre	***uhv*-ruh**
I	Jeg	**yæh**
We	Vi	**vee**
He	Han	**hahn**
She	Hun	**hun**
It	Den	**den**
They	De	**duh**
You (plural)	Dere	**dare**
Good	Bra	**braa**
Bad	Dårlig	***daw*-rli**

English	Norwegian	Pronunciation
Wife	Kone	***koo*-neh**
Husband	Mann	**mahn**
Daughter	Datter	***dah*-tehr**
Son	Sønn	**surn**
Mother	Mor	**moor**
Father	Far	**faar**
Friend	Venn	**vehn**
Open	Åpen	***aw*-peh**
Closed	Stengt	**stehngt**

Days of the Week

English	Norwegian	Pronunciation
Monday	mandag	***mahn*-dog**
Tuesday	tisdag	***tees*-dog**
Wednesday	onsdag	***owns*-dog**
Thursday	torsdag	***torsh*-dog**
Friday	fredag	***freh*-dog**
Saturday	lørdag	***luhr*-dog**
Sunday	søndag	***son*-dog**

Months of the Year

English	Norwegian	Pronunciation
January	januar	**yahn-yoo-*aar***
February	februar	**feb-roo-*aar***
March	mars	**marss**
April	april	**ap-*reel***
May	mai	**mayy**
June	juni	***yoo*-nee**
July	juli	***yoo*-lee**
August	august	**aww-*guust***
September	september	**sep-*tem*-behr**
October	oktober	**okt-*ooh*-behr**
November	november	**noh-*vehm*-behr**
December	desember	**dess-*ehm*-behr**

Numbers

English	Norwegian	Pronunciation
1	en	**enn**
2	to	**toe**
3	tre	**tray**
4	fire	***fee*-rah**
5	fem	**fem**
6	seks	**sex**
7	sju / syv*	***shoo / seev***
8	åtte	***awt*-tuh**
9	ni	**ni**
10	ti	**ti**
11	elleve	***elva***
12	tolv	***tol***
13	tretten	***tret'n***
14	fjorten	***fyor-t'n***
15	femten	***fem-t'n***
16	seksten	***sy-st'n***
17	sytten	***suh-t'n***
18	atten	***ut-t'n***
19	nitten	***nit-t'n***
20	tjue / tyve*	***tyoo-eh /teeva***
21	tjue en	***tyoo*-eh-en**
22	tjue to	***tyoo*-eh-too**
23	tjue tre	***tyoo*-eh-tre**
24	tjue fire	***tyoo*-eh-feera**
25	tjue fem	***tyoo*-eh-fem**
30	tretti	***tret*-tee**
40	førti	***fur-ti***
50	femti	***femti***
100	hundre	***hun*-dreh**
1,000	tusen	***too*-sen**

* There are two different words for these numbers, and they are used interchangeably, although syv and tyve.

MENU TERMS

Basics

English	Norwegian	Pronunciation
Tea/coffee shop	Konditori	**koondittoo-*ree***
Restaurant	Restaurant	**reh-stewr-*ahng***
Breakfast	Frokost	***froo*-kost**
Lunch	Lunsj	**lurnsh**
Dinner	Middag	***mid*-dahg**

Meats

English	Norwegian	Pronunciation
Beef	Oksekjøtt	***ook*-seh-khurt**
Chicken	Kylling	***khew*-ling**
Fish	Fisk	**fisk**
Lamb	Lammekjøtt	***lah*-meh-khurt**
Pork	Svinekjøtt	***svee*-neh-khurt**
Reindeer	Reinsdyr	***raeins*-dewr**
Sausage	Pølse	***purl*-seh**
Shellfish (seafood)	Skalldyr	***skahl*-dewr**
Veal	Kalvekjøtt	***kahl*-veh-khurt**

Vegetables

English	Norwegian	Pronunciation
Asparagus	Asparges	**ah-*spahr*-ggehs**
Beans	Bønner	***bur*-nehr**
Beetroot	Rødbeter	***rur*-beh-tehr**
Cabbage	Kål	**kawl**
Carrots	Gulrøtter	***gewl*-ruh-tehr**
Cauliflower	Blomkål	***blom*-kawl**
Cucumber	Agurk	**ah-*gewrk***
Corn	Mais	**maayss**
Lettuce	Hodesalat	***hoo*-deh-sah-laat**
Onions	Løk	**luhk**
Peas	Erter	***aeh*-terr**
Potato	Potet	**poo-*tay*-t**
Red cabbage	Rødkål	***ruh*-kawl**
Spinach	Spinat	**spi-*nnaat***

Dishes & Condiments

English	Norwegian	Pronunciation
Bacon and eggs	Egg og bacon	**ehg og *bae*-ikehn**
Baked potato	Bakt potet	**bahkt poo-*tay*-t**
Beef stew	Lapskaus	**lahps-kouss**
Boiled potato	Kokte potet	***kook*-teh poo-*tay*-t**
Bread	Brød	**bruh**
Butter	Smør	**smuhr**
Cereal	Frokostblandi	***froo*-kost-blahn-ing**
Cheese	Ost	**oost**
Fish soup	Fiskesuppe	***fis*-keh-sew-peh**
French fries	Pommes frites	**pom frit**
Hamburger with onions	Kjøttkaker med løk	***khurt*-kaa-kehr mehd luhk**
Lamb and cabbage stew	Fårikål	***fawr*-ikawl**
Mixed salad	Blandet salat	***blahn*-eht sah-*laat***
Noodles	Nudler	***newd*-lehr**
Omelet	Omelett	**oo-meh-*leht***
Open sandwiches	Smørbrød	***smuhr*-bruh**
Pepper	Pepper	***peh*-peh**
Salad	Salater	**sah-*laa*-teh**
Salt	Salt	**sahlt**
Soup	Suppe	**sew-peh**

Preparations

English	Norwegian	Pronunciation
Boiled	Kokt	**kokt**
Beaded	Panert	**pah-*nayrt***
Fried	Stekt	**stehkt**
Grilled	Grillet	***grill*-eht**
Poached	Pochert	**poo-*shayrt***
Smoked	Røkt	**ruhkt**

Fruit

English	Norwegian	Pronunciation
Apple	Eple	***ehp*-leh**
Banana	Banan	**bah-*naan***
Grapefruit	Grapefrukt	***grayp*-frewkt**
Grapes	Druer	***drew*-ehr**

English	Norwegian	Pronunciation
Lemon	Sitron	**si-*troon***
Melon	Melon	**meh-*loon***
Orange	Appelsin	**ahpeh-*lseen***
Peach	Fersken	***faesh*-kehn**
Pear	Pære	***pae*-reh**
Pineapple	Ananas	***ah*-nah-nahss**
Strawberries	Jordbær	***yoor*-bæh**
Tomatoes	Tomater	**too-*maa*-tehr**
Watermelon	Vannmelon	***vahn*-meh-loon**

Beverages

English	Norwegian	Pronunciation
Beer	Øl	**uhl**
Coffee	Kaffe	***kah*-feh**
Juice	Juice	**yewss**
Milk	Melk	**mehlk**
Orange juice	Appelsinjuice	**ah-pehl-*seen*-yewss**
Soft drink	Leskedrikk	***lehs*-keh-dirk**
Tea	Te	**tay**
Wine	Vin	**veen**

Index

G

H

I

J

K

L

O

P

Q

R

S

T

U

V

NOTES